192-1/66 Unche 8.10

LEO XIII AND THE RISE OF SOCIALISM

LILLIAN PARKER WALLACE

LEO XIII
AND THE RISE
OF SOCIALISM

DUKE UNIVERSITY PRESS 1966

© 1966, Duke University Press
Library of Congress Catalogue Card Number 66-16033
Printed in the United States of America
by the Seeman Printery, Inc.

TO MY FAMILY

PREFACE

The aim of this book is to bring into juxtaposition for the first time two historical streams of the nineteenth century: the course pursued by the Catholic Church under Leo XIII, and the rise of Marxian socialism. The result has been to answer a question posed in the minds of many thoughtful people: Why did Marxism, which promised so much *here* and *now* to the dissatisfied workers, fail to sweep all before it in western Europe? It becomes evident as the story unfolds that the hand of Leo XIII was one of those strengthening the dike which held back the flood. It is also shown in these pages how Leo XIII not only made Catholicism intellectually respectable but also turned it toward a compassionate approach to the social problem of the industrial age. Following in Leo's steps the beloved John XXIII during his all-too-brief pontificate was able to build a revolutionary social program. John's first encyclical, *Mater et magistra*, found its source in Leo's *Rerum Novarum*. The feet of Paul VI are happily set on this same path.

The sources for the development of socialism are manifold. The socialist leaders were often journalists; they lived by the pen and what they wrote found its way immediately into print. There is no dearth of books based on socialist sources. On the other hand, all that is written about Leo XIII's pontificate is secondhand except for the accounts written by Eduardo Soderini and T'Serclaes de Wommersom. To these two prelates Leo opened the Vatican Archives that they might write a true account of his pontificate. The Belgian prelate wrote in French; Soderini wrote in Italian. The Pope's words, however, were known everywhere; his encyclicals were published at once throughout the Catholic world and his addresses to pilgrims or visitors appeared in print the following day. The sources are thus quite adequate for re-creating the public image of the Pope and his interaction with the socialist leaders.

Every effort has been made to avoid writing from an American, Protestant, twentieth-century point of view. Research was done in continental contemporary accounts, proceeding chronologically. The first three chapters are designed merely to sketch the development of the chief characters as a background for understanding the encounter when it arose. The greatest difficulty stemmed from the fact that meanings of words and labels changed constantly throughout the century. The chronological approach helped to clarify the shifting significance of the terms. In the final writing it proved to be impossible to present the facts intelligibly in simple chronological fashion. The method of the revolving stage was then adopted, showing first one of the antagonists and then the other, for they never met.

From my point of view the reason for undertaking this study was that my earlier studies (*The Papacy and European Diplomacy 1869-1878* [Chapel Hill, 1948], and "Pius IX and Lord Palmerston," in *Power, Public Opinion and Diplomacy: Essays in Honor of Eber Malcolm Carroll* [Durham, 1959], with William C. Askew as collaborating editor) had concluded with relations between the papacy and the European world in a parlous state. It seemed necessary to examine the rehabilitation of the papal image accomplished by Pius' successor, Leo XIII.

I wish to express my thanks especially to Professor Harold T. Parker of Duke University who read the manuscript very carefully and made helpful criticisms. Msgr. Joseph N. Moody of Ladycliff College also read the entire manuscript and made useful suggestions. For whatever weaknesses remain the author is entirely responsible. Bishop Vincent S. Waters very kindly located the portrait of Leo XIII used as a frontispiece: for permission to reproduce the painting in this volume we wish to thank the Right Reverend Msgr. E. B. Broderick of St. Joseph's Seminary and College. The list of members of the staff of the Duke University Library to whom I am indebted for numerous acts of kindness is too long to be included here. Mr. Ashbel Brice of the Duke University Press has been as always, helpful, encouraging, and wise. I wish also to thank the Southern Fellowships Fund for a grant which facilitated the collection of source materials.

LILLIAN PARKER WALLACE

Meredith College, 1965

CONTENTS

THE BACKGROUND

THE ARGUMENT

THE CONCLUSION

THE BACKGROUND

I. JOACHIM PECCI AND THE CHURCH

> *There is no religion on earth now, the human race cannot remain in this condition. Wait a little and the natural affinity of religion and science will unite them in the head of some genius. The appearance of this man cannot be far distant; possibly he has already appeared.*[1]
>
> DE MAISTRE

> *As those [the socialist reformers] had wished to place at the service of the Revolution the force of the Church, Leo XIII wishes to put at the service of the Church the force of the Revolution. Marvelous audacity! Unforeseeable about-face!*[2]
>
> MAURICE BARRÈS

Vincent Joachim Pecci, the future Leo XIII, was born in 1810 not many miles from Rome, in the village of Carpineto in the Papal States. Napoleon I was in control of most of central and western Europe at the time; his armies were everywhere. Crowns rolled from royal heads. Boundary lines of states were changed by strokes of sword and pen. Even the Papal States did not escape this confusion. The Pope himself, Pius VII, was Napoleon's prisoner.

Count Ludovico Pecci, Vincent's father, could trace his ancestry far back through an illustrious Sienese family; his wife, the Countess Anna, was descended from Cola di Rienzi, the popular hero of the Renaissance.

1. Quoted in Maximilian Harden, *Monarchs and Men* (London, 1912), pp. 61-62.
2. Quoted in Alphonse Opper de Blowitz, *Léon XIII devant ses contemporaines* (Paris, 1892), pp. 223-224.

Coming to Carpineto from Tuscany had been, figuratively, banishment for the Pecci line.

The uncertainty of the times was further accentuated by brigandage which harassed the countryside in waves. The Count and Countess Pecci were much concerned about the welfare of their offspring in the midst of this turmoil. Their older sons had been sent away to be educated at the University of Rome. Now Joseph, the third son, and Vincent must be provided for. As a matter of precaution they were sent to Rome to stay with their uncle, Countess Anna's brother, while waiting for an opportunity to be put into school. Joseph and Vincent,[3] after spending a year in Rome, were enrolled in the recently reopened Jesuit school at Viterbo.[4] Here the boys proved to be good students, Vincent especially. He could not be diverted from his study table by games or entertainment; he was praised by a fellow student for his "good conduct." Here the brothers received the tonsure.[5]

From the College of St. Ignatius at Viterbo, Joachim, as he must now be called, went to the Roman College, restored by Leo XII. From the beginning Joachim had devoted himself to his Latin exercises. By now Latin was for him a living tongue, opening doors to the learning of the past and enabling him to cultivate that elegant literary style which was later to characterize his public and private letters.[6] Here in Rome Joachim, to his great delight, met Leo XII in person.[7]

3. It was only in these early years that the youngest son was called "Vincent." After his mother's death he dropped the "Vincent" and became known as "Joachim." See A. J. Boyer d'Agen, *La Jeunesse de Léon XIII: de Carpineto à Bénévent 1810-1838* (Tours, 1896), p. 166. This account of Leo's early life was written from unedited letters in the archives at Carpineto. Facsimiles of the letters signed "Vincenzo" are included in the volume.

4. The Society of Jesus and all of its teaching establishments had been suppressed by Clement XIV in 1773. Pius VII, just returned from exile, reopened the college in 1818. See Boyer d'Agen, *La Jeunesse de Léon XIII*, p. 189.

5. Countess Anna had feared for her two oldest sons at the time of the Napoleonic levy. She had decided that they would be safer away at the university studying medicine. At that time Joseph and Vincent had been too young to be eligible for the draft. The danger did not disappear with Napoleon's fall. Count Pecci wrote: "You know . . . how much anxiety I have about my sons, especially in the matter of conscription." The Countess concluded that the Church would be a better protector for her younger sons. She tried to have the boys take the tonsure. The youths were not yet ready for it, so the matter was postponed. See *ibid.*, especially pp. 168-169, 190, 194, 196.

6. *Ibid.*, p. 52.

7. With a group of fellow students Joachim had gone to see St. Peter's. The group went into one of the courts of the Vatican to receive the papal blessing from a balcony

At the Roman College Joachim studied philosophy, chemistry, physics, and mathematics, achieving distinction in all fields. Significant in Joachim's education was his association with Father Piancini, a noted teacher alive to the new scientific discoveries of the time. Piancini early attempted, for example, to establish a parallel between the biblical six days of creation and the story told in the earth itself as revealed by archeological and geological investigations.[8]

Receiving the doctorate at the conclusion of his studies in 1832, Joachim Pecci entered the School of Noble Ecclesiastics to study canon and civil law; he became doctor of both laws (J.U.D.).[9] At the age of twenty-five he received his degree in theology *ad honorem*. His brother Joseph entered the Society of Jesus; Joachim chose a career among the secular clergy. Named a prelate of the household of the Pope by Gregory XVI,[10] he was ordained priest by Cardinal Odescalchi in December, 1837. On Christmas Day he wrote a letter to an elder brother to have a Mass said for him that the Holy Spirit might descend on him "with the plenitude of his gifts."[11]

The academic life had claimed Joachim Pecci up to this point in his career. Like St. Thomas Aquinas before him, he enthusiastically attempted to form a harmonious whole of secular learning and religious faith (the medieval synthesis). He had disciplined his mind to the logical processes of thought taught by Aristotelian philosophy and had walked in the ways of science, not only *scientia* as knowledge but the new science based on demonstrable fact. This he had done under his Jesuit teachers.

above. Then a deputation was invited to be presented to His Holiness. Joachim was not only a member of that deputation but its spokesman. It was the memory of this occasion that prompted him later to take the name "Leo" and become "Leo XIII." See T'Serclaes de Wommersom, *Le Pape Léon XIII, sa vie, son action religieuse, politique et sociale* (2 vols.; Paris, 1894), I, 38; hereinafter cited as *Léon XIII*. This is the most important biography written while Leo XIII was still alive. A third volume appeared in the twentieth century, after Leo's death. T'Serclaes, a Belgian, was one of the two prelates to whom Leo XIII opened the archives; the other was the Italian, Eduardo Soderini. These are the sources on which all subsequent biographies have been based. See also Msgr. Pio Paschini, *Lezione di storia ecclesiastica* (3 vols.; Turin, 1955), III, 501, hereinafter cited as *Storia ecclesiastica*.

8. T'Serclaes, *Léon XIII*, I, 35.

9. *Juris utriusque doctor.*

10. William J. Kiefer, S.M., *Leo XIII: A Light from Heaven* (Milwaukee, 1961), p. 7. For complete details see Boyer d'Agen, *La Jeunesse de Léon XIII, passim.*

11. T'Serclaes, *Léon XIII*, I, 52.

He had concluded that religious dictum and verifiable fact could not be in conflict if both were properly understood. He had as yet had little contact with the actual world of people, of politics, of economic and social pressures. These experiences were to come.

Father Pecci's baptism in good works to the suffering occurred just before his ordination. His adviser, the liberal and charitable Cardinal Sala,[12] was head of the sanitary commission in Rome, where cholera was raging. Joachim's brother Joseph already was distinguishing himself in the work of relief. None of the members of the Order were stricken although they ministered day and night to the sick. Joachim mentioned this fact in a letter home,[13] perhaps to relieve family anxiety at having two sons engaged in so dangerous a task. Joachim seemed to have no fear for himself and aided his adviser with courage and energy. He was not stricken.

Experience of a totally different sort came quickly. The province of Benevento was in turmoil and confusion, smuggling and banditry being carried on as regular commercial enterprises. Father Pecci was sent as apostolic delegate to re-establish order. After reforming his own troops the new Apostolic Delegate tackled the concealed and formidable power of the bandit ring. This was the more difficult because the organization of criminals was protected by the nobles of the area. Pecci was successful. The bandits were imprisoned or killed and the wealthy who protected them in order to share the spoils were defied. To one of the nobles who threatened to go to Rome and lay his case before the Pope the young Apostolic Delegate replied: "Very well, my dear Marquis, but remember that before going to carry your complaints to the Vatican you must pass the prison of Sant'Angelo."[14] His covert threat was understood. Such procedure, he wrote to his family, was scarcely conducive to making him popular with the nobility of the area; it did, however, bring him the title of "friend of Justice." The approval of his conscience and of the common people brought him satisfaction enough.

His mission in Benevento well accomplished, Joachim Pecci was trans-

12. It was to Cardinal Sala that he had dedicated at the age of twenty the theses which he must defend publicly in the process of securing his doctorate. T'Serclaes, *Léon XIII*, I, 49.

13. *Ibid.*, I, 49.

14. *Ibid.*, I, 62.

ferred to Perugia as apostolic delegate in 1842. Although Perugia was in a more enlightened area of Italy, where conditions of life were more agreeable than in Benevento, he was still on the fringe of things.[15] The ideas of nineteenth-century life had touched Perugia to the extent that secret societies desiring change made their headquarters there, but political reforms were impossible under the rule of Gregory XVI.

The sojourn in Perugia, although it proved to be of short duration, endeared the young cleric to the people. He was as successful here as he had been in all of his undertakings up to this point. He had shown intellectual ability, kindness, and firmness. There was no indication as yet of his capacities for dealing with people in broader fields, but now he was to be asked to perform in a larger arena.

In 1843, at the age of thirty-three, he was appointed by Gregory XVI to the post of papal nuncio in Belgium. He was designated Archbishop of Damietta *in partibus infidelium*, and was thus given rank in the hierarchy of the secular clergy without corresponding duties. He was ill prepared for the assignment in Brussels, knowing almost no French and being unfamiliar with the techniques of international diplomacy. One might almost say that, except for his study of science and archeology, he had stepped out of the classroom of St. Thomas Aquinas into the age of steam engines and the telegraph. As a product of Jesuit schools, however, he had perhaps learned that the world must be combatted on its own ground and with its own weapons. Characteristically, realizing that he was not prepared for his duties at the Belgian court, Archbishop Pecci made use of a providential illness. Interrupting his journey toward his new post, he studied the rudiments of French; thus armed he proceeded to Brussels. There is no indication in Pecci's letters to his relatives at this time of any selfless ambition to be successful for the sake of human society or for the Church. He wanted to bring distinction to the Pecci family and was willing to struggle to accomplish that end.[16]

The Nuncio's education in the human problems of the century might have progressed with rapidity. Belgium was a good place in which to

15. René Fülöp-Miller (*Leo XIII and Our Times*, trans. Conrad Bonacina [London, 1937], p. 45) speaks of the States of the Church as an "artificially preserved remnant of the Middle Ages."

16. T'Serclaes, *Léon XIII*, I, 81.

learn what the Industrial Revolution was doing to laborers. The metallurgical industry, from the mining of ore to the manufacture of steel and iron, was leaping forward, side by side with the textile industry. The progress of the industrial masses engaged in these undertakings was, however, in the direction of increasing misery. Frequently without work, they could not protect themselves against constant hunger and wretchedness. Even when employed, the workers existed in surroundings not fit for human beings. Child labor was common, and female labor was frequently employed on public works such as canal construction. Wages were low, hours were long, and the work was heavy.[17] A commission had inspected conditions in 1840, and in 1843 a large-scale investigation was undertaken. It revealed incredible living conditions among the laborers. Their floorless habitations were hovels of mud and filth, without sanitation.[18] The Belgian countryside was being rapidly transformed into a continuous workshop, belching smoke and fumes. It was in the same year as this investigation that the new Nuncio went to Brussels.

Archbishop Pecci (as the Belgians addressed him) must have been somewhat aware of the massive growth of industry. How much he learned about the sufferings of the poor workers is unknown. He probably read the papers (when his French improved), as he did consistently in later life, but he had no real contact with working people. Although he rode on trains, visited various cities, and marveled at gas lights, he left no record of any deep awareness of the wretchedness of the time. His contacts were with King Leopold and his court, the College of Ambassadors, the internationally famous University of Louvain, prominent citizens, and, of course, the higher clergy.

The Nuncio got on well with the Belgian ruler. Leopold found him agreeable, a man of "prudence and incorruptibility, with an awe-inspiring dignity."[19] As an indication of his esteem King Leopold conferred on Pecci the Cross of the Grand Cordon of St. Leopold, an order which the

17. Maurice Vaussard, *Histoire de la Démocratie Chrétienne*, I: *France, Belgique, Italie* (Paris, 1956), 138.
18. *Ibid.*, I, 159.
19. Justin McCarthy, *Pope Leo XIII* (2nd ed.; New York, 1899), p. 53. This is Ambassador Ratazzi's statement, based on a conversation with Leopold. Pecci created the same impression whenever he traveled abroad.

ruler had himself founded.[20] The Archbishop had an audience with Queen Victoria in London, and he was received by King Louis Philippe in Paris. The sojourn in northern Europe was the Nuncio's first contact with liberalism and his first experience with secular government. Having spent his life in the Papal States he had known only officials garbed in cassocks; he had had contact only with ultraconservative policies. It is not to be wondered at that he did not understand liberal government, but it was unfortunate for his diplomatic career that this was the case. He did not act to restrain the bishops in Belgium when they were endangering the state's liberal institutions, which had maintained the complete freedom of the Catholic Church as a religion and as a participant in educational activities,[21] as his predecessor, Msgr. Fornari, had done. Archbishop Pecci did not show up well in contrast with the experienced and able diplomat into whose shoes he had stepped. He was ignorant of the fact that he should keep aloof from any semblance of interference in party politics, and for this he has been much criticized.[22]

Pecci has been much praised, on the other hand, for settling a long-standing dispute between the University of Louvain and the Holy See over certain doctrinal interpretations.[23] In this matter he was on familiar ground. This was almost his only successful undertaking during his stay in Brussels.

Being intelligent, Pecci must later have reviewed his experiences in Belgium and have sought to account for his failures. He knew that Msgr.

20. Kiefer, *Leo XIII*, p. 26.

21. Lambruschini wrote to the new Nuncio: "The Catholic religion and the exercise of political authority enjoy in Belgium . . . a liberty enjoyed only early in other countries. It is the strict duty of the apostolic nuncio to protect this liberty. To attain this end the nuncio must not show himself animated by indiscreet zeal. . . ." See T'Serclaes, *Léon XIII*, I, 84.

22. Count Dietrichstein, as Austrian representative at the Belgian court, was an eyewitness. His account presents an unflattering picture of the Nuncio. See Fülöp-Miller, *Leo XIII and Our Times*, p. 55. See also T'Serclaes, *Léon XIII*, I, 71. The ultramontanist *Univers*, however, commented that Pecci was "noted" in Belgium for the "perspicacity of his judgment" as to the circumstances that were already "preparing the European revolution." See *Univers*, Feb. 22, 1878. For a more recent appraisal, see Francesco Magri, *L'Azione Cattolica in Italia* (2 vols.; Milan, 1953), I, 35. Magri recognizes that the criticisms of Pecci as a diplomat were not all without justification. Msgr. Pecci as a nuncio had little perspicacity and was not "adapted [says Magri] to cope with a post of such great responsibility."

23. T'Serclaes, *Léon XIII*, I, 71. As a Belgian prelate T'Serclaes was especially competent to judge in this matter.

Fornari had left Brussels to take the important post in Paris, whereas he, Joachim Pecci, was not transferred but removed from the diplomatic service. The Brussels post was his first and last assignment.[24]

The Nuncio was to become simply the Bishop of Perugia. Whatever he had learned of diplomatic protocol would be of little value during the next stage of his career. How much he had profited from his first contact with a truly nineteenth-century state time alone would tell. The very existence of Belgium as a sovereign state was one of the earliest evidences of rebellion against the reactionary world of Metternich and the Congress of Vienna. Pecci loved Belgium,[25] while reviling its climate, and continued throughout his life to demonstrate his affection for its people.

The first months of 1846 were spent by Archbishop Pecci in visiting London and Paris before going on to Rome. Gregory XVI was at the point of death when Pecci arrived. It was not until July that the new Bishop of Perugia was consecrated and sent on to his post. The appointment was a sore blow to his ambition; it was, in effect, banishment from the stage of public action.

When the Bishop of Perugia went to take over his duties in the Umbrian capital it was in a real sense a homecoming. He moved into the bishop's palace, where he was to reside for thirty years and more. He moved back into the hearts of his people. Here had been his first appointment after leaving Benevento. In this city where the secret societies congregated and the revolutionary spirit was rife, he had been very successful. The people remembered him for his constructive acts in improving economic and social conditions. It was he who had opened a savings bank, he who had emptied the prisons. Now he was at home again; he concealed his disappointment at the obscurity of his position and gave himself up to affectionate care for the welfare of his flock, serving them with a growing humility.[26]

For two decades Bishop Pecci remained in the Umbrian city of

24. Fülöp-Miller (*Leo XIII and Our Times*, p. 54) calls the nunciature, indeed, an "ignominious failure" showing nothing of the "lofty aims and views which were one day to characterize Leo XIII."

25. T'Serclaes, *Léon XIII*, I, 96. Although Joachim Pecci's stay in Brussels overlapped the residence there of both Marx and Engels, there is no evidence of mutual awareness.

26. Fülöp-Miller, *Leo XIII and Our Times*, p. 57.

Perugia, ministering to his flock. There seemed no hope of advancement; his fame was limited to a small area in a remote corner of the Papal States. The only distinguishing feature of his stay was that, in contrast to the general misconduct of affairs in the States of the Church, his corner was well tended. Instead of extorting money from his parishioners to use in advancing his own cause in Rome (as Italian clergy were all too often accused of doing), he used his time and his money to benefit his parishioners. Charity, education, health, and general welfare were fostered, and appropriate institutions for achieving these ends were established. The delinquent were helped to reform; schools for high and low were set up; a hospital for the chronically ill was opened; an educational institution of higher rank, the Academy of St. Thomas, was opened, with the assistance of his brother Joseph. When the Society of Jesus was dispersed in 1848, Joseph adopted the garb of the secular clergy and took the chair of philosophy at Perugia.

Bishop Pecci came to be regarded in the Umbrian region as the leader of the bishops of that part of the papal domains, where all government was in the hands of the hierarchy. Revolutionary waves which swept through Italy as the Risorgimento began to develop in the peninsula brought hordes of revolutionary soldiers through Perugia, but Pecci's parishioners had no reason to join revolutionary movements; his people were happy and not oppressed.[27] Tangible reward for his quiet good deeds came presently in the conferring of the "Red Hat" (in 1853) by Pope Pius IX, fulfilling the promise held out to Pecci by Gregory XVI. Bishop Pecci, now Cardinal Pecci, was honored by being made the Archchancellor of the Roman University and Cardinal Protector of the Franciscans,[28] noted for their good works. So the name of Pecci came to be associated with the highest intellectual and charitable activities of the Church. He went little

27. Bishop Dupanloup of Orleans, famous as a French liberal, visited Perugia and witnessed the regeneration of the diocese; he did not undertake any similar program in his own diocese in France, however, having other overriding interests. His visit to Perugia was a factor, nevertheless, in spreading the fame of Bishop Pecci as a social reformer. See Eduardo Soderini, "Per la genesi della 'Rerum Novarum' nel suo venticinquesimo anniversario," *Nuova Antologia*, May 16, 1916, p. 213.

28. The Third Order of St. Francis. Cardinal Pecci was pleased. He said this offered him a splendid opportunity to "bring a salutary remedy to so many of the ills which affect society" and to promote the "reign of holy charity." See T'Serclaes, *Léon XIII*, I, 168.

to Rome, however,[29] and was not drawn into the politics of the Sacred College. In his reform activities Bishop Pecci was liberal; in his support of the prerogative of the Bishop of Rome he was conservative.[30] This was to prove of great advantage to him later. Meanwhile he pursued his quiet, scholarly, and charitable way. He wrote a great deal during these leisurely years, developing a Latin style which was to be one of the chief adornments of his later pontificate.

Simple reforms and simple life might satisfy the Perugians, out of touch with the great world north of the Alps. Two revolutions, of which Joachim Pecci had had but a taste in Belgium, were changing, or threatening to change, every aspect of life more fundamentally and rapidly than anything that had occurred in the history of man. As student, as young cleric, as diplomat, and as bishop, his lifetime moved *pari passu* with the movements unleashed by these mighty revolutions: the French Revolution and the Industrial Revolution. The one spread outward from France, the other from England. Both became world revolutions. Both moved inexorably. In the name of human reason the French Revolution attacked revealed religion for its exercise of authority as an organized church; it denounced hereditary divine-right monarchy with its absolutism; it refused to recognize a class structure based on birth. This was war to the death on European institutions. This Revolution proclaimed and rendered glorious the principle of nationalism, as Fraternity; it declared the right of people to participate in their own control, calling it Liberty; it announced as Equality the right of all citizens to be regarded without distinction in the eyes of the law. Hope stirred in the hearts of the oppressed. Fear gripped those whose authority and position were threatened: the Church, the monarchs, the upper classes. These made common

29. He was kept away by the maneuvering of Cardinal Antonelli, the Secretary of State. (*Ibid.*, I, 167.) Forty years later the *Journal des Débats* (July 2, 1888) spoke of the stay at Perugia as an "exile" which the "animosity of Cardinal Antonelli" imposed upon him.

30. This keeping of one foot in each camp was the probable reason for his appointment as *camerlengo* by Pius IX. See S. William Halperin, "Leo XIII and the Roman Question," in Edward T. Gargan ed., *Leo XIII and the Modern World* (New York, 1961), p. 106. Only a Cardinal could be made *camerlengo*; only a Cardinal could become Pope. Cardinal Hohenlohe later told Leo XIII that by softening Antonelli's animosity, he had made it possible for the Bishop of Perugia to be made Cardinal and thus become eligible for the Triple Crown. See Francesco Crispi, *Memoirs*, trans. Mary Pritchard-Agnetti from the documents collected and edited by Thomas Palamengo-Crispi (3 vols.; London, 1912), II, 406.

cause in an effort to retain the existing order. But for Napoleon they might have stemmed the revolutionary attack. His military successes spread the seeds of revolution throughout continental Europe and solidified the legal gains, embodying them in the Napoleonic Code. Metternich was able at the Congress of Vienna temporarily to check the revolutionary tide by building sea walls of conservatism and reaction. One by one these walls crumbled. The Revolution struck at the defenses and would not be denied.

The Industrial Revolution, developing in England a half-century earlier than elsewhere, completely altered the life of the urban proletariat. The results were for the time being catastrophic. Working long hours for low wages in ill-ventilated factories and swarming in unsanitary slums, the workers (children, women, and men) were stunted and warped by their incredible environment. Spreading to continental Europe in the nineteenth century, the urban social problems seeped into the old conservative society, undermining it while it was still shuddering from the frontal attacks by the French revolutionary movements.

It was inevitable that these two revolutions should interact, no matter how different they were in nature or how far apart had been their motivation. This interaction adds a new dimension to the complex study of nineteenth-century life.

The Church, whose duty was the care of souls of all estates, was under attack from many directions during the course of the century. Furthermore, as an international institution, it was in a peculiar quandary. Secular rulers, in the era of divine-right monarchy, had brought it to a large degree under their own control. The rise of nationalism had abetted this regalist movement. Royal absolutism made it possible to remove education and other matters of human concern from the Church and place them under state control. Known in France as Gallicanism, this movement had for several centuries worried the Popes. In the eighteenth century a movement closely resembling Gallicanism had arisen in Austria under Joseph II.[31]

Under these circumstances, the attack of the French Revolution on

31. In Austria the movement was known as "Josephism." The term "Gallicanism" could not strictly apply anywhere else than in France. Leo XIII in his encyclicals always referred to the French as "Gauls."

royal absolutism might be advantageous to the Church, but at the same time the Revolution had struck directly at the Church itself, not only at its organization but at its property, which was seized to finance the Revolution. The Church was singled out as the stronghold of obscurantism by the "enlightened" revolutionaries. It was denounced for its hierarchical authority and for the privileged position in society held by its prelates. For these reasons the Church had to regard the Revolution as satanically inspired. The property loss was rendered less objectionable by the action of Napoleon in executing with Pius VII the Concordat of 1801, which recognized as a *fait accompli* the spoliation of the Church's wealth and made provision for the payment of the French clergy from the public treasury. This agreement lasted for a hundred years.[32]

The Church had been driven, nevertheless, as a fellow-sufferer at the hands of the Revolution, into a closer union with monarchy and the aristocracy. In France, then, the French Church throughout the century oscillated between two poles, now making common cause with all the reactionary elements, monarchy and aristocracy, now accepting any form of government which did not attempt to destroy the French hierarchy's control over its clergy as well as over the education, marriage, and burial of its members. All at the same time, the French Church managed to remain highly national, Gallican, and socially reactionary. This situation helps to explain the failure of Liberal Catholicism in France. The French higher clergy were "Gallican," that is to say highly nationalist, in Church matters. They were also monarchist, aristocratic, and opposed to the Enlightenment in all its aspects.[33] They were clinging tenaciously to the ideas of the Old Regime. Against them rose a group of Catholics who opposed these reactionaries and proposed to recognize the ideals of the Revolution in its political, social, and intellectual aspects. This new "liberal" group sought to go "beyond the mountains" to the head of the Church for authorization of their liberalism; hence they were called "ultramontanists." Some of them sought to revivify the Church

32. From Napoleon's time on, the trend was to define relations between the Church and the various Catholic states by concordats mutually agreed to by the states and the Holy See. This change is thoroughly explored in Robert A. Graham, S.J., *Vatican Diplomacy* (Princeton, 1959), pp. 253-259, 232-237.

33. See Thomas P. Neill and Raymond H. Schmandt, *History of the Catholic Church* (Milwaukee, 1957), p. 544.

through development of Christian charity. Frederic Ozanam,[34] representing this point of view, founded the charitable order of St. Vincent de Paul. Others, like Buchez,[35] labored to organize workers, who might gain strength by their solidarity in the social and economic struggle without leaving the ranks of the Catholic Church. These two were the forerunners of the "Social Catholicism" which was to flower much later in the century. A third group, seeking to defeat the "Gallicanism" of the clergy in the interests of democracy, turned also to the papacy for support. They too were "ultramontanists."[36]

A brilliant galaxy of stars appeared in this ultramontanist struggle against the aristocratic monarchism of the French clergy. Conspicuous were Lacordaire, the popular preacher of Notre Dame, Montalembert, Charles De Coux, and especially Lamennais. With Lamennais as editor, a journal, *L'Avenir*, brought out in 1830, analyzed French society in brilliant fashion and established itself firmly on the ground of Catholic Liberalism. The battle being thus inevitably joined between the Liberals and the French hierarchy, Lamennais appealed to His Holiness, Gregory XVI. The appeal was vain. The Pope blasted the hopes of the French Catholic Liberals in an encyclical, *Mirari vos*, a thoroughly reactionary document.[37] Lamennais left the Church and went over to the ranks of the anticlerical young intellectuals. Others remained in the Church but were disillusioned and frustrated.[38]

34. Joseph N. Moody (ed. and co-author, *Church and Society: Catholic Social and Political Thought and Movements 1789-1950* [New York, 1953], p. 129) states that Ozanam, in his course at the University of Lyons, outlined a doctrine that was later to form the "substance of the Social Encyclicals."

35. Vaussard (*Histoire de la Démocratie Chrétienne,* I, 29) writing recently, said that P. B. J. Buchez and his pupils were authentic precursors of the Christian Democracy of the second third of the nineteenth century. Buchez was a materialist who became a believer. It is difficult in reading the comments of later twentieth-century writers to realize how passionate were the struggles of the postrevolutionary era in Europe. Only in the day-by-day accounts coming from the presses of the time does the bitterness of the intellectual, religious, and social struggles become real. Of course they were prejudiced, on one side or the other, but they spoke out of desperate concern.

36. Michael P. Fogarty, *Christian Democracy in Western Europe 1820-1953* (London, 1957), p. 155.

37. Vaussard (*Histoire de la Démocratie Chrétienne,* I, 135) comments that in Belgium, which had just been established as a separate state with a liberal constitution, the bishops refrained from commenting on the *Mirari vos.* The encyclical was clearly inapplicable and meaningless in Belgium. Buchez, in France, called the encyclical "Italian nonsense." *Ibid.,* I, 30.

38. Henry C. Day, *Catholic Democracy* (New York, 1914), p. 6. See also E. Lecanuet,

But the voices of the Catholic reformers had not been stilled. When the revolutionary wave hit Paris and France in 1848, Lacordaire, Abbé Maret, Ozanam, and the rest founded a new journal, *Ère nouvelle*. In it they attacked what they regarded as the shortsighted policy of the reactionaries, whether clergy or laity.[39] Lacordaire was supported by the Archbishop of Paris, who made him vicar general as an evidence of confidence. He sat in the republican Assembly in the spring of 1848, but after the "June Days" he withdrew from active politics and resumed his preaching while continuing to edit the *Ère nouvelle*.[40] The Catholics, on the whole, rejected the republican revolution in 1848, and social reform with it. They went over to the cause of monarchy, supporting Louis Napoleon.[41]

Not all the efforts of the French Catholic liberal reformers were lost. They had planted a seed in the conscience of the privileged orders—a seed of realization of social duty toward the disinherited. It would take a long time to develop but it did not die. These reformers had been "ultramontanists." The name lived on. It became attached later to the reactionaries, appealing "beyond the mountains" for support in their struggle to resist change.

In Italy as well as in France, the French Revolution left in its wake a heritage which would never be dispossessed. A Kingdom of Italy, temporarily established during the Napoleonic regime, aroused the emotion of nationalism throughout the peninsula. The Pope recognized nationalism elsewhere as legitimate but would never agree that the principle should be applied among Italians. The Pontiff was not only the universal spiritual head over the international Church but also the temporal

---

L'Eglise de France sous la Troisième République 1870-1878 (Paris, 1907), pp. 2-3. Michelet, the historian, turned from devotion to hatred, regarding the Church as having reverted in its decadence "not only to paganism but even to fetichism." *Ibid.*, p. 6.

39. L. Veuillot, editor of *Univers*, wrote to a friend that the "enraged sheep," Ozanam and the rest, had founded a new journal in which they charged that "Montalembert and *Univers* have betrayed the cause of liberty, they are good only to be cast to the dogs." Lacordaire wrote to a collaborator of *Ère nouvelle* that these reactionaries, mentioning specifically *Univers*, would be responsible for the next uprising which would fall on the churches and the priests. "I do not wish [he continued] to have a part in this lamentable result. . . ." See Vaussard, *Histoire de la Démocratie Chrétienne*, I, 37-38, 40.

40. Gennaro Avolio (*I Democratici Cristiani e'il non expedit* [Naples, 1903], p. 28) said that "one man in France stood for the people—a poor brother . . . Lacordaire."

41. Moody (*Church and Society*, p. 130) calls 1848 the "year of decision for the Catholic Church in France."

monarch over the Papal States. A French revolutionary legacy of nationalism, popular sovereignty, and anticlericalism could never find favor with the Holy See. The collapse of the Napoleonic Empire enabled the papacy once again to set up its control over the States of the Church as a completely independent area. Against the desire of Italians to see a national Italy established, the Temporal Power of the papacy would need constant support from some great European power, presumably Austria, now, since the Congress of Vienna, in possession of portions of the peninsula.[42] Succeeding waves of national insurrection continued to threaten to engulf the Papal States. The papacy retreated into hopeless and rigid reaction against any sort of change.

Reforms in administration in the States of the Church were desperately needed. All government offices were held by clergymen. The minister of Pius VII, Cardinal Consalvi, had attempted some improvements but they were insufficient,[43] and his efforts to secularize the administration were completely unsuccessful.[44] Zeal even for improvement in purely material questions disappeared from view. There were no channels for the orderly expression of public disapproval or requests for reform. Older citizens looked back nostalgically to the more enlightened era under Napoleon. The young, unwilling to remain quiescent, were drawn into the secret societies: the Carbonari, the Freemasons, or others. The Carbonari, officially condemned in 1821, existed in many areas of Italy, including the Papal States. The society was particularly strong in Naples, the papal neighbor to the south.[45] Attempts of Leo XII[46] to create a counterrevolutionary society, the secret "Sanfedisti," met with little success.[47] The Freemasons, introduced into Italy by Napoleon's

42. Lombardy and Venetia were directly under Austria. The Kingdom of Naples, ruled by a restored Bourbon, was under Austrian protection. The independent duchies of Parma, Modena, and Tuscany were under relatives of the Habsburgs.

43. Before the advent of the French, Pius VII had begun a series of internal economic reforms by weakening monopolistic guilds in a series of acts. These reforms "dovetailed with other laws establishing freedom of commerce." See Maurice F. Neufeld, *Italy: School for Awakening Countries; the Italian Labor Movement in Its Political, Social and Economic Setting from 1800 to 1960* (Ithaca, N.Y., 1961), p. 59, hereinafter cited as *Italy*.

44. E. E. Y. Hales, "Cardinal Consalvi: the Tragedy of Success," *History Today*, X (Sept., 1960), 618-620.

45. Paschini, *Storia ecclesiastica*, III, 499.

46. Leo XII followed Pius VII. He reopened the Jesuit college which was attended by the Pecci brothers.

47. Neufeld, *Italy*, p. 85.

soldiers, continued to grow. The most important new society, of future rather than immediate significance, was "Young Italy," founded by Giuseppe Mazzini in 1831.[48]

Gregory XVI came to the papal throne in 1831[49] just after the July Revolution in France (1830), which ousted the Bourbons and set the Bourgeois Monarch, Louis Philippe, on the throne. Although the revolution ended Metternich's dominance in western Europe, it did not remove his control from Central Europe and Italy. The contrast between the growing enlightenment in the west and the venality and corruption in the States of the Church[50] increased the fury of the dissident. Gregory XVI was not moved to reform. A Memorandum presented to him (1831) by the Five Powers[51] of Europe detailed reforms urgently needed in his dominions. Instead of carrying out the reforms, Gregory issued the encyclical *Mirari vos,*[52] which blasted the hopes of the liberals in Italy as well as in France and destroyed any prospect of a liberal movement led by the Catholic Church.

The papacy remained, under Gregory XVI, the enemy of Italian nationalism. The chief obstacles to liberalism and nationalism in the peninsula were the presence of Austria, controlling Lombardy and Venetia in the north, the reactionary Bourbon Kingdom of Naples in the south, and the States of the Church in the center. Perhaps the best-governed Italian state was the Kingdom of Sardinia, under the House of

48. Paschini, *Storia ecclesiastica*, III, 500.

49. Nada quotes the Austrian Ambassador's private report to Metternich: "The Conclave is so discredited by the intrigues of which Rome is the witness that someone has aptly said that the 'Holy Spirit has adhered to the principle of non-intervention.'" See Narciso Nada, "L'Austria e la questione romana dalla Rivoluzione di Luglio alla fine della Conferenza diplomatica romana (Aug., 1830–July, 1831)," *Publicazioni della Facolta de Lettere e Filosophia della Università di Torino* (Turin, 1953), Vol. V. Pius VIII had a brief and negligible pontificate after Leo XII.

50. Narciso Nada (*Metternich e le riforme nello Stato Pontificio: Sebregondi a Roma 1832-1836* [Turin, 1957], *passim*) gives a complete résumé of the breakdown of orderly government in the Papal States. See also Giuseppe Montanelli, *Memorie sull Italia e specialmente sulla Toscana dal 1814 al 1850* (2 vols.; 2nd ed.; Turin, 1855), I, 258. Mazzini in an essay, "Gli Stati Pontifici," gives a detailed description of the mismanagement, confusion, and venality of the government. See Giuseppe Mazzini, *Politics*, Vol. V (1921) of *Scritti editi e inediti* (94 volumes; Imola, 1906-1951), 85-100.

51. Paschini (*Storia ecclesiastica*, III, 502) maintains that France spoke for England, which had no accredited representative to the Holy See, and that Austria claimed to speak for Prussia and Russia, as well as for Piedmont.

52. E. E. Y. Hales, *Pio Nono* (New York, 1954), p. 45. This is the encyclical in which Gregory replied to the ultramontane liberals.

Savoy. While unity was desired by many Italians, there was no unanimity as to the method to be employed in putting the various states together and no agreement as to the type of government to be instituted when unity should be achieved. Extreme liberals wanted a republic in which the people would govern themselves; moderate liberals would be content with constitutional monarchy under some legitimate dynasty. Many wanted a federal state which would preserve historic ideals and individual differences. Yet, all were agreed on the need to exclude Austria.

These two movements, toward national unification and the modernization of government, continued to develop in the Papal States during the pontificate of Gregory XVI. It may be remarked that in two small areas of the papal dominions there was no eruption of revolutionary activities. One was at Imola, in the Romagna, where the kindness of Bishop Mastai Ferretti warded it off; the other was in the Umbrian capital, Perugia, where the reforms of Bishop Joachim Pecci kept violence at a distance. Both bishops became Popes.

The death of Gregory XVI in 1846 brought matters to a climax. Much would depend on the person elected to occupy the Holy See. The choice of the Conclave fell upon the Bishop of Imola, a reputed liberal, who became Pius IX. Now the reforms demanded by the European powers in the Memorandum of 1831 might be carried out. Even the Protestant states joined in hailing the coming of a liberal man to the Holy See.[53] The granting of amnesty to political prisoners[54] emptied the prisons and brought exiles back to Rome. Thereafter, the Pope steered a course, probably doomed to failure from the start, between the excesses of the radicals on one side and the reactionaries of his own household on the other. Demands for change increased. Innovations such as gas lights and railroad trains would not satisfy. Pius IX extended his reforms into the

53. For his relations with Protestant England, see Lillian Parker Wallace, "Pius IX and Lord Palmerston," *Power, Public Opinion and Diplomacy*, ed. Wallace and William C. Askew (Durham, N.C., 1959), pp. 3-46.

54. For contemporary comment on the amnesty, see Prince Metternich's *Mémoires, documents, et écrits divers* (8 vols.; Paris, 1881), VII, 178, and Raffaele Ballerini, *Premières pages du pontificat de Pie IX* (Rome, 1909). Ballerini's account was written before the death of Pius and was read and marginally annotated by His Holiness. For more recent analysis, see Cesare Spellanzon, *Storia del Risorgimento e del unità d'Italia* (5 vols.; Milan, 1933-1950), III, iii. Pietro Pirri ("L'Amnistia di Pio IX nei documenti ufficiali," *Rivista di storia della Chiesa in Italia*, VIII [1954], 207-232) gives a detailed account of the amnesty.

political sphere. Public insistence went beyond the point which as ruler over the universal Church he could accept. When Pius IX issued his final reforming decree, the *Fundamental Statute for the Temporal Government of the States of the Church* (March 14, 1848),[55] the Revolution of 1848 was already under way in Paris;[56] King Louis Philippe was already in exile. The flame of this revolution was spreading like wildfire in Central Europe and the Italian peninsula and was getting out of hand. The movement was both national and liberal. Troops from the Papal States joined other Italian troops against Austria.[57] Metternich, the Austrian minister, fell from power and followed the stream of exiled reactionaries abroad. The day of moderate reforms was over. Pius IX, idol • of the Italian people, who thought he would lead them to their goal, began to draw back, rescinding some of his earlier orders.[58] The assassination of Pellegrino Rossi,[59] the Pope's liberal minister, produced a riot after which a republic was set up in Rome. Pius IX fled to Gaëta in the Kingdom of Naples.

Reaction followed swiftly. The Roman Republic was destroyed by French troops acting under executive orders issued by Louis Napoleon Bonaparte, elected to the presidency of their new French Republic by an overwhelming majority.[60] A disillusioned and chastened Pius IX returned to Rome, where he ruled the Papal States with the aid of the clever and unscrupulous Cardinal Antonelli, his Secretary of State.

Pius IX ceased to venture.[61] He assuaged his disappointment at the loss of popular acclaim by appealing from his exile for the rallying of the

55. Hales, *Pio Nono*, pp. 58-59, 61.
56. In its initial phase the Revolution of 1848 drew the approbation of the Archbishop of Paris, who said the Church never "insisted upon" nor "proscribed any form of government" and reminded his clergy that they were "ministers of God for the good of men." Veuillot, editor of *Univers*, also spoke up for the Republic and refused to defend the departing monarch. See *Univers*, Feb. 27, 1848. It was his dislike of Louis Philippe and not any attachment to republicanism that inspired Veuillot. To many reactionaries the Republic would be a "bridge" to legitimate monarchy.
57. Hales, *Pio Nono*, pp. 65-67.
58. Cesare Vimercati, *Histoire de l'Italie en 1848-1849* (2nd ed.; Paris, 1954), p. 14.
59. Pius IX, in exile, regarded the leaders of the revolutionary Roman Republic as "assassins" for having killed Rossi, "socialists," meaning Saint-Simonians, or "foreigners," meaning non-Romans. See Hales, *Pio Nono*, p. 127.
60. See below, chap. ii.
61. Pius IX restored the economic guilds which Pius VII had abolished. Although their abolition had been hailed by economic reformers as a proper step toward laissez faire, the return of the guilds met with popular approval. See Hales, *Pio Nono*, p. 162.

faithful.[62] After his re-establishment in Rome he turned to matters of theology. In 1854 he proclaimed the dogma of the Immaculate Conception of Mary, to the rejoicing of many Catholics.[63] The dogma was proclaimed on his sole authority. Ten years later he issued an encyclical, the *Quanta cura*, accompanied by a *Syllabus of Errors*, attacking liberalism and modernism in every form. In the *Quanta cura* Pius IX branded as fatal errors communism and socialism. In the *Syllabus of Errors* he listed, among many other errors, nationalism in religion and the abolition of Church courts. He denounced civil education, civil marriage and divorce, and in general the whole rational approach to religion and the liberal program for human society.[64]

The effect of the *Quanta cura* and the *Syllabus of Errors* on the relations between Pius IX and secular governments was disastrous. The documents seemed to array the Church as an obscurantist institution against the scientific, social, and political ideas of the modern world.

Many bishops in enlightened areas of Europe tried to soften the effect of the *Syllabus* by explaining it away in their pastoral letters, saying that it was not "universally applicable" or not an "article of faith," or by clothing it in philosophical subtleties.[65] Pius IX let the criticisms and justifications stand without comment.

One other long-considered project of Pius IX was carried to fruition in the summer of 1870. So many contradictory opinions had been expressed by members of the clergy that a group of 450 bishops suggested in 1867 that an ecumenical council should be held to clarify the issues.

62. *Acta et Decreta Sacrorum Conciliorum Recentorium, Collectio Lacensis*, (7 vols.; Friburgi Brisgoviae, 1890), IV, 2-4; 55-57, hereinafter cited as *Collectio Lacensis*. See also G. D. Mansi, ed., *Collectio Conciliorum Recentorium Ecclesiae Universae* (53 vols. in 57; Paris, 1903-1927), XL, 98. Pius IX painted a very touching picture of his plight. It aroused the sympathy of both Catholics and Protestants.

63. *Collectio Lacensis*, VI, 836-843. This is the encyclical *Ineffabilis Deus*. The names of the Pecci brothers, Joachim and Joseph, appear in the list of cardinal priests (VI, 848).

64. In this connection it may be remarked that the signature of Cardinal Pecci was appended (at the Vatican Council in 1870) to the *Postulatum* against one of these errors—Ontologism. *Collectio Lacensis*, VII, 849 ff. The statement of condemnation was applied to the proposition: "The immediate and direct knowledge of God is natural to man (*Naturalis est homini cognito Dei immediata et directa*)." This is not surprising. According to James Collins ("Leo XIII and the Philosophical Approach to Modernity," in Gargan, *Leo XIII and the Modern World*, p. 183) Pecci probably urged Pius IX to draw up a list of errors for the *Syllabus* and even named some of the topics to be included.

65. For the effect on Europe, see Lillian Parker Wallace, *The Papacy and European Diplomacy 1869-1878* (Chapel Hill, 1948), pp. 9-11.

None had been convened since the Council of Trent in the sixteenth century. This suggestion fitted in with the Pope's desire to centralize control over the Church through erecting into dogma the doctrine of papal infallibility. While considering other matters *de fide* this doctrine also could be laid before the assembled fathers. The Council was duly convened in December, 1869.[66] The dogma of Infallibility was adopted by the Council although a considerable minority, representing the most enlightened and educated areas, notably France and Central Europe, voted against it on the first ballot and subsequently left Rome before the final vote was taken.[67] Cardinal Pecci voted with the majority for the dogma.

The real significance of the Council was that it decreased the authority of the bishops and archbishops of the Church by subordinating them to papal control. The international character of the Church was further emphasized by this fact. Its effect upon governments in the secular states, still alarmed at the statements made in the *Syllabus of Errors*, was to excite them still further. Some states had concurred in laying a dignified but ineffectual protest by the French Ambassador before the Council.[68] Relations between the papacy and the secular states were at a low ebb in the summer of 1870. Pius IX was on the eve of the culminating tragedy of his career. He lost the Patrimony of Peter to the rising Kingdom of Italy and retreated into the Vatican.

By January, 1870, Italian unification had become a nearly accomplished

66. The Council in 1870 must henceforth be designated Vatican Council I inasmuch as Vatican Council II was called by John XXIII and convened in October, 1962.

67. There were also English and American (United States) bishops who belonged to this minority. They did not form a large group. In addition to the *Collectio Lacensis* and the Mansi, *Collectio conciliorum* already cited (see above, p. 21n.) the more important sources dealing with Vatican Council I are, *Civiltà Cattolica*, Series VII, Vol. V; Lord Acton, "The Vatican Council," *North British Review*, LIII (Oct., 1870), 97-120; Dom Butler, *The Vatican Council: The Story Told from Inside in Bishop Ullathorne's Letters* (London, 1930); the anonymously published *Ce qui se passe au Concile* (Paris, 1870); Émil Friedberg, *Sammlung der Achtenstücke zum ersten vaticanischen Concil* (Tübingen, 1872); Johannes Friedrich, *Tagebuch während des vaticanischen Concils* (Nördlingen, 1873); Cardinal Manning, "True Story of the Vatican Council," *Nineteenth Century*, I (April, 1877), 190 ff., 483 ff.; Émile Ollivier, *L'Église et l'État au Concile du Vatican* (4th ed.; Paris, 1879); James D. Hennessey, *The First Vatican Council: The American Experience* (New York, 1963).

68. Wallace, *The Papacy and European Diplomacy*, pp. 91-94, 96-101; reprinted in Ernst Helmreich, ed., *A Free Church in a Free State? The Catholic Church, Italy, Germany, France 1864-1914* (Boston, 1964), pp. 22-25; one in a series of "Problems in European Civilization."

fact in spite of the Pope's refusal to lead it. Austria had been driven out; the independent states had been absorbed by Sardinia; all of the Papal States except the Patrimony of Peter had been taken over by the House of Savoy, now ruling over the Kingdom of Italy. All of this had occurred earlier in the decade. Now, events of the Franco-Prussian war necessitated the withdrawal of the French troops who were guarding the Pope at Rome.

Visconti-Venosta, the Italian Minister of Foreign Affairs, hoped to secure the Eternal City by peaceful means. Knowing the warm nature of Pius IX, he thought a spontaneous approach by King Victor Emmanuel to the Holy Father might ease the situation. Marco Minghetti, the Italian Premier, though with "extreme reluctance," took the path of force and the Italian troops attacked the Papal Guard.[69] So Victor Emmanuel took Rome and made it the capital of Italy. Pius IX, refusing to recognize as legitimate the forcible seizure of his patrimony, disdained to accept the income provided in the Law of Guarantees unilaterally enacted by the government of Italy and proclaimed himself a "Prisoner of the Vatican." Not only did he refuse the proffered income, he refused to recognize the Kingdom of Italy by dealing directly with it or by stepping on its soil.

The closing years of the life of Pius IX brought an upsurge of respect and sympathy for the aging Pontiff. He was stronger in his weakness than in the days of his acclaim. His private life was irreproachable. The death of his much-criticized Secretary of State, Cardinal Antonelli,[70] was no spiritual loss. The essential kindliness of the Holy Father had an opportunity to shine through and correct the image created by his apparent change from liberalism to reaction. The public never understood either of these two phases of his pontificate. His mistakes were not errors

69. Federico Chabod, *Storia della politica estera italiana dal 1870 al 1896*, I, *Le Premesse* (Bari, 1951), 216. To Pius and most Catholics this seemed a calamity. Even at the time, however some predicted that this release from entanglement with Italian politics would enable the spiritual mission of the Church to be more adequately attended to. Chabod wrote (I, 259) that "the future showed how much in error it was to have believed that the papacy had been buried forever with the breach of Porta Pia." But Chabod wrote this three-quarters of a century after the event. The Catholic world at the time regarded the occupation of Rome by the Italian troops as a disaster of enormous dimensions.

70. Antonelli was commonly referred to as the "Red Pope" (this was, of course, before the days of Moscow); Father Beckx, head of the Society of Jesus, was spoken of as the "Black Pope"; Pius IX was called the "White Pope."

of the heart.[71] In the temporal sphere he bequeathed to his successor two tremendous problems, the quarrel with the Kingdom of Italy and the quarrel with the redoubtable Bismarck—the Kulturkampf. Both quarrels played vital roles in the war of the Church against socialism.

71. This aspect of the life of Pius IX is explored in Gian Ludovico Masetti Zannini, "La spiritualità di Pio IX prima del Pontificato," *Rivista di storia della Chiesa in Italia,* XIV (Rome, 1960), 283-298.

II. THE BACKGROUND OF SOCIALISM

"I went [said Proudhon to his trial magistrate after 1848] to contemplate the sublime horrors of the cannonade." "But [asked the magistrate] are you not, then, a socialist?" "Certainly." "Well, but what, then is socialism?" "It is [replied Proudhon] every aspiration toward the improvement of society." "But in that case [said the magistrate] we are all socialists." "That [said Proudhon] is precisely what I think."[1]

The background of socialism lies in the emergence of a "social problem" in continental Europe during the nineteenth century and the theories advanced by intellectuals for its solution. The problem became acute in those areas which saw the rapid growth of the factory system and the expansion of mining operations which provided the necessary fuel and iron for the machines. The area in which these developments occurred was—with the exception of the Ruhr in the Rhineland—primarily Catholic Europe. Here the study of social groups engaged in confronting the varied problems of existence became "sociology," "economics," and "political science." Here the theoretical proposals for the solution of the "social problem" came to be known as "socialism."

While theorists were developing their schemes, the workers themselves were daily struggling to improve their lot or at least to stay alive by whatever means came to hand. While theorists and workers were thus pursuing their separate ways, professors and students, gathered in the seminar rooms of German universities, were confronting philosophi-

1. Émile de Lavelaye, *The Socialism of To-day* (London [1885]), p. xv.

cally the nature of reality; they found in the history of the human race materials for their conclusions. Philosophers, social theorists, and workers all played vital roles in the development of socialism. It is very easy to lose sight of the workers and their activities and view the rise of socialism as merely rivalry of middle-class personalities or contests among specific panaceas. Nothing can be more misleading.

For the workers the question was not academic. Those who worked in the skilled trades belonged to craft associations of long standing. They formed the elite of the working class. Conditions of the unskilled workers were in no way comparable. They wanted the right to organize, to bargain collectively as to wages and hours, and to strike in support of their demands. The workers did not regard the upper classes as their enemies. It would take a great deal of teaching to get them as a whole to adopt the principle of the class war. They were disposed to continue their habitual attitude of attachment to religion and to the Church.

In the 1820's, 1830's, and 1840's, the center of the theoretical discussion of social problems was Paris. It teemed with disaffected intellectuals, each with his pet solution for society's ills. A few clung to a purely political solution—the extension of the suffrage under a parliamentary monarchy or the establishment of a republic with a president and single-chambered assembly elected by universal manhood suffrage—but others mingled proposals for both political and social reform. Some found the solution in the enactment of individual legislative measures either in a parliamentary monarchy or a republic. Such legislative acts might include legalization of trade unions, prohibition of employers' combinations, fixation of maximum hours and minimum wages, abolition of child labor, accident compensation, unemployment insurance, and old-age pensions.

Other theorists offered socialistic schemes. Such proposals for the creation of an ideal society through the abolition of private property were as old as Plato and had been put forward by eighteenth-century philosophers such as Gabriel Monnot de Mably and André Morellet. These proposals had been devised, however, for a handicraft society. Gradually during the nineteenth century in France, the evils and possibilities of a nascent machine civilization and especially the plight and potential power of the factory proletariat penetrated the consciousness of middle-class dreamers such as Charles Fourier, the Saint-Simonians, Louis Blanc, and Auguste Blanqui. These concocted among them a witches' brew of denunciations of the capitalist system operating in the media of free competition. In the socialist indictment nothing was overlooked: monotony of factory work, the filth and disorder of early factories, cyclical depressions which brought employer and employee alike to ruin, exploitation of factory labor, and the use of children. For the poor where was liberty, the free development of their faculties, and growth to full moral stature?

The early French socialists differed, however, as to the remedy. Fourier, a traveling salesman, proposed in 1808 a cure that was possible only in a handicraft culture. Let men work together harmoniously in agricultural, handicraft communities of 1,620 individuals, where life would be adroitly calculated to afford each member a pleasing variety of labor. For fifteen years Fourier waited each day in his room at noon for a philanthropist to step forward with a million francs to subsidize the first model community. Comte Henri de Saint-Simon, an aristocrat who had sided with the rebels in the French Revolution, had a feeling for the immense productiveness of modern industry if organized and directed rationally by leading scientists, engineers, and businessmen. His disciples, elaborating his vague, suggestive philosophy after his death, urged in the late 1820's state ownership of factories, farms, and other means of production. The nation would become a vast co-operative industrial enterprise directed by a managerial elite for the rational exploitation of nature and the welfare of all. Each individual would be given work suited to his capacities and be rewarded according to his product, but everyone would have enough and, released from poverty, could freely develop his faculties. To initiate the grand project, eager Saint-Simonians urged: the abolition of inheritance, which would pass to the state; government banks and loans to expand productive facilities; schools to train engineers for managerial duties; and the employment of the army on public works. Through journalism, the Saint-Simonians tried to win the public.

By the time Louis Blanc, a dwarflike journalist with a vivid pen, published his *Organization of Work* in 1840, republican ideas were in the air. He proposed that workingmen form a political party, win universal suffrage, a single-chambered legislature, and legislative dominance of the government, and then reorganize production. Co-operation would be used to kill competition. With money derived from general taxation and state railways, the government would establish in each industry a factory, or social workshop, operated by its workers. They would elect their foreman and manager and share in the profits. These factories, manned by willing labor, would quickly drive private concerns out of business until an entire industry would be composed of efficient, social workshops. As the population was educated out of individualistic selfishness, each worker would co-operate willingly according to his capacity and receive according to his needs.[2]

A contemporary of Louis Blanc, Auguste Blanqui—a perennial instigator of street insurrections and revolts—scorned the chatter of the Fourierists, Saint-Simonians, and Blanc. Let the elite of the proletarian leaders seize political power in Paris by violence and govern dictatorially for a few years, while introducing social reforms that should prepare the people for self-government in a socialist society. He spent half his life in prison under four different French regimes. His career of revolution and imprisonment was punctuated by periods of freedom provided by pardon or amnesty. Far more revolutionary[3] than any of the Utopians, Blanqui was one of the most powerful personalities in France. Seldom seen by the workers, whose idol he was, he was all the more powerful for not being intimately known. He was admiringly called "*Le Vieux*" (the Old One). Although an anarchist, he thought a republic would succeed in opening the door to freedom. The first step would be destruction; destruction of the old would liberate society from bondage to the past.[4] New forms would then work themselves out. Blanqui's refusal to tie himself to a ready-made program enabled him to avoid the divisiveness to which such

2. This summary of the early reformers is adapted from studies and lectures of Harold T. Parker. Permission to include these paragraphs is here gratefully acknowledged.

3. John Plamenatz (*The Revolutionary Movement in France 1815-1871* [London, 1950], p. 45) calls Blanqui the greatest revolutionary of the nineteenth century. See also Gabriel Hanotaux, *Histoire de la France contemporaine* (4 vols.; Paris, 1903), I, 154. Hanotaux, speaking of Blanqui's lack of formulated program, says he was neither communist, nor separatist, nor socialist—but basically anarchist. In a preface to Blanqui's *La Patrie en danger* (Paris, 1871), p. xi, Blanqui is spoken of as not "*a* but *the* honest man," and the writer continues: "the honesty of this bandit-type is so real that he has never had around him any but honest friends."

4. Adam B. Ulam (*The Unfinished Revolution* [New York, 1960], p. 9) places Blanqui and Fourier in striking contrast.

programs were so prone. Devotion was to him as a leader, not to a formula. Even death would not destroy the effectiveness of such a mission.

With Armand Barbès, already engaged in revolutionary club activities, Blanqui founded the Society of the Seasons. Assisted by this group Blanqui engineered an abortive insurrection on May 12, 1839, which resulted in his imprisonment under a life sentence.[5] Because his health deteriorated in prison he was freed, and returning to Paris he resumed his leadership of the Parisian workers.

The only intellectual reformer not bourgeois by birth was Proudhon, the philosophical anarchist. In spite of his origin, he was able to secure an education which permitted him to enter upon a career of writing and politics. As a complete nonconformist he abandoned tradition and confronted the problems of society afresh. He weighed Church, State, and Property in the balance and found them wanting. He not only abandoned the Church but all belief in God, proclaiming himself an atheist.[6] All this appeared in his writing; in his private life he was neither erratic nor extreme. Revolutionary anarchists might claim spiritual descent from Proudhon, but he was not one of them. The Utopian Socialists associated with Proudhon but he did not become one of them. Distrusting every form of compulsion, he feared the glorification of the State as much as he resented the power of the Church.

Most of the early French socialists sought the brotherhood of man and developed theories of social readjustment in a spirit that was charitably Christian. This was evident from the time when Comte Henri de Saint-Simon brought out his *New Christianity* (1825). The moderate attitude

5. The original sentence was death, but it was commuted to life imprisonment. Many of the persons implicated in the insurrection took up their residence in London, remaining in touch with their fellows in Paris and Brussels. It was at this time that William Weitling escaped to Switzerland, where he set up the Utopian community later visited by Michael Bakunin. Antonio Labriola, famous Italian socialist, contrasts (*La concezione materialistica della Storia* [Bari, 1946], p. 15) the failure of Blanqui's Society of the Seasons with the success of the League of the Just which led to the League of the Communists and Karl Marx. Labriola was writing at the end of the nineteenth century.

6. Pierre Joseph Proudhon claimed that God was "the universal force, penetrated by intelligence," and again, that "God may be considered indifferently as the essence of man or as his antagonist." See P. J. Proudhon, *Les Confessions d'un Révolutionnaire pour servir à l'histoire de la Révolution de février* (3rd ed.; Paris, 1851), p. 19; hereinafter cited as *Confessions*.

of the Utopian Socialists on the religious question is in sharp contrast
with the belligerence of the republican era of the French Revolution.
The Catholic Church had been so involved with the property issue that
the removal of the Church's wealth from clerical hands to place it in the
state's possession drove many of even the lower ranks of the clergy (the
"non-juring" clergy) into a position of complete hostility to the republican
regime. The Bonaparte accession modified this intransigence, as Napoleon
and the Pope adjudicated their differences in the Concordat (1801) which
was destined to last for a century. There was a possibility that the utopian
schemes for social betterment might not, in France, lead to an out-and-out
war between atheism and religion. Étienne Babeuf, who had proposed a
revolutionary "Manifesto of the Equals" while the Revolution was
attempting to dechristianize France, did not publish it,[7] and the excess
of atheistic zeal was laid aside in 1799 with the end of the First Republic.
Increased tension during the closing years of the Restoration tended to
make the Utopian Socialists more outspoken against the Catholic Church,
but not against religion, broadly interpreted. Saint-Simon's illustrious
pupil, Auguste Comte, actually incorporated a "church" into his scheme
of a proper organization of society, as the only agency capable of producing in each rising generation a willingness to subordinate individualism to the general welfare. The disciplinary value of religion was
recognized. Against the Catholic Church, however, the republicans and
socialists found their enmity rising throughout the period of the Bourgeois
Monarchy. They feared that the "black cloud" would rise and make
common cause with the Legitimists.[8] They did not, however, for the most
part, cease to believe in God. They spoke of Him with respect and even
accepted the Gospels as the "breviary of democracy." Some associated
Jesus with Rousseau and Robespierre. Barbès invoked Christ when he
was at death's door. Fourier's "phalanx," Cabet's "Icaria," and Pierre
Leroux's *Encyclopédie nouvelle* were primarily humanitarian in outlook.
There was a certain affinity here with early Christianity.[9]

7. M. Paul Janet, "Les origines du socialisme," *Revue des Deux Mondes,* XL (1880), 571.
This "Manifesto," never sent to the press by Babeuf, was found among his papers. His
Association of the Equals had been formed during the revolutionary days of the Convention.
8. Lecanuet, *L'Église de France*, p. 5.
9. It was Cabet, according to Plamenatz (*The Revolutionary Movement in France,* p.

Louis Blanc, although called a Utopian Socialist, turned away from philanthropic efforts. The goods to be produced in his "national workshops" would be of value in the economic market. Thus the enterprise, although originally set up at the expense of the state, would maintain itself on a sound economic foundation. This system, he insisted, would add to the national wealth; all would prosper; there would be no losers.[10]

All of these critics were French. It was natural that their ideas should grow on French soil. It was natural, too, that their criticism should be listened to in that whole area which had been freed from legal privilege by the Napoleonic Code: the Ruhr, the Rhineland, the Low Countries, northern Italy, northwest Spain, and France, especially the provinces which bordered the Rhine and the Rhone. It was precisely in this same area that the proletariat was growing most rapidly in numbers; it was here that the Industrial Revolution was changing the very landscape from day to day. The sons of the revolutionaries of '89 could not forget that for a moment the common man had made his voice heard and his presence felt. It was natural that Paris should become the center of discussion of the social problem.

Into this welter of discussion in Paris entered refugees from central, eastern, and southern Europe. Here they could carry on their writing and publishing; here they could gather nightly in the cafés for mutually stimulating talk or gather in their clubs for the maturing of their plans. Many of the exiles were in the "League of the Banished," where German was spoken. Some exiles learned in Paris to speak German before they learned French. The left wing of the "League of the Banished" split off in 1836 to form the "League of the Just." Into these organizations poured a steady stream of these disaffected exiles who had been educated in

---

42) who, along with Louis Blanc, was responsible for winning the Parisian workers to socialism. Cabet was against what he regarded as the Church's perversion. He believed in democracy and in communism as it was early understood. No advocate of class war, he was not an inciter to violence, saying, "If I held a revolution in my fist I would not let it loose, even if it meant my dying in exile."

10. This program is not to be confused with make-work jobs of the "boondoggling" type. Blanc called make-work jobs, "disguised alms." The influence of Blanc was lasting; it was a factor in the development of public ownership of public utilities, both on the Continent and in America, in the introduction of useful work into correctional institutions, and in the growth of public education.

German universities or under teachers educated there. The literary life of Paris[11] and the relative freedom of conversation attracted them.

It was the philosophy of the German universities that cradled the revolutionary ideas of the students who came to Paris from central and eastern Europe. The French philosophers, the *Philosophes* of the Enlightenment, had not been philosophers in the true sense. Voltaire and the rest had been enamored of science and reason; they believed in natural law in the physical world and were confident that natural law in human affairs could be uncovered, given a little time. They had become critics of the institutions of their day, convinced that these institutions were perverted and inimical to man's welfare. They did not set up any organized, systematic structure of thought, any logical method of arriving at truth as to the meaning and ends of existence. The *Philosophes* were rather the forerunners of political science, sociology, and economics. Their approach was essentially pragmatic. They helped to bring on the French Revolution and the subsequent revolutions of the first half of the nineteenth century.

In the German universities, on the other hand, the attempt was made to construct a system of thinking having universal validity and thus to arrive at a true and ordered concept of reality. This was especially true in the intellectual circle which formed around Georg Wilhelm Friedrich Hegel, professor of philosophy at the University of Berlin until his death in 1831.

For Hegel the intellectual, religious, and political situation in Protestant Germany provided an atmosphere in which he could freely develop his ideas and lecture on them to his students. The absence of any restraining hierarchical power, the concept of a *Rechtstaat* embodied in the political system, and the organization of the university along seminar lines seemed to provide a maximum of opportunity for free rational thought. In these surroundings Hegel developed his philosophy of idealism. By dialectic means he reached the conclusion that the universe existed in and of itself. In this view of the universe as process, Hegel

11. Some of the Russians, for example, had read the novels of George Sand. See Franco Venturi, *The Roots of Revolution: A History of the Populist and Socialist Movement in Nineteenth-Century Russia* (New York, 1960), p. 17.

found no need for a Divine spirit *outside* to call the world into existence. God was immanent in the process—indeed *was* the process.[12]

Hegel believed in a philosophical Supreme Being, which he termed an Absolute Spirit (or Absolute Self or Absolute Reason). The Absolute Spirit, in order to realize itself completely, projects itself as its opposite—reality, the world.[13] It thinks the world into existence. At any given moment of time it is thinking the world and its inhabitants and their ideas. A philosopher, or a student of philosophy, who examines the processes of his own thinking is examining the ways of thought of the Absolute Spirit. A student of Hegel would be thinking in terms of contradictions (antinomies) stated as thesis and antithesis, as pure, ineffable *being* (thesis) brings to mind *becoming* (anti-*thesis*). Out of a conflict of these opposites arises a synthesis, which contains and harmonizes elements from both the thesis and the antithesis[14] but is more than either. So the Absolute Spirit, in thinking the world and human history, may, for example, think through the minds of men a given literary movement such as classicism (Racine), which emphasized perfection of form and the elevated portrayal of the noble emotions and noble personages. The Absolute Spirit will then think the antithesis, romanticism (Victor Hugo), which gave itself, sometimes with laxity of form, to the portrayal of the everyday emotions of everyday men and women. The reconciling synthesis would be the realism of Flaubert, who in *Madame Bovary* described with a perfection of form that would have delighted a classicist the rather commonplace emotions of a provincial middle-class woman.[15]

12. Here lies the essential difference between Hegel and Thomas Aquinas, whom Joachim Pecci was studying with such enthusiasm during this time. Neither of these thinkers regarded faith and reason as irreconcilable; apparent conflict, to both, merged in truth. Aquinas, however, did not view God as immanent in the universe but as outside and above it.

13. Auguste Cornu (*The Origins of Marxian Thought* [Springfield, Ill., 1957], p. 15) says: "Concrete reality is the creation of the thinking subject [i.e., the Absolute Spirit] which is inseparable from it."

14. Cornu quotes Hegel: "[The new concept is a] higher richer concept than the preceding one; for it became richer by the negation of the preceding concept, by what was contrasted to it; it contains it, but also more than it, and is the unity of it and its opposite." See Cornu, *The Origins of Marxian Thought*, p. 122 n. The quotation is from Hegel's *Wissenschaft der Logik*.

15. Harold Parker uses this illustration, showing the applicability of Hegel's method to the field of literature. Others have shown how this doctrine of the clash of opposites is vividly portrayed in Goethe's *Faust*, and in Thomas Mann's *Doctor Faustus*.

Hegel's theory with respect to the operations of the Absolute Spirit was thus a theory of how social change proceeded historically through the reconciliation of opposites. Also, since he assumed the synthesis was always an improvement over the preceding thesis, his philosophy was a theory of progress. History was on a one-way incline upward. He had two reservations, however: Christianity was the religion which had reached the culmination of perfection and admitted of no further change, and the Prussian government was the ideal governmental form.

Students flocked about Hegel to study his method, feeling that he was taking the shackles off their minds, leaving them free to construct a logical universe.[16] The more conservative among them retained their traditional Lutheran beliefs, interpreting their philosophy in a theistic sense. The Young Hegelians, however, turned Hegel's processes of rational thought into new channels, abandoning not only orthodoxy but all theistic beliefs[17] as dust to be swept out of man's mind. Like Hegel they believed there was no dichotomy between Spirit and matter; unlike him they believed that all was matter. So the groundwork was laid for dialectical materialism. In between these two extremes appeared a wavering stream of those leaving the old orthodoxy behind but not ready to go all the way to the leftist position. In their hesitancy they tended to retain theistic beliefs by giving them symbolic interpretations.[18]

Hegel died in 1831, leaving to his students the task of passing his philosophy to the next generation. The dynamism of his views, even secondhand, stirred the young in the seminar rooms of the German universities. They emerged with widely differing views. Some Young Hegelians were conservative, content to employ the dialectic as a delightful and harmless exercise. They were proud of the tolerance which permitted the free discussion of ideas in their universities. Hegel's freedom to teach was proof of this fact. Others, however, envisioned using ideas for the benefit of society and dreamed of programs of action. These were the Left Hegelians, whose views ran the gamut from philosophical anarchism to some new form of collectivism. All, however, felt a new

16. Franz Grégoire, *Aux sources de la pensée de Marx: Hegel, Feuerbach* (Paris, 1947), p. 133.
17. Cornu, *The Origins of Marxian Thought*, p. 57.
18. Grégoire, *Aux sources de la pensée de Marx*, p. 134.

sense of freedom. The scales had been removed from their eyes. Religion now appeared to them as a man-made contrivance conjured up by myth-makers and sanctioned by governments. Most of them went through a series of stages in arriving at this emancipation from what they regarded as religious superstition. Those who derived their Hegelian philosophy from Feuerbach[19] became avowed materialists. So long as their discussion of the new ideas remained within intellectual circles no furor was created. It was not until the discussion escaped from academic confines and entered the political arena that the eyes of the public began to rest disapprovingly on the young critics. Attacking the trinity of State, Church, and Capitalism in newly established journals of their own, they advo-cated actionist programs. The result was to draw down upon their heads the wrath of conservative governments in Central Europe still (until 1848) under the influence of Metternich. So began the stream of émigrés. They went to the Western capitals: Geneva, Brussels, Paris, London. But most of all at this period they went to Paris.

A leading Young Hegelian was Karl Marx. Marx was born at Trier in 1818 (eight years after the birth of Joachim Pecci) into a family of Jewish rabbis; his father, however, was a lawyer. The area was agricul-tural; vineyards predominated. Many peasants owned their own land in small or large holdings, and the area was little affected by the Industrial Revolution. The social problem was therefore in no sense acute. This was in sharp contrast to the situation in the north and east of Prussia, where the landlords formed an aristocratic and highly conservative class. Here at Trier the liberalizing influence of the French Revolution, both under the Republic and the Empire, remained.

The rebellion of the Marx family was primarily an intellectual rebellion against Jewish orthodoxy. The abandonment of the Jewish religion and the turning to Christianity represented an intellectual

19. Auguste Cornu (*Karl Marx et Friedrich Engels: Leur vie et leur oeuvre*, I, *Les Années d'enfance et de jeunesse: La Gauche Hégélienne 1818/20-1844* [Paris, 1955], p. 291) insists that Feuerbach regarded reason and faith as "incompatible." For exposition of Feuerbach's views see also C. N. Starcke, *Ludwig Feuerbach* (Stuttgart, 1885). See also Werner Schelling, *Feuerbach und die Religion* (Munich, n.d.), pp. 14-17, 126, 130-134. All of this is true humanism. See also Constantin Franz, *Über den Atheismus mit besonders Bezugnahme auf Ludwig Feuerbach*, Vol. II of *Speculative Studies* (Berlin, 1844), 105. See also William O. Shanahan, *German Protestants Face the Social Question* (Notre Dame, Ind., 1954), p. 54.

emancipation. This occurred while Karl Marx was a small child. Christianity, all religion in fact, was more easily discarded by him as a youth, since he had fewer emotional roots in religion than most of his contemporaries. He was well brought up morally, and he had a high sense of responsibility for family and society. "History [he said as a youth] shows how the greatest among men are those who are ennobled by working for the welfare of all."[20] Marx oscillated between the romantic atheism—the wish to be God—of his age and the eighteenth century—the Age of Reason—which refused God because earth sufficed.[21]

As a student at Bonn, Marx came into contact with revolutionary political ideas which still lived on in university circles in spite of repressive decrees which kept them from open dissemination. He did not remain at Bonn, however, but moved on to Berlin to undertake the study of law. He was now eighteen years of age. At Berlin he took courses in anthropology and history. History was taught by a disciple of Hegel as an infinite, rational development. So intrigued was the young student by the philosophical approach to the whole past of mankind that he presently abandoned his law studies to devote himself exclusively to philosophy. He moved to Jena, where he received the doctorate in 1841. His revolutionary tendencies had found some outlet in the "Friends of Poland Club." Since most Poles were under the Russian Tsar, these clubs were able to survive the political repression of subversive ideas. He also frequented the "Club of the Doctors," whose habitués were all Hegelians.[22] Marx was at this time a radical searching for a satisfying philosophy. Of one thing he was confident: there was no God who had either made or controlled the world; he believed that the world was real (and not ideal, as Hegel taught) and that science would reveal its essential nature.[23]

Marx returned to Bonn to make his home and confronted the necessity of earning his living. He knew that he intended to be a writer. At this point he was offered a position on the staff of Arnold Ruge's *Rheinische Zeitung*, published at Cologne. He accepted the offer, although he con-

20. Cornu, *Karl Marx et Friedrich Engels*, p. 53.
21. Georges M-M. Cottier, *L'Athéisme du jeune Marx: Ses origines Hégéliennes* (Paris, 1959), p. 365.
22. Cornu, *Karl Marx et Friedrich Engels*, pp. 85, 87, 133.
23. Cottier, *L'Athéisme du jeune Marx*, p. 366.

tinued to live at Bonn.[24] He was presently made editor of the review and was permitted to occupy the post, in spite of his radical views which were already making him suspect, until 1843, when the journal was forced to suspend operations.[25]

After the closing of his Cologne review in 1843, Marx, accompanied by his bride, the well-born Jenny von Westphalen, went to Paris to edit the *Deutsch-Französische Zeitung*, designed for German exiles. Except among these German émigrés who had read the *Rheinische Zeitung*, Marx was an unknown. Paris was not aware of his coming. His name was not a household word; he was viewed neither as savior of the human race nor fiend incarnate; he was simply a highly intellectual young German member of a Parisian German group, speaking and writing in German. It would be a serious mistake for anyone arriving in Paris with Marx in 1843 to try to see the outlines of Moscow or Peking in the background. Karl Marx was not a Marxist in 1843; he was not even a socialist. He was twenty-five years old but already a thorough intellectual, exploring history philosophically in the manner of the German university professors. The French, less interested in academic subtleties, throughout the century had been concerned with the construction of programs that might extend and make real the promises implicit in the French Revolution. In Paris Marx found an actual proletariat already enjoying the fruits of an advanced economic development. Here were numerous workingmen and workingmen's societies. These were facts. Joined with these facts were theories that were already beginning to criticize the capitalist system and a revolutionary spirit willing to put theories to the test.[26] French socialists were reformers and humanitarians whereas the German exiles were ob-

24. Franz Mehring, *Karl Marx: Geschichte seines Lebens* (Leipzig, 1933), pp. 58-59. Ruge began publishing the *Rheinische Zeitung* at the beginning of 1842. In it he was attacking the Prussian state while trying to harmonize "reason and faith." See Cornu, *Karl Marx et Friedrich Engels*, p. 291. See also Sidney Hook, *From Hegel to Marx: Studies in the Intellectual Development of Karl Marx* (New York, 1936), pp. 127-128.

25. For the details of the internal political-religious struggle which made it possible to secure state approval of Marx's editing and writing, at least briefly, see Mehring, *Karl Marx*, p. 60. Mehring quotes from exchanges of letters among Marx, Ruge, Feuerbach, and Bakunin (pp. 83 ff.). A phase quoted by Marx was to become even more famous: one could "let a ship of fools (Narrenschiff) sail before the wind a good while," but its fate was still "determined," although the fools would "not believe it."

26. Cornu, *Origins of Marxian Thought*, p. 83. By this time Marx was abandoning Hegel and turning to one study only—economic history—and applying here Hegel's dialectic method. It was thus that historical materialism arose.

sessed with the idea of governmental power—authority—as exercised with varying degrees of rigidity in the German states. In Paris Marx learned of the various panaceas for society's ills and regarded them all as utopian. He learned here, too, of the importance of organization, whether of the mutual-aid associations or the conspiratorial revolutionary clubs.

At Paris, by 1844, Marx completed his basic intellectual development. Himself a genius, he recognized the Hegelian dialectic of thesis, antithesis, and synthesis as the product of genius. This Marx accepted. In the course of four years he diverged from the master on a succession of points. First, Hegel tended to become more conservative in his later years, and his philosophy could be interpreted as a defense of anything that exists. If the world is Absolute Reason realizing itself and if history is an upward spiral, then everything that is existing or has existed can be justified. Most Young Hegelians had come to terms with the world as they found it and settled down to enjoy philosophy—painlessly. The Left Hegelians had not been content with this. They pointed out injustices in the Prussian state and emigrated to Paris. To Marx, Hegel's philosophy had been the beginning of a new way of thought, not the end. Even as a university student Marx had been a philosophical radical. He with the other Left Hegelians asserted that the master's philosophy, if properly interpreted, was an instrument for radical attack on the existing order. To Marx, Hegel's philosophy might justify everything that existed but did not justify rejecting change. Change was continuous and desirable. Nor need change be gradual and painless. In the past, progress was frequently the result of tension between opposites which grew to a crisis and then burst into open revolution. Then and then only did the leap into the next stage occur. The plain duty of an idealistic philosopher was to promote such a revolution. By his writings Marx must change the climate of ideas and undermine respect for obstructive and useless institutions.

Second, Marx moved away from Hegel's cloudy disquisition of ideas to a positive consideration of social, economic, and political fact. Marx's position as editor forced that development. His reading of Feuerbach accelerated this change. Feuerbach attacked Hegel for building an edifice of words about words. Hegel always claimed that the events and institu-

THE BACKGROUND OF SOCIALISM

tions of an age were determined by the Spirit of the Age. Feuerbach inquired what the Spirit of the Age is unless it is the summation of the totality of the phenomena which compose it. To say that the phenomena of an age were determined by its Spirit was simply to announce that the totality of the phenomena was determined by the totality of the phenomena, an empty tautology. Hegel's Absolute Self (Spirit) was, similarly, either a tautological reformulation of what it was intended to explain or a disguised name for the personal God of Christianity and beyond the limits of rational demonstration. Feuerbach believed the phenomena, examined, would explain themselves. When this was done, he declared, it was apparent that the motive force of history was not spiritual or ideological but material. The sum of material conditions at any given time determined what men were and how they lived and acted. *"Der Mensch ist was er isst"* (man is what he eats) was his own caricature of his doctrine.

Marx was impressed: the philosopher must return to the social, economic, and political facts. Which facts in particular? As editor he had to review the works of Fourier and Saint-Simon. He had to consider contemporary economic questions, the social problem of misery in urban factory centers, and the proposed socialist solutions. After his paper was closed, he devoted almost a year to reading history and political economy. He conversed through the night with French socialists. He was converted to the solution of the Saint-Simonians—government ownership of the means of production—and to some of the means proposed by Blanc and Blanqui—a workers' political party, dictatorship of the proletariat, and then gradual introduction of reforms. Through reading Jacques Thierry, a French bourgeois historian, he became aware of classes. They and their struggles, not nations and states, were the primary elements of the historical process. Economic facts gave rise to classes which engage in the dialectical process[27] of thesis, antithesis, and synthesis. In the 1840's the class of machine capitalists formed the thesis, the exploited factory workers the antithesis; out of the conflict between the two would arise a

27. Sidney Hook (*From Hegel to Marx*, p. 60) remarks: "A witty Frenchman once said that Marxism like Christianity has its Bible, its councils, its schisms; its orthodoxies and heresies; its exegeses, profane and sacred. And like Christianity it has its mysteries of which the principal one is the dialectic!"

synthesis, a world Communist society which would have the machine of the thesis but not the capitalists, the factory workers of the antithesis but not the exploitation. Marx's basic intellectual development was complete by 1844.

Like other Left Hegelians Karl Marx regarded religion as a myth concocted by human beings and perpetuated through institutionalizing it. He cast religion aside lightly, for himself. It had had no deep hold on him at any time. He recognized in Lutheranism a support of the monarchist form of government in Germany and of the existing social order. He had no appreciation of the fact that religion might possibly be dearer to men—at least some men—than economic well-being. His attitude toward it was rather one of amusement or disdain. He did not expect man to be rational, but he did expect him to be moved primarily by economic considerations. As for the Catholic Church, he feared its international hierarchical structure. He regarded Catholicism as even more irrational than Protestantism because of its pilgrimages, its shrines, and all the public and private paraphernalia of religious mystery. Marx thought that the Church's power lay in its control of the afterlife. The keys of Peter would unlock the gates of heaven and rescue the man from hell. As an anchor against the adverse winds and storms of the here-and-now he misunderstood and underestimated it. In fact, he knew little at first hand about Catholicism and Catholic Europe. The papacy seemed to be losing its grip. The ultraconservative Gregory XVI was occupying the papal throne when Marx was in Paris in 1844. It appeared obvious that the Risorgimento would presently restrict the Pope's territories and weaken his powers still further. Paris was French and Catholic, but to the refugees it was cosmopolitan and indifferent.

It was here in Paris that the fateful friendships and enmities of the century had their beginnings; here would-be reformers met for the first time. Karl Marx was but one. There were other exiles of perhaps equal ability who might become either his supporters or his enemies. It is necessary at this point to pause long enough to introduce the most important of these potential friends or foes. First, there was a German, Friedrich Engels, who became the lifelong friend and partner of Karl Marx.

The background of Engels differed considerably from that of Marx.

Engels was born (1820) into a wealthy manufacturing family of the Ruhr, where mining and manufacturing dominated the economic life. Strictly brought up in a society which condemned the joy of life as immoral, he found the path of emancipation from what he came to regard as "hypocritical religiosity" harder than it was for Marx.[28] Here in the Rhine Valley the social problem of the industrial age was already acute. Here, too, the Pietism of the wealthy bourgeoisie provided a stronger barrier against social reform and a greater bulwark against French influence than in the agrarian areas of western Prussia. Calvinist influence had early spread from Switzerland down the Rhine to take deep root in the Low Countries. Its effect was to alter the form of Lutheranism, producing German Pietism in this section of the Rhineland. The doctrine of the Pietists was a narrow and harsh one which enabled the owners to pile up wealth without any feeling for the welfare of the workers. Engels observed that the Pietists among the manufacturers treated the workers the worst—always trying to cut their wages under the pretext of keeping them from drink.[29]

From criticizing Pietism Engels turned to criticizing the social conditions in the Wupper Valley. He described the miseries of the poor: "But the rich manufacturers have a broad conscience and to cause one child more or less to perish does not trouble the soul of a Pietist, especially when he goes to church twice on Sunday."[30] Then he began to attack orthodox Lutheranism as well. Less trained in philosophy than Marx, Engels had practical contact with the social problems of the day.

28. Cornu, *Karl Marx et Friedrich Engels*, p. 114.

29. *Ibid.*, p. 210. Mysticism predominated among the working classes, among whom it was displayed publicly in the manner of their dress, the shapeless cloak, and the parting of the hair. Mysticism gave not only the Christian promise of eternal heavenly bliss to the elect but provided for ecstatic experiences of direct divine in-dwelling. In the Catholic Church monasticism provided a way to shut out the world and commune with God. Many Calvinists, denied such refuge, sought the same result through adoption of a garb designed to keep the mind from worldly pleasures (and from dwelling on their woes as laborers). The costume itself was an adaptation of the garb of the medieval "lay monk." Mysticism was a phase of German Pietism.

30. *Ibid.*, p. 211. These comments were incorporated in a work: *Lettres de la vallée de la Wupper*. This behavior was of course a far cry from the original Pietism of the seventeenth and eighteenth centuries, which emphasized the importance of the upright life and the practice of religion in society to offset the sterile theological trends of later Lutheranism. Shanahan (*German Protestants Face the Social Question*, p. 55) nevertheless calls Pietism the "most important resource" in Germany for dealing with the "religious crisis" of the industrial age.

The shift from silk to cotton manufacture greatly expanded the manu-facturing interests of the family, not only in the German Rhineland but in Belgium and, presently, in England, at Manchester. Here Engels came in contact with Chartism and the ideas of the Utopian Robert Owen. These ideas and experiences, plus a financial stability which often proved to be of great importance, were the contributions which Engels was to make to the intellectual partnership presently to be formed with Marx.[31] Marx was cloistered in his study, formulating his world view; it was Engels who was in touch with the social and economic dissatisfactions of the workers and especially the peasants of western Europe, who were migrating in increasing numbers to the freer air and unlimited space across the Atlantic.[32]

Others among the German exiles in Paris taking part in the revolu-tionary discussions were: William Weitling, who adopted the views of the French Utopian Socialists and set up an experimental community in Switzerland; the poet Georg Herwegh, who not only wrote a widely read account of his life as a reformer but led a column of Paris-recruited Germans in an abortive insurrection in South Germany; the immortal Heine, whose zeal for social reform made him a "soldier of humanity" as he wrote revolutionary prose and superb lyric poetry; and Moses Hess, who tried in vain to work out a synthesis of German philosophy, religion, and social action.[33] For the Young Hegelians the philosophi-cal critique of religion was the stepping stone to a critique of society and the state. Bruno Bauer, of the radical anarchist wing of the Hegelian Left, denied that Jesus had been an actual historical person. But Bauer founded no school of thought. Those Left Hegelians who walked in the footsteps of Feuerbach, contemptuous or derisive of Christianity, became atheists or made of historical materialism a new religion. All were agreed that no compromise was possible with the Catholic Church.

31. But the writing of Engels is not to be dismissed lightly. Several important western European socialists became converts as a result of reading his essay against Dührung. His work in completing the unfinished Das Kapital of Marx is no small accomplishment.

32. Cornu, Karl Marx et Friedrich Engels, p. 224. Engels said of the peasant that he was "freed from serfdom yet not free"; he was weighed down with "hereditary services," as well as "feudal courts" which rendered "bitter his repast" and troubled his sleep, until at last he decided to "leave his native land."

33. John Weiss, Moses Hess: Utopian Socialist (Detroit, 1960), pp. 44-47. See also Hook, From Hegel to Marx, pp. 195-196.

Not all the émigrés from German soil were German. Attracted by the philosophical and scientific prestige of the German universities, restless young intellectuals from Poland, Russia, and southern Europe studied in German schools. They joined the groups of Young Hegelians and ultimately migrated to the west. Among the most important of these, playing spectacular roles in the rise of socialism, were the Russians Michael Bakunin, Alexander Herzen,[34] and Herzen's friend Nicola Ogaröv. Herzen and his group espoused a series of causes and theories but founded no society, so they did not become rivals of Karl Marx. Herzen in spite of his hatred of tyranny refused to advocate violence; rather, he believed in reform through propaganda, from university room to printing press.[35] Paris was the Mecca that drew them all. As Herzen testified in his *Memoirs*: "Those were the days when France and Paris still had a magic spell for us." He characterized Paris as a "sort of gathering place for the whole world" that thus "ceased to be a pre-eminently French city"; it had become "a world hotel, a caravanserai."[36]

More significant than Herzen for the development of European radicalism, and more important in the career of Karl Marx, was Michael Alexander Bakunin. Born of a noble Russian family in 1814, he was four years older than Karl Marx and four years younger than Joachim Pecci.[37] Bakunin received an aristocratic education, somewhat more influenced by the West than was typical. His father had been a rich diplomat assigned to leading posts in European courts. The fact that his mother was a Muraviev proved later to be unusually significant in the period of Bakunin's exile. She had much influence with the Tsar but was unable to protect her son from the effects of his immoral behavior;[38] he was denied

34. Hook (*From Hegel to Marx*, p. 74) thinks it was Herzen who called dialectic the "algebra of revolution."

35. Herzen edited *Kolokol* ["The Bell"], a journal for Russian émigrés. See his *My Past and Thoughts: The Memoirs of Alexander Herzen*, trans. Constance Garnett (4 vols.; Edinburgh, 1924), III, 258, hereinafter cited as *Memoirs*.

36. *Ibid.*, III, 258.

37. There was no indication in Bakunin's early life of those powers which were to enable him to dispute the leadership of labor with Marx and remain the implacable foe of the papacy as an institution. The only thing obvious at this early date was that he was an individualist. See E. H. Carr, *Michael Bakunin* (London, 1937), p. 437.

38. He had early in life, says Venturi (*Roots of Revolution*, p. 36) convinced himself that what "*he* wanted" was what "God wanted." His own will was to be the sole arbiter of his acts.

the privilege of a commission in the army. His studies in Hegelian philosophy brought him in contact with Herzen and Ogarëv,[39] studying under erudite Moscow professors who had been pupils of Hegel.[40] Bakunin never mastered Hegel's dialectic method of speculative thought. He first came to notice in the West by publishing an article in a German review.[41] The phrase which attracted attention might have served as the masthead of Bakunin's life; it ended: "the passion for destruction is a creative passion." This statement is the best clue there is as to his views or program, if he had any. There is no question as to Bakunin's capacity to influence people, but to what ends is not clear. He was opposed to practically everything: religion, morality, truth, government, subjugation of the Slavs by Western nations, war, law, or whatever came to hand. He approved of violence in any cause. He was fundamentally anarchist, but not like Proudhon. He was communist in the medieval sense of being opposed to outside interference in the conduct of the affairs of the towns (thus preferring distant royal authority to near-by feudal control). He was not a communist in the utopian sense. He proved to be a thorn in the flesh of Karl Marx. He was not to be taken lightly. Did he always tell the truth? Did he ever tell the truth? The question of Bakunin must be left hanging until the story of his exploits shall have been told. Then the reader must weigh the evidence (or did Bakunin manufacture the evidence?) for himself. His biographers can give no certain answers.

In Paris all of these exiles mingled with the French socialists. It was here in Paris that Engels instructed Proudhon in the elements of dialectical reasoning. It was Moses Hess who introduced Engels to socialism. Bakunin took Engels to a workingman's meeting.[42] Through

39. Herzen (*Memoirs*, III, 255) speaks of Bakunin's "striking personality, his eccentric and vigorous appearance."

40. *Ibid*. Of the professors Herzen commented: "They were trying at that time to solve historical questions of the day by the dialectic method; it was an impossible task, but it put the facts in a clearer light." See also Nicholas Riasanovsky, *Russia and the West in the Teaching of the Slavophiles: A Study of Romantic Ideology* (Cambridge, Mass., 1952), p. 37. Hegelian philosophical studies, according to Riasanovsky, were diffused in Russia in upper-class society and not merely in the universities.

41. The review, *Deutsche Jahrbücher*, was edited by Arnold Ruge in Dresden. Bakunin's article was entitled "Reaction in Germany: Note by a Frenchman." See Mehring, *Karl Marx*, p. 56. Herzen, in Moscow, read the article. The pseudonym (Jules Elysard) did not reveal Bakunin to him. See Venturi, *Roots of Revolution*, p. 15.

42. It was Engels who said that the working class movement was the heir to classical German philosophy. See Hook, *From Hegel to Marx*, p. 60.

Vorwärts, journal of the German émigrés, Bakunin became associated with the German leaders, including Marx. The émigrés were atheist; the French socialists were not. They criticized the Church for blocking social betterment and for supporting reactionary aristocracy and government. All agreed on the iniquity of the existing order—political, religious, and social.

This was the Paris of 1843 (the year Joachim Pecci went to Brussels). Here the French socialist spark ignited the German intellect.

Marx and Bakunin both attracted and repelled each other from the start, if their later words on the subject can be believed. Marx thought the Russian's interest in communism[43] was "entirely out of curiosity"; Bakunin's impression was that Marx's interest in the proletariat was "mixed with personal vanity." "Marx as a German and a Jew [he said] is authoritarian from head to foot."[44] Bakunin found himself more *en rapport* with Proudhon, champion of freedom.

Karl Marx and Friedrich Engels did not remain in Paris. When Marx was asked by Guizot, Louis Philippe's minister, to leave Paris (actually at the request of Prussia) he went to Brussels, where he was joined by Engels. In Brussels there was a "Democratic Society for the Union of all Countries." Marx and Engels became members of this society. So did Bakunin, who was also forced to leave France and seek refuge elsewhere when he learned that the Russian government had ordered the Russian Embassy in Paris to return him to Russia. The decree against him included deprivation of his possessions and exile in Siberia at hard labor. Bakunin did not remain in Brussels; preferring precarious existence in the West to Siberian exile, he moved from spot to spot in order to preserve his liberty. Condemned to death by a Saxon court for participating in an uprising in Dresden, he was transferred and again sentenced to death at Olmütz by an Austrian court. He might have been put to death but for the intervention of the Tsar. Nicholas I claimed his right to take him into custody. Since Russian troops had helped Francis Joseph retain his realm in 1848, the Austrian Emperor sent Bakunin back to Russia.[45]

43. Marx was referring to the utopian type of community, such as William Weitling's in Switzerland. Bakunin had visited it.
44. Venturi, *Roots of Revolution*, pp. 46-47.
45. Herzen summarized these experiences in notable words, and told how at last, after

While he was in prison, Bakunin wrote a remarkable and strange document which he sent to the Tsar as a "Confession."[46] He did not remain in prison. Sent to Siberia for perpetual exile, Bakunin was assigned to the governor-general of Eastern Siberia, Nicholas Muraviev, a cousin. Here he was given such latitude of movement that presently he was able to cross the border and take ship for Japan. By way of Panama and New York he proceeded to London, turning up there in 1861.[47] From first to last Bakunin's career was histrionic.

The Brussels society to which Marx and Engels belonged was in touch with a London branch of the League of the Just, which was in process of turning itself into a Communist League.[48] The partners were engaged in publishing pamphlets in which they subjected to merciless scrutiny the mixture of French-English socialism and German philosophy then current. It seems to have been Engels who suggested the idea of blending the English classical economics and French socialism with the Left Hegelian philosophy, which was based on historical study. The general tenor of the argument was that the Utopian system could not possibly succeed in the type of society that was emerging at the time. That is to say, what was occurring in the industrial areas of Europe was a social revolution.[49]

Both Marx and Engels attended a conference of the League of the Just

---

being tortured in Austria Bakunin had been deported to Russia, "where he vanished behind the terrible walls of the Alexeyevsky Ravelin," making him in Herzen's view "one of those individual figures which neither the contemporary world nor history can overlook." See Herzen's *Memoirs*, III, 255.

46. Michael Bakunin, *Beichte, aus der Peter-Pauls Festung an Zar Nikolaus I. Gefunden im Geheimschrank des Chefs der III Abteilung der Kanzlei der früheren Zaren zu Leningrad* [found in the secret files of the chief of the Third Section of the earlier Tsars]. Translated and with a foreword by W. Polonski; n.p., n.d. Polonski called it (p. xi) a "Macchiavellian masterpiece." In it Bakunin refers to the Central Committee of the German Democrats with whom he had a "complete understanding [so he alleges]," to the "preparations for a new revolution in Germany," and to his plans "especially in the Bohemian question" (p. 64).

47. Venturi, *Roots of Revolution*, p. 51. See also Karl Marx, excerpt from "A Contribution to the Critique of Political Economy," in Marx and Engels, *Basic Writings on Politics and Philosophy*, ed. Lewis S. Feuer (Garden City, N.Y., 1959), p. 43.

48. After the Blanquist rising in 1839 the League of the Just had moved to London. In London it ceased to be a secret organization. The Communist League was a successor to this organization. See G. M. Steklov, *History of the First International* (trans. and pub. in England, 1928), pp. 15-17. Steklov gave credit to Chartism and its journal the *Northern Star* as forerunner of the new movement.

49. Mehring, *Karl Marx*, pp. 165-166. Cottier (*L'Athéisme du jeune Marx*, p. 366) testifies to the English influence: "The theism of Malthus confronts the atheism of Marx and nourishes it."

in London in 1847 as representatives of the Brussels organization. Marx made a speech in which he called upon the participants to get together a Congress of Nations, a "Congress of Workingmen," to establish "liberty all over the world." He emphasized the point that the workers must not put their trust in the middle class, who were not really democratic at heart; they were merely seeking their own advancement and would not extend to the workingmen the benefits secured. "The Democrats of Brussels," he declared "and the Chartists of England are the real democrats, and the moment they carry the six points of their Charter, the road to liberty will be opened to the world. Effect this grand object, you workmen of England, and you will be hailed the saviors of the whole human race."[50]

Engels was instrumental in having Marx commissioned to write a manifesto to workers. He, too, suggested changing from the catechism form which they had been using in their pamphlets and calling the "confession of faith" simply the "Communist Manifesto." Since "more or less history must be related," he wrote Marx, "the earlier form just does not fit."[51]

After some delay, which caused the Central Committee of the League to threaten Marx that they would "take steps against him" unless he met the deadline or returned the papers, the writing was completed. So appeared the *Communist Manifesto*.[52] It was designed to be printed and handed around to the members of the League, which gave its approval to the document.[53]

That the document was directed against the Church no less than against principalities and economic systems was apparent in its very beginning. The Pope was named first among members of a "Holy Alliance" planning to prevent the rise and spread of "communism."[54]

50. Harold J. Laski, *Communist Manifesto: Socialist Landmark: A New Appreciation Written for the Labour Party* (London, 1954), p. 30.

51. Engels to Marx, Nov. 24, 1847. Quoted in Mehring, *Karl Marx*, p. 177.

52. The text and prefaces to earlier printings are included in Laski, *Communist Manifesto*, together with the letter from the Central Committee to Marx (Jan. 26, 1848). Antonio Labriola (*Concezione materialistica della storia*, p. 29) said late in the century that it was due to historical contingencies that the doctrine of the *Manifesto* found neither a "base nor a terrain of diffusion."

53. Steklov, *History of the First International*, p. 17.

54. Later Marx expressed the opinion that man would rid himself of religion as he came to take a rational view of himself and of nature.

There was no indication at the time that the *Manifesto* would prove to be a world-shaking document. In summary form it included the points Marx had developed in the early forties. Using the approach of dialectical materialism to interpret the developments in human history, the conclusion was reached that the advance of industrialism—with its inescapable effect of swelling and impoverishing the ranks of labor, while piling up and concentrating wealth in the hands of capitalists—would lead inevitably to a world revolution from which the proletariat would emerge triumphant. The proletariat and the Communist leaders would participate in this inevitable historical process by forming political parties, at times and in some places allying with radical bourgeois parties or parties socialist-tinged (but never with any party opposed to working-class parties) to make immediate and partial gains, the ultimate object to be the seizure of political power. With the disappearance of social classes, which would follow the centralization of all control of production in the hands of the entire people, political power would cease to exist since political power existed only as a defense of class power. The ultimate aim would be a world-proletarian Communist society.

Written in German, the *Communist Manifesto* was ignored by the press. Publication in the *Deutsche Londoner Zeitung* began on March 3, 1848. A thousand copies (in German) reached Paris in March and Germany in April. A French translation was made before June. It was two years before it appeared in English, in the *Red Republican*. The first Italian translation was not made until 1889, when it appeared in *Eco del Popolo*, of Cremona.[55]

In the meantime Marx, expelled from Belgium, returned to Paris (during the Revolution of 1848) but after a short stay went on to Cologne, where he took up again his editorial career with the publication of the *Neue Rheinische Zeitung*, which closed in 1849. As a result of the incendiary character of the publication, Marx was put on trial for his life. Acquitted, he returned briefly to Paris but was not permitted to remain (he might remain in France, but not in Paris itself); he proceeded to

55. Laski, *Communist Manifesto*, p. 27. Cf. Karl Marx, exerpt from "A Contribution to the Critique of Political Economy" in *Basic Writings*, p. 45. See also Neufeld, *Italy*, p. 116.

England, "the homeland of the good," breaking all connections with official German life. London now became his second home.[56]

The Revolution of 1848, substituting the Second French Republic for the Bourgeois Monarchy, flamed throughout Central Europe and Italy, fed by demands for nationalism, constitutionalism, and social change. By 1849 it had spent its force and was brought under control, leaving constitutions in Prussia and Sardinia as permanent political gains and the abolition of serfdom in Habsburg lands as the only actual social gain. In France itself it was hailed by nationalists, liberals, and labor reformers. Success in February was easy and seemed complete. A Provisional Government was established while a new republican constitution should be written. Even Louis Blanc, the socialist, was permitted to experiment with his "right to work" idea,[57] but allowed to employ the idle merely in boondoggling jobs. The withdrawal of pay from persons so employed produced a violent insurrection, the "June Days," which brought appropriate punishment upon all who took part.[58] The day of Utopian Socialism, of hoping for bourgeois philanthropy, was over, washed away in blood.[59] Blanqui had understood that the June insurrection was the turning point, even while he urged his followers to take part:

56. Mehring, *Karl Marx*, p. 258. See also M. Beer, *Social Struggles and Modern Socialism*, II, *The General History of Socialism and Social Struggles* (2 vols.; New York, 1957), 79n.

57. Louis Blanc, *Le Socialisme: Droit au travail*, p. 63. Later, in justification of himself, Blanc wrote that the reactionary party tried to turn public opinion against him by "making a travesty" of his ideas. Blanc's "Organization du travail" was the object of workers' demonstrations at the Hotel de Ville. Its basic idea had been to do away with competition; co-operation was thus to be substituted for laissez faire. Even more radical was his suggestion that each should contribute "according to his capacity" and receive "according to his need."

58. *Ère nouvelle* thought there were very real workers involved in the "June Days." See Vaussard, *Histoire de la Démocratie Chrétienne*, I, 39.

59. Proudhon said the failure of Utopian Socialism lay in taking "hypotheses for realities." See his *Confessions*, p. 27. Herzen attributed the failure of the Second Republic to people's uncertainty, for "behind their Republic stood socialism." "France," he said in 1849, "frightened of the future, immersed in a sort of stupor, now rejects all that has been gained by the blood and toil of the last seventy years." See Venturi, *Roots of Revolution*, p. 33. See also Aldo Romano, *Storia del movimento socialista in Italia*, I, *L'unificazione nazionale e il problema sociale (1861-1870)*; II, *La crisi della Prima Internazionale (1871-1872)* (Rome, 1954), I, 233. Romano says that any attempt to harmonize the interests of the petty bourgeoisie with the proletariat was inimical to the development of true scientific socialism. He was speaking, of course, of Italy, but if he was correct then one may argue that the Revolution of 1848 which broke this bond in

No weapons must be left in the hands of the bourgeoisie. We have to give way before bayonets. . . . Obstacles, hindrances, impossibilities, will all vanish if the proletarians are armed . . . but for workers who are content to amuse themselves with street parades . . . then there will first of all be Holy Water, then curses, then bullets. . . . Let the people choose![60]

The election of the ambitious Louis Napoleon Bonaparte to the presidency of France in a landslide vote before the year was out gave a forewarning of coming events. His dispatch of troops, against the will of the Provisional Assembly, to restore Pius IX to his temporal throne in Rome in 1849 brought on a second street insurrection in Paris; it was swiftly put down. Imprisonment and exile scattered the Parisian groups.[61] Napoleon, by several stages, moved to destroy the Second Republic; he inaugurated the Second Empire, becoming Napoleon III.

Proletarians—everywhere suppressed (even Chartism had ended in a complete fiasco in London in 1848)—must begin again to lay foundations for a more successful attempt. In Italy failure of the mid-century nationalist effort outweighed the proletarian failure. Potential proletarian leaders in Germany, with the exception of Lassalle, were in exile. French leaders were impotent for a generation.

As for Karl Marx, now safe in London, he saw that he must await a more propitious time to unite the workers of the world. Their numbers were growing steadily everywhere in western Europe, but they remained powerless as a class.

The refugees in London reconstructed the Executive Committee of the Communist League in 1849 and formed ties with groups in Germany and Switzerland, but it was all sterile.[62] Marx occupied his time with writing.

He wrote, but did not complete, *Das Kapital* (which was later com-

---

France was an important step toward socialism, and not a catastrophe for the Marxist movement.

60. Quoted in Arno Schirokauer, *Lassalle: The Power of Illusion and the Illusion of Power* (London, 1931), p. 124.

61. According to Marx (*Der Achzehnte Brumaire* [3rd ed., Hamburg, 1885], p. 14), 3,000 were killed and 15,000 transported. Blanqui was imprisoned; Blanc took refuge abroad; Proudhon, who had never advocated violence was spared. Commenting later (*Confessions*, p. 374) Proudhon said the Jacobins (Republican Left in the Provisional Assembly) represented the "last hope of authority." Marx called this the most "colossal event in the history of the middle-class war."

62. Steklov, *History of the First International*, p. 18.

pleted by Engels from Marx's notes), in which he developed the ideas whose germs were in the *Communist Manifesto*. It would one day be known as the Workingman's Bible, but that seemed visionary at the moment. Even though he regarded the triumph of the proletariat as inevitable, he was not content to let history take its own course without prodding. He wanted to organize on an international basis a society which should assist the blind economic forces.

During this era of restriction on organization, of exile of labor leaders, and of general disillusionment about the possibility of reforming society, when it seemed, indeed, that the whole international movement had fallen apart, Marx and the circle of émigrés who surrounded him found one factor in the situation which they could use. The era of international expositions had arrived. In the attempt to build up foreign trade to balance expenditure for the raw materials to feed the insatiable machines, England, France, and presently others, turned to this way of advertising their wares. England held an exposition in 1851, France in 1855, and these were only a beginning (even Commodore Perry's expedition in 1853 was but a floating exposition). For labor, in addition to reduced fares, the significance lay in the fact that though the leaders were exiles and could not return to the Continent, the continental workers could visit them in London. Other safe causes which might justify holding an international meeting, by the early sixties, were the cause of Polish freedom, emancipation of slaves (especially popular during the Civil War in the United States), or the always laudable cause of world peace. Labor leaders returned home to tackle with renewed vigor the task of labor organization.

Great expositions in 1849 and 1855 brought to Paris floods of people from all countries and every class. It was the London Exposition in 1862, however, that led to a new attempt to form an international labor organization. Some French manufacturers thought it would be a good idea to send a delegation of workers to the London Exposition. They could get to know the English workmen as well as see the Exposition.[63] English laborers held a banquet for the visitors.[64]

63. Emperor Napoleon III facilitated their going. This was a part of the liberalizing of the Empire which characterized the sixties.
64. E. E. Fribourg, *L'Association Internationale des Travailleurs* (Paris, 1871), pp. 5-7.

French workers also attended a meeting held in St. James's Hall in April, 1864. The purpose of the meeting was to express sympathy for the Poles.[65] This led to a decision to convene another gathering in the fall, to which representatives of other nations would be invited. An English committee was formed and a message dispatched to the French. In addition to the Polish question they wanted also to discuss how by organizing on an international scale they might prevent foreign labor from being brought in to replace striking domestic labor. If all stuck together, they thought, such importation would be impossible.

According to plan a meeting was held in September in St. Martin's Hall to hear the French reply to the message sent them in the summer. Professor Edward Spencer Beesly, who was in the chair, first had the English message read. It mentioned the matter of imported labor. Much was said about peace. The English wanted to put Polish freedom first on the agenda. The French answer was then read. Poland was high in favor with the French also. They concluded that in view of the increasing concentration of capital the world would be run despotically unless the workers in various countries could organize and form an international organization.[66]

A General Council was formed for the proposed organization, including representatives, or delegated exiles living in London, from the various national groups. All these exiled representatives were members of the Communist League.[67] It was through this League that Marx and

Fribourg, a participant, describes the scene in the Crystal Palace, with about five thousand French workers present. They found, after early suspicious attitudes were laid aside, that friendly discussions could be fruitful. The English worker, the French discovered, was "better paid and with shorter hours" but still producing more and at less cost. They discussed the problem of the coming of machines which would reduce, they were sure, the number of available jobs. See Laveleye, *Socialism of Today* [1885], pp. 148-150.

65. Fribourg, *L'Association Internationale des Travailleurs*, pp. 9-10. See also Carl Landauer, *European Socialism: A History of Ideas and Movements*, I, *From the Industrial Revolution to Hitler's Seizure of Power* (Berkeley, 1959), I, 112.

66. The report of this meeting is from the *Beehive* of October, 1864, where everything was given in fullest detail. See *Founding of the First International: A Documentary Record* (New York, 1937), pp. 7-9. This is a collection of the major documents from the archives of the Marx-Engels-Lenin Institute, Moscow, hereinafter cited as *Documentary Record*.

67. Major Wolf, for example, was representing Italy (and Mazzini's point of view); Eccarius represented Switzerland; Karl Marx represented the Germans, and so on. See *Documentary Record*, p. 18.

Engels got into the new workers' International. In France, and notably in England, labor meetings were organized and attended by workers.

When the General Council met, a long paper of general principles was presented. It needed abbreviation. A subcommittee was designated for the purpose. The following week the General Council met again and decided that the revised statement still needed to be reduced in length; they sent it back to the subcommittee for further editing. By this time Karl Marx had been appointed to the subcommittee.[68]

From the standpoint of Karl Marx the most objectionable feature of the material to be edited was that in addition to French socialist ideas it also smacked of Mazzini, the founder of Young Italy. The document was full of a spirit long since gone. Mazzini hated the idea of the class war; he was not opposed to Christianity. These Mazzinian ideas were the antithesis of Marx's views.[69] To Marx Christianity was dangerous; the Catholic Church was the most hated foe. He was determined to leave no word of the original in the finished document. He succeeded. In the end he alone drew up the statement.[70] It was a masterpiece of finesse, pleasing everybody. It was deliberately vague and undogmatic,[71] steering cautiously among the dissimilar views of the English trade unionists, the French followers of Proudhon and Blanc, the German followers of Lassalle, and the Mazzinian Italians. Marx made room for all of these ideologies. He described the misery of the working population brought about by capitalism, said a good word for the trade unions, praised the "mutual societies" of Proudhon, and had a friendly word for the national workshops of Louis Blanc, while insisting that all workers of every land must get together in "international solidarity."[72]

68. *Ibid.*, pp. 22-25.

69. Mehring, *Karl Marx*, p. 362. Mazzini was popular in England, and Marx would not dare make a direct attack on what Mazzini had written.

70. For the way in which Marx managed to get the whole thing into his own hands we have his own account in a letter to Engels on Nov. 4, 1864 (Marx and Engels *Briefwechsel* [4 vols.; Berlin, 1930], III, 194, 198), in which he says that the subcommittee met at his house; not until then had he had the papers in his hand, so he could not "prepare anything in advance." He managed to discuss the rules until midnight, when members had to leave, saying they would have to meet again, as they had nothing to present to the General Committee; Marx then offered to write the address.

71. Engels to Marx, Nov. 7, 1864, *Documentary Record*, p. 50: I "suspect that this new association will split very soon into the theoretically bourgeois and theoretically proletarian elements as soon as matters are made somewhat precise."

72. Marx had not wanted the words "justice and morality (*Recht, Pflicht, Wahrheit,*

Marx was pleased with the setting up of the International Workers' Committee. He had respect for the power of the English members who were heads of the trade unions and so the "actual Labor Kings of London." The French members he regarded as "undistinguished," but they were leaders of the Paris workers. Having stayed away from "organization" he now felt that the time had come to accept it.[73] Most of all he was pleased to have eliminated Mazzini's influence from the statement of principles, called thereafter the "Inaugural Address."[74] Vague as it was by Marx's deliberate design, it purported to set forth the basic assumptions of the newly created First International. In some respects the organization was less international than it seemed. The German signers, for instance, were exiles, not representatives coming from Germany. Mazzini's acceptance and publication of the document[75] did not mean that Italian backing was automatically assured to the organization. Marx had eliminated Mazzini's principles from the "Inaugural Address" but not from Mazzini's mind. Nor had Marx eliminated Mazzini from Italy.

Moral, und Gerechtigkeit)" to be included. He said to Engels in a letter (Nov. 1, 1864) that he had yielded to the subcommittee's wish to include them, but placed them "in such a way that they can do no harm." At the general meeting he also made no demur when the Council struck out the term "profit mongers." *Ibid.*, p. 50. Some twentieth-century writers on the International use the inclusion of these words as proof of Karl Marx's essential morality, unaware of the circumstances which dictated their inclusion. This writer is not questioning Marx's probity, but merely pointing out that this quotation does not prove it.

73. Marx to Wedemeyer, Nov. 29, 1864 (sending copies of the address). He emphasized the power of the London labor leaders by describing a monster meeting in St. James's Hall which prevented Lord Palmerston from declaring war on the United States, "which he was on the point of doing." *Ibid.*, pp. 51-52.

74. Engels wrote Marx (Nov. 7, 1864) that perhaps now there would be an "end to *Dio e popolo*" (Mazzini's slogan). *Ibid.*, p. 49.

75. It was published in translation in *L'Unità italiana* on Feb. 18, 1865. See Neufeld, *Italy*, p. 92.

III. THE EMERGENCE OF KARL MARX

"Socialism is dead; to speak of it is to pronounce its funeral oration."[1]

LOUIS REYBAUD

The International Workingmen's Association,[2] when organized in 1864, was far less imposing and far less international than the title would suggest. Aside from French and English members most of the persons who had subscribed to the "Inaugural Address" were refugees from the Continent or were merely individuals who could not be said to be "representing" anybody. Their ideas were in the main incompatible. Seeming unanimity had been secured more by skilfully avoiding bold pronouncements than by any genuine agreement. Marx's real commitment to class war would not find immediate acceptance.[3] Most of the French and English members belonged to trade unions, but were not authorized to speak for them. Each spoke really for himself. The differences in ideology among them were fundamental. The grounds of agreement were so small as to provide little hope for unanimity on anything. The future of the organization, in contrast to a British trade union, seemed precarious indeed. The internationalist Karl Marx was not in a position to quibble. He had a foothold in this organization and a degree of prestige.

1. Reybaud, writing the article on "Socialism" for the *Dictionnaire de l'économie politique*, so declared in 1853. Quoted in Lavelaye, *Socialism of Today* [1885], p. xiii.

2. *Association Internationale des Travailleurs* (A.I.T.). It is usually referred to as the First International.

3. See Dalsème, *Les Mystères de l'Internationale* (Paris, 1871). *Les Mystères* was published anonymously as a tract against the International. It called the labor organization a "new religion," and stated: "After the Christ who promised the poor the realm of heaven, it comes to offer them the Empire of the Earth."

Marx, moreover, was only one among the several powerful personalities in Europe. There were Mazzini and Garibaldi, heroes of Italian unification. There were the French Blanqui and Proudhon. And there was Bakunin, back from exile in 1861.

Ferdinand Lassalle, founder of the German labor party and no less grounded in Hegelian philosophy than Marx, had recently been killed in a duel, but his spirit still lived on in his workers' organization.[4] Marx and he had not been in agreement either as to methods or objectives. Of incredibly brilliant mind and engaging personality, Lassalle had seemed the very antithesis of Marx,[5] who worked quietly behind the scenes to make his views prevail. Lassalle had been in jail during the worst days of the uprisings in 1848 and had thus escaped deportation. His application for membership in the Communist League (forerunner of the First International) had been rejected, so he had not been implicated when the members of the League were tried in 1852. With his unusual oratorical gifts he had captured the imagination of the German workers, becoming their idol. They responded to his call to unite; they formed the General German Labor Association (*Allgemeine Deutsche Arbeiterverein*), which became the German Social Democratic Party. Lassalle was friendly to Bakunin and even had a tentative alliance with Bismarck for a time.

Although a Hegelian like Marx, Lassalle held very different views on economics and on the relation of the State to the solution of the social question. He believed that labor should be organized to work under state aid. This is the beginning in Germany of the idea of State Socialism. This desirable end would be attained through universal suffrage. Lassalle was thus opposed to the utopian type of community advocated in France, England, and Switzerland by reformers; his ideas resembled those of Louis Blanc. He felt, rather, that labor solidarity could be achieved by organization of workers into a workingman's party. Such a party would

4. G. D. H. Cole, *A History of Socialist Thought*; II, *Socialist Thought: Marxism and Anarchism 1850-1890* (4 vols.; London, 1954), 86. The mantle of Lassalle fell presently on Schweitzer, who was not equal to the task. See Gustav Mayer, *Johann Baptist von Schweitzer und die Sozialdemokratie: Ein Betrag zur Geschichte deutsche Arbeiterbewegung* (Jena, 1909), *passim*.

5. Marx grudgingly granted Lassalle's importance in organizing German labor but criticized him for his mistakes, especially for making a personal sect out of his labor movement. See Marx to Schweitzer, Oct. 13, 1868. Schirokauer, *Lassalle*, p. 11. Lassalle's visit to London (p. 242) had established no real bond between them. Lassalle's brilliant but sordid private life was in sharp contrast to that of Marx.

use the legislative process to secure reforms. This procedure would weaken the control of the bourgeoisie over labor by forcing the capitalist class to conform to codes set up and supervised by the state. Marx, on the other hand, feared the might of the German state and wanted to build up the new capitalist class as the only class capable of destroying the power of the monarchy, supported by the Church and the aristocracy.

Labor, according to Marx, must organize in Germany, but could not take control of the state until the power of the monarchy had been reduced. Marxian and Lassallean concepts were thus in violent opposition to each other, except that both included a belief in the necessity of organizing labor. Marx's plan for class war and proletarian dictatorship would be difficult to achieve in the face of Lassallean opposition. Yet the fact that Lassalle had actually organized the German workers would be of immense value if Marx could only get control of the organization. The strongest German labor leaders left were William Liebknecht and August Bebel. Both became Marxists.[6] The majority of German workers, however, remained Lassalleans. The battle in Germany would be long and the outcome uncertain.

Mazzini and Garibaldi, although they both had a feeling for the common man, were more concerned with uniting Italy into a national state than with the social problem. Garibaldi, the soldier of fortune personified, was more committed to monarchy than was Mazzini, who would have welcomed a democratic republic. Mazzini represented the aspirations of Italian youth (Young Italy) toward unification. The basic difference between them was the question of religion. Mazzini's motto was "God and the People." There was no room in Marx's philosophy for God, and none for what seemed to him the sentimental nonsense of nationalism which infected both Mazzini and Garibaldi. Marx wanted class war and the triumph of the proletariat. He would gladly have dispensed with both Garibaldi and Mazzini but for the fact that he had no other link with Italy. He would have to tolerate them until he could get rid of them. It would not be easy. Mazzini seemed the more serious obstacle to the spread of Marx's proletarian movement because of his belief in religion. Marxism was to be a religion of humanity. Other-

6. Bebel and Liebknecht attempted to increase their influence on the German workers by founding, in 1869, a journal: *Volkstaat.* See Oscar Testut, *Association Internationale des Travailleurs* (Lyons, 1870), p. 307.

worldly religions must go. Since the "romantic" Garibaldi called the papacy the "most pernicious of sects,"[7] Marx felt that Garibaldi might more safely be disregarded. The problem of Mazzini was more perplexing.

In France, Blanqui posed for Marx an almost insoluble problem: should he support Blanqui all the way or not? This would be a fateful decision. Proudhon actually aroused less hatred among potential leaders than anyone. His non-violent approach, his lack of deviousness, his compassion, were disarming. He could be ignored.

As for Bakunin—that was another matter. In the end the transplanted Russian presented a tremendous obstacle to the plans of Marx.[8] In the meantime Marx decided to use Bakunin to break the hold of Mazzini on the Italian labor movement.[9] Marx could not win in England against the trade unions and the steady growth toward democracy and reform.[10] His road to international success lay on the Continent. London could shelter his physical body. English labor did not really need Karl Marx.[11]

7. See James Guillaume, *L'Internationale: Documents et souvenirs 1864-1878* (4 vols.; Paris, 1905, 1907, 1909, 1910), I, 47. Garibaldi's proposal at the meeting of the Peace League (1867) to "abolish the papacy" was greeted with "frantic applause."

8. See Karl Marx and Friedrich Engels, *Karl Marx oder Bakunin? Demokratie oder Diktatur? Eine Kampfschrift gegen der Vorläufer des Bolschewismus* (Stuttgart, 1920), pp. 77-78. The preface to this work is by William Blos, who gives a historical summary (p. 3) of the clash between Marx and Bakunin and regards Bakunin—not Marx—as the true forerunner of the Bolshevik Revolution of 1917. The polemical nature of this work suggests some reserve in accepting at face value not only the conclusions of Blos but also the validity of some of the accusations made against Bakunin. Alexander Herzen, the Russian editor of *Kolokol*, who had known Bakunin before the trek to the West, continued to support Bakunin both ideologically and financially. He was able to exercise some restraint at times over Bakunin's tendency to go to excess in his plans and plots. Herzen was not only a highly important factor in the slowly developing Russian revolutionary movement (which must not be examined here) but also a key figure in the Western socialist story because of his association with reformers, Russian and Western. The mass of Herzen's works, his correspondence with Ogarëv, and his publications, are explored in Venturi, *Roots of Revolution, passim*, including notes.

9. Marx wrote Engels (*Briefwechsel*, III, 189) on Nov. 4, 1864, that he had just seen Bakunin for the first time in years. The Russian was now ready to give his entire attention (the Polish cause had collapsed in 1863) to socialist causes. "On the whole," said Marx, "he is one of the few people whom I find, after 16 years, not backward but forward looking."

10. Carl Landauer (*European Socialism*, I, 116) points out the importance of the backing of the Marxian movement by the powerful English trade unions. The English leaders were from the ranks of labor.

11. In Anglo-Saxon countries the open door of opportunity in both economic and political fields kept hope alive among workingmen. The development of law as a concept for the defense of the common man against arbitrary action by governmental agencies was another strong factor.

How Karl Marx could lead the continental workers toward his own goals of revolution and Communist dictatorship of the proletariat was not yet clear. The principal task of the moment was to destroy the movement of conspiratorial anarchism, which challenged his own authority. This meant in plain language the destruction of Bakunin. Marx came to this conclusion only gradually. In 1864 he had thought it safe to use Bakunin in Italy to undermine Mazzini's hold as patriot and social reformer. Marx recommended Bakunin to the Italian labor leaders.[12] By degrees he came to realize that this had been a mistake or was at any rate questionable; the cure was worse than the disease. It had seemed vital to draw Italian labor away from Mazzini whose motto was still "God and the People." The Italian was determined to make Italy republican. To this end he announced to his fellow-Italians: "We are founding in Italy . . . the republican alliance."[13] Mazzini's influence in Italy, however, was actually waning. After the exclusion of Austria in 1866 the major patriotic demands had been met, except for Rome. His attempt to turn the successful kingdom into a republic was somewhat coolly received by a majority of people. Other problems were now more pressing. Italians needed to become accustomed to political action, in which they had had little or no experience. The peasants in central Italy, and especially in the south, were suffering poverty and destitution. Illiterate and lacking in cohesion, it would be a long time before they grasped the idea of improvement by political means. Even brigandage seemed preferable to political sterility. This Bakunin understood and condoned. Mazzini blindly pursued his political plans and lost whatever chance he might have had with the peasants. He turned to the Masonic lodges in his attempt to make Italy a republic.[14]

12. Mazzini himself recommended Bakunin to his friends in Italy and asked them to receive him. See Mazzini, *Scritti*, LXXII, 167. Garibaldi, with his popularity, was no less an enemy of the International, regarding as dangerous and wicked its program of war on capital and its view of property and inheritance as theft. "But if the International [he said] tends to the moral and material amelioration of the working class . . . crushed by [those who enrich themselves] out of the poverty of others, I will be with the International." Quoted in Ernest Lémonon, *L'Italie économique et sociale* (Paris, 1913), pp. 258-259.

13. Mazzini, *Scritti*, LXXXVI, 45. His appeal was signed in September, 1866.

14. *Ibid.*, LXXXVI, 155, 287-296. There is some reason to believe that with the rise of more revolutionary organizations the Freemasons were beginning to seem too conservative and were declining in importance. See Romano, *Movimento socialista in Italia*, I, 176. A decade later Leo XIII did not seem to hold this opinion.

Bakunin was supposed to pick up the disaffected who for any reason, religious or otherwise, dropped away from Mazzini. Whether Bakunin's reports from Italy were true or not, certainly Marx got the impression that the Russian had accomplished the mission for which he had been sent into Italy and that Mazzini need be feared no longer.[15] He concluded that Bakunin had built up in the peninsula a machine strong enough to endanger the General Council's control of the International.[16] Marx's suspicions about Bakunin were aroused. He devoted himself from then on to ferreting out the inside story of the Russian's life and undertakings. If he could find any incriminating evidence he might use it in ousting him from the International. He was later to learn that in entrusting it to Bakunin he had let Italy slip from his grasp. Its future was uncertain but it would not be dominated by Marx.

In the meantime, before Marx's suspicions had matured, and even for some time after, while he feared making a frontal attack on Bakunin until he could be positive that it would be successful, he tried merely to build up the International, adhering to the program originally laid out. The organization had planned from the beginning to hold yearly congresses. This plan was carried out, at Geneva in 1866, at Lausanne in 1867, at Brussels in 1868, and at Basel in 1869. These congresses were attended by delegations from workers' organizations in the different countries or by persons holding individual cards, granted because the laws of such countries as Belgium and France prohibited their citizens from attending as delegates any such organizations as the International, although they might attend as individuals.

At Geneva (1866) the differences among the delegates were conspicuous. The French were divided among themselves.[17] The Blanquists

15. Romano (*Movimento socialista in Italia*, I, 358) quotes the well-known *mot*: "The Bakuninist organization is practically reduced to four persons, of whom two are at odds with the other two." The influence of Bakunin cannot, of course, be written off so lightly. Romano himself admits (I, 290) that the youth of Italy understood more easily Bakunin's romantic "preaching" than Marx's cold and logical thinking.

16. Bakunin's personal attempts to organize in Italy were brought to an end by the Italian authorities. Counterfeit money was involved in the affair. Although Bakunin was not tried for criminal action in the affair, he was expelled from the country. He went to Switzerland, which he made his home and the center of his operations until his death.

17. The French translation of the program of the International differed from the original text. Marx's statement was: "That the economic emancipation of the working classes is therefore the great end to which every political movement ought to be

were not permitted to attend.[18] Some French representatives wanted co-operative associations; some wanted to retain individual property. Various attitudes were maintained on the subject of wages. Marx wanted to emphasize the points of agreement and leave the others out.[19] The English wanted trade unions. There was a "lunatic fringe" that dreamed of some universal panacea, or opposed war, or favored the Poles, or wished to free the Slavs.

At Lausanne (1867) the main question was that of priority—whether to seek political or social reform. The Congress maintained that the two were inseparable; political emancipation was an absolute necessity.[20] Three members were elected to represent the International at the League for Peace which was to meet the week following the labor Congress. Notables who were to attend the peace conference were invited to be present at the Congress of the International. Bakunin was thus invited to attend the meeting of the International because he was a committee member of the League. He was not allowed to sit as a delegate because the peace league was not a member of the International.

Bakunin went on from the Lausanne meeting of the International to the meeting of the League for Peace, of which he was a prominent member. Here he was outshone by Garibaldi, who received a great ovation when he appeared. Garibaldi's popularity had waned (in Italy) because of the recent incident at Mentana. His sun had actually set in the peninsula. His movement had "died at Mentana."[21]

---

subordinated *as a means*." The words "as a means" were omitted from the French version. Italian and other programs copied from the French text were, of course, minus this phrase also. See Romano, *Movimento socialista in Italia*, I, 260. This meant political abstention. In the absence of political action only direct, sporadic attacks of anarchic nature would remain as a program, unless one organized merely to organize.

18. Landauer, *European Socialism*, p. 116.

19. Jean Jaurès, *Histoire socialiste*, X; Albert Thomas, *Le Second Empire 1852-1870* (Paris, 1922), p. 299. Marx was not present in person, but his views were presented.

20. James Guillaume, *L'Internationale*, I, 36. See also Thomas, *Le Second Empire*, pp. 312-313.

21. See Romano, *Movimento socialista in Italia* (I, 307), for the effect of Mentana on the Italian socialist movement. Garibaldi had made an unauthorized attack on the Pope's territory, causing widespread concern in Catholic Europe. His attack embarrassed the Italian government and annoyed Napoleon III, now constrained by his dependence on Catholic support in France to send troops once more to "defend" the papal territory. This had a chilling effect on Franco-Italian relations. It was one of the factors in the downfall of Napoleon III in France (1870).

Unable to persuade the League for Peace to adopt the social program he proposed, Bakunin left the organization (1868) and formed an Alliance of Social Democracy, with headquarters in Geneva. Claiming to have sections and branches in many countries, he made overtures to the International, hoping to have his Alliance accepted for membership. His earlier attempts to get the peace league in had been unsuccessful. Perhaps this new organization, composed of both workers and labor leaders,[22] would be more successful.

As Marx carried on his research into Bakunin's past he became more and more bitter. He found that Bakunin had founded not only an outward, visible Alliance, but was apparently head of a secret brotherhood which he used the Alliance to conceal. Marx came to the conclusion that Bakunin wanted to get into the International in order to secure greater scope for his secret activity and also to give it better protection. His bitterness grew. It took shape in a satirical indictment conceived in terms which showed both the scorn he felt for the institutions of the Catholic religion and the depth of his annoyance at Bakunin. He was more than annoyed; he was afraid. In a remarkable document he carried this bitterness and annoyance to sarcastic lengths. He likens Bakunin and his Alliance to the Pope and the Church; Locarno (Bakunin's headquarters) is called "Rome"; Bakunin is "Pope Michael" or the "Holy Father"; Fanelli (the Alliance emissary in Spain) becomes the "Antonelli of the Alliance"; Bakunin's letters are "briefs"; Jacobi (a Polish physician in Turin representing the Alliance) is a "Papal Legate." Marx's International poses as the "opposition" to the "Papal Infallibility" in Bakunin's "Church."[23] Bakunin, for his part, was not above indulging in the same sort of scornful vituperation against his alleged enemies. Bakunin claimed that a friend-turned-enemy was the originator of the secret brotherhood and was not above using any means to spread the society outside of Russia, adopting the "Jesuit system": "violence for the body, lies for

22. This Alliance was only one of many that Bakunin had sponsored after his reappearance in Europe. First he had made a great campaign for the freeing of the Slavs, publishing a manifesto to that end in Herzen's Russian journal *Kolokol*. Engels subsequently said this was a ruse of the Russian government to extend Russia's boundaries into Central Europe by freeing the Slavs of the Austrian Empire. See Marx and Engels, *Marx oder Bakunin?* p. 79. See also Bakunin, *Oeuvres* (6 vols.; 4th ed.; Paris 1902-1913), I, 209. (The Alliance is not to be confused with Bakunin's secret brotherhood.)

23. Marx and Engels, *Marx oder Bakunin?* pp. 26, 31, 36.

the soul."[24] Bakunin in one of his published works[25] spoke of Paul's "scandal of faith," his "divine folly," which restored human reason. The question would remain: faith in what? Marx thought Bakunin's hierarchy was designed to produce an elite which would be faithful and devoted to its own autocratic head—in this case, Bakunin. Marx called the top hundred in the pyramidal structure of the brotherhood the "Sacred College."

It had been decided at Lausanne that the General Council, charged with conducting the affairs of the International between yearly meetings, should sit permanently in London. This would make it easier for Marx to control the International's policies. While the Council was preparing the agenda for the Brussels meeting, to be held in 1868, Bakunin's request to have membership granted to his Alliance was received. It was refused by the General Council, which stated that membership in the International was to be accorded only to national groups and not to an international monolithic structure such as Bakunin had organized. If he would split it up, the various national segments might join.

The Brussels Congress, meeting in September, 1868, was well attended. Although more than half of them were Belgians, the delegates represented English, French, Swiss, German, Italian, and Spanish sections. Blanqui was present as an observer. Marx did not attend. César de Paepe took his place in the debates. The representatives discussed ownership of property by the whole of society, citing railroads as an example of property already coming under social control. The French and the Swiss voted against this idea, calling it "communism." They were overruled by English, Belgian, and Dutch votes.[26]

In December, 1868, Bakunin wrote Marx that in the future his first love would be the International.[27] When he learned that his request

24. Guillaume, *L'Internationale*, II, 62.
25. *Dio e lo Stato* (Milan, n.d.), p. 136.
26. Julius Braunthal, *Geschichte der Internationale* (Hanover, 1961), I, 146-147. The London *Times*, reporting this Congress, said the delegates were not just trying to bring about improvements but a complete reorganization of society and not in a single nation but in the whole of mankind. This was the most extensive aim, said the *Times*, ever contemplated by any institution, "with the exception, perhaps, of the Christian Church." Quoted in Steklov, *History of the First International*, p. iv.
27. Bakunin to Marx, Dec. 22, 1868. Guillaume, *L'Internationale*, I, 103. Carr (*Michael Bakunin*, p. 351) says Bakunin's letter was proof of sincerity and conversion "unless he is to be regarded as a consummate and calculating hypocrite."

had been turned down by the General Council he decided to decentralize his Alliance. The national sections were then admitted.[28]

So Bakunin achieved his ambition to get into the First International —to accomplish his own purposes.[29] This Marx believed. He recognized how widely disseminated the anarchist program was and how difficult it would be to destroy. Marx and Engels were still busily uncovering Bakunin's secret brotherhood,[30] which they were sure was Bakunin's chief concern. Bakunin, they said later, was undisputed head of this hierarchy reaching into every country. The "brothers" were sworn to secrecy and obedience; they knew only the members of their own particular cell.[31]

The visible Alliance made headway in Latin Europe, at least to the extent of preventing the International from organizing successfully in Italy[32] and in Spain.[33] Most of the Spaniards did not know there was

28. Guillaume, *L'Internationale*, I, 108-110. The International was growing rapidly. In France, by 1869, the number of members had reached 200,000. See Val R. Lorwin, *The French Labor Movement* (Cambridge, Mass., 1954), p. 12. The older English movement was growing with the rapid rise of industry. The working class was enfranchised there in 1867.

29. Romano (*Movimento socialista in Italia*, I, 125) says Bakunin's purpose was to "adulterate and destroy it."

30. Two letters of Bakunin (1870) are germane. "Russian affairs," wrote Bakunin, "I have in no way put aside; I have at last found good men and have founded a Russian section of our secret brotherhood." He goes on: "By the way, have you run into Marx, the secret leader of all my open enemies?" Marx, he said, had been gathering letters and documents to destroy him. There was no need to fear: "We will match our strength with his. The Spanish, Italians, French and Belgians stand with us." In a second letter, more than two weeks later, Bakunin wrote that Nechaev had "stolen his letters" and "betrayed him." Bakunin declared himself "flabbergasted." See Bakunin, *Sozial-politischer Briefwechsel mit Alexander Herzen und Ogarjov* (Stuttgart, 1895), pp. 229, 232. This correspondence was published the following year in Paris in a French translation, including preface and annotations by Michel Dragomanov.

31. Marx and Engels, *Marx oder Bakunin? passim*.

32. According to Bakunin, in other countries the proletariat was mentally on a par with the bourgeoisie and had the same attitudes; it was not so in Italy. "On the contrary," he wrote, "in Italy prevail that ragged proletariat of which Marx and Engels speak ['lumpenproletariat'], for which they, like the whole school of German social democracy, manifest their profound disdain." See Romano, *Movimento socialista in Italia*, I, 267. Romano (I, 268) says Bakunin rested his movement on the spontaneous, rural, poverty-stricken mass; and not upon the urban worker favored by Marx. Bakunin realized more clearly than Marx that the Risorgimento had represented social failure while scoring political success.

33. Lafargue, Marx's son-in-law, tried to counteract the Alliance in Spain without success. See Gerth, *The First International: Minutes of the Hague Congress of 1872 with related documents* (Madison, Wis., 1958), p. xv.

any difference between the Alliance and the International.[34]

The Congress of the International at Basel (1869) was attended by forty-eight delegates. They discussed practical questions, such as the abolition of inheritance, collectivization of property, credit, education, and other matters. The Congress declared itself in favor of political abstention[35] and was gratified at the growth in the number of French International groups.[36] Bakunin was present. Neither Marx nor Engels went. Bakunin made a great impression.[37] As the success of the Alliance with its program of violent insurrection became more and more obvious, the rivalry between the factions of Bakunin and Marx developed rapidly. Marx, successful behind the scenes in making his views prevail, had not as yet emerged as the accepted leader of the laboring man. He limited his message to the proletariat, rapidly becoming the most numerous class in the industrialized areas. Bakunin, on the other hand, with a less systematic program of stages in economic development, could appeal to all who were dissatisfied with their lot, whether peasant or proletarian, whether oppressed by landowner or capitalist, or, indeed, by the State or the Church. His espousal of direct and immediate action in brush fires anywhere gave him a decided advantage in southern Europe, including southern France.

A drastic change, however, was about to occur in the international scene. An image of Marx in the minds of the people, as champion of labor, was about to emerge as a result of the spectacular events taking place in France. Marx had not been one of the heroes of the Revolution of 1848 in Paris. His public trial and deportation had been on German soil. Denied shelter by France, unless he chose to retire to some out-of-the-way place and stay away from Paris, he had gone to London. Nevertheless it was a French event that enabled him to step into the limelight.

The Franco-Prussian war (1870-71) was the last important watershed of the nineteenth century in the general history of Europe. The destruction of the Second Empire, the creation of the German Empire under the

34. Hektor Zoccoli, *Die Anarchie: Ihre Verkünder—Ihre Taten* (Leipzig, 1909), p. 128. See also Guillaume, *L'Internationale*, I, 77; II, 54.

35. See above, p. 61 n., for the omission of the phrase "by other means" from the French and French-derived copies of the program.

36. Testut, *Association International des Travailleurs* (1870), pp. 158, 168, 169-170, 175.

37. Gerth, *First International*, p. xiv.

Hohenzollerns of Prussia, the occupation of Rome by the Italian troops of Victor Emmanuel—all these took place during the course of the war. The effects of these dramatic occurrences were to have a profound influence on the Church, the success or failure of socialism in gaining control of labor, and, specifically at this point, the outcome of the struggle of Karl Marx against rival claimants for leadership.

In the midst of the collapse of the armies of Napoleon III on the battlefield, a self-appointed committee of republicans set up a Government of National Defense which slowed but could not reverse the tide of German success. The city of Paris was invested. The capitulation of the capital necessitated the formation of an Assembly to arrange terms of peace with the victorious Germans. A plebiscite for this purpose was held and returned a majority of monarchists (not Bonapartists) to the Assembly, which did not sit in Paris. The loss of the Republic (hastily set up at the collapse of the Empire) seemed imminent. In this situation the proletariat of Paris, together with some republican bourgeoisie, rose, seized control of the city, and set up the Commune of Paris, which they separated from the rest of France. In this seizure the members of the International were in accord with the Blanquists, who had been quietly organizing for just such an opportunity.[38] There was now open war between the newly elected monarchist Assembly, representing the newly established Republic of France, and the Commune. The French troops so recently employed against the Germans were now fighting their fellow countrymen barricaded within the city, held by the Communards. The hostages in the city were put to death, including the Archbishop of Paris.[39] The Commune was defeated. Paris was restored to France. A white terror followed the red terror of the Commune. The leaders, banished, were sent to penal colonies or took shelter abroad in Switzerland, Belgium, or England. The International was proscribed in France, and the

38. This was a complete reversal of the position taken by the members of the International in Paris at the start of the war. They had at that time issued a manifesto (on July 15, 1870) in reprobation of war: "War over a question of preponderance or dynasty can only be in the eyes of workers a criminal absurdity." Quoted in Testut, *Association Internationale des Travailleurs* (1870), Appendix.

39. Blanqui was in control of Paris with popular support during the siege by the Germans. His *Patrie en danger* (Paris, 1871) was in the form of a diary which ended with his seizure. Although elected as a member of the governing group during the Commune, he was under arrest and did not participate. He was thus not involved in the execution of the hostages. Condemned to death, he was not executed but imprisoned.

police were vigilant. There were still some members in France, but they could make little headway under the circumstances. Letters from Marx, directing them what to do, laid them open to arrest.[40] The Commune had accomplished nothing in the way of cementing together the factions in French labor. Nevertheless they had participated in it in one way or another.[41]

Karl Marx, meanwhile, seizing the moment of the establishment of the Commune, came out on his own responsibility with his *Civil War in France*.[42] Lauding, in the name of the International, this revolutionary attempt, he declared that this should be the signal for a mass uprising of the proletariat in the other great capitals of Europe to seize dictatorial powers. Similar uprisings were going on in other French cities, such as Marseilles and Lyons. These attempts, largely inspired by anarchistic desires to halt the centralization of France and establish *communal* controls, were reminiscent of the communes of the Middle Ages. The movement, quite respectable when it represented the medieval bourgeoisie against the aristocracy of the country, was viewed as thoroughly disreputable when carried out by the proletarian "rabble," champions of the abolition of private property.[43]

Blanqui had led the Commune. Marx praised it. Mazzini denounced it. Bakunin had taken part in the communal uprising at Lyons.[44] Marx would not have been happy to see a whole series of communes throughout France. To him there could be only one central authority. But the Paris of the Commune was also the heart of France. He would have liked

40. Alexandre Zévaès, *De l'introduction du Marxisme en France* (Paris, 1947), pp. 57-58.

41. Jean Bourdeau (*L'Évolution du socialisme* [Paris, 1901], p. 30) said the movement began by trying to save France from the Germans, then the Republic from its enemies, and finally Paris from the Republic. He quotes Jules Guesde: "The Commune which they have tried to reduce to a movement born of siege and plight of the Republic was, in its program, its procedure and its results, the greatest socialist explosion of the century, for the universalization of property. . . . Its flag, fallen from the hands of the last soldier, was picked up by the proletarians for the entire world."

42. New York: International Library, 1933. Originally published in 1871.

43. Proudhon's views were closer to the medieval communal notions than to those of the *Communist Manifesto*. Blanquists, who dominated the Paris Commune, were neither communal nor communist, but were vaguely the product of both. See Bourdeau, *L'Évolution du socialisme*, pp. 27-28.

44. Bakunin's participation at Lyons had been almost farcical. He had taken over the city (permanently), had been locked up, rescued, and was on his way out—all in a matter of hours. Sacrificing his hair and beard for anonymity he made his way (illegally) by Genoa and Milan to Locarno, his old refuge. He was still under banishment from Italy. See Romano, *Movimento socialista in Italia*, I, 285-286.

to see the same uprising occur in Berlin and Brussels, European capitals. The downtrodden workers everywhere looked upon the Commune as a symbol of hope. That hope was associated with the name of Karl Marx, which was on everyone's tongue. The champion of labor, he was pointed out whenever he appeared in public.[45] His prestige was due more to the Commune and his *Civil War in France* than to the International. The International was less important to him, but still it must not be allowed to fall into Bakunin's hands.

Both Bakunin and Marx had profited by praising the Commune, whereas all forces of law and order everywhere had been profoundly shocked by events occurring within the city of Paris, and especially by the execution of the hostages. Mazzini by denouncing the Commune pushed the dissatisfied Italian laborers and peasants toward Bakunin.[46]

In Spain, Bakuninist influence gave impetus toward violent revolution, aroused by the spectacular Parisian attempt. In France, anarchist influence was sporadically successful. But Marx, the enemy of anarchism, had come out boldly on the side of a proletarian uprising. Similarity between these two leaders was only skin deep. Bakunin wanted to fragmentize society; he wished to destroy the State. Marx wanted to take over the State's powers; he would *socialize* the State, bringing all aspects of life under its control, destroying any institutions that opposed this idea. Marx had no intention of turning the hands of the clock back to the "simple life." Every new development of science or politics, or even of concentration of wealth, were steps in the right direction. This was the goal of the ages toward which history continued inevitably to move. He saw no anomaly in the fact that the spokesmen for the proletariat, those advocating their own leadership in taking over and subsequently controlling society, were themselves of the bourgeoisie.

The immediate task of Karl Marx was now to defeat and remove Bakunin from the International. This move he did not propose to leave to time and history. He would use his own knowledge and sagacity to accomplish this end. The weapon for the struggle was at hand; he

45. Gerth, *First International*, p. xii.

46. Engels, speaking of the dissimilarity of views among the groups in the First International, wrote that it "was inevitable that the first great success should break up [the] simple harmony of all the positions. The success was the Commune. . . ." Engels to Sorge (in New York), Sept., 1874. Quoted in Steklov, *History of the First International*, p. 253.

must pick it up and prevent Bakunin from using it against him. This weapon was the mandate system of controlling the decisions of the International.

The last Congress before the Paris Commune had been held in Basel in 1869. None was possible thereafter until 1872. Bakunin was aware that the showdown was approaching.[47] He must also have known that any systematic investigation of his past would yield ground for questioning his honesty as well as his veracity.[48]

Now, in anticipation of the Hague Congress, Marx made careful preparation. He must know in advance his exact voting strength, including the votes of those attending and the mandates they held. Writing to one of his henchmen in New York, he said: "At this Congress the life or death of the International is at stake. You yourself and at least one or two others must come. As regards sections who send no direct delegates, they can send mandates."[49]

The Congress was to be the scene of a life-and-death struggle.[50] Both Marx and Engels, who had not attended earlier congresses, would be there in person. Bakunin would not be present at The Hague. There was no way to reach the Netherlands without crossing either France or Germany; in either case he would have been apprehended. Cafiero, Bakunin's lieutenant, came to The Hague but did not attend the Congress, disavowing it for the whole of Italy.[51] Marx was armed not only with a list of votes and mandates he could count on but also with a letter, written

47. Bakunin to Herzen, Oct. 28, 1869. *Correspondance de Michel Bakounine: Lettres à Herzen et à Ogareff 1860-1874*, preface and annotations by Michel Dragomanov, trans. Marie Stromberg (Paris, 1896), pp. 291, 299n. Herzen died shortly thereafter (Jan. 21, 1870). There was no one now in Bakunin's life to counteract the evil effect of Nechaev. See Romano, *Movimento socialista in Italia*, I, 270.

48. An example of Bakunin's method appears in Guillaume, *L'Internationale*, I, 210. Bakunin claimed, according to Guillaume, that one of the German leaders (Liebknecht) had stated semipublicly that Bakunin was a Russian spy and that he, the alleged spy, being guiltless of any such enormity, had forced the German before a jury to substantiate his accusation. The jury had completely exonerated Bakunin (according to Bakunin) and forced Liebknecht to retract; Bakunin then burned the signed verdict (thus destroying the evidence).

49. Marx to Sorge, June 21, 1872. Gerth, *The First International*, p. xvi. The same sort of advice went out to all sections favorable to Marx, listing in the instructions those in whose name mandates might be made out.

50. Mehring, *Karl Marx*, p. 532.

51. Many Italians who were very anti-Marxist and favorable to Bakunin did not go to The Hague. This meant a great loss of votes for Bakunin. See Carr, *Michael Bakunin*, p. 429.

by Nechaev, which put Bakunin's honesty in question.[52] Marx's research had been successful in turning up this incriminating document *in the original*. The letter was fraudulently secured but it was genuine.

The outcome of the meeting hinged upon the acceptance or rejection of the mandates held by those in attendance. This was skilfully handled by Marx and his supporters so that all procedural and substantive matters went as Marx desired.[53] The opposition came from the Dutch, Belgians, Spanish, and Swiss.[54] All of these desired looser organization; they wished to remove power from the General Council. In a series of votes, all of which went as Marx expected, Bakunin and Guillaume were expelled from the International;[55] the General Council retained its powers;[56] the use of political activity to secure the powers of the State was approved.[57] As might have been expected the Blanquists proposed an amendment: "If the strike is one weapon in our revolutionary fight, the barricade is another, and is the most powerful of all." So Vaillant, the leading Blanquist, spoke for force. At the same time he gave his support to the measure favoring political action. Guillaume spoke, of course, for the anarchist view. He declared that the *Communist Manifesto* was the first step in an attempt to thrust the theories of the German communists upon the whole International.[58] The seat of the General Council was removed to New York.[59] An inconsequential group was chosen to direct the International's affairs from the other side of the ocean. The organization had been administered the *coup de grâce* by Karl Marx. This surprising move was dictated by several considerations. Marx wanted to get the control center established where it would be well out of the reach of his European rivals. The organization had been of service to his design in the beginning;

52. Gerth (*The First International*, p. xvii) gives an account of the affair. The Russian terrorist Nechaev, to help Bakunin, wrote a threatening letter to Bakunin's publisher's agent. In effect Nechaev told the agent to stop bothering Bakunin about the money the latter owed the agent. Marx used the letter to cast doubts on Bakunin's honesty and to suggest that he kept company with gangsters.

53. This is all perfectly obvious from the minutes. The volume of Gerth includes photographic reproductions of the entire German version (in manuscript), as well as reports sent out by William Barry to the English *Standard* and a report to the New York Council by Sorge. Guillaume also gives a day-by-day account of the transactions.

54. Zoccoli, *Anarchie*, p. 422.

55. Gerth, *The First International*, p. 231.

56. *Ibid.*, pp. 211-212.

57. *Ibid.*, pp. 285-286.

58. Steklov, *History of the First International*, p. 236.

59. *Ibid.*, p. 216.

now it had outlived its usefulness. He no longer needed it. In fact, it was getting in his way. His own position in the eyes of labor had reached such a point, as a result of his support of the French Commune in his *Civil War in France*, that he had outgrown the organization.

That the International was in reality dead after 1872 was soon apparent. An effort was made from the New York headquarters to set up a Congress for 1873, in Switzerland. Engels instructed Sorge, the new president, to arrange to throw out any Bakuninists if they should appear.[60] The meeting was a complete fiasco. Marx wrote that this was inevitable; he knew it as soon as he learned that no delegate was coming from America. This was the virtual end of the First International.[61]

The Bakuninists held a rival meeting in Geneva, calling it the Sixth General Congress of the International Workingmen's Association. Representatives were there from Great Britain, Spain, France, Holland, Italy, and Switzerland. They abolished the General Council (in New York); they discussed the incompatibility of anarchism and collectivism. "Anarchism," said the English Hales, "is the law of death; collectivism is the law of life."[62] The Bakuninist Eccarius summed up the history of the failure of Marx's International and the attempt to establish a new Bakuninist International:

The old International, the first stone of which was laid at St. Martin's Hall on the 28th of September, 1864 . . . has ceased to exist. That which we now establish is entirely distinct from it. . . . Already before the Congress of The Hague, the [General] Council was divided into two hostile parties, and when it obtained the right of exclusion, it gave the death blow to the Old Association.[63]

In the history of labor, the First International had not been without significance. It had helped to formulate ideas and practical demands of labor. It had given impetus to labor legislation and to the organization of labor unions.[64] It was the beginning of the legend of Marx. It was not the end of anarchism.

60. Guillaume, *L'Internationale*, III, 82-83.
61. Actually the Swiss were the only ones who did attend. *Ibid.*, III, 136.
62. Steklov, *History of the First International*, p. 287.
63. Lavelaye, *Socialism of Today* [1885], p. 183. The final step in the dissolution of the First International was taken in New York in 1876. The International was declared formally abolished.
64. Lewis L. Lorwin, *The International Labor Movement: History, Policies, Outlook* (New York, 1953), p. 15.

Bakunin, before the defeat of his representatives at The Hague, had tried to arouse the lethargic peasants in Italy. They were discontented but averse to new ways. Uneducated and essentially conservative, they submitted to the domination of the reactionary classes. The rural workers were especially susceptible to the guidance and leadership of the reactionary clergy. Bakunin understood this question as Marx did not. In 1872 the Russian anarchist wrote:

Today when the proletariat of the cities is waking up and organizing itself in a revolutionary way in Italy as in all other countries of Europe, the country, the compact mass of the peasants, has become the only basis on which reaction may rest for support, a basis so formidable that as long as we do not wrest it from reaction we can never triumph, we shall always be beaten by it. The whole question of the triumph of revolution is reduced to this: how to raise, how to revolutionize the peasants?[65]

The death of Mazzini eliminated not only a rival of whom Marx was anxious to be rid but also an obstacle from the path of Bakunin. The Commune in Paris had had a tremendous effect on the Italian workers. Bakunin's approval of the insurrection increased the glamour of his name. The seizure of Rome by the Italian monarchy left Garibaldi no platform of discontent from which he might arouse the crowds. His movement was an extinct volcano. Bakunin's devoted followers were few, but to Bakunin that was no obstacle, provided they were devoted. He believed that a few really committed persons had a tremendous power of leverage: "a heroic élite, with single-minded faith in the libertarian ideal" could carry the day. He compared such a conquest for social ideals with the conquest of the world for the Christian religion by the Twelve Apostles:

. . . because of the heroic madness, the absolute, indomitable, intractable character of their faith in the omnipotence of their principle and because, disdaining deception and cleverness, they waged open war, without transactions [sic] or concessions, on all who opposed religions and even those only differing from theirs.[66]

65. Bakunin to Celso Ceretti, March 29, 1872. Quoted in Romano, *Movimento socialista in Italia*, II, 378.
66. Richard Hostetter, *The Italian Socialist Movement*: I, *Origins 1860-1882* (Princeton, 1958), 90. "Deals" or "bargainings" would seem to translate Bakunin's "transactions" better.

The end of the First International left Italy free to organize its own version of socialism and make its own choice between the socialism of Marx and the anarchism of Bakunin. For the only ultimate rival of Bakunin still in the field was Marx, who would have to build slowly the less spectacular movement of workers' unions.[67] If the glamorous and public acts of Bakunin's movement ran into restraining action by the government, there was always a way to escape by retreating into the secret brotherhood, which Bakunin controlled. In 1874 the word went out from Switzerland, where Bakunin had taken refuge after the Lyons uprising, that Italians were to stage revolts all over the peninsula. These spontaneous, violent uprisings were doomed to failure, having no program other than destruction.[68] The populace failed to respond; the attempts were abortive, the leaders escaping or going to jail. The senseless deeds of violence brought a crushing weight of public opinion against the Bakuninist movement. Government action was taken against the leaders of the various insurrections. Costa and Cafiero were the principal adherents of Bakunin. Prosecution gave Costa an opportunity to transform the dock into a rostrum (*le tribunal en tribune*). In a brilliant speech which lasted two days before a crowded courtroom in Bologna, he developed the history of the movement, reading from many documents. The accused in that trial were all acquitted. In a letter of gratitude for a contribution from the parent organization in Switzerland, the group stated their belief that no compromise was possible between the reformers and the exploiters; they affirmed their intention to carry on the social revolution. "We are young [they wrote] and without any other merit

67. Guillaume, *L'Internationale*, III, 40, 55.
68. The tales of the individual risings, managed by small cliques, are almost impossible to believe. In our day (1965) we should expect a movie director to emerge from the shrubbery with an admonition to "Hold it!" The most absurd of the incidents (recorded in Neufeld, *Italy*, p. 102) involved two prominent Bakuninists, together with a "blond girl with green eyes," the three posing as an Englishman, the Englishman's cousin, and his secretary. They rented a villa and used it as headquarters for their attack. Being prematurely suspected, they tried to pull off their coup without waiting for reinforcements, from there on playing the entire affair *ad lib*. Aided by ten revolutionaries who had missed their train in Rome and so had not been taken in by the police, they seized two villages, distributed the money in the town hall to the happy villagers, converted the parish priests to their cause, and started out to seize other villages. Surrounded inevitably by troops, their enthusiasm as well as their powder dampened by rain, they were arrested and jailed. In jail, nevertheless, they organized a branch of their International Alliance among the prisoners.

than our love for the human race; but it is this which is our strength, and which sustains us in the difficult struggle in which we are engaged."[69]

Bakunin died at Berne in 1876.[70] Costa was among those who escaped from Italy when the sporadic acts of violence brought extreme repression on the part of the police.[71] The way was now open for the slow advance of Marxism, which was less violent. Acts of terrorism were less often resorted to, but did not cease. While Pius IX was in his last illness, a bomb was thrown into the funeral procession of Victor Emmanuel II, whose death preceded by a few days that of the Pontiff.

The Spanish workers, influenced by Bakunin's protégés on the one side and Marx's son-in-law, Lafargue, on the other, were still divided after the Hague Congress. The decision of the International at that crucial meeting permitted each nation to set up a controlling council for itself. The Madrid union was able to establish a national council at Valencia to try to resist the encroachments of the anarchistic followers of Bakunin.[72] Dissolution of the International by the new Spanish dictator, Castelar, wiped out the sections and the journals, but did not destroy the movement.[73]

Bakunin remains an enigmatic figure. Whether he inspired or merely rode conspicuously a wave of conspiratorial action is not certain. The only tangible evidences of his actual influence lie, first, in the careers of those who in the early years (before the Siberian episode) were moved by his essays, and, second, in the fact that Marx took him seriously as a foe to be feared. These are not substantial proofs. They demonstrate the power of the image rather than the actual power of the man. His alleged secret brotherhood could take credit for any unsolved crime, such as assassination. Such an organization can sometimes be brought into existence by claiming that it exists. Even his private letters offer no real proof. Mendacity ever shows through. He was adept at the destruction of evidence and boasted of its destruction when it could have supported his

69. Guillaume, L'Internationale, IV, 3.
70. Guillaume, at the funeral, spoke of how the Russian had been calumniated; Paul Brousse paid tribute to him in the name of the revolutionary youths of France. Ibid., IV, 32.
71. Neufeld, Italy, p. 103.
72. Marx and Engels, Marx oden Bakunin? p. 40. Four Spanish delegates had protested the decisions.
73. Guillaume, L'Internationale, III, 168.

allegations. This is disarming. It tends to blunt the sharp edge of the most critical mind.

The death of Bakunin[74] and the dissolution of his organizations removed the most serious international stumbling block from the pathway of Karl Marx. Nevertheless, all opposition to Marx had not come from delegates committed to Bakunin and anarchism. Some delegates had complained of the authoritarianism of the Marxists. The development of national unions on the Continent to replace the International might open the door to a host of younger, lesser leaders. Of the older opponents of Marx there was still in France one towering figure: the revolutionary Blanqui.

Marx and his lieutenants saw they must secure control over the whole proletarian movement. His ideas must be made to prevail. What those ideas were, expressed as basic philosophy, had been laid bare for inspection in the *Communist Manifesto*. The growth in numbers of the proletariat while becoming ever more poverty-stricken, the increase and concentration of wealth in the hands of the bourgeoisie, the development of industry in size and organization, the heightening of class conflict to the point of explosion, the subsequent taking over of the powers of the state by the leaders of the proletariat, the assumption of control over the economic structure under "proletarian dictatorship," the resulting abolition of private property—all these were predicted as inevitable. The enemies of the proletarian movement were identified: the Christian religion (especially the Catholic Church with its hierarchical structure under the papacy), the bourgeoisie, and the political state. What was not so clear was the method by which the proletariat was to accomplish the destruction of this triple-headed opponent barring its path. Seizure of the powers of the state by violent revolution would eliminate two (as well as the

74. The influence of Bakunin was passed to the Russian Kropotkin in Switzerland; through him it was introduced into the Russian group of intelligentsia who turned their backs on any program to secure constitutionalism and instead decided to go to the workers and the peasants. The question of Marx or Bakunin was left in abeyance. This Russian movement, while falling within the chronological limits of this study, is not vitally connected with the central theme: the relations between socialism and the Catholic Church under Leo XIII. This Russian phase of the rise of socialism may be profitably examined in Venturi, *Roots of Revolution*, pp. 478-506. One comment of Kropotkin, who remained in the West, is pertinent: "I was profoundly influenced by the theories of anarchism, which were beginning to be formulated in the Jura Federation, mainly through the work of Bakunin; and also by criticism of state socialism which threatened to develop into an economic tyranny even more terrible than political despotism. . . ."

property of the third). But devotion to religion was not conquerable by force. The Church, then, would be the ultimate foe. If the Church continued to ally itself with the bourgeois state and bourgeois economic and social ideology against the rising tide of proletarian hopes, revolution might overturn the whole social structure.

It was at this point that Catholic Europe saw a new personality mount the throne of Peter. Joachim Pecci was about to become Leo XIII. Would this make any difference?

THE ARGUMENT

IV. THE ELECTION OF LEO XIII

Annuntio vobis magnum gaudium: habemus papam eminentissimum et reverendissimum dominem Joachim Pecci qui sibi nomen imposuit Leonis XIII.

CARDINAL CATERINI[1]

Pius IX was already an old man when he became "Prisoner of the Vatican" in 1870. By the following year he had "seen the days of Peter,"[2] which no occupant of the Pontifical Throne had until then accomplished. The responsibilities of the office demand a man of proven capacity; the choice must fall on a member of the Sacred College; inclusion in this body guarantees in itself that one has lived long enough to demonstrate his capacities and to acquire a reputation as a leader. Popes are thus usually men of advanced age before assuming the papal crown, and the cares of office are burdensome. To the astonishment of the world as well as the Church, Pius IX remained Pope for thirty-two years.

Cardinal Pecci, in Perugia, pursued his quiet way far from the public eye. To all intents and purposes he had been "banished" by Cardinal Antonelli, Pius IX's Secretary of State. The Bishop of Perugia found himself at the antipodes from Antonelli in temperament and in the way he judged the events of the time.[3] By 1876 Cardinal Pecci had already been thirty years in continuous residence in his diocese. He had

1. Cardinal Caterini announced the election of Leo XIII to the waiting Romans.
2. St. Peter had been Bishop of Rome for twenty-five years. No Pope before Pius IX had ever occupied the Papal Throne for so long a period of time, thus "seeing the days of Peter." Two Popes have now done so: Pius IX and his successor, Leo XIII.
3. Eduardo Soderini, *Il Pontificato di Leone XIII* (3 vols.; Milano, 1932-33), I, 177. An exchange of letters reproduced in Soderini (pp. 178-180) showed Pecci what Antonelli's attitude was.

been a member of the Sacred College since 1853.[4] Studiously and charitably inclined, he had tried to administer the Perugian diocese to the
advantage of his flock in a rapidly changing world. Echoes of the sweep-
ing alterations produced by the new science and technology, as well as
reflections of the new social and economic theories of the nineteenth
century, reached his thoughtful mind. Neither the dubious programs
of the secret sect nor the sporadic acts of violence of Bakuninist cells
could escape his attention. His pastoral letters exhibited an increasing
concern that the Church meet the challenge of the day and cease to take
refuge in obscurantism.

The most notable among these pastoral letters was sent out as a
Lenten message, in 1877.[5] The Bishop of Perugia begins, in this letter,
by saying that it is unbelievers who insist that the Church and civilization
must inevitably be irreconcilable enemies of each other. The so-called
"struggle for civilization"[6]—a vague phrase—means, to some, immodest
theaters, the decline of churches, the removal of curbs on usury, filthy
press, and corrupting art. Most of the good in civilization, asserts the
Cardinal, has come through the Church. Man's wants, on various levels,
are met by various institutions: economic organization for physical needs,
lawyers for defense of rights, social organization (society) for the provision of schools, books, and publishers, the clergy for spiritual needs.
The nineteenth century, he continues, has added vast improvement in material things, such as houses and equipment. Men in society produce,
by successive developments, civilization. Does this fact necessitate throw-
ing over the Church? Does the Church want man to remain barbarous?
He quotes Montesquieu: "The Christian religion, which seems to have
no other end but to secure our happiness in a future life, also ensures
our felicity on earth." He goes on to contrast the high regard in which

4. According to Cardinal Hohenlohe, Pius IX, because of Antonelli's machinations, had
been unwilling in 1852 to receive the Perugian bishop; Hohenlohe had softened Antonelli's
animosity, he claimed, and thus was responsible for Pecci's entrance into the Sacred
College. Hohenlohe was thus virtually claiming that he alone had made it possible for
Pecci to become Pope. See Francesco Crispi, *Memoirs*, II, 406. See also Egidio Vagnozzi,
"Leo XIII and the Problem of Human Liberty," in Gargan, *Leo XIII and the Modern
World*, p. 89.

5. *A Pastoral Letter for Lent by Cardinal Pecci, now Leo XIII*, Feb. 6, 1877 (Dublin,
1878), Treasure Room, Duke University Library.

6. This is the term used to describe the quarrel in Prussia between the Church and
culture: the Kulturkampf. The specific German quarrel is referred to by historians under
its German name. Cardinal Pecci is speaking in more general terms.

labor is held by the Christian Church with the pagan scorn of it; he points out the tendency even in France of some to bow to the rich. Depicting the workingman's life of toil, even the toil of children, he criticizes the rapacity of those who are responsible for it and insists that Sunday should be a day of rest, enjoyment, and of hearing the words of the minister in church. Science has harnessed the forces of nature, freeing man from hardship; the Church cannot be an enemy of nature or of attempts to study its forces; the universe is a book. Labeling that which "calls itself civilization" as the true enemy of progress, he characterizes it as the civilization which seeks to take the place of Christianity. The Cardinal thus interprets and defends the *Syllabus*[7] of Pius IX. He inveighs against research that destroys the Bible, levels man to the brute, and shakes the foundations of moral, social, and political order. Earlier attempts to explain the *Syllabus,* Cardinal Pecci insists, were motivated by a desire not to stir up discord between State and Church over questions of nationalism, democracy, and other politically thorny matters. The Cardinal makes no mention of politics except in this indirect reference. Rather, he goes to the basic question of the relation of man to nature, knowledge, God, and the Church.

Cardinal Pecci was undoubtedly trying to pour oil on the waters troubled by the *Syllabus,* Vatican Council I, and the Kulturkampf in Germany, which was part of the aftermath of the Council.[8] To be sure, thirteen years had elapsed since the issuance of the *Syllabus,* and issues that had sharply divided the Church from the secular states had partially subsided, except in Germany. The Franco-Prussian war, in which a Lutheran state defeated a Catholic country, was partly responsible. World sympathy for Pius IX as a "prisoner" also contributed to the softening

7. The defense of the *Syllabus* by Pecci on the eve of Pius IX's death is an important fact. The Cardinal was showing how the Church protested against the moral laxity which accompanied the increasing luxury of modern living, brought about by scientific invention. He was not attacking science or invention. The encyclical thus won the admiration of the social reformers without offending Pius IX, who presently called him to Rome. Raymond H. Schmandt ("The Life and Work of Leo XIII," in Gargan, *Leo XIII and the Modern World,* p. 19) says that the Provincial Synod at Spoleto twenty-eight years earlier (1849 [Bishop Pecci had played the leading role here]) had laid the groundwork not only for the Pope's issuance of the *Syllabus* but also of his definition of the dogma of the Immaculate Conception of Mary and (in 1870) of the dogma of Papal Infallibility. Schmandt asserts that Pecci was one of thirty-four bishops consulted by Pius IX about the summoning of Vatican Council I to consider the latter dogma.

8. Wallace, *The Papacy and European Diplomacy 1869-1878,* p. 255.

of the mutual antagonism. Yet it still seemed that the Catholic Church was in a "losing feud with the whole modern world, intellectually, politically, and morally."[9] The notable thing about the Cardinal's letter was its spirit of reconciliation in combination with a sense of realism and a respect for the accomplishments of man in practical and intellectual fields.[10] This spirit, this new attitude, attracted attention, not just in the diocese of Perugia, but far beyond. As a result of this letter, Cardinal Pecci emerged from obscurity; the eyes of the Church were upon him. The letter was the turning point of his life. The power of the written word was demonstrated again in this event, as it had been demonstrated a few years earlier by Karl Marx's *Civil War in France*.

The most immediate result of the appearance of the pastoral letter was the summoning (in September, 1877) of Cardinal Pecci to the Vatican to replace Cardinal de Angelis as *camerlengo*, papal chamberlain. In this position he would be head of the Apostolic Chamber. He came to Rome and took up his residence in the Falconieri palace.[11] It would be he who would remain, by virtue of his office, close to the person of Pius IX until death should remove the Pontiff. It would be his duty to tap the forehead of the dead Pius three times with the silver hammer, pronouncing his name each time, and to proclaim: "The Pope is really dead." He would be the one to take the Fisherman's Ring from the lifeless finger. It would fall to his lot to take charge of the papal household and arrange for the holding of the Conclave. It would be his duty to bring the Ring to the Sacred College, so that, when broken, the authority over the Church would pass into that body for the duration of the Conclave. Cardinal Pecci would himself represent the Temporal Power as the whole Sacred College would represent the Spiritual Power. Money coined during the vacancy of the Holy See would bear the arms of the Pecci House. The Papal Chamberlain also would be in charge of the Swiss Guards. All administration would be in his hands, with rotating

9. Carleton J. H. Hayes, *A Generation of Materialism 1871-1900* (2nd ed.; New York, 1947), pp. 141-142.

10. Gabriel Hanotaux, *La France contemporaine* (4 vols.; Paris, 1903), IV, 271.

11. As a Cardinal, Pecci had appeared to side with neither faction in the Sacred College, intransigents or moderates, but maintained a position between the two, thus keeping a foot in both camps. See S. William Halperin, "Leo XIII and the Roman Question," in Gargan, *Leo XIII and the Modern World*, p. 106.

groups of three cardinals assisting him.[12] All of this meant that from the moment of his appointment as chamberlain all eyes would be turned in the direction of the former Bishop of Perugia.[13]

In December Pope Pius IX was taken gravely ill, and, although he rallied in January, it became apparent that he would not survive. One typical final gesture of His Holiness must be recorded. King Victor Emmanuel II suddenly fell ill and was on his death bed. Pius, distinguishing between Victor Emmanuel as man and as king, sent a priest to administer the last rites and gave permission for the burial to be in consecrated ground. The Pontiff, himself approaching his end, is reported to have said on receiving news of the King's death, "He died like a Christian, a king, and a gallant gentleman."[14]

Pius IX did not survive the Italian ruler long. His last days were saddened by the accession of Humbert I to his father's throne as king of Italy, which seemed to sanction and make permanent the removal of the Temporal Power from the Pontiff's hands.[15] He died in the thirty-second year of his pontifical reign,[16] leaving many unresolved questions in the relations of the papacy with the secular states. These issues would be waiting for his successor. On the other hand, he left an increasing respect on the part of the non-Catholic world for his sanctity.[17] The purity and devotion of his life were unquestioned.

12. *Siècle* (Feb. 8 and 9, 1878) followed an account of the life of Pius IX with a minute description of this procedure.

13. Quite different is Gambetta's description (Paul Deschanel, *Gambetta* [Paris, 1919], p. 215) of the summoning of Cardinal Pecci: ". . . from whom the old Pope, Pius IX, jealous, had tried, dying, to snatch the tiara . . . by making him *camerlengo*. . . ."

14. Friedrich Nielsen, *History of the Papacy in the Nineteenth Century* (2 vols.; London, 1906), II, 463. The memory of Pius IX was damaged unworthily by an action of one of the intransigent clergy. Pius IX had once had occasion to commend the man, a publicist. This intransigent now, as Pius was approaching death, published a violent diatribe against the Archbishop of Milan for recommending King Victor Emmanuel to the prayers of the faithful. When protest against this diatribe was made, the journal published the old letter from Pius IX, which had no connection with the current incident, making it appear that the Pope had approved the attack. See *Journal des Débats*, March 7, 1878.

15. Pius IX rallied his strength and protested the "rights of the Church to its ancient domains." Lecanuet, *L'Église de France*, p. 555.

16. Cardinal Antonelli had preceded him in death by a little over a year, having died in November, 1876. The scandal caused by the suit started by his daughter, Countess Lambertini, to secure his fortune doubtless was in Pius IX's mind when he said, "Do not speak to me any more about him."

17. The ultramontanist (and legitimist) daily in Paris (*Univers*, Feb. 10, 1878) said at his death that there were only two completely honest men in Europe, Pius IX and the

Two days after Pius IX's interment, and three days before the Conclave, Cardinal Manning met with Cardinal Franchi and some others to consider the question of the late Pontiff's successor. It was apparent to them that to choose a Pope who would reconcile the papacy to Italy would be a matter of vital necessity. They agreed on Cardinal Pecci and proceeded to work for his election.[18]

The Sacred College met daily until the Conclave. The traditions of the Church were carried out with all customary pomp. Mass was said each day for nine days (the first day being the third of the Pope's death) beginning with the Cardinal Dean as celebrant. Cardinal bishops and priests followed on succeeding days. The costumes worn by the various ranks of the clergy were somber, mostly choir robes over black serge, without lace. The Cardinals, however, wore violet mantles. According to custom the Ring was broken, as were the forms of the lead seals. The Pontiff's body lay in state, that the thousands of the faithful might pass by and kiss his feet; it was then interred temporarily, while the permanent resting place was being prepared.[19] A note was sent out to secular governments announcing the death of Pius, pointing out the heavy duties laid on the College of Cardinals, and asking for protection and assurance of tranquillity for the Conclave in selecting a successor.[20]

Count of Chambord; "now there is only one." The *Daily Telegraph* (Feb. 8, 1878) commented that Pius IX would be remembered as one of "the best of those who have worn the Triple Crown." The London *Times* (Feb. 8, 1878) attributed the importance of Pius IX as "Pope-Martyr" to the calamities through which he had passed—conspiracy, rebellion, dethronement, exile, captivity—but gave a less flattering estimate as to his capacity. The *Pall Mall Gazette* (Feb. 9, 1878), quoting the *Spectator*, pronounced Pius IX "the most successful Pope of modern times. . . ." The French press expressed views varying from eulogy to denunciation, Louis Veuillot of *Univers* (Feb. 9, 1878) going into paeans of praise. *Provinzial-Correspondenz* (Feb. 8, 1878) merely stated that Pius IX had been the first Pope to enjoy fame under the dogma of Infallibility and the last Pope to exercise temporal sovereignty.

18. Edmund Sheridan Purcell, *The Life of Cardinal Manning* (2 vols.; London, 1896), II, 551. As *camerlengo* Pecci had said to the dying Pontiff, "Holy Father, bless us all in the Sacred College, bless the whole Church." Pius IX replied: "Yes, I bless all the Sacred College and pray God may give you light that you may be able to make a good choice." See Soderini, *Il Pontificato di Leone XIII*, I, 8.

19. The removal of the bones of Pius IX to the Church of San Lorenzo Fuore le Mure in 1881 brought about an unfortunate incident. It was accomplished at night, but not without attracting a large crowd, mostly hostile. Some of them wanted to dump the bones into the Tiber. At a protest meeting against the papacy one of the extremist antipapalists said: "I spit upon the decaying corpse of the papacy." Soderini, *Il Pontificate di Leone XIII*, I, 5.

20. There had been some suggestions of going elsewhere to hold the Conclave, because

This was the first election since the loss of the Temporal Power. The Sacred College was not master in Rome.

When the Conclave assembled,[21] there was keen interest throughout Europe, not only on the part of the devout and the idly curious, but on the part of members of other faiths as well. The well-informed of whatever faith (or lack of faith) were aware of the serious nature of the problems which the new occupant of the Chair of Peter would find confronting him. The suspense was not prolonged. In two days the decision had been made. The first scrutiny produced no results; in the second, Cardinal Pecci had thirty-four votes; in the fourth he received forty-four. All then acceded.[22] The canopy remained over the throne of Cardinal Pecci; the others were removed. All the Cardinals, except the successful one, concealed their crosses under their robes.[23]

From the balcony of the Vatican, Cardinal Caterini announced the result of the election to the waiting crowd. There was a new Pope,

---

of the fear of interference. In the end the decision was to hold it as usual in Rome. See Sigmund Münz, *Aus Quirinal und Vatikan* (Berlin, 1891), p. 147. Baron Haymerle (Austro-Hungarian Ambassador to Italy [Quirinal]) wrote the Austrian government (Dec. 12, 1877): "The Italian government is determined that the future Conclave shall be free, independent and secure." The message was sent by the Austrian government to Jacobini, nuncio at Vienna. Jacobini not only wanted the Conclave to be held at Rome but wanted it to elect an Italian, a moderate, not a member of a religious order. The French Foreign Minister wrote Meglia, the nuncio at Paris, that he was persuaded that the Italian government, in its own interests, would maintain perfect order. See Soderini, *Il Pontificato di Leone XIII*, III, 39-40. On the other hand, since Crispi was in power as Minister of the Interior, it was recalled that he had said, discussing the Law of Guarantees, that the officials of the civil authority could be introduced into the papal residence if furnished with a decree from the supreme judicial magistrate (Soderini, III, 45); the Italian government let it be known, however, that it was ready to place at the disposal of the Sacred College whatever armed force it might wish (p. 46).

21. Humphrey Johnson (*The Papacy and the Kingdom of Italy* [London, 1926], p. 112) points out the change in the character and composition of the Sacred College, the beginning of its democratization indicated by the absence of many names of prestige: Medici, Farnese, Este, Guise, Lorraine, or Habsburg. There were others, of course, to take their place: Hohenlohe, Bonaparte, and Schwarzenberg.

22. The process known as *accessit* involves no ballot. Individuals announce that they are changing their votes to the one who seems to have a chance to win. The balloting itself is secret, so the successful candidate does not know who have supported or opposed him. In the days of Renaissance corruption there was a good deal of significance in this open avowal of support. The one who started the landslide would be well rewarded with appointment to various lucrative positions, largely sinecures. In modern times such corrupt practices have ceased to exist, but the process of *accessit* remains. When, as in this case, *all* have acceded, a spirit of harmony and good feeling is established.

23. During the Conclave all are on the same footing; all are equal. Each occupies a canopied throne; each wears his pectoral cross visibly; they sit in a circle, in which there is no head. The successful Cardinal now immediately becomes ruler.

Joachim Pecci, who had chosen "Leo" as his name for the duration of time; he would be Leo XIII.[24]

Cardinal Pecci was already sixty-eight years old when he was chosen to be Supreme Pontiff over the Church. He was also frail. When he received the homage of the Sacred College he was overcome. How could he confront the duties laid upon him by the Conclave? "I am a feeble old man," he protested; "I cannot assume so immense a burden! I shall collapse under it in a few days!" His tears, in fact, had rained down when he heard his name reiterated again and again as the scrutiny progressed.[25] Cardinal Franchi, then Secretary of State, and the English Cardinal Manning had been successful in persuading the Conclave to elect the one who they thought would be able to reconcile Italy and the Holy See. These supporters were afraid that the new Pope would not last the day out. Within five months Cardinal Franchi was dead; the frail Pope lived twenty-five years.

On the day of his election Leo XIII chose his arms, with the Pecci family device and the words *Lumen in coelo*.[26] On the same day he wrote a letter, his first as Pope, to his brothers, to tell them of his election to the Chair of Peter; he sent them the Apostolic Blessing and asked for their prayers.[27] These were personal acts. His public acts would be eagerly awaited by the general populace. From the moment the announcement was made that the Conclave had finished its work, and before the coronation could be held, speculation was rife. His first acts and utterances would be a clue as to the general character of his pontificate. The excitement was all the more intense because of the long lapse of time since a monarch of the Church had been crowned. It was still greater because so much depended on the attitude he would take toward the Kingdom of Italy. While the preparations were going forward for

24. Fülöp-Miller, *Leo XIII and Our Times*, p. 37.

25. Soderini, *Il Pontificato di Leone XIII*, I, 223. Cardinal Calenzio told him it was the will of God. It was from Calenzio's diary that Soderini took the description of the election.

26. *Univers*, Feb. 24, 1878. An ancient legend embodying a lion, a tree mounting to the blue sky, a star, seemed to some to be a prophecy of Malachi come true; the Pecci arms, the motto, and the name *Leo* contained all of the elements. *Univers* (July 8, 1878) discussed the legend.

27. Boyer d'Agen, *La Jeunesse de Léon XIII*, p. 22. One may imagine the pride with which he wrote: "From the Vatican."

the coronation the first wave of public opinion began to be registered. The initial response was good: the new Pope's reputation as a man of learning and moderation predisposed both conservatives and radicals to regard him in a favorable light. In the basilica, on the occasion of the election, the Italian leaders were applauding; even the Free-Thinkers and many Freemasons joined in the applause. The Italian journals took the same position of approval.

The universality of the approval does not mean that differences of opinion ceased to exist among the Romans or even among the members of the Pope's own official household. These cleavages were wide and deep. Leo was hampered in handling the crucial Italian question from the start by the pressure of those around him who had personal reasons for feeling vindictive toward the Kingdom of Italy. They could not compel him but they would try to mold him. The intransigent group in the Sacred College, who wanted the Italian question left unsettled, succeeded, after much discussion, in having the coronation ceremony set for the Sistine Chapel rather than the Vatican. The basis of their argument was that there was no real tradition to go by. No one had succeeded to the Triple Tiara since the loss of Rome. Leo chose the Sistine Chapel, as being more suitable to the times than St. Peter's.[28] According to tradition the cannon should have sounded from the Pope's fortress of Sant'Angelo and the new Pope, wearing the Triple Crown, should have appeared on the balcony of the Vatican overlooking St. Peter's Square. When the day came for the coronation the cannon did not sound; the Pope did not appear. His own account, given later in life, shows the reason:

As soon as I had received the obedience of the Cardinals I left the Sistine Chapel in order to give the blessing. The two Cardinals nearest me, Bartolini, and, if I remember correctly, Oreglia, told me it was thought best for the benediction to be given from the inner logia of the Hall of Beatification and added that the French Ambassador too was of this mind. . . . When I reached the hall I found that all had been already prepared.[29]

28. So states Eugène-Melchior de Vogüé ("Affaires de Rome," *Revue des Deux Mondes*, III [1887], pp. 815-816). It was thought by many that this coronation would be a small affair, perhaps the last such event; certainly it could not compare with the coronation of a new Italian king—in Rome itself.

29. Soderini, *Il Pontificato di Leone XIII*, II, 9. Soderini says he brought the question up with Leo in 1901; Leo gave the above account of the events of the day.

The crowd in St. Peter's Square was disappointed at not seeing the Pope. The general assumption was that Leo XIII had made the choice deliberately and had thus dampened the hopes of reconciliation.[30] The intransigents had had their way about the benediction, determined that Leo XIII should remain Prisoner of the Vatican. They pretended that there was danger of some disrespect from the waiting crowd if he gave it from the outside loggia. The Italian government claimed that if he had come out he would have found the entire Italian army on their knees before him.[31] There was actually some disorder, because of the vastness of the crowd, in spite of the efforts of the soldiers and the police. Each side blamed the other: the clergy said the disorder was the fault of the government; the Italian papers said it was all due to the clergy, trying to stir up confusion in order to persuade Europe that the Pope was not really free in spite of the protestations of the government.[32]

Unhappiness reigned in Rome because of the Pope's failure to appear. The poor of the city, too, were keenly disappointed, since there was no distribution of largesse by the Pope. Sums were collected from the government, ambassadors, and others, to keep down the expressions of discontent.[33]

The other traditions connected with the coronation were carried out: the flax was burned, the words were spoken: "Holy Father, thus passes away the glory of the world."[34] At the Vatican, on March 28, Leo XIII made the customary profession of faith and took the oath to observe the Apostolic Constitutions.[35] Two of these were especially significant, one promulgated in 1564 by Pius V and the other in 1660 by Alexander VII; they forbade the alienation of the territories of the Roman Church in any manner whatsoever.[36] The question was as to Leo's interpretation

30. G. Mollat (*La Question Romaine de Pie VI à Pie XI* [Paris, 1932], p. 372) takes this for granted.

31. *Journal des Débats*, Feb. 26, 1878. See also Soderini, *Il Pontificato di Leone XIII*, II, 6.

32. Dispatch from Rome, March 4, 1878. *Univers*, March 7, 1878. The dispatch went on to say that this stirring up of confusion was not a new move, but usually successful; it will always be claimed that "the lamb [the Church] troubles the water of the wolf [the world]."

33. *Journal des Débats*, March 2, 1878.

34. *"Pater Sancte, sic transit gloria mundi."* Joseph E. Keller, S.J., *The Life and Acts of Pope Leo XIII* preceded by a *Sketch of the Last Days of Pius IX* and *The Origin and Laws of the Conclave* (New York, 1879), pp. 259-267.

35. *Ibid.*, pp. 299-300.

36. Wallace, "Pius IX and Lord Palmerston," in Wallace and Askew, eds., *Power, Public Opinion, and Diplomacy*, p. 11.

of this obligation. Would he feel that he must recapture the Temporal Power? Would he regard the matter as a *fait accompli*? Would he continue to assert his claim but take no steps to recover the lost territory? All these questions required delicate handling. The Italian Ministry had made no move to influence the Conclave toward choosing a Pope lenient toward Italy. The usual explanation for this forbearance is that Italy was trying to prove to Europe (and the world at large) that the Italian government would both protect the Conclave and leave it free, thus demonstrating that the Temporal Power was not necessary for the Church's independence. Another explanation is that the sudden death of Victor Emmanuel II of Italy and the Russian war with the Turks endangered the cause of liberalism in Europe; this would be no time to jeopardize it still more by stirring up a new quarrel with the Church.[37]

Leo XIII realized from the beginning that there were two groups of Italians who were united on the point of wanting Rome to be the capital of a national Italy. One of these groups was still religious and devoted to the Pope as head of the Catholic Church; the other was determined to destroy the papacy and all religion.[38] Many Italians felt, however, that the Pope had been, in a sense, the prisoner of the various religious houses that filled Rome and that the right of the Pope to speak untrammeled on any question had been smothered by their presence. Italians, generally, regarded the seizure of Rome by the House of Savoy as a simple annexation of national territory similar to the French annexation of Nice and Savoy or the Prussian annexation of central Germany.[39] The view of Pius IX had been that the act was an illegal and violent seizure of property over which the papacy had ruled for a thousand years. He regarded it as a catastrophic event. There were some both inside and outside Italy who realized that rather than a catastrophe it was a blessing, however improperly it had been carried out. The Pope was released from ruling over subjects demanding nationalism and democracy, which he could not grant. Further, the problems of Roman citizens, whether lay or clerical, as citizens were now the responsibility of the secular govern-

37. Carlo Bonacina, *Storia universale della Chiesa Cattolica durante il Pontificato de Leone XIII* (Turin, Rome), p. 23.
38. Soderini, *Il Pontificato di Leone XIII*, II, 4.
39. D. Pantaleoni, "L'Italia e il Papato Spirituale," *Nuova Antologia*, XV (Nov., 1870), 464.

ment. The papacy could now stand above and apart from these irksome questions and take a world view.

In the Italian government there was a difference of opinion, not as to the right of the nation to take the States of the Church, but as to the proper relation between the Church and the new kingdom. The Right (*Destra*) continued to adhere to Cavour's doctrine of separation of Church and State: the Church should remain in control of faith and morals; the State should control secular matters; questions arising between them should be compromised after discussion. The Left (*Sinistra*), on the other hand, wanted to return to the old doctrine of regalism, a doctrine subordinating the Church to the State and making it a mere agent of the government. In other Catholic states in the nineteenth century, this regalist doctrine was being laid aside, and relations between Church and State were being defined in concordats.[40]

The acts and words of Leo XIII were scrutinized from the beginning to see how he would stand on the question of relations with Italy. On April 20, 1878, he made his reply to the traditional address of the Sacred College. He had now occupied the Holy See for two months and had had time to prepare his utterance. Cardinal de Pietro, papal chamberlain and dean, felicitated Leo and the Holy See on confounding their critics who had prophesied the utter destruction of the pontificate at the death of Pius IX. In his reply Leo XIII called attention to history which proves that human attacks make the situation painful and difficult but cannot destroy the institution; one should treasure no illusions, however, for the war against the papacy, he said, "continues today more implacable on every front, and uses the most unworthy and disloyal weapons."[41] He showed the same humility and fear of physical weakness which had found expression on the day of his election. He spoke of the weight of the Sovereign Keys, and said with David: "Who am I, Lord God, that Thou hast led me hither?"[42] Then, trusting that if it is God's will

40. For a view of the period under study, see D. Pantaleoni, "Libertà o giurisdizione nel regime della chiesa," *Nuova Antologia*, XXXI (Jan., 1876), 159. For a twentieth-century view, see Samuel William Halperin, *Italy and the Vatican at War: A Study of Their Relations from the Outbreak of the Franco-Prussian War to the Death of Pius IX* (Chicago, 1939), p. 30.

41. *Univers*, April 24, 1878.

42. *Quis sum ego, Domine Deus, quis adduxit me huc usque?* See T'Serclaes, *Léon XIII*, I. 196.

strength will be provided, he says confidently: "He chooses the weak of this world that he may confound the mighty."[43]

The first encyclical, *Inscrutabile Dei,*[44] characterized by a superb Latin style, set the tone for his pontificate. He bewails the evils of the day, ascribing them to the rejection of the authority of the Church: unwillingness to submit to legitimate authority, internal and bloody dissensions, insatiable desire for things temporal to the neglect of things eternal, treasonable acts committed in the name of liberty and right that lead to new revolutions. "The enemies of public order have understood this" and have concluded that the best way to "overturn the foundations of society" is to "attack the Church of God" with unflagging determination, to "render it odious and hateful," depicting it as the "enemy of true civilization." They strike also at the "supreme power of the Roman Pontiff," guardian of the "immutable laws" of welfare and justice. From this fact spring these laws in most countries which attack "the divine constitution of the Catholic Church." He deplores the confiscation of material wealth which supports the clergy in their work, and which has resulted in putting under public control the charitable institutions. He bewails the "unbridled liberty of teaching and publishing," which violates the "right of the Church to educate youth."

Leo XIII continues in the encyclical to expatiate on the service of the Church to human society in bringing it out of barbarism, abolishing slavery, protecting and encouraging the sciences and arts, especially philosophy, which he maintains is the only foundation for true interpretation of other branches of knowledge. It was the glory of the Roman Pontiff, he declares, to have been a "rampart" to protect society from falling back "into superstition and barbarism." Those who broke away from the Holy See, he asserts, such as the Orientals (the Greek Orthodox) experienced the decay both of their reputation in science and letters and of the dignity of their empire. The glory of Italy he attributes to the Roman Pontiff.

With reference to the Temporal Power, he recalls the occupation of the States of the Church by Italy and insists that the Spiritual Power, defender of liberty, must rest upon the Temporal Power. Like his prede-

43. *Infirma mundi eligit, ut confundat fortis. Ibid.,* I, 196.
44. "When by God's inscrutable design." Encyclicals are known by their first words or phrase.

cessors, especially Pius IX, he must "reprove errors" and "condemn them by apostolic censures." He defends Christian marriage and the family, in which true education must begin; he criticizes the laxity of the modern state in this regard. He predicts that the human race, in the face of so many evils and calamities, will seek "safety and prosperity in the Church," and in the "infallible authority of the Apostolic See."[45]

By "enemies of the public order," referred to in the encyclical, Leo XIII undoubtedly meant advocates of socialism, anarchism, secularism, and other groups such as the Masonic Order, although he did not specifically name them. All these were regarded by him as revolutionary. Some thought he was condemning modernism in general, and the paean of praise from the liberal press which first greeted the news of his election was replaced by less extravagant utterances. A moderate journal put it thus:

The new Pope does not resort to imprecations, he does not curse, he does not, so to speak, threaten, and in this there is a perceptible (and perhaps the only) difference from the former. But as to the condemnation of all the conquests of the modern spirit, he is absolute, decided, inexorable, almost cruel, quite as the one he succeeded. . . . The form is sweet but the substance is absolute, hard, intransigent. . . .[46]

The open war between the Church and the revolution indicated in the encyclical brought no comfort to the revolutionaries; even the moderates really found no specific mention of what they were most anxious to hear: a modus vivendi, which would permit them to be both Catholic and Italian. There was no such proposal in the carefully worded statement.[47] The breadth of kindliness and liberalism of spirit which permeated the entire encyclical, on the other hand, did not please the intransigents. The words might praise Pius IX but an attitude of recognition and acceptance of change lay beneath the words.

45. English text in *The Great Encyclical Letters of Leo XIII*, ed. J. J. Wynne (New York, 1903), translations from approved sources. Schmandt ("Life and Work of Leo XIII," in Gargan, ed., *Leo XIII and the Modern World*, p. 22) labels the *Inscrutabile Dei* "unexciting platitudes."

46. *Riforma*, quoted in T'Serclaes, *Léon XIII*, I, 213-214.

47. The *non expedit* (it is not opportune) of Pius IX had been endorsed personally by the Pontiff in 1874, at the time of the founding of the *Opera dei Congressi e dei Comitati Cattolici*. See Fausto Fonzi, *I cattolici e la società italiana dopo l'unità* (2nd ed.; Rome, 1960), p. 32. It was natural that the Catholics should await official utterance from the new Pope as to the retention or abandonment of this prescription.

Since Leo XIII had not *specified* any errors, however, the moderates continued to hope that a mild path might be pursued in his policies. For clarification of his attitude on the "neither elected nor electing" (*nè eletti nè elettori*) the Catholic Associations asked Leo his views on this dictum of Pius IX. Must they still refrain from participation in national elections, engaging only in municipal and provincial balloting?[48] Leo in reply exhorted them to continue in the same path and use "all means of press, and so forth [Leo did not specify the other means] to carry on their program."[49] This refusal to change, this clinging to the old prohibition against participation in national affairs, dampened the spirits of the moderates who had looked for a new policy.

Leo XIII had no channel of direct communication with the Italian government, but through unofficial channels some things did get done. Since Catholicism was the state religion, all appointments to ecclesiastical office and all use of property for ecclesiastical or educational purposes were under government control. Sees might remain vacant, churchmen might await appointment indefinitely, if the government did not take the trouble to act. The Church's preferences could not be made known officially. In some cases this resulted in unconscionable delay in receiving state authorization. In areas of Italy which had never been a part of the States of the Church matters might continue to be handled amicably as before. In other places it was sometimes haphazard, depending on unofficial communication between friendly persons who conveyed the Church's wishes in the matter of appointment. Through these unofficial channels there was some easing of the situation.[50]

The chasm between the papacy and the Kingdom of Italy during the lifetime of Pius IX and now under Leo XIII showed no promise

48. In December, 1866, a rescript of the Holy Penitentiary had admitted that Catholics could sit in Parliament if in taking the oath they added: "divine and ecclesiastical laws reserved," in a low voice, distinctly audible to their immediate neighbors (as eventual witnesses). One, who added it aloud, brought the expulsion of the Catholics from the Chamber, except for the liberals, who did not add the formula at all, thinking that in "the purely political field they did not need instructions from the Holy See." See Vaussard, *Histoire de la Démocratie Chrétienne*, I, 220. For Leo's refusal to alter the *non expedit*, see Angelo Gambasin, *Il movimento sociale nell'Opera dei Congressi 1874-1904. Contributo per la storia del cattolicismo sociale in Italia*, Vol. XCI, *Analecta Gregoriana* (Rome, 1958), p. 50.

49. See *Univers*, June 13, 1878. Leo XIII did not describe the program. It was, in general, religious, educational, and charitable.

50. Neufeld, *Italy*, p. 87. See also T'Serclaes, *Léon XIII*, I, 216.

of being bridged and permitted a much more rapid laicization of the state than would otherwise have been possible. The questions involved dealt primarily with religious orders, charitable institutions, public education, and civil marriage.[51] The papal exhortation to abstain from politics thrust the functions of government into the hands of radical parties. With a leftist government in control, the controversy with the Vatican would become more severe and move at a faster pace. The transfer of responsibility for secular life in Rome from the Pope to the Kingdom of Italy left charity in the Pope's hands but made social welfare the obligation of the government. Leo XIII was free to dispense charity—no one was ever turned from his door[52]—but did not have to see to it that all had work, or that housing conditions were improved, the laws obeyed, the workers protected in their right to form unions. It is doubtful whether Leo appreciated the significance of this fact.

Rumors spread that His Holiness was seeking a way to receive the financial payments provided in the Law of Guarantees. The rumors were categorically denied by *Osservatore Romano*, but there must have been some ground for them. At any rate the following year (1879) when the new Cardinals[53] gathered at Rome to receive their Red Hats the rumors reappeared. It was said that Leo was getting together a commission of Cardinals to examine the possibility of receiving the subsidy without damaging his spiritual mission. Again the rumors were denied.[54] Certainly nothing came of it. Undoubtedly the pressure of the same intransigents who had prevented Leo XIII from appearing before the Roman people on the day of his coronation continued to operate against any softening of the papal position. They wanted him dramatically rescued by the sword of an outside power which would defeat Italy and forcibly restore Rome to the Pope. Such a plan was actually cherished by the reactionary classes of France, if they could come to power.

There were some hopeful signs to encourage liberals that Leo XIII

51. Four hundred convents and the dwellings of the heads of the religious orders were confiscated. See Lecanuet, *L'Église de France*, p. 169. This was taking a long step in the direction of laicizing the schools, hitherto in the hands of the religious.

52. *Journal des Débats* (March 3, 1878), speaking of the poverty and misery in Rome, commented: "The Pope is no longer sovereign in Rome, but there is no obstacle to his being its benefactor." Thus he might have acquired greater prestige than the most skillful policy could have given him.

53. The nuncios to Paris, Madrid, Vienna, and Lisbon had been made Cardinals.

54. Letters from Rome, Oct. 4, 6, 1879. *Univers*, Oct. 5, 7, 1879.

would at least follow the path of moderation. One such sign was the publication and dissemination of his recent pastoral letter (written at Perugia) on "The Church and Civilization." Another hopeful sign appeared in his early discourses with groups of learned men who came to congratulate him on his elevation to the pontificate. He was himself a learned man, boldly attacking intellectual problems. Aware that the very words "Catholicism" and "obscurantism" had become synonymous in the public mind, he recognized a field in which the image of the Church could be altered to the great advantage of religion. His interest in archeology and natural science, aroused during his years as Viterbo and at Rome, would stand him in good stead as Pope. Anthropology and archeology had been pushing back the dawn of man's existence on earth. During the century an inevitable clash between science and religious dogma had occurred. The struggle was mounting in intensity. The adherents of science were not only anticlerical but became successively anti-Catholic, anti-Christian, antireligious, and finally atheist. Leo XIII did not fear scientific truth. He did not shut himself within a wall of dogmatic rejection of scientific change. It is typical of him that he received among his earliest visitors the archeologists and other scholars of his day. Of the inevitable triumph of truth over error, of the faith over the world, he had no doubts. He reverted constantly to the theme. One day he would lay these views before the world in an encyclical, but before undertaking this intellectual work there were other tasks that could not be deferred.

Through diplomacy Leo XIII must begin to re-establish the Church's prestige, which had suffered grievously in recent years. It was no less essential that he should denounce the Church's most powerful opponent: socialism. For socialism likewise claimed that truth must inevitably triumph over error, that its program would inevitably conquer the world.

V. THE NEW POPE AND HIS PROBLEMS

"Since Gregory VII and Boniface VIII never has a Pope left to his successor a heavier task."[1]

ANATOLE LEROY-BEAULIEU

Diplomatic courtesy demanded that the election of Leo XIII to the Holy See be communicated to the world through proper channels. Where concordats existed, communication would be either through ambassadors at the Vatican or nuncios in the various capitals. Where no such arrangements existed other channels must be sought. Since relations with both Catholic and non-Catholic states had been none too cordial since Vatican Council I, the letters of announcement might be an opening wedge for establishing more harmonious relations. It was the duty of the Cardinal Secretary of State to conduct the mass of correspondence. Cardinal Franchi, one of the principal supporters of Cardinal Pecci at the Conclave, was chosen by Leo XIII to occupy this important position, with Msgr. Vannutelli as deputy. The appointment was well received.

In a circular to the nuncios, the new Pope sought to discover how foreign governments would react to a firm but less aggressive policy on the part of the Vatican. In the case of two non-Catholic states, Russia and Germany,[2] diplomatic relations once existing with the Vatican had been severed under Pius IX. Both of these governments said that a change in policy would make re-establishment of relations easier. Leo XIII was anxious to take steps to improve the situation, although his suggestion of sending a special envoy to the German Emperor was frowned on by

1. "Un Roi et un Pape," *Revue des Deux Mondes* (May 15, 1878.)
2. Relations with Germany were disrupted as a result of the quarrel between Bismarck and the church.

certain Cardinals. In spite of this, the new Pope persisted in the attempt to open up diplomatic channels.[3]

Letters began to go out at once from the Vatican to the various heads of state. To the President of the Swiss Republic Leo XIII wrote on behalf of the Swiss Catholics. The reply stated that Catholics enjoyed, "like all faiths, a liberty guaranteed by the Constitution." The Pope wrote in similar vein to the King of Belgium and to the Tsar of Russia, especially (in the letter to Alexander) on behalf of the Polish Catholics. From the Tsar he received a reply thanking him for providing the opportunity to enter into negotiations with regard to the Poles.[4]

In the case of Italy the problem of notification would be difficult, since there was no direct communication. How was the letter to be addressed? If it were sent to the Quirinal, addressed to the "King of Sardinia," Humbert would not receive it; if it were addressed to the "King of Italy," Leo would not sign it. Someone suggested that it be sent to the Pantheon, and say simply, "To the King."[5]

Especially important was Leo XIII's letter to William I, Emperor of Germany.[6] In it he announced his accession to the "See of the Prince of the Apostles," deeming it a duty to make it "known to His Royal and Imperial Majesty," under whose "glorious sceptre live so large a number of those who profess our religion."[7] He found it cause for sorrow, he

3. Correspondence from Rome, March 8, 1878. *Univers*, March 12, 1878.

4. Correspondence from Rome, March 12, 1878. *Journal des Débats*, March 14, 1878. The exchange of letters between the Pope and the Tsar was followed, five years later, by a second move on Leo XIII's part, when Vannutelli, Deputy Secretary of State, represented the Pope at the coronation of Alexander III. A decade later, through continued negotiations at Vienna, relations were re-established between the Holy See and the Russian court. See Robert A. Graham, *Vatican Diplomacy* (Princeton, 1959), p. 69.

5. *Journal des Débats*, Feb. 28, 1878. Another diplomatic problem was the result of Pius IX having refused to receive anyone who had first gone to the Quirinal. Without reversing this precedent set by his predecessor, Leo XIII found a quiet way out of the difficulty; the Prince Imperial of Germany when calling on the Pope went from the Quirinal to the German Embassy (which was German territory) in an Italian carriage and from there to the Vatican in a German conveyance. Leo XIII received the Shah of Persia, although the purpose of his coming to Rome was to felicitate King Humbert. See *Journal des Débats*, April 22, 1878. See also Anatole Leroy-Beaulieu, *Papacy, Socialism and Democracy*, trans. B. L. O'Donnell (London, 1892), p. 39. Leroy-Beaulieu's name is signed to the lead articles of the *Débats* during this period.

6. Leo's letter of announcement was sent through the Catholic King of Bavaria, since there was no nuncio in Berlin and no ambassador in Rome.

7. William was King of Prussia as well as Emperor of Germany. Rhenish Germans annexed at the Congress of Vienna brought the number of Catholics to about two-fifths of the total population of Germany.

went on, that the good relations which once existed between the Holy
See and His Majesty had ended, and asked him to restore "peace and
tranquillity of conscience" to "that portion of his subjects." He implored
God, he said, to unite the Emperor and himself in the "bonds of Christian charity."[8]

This was the opening move to alter the relations between Germany
and the Holy See. The tone of the letter was mild and courteous and
made no mention of the Church's retracting anything said or done under
Pius IX. More important than anything said—or left unsaid—was the
Pope's assumption of the initiative.

William's reply was couched in friendly language. He congratulated
Leo on his election.[9] Later, on the occasion of an attempted assassination of the Emperor (by a socialist acting on his own initiative), Leo
took advantage of the incident to write another letter, expressing his
sympathy. Frederick, the Prince Imperial, replied.[10] It is claimed that
in Leo's letter was enclosed a copy of the *Syllabus* of Pius IX with its
denunciation of socialism. Friendly exchanges of letters cleared the air
but could not settle the fundamental issues of the quarrel between the
German government and the Church.

Cardinal Franchi lived only five months after Leo's election.[11] Cardinal
Nina succeeded him as Secretary of State. Leo XIII's letter of instructions
to his new Secretary illuminates his attitude toward the secular world
of his day, the world in which the Cardinal was to act in the name of
the Holy See. Recalling once again as in his first encyclical, *Inscrutabile
Dei*, the errors and discords in secular society, he attributed them to
the apostasy of society from Christ and His Church, the historical beacon
and only refuge promising tranquillity and salvation. The Church, he

8. Keller, *The Life and Acts of Pope Leo XIII*, p. 276. The letter is also reproduced in
the Appendix to Édouard Lefèbvre de Béhaine, *Leo XIII et le Prince de Bismarck; Fragments d'histoire diplomatiques avec pièces justicatifs* (Paris, 1898). Lefèbvre de Béhaine
was in the French diplomatic corps in Rome.

9. The original letter was in Latin. In a French version it appears in Lefèbvre de Béhaine,
Léon XIII et le Prince de Bismarck, Appendix, and in *Univers*, July 4, 1878.

10. Prince Imperial to Leo XIII (Berlin), June 10, 1878. Lefèbvre de Béhaine, *Léon
XIII et le Prince de Bismarck*, Appendix, pp. 294-295. The letter was countersigned by
Bismarck.

11. Ultramontane *Univers* (Aug. 3, 1878) attributed his death to the Italian revolution;
in making Rome the capital of Italy and thus forcing the Pope to become a prisoner, the
Italian government had made it impossible for the papal household to occupy the summer
palace in the Quirinal, where the air was more salubrious; thus Cardinal Franchi con-
tracted Roman fever and died.

insisted, still had all the necessary strength to cope with "the moral and intellectual corruption" which was poisoning society. His desire, continued Leo, was to call upon the heads of the nations not to refuse in these necessitous times the aid of the Church. Urged, he said, by apostolic charity, he wished also to extend the invitation to non-Catholic rulers, anxious that their subjects might "enjoy the beneficent influence of that divine institution." He went into the attempts to solve the German quarrel and then called attention to the problems confronting the Church elsewhere in Italy and in the East. The government of the Church was proving "most difficult" because he was "hampered by existing conditions," when he needed, as head of the Church, to "enjoy the fullest liberty" in order to carry the "beneficent action of the Church and the papacy into the heart of the society of the present day."[12]

With Protestant England there was no diplomatic contact on a regular basis; formal relations had ceased in the sixteenth century, although at times special missions had been sent to confer with the Pope.[13] Informal relations remained amicable during the nineteenth century except for a brief period following the establishment of a Catholic hierarchy there[14] and a chilling atmosphere after the promulgation of the dogma of Infallibility by Vatican Council I. Neither of these displays of irritation had any official sanction.[15]

Outside Europe the Vatican had relations with Latin America, which was Catholic, and with the colonial possessions of such Catholic states as were linked by concordats with the Holy See. This also included the colonial possessions of Italy. Leo's handling of the problems connected with these areas early established and maintained his high reputation as a diplomat.

12. Leo XIII to Cardinal Nina, Aug. 27, 1878. Keller, *The Life and Acts of Pope Leo XIII*, pp. 314-324. *Univers* (Sept. 29, 1878) also carries the letter. This is one of the important documents of Leo's pontificate.

13. An attempt to establish relations on a regular basis had been made at the beginning of Pius IX's pontificate. After extensive debate in the House of Lords such a bill was passed. So many restrictions were placed, however, around the type of person who would be acceptable in London as the Pope's representative that Pius IX sent no one. See Wallace, "Pius IX and Lord Palmerston," Wallace and Askew, eds., *Power, Public Opinion and Diplomacy*, pp. 24-25.

14. *Ibid.*, p. 45. This occurred in 1850. An Ecclesiastical Titles Bill was brought in: "To Prevent Assumption of Certain Ecclesiastical Titles in respect of Places in the United Kingdom." It was passed but not enforced and was subsequently repealed.

15. Gladstone waited until he was out of office before publishing his views on the Council. See Wallace, *The Papacy and European Diplomacy*, p. 172.

Even while the *Te Deums* were sounding at his election to the Chair of Peter the diplomatic Congress of Berlin was being convened. At this Berlin Congress, Tsar Alexander II was forced to relinquish most of his recent acquisitions won in the Russo-Turkish war. The Treaty of San Stefano, between Turkey and Russia, highly favorable to the latter, was set aside by action of the major powers of the Continent and a new agreement, less to Russia's liking, substituted. Among the questions discussed at Berlin were two of vital concern to the papacy. They show how closely the Vatican was tied into the general course of events in Europe. One question revolved around the presence of many Catholic Christians in the Near East. Their traditional protector was France. Although these eastern Catholics had fared none too well under the Turks, the papacy could not view with complacency the expansion of the Orthodox Tsar Alexander II into this area. The difficulties experienced by the Poles under Russian rule did not augur well for good treatment of additional Catholic subjects. Viewed from this angle, the Tsar's courteous reply to Leo's letter announcing his election takes on new meaning.[16]

The second question had to do with Italy. In the general scramble for territory which took place in Berlin, Italy was in an excellent position to bestow its approval upon the acquisitions of other states in exchange for recognition of Italy's occupancy of the Pope's domains. To Italy, possession of the Pope's former territories represented "rights"; to the Vatican, the same fact was regarded as high-handed seizure, never to be tolerated.[17] Bismarck refused to guarantee support to the Pope in recovering Rome. On the other hand he refused to guarantee possession of the city to Italy.[18] He would be willing to see Rome restored to the Pope by peaceful negotiations. Catholics in the German Empire

16. Fülöp-Miller, *Leo XIII*, p. 92.

17. E. L. Woodward, "The Diplomacy of the Vatican under Popes Pius IX and Leo XIII," *Journal of the British Institute of International Affairs*, III-IV (May, 1924), 132.

18. The Italian people were unhappy that Italy came away from the Congress of Berlin "empty handed" when others had received so much. They did not understand that the Italian representatives were trying to prevent other states from acting against Italy because of the "seizure of Rome." See Maurice Vaussard, *Histoire de l'Italie contemporaine* (Paris, 1950), pp. 36-37. On the other hand the French Foreign Minister, William Henry Waddington, boasted that France had come out with "empty hands," as though this were France's policy. See Albert de Mun, *Combats d'hier et d'aujourd'hui* (4th series; Paris, n.d.), III, 178. This policy of abstention from empire grabbing did not meet with the highly patriotic de Mun's approval.

had been eager for Bismarck to undertake a crusade on behalf of the papacy in its claims against Italy. Instead, the Chancellor had managed to become embroiled with the papacy in the Kulturkampf. Now he was refusing to guarantee that Italy could keep Rome, so the question was left dangling. This unresolved problem was damaging both to Italy and to the Church.

During the political and diplomatic turmoil of the Congress of Berlin Leo XIII inducted his new Secretary of State into office. A brief survey of the political scene in Catholic Europe will make clearer the diplomatic problems confronting His Holiness and Cardinal Nina.[19]

The most northerly Catholics in continental Europe were the Poles. By the time of the French Revolution they had ceased to exist as a political entity. The part added to the Habsburgs remained under Catholic control. The Poles under the Hohenzollerns were subjected to attempts to Prussianize them. While there was no deliberate attempt to interfere with their religion as such, they were very much involved in the quarrel which developed between Prussia and the Church. The major share of Poland had passed to the Romanovs. Under the rather mild personal rule of the Tsars they had not necessarily suffered as much in their religion as in the frustration of their national pride. Revolting in 1863, they were severely repressed and their situation became worse. The constant drive of Russia southward toward the Straits against the weakening Ottoman Empire was checked by Austria, but not without the assistance of two non-Catholic powers, England and Germany, at the Congress of Berlin. On the other side of Germany the Catholics of Alsace and Lorraine had passed into the hands of Prussia with the Franco-Prussian war, as had, voluntarily, the Catholic states of South Germany: Bavaria, Baden, Württemburg, and Hesse, although these last had become states of the German Reich and not Prussian possessions. Since the Empire (Reich) was set up as a federated state, these Catholic states in the south operated internally under their own laws, which were not identical with those of Prussia. All were represented in the Reichstag, the parliament of the Empire. These facts are of importance not only in discussing relations with the Catholic Church but also in

19. In later chapters such of these questions as have an important relationship with the struggle between the Catholic Church and the socialists will be examined more carefully.

examining the rise of socialism in Germany. Leo XIII, for example, could handle negotiations with the Hohenzollerns through the Bavarian nuncio, who was accredited to the Bavarian king. A socialist outlawed in Prussia might sit in the Reichstag from Baden.

The absorption, virtually completed by 1870, of the various independent states of Italy by the House of Savoy left the papacy with no direct diplomatic channel to any of these Italian areas. Formerly the papacy had had a nuncio at the court of the Bourbon King of Naples in the south, as well as at the courts of the other independent rulers in the peninsula; the Habsburg court controlled Lombardy and Venetia in the north, so the papacy had contact with them through Vienna. The unification of Italy thus produced a major change in the relations between the Vatican and the outside world.

The Iberian states were in direct diplomatic contact with the papacy. The nunciatures at Madrid and Lisbon were regarded, along with those at Paris and Vienna, as top-ranking.[20] In spite of their losses in Latin America, both Iberian states had extensive colonial possessions where Catholic missionary enterprises were actively promoted.

Belgium (as well as neighboring Luxemburg) was Catholic. Here Leo was on familiar ground. Here, where he had been nuncio, he had gained sufficient understanding, with all his mistakes as to parliamentary matters, to be able to ward off bitter controversy between Church and State.

In France Leo's diplomatic skill would be put to the severest test. In France Leo XIII and the Church would encounter all of the problems of the new age in their most developed form. France, the intellectual center of Europe, teacher of democarcy and nationalism to continental Europe, birthplace of social criticism and of socialism, was the eldest daughter of the Church. Here violent extremes met and clashed. Here the great decisions of the Western world might well be taken. The Commune of Paris was destroyed, the war with Prussia lost, the Second Empire brought to an end. France was for the moment republican by force of circumstances. The Assembly at Bordeaux, elected to bring the war to a close and arrange terms of peace with Prussia, was monarchist.

20. Graham, *Vatican Diplomacy*, pp. 122-123. The nuncios in these four capitals traditionally received the Red Hat. Leo XIII had wasted no time in appointing these representatives and in making them all Cardinals.

The French Church favored the cause of monarchy. Its leaders wanted to bring the temporary Republic to an end and set up a more conservative governmental form. The most extreme among them cherished the hope of an expedition into Italy to restore Rome to the Pope and release him from his "imprisonment" in the Vatican. The aristocracy agreed. Even the new capitalists feared republican innovations. The only question was which monarchist line to restore. The Bonapartists were discredited by failure in the war and so were not running for the moment. The monarchist Assembly was split between adherents of the Legitimists, who wanted the direct Bourbon line, and the Orleanists, favoring the descendant of Louis Philippe. A compromise agreement reached could not be carried out; the Bourbon Count of Chambord would not come without his white flag. To abandon the tricolor was obviously impossible for France. The monarchists would have to wait until the death of Chambord (who had no heirs) should enable the Count of Paris to be crowned. A sketchy constitution was devised to carry the country along until that moment should arrive. Elections held under this constitution returned a republican majority to the Chamber of Deputies. The Senate was monarchist but apparently could not remain so. France seemed about to slip from monarchist hands. Republicans feared that the President of France, a monarchist, might attempt some coup d'état. This was the situation when Leo XIII was chosen by the Conclave to become Pope. The Count of Chambord sent his felicitations to Leo; the Count of Paris attended the obsequies of Pius IX.[21] The alignment of the clerical party in France with the monarchists made the attitude of the new Pope a matter of vital importance.

Almost at once the clericals clashed with the Republic, which they still regarded as a makeshift. The clashes centered upon such questions as education, marriage, and religious orders.[22] In spite of the fact that the provisions of the Concordat of 1801 bound the French clergy to the government, which guaranteed financial support, and in spite of the common interest of the leaders of both Church and State in the imperialist adventures of the Republic, the clashes over internal problems continued without abatement. The government was more favorable to the religious

21. *Univers*, Feb. 23 and March 3, 1878. *Univers* was not only Catholic but frankly monarchist.

22. Evelyn M. Acomb, *The French Laic Laws 1879-1889* (New York, 1941), p. 65. Gambetta said in 1879 that there "are only republican and religious questions."

orders in their missionary activities than to their presence on the home front.[23]

How long the Pope could remain aloof from the French question was problematical. It would be a thorny one to pick up. So long as he cherished the notion that his rescue in Italy might come from the faithful in France, the tendency would be to delay any direct interference in the political behavior of the French clericals. To lay aside the hope of recovering Rome would bring the wrath of the intransigents in the Papal Curia.

The most pressing diplomatic problem was the one with Bismarck. The German Chancellor had refused to intervene in the First Vatican Council when the question of Papal Infallibility was under discussion. He said it was no concern of his what the Church adopted as belief unless it invaded the world of the State. Döllinger, the famous Bavarian theologian who had worked to prevent the adoption of the dogma on the grounds of history,[24] broke with the Church as a result of the issue. He decided that he could not remain in obedience to the "New" Catholic Church created by the decisions of the Council with regard to the dogma of Infallibility; he said he was still a member of the Catholic Church—the "Old" Catholic Church—and as such would deal no more with Rome and the papacy. He persuaded a number of Bavarian churchmen to go along with him in this matter,[25] and the movement spread somewhat, although strongly opposed by other churchmen who remained loyal to Rome. Treatment of Catholic communicants in Prussia was more liberal than anywhere else in Europe. The salaries of the teachers in the schools were paid by the state, whether the schools were Catholic or Protestant. There was no interference with their teaching of Catholic doctrine[26]

23. *Ibid.*, p. 65. The Opportunist Government hoped the wealthy bourgeois would support the "republic if they were promised peace and profit."

24. A good part of the opposition to the adoption of the dogma was based on the grounds that it was not opportune. Döllinger, however, was among those who denied its validity; he was the writer of the Quirinus letters, so critical of the Council. Döllinger maintained that a Pope (Honorius) had rendered a decision touching the faith, which had been subsequently rejected by an ecumenical council. The question was whether Honorius was or was not speaking *ex cathedra* when he made the error in a letter. For a discussion of the original question, see Paschini, *Storia ecclesiastica*, II, 62-63, 66, and especially 73. We are concerned here, not with the theological question, but with the historical movement growing out of Döllinger's view.

25. Döllinger signed a letter of protest together with other theologians. See Hahn, *Geschichte der Kulturkampfes*, p. 39. For the bishops the question was not academic but practical. They were the shepherds of their flocks.

26. Emperor William I in writing to the Empress Augusta (*Die Vorgeschichte des*

until the split between the "Old Catholics" and the Church occurred. Bismarck refused to dismiss the "Old Catholic" clergymen teaching in the schools; they had previously been acceptable both to the Catholic Church and to the State; Bismarck said he could see no change in their qualifications and refused to dismiss them. An open quarrel thus developed between Bismarck and the Catholics adhering to Rome. Rome, of course, supported her loyal followers.

Another source of annoyance to Bismarck was the appearance of a Catholic party—the Center Party—in the new German Reichstag, parliament of the Empire as a whole.[27] The citizens of Alsace and Lorraine sent only bishops to represent them in the Reichstag to show their disapproval at having been snatched away from Catholic France and put under Protestant Prussia. Their displeasure was primarily nationalist. Together with Polish representatives, this group was committed from the beginning to a program of helping the Pope to recover his possessions in Italy.[28] Failure of the German Empire to intervene on the Pope's behalf, together with nationalist sentiments on the part of Alsatians and Poles, developed into a consistent controversy between the Catholics and Bismarck. The rise of the Old Catholic movement added an explosive element to the situation. Bismarck undertook to chastise the Prussian Catholics, over whom he had control. Before he could secure the passage of any laws against them in Prussia he had to alter the Prussian Constitution, which guaranteed complete freedom to all religious communities in the regulation and administration of their affairs. Article 15, which

Kulturkampfes; Quellenveröffentlichen aus dem deutschen Zentralarchiv [ed. Adalheid Constabel; Introduction by Fritz Hartung; issued by the Democratic Republic of 1949 through its State Archives Section of the Ministry of the Interior], p. 34n) spoke of the parity in Prussia, in the state's dealing with the two confessions, which existed in no other state; hereinafter cited as *Vorgeschichte.*

27. In the beginning Bismarck favored the formation of the Center Party as a conservative party which would help maintain control by the Right against the liberal or radical demands of the parties of the Left, which included the Social Democrats. This approval changed to hostility as events moved toward the initiation of the Kulturkampf. For these shifts of position (and ultimate return to partnership with the Center), see Federico Chabod, *Storia della politica estera Italiana dal 1870 al 1896,* I, 165.

28. *Vorgeschichte,* pp. 29, 30, and *passim.* Empress Augusta in several letters (Sept. 8, 1870, and later) tried to persuade William to intervene in Rome in behalf of Pius IX. William in reply (Sept. 26, 1870) reminded Augusta of what he had often told her, that the Church was out of step with the progressive age; the Council and the declaration of Infallibility had been the ultimate damaging proof ("knocked the bottom out of the barrel [*dem Fass den Boden ausstiess*]"); the Pope's power would increase if he remained in Rome as "Prince of the World" and not "Prince of the Church."

contained this guarantee, was altered by adding the words: "but remain subject to the laws of the state, and to the supervision of the state as defined.by law." Article 18, in which the state had abolished its right to control the filling of ecclesiastical offices, was altered by adding: ". . . the competence of the state in regard to the preparatory education, to the appointment and to the dismissal of clerical persons . . . will be determined by laws which will likewise fix the limits of ecclesiastical discipline."[29] The Society of Jesus was expelled from Germany; other orders (unless engaged in the care of the sick) were later expelled. The way being paved by the alteration of the Constitution of Prussia,[30] a series of laws was enacted in successive May sessions of the Prussian Landtag. These laws, subsequently extended to the whole of Germany, were called the "May Laws," from the month in which they were enacted, or "Falk Laws," from the name of the Minister of Public Worship.[31] The May Laws provided that the state should control the education of all clergy through the gymnasium and university and examine them at the end of the course; they gave the state authority to veto clerical appointments; they prohibited the Church from using any means of punishment except in the spiritual sphere; they permitted the state to imprison or expel recalcitrant clergymen. A special tribunal was set up to handle cases arising from these laws.[32] Without bishops in several sees, pulpits in many areas remained vacant. Thousands of German

29. Günter Dettmer, *Die Ost-und Westpreussischen Verwaltungs behörden im Kulturkampf* (Heidelberg, 1958), p. 52. The articles were altered in 1873 and were removed from the Constitution in 1875. The privileged position of religions was ended. See also Kurt Eggers, *Rome gegen Reich* (Stuttgart, 1937), p. 43. See also Wallace, *The Papacy and European Diplomacy,* pp. 207-208. Bismarck, in the effort to get the upper house (*Herrenhaus*) to make the constitutional changes, said (May 10, 1873) that the papacy had become a world political power mixing spiritual matters with secular affairs. He insisted that the quarrel was between the Pope and the Emperor.

30. These articles of special privilege had never been incorporated into the Constitution of the Empire. Therefore no changes in it were required.

31. Bismarck called Falk to replace Mühler as Minister of Public Worship when he decided to press the issue against the Catholics, in order to "re-establish the right of the state over against the Church and to do so with the least possible noise." See Renate Ruhenstroth-Bauer, *Bismarck und Falk im Kulturkampf* (Heidelberg, 1944), p. 23. Empress Augusta had warned the Emperor early in the struggle (May 21, 1872) that an attack on the religious orders would be interpreted as a further attack on the Church, and thought it necessary "to take into consideration the whole situation and the dangers of the future." *Vorgeschichte,* p. 250.

32. Archbishop Ledochowski of Posen was imprisoned; Conrad Martin of Paderborn was deprived of his See; religious orders were dissolved.

Catholics were presently without religious care. In many places there was no one to administer the sacraments.

Another source of irritation arose over the question of Prussia's ambassador to the Holy See. Bismarck's attempt to appoint Cardinal Prince von Hohenlohe did not meet with approval at the Vatican and the post was left vacant.[33]

There was no debate between the Holy See and the German government. There was no channel for any such debate, or for any communication. There was no nuncio in Berlin, no ambassador from Germany at the Vatican. Prussia, or the German Empire, passed laws; the laws were enforced; the German bishops refused to follow new rules laid down without consultation between Germany and the Holy See. No new appointments were made to vacant sees, no teachers to vacancies in the seminaries. The training of new clergy was practically halted. The Pope knew what Bismarck was saying because the Chancellor's speeches in the Landtag or Reichstag were reported in the papers. Addresses made by the Pope to groups of pilgrims at the Vatican were similarly reported in the press. Pius IX did make one effort to halt the struggle: he wrote a private letter to the Emperor, saying that he understood the legislation enacted in Germany had not met with the Emperor's approval. William I replied courteously, saying that to his deep regret his Catholic subjects for two years had been maintaining an organized political party, supported by the higher clergy, and had taken a position of defiance against the laws of the state. The Emperor added that the controversy had been started by the Pope's own supporters.[34]

The name "Kulturkampf" was first given in a speech in the Prussian Landtag on January 17, 1873, by a Progressive member; it was to be a struggle of modern, liberal, scientific culture against ecclesiastical slavery and medieval obscurantism. The name was not used by the government or official press until much later, because of reluctance to admit that the war was against the Catholic Church itself.[35] The quarrel was much too broad to be confined to an altercation among Germans. As he

33. *Memoirs of Prince Chlodwig of Hohenlohe-Schillingsfürst*, ed. Friedrich Curtius (English ed., ed. George W. Chrystal; 2 vols.; New York, 1906), II, 72; hereinafter cited as Hohenlohe, *Memoirs*. See also Ludwig Hahn, *Geschichte des Kulturkampfes im Preussen* (Berlin, 1881), p. 71.
34. Letters quoted in Hahn, *Geschichte des Kulturkampfes*, p. 131.
35. Wallace, *The Papacy and European Diplomacy*, pp. 187-210.

warmed to the struggle Bismarck said for all the world to hear: "To Canossa we will not go. . . ."[36] Pius's reply, delivered before the German reading club in Rome, contained the words: "Who knows if a little stone may be detached from the heights to break the foot of the colossus."[37] Since neither side showed any inclination to modify its position it became obvious that solution would have to wait until either Bismarck had a change of heart or Pius IX should die. The "Josephism" of the eighteenth century had reappeared in the nineteenth. Once more the State proposed to control the Church.[38]

Pius IX viewed the imprisoned German bishops as martyrs. In an encyclical issued on February 5, 1875, he castigated the German May Laws:

For it is not to the powers of the earth that the Lord has submitted the bishops of His Church, but Peter to whom he has entrusted his sheep and his lambs. That is why no temporal power, however high, has the right to despoil of their episcopal dignity those who have been named by the Holy Spirit to administer the Church. . . . It is necessary to obey God rather than men.[39]

Bismarck, in a speech before the upper house in Prussia on April 5, 1875, bitterly attacked the Pope. He said the Church was now the Pope and nothing else. Before Vatican Council I the bishops had had a right to think for themselves independently of what the Pope thought. Since the Council, however, they had become prefects of the Pope. He compared the Pope with Peter, saying that he was not really Peter's successor for Peter was not infallible; he had sinned, repented, and wept bitterly. Bismarck ended with the words: "From the Pope, I think, we need not expect that."[40]

Conditions in Germany went, indeed, from bad to worse. German

36. *Stenographische Berichte über die Verhandlungen des deutschen Reichstags,* 1st Leg. Per., May 14, 1872, XXIV, 355f; hereinafter cited as *Verhandlungen des deutschen Reichstags.* Reference is, of course, to the famous medieval scene of the German Emperor, Henry IV, waiting in the snow, barefoot, before the Pope's door at Canossa.

37. In debating a money bill, opposed by the Catholic Center, the religious quarrel was brought in. One member (Treitschke) demanded to know from what source the threat had come of the stone which might be dislodged from the height, etc. See *ibid.,* April 14, 1874, XXXI, 780.

38. Heinrich Geffcken, *Church and State: Their Relations Historically Developed* (2 vols.; London, 1877), I, 513.

39. Emile Ollivier, *L'Église et l'État au Concile du Vatican* (4th ed.; Paris, 1879; 2 vols. in one), p. 433.

40. Geffcken, *Church and State,* I, 177 f.

laws were passed; the Church condemned them all; Germany condemned the condemnations. Under these acts of persecution the Catholics
clung more tenaciously to their faith than ever. They gathered together
under the leadership of Ludwig Windhorst, who defied Bismarck: "You
have power to torment us, to wound our hearts, you do not have power
to take our faith from us. When you have closed all our churches we
shall assemble in the forests. . . ."[41] In the beginning the Liberal Catholics
had approved the removal of the Jesuits from the German scene. Prince
Hohenlohe, whose brother was a Cardinal, objected to the anti-imperial
activities of the Society of Jesus, and insisted that he was a "Ghibelline"
and would be "till the end of the chapter";[42] later he said, "When the
Osservatore Romano, conducted by Jesuits, reminds us that no heretic
can be Emperor of Germany," that the Pope "must dethrone him and
the people drive him away"—then these are no "rash journalistic excesses," but facts of such importance that "no one can shut his eyes to
them."[43]

The later, more severe and repressive laws drew the Liberal Catholics
to the side of the Church. The bishops, for example, were now required
by oath to keep conscientiously the state's laws without reservation and
without condition. Civil marriage was now made compulsory in Prussia.
Schools conducted by the clergy were suppressed in Alsace.[44] The climax
of the struggle came when the Church ordered the clergy not to adhere
to the state's regulations, while the state, on its side, refused to pay
salaries to any who did not adhere.[45]

41. Ollivier, *L'Église au Concile du Vatican*, II, 430.

42. Prince Chlodwig zu Hohenlohe-Schillingsfurst to Prince Karl zu Hohenlohe-
Waldenburg, quoted in Hohenlohe, *Memoirs*, II, 78 ff. Imperialists were "Ghibellines" and
papal followers were "Guelphs" in the medieval quarrel between emperors and Popes.

43. *Ibid.*, II, 84 ff.

44. It is not the intention of this volume to explore—much less to settle—the eternal
question of ultimate authority as between Church and State. In the nineteenth century
the question was assuming a new aspect. The horror of twentieth-century reversions to
absolutism in a far more awful form than ever previously conceived was not yet upon
the horizon and should be excluded from our thinking. Each side, in the nineteenth
century, claimed to base its position on liberty. The Church insisted that only in truth
could liberty survive; the State maintained that only under its aegis could man be free
from obscurantism, which it said the Church interposed as an obstacle in the way of a
rational and scientific approach to the human problem. There were perfectly sincere men
on each side of the controversy; there were others who used the controversy for unworthy ends.

45. Lefèbvre de Béhaine, *Léon XIII et le Prince de Bismarck*, pp. 77-78.

The Kulturkampf was one of the most tangled series of events in the nineteenth century, involving almost every aspect of life. Politically it represented an uneasiness on the part of the Catholic south German states which had so recently joined with Prussia in creating the German Empire. They feared the might of the Prussian state, monarchist and almost absolutist, dominated by Bismarck in the name of the Hohenzollern Emperor.[46] Only the granting of universal suffrage for representation in the Reichstag had persuaded them to come in. Intellectually the Kulturkampf was an expression of mutual fear. Prussian learning in philosophic and scientific fields was pre-eminent in Europe. The "scientific view" that all questions should be subjected to rigorous intellectual investigation and rest upon research and proof was terrifying to simple souls who clung to faith; it seemed to threaten the whole structure of organized religious belief. Not only did the Catholic Church strike back, but other faiths, especially in western and northern Europe, experienced shock. Bismarck's attempt to internationalize the struggle broadened the area of direct involvement in the contest between two mighty forces. Europe resounded with the "noise" that Bismarck had been so anxious to avoid when he appointed Falk to be Minister of Public Worship. The two leaders of the antagonistic forces came to be the Iron Chancellor and the Pope.[47]

This was the intolerable situation which confronted Leo XIII upon his accession; it explains why his letter of announcement to the German Emperor was far more than a mere routine matter of courtesy. Leo was trying to find a soft spot in the state's armor by approaching William. The Emperor had been dubious about the Kulturkampf from the first. The Empress had been more than dubious.

During the first year of his pontificate, Leo XIII was discovering how manifold were the duties of one who headed so farflung and powerful an institution as the Catholic Church. No question could be picked up, examined, acted upon, in and of itself. Any tentative step anywhere on the globe would alter the internal situation in other areas. For example, the Holy Father could not consecrate a bishop to minister to the

46. Differences between the Chancellor and the Emperor were invariably resolved by Bismarck's threatening to resign, on the grounds of his "health," and his "sleepless nights." See Hohenlohe, *Memoirs*, II, 73.

47. The involvement of the socialists in this affair will become apparent in the next chapter.

Chinese, establish a hierarchy in Scotland,[48] write a letter to a German ruler, or mention St. Thomas without having the act scrutinized by French imperialists, English no-popery enthusiasts, diplomats creating new alliances, or university professors preparing their lectures. With so much hanging on every word and deed, nothing could be undertaken hastily. And yet encyclicals must be written.[49] In one which appeared before the year was out Leo took up the cudgels against the socialists.

The *Quod apostolici* appeared on December 28, 1878. The question of socialism could not be put off. Other questions might be handled through diplomatic channels, other hindrances to the Church might be tolerated for the time, but not socialism. Socialism struck at the very roots of religion.

Socialism, Leo XIII said in the encyclical, attacked "all that has been wisely decreed by human and divine laws for the protection and adornment of life." He rejected the socialist view of the equality of all men and objected to the suppression of property: ". . . they wish to snatch away and hold in common all that has been acquired by legitimate inheritance, by labor of brain or hands, and by economy." He strongly disapproved of the socialists' attitude toward marriage and refusal to recognize the sacredness of the union as an indissoluble bond, founded on the law of natural rights. In this family bond the mutual duties and rights between parents and children, masters and servants, could find fulfilment. He mentioned the attacks on the lives of kings which stemmed from this socialist group who hated royal authority. It was the religious wars of the sixteenth century, he declared, that began the attempt to "overthrow the supernatural order" and "subvert all revelation" "rationalism [of the eighteenth century] contributed to its worsening"; then "by a new impiety, unheard of even among the pagans themselves, they established governments without any regard for God and the order established by Him"; they sought the bases of their laws, not in God, but in "the multitude of the people, who, believing them-

48. The question of the hierarchy in Scotland had been arranged before the death of Pius IX; it was announced under Leo XIII.

49. The Pope was a very busy person. He never neglected private religious devotions. Audiences, not only with ambassadors and heads of state but with plain people, consumed an ever-increasing amount of time. Improvements in transportation, and in a time of general peace (no major wars were fought during Leo's pontificate) brought hordes of pilgrims and sightseers to Rome; all wanted to have an audience with the Pope. There would be little time for relaxation in writing Latin poems.

selves free from all divine sanction, have no longer wished to tolerate the imposition of laws which could be pleasing to Him." Leo declared that their system would exclude Christ from the schools and from human life; people would forget the punishment to come, and desire only happiness; this would arouse in the poor a desire for the goods of this world. "So it is not astonishing," he said, "that there is no longer tranquillity in public or in private life, and that the world has arrived almost at its utter ruin." It was the Church that protected public peace, and it was the Church's precepts which destroyed "at the root the bad seed of socialism." He believed in inequality of rights and power (not arbitrary power); he called obedience "noble," and denied the right of revolution against authority. He regarded social class distinctions as established by Providence; he described the right of ownership of property as a natural right and put robbers of property in the same category as idolaters and adulterers. The poor, according to the encyclical, should be held in honor and helped by the rich. The encyclical goes on:

Who does not see that [in paternalism] lies the best means of appeasing the long-standing conflict which exists between the poor and the rich? Reason and factual evidence show that if one neglects or rejects this means, it must necessarily follow, either that the majority of the human race may fall into deplorable condition under paganism, or that human society will be agitated by continual uprisings and saddened by these occurrences of rapine and brigandage whose spectacle has afflicted us for a long time.[50]

The encyclical becomes more positive and specific and opens up a real channel for the improvement of the lot of the worker, thus rendering him less susceptible to the blandishments of the agitator:

It is fitting to foster societies of artisans and workmen, which, under the tutelage of religion, may render the members content with their lot and lead to a quiet and tranquil life.[51]

Papal sanction was thus given in the *Quod apostolici* for the formation of unions *under the tutelage of the Church*. So Leo on the one hand

50. One recalls that Leo early in life had dealt with brigandage and rapine.
51. "*Opportunum videtur, artificum atque opificum fovere. . . .*" This is the most important clause in the encyclical; Msgr. Justin Fèvre, Protonotary Apostolic, quotes it in a letter to the nuncio in Paris, Msgr. Ferrata. See Fèvre, *La Défense de l'église en France sous Léon XIII* (2nd ed.; Paris, 1894), p. 100. Most of the encyclical is given in T'Serclaes, *Léon XIII*, I, 244-246. For a German translation see Leopold Lentner, *Der Christ und der Staat* (Vienna, 1952), p. 38.

condemned the agitators and on the other issued admonition to the Church not to neglect the problems of the poor. Leo's predecessors had condemned and denounced revolutionary agitators who wooed the worker away from obedience to Church, State, or family authority. Leo emphasizes the duty of the father to maintain discipline over the wife, while both maintain it over the children. He emphasizes the duty of those who have possessions to have concern for those who do not. This interjection of paternalism strikes a new note.

Leo XIII's encyclical, the *Quod apostolici*, drew a direct answer from the ranks of the socialists. Jules Guesde, the leading Marxist of France, wrote a reply. Addressing it

To Monsieur Leo XIII, Pope of his state, in his palace of the Vatican, at Rome. Sir: It is a socialist who addresses you, one of those "perverse men" against whom is directed . . . your "encyclical" letter, and who far from complaining about the denunciations with which you attack his "accomplices" in governmental Europe, experiences the need, as much in the name of the latter as of himself, to congratulate you on your latest epistle.

Guesde pays tribute to Leo XIII's sagacity and profound knowledge of his time. He congratulates the Pontiff also for having perceived more clearly than the political leaders of the time, that socialism is not "dead," as they have pronounced. The Pope has, rather, put the social problem in the first rank, where it belongs. Even more, he has, says Guesde, "defined socialism instead of calumniating it." It would be the basest ingratitude not to thank him for this. He applauds also Leo's understanding of the basic difference between the "community of goods" practiced by the early Christians, based on scorn of worldly wealth, and the " 'communism' or 'collectivism' of today, exclusively preoccupied with assuring to each the enjoyment of the fruits of his labor," and thanks him for explaining so clearly the difference between the Church's authoritarian, hierarchic family with the socialists' equalitarian concept based on freedom, which, says Guesde, it "could only profit you to leave in its present state of confusion."

In more direct terms Guesde, quoting passages from the *Quod apostolici*, goes on to state that the Pope is right—there are only two answers to the social problem, socialism or Catholicism, but he claims that Catholicism's answer places the burden on heaven to make up for the ills of the poor while on earth. Again Guesde quotes from the encyclical: "If the ordinances of legislators and princes sanction or command anything contrary to divine or natural law, the dignity of the Christian name, duty, and the apostolic precept proclaimed that it is necessary to obey God rather than man." This, says Guesde, is proclaiming the right of revolution, and is precisely the right claimed by the socialists.

The whole tone of Guesde's letter, designed obviously for publication rather than transmission, is one of raillery. Yet underneath the raillery is the suggestion that, however much they may differ from each other, both Leo XIII and the socialists are on the side of man in the struggle against "legal tyranny."[52]

Leo XIII's encyclical on socialism and Jules Guesde's reply in his open letter are the most direct verbal confrontation between Marxian socialism and Leo's Catholicism. The ideological chasm between the two was very deep. One was founded on the conviction that God existed. The other rejected the idea of any power higher than man. One was founded on compassion for man in this vale of tears, but more especially for his eternal soul. The other had compassion for exploited man, whose death would be his end. There would be no future life to restore the balance. One taught love; the other taught class war. Such an analysis is, of course, an oversimplification of the collision between the two antagonists. It would probably be truer to say that two world views were in a contest to win the allegiance of the mass of mankind.

In 1878 it would have been foolish to predict the outcome of the struggle. Leo XIII was just at the beginning of his mission as leader of the Catholic forces. A quarter of a century lay before him in which to develop his ideas and work out his programs. Marx, on the other hand, was near the end of his life. His work was almost done. He had largely completed his analysis of the trends of historical economic and social forces. He was convinced that sooner or later certain social results would inevitably appear. The attempt to organize the rank and file of the working class in readiness for the inevitable day must be left to his lieutenants.

Leo XIII's primary responsibility was to be the spiritual leader of all Catholics everywhere. It would be no simple task. The spiritual bonds

52. The letter is reproduced in Compère-Morel, *Jules Guesde: Le Socialisme fait homme 1845-1922* (Paris, 1937), pp. 143-145.

between him and his widely spread flock were inevitably intertwined with political and diplomatic problems. No easy solutions would be possible in these complex situations. The simplest event would have far-reaching ramifications. The assassination of Tsar Alexander II, for example, at the hands of a nihilist, smoothed the path of diplomacy between the Holy See and Greek Orthodox Russia. Both were facing a common foe in the various subversive societies. The darkening cloud of socialism in Germany would make Bismarck come to terms with the papacy in the Kulturkampf.

The new Pope understood neither democracy nor nationalism. He had had no experience with either. He regarded imperialism as a noble undertaking. Although Marxism claimed to support the legislative path to power, it rejected nationalism completely. Religion and nationalism, said socialism, merely blinded men's eyes to their real interests. As for imperialism, socialism branded it as wholly evil. Both antagonists were at the outset handicapped by their lack of understanding of these political trends. A more serious handicap for the Church was its traditional alliance with monarchy, aristocracy, and property. These allies were to be of no service to Leo XIII in any attempt to solve the social problem and keep the workingman from adopting Marxism as his religion.

It is sufficient at this point to get some idea of the seriousness and scope of the struggle between the two contestants. Montalembert had said in 1850: "There is no middle ground. Today one must choose between Catholicism and socialism." It was true. There was no middle ground. Now in 1878 there was a new Pope, learned, diplomatic, and concerned for the welfare of human society. Would he find a new method of accommodation?

At this point it is better not to seek definitive answers to any of these puzzling questions. Appraisal must wait until the events of the next decades have been depicted in a series of shifting scenes. The first of these scenes to be examined is the struggle going on in Germany between the German Empire and the papacy: the Kulturkampf.

VI. THE KULTURKAMPF

"To Canossa we will not go."

BISMARCK

The struggle between Bismarck and the Holy See is completely interwoven with the rise of socialism in Germany. Socialism was not a major
issue when the Chancellor embarked on the stormy waters of the attack
on the Catholic Church. As the dispute reached more and more alarming
proportions, the opponents, although natural allies in many ways, were
prevented from taking any concerted action against the development of
the socialist movement. Leo XIII and Bismarck both held socialism an
anathema; yet here they were in opposing camps in the Kulturkampf.
The new Pope had inherited the quarrel from his predecessor, Pius IX;
Bismarck had undertaken it deliberately and found himself wading in
deeper and deeper, first at home and then abroad, as he drew up the
principles of his international diplomacy.

The public moves in the contest were made in the course of the
debates in the Prussian Landtag[1] and in the Reichstag. Behind the scenes
diplomatic moves were made. Bismarck was rated the ablest diplomat
in Europe; Leo XIII's diplomatic ability was as yet unknown. His first
diplomatic ventures, in Belgium, had not been notably successful, probably not through lack of native ability but because of lack of knowledge
of the rules of the game, especially in a parliamentary state. A quarter
of a century had elapsed since then, during which Joachim Pecci's skill
and knowledge had had time to develop.

The quarrel with Germany could not be ignored; archbishops and
bishops were actually deprived of their sees or languished in prison; the
May Laws had been enacted and were in force; the Constitution of

1. *Herrenhaus* and *Haus der Abgeordneten* (House of Lords and House of Representatives).

Prussia had been altered; religious orders had been expelled or prevented from teaching; endowments on temporalities granted by the state to the Catholic Church had been suppressed.[2] The matter could not be allowed to rest there.

The first conciliatory move had been made: the letter of announcement of Leo's accession sent to the Emperor (via the King of Bavaria because of the disruption of relations between Prussia and the Vatican). The letter referred to the cordial relations once existing between the Holy See and the Germans. William I in his reply picked up this reference and said that peace had been obtained when the Christian subjects remained in obedience to the "authorities of the country." He hoped that Leo would use the "powerful influence" accorded by the Constitution of his Church over all its members to the end that those members hitherto neglectful of their duty might in future "be obedient to the laws of the country which they inhabit."[3]

Acknowledging William's reply of congratulations, Leo addressed a second letter to him. In it he said that churchmen would obey the nation's laws if they did not contravene their sacred obligation to the laws of the Church. He went on, ". . . for it is an incontestable maxim of our holy religion that the accomplishment of the most exact of the religious duties is united, when no obstacle is interposed, with obedience and respect for the authorities and laws of the State." The present laws, he pointed out, suppressed earlier laws guaranteeing the complete independence of the Catholic Church. The Catholics in Germany, therefore, found themselves with the "unhappy alternatives" either of refusing obedience to the new laws, or of failing in the "sacred duties which have been imposed upon them by the law of God and of the Church." He urged William to return "magnanimously to that earlier arrangement."[4]

This exchange was followed by another on the occasion of the attempted assassination of the Emperor. Leo's letter on this occasion was answered by the Prince Imperial, countersigned by Bismarck. Prince Frederick said the May Laws could not be withdrawn, for no ruler of

2. The state granted income but not ownership. Salaries paid to clergymen were a state obligation.
3. William I to Leo XIII, March 29, 1878. The letters are reproduced in Lefèbvre de Béhaine, *Léon XIII et le Prince de Bismarck*, Appendix. The originals are in Latin.
4. Leo XIII to William I, Emperor of Germany. *Ibid.*, pp. 292-293.

Prussia could yield to outside pressure in the matter of legislation; it thus lay beyond the power of the Prince Imperial and of His Holiness to appease the "war of principles"; these principles had been maintained in Germany for a thousand years; nevertheless, he was ready to negotiate as to "the difficulties stemming from this conflict" in the spirit of conciliation and peace "which the Christian faith inspires."[5] Bismarck was evidently hopeful that with the new Pope a more reasonable attitude might prevail at the Vatican. He did not intend to make a move for peace; he might listen to a proposal.

More than diplomacy was involved in the quarrel between the German government and the papacy. The right of universal suffrage first granted to the North German Confederation (before the birth of the Empire) had been extended to all Germans when national unification was achieved by the Franco-Prussian war.[6] This enabled the representatives of Alsace and Lorraine to adhere to the anti-Bismarckian Center Party. As has already been explained, one of the early points of solidarity in this group was resentment against the seizure of the Pope's possessions in Italy. As Catholics they remained devoted to the "Prisoner of the Vatican" and hoped to influence the German state to rescue him. The May Laws, when enacted, furnished another strong motive for cohesion. The center group, led by Windhorst, provided Leo XIII with an organized army of legislators, who voted as one on all measures. Windhorst could pour floods of oratory into the ears of the deputies.[7] New administrative measures against the Catholics simply increased their zeal and solidarity. Dr. Falk, the Minister of Public Worship appointed by Bismarck to carry on the struggle, became the symbol of their persecution. He could not conquer them by telling them how injurious their ways were to the welfare of the state. "The power of the Catholic clergy is so great," he had said back in 1873, "that not a word of what the Government says against them is believed by the masses."[8]

The members of the Center Party were conservative but not reactionary. As Catholics, those who had been forcibly included in the German

5. Prince Imperial to Leo XIII (Berlin), June 10, 1878.

6. Without universal suffrage the South German states would not have come in.

7. Wallace, *The Papacy and European Diplomacy*, pp. 190, 206-207. See also Geffcken, *Church and State*, II, 513.

8. Geffcken, *Church and State*, II, 513. Geffcken rightly interpreted the Falk Laws as a renewal of "Josephism," to subordinate the Church to the State.

Empire felt closer to the Catholic Church, which was international, than to the national state; their devotion as misplaced Poles or Frenchmen lay beyond the borders of Germany.[9] Those who belonged to states which had voluntarily joined the Empire were still to a large degree "particularists," more devoted to the individual state than to the Empire as a whole. They were more Catholic than German. As Catholics they would not tolerate atheistic philosophies. As Catholics they believed in peaceful procedures and were averse to anarchistic programs. As Catholics they would not consent to the abolition of private property. In their social outlook, however, they did not conform to the Conservative pattern. They frequently tended to support the claims of the workingman, partly, at least, because of charity, partly because the bishops as well as the other aristocrats were inclined to resent the rapidly rising wealth and power of the emerging industrialists.

The German Center continued to grow in the face of persecution, and Leo XIII encouraged its members to stand firm. At the end of May, 1878, in receiving a group of them he commended them for their faithfulness under oppression: "Do not allow yourselves to be conquered or split by violence or the long duration of the ills you are suffering; they will turn out in the end to the greater glory of the Church." In the July election of that year the Center Party increased its representation from 95 to 103 in a Reichstag of 397 members. Through the exchanges of letters with the royal family Leo XIII was at that time beginning the diplomatic effort to ease the situation; in his reply to the Prince Imperial he suggested that discussions be held at Rome. This seemed to Bismarck a little too much like "going to Canossa"; the Chancellor thought they should be carried on at Berlin by an envoy of the Pope.[10] The decision reached was to hold preliminary talks at Kissingen, in Bavaria, the Belgian Nuncio being empowered to represent the Church, Bismarck him-

9. The situation changed somewhat, however, when the French Republic began to adopt anticlerical laws. The day Gambetta said, "Clericalism, there is the enemy!" a great many voters in Alsace and Lorraine changed their minds and their votes in the Reichstag. See Saint-Vallier to Waddington (confidential), Berlin, May 25, 1879. *Documents diplomatiques français*, 1st Ser., II, 504-506; hereinafter cited as *D.D.F.* Saint-Vallier was Ambassador, Waddington was Foreign Minister of France. Alsace and Lorraine did not constitute a separate state in the German Empire. They had, in consequence, no legislature of their own. Nor were they a part of any separate state in the Empire. They were, however, represented in the Reichstag as citizens of the Empire.

10. Lefèbvre de Béhaine, *Léon XIII et le Prince de Bismarck*, p. 85.

self representing Germany. The Chancellor was sincerely trying to yield a little in diplomatic fashion. He tried to find some law that could conveniently be "allowed to sleep." To abrogate the May Laws would be giving up too much; they were a "matter of principle." Besides, what would the "Holy See give for such a complete change?" "It would give tranquillity of conscience to South Germans," replied the Nuncio, "and hence religious peace: an immense good which would permit the uniting of all the forces of honest persons against the enemy." Bismarck agreed that such a peace would be worth having "at any cost."[11]

While discussions were going on at Kissingen there the news arrived of the death of Cardinal Franchi and the appointment of Cardinal Nina to the office of Secretary of State. Bismarck was unhappy about Franchi's death. In talking with the Nuncio he wondered whether Leo XIII's policies would be altered by the necessary change of secretaries.[12] When Cardinal Nina's letter came it stated that the Pope wanted the situation of 1848 restored. Bismarck read the letter and commented to the Nuncio: "I am ready to give you much and *also to make you a little Canossa* . . . already it is being said that I am on the way and that if I have not gone to Canossa, it has come to me." He thought the Pontiff was offering very little in exchange.[13]

Bismarck wrote to Cardinal Nina that he hoped there might be mutual concessions; the Sovereign would never agree to alter the Prussian Constitution (at the behest of any power outside the state).[14] The Germans were seeking a modus vivendi, not a real settlement. The Nuncio pointed out that Mass was not being said because priests were in prison; religious orders were no longer able to function; socialism was not being combatted.

The possibility of peace between the Pope and Bismarck was a matter of general interest; it could not go unnoticed and was widely discussed. There was much guessing as to motives and prospects. Only two persons really knew: Leo XIII and Bismarck. The question of motive was generally viewed as connected with the rapid growth of socialism in Germany, but socialism was not the only factor. Bismarck, much later,

11. Soderini, *Il Pontificato di Leone XIII*, II, 124. The nuncio was Aloisi.
12. *Ibid.*, II, 129.
13. *Ibid.*, II, 140.
14. *Ibid.*, III, 185.

looking over these experiences, said he was in part constrained to soften his position by the fact that the quarrel was distasteful to both his colleagues and the Emperor; unwelcome cabinet crises occurred.[15] As to prospects of success in bringing about a pacification in the affair, and as to which contender would yield, opinions were as far apart as the poles. The *Journal des Débats* asked, "Will the Iron Chancellor go to Canossa?" and answered immediately, ". . . although no word has come out of the Kissingen negotiations, it is well known that the German Chancellor is not at all disposed to humiliate the crown before the tiara. To free the individual from the yoke of the State," continues the liberal journal, "as the Church purports to do, what a liberal and beautiful undertaking! The Prussian state replies that history offers no example of an empire which has ever been founded or endured by admitting such a revolutionary principle. . . . The Prussian Government has applied these theories [of the state's ultimate authority], perhaps a little brutal, but incontestably sane."[16]

On the other hand, the *Norddeutsche Allgemeine Zeitung* came out flatly:

It would be a proof of profound ignorance to believe in any change of policy on the part of the new Pope. The Pope is not buying an entente by abandoning principles on which the papacy rests. Leo XIII is renouncing nothing, not even the Temporal Power, snatched from the papacy. No more than his predecessor does he accept the revenues offered in the Law of Guarantees, although the journals allege that financial poverty is making itself felt at the pontifical court.

The journal pointed out the militant character of the Center Party, waiting for the word from Leo that he wanted peace; it was obviously Bismarck who was suing for peace because of his need for the Catholic deputies.[17]

What Leo XIII wanted was not only a return to the highly favorable conditions before the Kulturkampf began but also a vindication on the basis of principles. He was sure that time was on his side. The factors operating to drive the Conservatives into a recognition of their need for the hundred votes of the Center Party were not likely to diminish but

15. Otto von Bismarck, *Gedanken und Erinnerungen* (2 vols. in one; Stuttgart, 1898), p. 479.
16. Quoted in *Univers*, Sept. 8, 1878.
17. Quoted in *Univers*, Oct. 9, 1878.

rather to increase. The growth of socialism in Germany and the violence of the times, as evidenced by attempted assassination of rulers (an attempt had just been made on Bismarck's life), put increasing pressure on the Chancellor. The Center Party, approached by the Conservative Party to give support to its program, was willing to co-operate provided it were understood that the Catholics would not be expected to endorse any type of omnipotent state that was founded on the police rather than on law; the Center was defending the traditional rights of the Church and the state. Windhorst[18] thought that in the negotiations under way between Germany and the Church the government was not really trying to end the Kulturkampf but to destroy the Center Party.[19]

The talks going on at Kissingen revealed how far apart on matters of principles the two contenders were, and the talks soon lagged. To negotiate a peaceful settlement was not to be as easy as it had seemed. Leo XIII, however, did not limit his diplomatic moves to the Kissingen talks. He opened up other channels of communication. One such move was to instruct Msgr. Czachi, a member of the diplomatic corps, to go to the Belgian Ambassador in Rome and dictate a note expressing the Pope's pacific views; this note was to be communicated by the Ambassador to the Belgian Foreign Minister, Baron Nothomb. Czachi did as requested and the note reached Brussels. The communication outlined the steps Leo expected to take in the solution of the Kulturkampf. Baron Nothomb sought the advice of his Prime Minister before taking any steps to have it conveyed to Bismarck; he was instructed not to do so. There the matter rested.[20]

In Germany the educational problem was very real as a result of the Kulturkampf. How real and how rigid the parties were in adhering to their views was voiced by *Kölnische Zeitung*: ". . . the Prussian statesmen will never turn the schools over to the Catholic Church."[21] The Prussian Constitution of 1850, before its modification in 1850 by the Kulturkampf, not only granted freedom for religious orders but allowed the different

18. Bismarck remarked in this connection: "See what a misfortune it is to have for head of a religious party one who represents a political party." See Soderini, *Il Pontificato di Leone XIII*, II, 130.

19. Telegraphic dispatch from Berlin. *Univers*, Oct. 26, 1878.

20. Georges Goyau, *Bismarck et l'Église: Le Culturkampf 1870-1887* (4 vols.; Paris, 1922), III, 40. Thirty-five years later when the note was read it was seen to have outlined the course which the negotiations actually took.

21. Quoted in *Univers*, Dec. 5, 1878.

faiths to control education. The state paid the salaries of the teachers but left the determination of organization, personnel, and instruction to the Lutheran Church in the Lutheran part of Germany and to the Catholic bishops in the Catholic areas. Catholic religious instruction was given by Catholic priests educated in the seminaries, whch were controlled by the Catholic Church; these Catholic priests received their salaries from the state. No separation of Church and State existed in Germany. Bismarck, in 1879, described the situation to the French Ambassador in discussing how it was related to the unification movements which produced the German Empire. The Catholic areas included, in addition to the Poles, who had been taken in during the eighteenth century, some enclaves added in 1867 when Austria was excluded from the Confederation, Alsace and Lorraine taken from France in 1871, and the South German states which were in the federal Empire. The exclusion of Austria even if shorn of its non-German elements (Hungarians and Slavs) was dictated, explained Bismarck, by the desire to retain Protestant preponderance in the new Empire; he undertook the Kulturkampf, he said, in order to secure unity—out of necessity.[22]

While diplomacy was dragging along, Bismarck found himself more and more frustrated by the solid block of votes cast against him in the Reichstag by the Center Party. In May, 1878, his first bill against the socialists had been defeated by a combination of Catholic Center and the National Liberals.[23]

The important practical issue standing in the way of fruitful negotiations was the matter of clerical appointments. If the Church would agree to notify the state as to vacancies, then the state would certify the candidates and the pulpits would be filled. This filling of the pulpits would be a great and visible gain to the Catholics. After weighing the matter Leo and the Cardinals decided against it. What Bismarck had to offer, abandonment of the Old Catholics (who were no longer important, having no cohesive core) and abolishment of the ecclesiastical tribunal,

22. Saint-Vallier to Waddington, Varzin, Nov. 14, 1879, *D.D.F.*, 1st Ser., II, 582. Bismarck explained to the French Ambassador: ". . . I ask you what the Kulturkampf would have been with ten million more Catholics. . . . I would have been broken in the struggle, and the state with me. . . . I would have made real the chimæra longed for by Napoleon III, two hostile Germanies, papist in the South, Huguenot in the North."
23. The socialist Liebknecht had admitted at Ghent the previous year that the growth of the Socialist Party was in some measure due to the Kulturkampf. See Soderini, *Il Pontificato di Leone XIII*, II, 130.

were not enough. There seemed no advantage then in prolonging the
Kissingen talks. The negotiations came to a halt. As long as the Center
Party held firm, more could be gained later than Bismarck was yet
ready to concede.

In the autumn of 1878 when Bismarck was devising new moves
against the socialists, the Center Party stood squarely in his way. In the
parliamentary commission which was examining a bill to be introduced
into the Reichstag, the representatives of the Center Party sided with
the Progressives against the Conservatives and the National Liberals.
When the commission brought in its report, the Government took up
the cudgels against the socialists; the Center opposed the Government
moves. Windhorst asked the difference between "social" and "socialists";
he said he was not satisfied with the Chancellor's statement that everyone knew who a Social Democrat was and who was not; Windhorst
observed that the deliberation going on at that moment could be regarded as socialist-tinged.[24] During the course of the discussion one
deputy accused the Center Party of being in alliance with the socialists;
he said they were voting with them, and read from a placard showing
the Social Democrats how to vote for Center candidates.[25] Another
deputy took the same line two days later; he read from a handbill:

> Social Democrats! all to the polls!
> In Elberfeld our candidate won by 15,104 votes,
>   in Prell by 14,176!
> For this victory we are indebted to the Ultramontane
>   Party!
> They kept their word to us. So elect Dr. Christopher
>   Morfang![26]

Windhorst insisted that there was no alliance; he claimed the Kulturkampf had contributed to the agitation; any party had the right to take
votes wherever it could find them; he was of the opinion that adoption
of universal suffrage was responsible for the trouble.[27]

The Berlin *Post* and the *Norddeutsche Allgemeine Zeitung* maintained that Windhorst, with the aid of the clerical faction of the court,

24. *Verhandlungen des deutschen Reichstags*, 4 Leg. Per., I Sess., 1878, 10 Sitz., Oct. 11,
1878, LI, 202, col. 2.
25. *Ibid.*, LI, 234, col. 2.
26. Deputy Dernburg, Conservative. *Ibid.*, LI, 261-262.
27. *Ibid.*, LI, 263, col. 1.

was pretending to be conservative in order to defeat the Chancellor; Windhorst was only a Guelph (papal) *agent provocateur*; once Germany was reconciled with the Pope, the party would have no reason for existence.[28] Windhorst, in speaking against the Government bill, confronted squarely the question of socialist atheism. If the love of God and belief in a future life were implanted in people's hearts, there would be no success for socialism.[29] He and the Center Party continued to vote with the socialists, but were unable to prevent the passage of the antisocialist measure.

Diplomatic negotiations might be carried on in secret; the public hammer blows came in the debates in the Reichstag and in the Prussian Landtag, where also the voice of Windhorst led the Church's cause. Here in the Landtag he moved to restore the articles in the Constitution of 1850 which had been removed. Dr. Falk, author of the May Laws, on behalf of the Government asked for a vote of *No*. Windhorst's motion was voted down; he said, "If an entente were concluded between the Government and the Roman Curia,[30] we would submit completely to this arrangement, even though we should consider the concession to the state as very considerable."[31] Falk retorted that he was not talking about a concordat; modifications would be made with regard to religious orders; not a single backward step would be made in the matter of the schools. The Center did not want peace, he went on, it was fighting for the sake of the struggle; the state and the Pope wanted peace, but it could not be accomplished in the blink of an eye.[32] Windhorst's attempt to restore the situation existing before the quarrel started, although unsuccessful, actually helped the negotiations between the Vatican and the Empire because of the promise his speech had contained that whatever agreement was approved by the Pope would be accepted by the Center Party. In Rome the Curia was counting on the Emperor's favorable attitude and Bismarck's skill in finding a way out that would suit the Pope.

28. *Univers*, Oct. 20, 1878.
29. *Verhandlungen des deutschen Reichstags*, 4 Leg. Per., I Sess. 1878, 10 Sitz., Oct. 11, 1878, LI, 203, col. 1.
30. The Roman Curia is the body of congregations, tribunals, and offices through which the Pope governs the Roman Catholic Church.
31. This statement of Windhorst was a promise that the Center Party would accept any compromise agreeable to the Pope.
32. Agence Havas, Berlin, Dec. 11, 1878. *Univers*, Dec. 13, 1878.

The Center Party was momentarily encouraged in the following year by the fall of Dr. Falk, detested by the Catholics. Bismarck and Falk did not agree on an economic question relating to protectionism, a matter on which the Center had been in agreement with the Chancellor. The Reichstag voted to set up a customs barrier, the Center casting its votes for the bill. Falk was allowed to resign, ostensibly on this issue; he was replaced by Puttkamer as Minister of Public Worship. The Catholics were elated.[33] No less pleased was Bismarck. He took occasion to proclaim publicly, with reference to the Kulturkampf: "I do not ever consider conflicts as an institution which it is necessary to perpetuate, and if ways and means present themselves for sweetening the bitterness of the antagonism without involving the principles in the question . . . and if mutual knowledge gained through common action toward a common goal were achieved I would not close the opening door and refuse to enter."[34] Again he remarked: "I am not a *Kulturkämpfer* by profession." He understood that the Pope and the German state were approaching the question from entirely different points of view. He said later, in recounting his efforts to come to some solution of the quarrel, that Rome (meaning the Vatican) regarded the Evangelical dynasty and Evangelical Church as an aberration and disease which it was the task of the Catholic Church to stamp out, while he regarded the quarrel as a diplomatic struggle in which the usual procedures would be employed and a compromise worked out.[35]

It is true that Cardinal Nina, the Secretary of State, completely misunderstood the situation in Germany; he thought that the German Reichstag was entirely under the control of Bismarck; such was not the case. In the Prussian Landtag, Bismarck had a powerful voice. In the Reichstag, the parliamentary body of the Empire, whose members were chosen by universal suffrage, constitutional procedures were followed. Bismarck might persuade; he could not override.[36] He was careful, therefore, never

33. They soon decided that the new minister was no better than Falk and was just as opposed as his predecessor to altering any regulations with regard to education and the Church. See correspondence from Berlin, *Univers*, Sept. 14, 1879.

34. Goyau, *Bismarck et l'Église*, III, 81.

35. This example of hindsight occurred in 1886. See Bismarck, *Gedanken und Erinnerungen*, p. 481. Bismarck used the word "curse"; "curse" would be offensive to the twentieth-century ear; "stamp out" seems preferable.

36. In the imperial house (*Bundesrat*) Bismarck cast the seventeen Prussian votes, usually decisive.

to take a position where he could be defeated. If such an event occurred he could prorogue the Reichstag; this would be his only recourse.[37]

Since it was in the Prussian Landtag that the constitutional changes had been made and the May Laws originally passed, it would be practically impossible—against Bismarck's will—to revert to the old situation so favorable to the Catholic Church. When the Kissingen discussions came to a dead end because the Nuncio and the Chancellor's representative[38] had insufficient authority to effect any real changes, negotiations were moved to Gastein to be carried on by the Nuncio at Vienna, the very capable Cardinal Jacobini, and Bismarck himself, who was there in connection with the signing of the Austro-German treaty of alliance. Windhorst consulted Jacobini as to procedure. In the Landtag he would get no more and no less than Bismarck should choose.[39] Should he ask for everything and hold on to it, or should he compromise? In other countries the Church tolerated things not according to canon law—why not in this case? Windhorst was willing to be guided in his decisions by what the Church wanted him to do.

At Gastein agenda were worked out to be pursued in Vienna by Jacobini and the Prussian Commissioner of Public Worship. Once more the negotiations ran into irreconcilable differences on matters of principle. They broke off toward Christmas.[40] Leo XIII had relaxed on one point: communication to the Government of the names of assistants to the bishops before their installation. His Holiness knew how to relinquish a pawn in order to prevent a stalemate. Bismarck was used to maneuvering with the might of Germany behind him; his diplomacy was always made possible by the strength of the German army. Leo XIII's army was

37. This does not mean that the Reichstag controlled the cabinet or Government operations. The Government was above parties and not responsible to the legislative branch. Party power was strictly limited to the legislative process. It had no authority either to prorogue itself or to continue to sit. Such a decision would be made by Bismarck. He was too good a politician and too good a diplomat to interfere in the actual legislative process. The formation of the federal Reich had been too difficult and too costly to endanger by maladroitness. Among the cross waves, the Kulturkampf and his imperial expansion plans, he found his ship difficult to steer. See Georg Franz, *Kulturkampf: Staat und Katholische Kirche im Mitteleuropa von der Säkularisation bis zum Abschlüss des Preussischen Kulturkampfes* (Munich, 1954), p. 277.

38. Bismarck had personally conducted the negotiations during the summer; in the autumn he left matters to a substitute.

39. Goyau, *Bismarck et l'Église*, III, 104-105.

40. T'Serclaes, *Léon XIII*, I, 317.

the legions of the faithful; his weapons, those of the spirit, and he made haste to use them. Through the German bishops he succeeded in getting Catholic flocks to pray publicly for cessation of the Kulturkampf. One big meeting was assembled at Dortmund, another at Cologne, and still others in various sections of Prussia.[41] Silesia, Hanover, Poland, Eastern Prussia, and Nassau all held meetings.

Another move on Leo's part had been to communicate with the Germans through Archbishop Melchers, exiled from Cologne. This was a much more dramatic approach than to express his views through a bishop in one of the South German Catholic states, which could easily have been done. Leo XIII wrote the Archbishop a letter in which he explained how the Church was hampered and fettered and thus prevented from exercising its salutary mission in a society confronted by so many dangers. It was for this reason, he said, that he had undertaken "to call princes and peoples back to peace and friendship"; he was directing his efforts to see the end of dissensions in the "noble nation of Germans" and secure the blessings of peace "without injury to the rights of the Church"; he said he could not rest while "pastors of the Church" were "condemned or exiled," with the ministry of the priesthood "fettered in every way," the "religious communities and pious congregations overthrown and scattered, and all education, not even that of the clergy being excepted, withdrawn from the watchful care of the bishops." Parishioners, he maintained, would show themselves obedient to the laws (not inconsistent with the faith and duty of a Catholic). He implored God "to incline to more gentle counsels the illustrious and powerful Emperor of Germany," and the "distinguished personages" who were his advisers.[42]

Not only did Leo's words reach the Germans through the publication of this letter but also directly through the Archbishop himself, who went in disguise into Germany to confer with Catholic negotiators. He ran great risk of arrest in doing so. His opinion was that Bismarck would never make concessions, but that time would bring a change; when the Emperor should die he would be followed by the Prince

41. *Univers*, May 9, 1880.
42. Leo XIII to Archbishop Melchers, Dec. 24, 1878. Lefèbvre de Béhaine, *Léon XIII et le Prince de Bismarck*, pp. 332-334. Melchers was well known as a prelate suffering exile as a result of the May Laws.

Imperial, which would alter the situation, thanks to the influence of his wife, the Princess Frederick.[43] Then, thought the Archbishop, the Church would be let free, in Prussia as it had been in England.[44]

No tangible results appeared from the Gastein negotiations, but they were not abandoned. Whenever they slowed to a standstill they were gently prodded into activity again. Bismarck had his limits beyond which he did not want to go. Leo had his limits too; he did not expect to be defeated by the Chancellor and planned to get all he could out of the bargaining. He reminded a group of German pilgrims (in an audience in the Vatican) of his attempts to negotiate for peace; he was bound by his oath to the Constitutions of the Church, however, not to accept conditions incompatible with it; what he wanted was merely *quod Caesaris Caesari, quod Dei Deo*; the two powers must live in accord for the welfare of mankind.[45] Leo XIII was in a better position than the Chancellor; so long as the Center should stand firm he had a mighty weapon in his hand. He was amiable, patient, and persistent. Bismarck was more impatient. Each day saw his problems increase; he needed the Center Party votes.[46]

By now three years of Leo's pontificate had elapsed and still no solution of the Kulturkampf had been found. Both sides remained pleasant but unmoving; sees were still vacant; bishops were still in exile. The Pontiff had given in on one minor point and Germany was administering the laws with less harshness, but that was all.

On the anniversary of his election, when the Sacred College came to pay their compliments, Leo XIII replied by bewailing the parlous state of affairs with regard to the Church in all parts of the world and then announced that since help could come from no other source but heaven it was an appropriate time to emphasize progress and good works, so he was proclaiming a year of jubilee; the Church "must labor much and

43. Victoria, daughter of the Queen of England, a strong believer in constitutional monarchy. She dominated Frederick's thinking. See Frederic B. M. Hollyday, *Bismarck's Rival: A Political Biography of General and Admiral Albrecht von Stosch* (Durham, N.C., 1960), p. 41.

44. Goyau, *Bismarck et l'Église*, III, 40.

45. Dispatch from Rome, May 27, 1880. *Univers*, May 28, 1880.

46. Bismarck in abandoning the laissez-faire economic doctrine was losing the votes of the National Liberals but gaining support from the Catholic Center. See Fülöp-Miller, *Leo XIII and Our Times*, p. 109.

much contend."[47] Now the whole world would be praying for the establishment of peace in Germany.

Bismarck had one strong diplomatic arrow in his quiver, the question of the Italian Law of Guarantees so resented by His Holiness. The Berlin *Post*, Bismarck's own mouthpiece, published a series of articles which claimed that the Law of Guarantees was an instrument of absolutely international character and called for Italy to make new propositions to the Pope and to Europe, or, failing that, to convene a European congress to discuss the question.[48] In putting out this "feeler" Bismarck was trying to win the Pope over to greater promptness in coming to terms and thus persuade the Center Party to cease acting as a party of obstruction. This was the interpretation generally put on Bismarck's move by the press. *Osservatore Romano* thought such a plan would help Italy in two ways: one, by reducing the danger of republicanism (the seizure being the work of the House of Savoy), and two, by removing from Italy the hostility felt toward her by the Catholic world.[49]

Windhorst, having tried without success to get Prussia to lay aside the articles in the Constitution which were the basis of the whole Kulturkampf, returned to the attack in the Reichstag, whose laws covered the entire Empire. He was not satisfied with mere changes in administering the laws and relaxation in harshness of carrying them out. Mild administration was no safeguard. At the beginning of 1882 he pointed out this fact, stating that a "fixed law even though limited is worth more than a discretionary power." He also insisted that the Reichstag was perfectly competent to settle the Kulturkampf; it was not necessary to wait for the Prussian Landtag. In a very forceful speech he pointed out the necessity of settling the question in the interest of the consolidation of Germany; to relax the law in individual cases was no solution; the Catholics were still unhappy, and could not forget the rigors of the

---

47. ". . . *multum laboret necesse est multumque contendat.*" *Univers,* March 19, 1881. Encyclical of the Extraordinary Jubilee.

48. *Télégraph* (Opportunist), quoted in *Univers,* Jan. 7, 1882. It created quite a stir—"At Madrid as at Berlin, at Vienna as at London, there is talk of nothing else."

49. Quoted in *Univers,* Jan. 9, 1882. The addition of Italy to the Austro-German alliance to form a Triple Alliance in 1882 weakened if it did not remove this diplomatic weapon from Bismarck's hand. Nevertheless, the Triple Alliance remained in several respects an uneasy one, owing chiefly to disagreements between Italy and Austria. See William C. Askew, "Austro-Italian Antagonism," Wallace and Askew, eds., *Power, Public Opinion and Diplomacy,* pp. 172-173.

Kulturkampf. He asked, said Windhorst, only that the re-establishment of religious liberty for all faiths be explicitly recognized. Addressing the Conservatives directly, he went on: ". . . how do you expect conservatism to prosper when the institution which could develop the true principles of social conservatism is paralyzed?" He objected to the police character of the laws, the singling out of specific groups, not citizens as a whole, for surveillance. "Even the law against the socialists," he asserted, "against which I protested, furthermore, does not go much beyond that. But the Government thought that everything was permissible against the Catholics. . . . This exceptional legislation is generally condemned." Even more strongly he stated that the "Church of God" could not be made dependent "on the arbitrary acts of men." The Catholics did not want "adjustment" but "fundamental liberty"; they were all "equal before the law."[50]

The Conservatives would not be won over. They were willing to modify but not abrogate the laws. After all, the world had moved on. Other Catholic states had long since abandoned any such position as that maintained in Prussia in 1850.

By this time a new channel of communication had been opened up through the re-establishment of diplomatic relations with the Vatican. Dr. Schlözer was first sent as German Ambassador Extraordinary and Plenipotentiary; when in May the Prussian Landtag voted the funds for reopening the Prussian Embassy he was made Prussian Ambassador to the Vatican.[51] Things still went slowly, however, and negotiations through this channel tended to bog down.[52]

The announcement toward the end of March that Leo XIII had nominated three bishops to vacant sees in Germany was taken as an

50. *Verhandlungen des deutschen Reichstags*, 5 Leg. Per., I Sess., 1882, 22 Sitz., Jan. 11, 1882, LXVI, 533.

51. A Progressist, at the time when Dr. Schlözer was sent, remarked that the Chancellor, having a choice between "going to Canossa or going to Rome, chose the latter." See *Univers*, March 9, 1882. This move had been suggested back in 1879. The Chancellor even spoke of establishing a nunciature in Berlin; to this the Emperor was opposed. See Franz, *Kulturkampf*, p. 209.

52. Leo complained: "To all my remarks M. Schlözer replies by saying that Prince Bismarck is a man of iron who will not yield, and in whom it is necessary to show confidence. When I evince arguments which he cannot contradict he replies that his instructions do not permit him to discuss them; on my side, however, I am not afraid to change on certain points and I shall have to continue to battle foot-to-foot against the *man of iron.*" Quoted in Lefèbvre de Béhaine, *Léon XIII et le Prince de Bismarck*, p. 167.

indication that attempts at compromise and conciliation were making some progress.[53] When the question was brought up for debate in the *Herrenhaus* of the Prussian Landtag, a compromise was reached which was accepted by the lower house (*Haus der Abgeordneten*). The law passed was discretionary, not spelled out in much detail; the purport of it was that the bishops could return to their dioceses. Windhorst discussed the whole affair in a speech at the end of the year.[54] Bismarck had come a long way toward Canossa; he had not as yet stood in the snow.

During these years since the election of Leo XIII in March, 1878, German socialists and Catholics had been, inevitably, allies, however much both parties might wish to deny the charge. They seemed strange companions, because of the rejection of God by the socialist leaders. The deification of man was to them the turning point of world history.[55] "Socialism and atheism are one," said a Dresden journal, "for social democracy is itself a religion." Social Democrat Deputy Most, while in Berlin, announced to two Lutheran ministers: "The days of Christianity are numbered, and the day is not far off when one will say to the priests; 'Make your peace with heaven, for your hour is passed.' "[56]

After the partial success registered in 1882, no further progress was made immediately toward ending the Kulturkampf. Pressure toward further ameliorative steps came in the spring of 1884 when Bismarck was pushing for the retention of the law against the socialists. The outcome would depend on the votes of the Center. When the debates opened Windhorst proposed several amendments and spoke strongly in favor of modifying the bill. He did not attack the principle of the law as such but the arbitrary police power wrapped up in it. The Catholic Workingman's Clubs, he said, could, under the proposal (against the socialists), be attacked on the pretext that the cohesion of their members constituted a danger of socialism. He wished the previous arrangements to be restored, whereby the socialists would have a right to hold meetings and

53. Letter from Rome, March 30, 1882. Quoted in *Univers*, April 2, 1882.
54. *Verhandlungen des deutschen Reichstags*, 5 Leg. Per., II Sess., 1882, 27 Sitz., Dec. 13, 1882, LXVIII, 749, col. 2. Windhorst said the bill had passed the *Herrenhaus* by an overwhelming majority.
55. Werner Sombart, *Der proletarische Socialismus* ["Marxismus"] (2 vols.; Jena, 1924), I, 249.
56. *Univers*, July 10, 1878. See also Shanahan, *German Protestants Face the Social Question*, p. 347.

the police would no longer be permitted to expel anyone on the ground of genuine or pretended danger. Windhorst knew that Bismarck could not carry his bill without the Center votes.[57]

On the next day Windhorst withdrew his amendments and the law passed, 189 to 157. It received 39 votes from the Center, but 53 of the Center voted against it.[58] Without the 39 Center votes supporting the Chancellor the measure would have failed. In 1878 the Center had been unanimously opposed; in 1881 16 members were *for*; this time the number had risen to 39. One of the Alsatian deputies, Winterer, who was one of the 39, said that all conservative forces everywhere should get together and apply an international remedy for socialism; the Kulturkampf would have to be brought to an end.[59]

After the third reading of the bill it became law. Windhorst immediately moved to take up the question of the Kulturkampf, but his motion was rejected. The Landtag had taken no steps in revision and no other moves were in progress to settle the issue.[60]

The victory of the Chancellor had been made possible by the Center votes and he knew exactly where he stood. Had he received no votes from the Center he would have had to dissolve the Reichstag. This meant that his social legislative program had also been in the balance while the bill against the socialists was pending. The interrelation among social legislation, socialism, and the Kulturkampf was clearly demonstrated. Since the bill against the socialists was not in itself a religious one the members of the Center were not under strict orders in their voting. Nevertheless, it was obvious that Bismarck could not count on the continuous support of even the minority in the Center Party, unless he showed some effort to bring about a real settlement of the religious issue.

Personal relations between Leo XIII and the German court remained amicable. The Prince Imperial's visit was pleasant, if not productive. The Emperor, never having wanted to see the Kulturkampf started, would

57. *Verhandlungen des deutschen Reichstags*, 5 Leg. Per., IV Sess., 23 Sitz., May 9, 1884, LXXVIII, 481, col. 2. See also Agence Havas, Berlin, May 9, 1884. *Journal des Débats*, May 10, 1884.

58. *Temps* (dispatch from Munich) quoted in *Univers*, May 14, 1884.

59. *Verhandlungen des deutschen Reichstags*, 5 Leg. Per., IV Sess., 1884, 24 Sitz., May 10, 1884, LXXVIII, 466-467, col. 1.

60. Letter from Berlin, *Journal des Débats*, Oct. 8, 1884.

have been delighted to see it ended; the negotiations were in Bismarck's hands.[61] Were the German bishops more obstinate than the Pope?

In the Landtag debates on religion continued in 1885; here various specific issues were debated. Again Windhorst's voice was heard: "The State must, of course, when it is necessary, help the Church, with that I am in complete agreement. We Catholics want from the State, not money but freedom, and when we have that we shall make no further demands on the State, which never confers benefits without securing itself a greater lion's share of independence in return."[62]

There was some easing of the situation; the assignment of Archbishop Melchers (formerly of Cologne) and Ledochowski (of Posen) elsewhere and the appointment of new bishops for these posts had relieved the tension somewhat, although a third bishopric was still under dispute and still unsettled a year later. Windhorst did not like concessions "drop by drop."

In order to encourage Leo XIII to put a restraining hand on the German bishops, Bismarck asked him to mediate the dispute in Spain in the matter of the Carolines.[63] This Leo did in a manner which was eminently fair to both Spain and Germany. Leo XIII wrote to Bismarck making him a Knight of the Order of Christ and presented him with the insignia of the order.[64] The publicity attending the affair mortified King Humbert I, who had offered to mediate.[65]

Progress now became evident in the negotiations over the Kulturkampf. On January 6, 1886, the Pontiff wrote to the German bishops

61. T'Serclaes (*Léon XIII*, I, 409) says: "The Prussian eagle, so much a symbol of war against religion, had lead in its wings but they were still violently fluttering." The French pun is impossible to translate into English: *se débattaient* means not only that they fluttered but that they "kept on talking."

62. *Verhandlungen des deutschen Landtages*, Berlin, Feb. 20, 1885. Reproduced in *Kölnische Zeitung*, Feb. 21, 1885.

63. T'Serclaes, *Léon XIII*, I, 404.

64. Leo XIII to Bismarck, Dec. 31, 1885. Lefèbvre de Béhaine, *Léon XIII et le Prince de Bismarck*, p. 374. Leo told Bismarck that he had informed the Emperor of his great pleasure in carrying out the task but wished to express his sentiments to the one (Bismarck) who had suggested the Pope's mediation and subsequently so ably seconded Leo's efforts in the matter. Such a request had not been made of the Holy See for a long time. After complimenting Bismarck on his wisdom which was a principal factor in the strength of the Empire, Leo spoke of the force of the papacy when allowed perfect freedom. He thanked Bismarck for the progress made in seeking peace and expressed the hope that the future would bring further successes.

65. Mollat, *La Question Romaine*, p. 379.

assembled at Fulda, expressing his hope that in Germany Divine Providence might bring better things and explaining that the chief points of concern were for the complete freedom in the matter of educating the clergy in the seminaries,[66] for the maintenance of the authority of the bishops over their flocks, and for the assurance of freedom for Catholic missions in the colonies. He did not yield on any vital point: "However much We may be constrained by a desire for peace," nevertheless, "for those things which have been divinely constituted and sanctioned, . . . We shall not hesitate to endure in the example of Our Redeemer, any extremities whatsoever."[67]

The discussions between the Vatican and Germany now got down to specific matters and the ironing out of troublesome details on issues long in dispute. Emperor William had settled one issue by returning one bishop to his diocese by royal decree; now he appointed Msgr. Kopp, of Fulda, to the Prussian *Herrenhaus*. In the lower house Bismarck stated that there never would have been a Kulturkampf if his personal opinions had prevailed.[68] An Italian journal announced with fright that Bismarck's concessions as to the education of the Catholic clergy, on which he had "treated with the Jesuit General," indicated that the Chancellor was preparing to go not only to "Canossa but even to Loyola."[69] A bill was prepared to remove state examinations for ecclesiastical office, reopen Catholic seminaries, and put educational institutions under merely general supervision of the state. It proposed to suppress the special tribunal for religious affairs. Supplementary articles provided for removing vexing questions as to sacraments.[70] This bill would pass the Landtag only if Leo on his side would concede, permanently, that notification of appointments to ecclesiastical office would be made to the Prussian government.[71]

66. The need is to revise those laws *quae libertatem impediunt Episcoporum propriam, Ecclesias suas regendi ad normas divinitus constitutas, atque instituendae in, sacris Seminariis ad canonicarum sanctionum praescripte juventutis.* Latin text in *Univers*, Jan. 19, 1886.

67. ". . . *extrema quaeque perpeti, exemplo Decessorum Nostrorum non dubitaremus.*" This is the *Iampridem Nobis.* The Latin text in *Univers*, Jan. 19, 1886. Leo expressed delight in the way the sons of the Church held fast to the faith of their fathers ("*fidem patrum suorum integre fermiterque tenere*").

68. *Norddeutsche Allgemeine Zeitung*, quoted in *Univers*, Feb. 6, 1886.

69. Letter from Rome, quoting *Gazetta del popolo. Univers*, Feb. 13, 1886.

70. T'Serclaes, *Léon XIII*, I, 412.

71. Agence Havas, Berlin, April 9, 1886. *Univers*, April 11, 1886.

In the debate on this bill in the upper house (*Herrenhaus*) Msgr. Kopp, who was now a member as Windhorst was a member of the lower house, asked for a definitive commitment that the May Laws would be removed. Bismarck did not agree; he would be willing to modify them; he still believed they had been necessary at the time they were enacted. "But it is entirely erroneous," he said, "to believe that these May Laws are to be the palladium of the Prussian state, and that one may never tamper with them"; he went on to remark, however, that the Progressist journals seemed "unwilling for Prussia and the Church to settle their controversy and live in peace."[72] The upper house agreed to revision of the controversial laws.

While these discussions were going on, Schlözer, in Rome, sent the Pope an autograph letter from Emperor William and a magnificent pectoral cross ornamented with diamonds.[73]

At the beginning of May a German translation of a note from Cardinal Jacobini, to which William as King of Prussia had already sent a friendly reply, was laid before the Landtag: the essential feature of the note was that the Pope would accept the promise of the Prussian government to change its laws; he, on his part, would notify the government of any nominations to parishes vacant at that time.[74] The members of the Landtag were inclined to retain the May Laws, not through enmity toward the Catholic Church but on purely objective grounds: the nature of the Church, with its historical development of political power; its intolerance toward other confessions. Freeing the Catholic Church completely, they thought, would put German unity in question, since Germany was divided into two confessions. The Liberals were pretty stormy over the suggestion of abolishing the laws. Bismarck said the Curia merely wanted them to rethink and modify them. The Conservatives were willing to modify. Religious peace, according to some of the speakers, would be desirable.[75]

The cabinet had agreed that, if Leo would agree to the nomination of clergy, the Prussian Landtag would make the desired changes in the laws. The Pope's willingness to accept the *promise*, and his promise in return to make the notifications in the future, now left Bismarck with

72. *Ibid.*, April 14, 1886.
73. Dispatch from Rome, April 27, 1886. *Ibid.*, April 28, 1886.
74. *Kölnische Zeitung*, May 4, 1886.
75. Telegram from Berlin. *Kölnische Zeitung*, May 4, 1886.

the difficult task of pressing the changes through the Landtag. The upper house had not been difficult, but he was running into trouble in the lower house. The debate went on, and here was Bismarck trying to get the *Haus der Abgeordneten* to do the reverse of what he had been urging on it a decade earlier. The realism of Bismarck's political policies was never more clearly displayed—he must have peace with the Vatican. He tried to persuade the members that the Curia would have made the *whole* promise that was expected had they been sure that the Deputies would go along with the decision of the *Herrenhaus*; there was no doubt that once modifications were carried out the Pope would fulfil his promises.[76]

During the succeeding days some changes were worked out, but not all the changes the Pope had asked for were made; the religious orders were to be restricted as to the type of persons whom they served; some orders, Benedictines and Franciscans, were permitted to return, and the situation gradually improved,[77] but there were still difficulties in the way. How could Prussia permit the return of the Jesuits, for example, when they were interdicted in Catholic Bavaria? The pro-Bismarck *Kölnische Zeitung* remarked at the end of May, after discussing the May Laws: "And in other political questions there has been no noticeable evidence of the hoped-for change in the Center [in the Reichstag]."[78] It was still acting as a party of obstruction.

The filling of the vacant sees and the return of the bishops brought general satisfaction to the Catholics, and even Protestants rejoiced that peace with the papacy was returning.[79] The rejoicing was not universal. One Slavic Ultramontane journal viewed the prospect of "peace between the Pope and the Emperor as the greatest of horrors."[80]

76. *Kölnische Zeitung*, May 5, 1886.
77. Lefèbvre de Béhaine, *Léon XIII et le Prince de Bismarck*, p. 198. Many of the important documents are reproduced in the Appendix.
78. *Kölnische Zeitung*, May 27, 1886.
79. T'Serclaes, *Léon XIII*, I, 418. T'Serclaes quotes *Echo der Gegenwart*: "The State has been not to Canossa but to Rome." Bismarck's about-face, surmised T'Serclaes, might be due to his belief in the old adage: 'Who eats of the Pope dies of it (*Qui mange du pape en meurt*).'" The *Preussische Jahrbücher* said of Bismarck: "He does not seek glory but he does seek the most appropriate means to accomplish what is possible." Quoted in *Kölnische Zeitung*, May 3, 1886.
80. This was because of the national question. Prussia used the schools to Prussianize the Slavs, who were Catholic. Frankenburg (a member of the Prussian *Herrenhaus*) mentioned this in a letter to the Berlin *Post*. The sheet in question was the *Schlessische Volkszeitung* of Breslau. Quoted in *Univers*, April 7, 1887.

The situation in Germany was changing. The solidarity of the Center was beginning to crumble. Acting as one on any measure purely in defense of religion, they were starting to defect on other questions. Leo XIII had expected to gain all his ends by outwaiting Bismarck and opposing him on all measures. Up to 1886 this had been a highly successful policy. The first sign of warning had come in the vote on the socialists in 1884. The matter came to a head in 1887.

Jacobini wrote to the nuncio at Munich that the Holy Father, in view of the approach of the revision of the politico-ecclesiastical laws, desired the Center to support the military budget (the Septennate). The Pope had reason to believe, said Jacobini, that this was necessary because a refusal to support the military expenditures bill would make the Catholics seem antipatriotic, a dissolution of the Reichstag would take place, and the friendly relations established by the Holy See with the German Government would be damaged; all this would be reflected in the Government's attitude when the revision of the ecclesiastical laws came up. On the Pope's behalf he was to work on the Center. Frankenstein, of the Center, wrote the nuncio that he was always glad to take the Pope's suggestions in religious matters, but the Septennate was different, not being a question of religion. He said it would be a misfortune to ask this of the Center; a demand for support would force his resignation and that of many of his colleagues.[81]

The nuncio at Munich sent Frankenstein's letter to Jacobini, who replied that the Pope still regarded the work of the Center as not yet completed; support for the Septennate would work in the interests of religious peace by "making the government of Berlin debtor to the Holy See," and consequently constraining it to be "more favorable to the Catholics." The Holy See, furthermore, could not let slip such an opportunity to be "agreeable to the Emperor of Germany and to Prince Bismarck," in order to incline them toward "amelioration of the situation of the Holy See."[82]

A great furor was created when the letter (containing the instruc-

81. Frankenstein to Msgr. di Pietro, in Lefèbvre de Béhaine, *Léon XIII et le Prince de Bismarck*, p. 445. Frankenstein was president of the party.
82. This is a reference to Leo XIII's desire for help from Germany in the matter of the Temporal Power. Upon learning of this step Cardinal Ledochowski, a Pole, left the Vatican and took up his residence in the Mattei palace. See Rafaele de Cesare, "Il Dottor Schloezer e la fine del Kulturkampf," *Nuova Antologia*, CXXXVI (1894), 29 ff.

tions for the Center) was published; it was supposed to be confidential, so the phraseology had not been carefully protected against misrepresentation. *Osservatore Romano* commented that the liberal press was treating the letter as "a flag captured from the enemy." The reference in the letter, went on the Roman journal, to the situation of the head of the Church in Italy "aroused in the liberal press its habitual vice of believing that the Pope thinks of nothing else than his situation in the peninsula, and that for him the Alps are the limit of the world." They should realize that there was another objective in the letter: "obtaining religious peace in Germany."[83]

There was much criticism of several aspects of the letter. In the first place, said the critics, it was politics pure and simple—not religion. It was also militaristic in its suggestion of supporting Germany's proposals for vast military expenditures when the papacy was supposed to support peace. Finally, it was an unfriendly act toward France, for the military projects of Germany were directed against France. *Osservatore Romano*, in replying to these criticisms, declared that the charge of politics was simply not true: "The Holy See does not occupy itself with either domestic or foreign affairs of nations but with matters which are religious or moral, and those which by their nature or because of circumstances are related to religious or moral interests. . . ." The letter in question "treated of religious and moral issues [only] under the special aspect of the Church and the papacy." As to unfriendliness to France and support of militarism, the journal stated: "On the contrary, as even the republican journals of that nation [France] recognize and those least suspected of impartiality for the Apostolic See, the Sovereign Pontiff has worked for the greater good of France and Europe, in the present circumstances, in working for peace since [as Bismarck had asserted] the Septennate was the easiest means for the preservation of peace and the surest obstacle to the explosion of war."[84] As a result of the opposition of the Center to voting, as the Pope wished, for the military bill, the Reichstag was dissolved by Bismarck and new elections were held. The Septennate was then passed.[85]

83. *Osservatore Romano*, quoted in *Univers*, Feb. 11, 1887.
84. *Osservatore Romano*, Feb. 10, 1887, quoted in *Univers*, Feb. 12, 1887.
85. Goyau, *Bismarck et l'Église*, IV, 130. The Liberals were scandalized. Bismarck said: "I rejoice to see the two authorities, the temporal and the spiritual, combatting

Bismarck in the *Herrenhaus* spoke on the question of the return of the religious orders. "The essential thing," he said, "is that peace be re-established in the state and the projected law presented to you tends to that end. . . . If the Catholics declare that they cannot live in peace with us, I cannot understand their point of view, but no more can I impose my way of looking at things on them. . . ."[86] The proposed law passed the Prussian upper house by a large majority on the following day.[87]

The crucial debate would take place in the lower house. Msgr. Kopp declared that he and the other bishops had voted in the *Herrenhaus* for the passage of the ecclesiastical law even though he did not like the bill as it was; he hoped it would be altered in the lower house. To prevent attempts to change the bill Leo XIII wrote to the Archbishop of Cologne urging acceptance of the proposed law. He enumerated the gains that had been made, the filling of the vacancies in the parishes, the appoint-ment of bishops to the vacant sees, the opening of four new seminaries under Catholic direction for the education of the clergy, and the recall of some of the religious orders. Duty and prudence warned him "to prefer the present and attainable goal to a doubtful and uncertain hope." He said he had promised the preceding year that he would accept the reforms offered by Prussia and must keep the promise. He regarded it as a great thing that now essential services could be carried on, in the light of day, without interference; this was a great gain. The matter of communicating the names of the clergy to the Government could be arranged between the Holy See and the German Government in amicable exchange of letters. What remained of the old laws could be "tolerated." He instructed the Archbishop to inform all of his colleagues of his wish that they accept and vote for the law.[88]

---

democracy by common agreement." De Vogüé, "Affaires de Rome," *Revue des Deux Mondes*, III (Paris, 1887), 828. De Vogüé adds: "And no one protested."

86. Bismarck in the *Herrenhaus*, March 23, 1887. Quoted in *Univers*, April 10, 1887.

87. At a dinner at the house of the Duc de Ratibor that night a telegram was sent by the Duke, Msgr. Kopp, and Galimberti, to the Pope to apprise him of the fact; "He will sleep better"; *Univers* (April 7, 1887) quoting the Berlin *Post*. Ratibor was president of the *Herrenhaus*; he gave the dinner in honor of Msgr. Galimberti and the Bishop of Fulda (Kopp), before going on to a *soirée* of the Emperor and the Empress.

88. Leo XIII to the Archbishop of Cologne, April 6, 1887. Published in *Univers*, April 19, 1887. How interrelated were the affairs of religion, politics, and social questions in the nineteenth century is illustrated in this letter. Part of it dealt with the question of the relationship of the Holy See to Italy and the hope that Emperor William and Bismarck might support him in this direction; this brought up the question of the Triple Alliance.

The publication of the letter of Leo XIII to the Archbishop of Cologne left no room for doubt as to where His Holiness stood on the question of accepting the new ecclesiastical law. The members of the Catholic Center in the Prussian lower house[89] met and decided that the voice of the Pope must be obeyed.[90] They appointed Windhorst to give their adhesion. When the debate was resumed in the lower house the National Liberal Party attacked the bill. Windhorst replied, without comment, that the Holy See found the law as passed by the *Herrenhaus* could be tolerated. This meant the passage of the bill into law (the Center members voting for it since Leo approved it) and the formal end of the Kulturkampf.[91] Its ending was hailed with relief by most Catholics, but not by all. Rome (the Curia) had wanted all or nothing. Leo would take what was possible and immediate. Non-Catholic socialists feared the alliance of Bismarck with the Catholics. The socialists were now the ones in Germany who could not propagandize their ideas in "the light of day." The Kulturkampf had accomplished much in the sixteen years since it had begun to take form in the German Empire. The Church during its period of persecution had been watched with sympathy and admiration everywhere, by Catholics and other Christians. Nothing had

---

The alliance was defensive; any attack on Italy in the interest of restoring the Temporal Power would supposedly have to be answered by the mobilization of German and Austrian troops in defense of Italy. On the other hand the religious question was interwoven with the rise of socialism. Both of Bismarck's plans for handling the social question necessitated the support of the Center Party.

89. They were also deputies in the Reichstag, where the name "Center" properly belonged.

90. *Kölnische Zeitung*, quoted in *Univers*, April 21, 1887. The meeting was on April 19.

91. See Wallace, *The Papacy and European Diplomacy*, p. 255, for an estimate of the Kulturkampf in its broader European setting. One modern German view (Franz, *Kulturkampf*, pp. 276-278) is that while with Bismarck it was merely a weapon in a shifting policy of opportunism, with the National Liberals it was a deliberate and unalterable policy of "shaping a national church" under the supervision of the national state. The liberal Left wanted the Church done away with and the state run on the basis of secularism and culture of a new age. Another German view (Ruhenstroth-Bauer, *Bismarck und Falk im Kulturkampf*, p. 92) is that the Kulturkampf was laid aside by Bismarck because he needed the Center votes in carrying out his internal reforms. The most commonly held version is that Bismarck gave up the Kulturkampf in order to fight the socialists. These various views are not necessarily mutually exclusive; they merely shift the point of major emphasis. The only valid conclusions are to be arrived at by placing the question in the midst of the totality of the European diplomatic scene. Bismarck's sight was never limited to Germany alone. G. Valbert ("L'Allemagne nouvelle jugée par un Allemand [Bruno Bauer]," *Revue des Deux Mondes*, XLI [1880], 700) pointed out while the Kulturkampf was still in progress that it was "not alone against the keys of St. Peter and the Tiara that the Berlin Caesar was struggling."

done more than this to make liberals forget the First Vatican Council and the *Syllabus*. What remained of the legal enactments included the retention of the Prussian Constitution as modified by the removal of Articles 15, 16, and 18, which were not restored, the continuance of the law of expatriation of priests, the retention (by the state) of the sums withheld from the clergy during the struggle; and the declaration that the state had the right to set the boundaries between the two powers, a right which the Church has always claimed for itself. Most of these points of disagreement were merely buried, not solved, in the effort of both the Pope and Bismarck to clear the air and not compel people to suffer the lack of spiritual solace while every detail of abstract theory should be fought out. His Holiness was pleased that peace with Germany had been attained. He discussed it in an allocution on May 23, contrasting the situation in Italy with the accord reached by patience and good will in Germany.[92] The following year, William II (who had succeeded to the German throne following the death of William I and, ninety days later, of Frederick, the Prince Imperial, in 1888), as King of Prussia, in his speech from the throne to the Landtag, said he was especially pleased that the politico-ecclesiastical legislation had succeeded in modifying "the relation of the State with the Catholic Church and its spiritual head, so as to make it acceptable to both parties." He said he would attempt to maintain religious peace in the country.[93]

A further compromise was worked out later, somewhat less heralded, in questions unsettled at the time of the pacification in 1887. Windhorst in 1890 introduced a bill to restore the payments withheld from members of the clergy who broke the laws during the Kulturkampf. The government had been paying for several years interest on the sum; now they were asked to pay the principal; the Emperor yielded and paid the amount. The Pope yielded on a question of nomination.[94]

92. *Univers*, May 27, 1887. Leo said of the end of the Kulturkampf that an end had been made "to this violent conflict which afflicted the Church without profiting the State."

93. *Journal des Débats*, June 28, 1888.

94. He agreed to the German Government's wish in the matter of the nomination of a bishop to the bishopric of Strasburg. So asserted the Berlin correspondent of the *Journal des Débats*. It was suspected, said the correspondent, that a factor in the compromise was the matter of a commercial treaty with Austria, opposed by the Conservatives but desired by Bismarck; with the help of the Center Party, acting under instructions and somewhat reluctantly, the treaty was enacted. See *Journal des Débats*, Jan. 21, 1891.

The Center remained the most compact party in the Reichstag, although there was no clear-cut issue on which to campaign.[95] Members of the Center were still co-operating with the government in the hope of securing further changes in the religious laws (only one further change was actually made, in 1902). With their assistance a navy appropriation bill was passed.

The most significant results arising from the solution of the Kulturkampf lay in the fields of diplomacy and the rise of socialism. The first, leading up to World War I, would take us too far afield. The second will be considered in a later chapter.

95. This was especially true in 1898. In spite of the lack of issues the Center gained 7 seats, and returned 105 deputies. The socialists had 56 and the National Liberals 46. These were the only parties of substantial size. See *Univers*, June 27, 1898. Before the election so many deputies went home to campaign that a quorum could not be secured. See *Univers*, April 27, 1898.

VII. MARX AND SOCIAL-IST DIVISION

"You have, Sire, contrary to what we have become accustomed to here, explained, defined socialism instead of calumniating it."[1]

JULES GUESDE

When Karl Marx eliminated the anarchist Bakunin from the First International it was not with the idea of strengthening the organization but rather of removing a weapon from the hand of his opponent. The greatest obstacle immediately in the path of Marx was fractionalization at the community level. This was what anarchism fostered: sporadic acts by groups who opposed the structure of society in all its organized forms. Marx wanted a developed economic order to remain until his movement was strong enough to take it over as an operating concern. The first task before him was to secure the quiet demise of the First International; he had outgrown it. This goal was easily attained by removing its headquarters to New York. He, of course, remained in London. The second task would be to imbue his lieutenants with a deep and permanent devotion to his ideas. In their respective countries they were to insinuate themselves into organizations arising spontaneously among the discontented and take control of them. The number of the discontented and the depth of their dissatisfaction Marx thought he could predict: the forces of history were operating on his side.[2]

1. Open letter to Leo XIII. Compère-Morel, *Jules Guesde*, p. 143.
2. Werner Sombart (*Der proletarische Sozialismus* ["Marxismus"], II, 248-252) says that socialism began as a religion of man; it became a religion of hate, the proletarian saying, "We will love our enemy . . . only when he lies helpless on the ground." It did not necessarily mean violence, although its exponents may have regarded violence as inevitable.

The political boundaries of European states seemed permanently established with the German victory at the end of the Franco-Prussian war. The decision of Marx and his adherents at the Hague Congress fell in line with this reality by conceding that socialism should develop on a national basis; the members of the International in the various countries were to give one another a helping hand.

The story of socialism in these years following the Hague Congress becomes, then, not a single account but a raveled thread running through the fabric of the nations. In all of these countries, although not with the same speed, the political trend was toward constitutional government.[3] The problems confronting Marx's lieutenants would vary from country to country. Some factors were present in different degrees in all: the growth of industrialism, the phenomenal march of science, colonialism, and, throughout Catholic Europe, the international character of the Church. Leo XIII, as Pontiff, had lost little time in declaring the opposition of the Church to socialism.[4]

MARXISM IN GERMANY

Even after unification Germany was not ready for the Marxian program. The power of the feudal aristocracy had not been broken, as it had been in the areas where the French Revolution had swept the boards and facilitated the rise of the capitalist class. Furthermore, the workers' movement, founded by Lassalle, was not socialist. Marx and Engels, although imbibing their philosophy from the German fountain, had become socialist through their contacts with the French during their sojourn in Paris. Marx's social theory was founded on the Hegelian philosophy but its socialist content was not a German product. His theory called for the growth of a capitalist class, organizers of large-scale production, from whose hands socialist labor would wrest control when it became fully conscious of its needs, its enemy, and its own determination. This would come about in the fullness of time, when conditions in Germany should be right.

3. This trend, in general, was more pronounced in Protestant Europe, although there were exceptions.
4. In the *Quod apostolici*, issued during the first year of his pontificate. Guesde's letter had been a reply to this encyclical.

Attempts of the Lassallean German Workers' Association to press for immediate reforms of the capitalist system were premature, or so thought William Liebknecht and August Bebel, Marx's lieutenants. They believed the workers should ally with the middle class to win civil liberties and representative institutions from the feudal aristocracy. Marx backed them in this view. The difficulty was that the influence of Lassalle lingered on after his death and hampered the efforts of Marx's stalwarts to take over the labor organization. The Association was brought into the International, largely through the urging of Liebknecht and Bebel, but fell into the hands of Johann Schweitzer (until 1871), who founded a journal, the *Sozialdemokrat*, in which he ran articles supporting Bismarck's parliamentary development in the German Empire. Although Marx had originally given grudging approval to the establishment of the journal, he soon regretted it. He had no desire to build up "Caesarism" and the glorification of the Prussian state. When the Reichstag of the North German Confederation met in 1867 both Schweitzer and Liebknecht sat as representatives. The difference of view between them became more pronounced as time went on. In 1867 Schweitzer had been elected head of the Lassalleans. Marx sought to win them away from Schweitzer. His moves were partially successful. Amalgamation of the factions began at Eisenach in 1869[5] and was furthered at Gotha in 1874. The Lassalleans were nationalist and reformist; Liebknecht and Bebel, as Marxist disciples, were revolutionist. The nationalist concept had been accepted by the Marxists in coming to terms with the Lassalleans, but only out of necessity. The workers were not ready for the revolutionary program; the Marxists were too few in number to dictate. The Gotha Program, to which both groups assented in 1875, included many views quite foreign to Marx's beliefs, or views accepted merely as temporary expedients on the march toward a classless society which should own all things *as a society*. Such notions as the "iron law of wages," the right of each laborer to the "whole product" of his labor, the desirability of

5. Marx's confidential advice to Liebknecht and Bebel was to prevent Bakunin's followers from stirring up the old animosities between the Marxists and Schweitzer; it might destroy socialism in Germany. See Romano, *Movimento socialista in Italia*, I, 264. Gunter Nollau (*International Communism and World Revolution: History and Methods* [New York, 1961], p. 13) attributes Marx's apparently new attitude to the failure of the Revolution of 1848. The revolution was in harmony with the predictions in the *Communist Manifesto*; it failed to produce a proletarian victory. Marx saw that bourgeois reforms had to come first.

"equitable distribution of the proceeds of labor," the belief that the capitalists were "sole exploiters of labor," were all completely rejected by Karl Marx. In disapproval he wrote his *Critique of the Gotha Program* to inform his German lieutenants of his views. They insisted that his critique should not be published; the program would have to be accepted for the time being as the only way to produce unity in the ranks of German labor.[6] The Gotha Program, although largely taken from the old Lassallean program, included much that was Marxist in origin. On the surface it seemed a complete victory for the Lassallean majority. The revolutionary minority would have to bide their time. Lassalle was in his grave but his spirit was still alive in the German Workers' Party.[7] Liebknecht and Bebel, however, exercised their leadership more effectively than did Schweitzer, who was president of the party. Schweitzer's image as a leader continued to be plagued by scandal connected with his earlier career. The qualities of leadership in Liebknecht and Bebel became increasingly apparent.[8] Their followers were numerically too small to wrest the presidency of the party away from the Lassalleans, but the voices of their orators in legislative debate began to change the situation. The opening of the Reichstag provided an opportunity for the dissident minority. Universal suffrage together with the federal structure of the Empire permitted the seating of socialists who could live legally in one of the other federated states even though barred from residence in Prussia.[9] The German socialists found that they needed representa-

6. Gay, *The Dilemma of Democratic Socialism: Eduard Bernstein's Challenge to Marx* (New York, 1950), pp. 21-23. In Gay's opinion the evolution of this newly consolidated party toward "complete adoption of Marxism was only a question of time" (p. 24).

7. Even their songs commemorated the workers' dead hero. See Braunthal, *Geschichte der Internationale*, p. 267.

8. Harry Schumann, *Karl Liebknecht: Ein Stück unpolitischen Weltanschauung* (Dresden, 1923), p. 11. Schumann says the group of Marx's lieutenants was one of his "Foreign Legions" which was split off from the parent International stem to pursue their own national aims. Schumann agrees that the main purpose of the splitting off was to give Marx a free hand in making decisions. There was no General Council to restrain him; the International was fragmented and dying. Marx's name was more widely heralded and he was stronger than before.

9. Bebel represented at first Glauchau, in Saxony, later Dresden. Nationwide laws adopted by the Reichstag would affect their activities but would not prevent them from sitting as deputies. Since the Constitution of Prussia, with its three-class voting structure, was much less liberal than the Constitution of the Empire, the socialists could not hold a party Congress on Prussian soil. The socialist Reichstag deputies were able, however, to convene a Congress of German socialists at Gotha (August 19, 1878), which was not in Prussian territory. See Guillaume, *L'Internationale*, IV, 22.

tives who could hold their own in debate against highly educated deputies of the other parties. This Liebknecht and Bebel could do, rivaling even the mighty Windhorst, spokesman for the Catholics.

Liebknecht, first meeting Marx in Paris, was subsequently with him for many years in London. He was editor of the socialist journal *Volkstaat*. Liebknecht met and influenced the younger Bebel. These two sat in the Reichstag almost continuously. Both had come from Evangelical backgrounds; Liebknecht admitted that his family boasted descent from Martin Luther.[10] Bebel's interest in the salvation of the working class had been aroused by a Catholic priest in South Germany. The names of the two orators were known everywhere; their speeches received wide publicity in the press.[11]

Bismarck was aware of the danger[12] presented by the growing popularity of the Social Democratic leaders and the increase in the number of Social Democratic deputies in the Reichstag,[13] but there was really little he could do. He did not attempt to alter the electoral laws as a means of preventing the socialists from electing representatives. In order to get the South German states to enter the Empire he had had to confess himself a convert to universal suffrage. The Rhineland also had been deeply affected by these liberal ideas, implanted during the revolutionary and Napoleonic era and reinforced during the Revolution of 1848. By tampering with the suffrage laws Bismarck would have endangered the imperial structure so painfully won. All moderate and liberal parties in the Reichstag would have opposed him. Rather, he made a direct attack on the socialists, introducing a bill against them on May 28, 1878. It would have given the police almost discretionary powers over the social-

10. Schumann, *Karl Liebknecht*, p. 8.

11. Important speeches in the Reichstag were quoted in the daily papers in Paris or in London as in Berlin. Marx's writings were not known to the Germans until much later, when they were introduced by Karl Kautsky. See Beer, *History of Socialism*, II, 147.

12. Bismarck told Busch, the publicist, that his enmity toward the Social Democrats began when he heard one of them, Bebel or Liebknecht, he did not remember which, extol the Paris Commune. See Moritz Busch, *Our Chancellor* (Leipzig, 1884), p. 198. It was actually Bebel who made the statement.

13. The rise of socialism up to May, 1878, was summarized in an article in *Univers*, July 10, 1878. Socialism was described as moving from France to Germany and there making a phenomenal growth. The number of German socialist journals rose from six in 1869 to forty-seven in 1878.

ists and the socialist press. The measure was, however, defeated, the Catholic Center Party voting with the National Liberals against it.[14]

The war against the socialists was pressed on other fronts as well. Bismarck sent out a circular inviting the European powers to "employ all means at their disposal to repress the action of the socialists and internationalists."[15] All attacks on rulers were attributed to agitators.

The situation was, indeed, difficult for Bismarck. Money bills required Reichstag assent; this meant debates. He feared Bebel's tongue and his uncanny ability to bring up points out of Bismarck's past which the Iron Chancellor would have preferred to leave buried. When debates on new measures proposed against the socialists were resumed in the fall of 1878,[16] Bebel in a notable speech made a personal attack on Bismarck, rehearsing the relations between Lassalle, the magnetic founder of the labor movement, and the Chancellor. Going through the rapprochement (1863-1864) chapter by chapter, he put the worst possible construction on Bismarck's actions and motives, even implying that the Chancellor's relations with the Countess Hatzfeldt (Lassalle's client and reputed mistress) had not been above reproach.[17] Bismarck replied with lofty aplomb. Assuring the Reichstag that against his will he held his position at the insistence of the Emperor and could not resign without permission (the German cabinet was not at the mercy of parliamentary majorities) he declared Bebel's statements to be a mixture of truth and falsehood. He denied all implications of impropriety; he said the conversations were sought by Lassalle, and not by himself, and he could not

14. *Verhandlungen des deutschen Reichstags*, II Sess., 1878, May 23, 1878, XLVIII, 495, col. 2. Bismarck had thought the time propitious because of the recent attempt to assassinate the Emperor. The assassin, who had in his possession a number of membership cards in different Social Democratic societies, together with a quantity of socialist literature and the portraits of Liebknecht and Bebel, claimed to be an anarchist. See Agence Havas (Berlin), May 12, 1878, *Univers*, May 14, 1878.

15. *Univers*, June 12, 1878. The article states that Favre, in 1871, had sent out a similar kind of circular, an appeal about the desperate system which was threatening Europe, a handful of despotic leaders trying to "gain control of the multitude and turn the land into an immense workshop [the Commune]." The article goes on that Bismarck was pleased *then* that France was being destroyed from within—it would be easier to defeat; now these ideas had "jumped the Rhine," to Bismarck's discomfiture.

16. The Social Democratic representation was much reduced by the election which had just occurred, but Bebel's voice was enough for an army.

17. *Verhandlungen des deutschen Reichstags*, 4 Leg. Per., I Sess., 1878, 4 Sitz., Sept. 16, 1878, LI, 41, col. 2.

have known how to reach him, not "having the honor of the Countess Hatzfeldt's acquaintance."[18]

Bebel in his condemnatory speech also explained the socialist platform: the Social Democrats took their stand on the Gotha Program.[19] He described the International Workers' Association, with its subsidiary chapters and individuals, bound together on the foundation of truth and right, without regard to creed, color, or nationality; their Congress[20] thought it the obligation of man to provide "the rights of man and the citizen, not for himself, but for every man who did his duty.[21] No rights without duties; no duties without rights." In states where the suffrage existed, it must be exercised and representatives elected; where it did not exist, the objective must be to secure it.

Even a few representatives could stir up agitation. Liebknecht had admitted in 1874 that the Social Democratic Party was a revolutionary party; participation in elections was solely with the object of agitating. Their elected representatives would have a wide audience. "We only mount the rostrum of the Reichstag," he said, "in order to speak to the people."[22] No attempts were made to conceal the revolutionary intentions of the party. One of the songs sung at the rallies was the "War-Lay of Mankind":

Happy we! the tinder is piled up, the world torch flares skyward! The battle sword is brandished, the bullet whistles, all around us is the savage clamor of battle. Look! See how thrones tumble down and the holy stools tremble![23]

The bill to be proposed against the socialists was in the hands of a parliamentary commission, on which all parties were represented. During the debate in the commission on such matters as management of savings funds of the socialists, infraction of the Association Law (which so

18. *Ibid.*, 5 Sitz., Sept. 17, 1878, LI, 67, col. 2. Bismarck's reply came the day after Bebel's attack.

19. *Ibid.*, 4 Sitz., Sept. 16, 1878, LI, 44, col. 2. Bebel's statement was, of course, made for effect. He had no intention of standing on the Lassallean "Gotha Program." Acceptance of the program had been merely tactical.

20. The International Congress held at Ghent in September, 1877. The Belgian socialists had invited socialists from everywhere to attend this "Sozialistische Weltkongress." It had not led to any permanent international organization. See Braunthal, *Geschichte der Internationale*, p. 197.

21. *Ibid.*, LI, 49, col. 1. Here is exhibited the ideological tie with the era of the French Revolution and Napoleon.

22. *Volkstaat* (Liebknecht's socialist journal) quoted in Busch, *Our Chancellor*, p. 204.

23. Quoted in Busch, *Our Chancellor*, p. 204.

particularly incensed Windhorst, who said it could be used against religious groups), and interdicting socialist writings, the Center Party and the Progressists lined up against the Conservatives and the National Liberals.[24] The progress of the commission was followed with interest everywhere, with journals outside Germany expressing their views. *République française*, criticizing the campaign against the German socialists, drew this reply from the Berlin *Post*: "The French republicans should remember . . . [that] if the German Government had lent the slightest support to the Sixteenth of May [*Seize mai*],[25] France would not yet have shaken off the [monarchist] régime, the Republic would not yet be consolidated. The republican press should show more regard for the all-powerful Chancellor and his precious 'reptiles,' from which they extract long articles every day."[26]

When the commission brought in the report recommending adoption of the antisocialist measure, the Center Party opposed its proposals. Windhorst, asking the difference between "social" and "socialist," took the rostrum and debated against the various articles as they were proposed. Deputy Ludwig Bamberger (Liberal) accused the Center Party of being in alliance with the socialists.[27] Deputy Dernburg (Conservative), arguing against allegations in Bebel's prosocialist speech, said the English socialists were establishing themselves successfully because they remained within the law, and the general public was convinced that they would not depart from this legal path.[28]

One phrase in a speech of Bismarck's early in the debate drew acrimonious comment from French papers. After criticizing the influence the French proponents of "revenge" exercised over the *Frankfurter*

24. The Progressists (Fortschritt party) were left of center; the National Liberals were rightists (the party of big business); the Conservatives (the old Junker party) formed the extreme right. The fate of the proposed legislation would seem to hang on whether, for practical considerations, some members of the opposition might be persuaded to support the Government. *Norddeutsche Zeitung*, Sept. 23, 1878, quoted in *Univers*, Sept. 25, 1878.

25. This was the day on which MacMahon arbitrarily dismissed Simon and put Broglie in his place. For the debate on the ministerial crisis see *Annales de la Chambre de Députés*, 1877, III, 24-25.

26. Berlin *Post*, quoted in *Univers*, Sept. 6, 1878. In the "reptile press" Bismarck aired his views, without ostensibly doing so.

27. It was at this point that Bamberger showed the voting placards, urging the socialists to elect Center Party representatives. Windhorst denied that an alliance existed.

28. *Verhandlungen des deutschen Reichstags*, 4 Leg. Per., I Sess., 1878, 12 Sitz., Oct. 14, 1878, LI, 261-262. The connection with the Kulturkampf was obvious.

Zeitung,[29] he asserted that the Commune had rid France of socialism, after which it had moved into Germany.[30] Windhorst agreed with this view, and criticized the development of philosophy in the German universities, regarding it as responsible for the shift toward atheism. Windhorst said categorically that people would either return to religion or become Social Democrats.[31]

In spite of opposition from the Center and the Liberals the bill against socialism was adopted and passed into law on October 19, 1878. Article 28 permitted the police to prevent a gathering of more than three people without authorization and forbade the distribution of brochures and broadsides on the streets. It permitted the police to expel anyone suspected of endangering public safety. Weapons were not to be carried, the authorities declaring that they had uncovered evidence of a vast association, reaching into Paris, London, Naples, Rome, Vienna, Kiev, Odessa, Moscow, and St. Petersburg. (They had evidently uncovered Bakunin's secret literature.)

Laws against the socialists provided no solution for the social problem, which grew constantly worse as the rapidity of industrial growth brought people from the countryside into the cities. It was here that unprotected labor suffered most severely and was most separated from the consolation of religion. No public system of charity was present to cope with the swelling tide. Charity exercised by both Protestants and Catholics tried to help. In Berlin, for example, there were three hundred thousand proletarians, outside the Church, whose children were growing up to hate the society that was responsible for their misery.[32] The socialists offered these masses a way of aiding themselves. The Social Democratic Party in the Reichstag championed their cause. The Center Party, because of its opposition to the Chancellor, was in a strange alliance with them, an alliance which would last as long as the Kulturkampf endured.

29. The representatives from Alsace-Lorraine were urged to oppose and discredit Bismarck on every issue coming up in the Reichstag.

30. Moüy (chargé d'affaires), telegram to Waddington, Berlin, Oct. 10, 1878. *D.D.F.*, 1st Ser., II, 387.

31. *Verhandlungen des deutschen Reichstags*, 4 Leg. Per., I Sess., 1878, 10 Sitz., Oct. 11, 1878, LI, 203, col. 1. The entangling of religion with the state in Germany had hindered the "development of social teaching," emphasizing conservatism instead; the elements of a social program had been present in the sixteenth century in Luther's teaching. See Shanahan, *German Protestants Face the Social Question*, p. 6.

32. Correspondence from Berlin. *Univers*, Dec. 6, 1878.

The voice of Windhorst continued to criticize the turning of socialist activities over to the supervision of the police.

Bismarck came to realize that the urban social problem could not be ignored and could not be cured merely by laws passed against the socialists. The social problem was the ground from which socialism sprung. He was aware that the solution could not be left to charity nor to the benevolence of factory owners. He believed also that collective bargaining through trade unions was not the answer for Germany. Such a solution might be all right for democratic England, where monarchy enjoyed a purely symbolic role and where labor unions were successful both in collective bargaining and in securing labor legislation. Such procedures, slow at best, depending on the efforts of workers themselves, would not be appropriate in Germany, where monarchy was still powerful. In the German situation, Bismarck thought, helpful legislation must be proposed and supported by the state itself.[33] He was confident that the leaders of the Social Democratic movement, as Marxists, wanted social revolution—not reform. He might spike their guns by introducing a program directly beneficial to the workers and immediately realizable. Emperor William I, in his speech from the throne a month after the passage of the antisocialist law, said proposals would be made to create associations for the amelioration of the lot of the workers and to establish agricultural banks. Bismarck expected that both the Progressists and the Center could be counted on to support such a program.

The part played by the Chancellor in the campaign for positive action was described by him later (with a few minor errors as to sequence of events) in conversation with Busch, giving himself due credit in the telling. According to Busch's account of the interview, Bismarck rejected the whole idea of the socialist state as expounded by Bebel. The socialist orator claimed that there would be no wrong-doing in a socialist state, because only class exploitation produced evil conduct. Bismarck asked who "would be warden in the Universal House of Correction?" He thought workers ought to be provided with incomes when they lost

33. Bismarck's position as Chancellor of the Reich was unshakable. The ministry over which he presided was not subject to parliamentary control. He could arbitrarily dissolve the Reichstag at any time. He was constrained merely by the fact that the Reichstag must assent to the military appropriations bills. This was what had given the Center its power. This same principle of the strong monarchy meant that Bismarck could move rapidly with his social program—more rapidly than would have been possible in England.

their jobs. "To attempt anything of the sort on a large scale," he went on, "might entail an expenditure of millions, but the notion does not seem to be intrinsically an absurd or silly one. We make experiments in agriculture and manufacture; might it not be as well to do so with respect to human occupations and the solution of the social question?" He later said he would spend three hundred million marks to get contented workers.[34] He proposed "practical Christianity" as an appropriate enterprise on behalf of labor, saying that "unless you put your hands into your pockets and into the state exchequer you will not do much good."[35] He succeeded in getting a bill for compulsory accident insurance recommended by the Federal Council (*Bundesrat*), but the Reichstag passed it in such altered form that the Council would not accept it.[36]

Bismarck's failure in this first attempt at State Socialism, or the "social state,"[37] was attributed to the antagonism of the Center Party to anything he might propose while the May Laws against the Catholics were still in effect. The Catholic Center was, however, interested in justice and fair play. They applauded a thoughtful speech in the Reichstag by Georg von Hertling, a Catholic deputy, at the beginning of January, 1882.[38] Hertling pointed out that as a result of modern industrial development in all lands the workers' labor was a *commodity*, subject to market fluctuations; the worker himself was the *seller* of his labor according to the economic law of the tendency of wages not to rise above the level of subsistence.[39] The results were shocking, and necessitated not only the investigation of researchers but the earnest consideration of statesmen. Hertling went on that he and his friends had decided to break with the doctrine of laissez faire (a bold statement to make in 1882) and to see to it that legislation and the power of the state were used in the industrial realm for the higher aims of mankind. He spoke of Sunday labor,

34. Busch, *Our Chancellor*, pp. 197-198, 218.

35. *Ibid.*, p. 223.

36. *Ibid.*, p. 224. The measure was debated in April, 1881.

37. The "social state" should not be confused with the socialists' "socialist state." In the "socialist state" the working class would theoretically be in control.

38. The laws against the socialists passed in 1878 had been renewed in 1881.

39. This is the "iron law of wages," viewed as inevitable by laissez-faire economics. Hertling was showing that the laborer was hit by two economic laws because of his dual capacity as a commodity and as a seller, competitively selling his labor. Hertling was a prominent member of the Reichstag and of the Center Party; he was Prime Minister of Bavaria. Later he was to become Chancellor of the Empire (1917-1918). See Moody, *Church and Society*, pp. 465-466.

of women in factories, and of private industries which worked their employees two to four hours a day above the twelve-hour day. "This is a case where state intervention is indicated as necessary and indispensable."[40] Hertling supported the Church's teaching that the employer should not regard the worker simply as a factor in his profit, but as a "personality made in the image of God." He should impress on the worker his "worth as a man."[41]

Bismarck also spoke, undeterred by his failure in the previous year to get the social program going. He emphasized specific points of needed reform. He argued that accident insurance could be handled only through closed workers' organizations—"centralization would be useless in this matter." He mentioned that the Emperor was anxious that an attempt "to solve the social question should be begun before his death." Bismarck wanted it publicized that it was the workers who were rejecting the Government's plans; then it would be clear that he had done his duty. It need not all be carried out by legislation—"Christianity is and will remain the basis of our social life." It would be necessary to take measures against lowering wages and to see that certain industries were not overburdened with import duties. Limitation on the hours of labor, he said, and restriction on the work of women would require study. The lessening of import duties would help to "attenuate the ills from which the working classes were suffering."[42]

Accident and sickness insurance were still under discussion in the Reichstag in May, 1882. Karl von Bötticher, State Secretary of the Interior, speaking on behalf of Bismarck, discussed the proposed law, which had already been examined and approved by the Emperor. Bötticher gave statistics with regard to the number of mutual insurance groups in recent years which showed their decline. Obviously this voluntary arrangement was not the answer to the problem; an obligatory measure set up by the state would be essential.[43]

With the Emperor's approval and the support of the Center, if the Kulturkampf were really buried, Bismarck could get this legislation through. Whether by this means he could destroy the hold of the Social

40. *Verhandlungen des deutschen Reichstags*, 5 Leg. Per., I Sess., 1882, 20 Sitz., Jan. 9, 1882, LXVI, 480-483.
41. *Ibid.*, LXVI, 484.
42. *Ibid.*, LXVI, 485, col. 2.
43. *Ibid.*, 5 Leg. Per., II Sess., 1882, 10 Sitz., May 15, 1882, LXVIII, 200, col. 1.

Democrats over the workers was still, and would be for a long time, an unanswered question.

The law against the socialists, enacted in 1878 and renewed in 1881, was again up for renewal in 1884. Windhorst introduced amendments and tried to modify the bill; he based his objections on the police power wrapped up in the existing law. Left-Liberal Deputy Eugene Richter said the law was useless; it had not put an end to criminal acts (the implication being that socialism was responsible for all violent crime). Puttkamer replied for the Government that without the law there would be torrents of blood. "All the states which have no such law," he insisted, "are corroded with anarchism, which is the result of socialism. The Government does not disparage the benevolent intention which has inspired the Windhorst proposals, but the responsibility which is incumbent upon it prevents it from accepting them." Bismarck came in and spoke; he referred to the attempt of Windhorst to get measures adopted against regicide (1881); he read the Emperor's letter written on the occasion of the assassination of Alexander II, taking the same view; he explained that Russia and Austria were agreeable to holding a conference on the question, but that France's acceptance was conditioned on England's, and England refused; later Austria withdrew, so only Russia and Germany conferred. The Chancellor went on to say that the law against the socialists could not be softened; the Government hoped by social reforms to give the workers what they needed: work when able, and aid when they could not work.[44] The debate was a fiery one, with the threat of dissolution hanging over the Reichstag. When Windhorst withdrew his amendments, enough Center votes defected to the Chancellor to give him a victory by an uncomfortably small margin.[45]

The capitulation of the Reichstag was the event of the day. In the course of the debate the Chancellor had used the words: "right to work"; the Berlin correspondent of *Univers* reported: "evidently Bismarck has not thought what consequences one could derive from such a theory."[46] An Alsatian deputy, who voted *for*, said it was the international character

44. *Ibid.*, 5 Leg. Per., IV Sess., 1884, 23 Sitz., May 9, 1884, LXVIII, 481, col. 2. Dissolution would be Bismarck's only recourse unless enough Center votes came to his side to pass the bill.

45. The socialists at Munich, to express their defiance or disappointment, made a demonstration. See telegram from Berlin, May 10, 1884, quoted in *Journal des Débats*, May 14, 1884.

46. Correspondence from Berlin, May 11, 1884. *Univers*, May 15, 1884.

of socialism that made it dangerous; Bismarck's projects for reform would not stop it; what was needed was an international remedy. The Alsatian then linked the question with the Kulturkampf. Another Alsatian who had defected, Baron Zorn zu Bulach, wanted it made clear that on matters touching Alsace-Lorraine they were all of one accord; he had merely joined the Chancellor on the one issue of socialism.

Meanwhile Bismarck's program of social legislation had been held up pending the outcome of the bill against the socialists. New social measures were now up for discussion. The bill on sickness insurance having been accepted,[47] the question of compulsory accident insurance was next. A book on State Socialism (*Socialisme de l'état*) by Léon Say was quoted approvingly in the Reichstag. The laissez-faire advocates were of course opposed to all such social legislation, which Bismarck was insistently promoting. Each measure had to be worked out by a commission, in which modifications, if any, were made before the bill reached the Reichstag. It was this program of reform legislation, already examined and ready for debate, that was held up by the discussion of the antisocialist bill; the threatened dissolution would have postponed it indefinitely.

Before the passage of the antisocialist law in 1878 the growth of the socialist party had been rapid. After the activities of the party were made illegal, the socialists were hampered in recruiting laborers as members of their party organization. At the same time the ideas of the Marxist minority in the party became better known, publicized as they were by the Reichstag debates. As a result, within the party the Marxist minority made progress against the Lassallean majority.[48] Liebknecht and Bebel worked to make Marx's views prevail. They attacked Christianity, whether Catholic or Protestant,[49] but were skilful enough not

47. The bill on sickness insurance was adopted on June 15, 1883; accident insurance became law on July 16, 1884. There was a gradual extension of applicability to army, navy, transportation, building, navigation, and maritime occupations. Disability and old age laws came on June 22, 1887. See Francesco S. Nitti, *Catholic Socialism*, trans. Mary Mackintosh (3rd ed.; London, 1911), p. 10. The original Italian edition was published in 1895.

48. Lassallean ideas never wholly died out. They laid a groundwork for later Revisionism. This will be considered in a later chapter. See Shanahan, *German Protestants Face the Social Question*, p. 345.

49. On the other hand, a booklet by a Catholic author (R. P. Felix, S.J., *Le Socialisme devant la société* [Paris, 1878]) attributed the rise of socialism in Germany to Lutheranism and quoted once more Luther's oft-quoted words: "Rome—it is Babylon; the papacy—it

to push the attack too far and too fast. They recognized religion and nationalism[50] as the two most redoubtable foes of Marxian socialism.

The virtual ending of the Kulturkampf in 1887 gave Bismarck allies in his antisocialist program and in his plans for social betterment. He knew that he had lost valuable time by delaying his rapprochement with Leo XIII.

BELGIUM: SOCIALISM OR ANARCHISM?

Socialism in Belgium had the advantage (also present in England) of complete freedom of publication. Brussels was one of the chief centers for contact among reformers. Marx, Engels, Bakunin—each had been in Brussels before the publication of the *Communist Manifesto*. De Paepe, a Belgian, had heard Marx's address at the founding of the International Association of Workers in London. Belgium had had its own version of Utopian socialism.[51]

Now, Belgian workers were interested in protecting their own jobs by preventing the importation of labor. One of the avowed purposes of the First International had been to prevent such importation of cheap labor. In consequence, sections of the First International were formed without much difficulty in Brussels, Ghent, and other cities. The International, however, disapproved of strikes, and ruled that money paid into the general treasury was not to be used to support them. The Belgian workers, on the other hand, felt that in the absence of universal suffrage strikes were their most effective weapon. In spite of these differences of opinion the International made a significant beginning. It was ably led by César de Paepe and Henry van den Abeele, who kept Marx's authoritarian views alive even while they lent an ear to Bakunin's proposals. Édouard Anseele, differing from them, favored Bakunin's direct action. De Paepe participated actively in the congresses of the International where the theories of international socialism were beginning to be more

---

is the prostitute!" The author put Voltaire and Mirabeau as Church critics in the same category as Luther. The book was reviewed in *Univers* (July 18, 1878). An editorial (Aug. 3) took cognizance of the growth of atheistic socialism in the ranks of labor.

50. Both Liebknecht and Bebel had been sentenced to imprisonment for their failure to co-operate in the Franco-Prussian war. See Nollau, *International Communism and World Revolution*, p. 17.

51. G. D. H. Cole describes (*Socialist Thought*, II, 59-69) some of these versions: those of Kats, Colins, and de Keyser.

clearly defined. The more clearly the definitions were stated the wider grew the cracks between the various groups. De Paepe always argued against seeking "political liberties first." Yet in general he supported Marx's plans, and took the floor for him when Marx was not present in person.[52]

At the Hague Congress, where all decisions had gone as Marx wished and where Bakunin's emissaries had been barred, the question of socialism *vs.* anarchism had not been answered. War, rather, had been declared between the rival ideas. The Belgian leaders were disposed to drift away from the remnants of the International and go over to the new organization, founded by Bakunin, which claimed to be the continuation of the old Association. These Belgian leaders were restrained from outright adoption of the whole anarchist line by the force of changes occurring in society around them. De Paepe began to comprehend that the scientific elements in the Industrial Revolution would produce such a network of operations that central government would become the organ of scientific unity and localism would be impossible. With remarkable foresight he saw that because of new developments in manufacture craft organizations would disappear. At the Brussels conference (1874) he said: "The worker will no longer be tied for life to one particular kind of labor but will be free to engage simultaneously or successively in a number of different occupations."[53]

Anarchism continued to pose a threat to the followers of Karl Marx in Belgium, especially in the south. It had not been a real problem in Germany, for it gained little foothold among Germanic people, but from southern Belgium on to the Mediterranean, anarchistic tendencies appeared in much greater measure.[54] They remained a thorn in the flesh of Marx's adherents until the end and helped to sow discord among the various socialist groups which convinced Marxists were trying to weld together. Bakunin stirred the fires of anarchism[55] until his death

52. The French members of the International complained that leadership had moved from France to Belgium, where it had become authoritarian (i.e., Marxist). See Fribourg, *L'Association Internationale des Travailleurs,* p. 4.

53. Steklov, *History of the First International,* p. 295.

54. Georges Weill, *Histoire du movement social en France 1852-1914* (Paris, 1924), p. 263.

55. Both Proudhon and Bakunin have been called "anarchists" but they were very different from each other. Proudhon was a "mutualist," while Bakunin was a "libertarian." To follow the shifting meaning of these terms see Jean Maitron, *Histoire du mouvement anarchiste en France 1880-1914* (Paris, 1951), pp. 11, 43, 59, 111.

in 1876.[56] A group of able and militant disciples took up the work and continued to carry it on with spectacular methods that made the headlines.[57] The refusal of anarchists[58] to submit to regimentation in any form made organization among them difficult and ultimately impossible. The movement as an idea, furthermore involving *acts*, was far more important than the lack of cohesiveness among anarchists would tend to suggest. Every anarchistic act of violence sowed seeds of violence among those who found society oppressive. Anarchism rejected the political path. Authoritarian socialism made the conquest of the political powers the fundamental plank in its platform. The real question remained: to which leader would the workingman respond?

SOCIALIST DIVISION IN FRANCE

In France, the clear-cut victory of Marx at The Hague was not reflected. The strongest supporters of the Marxist program were ultimately Jules Guesde and Marx's son-in-law, Lafargue. Even Guesde came only by slow stages to the point of adopting Marx's views. The Hague meeting, which had taken the First International away from Bakunin, had simplified nothing in the French socialist movement. Left to their own devices by the decision to split up into national groups, French socialists were driving in every direction. Not all the groups were really socialist.

56. Bakunin, near the close of his life, thought the revolution (open revolution) was, for the moment, dead; it would be necessary to revert to subterranean, invisible revolution; the masses lacked revolutionary zeal; they could be saved only by organizing them to carry out a great revolution. But how to organize them? "Propaganda alone remains." Quoted in H. E. Kaminsky, *Michel Bakounine: La vie d'un révolutionnaire* (Paris, 1938), p. 342.

57. Most notable among the followers was the Russian, Prince Peter Kropotkin, first a famous geographer, then an anarchist, and then once more a geographer. Famous also were the brilliant Eliseé Reclus (also a geographer) and Louise Michel, the "good Louise," heroine of the Commune. Both Bakunin and Kropotkin were prosecuted for recruiting in France. Reclus went back to Switzerland, where he remained. Kropotkin returned to England and lived the life of a scholar. His trial in France gave publicity to his views. See Weill, *Histoire du mouvement social en France*, p. 263. The article on "anarchism" published in the *Encyclopedia Britannica* (1946 ed.) was written by Kropotkin.

58. Both Marxists and anarchists used the name "communist." Utopian socialists and mutualists had been "communist" too. The term had been used in the Middle Ages to describe the organization of urban communities to rebel against feudalism and set up towns independent of feudal interference. This element had also been present in the Paris Commune. It seems better to avoid the use of the term, at least until after socialist "Revisionism" developed.

All disapproved, in one way or another, of the existing social order. That was as far as unanimity went. They were well supplied with leaders, but the leaders were in disagreement on practically all points. In the course of time groups gathered around the most forceful, or vocal, or persuasive, of these leaders and formed small groups of adherents, designated by the names of their chiefs.

To make matters more complex, the leaders themselves did not always adhere throughout the 1870's and 1880's to the same program or platform with which they had started out; they sometimes shifted to new views, often radically different from the ones they had earlier held. All who had been involved in the Commune were in exile[59] or were banished late in the seventies for international activity. As if this were not enough, the confusion was still worse confounded by the fact that the workers—the actual workers—were members of their own unions, their *syndicats*, and were much more interested in the tangible improvement of their situation and in methods of still further improvement, than in developing theories or forming political parties. They were not committed to a socialist point of view. The program they supported without exception was the program of the French Revolution. They were revolutionaries, opposed to monarchy, aristocracy, and religious coercion. In this path they would gladly follow Blanqui, or the anarchist Bakunin, or Proudhon, whose spirit still lived on in the *syndicats*, or new young leaders arising from their own ranks. The *syndicats*, terribly damaged by the crushing of the Commune, in 1871, were groping for ways to improve their legal as well as their economic position. Never unified in their views, in general they believed in co-operatives, mutual credit associations, and strikes—including the revolutionary general strike. They had supported the candidacy of workers to speak for labor in the National Assembly and continued to support such candidacy for the Chamber of Deputies. They believed also in State intervention in questions of labor organization.[60]

59. A member of the First International complained that all members were being treated as though they had been responsible for the acts of violence committed by the Commune. Marx's letters to French members, directing them what to do, laid them open to arrest. See Zévaès, *Marxisme en France*, pp. 57-58. See also Fribourg, *L'Association Internationale des Travailleurs*, pp. 1-4. Fribourg was one of the founders of the International.

60. Bourdeau, *L'Évolution du socialisme*, p. 31. Although of medieval origin as guilds of journeymen, the *syndicats* developed and increased in numbers and significance under

The objective of the socialist leaders was to secure control over the thinking and activity of the workers. On the ground that writing was also labor they insinuated themselves into the central labor organizations where workers of different trades were gathered together. This process of insinuation would be regarded as evil or as good depending on whether one were in sympathy with or at enmity with the ideas thus introduced. Had the socialist leaders been of one mind this self-appointed task would have been much simpler. Their strength lay in their journals. In these they preached the word of socialism. The workers read the journals. The difficulty lay in the fact that the leaders differed among themselves as to the path to be followed in reaching the socialist goal. Coteries formed around the important socialist leaders, who indoctrinated their followers through the editorials in the journals. Leaders and workers, actually united only on the common ground of disapproval of the existing order and fear of resurrecting an order less to their liking, flowed together and apart, dividing, uniting, disputing, but always recognizing that the unity which proved so elusive would be necessary if they were to transform society. France could not be made socialist unless the mass of workers were won over to a single socialist viewpoint.

The setting up of a Republic while the Franco-Prussian war was in progress was approved by all the dissident. The sending of the Republic's military forces to put down the Commune of Paris brought disillusion.[61] The number of those opposed to any government increased. This opposition enlarged the ranks of the Blanquists and anarchists and hampered the socialists in their attempt to capture labor. The thing most feared by nearly every dissident, however, was the possible overthrow of the Republic by the monarchists. Such fears were not without justification. The history of France in the first years after the Commune was the

the Third French Republic. They were made up of skilled workmen, organized according to their craft, in syndical chambers. As a group they were averse to forming a political party. See Bernard Georges and Denise Tintant, *Léon Jouhaux: Cinquante ans de Syndicalisme*, I: *Des Origines à 1921* (Paris, 1962), 14-15n. The book is based on Jouhaux's notes and documents. Syndicalism as a movement cannot be said to have existed before the nineties, but the *syndicats* were nothing new.

61. The commune had moved from mild socialistic reforms to murder and pillage, execution of the hostages, and the burning of Paris. The Church sided with the Republican forces against the Commune. See Lecanuet, *L'Église de France*, pp. 133, 141.

story of attempts to take over the Republic and transform it into a monarchy. The first of these crises occurred in 1877.

All the people had participated in the election held while the war was going on. The Assembly thus elected governed France until permanent forms could be worked out. It was monarchist by virtue of the fact that the election turned, not on rival political views, but on the question of peace or war. Peace won, and the monarchists who had favored bringing the war to an end were the ones who had seats in the Assembly. They were not averse to social change in moderation. They retained social legislation passed in earlier regimes[62] and restored the syndical chambers. They even discussed eliminating laws under which the socialists were being penalized. Nothing, however, came of that.[63] Neither the extreme Left nor the intransigents of the extreme Right were pleased with this moderation. The members of the Assembly recognized that their retention of power was only transitory and temporary. Control was supposed to pass to a new monarchist government under one of the rival dynasties (Bonapartist, Legitimist [Bourbon], or Orleanist) that at one time or another had reigned in France. For the moment the Bonapartists were least in favor, having lost the war. Many of the monarchists in the Assembly were ultramontanists.[64]

Failing to overcome the intransigence of the Bourbon claimant (the Count of Chambord) with respect to adoption of the white flag, the Assembly was forced to put together a makeshift republican constitution, whose presidency could be easily exchanged for monarchy when the count died. To the clericals[65] this temporary arrangement was merely providing a caretaker government until the monarchist restoration should be brought about.

62. Measures passed under Louis Philippe and the "Liberal" Empire of Napoleon III were kept. See *ibid.*, pp. 130-132.

63. Landauer, *European Socialism*, I, 286.

64. By this time the term "ultramontanism" had altered in meaning. Before 1848 it had meant an appeal of liberals in the Church to the papacy to endorse their program of reform, blocked by the rigidity of the French hierarchy. The Revolution of 1848, the Commune of 1871, and the seizure of Rome by Italy had intervened. Now ultramontanism was a watchword of extreme Catholics who wanted a restoration of monarchy in France and who intended to restore Rome to the Pope.

65. Not all the clergy were ultramontanists. Bishop Dupanloup was leader of the liberals. He took a successful stand against an attempt to turn the Assembly into an ultramontane agency. See Lecanuet, *L'Église de France*, p. 161. See also *Univers*, April 6, 1872. Ultramontane *Univers* compared Dupanloup to "Pilate."

After the constitutional measures were adopted in 1875, France was a republic under a president. Elections, which were held under the constitutional provisions, promptly returned a republican majority in the lower house, the Chamber of Deputies. France prospered during these years, recovering prestige lost by the debacle of Sedan in 1870. Marshal MacMahon produced a crisis by arbitrarily dismissing the Simon[66] cabinet on May 16, 1877, the *Seize mai* over the clerical issue, and persuading the Senate (still monarchist) to dissolve the Chamber of Deputies. The Chamber, strengthened by election results, refused to support a cabinet appointed arbitrarily; MacMahon yielded. The country was fearful for a while that MacMahon would execute a coup d'état. He did not do so. The principle of responsible ministries was observed from then on. The threat of a coup d'état drew together all factions except the intransigent Right monarchist and ultramontanist. The workers were strongly republican. Their political ambition was to be permitted to organize and hold their meetings free from interruption by the police.

In the absence of any single party with majority strength, France was governed from this time on by coalitions put together from parties of somewhat similar views. These coalitions, just to the right or left of center, were opposed by the clerical-monarchist extreme Right and the radical and socialist Left. The group in power, avoiding extremes in either direction, was so pragmatic in its approach that it was always referred to as "Opportunist." Gambetta was the outstanding leader of this bloc.[67]

Although there were many socialists in France under the Third French Republic, there was no single French leader disposed and able to carry the Marxist banner as Liebknecht was doing in Germany and de Paepe in Belgium. The Marxist movement got its real start in France through the efforts of Paul Lafargue, Marx's son-in-law. Overwhelmed in Spain by the anarchist tide, Lafargue shifted the scene of his operations to France. The most notable of his successes here was winning Jules Guesde, editor of *Égalité*, to the Marxist cause. Like most of the other

66. Jules Simon had greatly offended the Pope (Pius IX was still alive) by saying that the Vatican was not a prison. "Someone," said Pius, "who directs a great state has said that the Pope lied. I do not wish to know who said it, but it was said." Quoted in Daniel Halèvy, *La Fin des notables*, II: *La République des ducs* (Paris, 1937), 267-268.

67. It was Gambetta who quoted in the Chamber: "Clericalism—there is the enemy!" Deschanel, *Gambetta*, p. 202. Cf. *Annales de la Chambre de Députés*, 1877, III, 24.

potential leaders, Guesde was in exile. Domiciled in Italy, he sent his articles to Paris for publication in *Égalité*. Returning from exile he resumed his position as editor. Still not a Marxist at the time of his return, he began reading the works of Marx and found himself drawn more and more toward the Marxian position. Lafargue persuaded him to visit Marx in London (1880).[68] This visit completed his conversion and gave him a program. From that point Guesde and Lafargue worked together to gain control over French socialists and French labor.

The chief lions in the path of Marxism, even if all socialists could be persuaded to get together, were anarchism and Blanquism. Blanqui was still in exile, but his devoted followers were numerous in France. Because Blanquism was a "personality cult," it would be incompatible with socialism. Yet it could not be ignored. The popularity of anarchism rested on its theories of "direct action" and the "general strike." These dream theories fascinated the rank and file of laborers, gathered in their *syndicats*. The Marxists (and other socialists) rejected the idea of a general strike. They preferred to put their trust in the political path, winning legislative control by electoral means.

In the year in which the First International was formally dissolved,[69] the year also in which Jules Guesde returned from exile, a delegation of French workers attended the Philadelphia Exposition of 1876. They came back with determination to hold a congress of workers to examine the problems of labor and confer as to the best methods of solving those problems.[70] They got together in Paris and discussed such subjects as restrictions on labor of women and children, retirement benefits, and removal of police surveillance of the *syndicats*. They concluded that an international gathering would be helpful. A commission was appointed to make arrangements for holding such a meeting in Paris in 1878. The year 1878 was chosen to coincide with the Paris Exposition held in commemoration of the death of Voltaire.

68. Marx and Guesde worked out a minimum program for French socialism. Emphasis was to be on organization and discipline. These factors, so ably developed in England by the trade unions, had been conspicuously absent among the radicals during the Commune in France. Guesde had noted the same lack in Italian socialism during his exile there. After the London trip he proposed to follow the English lead—organize—and stop tearing up the paving blocks to build barricades. See Maitron, *Histoire du mouvement anarchiste en France*, p. 94. See also Compère-Morel, *Jules Guesde*, pp. 98-99, 119.

69. Braunthal, *Geschichte der Internationale*, p. 197.

70. Steklou, *History of the First International*, p. 324.

Meanwhile the *syndicats* continued to hold local meetings. Views of every kind from anarchist to authoritarian Marxist were aired at these meetings. A meeting held at Lyons in 1878 exhibited all of these features. Some members suggested suppressing the machines, viewing them as the main cause of unemployment. They debated the issue of collectivism, but a motion of endorsement received only ten favorable votes. The question of greatest interest to the majority was that of freeing their associations from restrictions. They had no legal existence and no legal right to strike.[71] In spite of coming to no conclusions about anything (except their lack of enthusiasm for the Marxist program), they still thought they should report their discussion to the international workers' meeting planned for Paris later in the year.[72] At that meeting, as usual, there were *syndicat* members and social theorists, ranging from Guesdists to Blanquists. The rank and file of *syndicat* members were proletarian. Middle-class theorists, whether socialists, mutualists, or whatever, joined *syndicats* in order to attend meetings and get a foothold among the workers. Only among *syndicat* members were there enough actual bodies (in the physical sense) to carry out a revolution or win an electoral battle. The meeting at Lyons was covered by a Catholic reporter who sent his description to *Univers*. They were making, said the reporter the "same crude, sterile speeches" as before, having no more practical solution for the social problem than the "organization of a banquet at which they have drunk and sung to the wiping out of pauperism, the emancipation of the workingwoman, the representation of the proletariat, and so forth." They suggested solutions, according to the reporter, to stop competitive prison labor, stop piece work (the piece-worker worked longer hours), and to return to the system of the workers' owning their tools.[73] Solutions such as these were scorned by the Marxists; they were met with derision also by the conservatives. The conservative derision, however, was mixed with fear.

The centenary of Voltaire was duly celebrated; the Paris Exposition proceeded as scheduled; it was the plans of the socialists that ran into difficulties. The commission appointed by the *syndicats* to make the arrangements was stopped by the announcement that the French govern-

71. Compère-Morel, *Jules Guesde*, p. 133.
72. Maitron, *Histoire du mouvement anarchiste en France*, pp. 88-89.
73. *Univers*, March 8, 1878.

ment would not permit the Congress to meet in Paris. Confronted with this refusal, the commission drew back. They were in an embarrassing position. Seventy of their *syndicats* had made arrangements to send delegations, to join with socialists from far and near. The Marxist group, headed by Guesde,[74] was unwilling to drop the idea, in view of the expected attendance from within and without France. Not all of the groups on foreign soil, however, were able to send delegates. A Madrid group and one from New York, bewailing their exile, asked Massard in Paris to represent them. The Madrid group claimed to be "social revolutionaries, federated collectivists" (devoted to the Commune of 1871). The New York group was of the same general mind, but was troubled by internal squabbles; it wanted to go on to the "conquest of complete power over the Jesuits and the bourgeoisie."[75]

The Marxist group decided to proceed with its plans anyway, but to hold the meeting in a private dwelling and to permit only workers to attend, in order to circumvent the refusal of authorities to authorize the meeting. The leaders barricaded the house, as an extra precaution. When the delegates arrived they were met at the door by the Commissioner of Police. Arrests followed. The members were haled into court; their punishments ranged from fines of fifteen francs to six months' imprisonment. Jules Guesde was one of those drawing heavy sentences.[76] In his verbal defense in court, Guesde said the Prefect of Police, apparently without suspecting that there were laws against *conditional threats*, had threatened the treasurer and secretary with prosecution for illegal association unless they gave up their plan to hold the international meeting. They decided to go ahead with the meeting and put the law to the test, whether "all are really equal before the law—or whether it prohibits to the poor what it permits to the rich. French capitalists of all sorts had been able to hold . . . under the shelter of the Universal Exposition, their

74. As the result of an article by Guesde in *Égalité* (June 2, 1878) on the subject of the Centenary of Voltaire stating that while Voltaire had voted for confiscation of the goods of the clergy "he had invented the budget for religion; if he had chased the priest from the public square, instead of expelling him from everywhere and forever, he was content to close him up in a temple built and maintained at our expense," *Égalité* was suspended for a year. The journal reappeared in 1880. See Compère-Morel, *Jules Guesde*, p. 136.

75. Both letters in *Univers*, Oct. 29, 1878.

76. Léon Blum, *Les Congrès ouvriers et socialistes français* (2 vols.; Paris, 1901), I, 33; hereinafter cited as *Les Congrès*. Blum publishes a résumé of the minutes of the meetings.

international congresses and to take measures that were international in character. . . . Was labor alone to be excluded from such a right?"[77]

Some of the members of the French Chamber of Deputies were disturbed by the refusal of the authorities to permit the meeting; Louis Blanc wrote a letter of protest. The President of the Council said the law (of 1831) had been scrupulously obeyed; he refused to have the subject put on the agenda for discussion.[78]

Although the attempt to hold an international meeting had turned out to be a fiasco, slowing down Guesde and his Marxist group in their effort to get control of the *syndicats*, preparations were going forward to hold a French labor congress at Marseilles. The arrests made at Paris aroused special interest in this new attempt.[79] In addition to representatives from syndical chambers and professional associations,[80] unorganized socialist groups and social-studies circles were represented. It was a heterogeneous gathering. The hall was decorated with the customary posters: "No rights without duties; no duties without rights"; "Work for all"; "Land for the peasant"; etc. They adopted a name: the Worker's Socialist Congress of France (*Congrès ouvrier de France*).[81] On the whole the Congress was a triumph for the Marxist Guesde. Although the Congress did not yet recommend the abolition of the wage system, it approved resolutions endorsing collectivism, the immediate nationalization of mines and railways, and the establishment of a French Socialist Party.[82] The Congress, which at its Lyons meeting in 1878, the preceding year, had said, "Let the master and disciples of collectivism find some other speakers' platform than that of the national congress of French labor,"[83] now was approving what it had shortly before rejected. Though approval was sought for both consumers' and producers' co-operatives, which could be useful propagandizing agencies, the idea of revolution was uppermost in the minds of the delegates. The stand of Louis Blanc, who

77. Compère-Morel, *Jules Guesde*, p. 131.
78. *Univers*, Sept. 19, 1878.
79. Maitron, *Histoire du mouvement anarchiste en France*, p. 91. See also Blum, *Les Congrès*, I, 33.
80. One for every twenty-five members, except in larger cities, where the ratio was one for every thirty members. "Syndical chamber" is the technical term applied to an organized local craft union, or *syndicat*.
81. Maitron, *Histoire du mouvement anarchiste en France*, p. 93.
82. *Parti des Travailleurs Socialistes en France*. See Blum, *Les Congrès*, I, 44.
83. Blum, *Les Congrès*, I, 26.

had expressed in a letter to *Figaro* his horror at the current incendiarism, pillage, and assassination, was attacked in a speech that exhorted members to remember that their brothers were those in other lands—Russia and Germany—who were united in crying: "Long live the universal social revolution."[84]

French journals attacked the decisions of the Marseilles Congress. Guesde, in *Revue socialiste*, defended the program. "Collectivists . . . are not communists in the accepted sense of the word in France. They have never advocated the sharing of the fruits of labor, objects of consumption. . . . They do advocate collective appropriation of the means of production."[85]

After the Congress of Marseilles, the out-and-out anarchists did not attend the congresses. The year following, at Le Havre, their credentials were not validated. They simply stayed away from the meeting at Reims (1881). They thought the socialists were as bad as the parliamentary bourgeoisie. Failing to get up an organization of their own, they resorted simply to anarchist acts.[86]

Although Guesde triumphed in successive labor congresses, factional diversity continued among the leaders of the French working class. Diversity was encouraged by the consolidation of the Third Republic. Republicans gained control of the Senate and then, with the resignation of the monarchist MacMahon, of the presidency. The preservation of the Republic had momentarily united bourgeois and labor groups in a common cause. Now that its future seemed assured, the various groups were freer to seek the realization of their own special aims. Diversity was also promoted by the release of left-wing labor leaders from prison. They resumed agitation for their ideas. Besides, the spirit of anarchism was not dead. The Marxists could use it as a wave to carry them forward, but in the end they must bring it under control or lose their program. Yet to destroy anarchism would be impossible, for by its very nature it was not subject to sudden death, because of its abhorrence of organization and lack of authoritarian ideology. In addition (a further diversity), not all of Guesde's associates had experienced change to

84. *Ibid.*, pp. 37-38.
85. Compère-Morel, *Jules Guesde*, p. 157.
86. Maitron, *Histoire du mouvement anarchiste en France*, pp. 101-102. Their meetings became increasingly chaotic.

authoritarian Marxism. Paul Brousse[87] declined to follow Guesde's lead. He and Guesde were becoming rivals. And there was the spirit of the exiled Blanqui, still living among his followers.

One of the first acts of the now thoroughly republican government in France was to take steps toward the return of the exiled Communards. Partial amnesty was granted at once. Blanqui had been elected to represent Bordeaux even while he was in exile. On his return he was chosen by a large majority of voters, but his election was not validated.[88] He would be a candidate again, content to substitute ballots for barricades.

The convoys were returning as a result of the partial amnesty. The second convoy was met in Paris by Louis Blanc, in spite of the fact that he had squarely condemned the Commune in 1871. Now Blanc and Blanqui were taking bows together. Victor Hugo joined Blanc in the demand for complete amnesty.[89] This became a popular topic for fiery political speeches by those trying to get the deported elected. Even the Catholic journal *Univers* thought partial amnesty called for full amnesty; it was difficult to understand how Rochefort could remain in exile when Gambetta was "enthroned at the Palais-Bourbon." Perhaps the most dramatic case was that of Sylvain Humbert. A letter from Rochefort (still deported) was read to the voters in an attempt to get Humbert elected:

It was there, six thousands leagues from home, that more than four hundred of the condemned underwent their punishment, in the midst of robbers, assassins, and parricides. Humbert was among them, and when I heard the roll of the drums designed to cover the cries of the punished, I would say to myself: "Perhaps it is Humbert they are beating."[90]

87. Paul Brousse was a medical student originally sponsored by Guesde, before the latter's conversion to the Marxian school. Brousse was one of the supporters of the revolutionary movement driven in France to *sub rosa* meetings in darkened cellars and to sending out their journal (*La Solidarité*) in boxes of wine. In Switzerland their brochures were easily published. Among these were: "*The Crimes of the Popes*, by One of the Damned; *The Knavery of the Bishops and Priests*, by An Apostate," and others, some of them directed against property owners and the army. See Maitron, *Histoire du mouvement anarchiste en France*, p. 80.

88. Since Blanqui was an unofficial (what Americans would call a "write-in") candidate, his total number of votes would be "against the book" and must represent a quarter of the number of registered voters, not of the number of votes cast. Although he received more votes than both of his competitors put together, he thus lost the election.

89. *Marseillaise* said the deportees came back in rags, with foreign wives; someone called deportation the "dry guillotine." Quoted in *Univers*, Oct. 9, 1879.

90. *Siècle*, quoted in *Univers*, Oct. 12, 1879. Sylvain Humbert, a journalist, subsequently became a leader and historian of the labor movement.

Humbert was elected!

The law granting complete amnesty was passed in June, 1880.[91] This brought back more deportees and produced a substantial revival of Blanquist influence. The Blanquists set forth their intentions in a lengthy manifesto; its principal tenets appealed strongly to the workers in highly industrialized areas where the votes of this class were a determining factor in election outcomes. The Blanquist manifesto, born of the bitterness and suffering of exile, of the galleys and prisons, of the blood of the executed, was a defiance of God and man, a wail demanding revenge, a promise of a new society that would emerge after an initial period of proletarian dictatorship and bring an end to all exploitation of man by man. It called upon the proscribed to form a new party, "the Revolutionary Commune," which should be atheist, for "man would never be free" until he should have "driven God from his intelligence." This "monstrous idea of a being . . . outside the world and man" was the "principal obstacle to his liberation"; this error must be denied "before all others" because for centuries it had been the root of all actions which "curbed, enchained, despoiled, and martyred men"; in the Commune every priest, every religious organization "must be proscribed." The struggle was not alone against the Church, the manifesto stated, but against the bourgeoisie because the capitalists allowed the workers "just enough to prevent starvation." There must be no room for "compromise, which by delaying victory would merely prolong slavery; by the abolition of property the annihilation of classes could be carried out"; universal instruction would lead to "intellectual equality," necessary for material equality. The movement must be "communist" and "revolutionary," overturning by force a society maintained by force; the "commune" was simply the "military force of the Social Revolution." The "radicals" (supporters of the Opportunist Government) would be the last defenders of the "dying bourgeois world"; against the people "radicals and Jesuits were in accord." Particularly to be avoided were those who would substitute for rapid revolution the slower process of "evolu-

91. The return of the amnestied brought back to Paris Charles Longuet and his wife Jenny, Marx's daughter. Marx visited them subsequently in Paris. Marx died in London in 1883. Engels carried on his work of publication. His son-in-law Lafargue carried on his program in northern Spain and France. Another daughter, Eleanor Marx-Aveling, supported Marx's program. Longuet, a serious student of economic and social problems, began to modify his early views in the light of observable facts.

tion." Hurling its defiance against society, the document boldly accepted the incendiarism and the execution of the hostages carried out by the Commune.[92] It was a remarkable document, calculated to arouse hatred, courage, and determination, or fear, disapproval, and disgust; compassion would be the last emotion one would expect to be aroused.[93]

The returning Communard exiles founded a Central Revolutionary Committee which opposed the French Workers' Party[94] that had managed at Marseilles to put under one roof for the time being the many disparate elements among the dissident.[95] This new committee lacked cohesiveness, desiring as it did to engage in special revolutionary projects. The Blanquist elements were brought somewhat in line through the organizing efforts of Éduard Vaillant.[96]

Blanqui did not live long after his repatriation. He died January 1, 1881. There was some fear that a struggle might occur at his funeral, the die-hards having announced their intention to attend with the red flag of the Commune, but no disturbance took place. On the way to the Père Lachaise cemetery there were cheers for the social revolution, for Rochefort, and for Blanqui; the marchers carried the red flag; they doffed their hats in passing the Statue of Liberty in the square of the Bastille; they did not lay the flag on the casket. Police made no attempt to stop any of this.[97]

The influence of Blanqui could not be buried with him. Clemenceau, for example, who had just been elected head of the Extreme Left (in the Chamber of Deputies), had been deeply stirred by him.[98] To two generations of workingmen and eager young intellectuals "Le Vieux" had been the spark that moved them from apathy to action. Now they were

92. Printed handbill of the manifesto, n.d. It was signed by Da Costa and Vaillant.

93. And yet, one of the original Communards, wounded and pitiful, started a faithful son of the Church on a life-long quest to help and solace the unfortunate. The career of this compassionate man, Albert de Mun, will be recounted in the next chapter.

94. Albert Orry, *Les Socialistes indépendants*, Vol. VIII of Jaurès, *Histoire des parties socialistes* (Paris, 1911), pp. 3-4. See also Zévaès, *Marxisme en France*, p. 52.

95. John Labousquière, *La Troisième République*, p. 232.

96. Landauer, *European Socialism*, p. 291. It was Vaillant who with the Italian Da Costa signed the Blanquist manifesto.

97. *Univers*, Jan. 6, 1881. Blanqui's grave became subsequently a rallying point for the dissident.

98. As a young medical intern Georges Clemenceau had visited Blanqui daily in his prison (Sainte-Pélagie) in the sixties; he himself was the son of a deportee to Algeria. See Lecanuet, *L'Église de France*, p. 39.

turning to legislative halls where under the Third French Republic representatives could "blow off steam" for themselves and their constituents.

The French Workers Party was split into two wings as a result of the fight developing between Guesde and Brousse. Guesde's collectivist wing clung close to the program of Marx and Engels;[99] this group alone maintained close ties with Marx in London and subsequently with Engels. The Possibilists,[100] under Brousse, had no such ties. Guesde, under the guidance of Marx, was trying to centralize the workers' organization and make it answerable to Marxist authoritarian policies. Brousse detested this "German" authoritarianism.[101] The opponents of Guesde's Marxist program thought it was too abstract, too full of "political economy," of which the mass of workers knew nothing; most of all they resented attempts to subject them to rigid control.[102] Guesde saw that a break with Brousse was inevitable.

It would be a mistake to think that the platform of any group or leader was fixed and final. The changing economic and political scene brought questions as to how an egalitarian society could be achieved. In public discussions leaders were forced to clarify their pronouncements and even to admit the necessity for change in their tactics. One such occasion (in 1881) was especially illuminating. A debate was held in public between Guesde and Charles Longuet, Marx's son-in-law. Several other labor leaders and many workers were present. Longuet stated that he had some reservations about the immediate appropriation of the soil; this aspect of the party's program he found unacceptable; there were

99. Guesde resented being called an anarchist; he claimed that he was an adversary of Bakunin, but not an adversary of anarchists as people; he disapproved of their acts and doctrines; he found absurd their notion that the State with its repressions was the only obstacle to the realization of an egalitarian society. See Compère-Morel, *Jules Guesde*, p. 147. See also Bourdeau, *Évolution du socialisme*, p. 37.

100. The word "Possibilism" was first used in *Prolétaire* (Nov. 19, 1881): "It is necessary to split up our objective in order to render it ultimately possible." See Sylvain Humbert (*Les Possibilistes* [Paris, 1911], Vol. IV of Jaurès, *Histoire des partis socialistes*, p. 7) for Malon's comment: "It is almost always its enemies that give a movement its name." Brousse, recounting earlier anarchist victories over the Marxists, declared: ". . . but we were isolated and we lacked energy in the conflict with the bourgeois mass." He claimed that the bourgeoisie were united against the working class. See Steklov, *History of the First International*, p. 347. Now Brousse was trying to fit his program to political facts.

101. Marx used the term "German socialism" as the equivalent of "modern scientific socialism." See Marx to Sorge, London, Nov. 5, 1880. Quoted in Zévaès, *Marxisme en France*, p. 113.

102. Orry, *Les Socialistes indépendants*, p. 4.

too many obstacles to surmount. He thought this proposal, which did not regard the peasant as a serious impediment to immediate communizing of the soil, could not be realized during their lifetime. The peasants would never be converted by propaganda—only by actual fact. Industry, he continued, was much more advanced, but if a "magic wand" could turn it over to the revolution, "how would the proletariat handle it?" The existing organization could not be replaced at one fell swoop by another. The revolution should proceed by degrees. It might start, for example, nationalizing the railroads.

Guesde, in reply, said he did not expect industry to be turned over to the revolution by a "magic wand"; he protested that there was no thought of expropriating the land of the small peasant proprietor; he even admitted that he himself was evolutionary and not revolutionary. He went on to assert that the actual direction of industry was already in the hands of workers, the employers being idle. Guesde complained that the French Revolution had raised the Third Estate by dispossessing the First and Second, and had then proceeded to close the door to prevent the rise of the Fourth. Longuet rejoined that partial reforms were possible—such as shortening the hours of labor. The International had never imposed a credo; now Guesde's party, he declared, was trying to impose a program. In the general discussion which ensued it was proclaimed that power must be snatched from the bourgeoisie; the ballot must be supported by the gun; it must be peace or war. Once more Longuet took up the argument; the bourgeoisie could make reforms, and not through disinterest; furthermore, the Workers' Party represented only a small minority of the workers, having only some fifteen thousand members. This Guesde denied.[103]

The disagreement between Brousse and Guesde became an open quarrel at the Congress of St. Étienne (1882).[104] Unable to get control of the French Socialist Workers' Party (*Fédération des travailleurs socialistes*) at the Congress, Guesde and twenty-two others walked out to hold a

103. Compère-Morel, *Jules Guesde*, pp. 190-195. Guesde wrote to Clemenceau, editor of *Justice*, after the debate with Longuet, that he did not expect to socialize agriculture until "industrial and financial property, then commercial property," had been taken. *Ibid.*, p. 197.

104. Orry, *Les Socialistes indépendants*, p. 7. At Le Havre in the intervening year, a bitter fight had broken out, but the body remained together for another year.

rival meeting (at Roanne) as the French Workers' Party (*Parti ouvrier français*).[105]

The eighty-eight socialists who remained after Guesde's walkout included Brousse and his Possibilists, and also Malon,[106] who did not see eye to eye with Brousse on all points. They kept the original party name, Federation of Socialist Workers: *Fédération des travailleurs socialistes*, usually called "Possibilists."[107] This group drew up an indictment against Guesde, accusing him of being "bourgeois," of having destroyed the First International, and of having made a travesty of Brousse's opinions. Brousse said Guesde wanted to impose Marxism in every detail. The report went on to ask the Congress whether they wanted in their midst "popes or infallibilists, making use whenever they wished of censure and excommunication." From now on the two groups held separate congresses and appeared as rivals on all sorts of occasions.[108]

Although the Possibilists were numerically stronger than Guesde's authoritarian group (which walked out in 1882) they did not present a united front on basic questions. Brousse and Jean Allemane differed on the matter of co-operation with bourgeois parties, although they were agreed on Possibilism as a general program. Left-wing Allemane frowned upon co-operation, while Brousse favored it. Another source of dispute was the general strike, disapproved by Brousse but endorsed by Allemane. These differences were not resolved. They would lead later to an actual break.[109] For the time being the Possibilists, meeting in Paris in 1883, turned their attention to electoral procedures[110] and local elections.

Guesde's *Parti ouvrier* at their meeting discussed basic theory. The

105. Blum, *Les Congrès*, I, 78. One element in the quarrel concerned whose journal, Guesde's or Brousse's, had the right to speak for labor. Brousse's *Prolétaire* had been founded while Guesde's *Égalité* was under suspension. Now they were competitors.

106. Benoît Malon, who had educated himself by incredible labor and self-denial, became a revolutionary. Taking refuge in Switzerland after the Commune, he associated with Blanquists, but contributed to Guesde's *Égalité*. He remained friends with Guesde in spite of the break at St. Étienne. See Weill, *Histoire du mouvement social*, p. 268. See also Compère-Morel, *Jules Guesde*, p. 121.

107. Humbert, *Les Possibilistes*, p. 3. See also Zévaès, *Marxisme en France*, p. 124.

108. Blum, *Les Congrès*, I, 80, 89. Engels said (Oct. 22, 1882): "The incompatible elements have separated, and that is good." Brousse said: "If the Marxists are right the laborers will go over to them."

109. Braunthal, *Geschichte der Internationale*, p. 217.

110. *Scrutin de liste* (choosing representatives from a total list rather than each district voting for its own representative). This procedure, which the Possibilists approved, permits a minority to elect at least a few representatives.

consensus was that revolution could not be predetermined. Rather it would be the "fated consequence of the general movement elaborated in modern society"; the task of the party would be to educate the working class and prepare them "through universal suffrage" to transfer the struggle to the political domain; it would be carried out under a single program in which the party would act dictatorially, with the aim of seizing the public powers; subsequently the party, as a class party, would disappear, having no longer any reason for existence.[111] They predicted that the state would disappear as Engels said; its last act would be the taking over of the means of production.[112]

The leaders of the various parties might discuss practical politics or fundamental theory, but if they were going to make any progress they must woo labor, whose *syndicats* were opposed to political parties.[113] Each local *syndicat* was completely autonomous. It handled its own local problems, from collective bargaining and calling a strike to the arrangements for its own social gatherings. Representatives of these *syndicats* attended various syndical congresses, listened to speeches, discussed hours and wages, followed popular leaders in their disagreements, but went home to make real decisions. They might be swayed by oratory or influenced by journals, but they were not bound by decisions of any central body or compelled to submit to its dictates. They were a series of cells—not a honeycomb cemented together.

One factor which slowed the development of syndical strength was the relative absence of large-scale industry; in France the customary place of work was shop rather than factory. Each industrial or mining enterprise was likely to be owned by a family.

The *syndicats* had been tolerated rather than legalized until 1884. When legalization came in that year, under the Waldeck-Rousseau law,

111. Blum, *Les Congrès*, I, 94.

112. *Ibid.*, I, 96. The minutes of the meetings make dry reading. More lively are the newspaper accounts. At the Workers' Party meeting in 1884 at Roubaix a considerable fracas occurred in which some German proletarians tried to overturn the Vendôme column, a proceeding which some three hundred students tried to stop. See Jules Guesde in *Cri du peuple*, quoted in *Univers*, Feb. 19, 1885.

113. Lewis L. Lorwin, *The International Labor Movement: History, Policies, Outlook* (New York, 1953), pp. 30-31. Victor G. Chaulnes, writing at the time (*Univers*), attributed the rise of the *syndicats* to the laissez-faire economic theory—its "liberty to work," which gave the workers no protection, resembled asking a baby left alone in the desert to "celebrate his liberty"; the workman's only recourse was to form associations; the *syndicats* were "born of these aspirations, legitimate in their origin."

the non-socialist *syndicats* readily constituted themselves as legal organizations. The socialist *syndicats,* which had fought against the passage of the bill, preferred uncertain toleration to legalization with police surveillance.[114] They came to take an increasing interest in electing representatives, at the national and local level, who showed sympathy with their aspirations. Sporadic acts of violence punctuated their history. These were largely spontaneous acts growing out of local situations. In areas where Catholic reformers had been more successful in organizing clubs under clerical guidance there was much less violence, the Church acting as a conservative force.

No one was more aware than Jules Guesde of the importance of gaining the ear of the workers in the *syndicats* if the socialist cause were to prosper in France. The objective of his *Parti ouvrier* was the conquest of the public powers of the state. "Syndicalism," he stated, "independent of political parties, is absolutely incapable of leading the workers to their emancipation." Guesde's intention was to establish an "indissoluble union" between the workers' movement and socialism, "subordinating economic action to political action," and viewing the *syndicats* as a good field for "socialist recruiting."[115] Members of Guesde's *Parti ouvrier* joined various *syndicats* to spread the authoritarian socialist word. They helped in the organization (in 1886) of a federation of *syndicats,* which soon became a sort of annex to the *Parti ouvrier.* In the same year the Labor Bureaus[116] were set up in connection with local *syndicats.* The leaders of these bureaus viewed with alarm this extension of the Marxist *Parti ouvrier* into the ranks of labor. Whether the federation of *syndicats* would regain its independence or remain under the wing of the Guesdist party was for the time being an unanswerable question. Uncertainty in this matter added an extra element contributing to the growing confusion in socialist ranks, already split three ways by the defection of the Possibilists and by the increasing lack of harmony between the Possibilists Brousse and Allemane.

114. There were 400,000 members of the *syndicats* in 1884. Bourdeau, *Évolution du socialisme,* p. 37.
115. Georges and Tintant, *Léon Jouhaux,* p. 15.
116. These were Labor Exchanges, usually aided by financial grants from the municipalities in which they operated as semipublic institutions. Some labor extremists were prejudiced against them because of this acceptance of funds from the public authorities. The function of the bureaus was to secure labor for employers and employment for idle laborers. They also did some work in training workers for prospective employers.

The federation of *syndicats* favored the strike as a weapon. Although local strikes were decided by local *syndicats*,[117] there was no belief that local strikes could really solve the workers' problem; only the general strike could do that. In 1888 the federation adopted a resolution to this effect: "Only the general strike, that is to say the complete stoppage of all work, or Revolution, can lead the workers toward their emancipation."[118] This was anti-Marxist doctrine. Guesde and his *Parti ouvrier* still believed that socialism could win only through conquest of the public powers by entering the political arena. They found that the *syndicats* by espousing the general strike were slipping from their grasp.

SOCIALISM *VS.* ANARCHISM IN ITALY

Bakuninist influence presented in Italy a greater obstacle to the apostles of Marxian socialism than it did anywhere north of the Alps. In the period from the death of the First International[119] to the founding of Italian socialism in 1890, the peninsula was the scene of episodic rebellions and unrelated anarchistic acts of violence. As the famous Anna Kulishov declared in open court in Florence: "Socialism does not create armed bands, but it is ready to direct those that are thrown up naturally by social conditions."[120] The development of a controlled, centralized authoritarian, socialist movement in Italy seemed impossible of attainment.

The Risorgimento with its excitement and ultimate political victory, culminating in making Rome the capital of united Italy, had pleased the people of all classes, even the humblest. Now, they thought, would come long-expected improvements in day-by-day living. The improvements failed to appear.[121] The fires and illuminations in honor of na-

117. Most serious of these was the one at Decazeville, in 1886, where violence occurred on both sides. Rothschild was reported as saying to President Grévy and Premier Freycinet: "Rid me of this Decazeville strike or I will kill your loan along with your credit." See *Univers*, April 5, 1886, quoting *Cri du peuple*.

118. Blum, *Les Congrès*, I, 111.

119. Recruitment for the First International was carried out in Italy by Cafiero, who tried to get a Central Committee for Italy and then to establish a national section of the International. He was assisted by Gambuzzi. See Romano, *Storia del movimento socialista in Italia*, II, 86, 98.

120. Neufeld, *Italy*, p. 108. Expelled from France in 1877, she had turned up in Italy, where she became associated with anarchists. Her companion, Andrea Costa, had been imprisoned, and returned to Italy after his release (1879).

121. Giovanni Spadolini (*Lotta sociale in Italia* [Florence, 1948], p. 31) speaks of the Risorgimento as a "social failure."

tional triumph cooled to ashes, leaving the mass of people worse off than before. The mood of the Italian people became one of disillusionment. On the eve of the War of Liberation, King Victor Emmanuel II had declared: "We are not insensible to the cries of misery which are raised toward us from so many parts of Italy."[122] It is true that the old feudalism had been made illegal, which seemed a gain, but a new, actual feudalism—an administrative feudalism—controlling police action, had taken its place. Against it the ignorant peasants were defenseless.[123]

The "cries of misery" were still being raised, but in vain. In the effort to bind the state together and restore it to something of its ancient prestige, expenditures were made which necessitated increased taxation. Economic conditions, especially in the south, went steadily from bad to worse. Denuded of forests,[124] the soil was lost by erosion. Agriculture, the mainstay of southern Italy, became less productive. Unemployment increased, relieved only by emigration to the Americas.[125] It was in the southern area that anarchism had at first its greatest appeal. However, anarchism had spread from the south to the north,[126] where it made more rapid gains. The split at The Hague in 1872 had been demoralizing to the Italian leaders. They were inclined to join Bakunin's International Alliance.[127] The anarchistic tendency never disappeared from the Italian labor scene. Garibaldianism and Mazzinianism had both fed its fires by their agitation for political liberation[128] and social reform.

Industrial development in the north was proceeding with rapidity. Here the old craft guilds had laid foundations for a modern labor movement. A *fascio operaio* (union of laborers) had been founded by workers themselves.[129] No one was permitted to join who was not actually a

122. Lémonon, *L'Italie économique et sociale*, p. 265.
123. Giocchino Volpe (*Italia moderna 1815-1915* [Florence, 1945], p. 221) says they found relief only in "explosions, violent and sterile."
124. *Ibid.*, p. 83. Timber was used in construction of roads.
125. Romano, *Storia del movimento socialista in Italia*, I, 53-54. See also Giuseppe Toniolo, *Capitalism and Socialism* (Vatican City, 1947), p. 389.
126. Lémonon, *L'Italie économique et sociale*, p. 338.
127. Ivanoe Bonomi, *La politica italiana da Porta Pia a Vittorio Veneto 1870-1918* (Turin, 1944), p. 116.
128. The death of Mazzini in 1872 produced a gradual dissolution of his movement. See Cole, *History of Socialist Thought*, II: *Marxism and Anarchism 1850-1890*, 123.
129. The workers of the north were literate, competent, and industrious. One of the reasons for calling the London meeting (1864) had been to prevent the importation of labor to compete with native labor in any country. Those most frequently imported (and not only on the Continent) were the Italians. The records of strikes in French industry contain many references to this importation.

worker. Here was another obstacle in the path of Marxism. Marxist theorists, including Marx and Engels themselves, were middle-class intellectuals attempting to organize and direct the workers, but were almost never, even in origin, members of the working class.[130] The Italian clergy, on the other hand, were not middle class but peasant in origin.[131]

The return of Andrea Costa to Italy in 1880 after his release from French incarceration marked a step, not only in the development of socialism as opposed to anarchism, but also in the turning of labor leaders toward the path of change through parliamentary procedure. Costa was won over to this method of securing reform. This was true also of Enrico Bignami and Oswaldo Gnocchi-Viani, who chose the parliamentary path. They tried to establish socialism on a legal footing.[132] The workers, however, were unwilling to support the socialist candidates and ran their own. This practice further divided the forces of the Left.

It would take time for the people of Italy to distinguish the differences among the various proposals for reforming society. Nihilism, communism, socialism, anarchism, were all equally suspect, interchangeable, in fact, in their eyes. If an outrage were committed and the suspect could not be identified, all Marxist socialists who were handy were arrested and brought to trial.

In turning to the path of legislative reform all moderate and leftist parties were hampered by the absence of any real parliamentary procedure. King Humbert's[133] idea of cabinet government was more nearly like that of the Hohenzollerns of Prussia. The problem of political evolution toward democracy would slow the process of confronting the social

130. The Italian socialists Enrico Bignami, Osvaldo Gnocchi-Viani, and Andrea Costa were middle-class Marxists, although Costa had started out as a Bakuninist. Constantino Lazzari, a glove maker, who ultimately became the secretary of the Socialist Party, was one of the few socialists to rise from the ranks of the working class. See Neufeld, *Italy*, pp. 105-109.

131. Robert Michels (*Italien von Heute: politische und wirtschaftliche Kulturgeschichte von 1866 bis 1930* [Zurich and Leipzig, 1930]) asserted that the clergy in spite of their "hierarchical structure" were genuinely Italian in their feeling. This Bakunin had discovered; Michels reiterated it.

132. Lémonon, *L'Italie économique et sociale*, pp. 342-345. Malatesta urged boycotting the legislative path. Cafiero, who had in the beginning sold his patrimony and given it to the workers' movement, was ultimately won over from anarchism to parliamentary socialism.

133. After the death of Victor Emmanuel II, Humbert I had succeeded to the throne in 1878, just at the time of Leo XIII's election. His coronation was one of the "affronts" to the new Pope. The year was marked by bomb outrages, especially directed against the royal family, and celebrations held in their honor.

problem realistically, and yet such a development of political liberalism was a necessary prelude to any successful attempt to develop socialism. The reactionary state must first be defended and made liberal.[134]

No description of the rise of socialism, no picture of the social problem, no recounting of efforts to stir the Italian masses to organize or to resist the heavy hand of the property owner or employer, can be drawn in Italy. Conditions varied too much from area to area in a country whose parts had for so many centuries been divided into separate political units. Such statistics as are available[135] are completely inadequate and misleading. One is safe only in saying that in general the north led the south, the urban far outdistanced the rural, and that examples of benevolence in attitude toward workers were so rare that they were suspect when demonstrated. Poverty was incredible; ignorance was complete; hope was almost non-existent; police repression was unbelievable. Co-operatives and mutuals, wherever they existed, offered a single ray of hope. There was no fertile ground for sowing seeds of Marxian organization and militancy. Such concepts were completely out of reach. Workers needed to be helped. Employers needed to be converted. That the Church was not wholly blind to the social problem will appear in the next chapter.

134. Spadolini, *Lotta sociale in Italia*, pp. 211-213.
135. Neufeld (*Italy*, chap. v) gives as complete a coverage of statistical evidence as is possible to put together.

VIII. THE WORKINGMAN AND THE CATHOLIC REFORMERS

"If Catholics in name were Catholics in fact the social problem would be resolved."[1]

GEORGES CLEMENCEAU

A young officer of the French army was standing with his superior watching a convoy of Communards led away in 1871 from the Paris they had left in flames. Among them he saw a bleeding, dying man who said: "The Insurgents—it is you." "The convoy moved on," said the officer later, "but the sight remained with us. Between these insurrectionists and the legal society of which we were the defenders, an abyss appeared which this legal society had made."[2] The young officer was Albert de Mun. He was twenty-nine years old at the time of the Franco-Prussian war. That day, unable to get the dying man out of his mind, this fervent Catholic embarked on a lifelong career of effort to solve the social problem in and through the Church. He found that there had been others before him equally disturbed. Notable among these were members of the charitable order of St. Vincent de Paul. To them he turned for advice. He was directed to Bishop Ketteler in Germany.

Baron Wilhelm von Ketteler, Bishop of Mainz, was the outstanding figure among German Catholic reformers. The area of his life and labors was the Rhineland, where idustrialization brought on the social problem early in the century. Here the influence of the Pietists had been strong.[3] Here social reform had been first directed to the needs of orphans

1. Quoted in Henri Rollet, *L'Action sociale des Catholiques en France 1871-1914* (Paris, 1947), p. 335.
2. Adrien Dansette, *Les Origines de la Commune de 1871* (Paris, 1944), pp. 168-169.
3. The influence of Pietism on Engels has already been noted.

left destitute by the revolutionary and Napoleonic wars.[4] Ketteler entered the priesthood and was ordained priest in 1844. He studied under the greatest Catholic theologians of his day: Döllinger and Haefele.[5] From the beginning he concerned himself with the problems of want and charity, distributing his entire patrimony in alleviating the distress of the poor.[6] His fame rested, however, not on his personal charities but on his clarion call to Catholics to take cognizance of the urgency of the social problem. In 1848 at Mainz, while still a parish priest (he was made bishop two years later), he preached a series of sermons which aroused widespread interest: "The Great Social Questions of the Present."[7] Ketteler's most arresting statement dealt with the nature of property. He criticized the Liberals' laissez-faire doctrine of "unlimited competition in an atomized society"[8] and claimed that the "false doctrine of the absolute right of property" was a "continuing crime against nature." He asserted, on the other hand, that the famous words: "Property is theft!" were both false and true. From the falseness of the doctrine of property was born "the false doctrine of communism."[9] But the statement was not wholly false, for property could not be regarded "as exclusively one's own."[10] Believing that all ills were due simply to lack of faith,[11] Ketteler addressed himself to the individual. He did not, as did the socialists, assign to society in general responsibility for the plight of the laborer; he did not plan to organize labor nor to start legislative reforms; what he did was to arouse an undying concern over the social problem. He became interested in Lassalle's movement and corresponded with him for some time. Becoming dissatisfied with Lassalle's emphasis

4. Shanahan, *German Protestants Face the Social Question*, p. 66.

5. Döllinger was the founder of the Old Catholics in Germany, following Vatican Council I in 1870.

6. Avolio, *I Democratici Cristiani e'il non expedit*, p. 7. Ketteler was sent as representative to the Frankfort Parliament in 1848, where he took an important part in claiming for Germany "liberty of religious associations of every confession" and "autonomy in scholastic matters."

7. ". . . the social question," said Ketteler, "looms larger than ever, demanding solutions more harshly than ever." William von Ketteler, *Die grossen socialen Fragen der Gegenwart* (Mainz, 1849). There are six sermons in the series; the quotation is from the second sermon. See also Moody, *Church and Society*, pp. 407-409.

8. Fogarty, *Christian Democracy in Western Europe*, p. 164.

9. Avolio, *I Democratici Cristiani*, p. 12.

10. Melvin J. Williams, *Catholic Social Thought: Its Approach to Contemporary Problems* (New York, 1950), p. 22.

11. Shanahan (*German Protestants Face the Social Question*, p. 184) quotes from Ketteler's papers: "Lack of faith appears to me as the only source of corruption."

on co-operatives, self-help societies, and other types of social reform for factory workers, Ketteler sought advice from Victor Huber, a Protestant[12] and Conservative. While Huber held many views similar to Lassalle's he went further in the attempt to find a Christian approach to the social question. He became interested in the work of Father Kolping, a Catholic priest, who was actively engaged in a movement to organize labor along Christian lines. Huber spoke at some of Kolping's meetings. The priest believed that the Church held the solution of the social problem and was willing to put his belief to the test in his workingmen's circles.[13] Huber's own ideas had been derived from study and inspection of the English situation, where the factory system was much more thoroughly developed and where the co-operative movement of Robert Owen was initiated.

Ketteler, through Huber, became aware of Kolping's circles. He was impressed with Kolping's approach to the question. The circles furnished Ketteler a means for spreading his ideas as to the proper relation of the Church to labor. His published view on the subject[14] was a refutation of the position taken by Lassalle. Ketteler did not want to see the workers swept by their misery into this godless stream. He viewed the liberalism of the day as deifying the State:

> The State without God
> The State itself God
> War against the true God through the State.

He thought liberalism[15] laughed at eternity and said the socialists laughed with them, declaring: ". . . we laugh with you, but if this life is all there is, why should ninety per cent be excluded from enjoying what the ten per cent possess?" The liberals talked about equality, but only in nationalism did they realize it; in property they rejected it. The socialists, on the other hand, said all men were and must be equal. Ketteler's belief was that the Church resolved this question of equality by provid-

12. Fogarty, *Christian Democracy in Western Europe*, p. 165. There were other Protestants in Germany who were interested in the social problem. Pastor Stöcker, for example, set up a "central Union for Social Reform." See Laveleye, *Socialism of Today* [1885], p. 107. Except as their efforts contributed to Bismarck's State Socialism covering all Germany these Protestant efforts cannot be considered here.

13. Kolping's motto was: "Let there be no vain words, they irritate wounds; charity alone can accomplish all." See Nitti, *Catholic Socialism*, p. 11.

14. Avolio, *I Democratici Cristiani*, p. 14.

15. This is laissez-faire liberalism, with unrestricted competition.

ing equality in the higher good.[16] However, whatever program Ketteler had was largely negative. He was inclined to lay the ills of labor at the door of the liberals and Freemasons. He called Germany the "slave market of our liberal Europe." These new industrial capitalists whom he called liberals had no positive program of reforms to offer labor except to amass savings and form mutual co-operative associations.[17] Although some workers were turned from socialism to the Church by Ketteler,[18] Lassalle's positive program of organizing labor into a party proved to be more enticing to the rank and file of workingmen. They turned toward Lassallean organization along political lines, moving gradually in the direction of Liebknecht and Bebel. Yet the religious movements were not wholly without influence. At the time when the Lassalleans and the Marxists were drawing together at Eisenach (1869)[19] with a program of action, Ketteler had modified his view of favoring legislation to protect labor. The boots by which he had advised the laborer to pull himself up had had no straps. He began, therefore, to advocate measures to improve hours and conditions of labor, prevent child labor, and protect the labor of women; he said such laws should be enforced by government inspection.[20] In 1871, when Hesse became a part of the German Empire, Ketteler had a seat in the Reichstag which he presently resigned. He also had a right, by virtue of his official position as Bishop of Mainz, to a seat in the upper house but did not occupy it.[21]

16. Wilhelm von Ketteler, *Liberalismus, Socialismus, und Christenthum* (Mainz, 1871), pp. 11-16. This is good Hegelian dialectic turned in favor of the Church, as Marx turned it in favor of socialism. Ketteler said (p. 19) that the liberal doctrine of free individuals in economic competition with one another could not produce a system of true authority, but only an "assemblage of conflicting interests."

17. Thomas Parker Moon, *The Labor Problem and the Social Catholic Movement in France* (New York, 1921), p. 123.

18. Avolio (*I Democratici Cristiani*, p. 14) says "many" were turned.

19. Marx's reaction to Ketteler and clerical reformers generally was that "Whenever they think fit . . . they flirt with the labor question." Engels took Ketteler more seriously and quoted from the Bishop's works in writing his own *The Situation of the Working Classes in England*. See Edgar Alexander, "Church and Society in Germany; Social and Political Movements and Ideas in German and Austrian Catholicism 1789-1950," in Moody, *Church and Society*, pp. 414-415.

20. Moon, *The Labor Problem and the Social Catholic Movement*, p. 125.

21. See above, for the legislative problems in the Reichstag while the Kulturkampf lasted. Bismarck was anti-Center and pro-social reform. The Center would not support him in his social program until he gave up the quarrel with the Church. Canon Morfang, who sat for Hesse in the Reichstag, was a staunch member of the Center Party.

Although Bishop Ketteler had not solved the social problem nor prevented the rise of socialism in Germany, nevertheless he affected others who would take up the work there, as well as in Austria, Belgium, and France. He had met Baron Karl von Vogelsang in Berlin. Through the Baron and his associates Austria and Central Europe would later be aroused. At the Catholic congresses other Catholic leaders were reached and impressed. Abbé Winterer, of Belgium, thus became an indefatigable worker for social reform through the Church. "The social question," said the Abbé, "is intimately tied to the religious question." He knew that the Church had not ignored the question of slavery; no more could it ignore the question of wages or the agrarian question.[22] How far the fame and influence of Ketteler extended may be judged by the fact that the future Leo XIII while still at Perugia was familiar with his work.[23]

The influence of Ketteler's life on Albert de Mun was a prime factor in arousing the young French officer to take up the cause of social reform in a Christian spirit. It was in the Society of St. Vincent de Paul that de Mun found the opportunity to begin his self-appointed task. The Society of St. Vincent de Paul was the work of Frédéric Ozanam, who early in the century at the age of eighteen had written a pamphlet: *Reflections on the Doctrine of Saint-Simon.* The pamphlet called upon Christianity to apply its principles, not merely to discuss them in theoretical terms. "True Christianity," wrote Ozanam, "should render man happy not only in heaven, but also on earth. . . ." The churchmen should not only preach that "the poor are the beloved children of God," but bring about a "speedy improvement in the moral and physical condition of the most numerous class. . . ."[24] Ozanam criticized economic liberalism as degrading the human dignity of the worker, subjecting his wages to the economic ("iron") law of supply and demand, and regarding him as a "commodity" in the market.[25] Ozanam, however, did not stop with criticism; he took action.

22. Eugène-Melchior de Vogüé, "Affaires de Rome," *Revue des Deux Mondes,* III (1887), 841.

23. Eduardo Soderini, "Per le genesi della '*Rerum Novarum*' nel suo venticinquesimo anniversario," *Nuova Antologia,* May 16, 1916.

24. Moon, *The Labor Problem and the Social Catholic Movement,* p. 26.

25. J. N. Moody, "Catholicism and Society in France: Catholic Social and Political Movements 1789-1950," in Moody, *Church and Society,* p. 93.

Impressed no less by Saint-Simon than by the insurrection of laborers at Lyons in 1831, who went berserk and struck out blindly against their oppressors under the slogan "Live working or die fighting," he resolved to found a society for their relief. Within two years he had established his organization. It was appropriately named the Society of St. Vincent de Paul, commemorating the noble efforts of that great spirit of the seventeenth century. Ozanam associated himself with Lamennais, Lacordaire, and Montalembert, all liberal Catholics who were trying to reconcile the Revolution with Christianity. He was one of the founders of the *Ère nouvelle*, to preach the alliance of religion and the Republic in 1848.[26] The liberal Catholic movement failed of its purpose but Ozanam's Society of St. Vincent de Paul lived on.[27]

The young lay member of the society whom de Mun had met was Maurice Maignen, director of a Catholic club of young apprentices on the Boulevard Montparnasse. The director helped them with their everyday problems as well as with their spiritual life. In these contacts Maignen came to the same conclusion as did the dying Communard: the basic struggle of labor was a class struggle; he laid the blame at the feet of the well-born. Even the excesses of the mob in Paris at the time of the Commune he attributed to the upper classes who had rejected labor: "The responsible, the truly responsible, it is you, the great, the rich . . . the happy."[28]

Maignen's club grew and prospered until the fall of the Empire, but the war and the Commune dissipated his resources. He resorted to prayer. He presently sought a young nobleman who as an officer in the army had been imprisoned by the Germans after the Battle of Metz. The officer was René de La Tour-du-Pin Chambly, whose companion in prison was Albert de Mun. When Maignen went to see La Tour-du-Pin he met de Mun also. The two officers agreed to assist. On December 10, 1871, de Mun visited Maignen's Montparnasse Club and captivated everyone with his oratory.[29]

Albert de Mun began promptly by founding the Association of Cath-

26. See above and Lecanuet, *L'Église de France*, p. 11.
27. Moon, *The Labor Problem and the Social Catholic Movement*, p. 26.
28. Rollet, *L'Action sociale*, p. 15.
29. Lecanuet, *L'Église de France*, p. 393.

olic Workingmen's Clubs.[30] He was presently astounded at the warmth
of friendship shown him as a result of embarking on this undertaking.[31]

The organization of the clubs was to be under the supervision of a
committee presided over by Paul Vrignault, Chief of the Bureau at the
Ministry of Foreign Affairs. Its members, in addition to Maignen, Albert
de Mun, and Albert's brother Robert, included two deputies (Keller and
Baron Guiraud), Léon Gautier (a professor), Armand Ravelet (a lawyer),
and La Tour-du-Pin. Their first task was to inform Pope Pius IX of their
action. Their letter began by declaring their complete adhesion to the
Syllabus; their aim was to bring about the devotion of the directing class
to the working class; the organization's principles would conform to
whatever His Holiness might prescribe not only in religious but also in
secular matters; the proposed form of the new organization was an "association of workingmen's clubs."[32] At the same time the committee drew
up a manifesto which was broadcast in every section of Paris asking men
of good will to join in the undertaking to found, not one, but hundreds
of such Workingmen's Clubs, dedicated to God and France. What if it
cost a million francs? Had not the Commune cost France more?[33]

The first club was founded at Belleville, where two hundred people
came to see the flag of the cross raised "on the hill made bloody by
crime."[34] Other members of the committee established clubs, each in a
different quarter of Paris. Subsequently clubs were established throughout
France. At Poitiers Msgr. Pie complimented Albert de Mun and adjured
him "never to make peace with the enemy."[35] The movement became
fashionable. The workers in the craft shops were brought in, perhaps
because there was less hostility among them against their employers. The
workers in the great industries were more inclined to hold aloof.[36]

30. *Oeuvre des Cercles Catholiques des Ouvriers.* The association was founded on
December 23, 1871.
31. Vaussard, *Histoire de la Démocratie Chrétienne,* I, 35.
32. In actual fact the clubs were to include the managerial class as well as the workingmen. See Lecanuet, *L'Église de France,* p. 394. See also Rollet, *L'Action sociale,* p. 15.
One member of the committee became Minister of Agriculture in the Broglie cabinet. See
also Marc Sangnier, *Albert de Mun* (Paris, 1932), p. 24.
33. Lecanuet, *L'Église de France,* pp. 394-396.
34. It was here that the hostages of the Commune had been executed. De Mun is quoted
in *ibid.,* p. 397.
35. ". . . ne hostibus reconciliarentur." He was quoting from the Book of the Maccabees.
Ibid., p. 399.
36. Vaussard, *Histoire de la Démocratie Chrétienne,* p. 36. Vaussard denies (pp. 35-36)

So was launched the Catholic movement to save the workers, body and soul, to stave off socialism, and to glorify France. A number of military officers joined the group. Msgr. Mermillod, preaching at Sainte-Clotilde, praised the organization as he appealed for financial support and members. "The young officers, he said, have carried your flag, your standard, your sword; they have been the honor of your country, and now they come to the people as they went to the enemy . . . not with arms . . . but with blessings. . . . To rent one of your theatres would cost 300,000 francs, and for twenty Clubs 300,000 francs will suffice. Will it be said that in the city of Paris not enough money could be found to establish twenty clubs?"[37] The people responded. Not only did the money come in but persons of position as well as workingmen joined the movement. If only one worker showed up to form a club—no matter! a parade would be held just the same, the lone worker carrying the banner and the rest of the people marching behind with pomp and ceremony. The club was established; it would soon be overflowing with members.[38] The first general assembly of the clubs was held in Paris in May, 1873. The members came by trainloads.

The young officers had indeed joined the movement. This fact led to suspicion on the part of the republican government, for the military were monarchists. Their facile flocking into the new organization of de Mun, who became Secretary General of the Association of Workingmen's Clubs, would bear watching. He himself never forgot his military days; he remained always at heart the French officer.[39]

The danger of a union between the clubs and the cause of monarchy was very real. The Count of Chambord, pretender to the throne of France, wrote to de Mun asking the young orator to be his interpreter to the "dear workingmen" who were the "constant object" of his attention. De Mun was willing; he became the spokesman not only for the Church

the assertion of an ex-Jesuit, Emmanuel Barbier (*Histoire du catholicisme libéral et catholicisme sociale*), that the only members they got into the circles were the "sextons, the houseporters, and the office boys." Fogarty (*Christian Democracy in Western Europe*, p. 170) concludes that the "pious and meek" among workers joined the Church's paternalistic organizations while the "militant" turned to the socialists.

37. Lecanuet, *L'Église de France*, p. 398.
38. *Ibid.*, p. 407. See also Rollet, *L'Action sociale*, p. 20.
39. Albert de Mun, *Combats d'hier et d'aujourd'hui* (4th series; Paris, n.d.), IV, 160-167. De Mun always justified the war of 1870 against Prussia, but did not justify the appeasement which had preceded it, which made it "no less inevitable but impossible to win."

but for the restoration of monarchy.[40] Elected to the Chamber of Deputies in 1876, although promptly excluded, the Chamber not validating his election, he was re-elected, took his seat, and was perennially re-elected thereafter. Here in the Chamber as well as in the regular assemblies of the clubs his oratorical ability had full opportunity for development. He had no peer in France. His voice was always raised on the side of the Church.[41] Albert de Mun was a monarchist, but the Church was the passion of his life. He was called *"cuirassier mystique."*[42]

De Mun's program was forthright and unequivocal:

It is time to break with the fatal tactics which, little by little, relegate Catholicism to the last rank of the social movement like an ambulance convoy at the rear of an army to bring relief in the name of charity to the wretches strewn along the road.

Even more explicitly he said:

It is our task to clear the Church of the charges hurled against it and without abandoning a word of its social definitions to show that there are within it resources sufficient to meet all the legitimate aspirations of the worker, to satisfy all his needs, and to harmonize his material well-being with the safety of his soul.

He wanted to instil these concepts in large-scale industry, to persuade the owners to examine the social question, and to restore a society based on Christian principles.[43]

The movement to found the clubs coalesced with another organization already in existence, that of a factory owner named Harmel. Harmel's groups were founded on a paternalistic basis, regarding the duties of the managerial class toward the worker as similar to those of a father to his family. One prominent feature of Harmel's movement was the regular planning of pilgrimages, which combined relief from the monotomy of labor with religious aspects; they were nineteenth-century substitutes for Canterbury pilgrimages or Crusades. Since the founders were antirepublican these journeys took on political overtones. When conducted on foot, the procession passing through a village might raise the cry of "Henry

40. Moon, *The Social Catholic Movement*, p. 98.
41. *Ibid.*, pp. 87-88.
42. Luisa Riva Sanseverino, *Movimento sindacale cristiano, dal 1850 al 1939* (Rome, 1950), p. 70.
43. Rollet, *Action sociale*, p. 57.

V."[44] As the railroads developed, the pilgrims traveled to much more distant spots, even going to Rome to visit St. Peter's and have an audience with the Pope. Such was the situation when Leo XIII began his pontificate in 1878. Albert de Mun was making stirring speeches on every occasion; Harmel was conducting his pilgrimages. The homage of the Association of Workingmen's Clubs was carried by de Mun to His Holiness. Reporting on this event to the Sixth General Assembly of the organization, de Mun said that Leo XIII had given his blessing to the society and made de Mun promise to be a faithful defender of the Church. The orator concluded with these words: "This pledge I took from the bottom of my heart not for myself but for all of you, for the entire Association and for all those who belong to it."[45]

Although de Mun thus spoke as a conservative, or reactionary, some called him a socialist. The republican *Journal des Débats* so labeled him. "M. de Mun," said the journal, "flatters the worst passions of poverty, often engendered by vice. He, too, declares that the worker is exploited. He, too, denounces the laws of modern labor."

Trouble was in store for de Mun's association. Needing government approval to be authorized, according to the law, it must avoid arousing any suspicion. At the meeting at Chartres, in September, 1878, all went well in the beginning. There was certainly nothing subversive about Harmel's remarks. He likened an industrial enterprise to a family having mutual obligations. He praised the Church, which, he said, had found the "worker a slave; recognizing in him the brother of Jesus Christ," it had "taken him by the hand . . . drawn him from his abasement, and placed on his head the royal crown of the children of God." In addition to references to charity and justice, Harmel's resolutions included a plea that young supervisors and technicians should be educated to care for the moral and material well-being of the workers' families. "The Catholic Church alone," he declared, "effectively opposes its three affirmations

44. Wallace, *The Papacy and European Diplomacy*, pp. 177-178. See Duc de Broglie, "Mémoires," *Revue des Deux Mondes*, VII (1932), 147. Broglie says: "The cause of religion, of the Pope's Temporal Power, and of the restoration of Henry V were too frequently put in the same order, as destined to triumph the same day and by the same means."

45. Quoted in *Univers*, Sept. 14, 1878. In the lead article (signed by Arthur Loth) *Univers* said the *Débats* was trying to put de Mun in the same category as the various social revolutionaries, Blanqui and the rest, whose meeting in Paris the police had just refused to authorize.

[religion, government, property] to the three negations [atheism, anarchy, communism]." He recommended a study of the labor of women and children, noting with approval the Swiss law of January 1, 1878, and the English law of May 27, 1878. A similar law, he thought, should be passed in France.[46]

The governmental authorities would certainly not criticize Harmel's speech. Criticism would come from enemies of the Church who regarded these tactics as an attempt to divert labor from its own real interests, to be attained, said the enemies, by resisting Church, State, and Property.

Neither did the reading of a letter from Leo XIII cause any disturbance. It was the highlight of the Chartres gathering. The letter, sent to the Bishop of Chartres, contained the papal blessing which the organization sought. The reading of the letter was public acknowledgment, from the highest source, of the value of the association and its individual clubs. The people responded: "Long live Leo XIII!"[47]

It was the juxtaposition of the reading of the Pope's letter and Albert de Mun's speech that did the damage. Summing up the evils of the time, de Mun concluded that society could only be cured by substituting for the revolutionary theory of the "rights of man," the *Counterrevolutionary* theory of the "Rights of God."[48] In the popular mind the Counter-Revolution and the Old Regime were synonymous. Here, apparently, was subversion; laborers under the banner of the Church might well be using the local clubs to foster a movement to restore the Old Regime! And in the same meeting Leo XIII was blessing the organization! Governmental reaction registered alarm. Nor was this the sum total of the damage done. Whatever may have been in de Mun's mind, his choice of time, place, and words created havoc. He was a known monarchist. This was not proof that he wanted to restore the Old Regime, but young laborers were inclined to believe on the face of it that he was; they turned their backs on him and his movement. The association was hampered in its growth as a result. It continued to serve a useful function, however, and fostered discussion of very practical matters in the local clubs. Production, consumption, and credit were debated. Pleas were made to study savings and credit, free service of an employment bureau, people's banks,

46. *Univers*, Sept. 13, 1878.
47. *Ibid.*, Sept. 14, 1878. Leo XIII in *Quod apostolici*, to be delivered at year's end, was to mention his approval of the formation of the clubs.
48. *Ibid.*

family savings to cover illness, and apprenticeship.[49] At the general meeting at Angers in September, 1879, where these matters were brought
up, a letter from His Holiness was read, again emphasizing his approval
of what the association was trying to do.[50]

Two years later, in 1881, the Pope again sent a letter (to Cardinal
Marino) to be read at the meeting of the association. This time, however, a new note was introduced into the situation. Leo wrote:

We approve especially, and this will contribute notably to harmony and
prosperity in the Association, that you submit all your projects and works to
the pastors of the churches whom you wish to have as presidents [of the clubs].
It is, in fact, divinely ordained by the Church that it is the right and duty of
the bishops to dictate the rules and to march at the head through doctrine and
example, while it is the part of the faithful to follow the footsteps of the pastors,
to obey with docility their precepts and to witness to them their filial love while
giving them in abundance their practical assistance.

The general effect was to throw a wet blanket over the movement. The
clerical and monarchist imprint was too plain for the average workman.
The clubs were not prospering as they had at the beginning, when a
burst of enthusiasm carried them on.[51] A number of factors were involved in this decline. Many owners became suspicious of the clubs.
The clergy did not rally, or if they did they threw a damper on the
young workers, who hesitated to express themselves in the local clubs
in the presence of persons so much better educated than they.[52] The
lesser clergy resented the movement because it went beyond the limits
of the parish and diminished the authority of the parish priest. The
bishops frequently thought they had done enough for the cause when
they sat benignly on the platform with de Mun. Part of it was pure
apathy and preoccupation with other duties. The clergy, in general, were
not fired with de Mun's zeal. They never gave the workers elbow room
to develop.[53]

49. *Ibid.*, Sept. 8, 1879. *Univers* endorsed the movement: "Since we are confronted with
the alternatives of choosing between the Christianization of business enterprise by the
clergy and the de-Christianization inaugurated by scientific opportunism, we do not hesitate to put our sympathies freely on the side of the Christianizers."
50. *Ibid.*, Sept. 3, 1879.
51. In a speech in 1882 de Mun spoke of beginnings of the movement "launched with
youthful ardor into the great enterprise of reestablishing Christian order in the world of
labor." Quoted in *ibid.*, May 10, 1882.
52. Rollet, *Action sociale*, p. 37.
53. Vaussard, *Historie de la Démocratie Chrétienne*, p. 36.

There were other factors of a more disquieting nature. The French government, now thoroughly republican, became still more suspicious. Not only the unfortunate affair at Chartres but also the continued interest of military men of rank made the government apprehensive. The government ordered the officers to withdraw themselves from the movement and take no part in politics. The governmental attack on Church control of education and against the religious orders was beginning. The Church needed to bury all factors tending to divisiveness. The *Syllabus* of Pius IX was one of these factors. Future Popes were not expected to denounce it, but the divisions it had caused at the time of its promulgation were better laid quietly to rest; de Mun, instead, had taken his stand boldly and publicly on the unpopular document.[54]

The government became still more suspicious because of the clerical control over the meetings of the clubs. Some of them were ordered to disband. Seeing the handwriting on the wall, de Mun called off a scheduled regional meeting.[55] He tried to keep the movement alive by changing the character of the clubs into organizations for professional improvement. Their growth was hampered, but they did not go out of existence. They had already done some good. The close contact which obtained for a while between the laborers and the clergy had kept many of them within the Church and had taught the clergy that there was a "social question."

Many sincere Catholic workingmen still did not lose hope that the Church might save them. One such group, received by Leo XIII, said they "saluted in the Apostolic See the strongest defense of popular rights; they hoped for a remedy for their present ills, not from deceitful promises made them for almost a century, but from action of the Church and from protection of the Holy See, which alone could bring about the material and moral relief of the working people."[56]

The Council of Studies, a section of the parent organization, con-

54. When Bishop Dupanloup, of Orleans, had interpreted the *Syllabus* in a mild and liberal sense, 630 bishops wrote to congratulate him. Others, however, including notably Msgr. Pie, wished to interpret it literally. So the French clergy had been seriously divided. See Lecanuet, *L'Église de France*, p. 419. See also Wallace, *The Papacy and European Diplomacy*, p. 67.

55. Rollet, *Action sociale*, p. 48.

56. *Journal de Rome*, quoted in *Univers*, April 15, 1882. The pilgrimage to the Holy See was from Paris.

tinued to study the social question from every angle and slowly to formulate principles with regard to the relations between the Catholic Church and the workingman. In the matter of legislation in the Chamber of Deputies, the procedure of the study group was, first, to discuss the question in their own council, and then to formulate a measure for presentation by one of their number who was a deputy.[57] De Mun recognized that careful and exact study of every question was a necessity. Reporting to the association, he described the growing interest and feeling of responsibility exhibited in the Chamber of Deputies. Almost every day the Extreme Left (the Independents) brought up such questions as accidents, sanitation, and old age assistance.[58] As a preparation for a bill which proposed to extend the rights of "mixed *syndicats*"[59] (including workers and employers), members of the Council of Studies sent out to conservative journals a request for signatures to a petition and conducted a campaign of conferences and meetings. "We proposed the right of syndical association with all its consequences," said de Mun. "We demanded that it should be the point of departure for social reorganization which would substitute the corporative regime for the individualistic regime."[60] This attempt to go back to the medieval system met with a cold response on the part of the owners, especially in the north of France. Some called it "legal communism," some "Utopian," and some simply labeled it "nonsense." Owners were cynical about meeting democratically with their employees. From the thirty-five thousand members in the clubs only seven thousand signatures were secured. The measure was turned down by the Chamber of Deputies.[61]

Albert de Mun began to see that international action would be needed if some of the worst ills of labor were to be cured. In the Chamber he raised his voice, and it was the first time anyone had mounted the tribune to speak on such a subject. "There was formerly in the world," he said, "a mediating power, it was the Catholic Church which was recognized and accepted by all; it imposed limitations on the abuse that one could make of the energies of man." He asked what was to be put in

57. Moon, *The Social Catholic Movement*, p. 158.
58. Rollet, *Action sociale*, p. 148.
59. *Syndicats* of all sorts were still without legal basis.
60. De Mun, *Combats d'hier et d'aujourd'hui*, II, 281. See also Sangnier, *Albert de Mun*, p. 39.
61. Vaussard, *Histoire de la Démocratie Chrétienne*, p. 50.

its place, if not the concert of civilized states. He called to mind the international convention to regulate the laws of war, the transportation of mail—why not regulate the conditions of labor?[62] This idea had not been de Mun's originally. He was not basically a theoretician, preferring to leave such matters to others. It had been La Tour-du-Pin who argued for a reversion to medieval forms. Violently opposed to liberalism with its doctrine of economic competition, La Tour-du-Pin did not foresee the great industrial concentration which was on the horizon, and sought to turn back toward a simpler type of organization, the medieval corporation. This seemed to him the surest defense against revolutionary syndicalism.[63] In spite of competitive practices which weighed heavily upon them, some proprietors felt their social as well as moral responsibility and established a Society of Christian Proprietors, which exercised no compulsion over its members but developed a community of principles, leaving the method of application to each individual.[64]

In 1884 the Waldeck-Rousseau law legalized labor organizations, under restrictions which the Marxists feared (requiring that membership lists be deposited with the police). This legislation was regarded as an important step in labor reform. Without giving up his Association of Workingmen's Clubs, which were no longer prospering, de Mun pressed more strongly toward legislative action; he tried to infuse the Christian spirit into the debates on labor problems. The Council of Christian Studies, in agreement on this matter, put it thus: "Christian charity is necessary; it does not suffice to guarantee to the worker, or to the master, the fulness of his right. . . . Justice is indispensable; for it has as its direct object the *rights of others.*"[65]

Leo XIII, in order to give stronger support to the movement of the clubs and also to open up a channel through which he might restrain the outspoken de Mun (who always brought monarchy into his speeches), appointed Cardinal Parocchi as Protector of the Association.[66] De Mun, encouraged by receiving the Grand Cross of the Order of St. Gregory the Great and by the success of Harmel's recent great pilgrimage to Rome and emboldened by the success of the Catholic Party of Belgium

62. Quoted in Rollet, *Action sociale*, p. 172.
63. Vaussard, *Histoire de la Démocratie Chrétienne*, pp. 47-48.
64. *Univers*, June 1, 1884.
65. *Ibid.*, March 1, 1885.
66. *Ibid.*, June 24, 1885.

(in the election of 1884), contemplated the formation of a Catholic political party in France. By means of this he could defend the Church and carry out social reforms. He was advised through the nuncio in Paris by Leo XIII that such a move would be unwise.[67] He dropped the idea.

His Holiness continued his support of the clubs, never ceasing to reiterate to groups of workers who sought him out that the workers' "Association had been born and flourished under the inspiration of the Church."[68]

In spite of the gentle rebuff administered to de Mun in the matter of the political party, he did not cease to press the cause of social reform. Speaking at one of his association meetings, he said that the Revolution of 1789 had a doctrine, which he had been denouncing for years, and an instinct; the instinct was true; it was the need for justice.

There was [he went on], at the end of the last century . . . an immense and universal desire for justice. . . . Who would bring it to the drained-out world? That is the question on which the destiny of the century has hung and it is through having understood this . . . that the disciples of Voltaire and Rousseau have been able to push the people into the road where they wanted them to walk, and where they found, not release from bondage, only a new slavery. . . . The dream of justice was awakened in the soul of the people; it will never be extinguished.[69]

Quoting the famous words of Turgot at the time of the French Revolution: "It is not a question of knowing what has been but what must be," de Mun showed that he was looking to the future, not justifying the past. He continued to support labor legislation in the Chamber of Deputies. He sponsored a bill to cover workers' accidents and sickness and old age insurance[70] but in vain. He tried to get a bill against night

67. Rollet, *Action sociale*, p. 185. De Mun did not understand that the Pope could not be officially in contact with a party opposed to the governmental regime. His own brother-in-law in Belgium (the Duc d'Ursel) warned him that he would split the Catholics by any such move; people might agree on some matters who would be completely at odds over others.

68. Leo XIII to a group of industrial workers. *Univers*, Feb. 27, 1885. Two years later he received a delegation of 1,400 workingmen, 100 heads of industry, and 300 of the clergy. The delegation was led by Cardinal Langénieux and Albert de Mun. The Pontiff was giving the French movement all possible support. See Soderini, "Per le genesi della 'Rerum Novarum' nel suo venticinquesimo anniversario," *Nuova Antologia*, May 16, 1916.

69. Feb. 21, 1886. Quoted in *Univers*, Feb. 26, 1886.

70. Acomb, *The French Laic Laws*, p. 71.

work for women.[71] He did succeed in getting weekly rest for women and children and forbidding heavy manual labor for boys under sixteen unless they secured a medical certificate.[72] Perhaps the seeds sown by his inimitable oratory would some day take root, but for the moment they seemed to have little effect.

There was a growing feeling that goods produced for international trade should not be restricted or hampered by economic or social measures in a single country. Such legislation would price the goods completely out of competition in the international market. Such questions, it was thought, ought to be discussed by an international gathering.[73] The classic doctrine of laissez faire was beginning to draw criticism, not only from the ranks of labor, more and more advocating international organization and the eight-hour day, but also from industrialists and social reformers. They were getting little help from the clergy. Here and there a clergyman, like the Cardinal Archbishop of Paris, was sincerely concerned about the problem of labor and the welfare of the laborer. Too many of them were so much interested in the destruction of the Republic that they gave scant attention to social reform and legislation. Albert de Mun was interested in both. "Individualism," he said, "is falling under ruins which it has made. Social reform has begun; it will no longer be halted."[74] He told French youth, however, that the Revolution of 1789 was bankrupt, played out. "There is a lamentable victim. . . . It is the people . . . whom the upper classes have abandoned after leading them astray. . . ." He proposed as a slogan for the time: ". . . the service of the Church and the people! That is what must be written on your flag!"[75] He castigated the Republican Party in the Chamber of Deputies for having by its religious wars made two separate nations of France: a radical, irreligious nation, and a nation made up of believers and all people of good will.[76]

The speeches of de Mun were carried, or quoted from, in the leading journals of France. *Justice*, for example, commented on one: "the dis-

71. Rollet, *Action sociale*, p. 145.
72. Vaussard, *Histoire de la Démocratie Chrétienne*, p. 52.
73. Rollet, *Action sociale*, p. 146.
74. Albert de Mun at the Catholic Congress. *Univers*, May 6, 1887.
75. *Ibid.*, May 2, 1887, May 6, 1887.
76. Albert de Mun in the Chamber of Deputies, June 8, 1889. See *ibid.*, June 10-11, 1889.

tinctive trait of M. de Mun's socialism" is that "it sets the rights of God as the necessary basis of institutions, laws, customs. That is what creates an abyss between the republican socialists and the Christian socialists."[77] The bitterness of the religious war was one of the factors which prevented France from making as rapid progress in social lgeislation as was being made among her northern neighbors.

There was no doubting de Mun's interest in this Christian development; the difficulty lay in his preoccupation with the monarchist cause. A writer for the *Pall Mall Gazette* interviewed him, characterizing him as the "most eloquent of living Frenchmen." The interviewer was much impressed; de Mun did not seem like an ordinary politician who thought that anyone differing from him was "capable of stealing spoons"; rather, he "combined the convictions of the medieval crusader in theology with the humanitarian zeal of a modern socialist." De Mun told the interviewer that the Catholics in France ought to get out of the political parties and concentrate on the problem of religion. "If only they would follow the example of Cardinal Manning in England the movement would be irresistible. I believe that Pope Leo XIII, who is keenly solicitous concerning social questions, and who has loudly praised Cardinal Manning for his action in the dock-laborer's strike, would be only too glad to encourage the bishops, the clergy, and the Catholics of France."[78] De Mun was undoubtedly right about Leo XIII; whether the *Pall Mall* interviewer was right about de Mun only time could tell. His public speeches did not give an unequivocal answer on that point; they continued to be full of references to the glories of monarchism. The Republic, which he called the "alliance of all the dissatisfied,"[79] seemed to him to be the real enemy of the Church.

The movements of de Mun and Harmel continued to receive the Pope's approval and support.[80] To a pilgrimage of workers from France Leo delivered an address expressing his love and concern for their welfare. He explained that slavery was a characteristic of pagan society but was abhorred by the Church, which says: "You are all by the same title sons of the Heavenly Father; you have all been ransomed at the same

77. *Ibid.*, July 2, 1889. The editor of *Justice* was Alexandre Millerand.
78. *Pall Mall Gazette*, Oct. 9, 1889.
79. *Ibid.*
80. Nitti, *Catholic Socialism*, p. 371. Nitti was writing in the early nineties.

price."[81] His Holiness did not mean, however, in stressing their equality as sons and brothers, that social classes had ceased to exist under the Church. His admonition to the workers assembled before him was to be submissive to their employers, to refrain from acts of disturbing the peace, and to let Christian ideals control them in the formation of their craft guilds.[82] He recognized, on the other hand, that employers and even the state had duties to perform: "You, owners, have the duty of considering the worker as a brother and ameliorating his lot as much as possible . . . and you, custodians of the public powers, do not count, in the conflict of social interests, on repression by force of arms. . . .Let the welfare of the worker be provided for."[83]

The pilgrimages were getting larger. One numbered ten thousand. It was no small task to find lodging for so large a group. The Pope could not receive so many in audience at one time.[84] Something needed to be done to reorganize the whole movement, reducing the group to echelons of smaller size. Preparations were going forward, nevertheless, for an even larger pilgrimage in 1891 when an incident in Rome brought the project to a halt. One of the echelons, sightseeing in the Eternal City, visited the Pantheon and inscribed in the visitor's book: "Viva the Pope-King!"[85] This act produced a storm of disapproval in Italy. A great uproar occurred in the streets, the people shouting, "Down with the Pope! Down with France! Viva Sedan!"[86] They demanded the abolition of the Law of Guarantees.[87]

These unfortunate incidents had an adverse effect not only on the pilgrimages but on the Workingmen's Clubs. The Pope had regarded the pilgrimages as useful. To Harmel he spoke of the credit due them

81. Dispatch from Rome, Oct. 21, 1889. *Univers*, Oct. 22, 1889.

82. Leo XIII was not aware that industrialism had gone too far to permit a return to medievalism and the class structure of the Middle Ages.

83. *Univers*, Oct. 23, 1889.

84. Rollet, *Action sociale*, p. 260. It was also impossible to keep politics out. The circulars carried announcements: "Rome pagan. Rome Christian. The Pope a prisoner." This was ominous for good relations between Italy and France.

85. In Paris the Minister of Public Worship sent a circular to the bishops to discourage such manifestations.

86. Sedan was the battle which had marked the triumph of Prussia over France in the Franco-Prussian war. Germany was now an ally of Italy.

87. Rollet, *Action sociale*, p. 261. Leo XIII sadly confided to Harmel after this affair: "I was a prisoner; now I am a hostage."

for helping with the Church's struggle against atheistic science and anarchic socialism. He eulogized Albert de Mun's work also.

The decline of the clubs was welcome to the Marxists and the revolutionary socialists. Nurtured in atheism, they despised all religion, especially Catholicism. The growth of French "religiosity" (as they termed it) was most unwelcome, hampering them in their own work of organizing labor for socialism. They still regarded the Church as their most redoubtable foe. The Church viewed socialism in the same light. Most of the journals of the Left as well as those of the monarchist-clerical Right would still echo Montalembert's words of 1850: "There is no middle ground; today one must choose between Catholicism and socialism." And one would still repeat a decade later the words of Émile Deschanel: "We too, no less believe that the struggle is henceforth between these two principles and that it must end only by the annihilation of one or the other."[88]

In Italy the need for social reform was present long before the development of the Industrial Revolution there. Reform had not come. Poverty and illiteracy were endemic in the agrarian south.[89] The masses of laborers on the estates or in the sulphur mines belonging to laity or clergy[90] were aroused for a moment by desire for a united Italy free from foreign intervention. Later they took fire here and there from the revolutionary message of the Bakuninists. In the end they sank lower than before.[91] Even the Marxian socialists had been unable to make headway among them. It was a period of terror.

88. Quoted in *Univers*, Oct. 17, 1870. Deschanel wrote these words in No. 27 of *Liberté de pensée*. He chose not to be Catholic. It is interesting to note in contrast that Barnabé Chauvelot, who had been Proudhon's secretary and suffered along with him the judicial consequences, turned back toward the Church and regained his Christian faith. He became one of the collaborating editors of *Univers*. See the issue of Aug. 19, 1879, at his death.

89. Avolio, *I Democratici Cristiani*, p. 20.

90. Romano (*Movimento socialista in Italia*, I, 54) related the encounter of a Garibaldian with a southern monk. To the Garibaldian's praise of the future Italy, united, free, and provided with schools, the monk replied that "liberty is not bread, nor schools either. They may be enough for you Piedmontese but not for us." "What do you want?" "Not a war against the Bourbons [foreigners, sitting on the throne of Naples], but of the oppressed against the oppressors, great and small. . . ." "Then also against you friars, who have convents and lands where there are houses and fields." "Also against us, even before any others. . . ."

91. National unification brought no economic relief. In the 1860's the closure of religious congregations and the confiscation of Church lands ended in the sale of these properties to land speculators whose policies were more oppressive than those of the former owners. See Neufeld, *Italy*, p. 78.

In the north of Italy the proletariat grew and awakened to class consciousness. Here they had changed masters; the new bourgeoisie of money had moved into the forefront to join the aristocracy of the court. These new classes represented a political liberalism which aimed to dissolve all social organization as the new technological economy of the Industrial Revolution and the competitive doctrine of laissez faire became dominant.[92] After the seizure of Rome, which resulted in abstention of Catholics from voting, and under the restricted franchise, there seemed little hope of reform through the legislative process.

It was by the young in Italy that the first steps were taken to stir Catholic society to action. In February, 1867, at Bologna, was founded a "Society of Italian Catholic Youth," whose motto was "Prayer, Action, Sacrifice."[93] In October, 1871, Catholics at Venice, there to celebrate the victory over the Turks in the naval Battle of Lepanto three hundred years earlier, heard the announcement that the Catholic Youth Society was proposing to call an Italian Catholic Congress.[94] So was created in 1874, at Venice, the first of the *Opera dei Congressi e Comitati Cattolici*. They were seeking, said one of the constituent groups, a "solution of the social problem, caused and compromised by the revolution," which had "created pauperism." Catholic banks and Catholic mutual aid societies might rescue the workers from "irreligion and pauperism."[95] The meetings were to be held annually. In 1875, at Florence, Count Paganuzzi was elected president of the organization.[96] The following year there were some anticlerical demonstrations and the meeting was ordered to close.[97] At Bergamo, during the next Congress, the Catholics started the *Opera di Carità*, following a papal brief of Pius IX. They got down to some practical discussions on women and hard labor, hours, housing, and corporative organization.[98]

92. Giuseppe Toniolo, *Capitalism and Socialism* (Vatican City, 1947), p. 390. Msgr. Toniolo was professor of economics at the University of Pisa. His reputation as a theorist attracted youth to his classes. He and later these students were able to carry the message of Christianity into public life.

93. Giovanni Acquaderni was the first president. See Fonzi, *I Cattolici e la società italiana dopo l'unità*, p. 31.

94. Vaussard, *Histoire de la Démocratie Chrétienne*, p. 221. See also Magri, *L'Azione cattolica in Italia*, I, 12.

95. Gambasin, *Il movimento sociale nell'opera dei Congressi*, p. 129. The speaker was Dr. Cesare Pecci.

96. Sanseverino, *Il movimento sindacale cristiano*, p. 111.

97. Magri, *Azione cattolica*, I, 21.

98. Sanseverino, *Il movimento sindacale cristiano*, p. 111.

By the time the next Congress was held Leo XIII had mounted the pontifical throne and the question foremost in Italy was the question as to whether the liberal Pope would be reconciled with the Kingdom of Italy and permit the Catholics as citizens to participate in the full political life of the state. Leo XIII's conciliatory gestures toward the European states gave them hope that conciliation would rule at home. The "transigents," while clinging to religious orthodoxy, rejecting the heterodox tendencies which had developed in Europe during the Revolution of 1789, nevertheless felt that changed conditions must be recognized; only thus could an "effective work of Christian restoration be accomplished."[99] In this attitude the majority of the Italians concurred. The "intransigents" did not accept this point of view. The division was present in the Sacred College as well as in the *Opera dei Congressi*. In the latter the struggle was between the intransigents and those who favored freedom for the Catholic youth to pursue their work of study and organization for social reform unimpeded by the conservatism of the faction in authority. The reactionary intransigents prevailed, meeting new proposals with "imprecations."[100] The clergy kept a firm hand on all activities of the associations of laborers which the committees of the clergy were engaged in getting up. The views expounded by the forward-looking theorists were too far in advance of their time.[101] From this time on until 1889 there was a decreasing enthusiasm in the organization, initially so successful.[102] The intention of the intransigent, abstentionist, reactionary Catholics had been from the start to control and smother the modernist aspirations of the Catholic youth societies and place a damper on the work of the Catholic Union for the Social Studies. One unexpected result of this attempt to combat liberal tendencies in the new unitary Italian state by organizing the masses under the watchful eye of the Church was that in the end the organization contributed to unification of the peninsula by drawing groups from all regions together.[103]

The Pontiff rescued the Society of Catholic Youth from the smothering embrace of the *Opera* and moved it to Rome as an independent

99. Fonzi, *I cattolici e la società italiana*, p. 35.
100. Magri, *Azione cattolica*, I, 22. Abstention from voting remained the rule.
101. Neufeld, *Italy*, p. 183. Marquis Achille Sassoli-Tomba published two important books in 1878 and 1879 on labor co-operatives and housing, and on the agrarian question.
102. Gambasin, *Il movimento sociale nell'Opera dei Congressi*, p. 117.
103. Fonzi, *I cattolici e la società italiana*, p. 60. See also Gambasin, *Il movimento sociale nell'Opera dei Congressi*, p. 117.

study circle.[104] Leo XIII had earlier said, "I wish the younger generation of Italians to destroy the prejudices of their elders, that the sons, in short, may lead their fathers back to the right path."[105] This wish of the Pope had not been fulfilled. Instead of infusing modernism into the *Opera dei Congressi* the youth had been swallowed by their elders. The gulf between them was too deep. The elders were too conservative, except for a few, and refused to recognize that religion alone was not enough for the workers. Socialists were promising them much more. Young Dom Romolo Murri, a reformer passionately devoted to religion, saw that socialism was the great threat[106] and that its program was based on opposition to the Church and to all religion except its own religion of "man." He saw that many adopted socialism as a whole world view. To Murri this socialist philosophy, which he rejected, was essentially that of a world self-created, self-contained, and without responsibility to anything but itself. In such a world man was no longer regarded as accountable; he was the helpless product of the past of the human race.

The attempts of the Catholic reformers to do something about the social question in Catholic Europe do not seem on the surface to have accomplished a great deal when the results are summed up. The efforts should not be written off, however, as valueless. The high hopes that attended the beginnings did not develop as their authors expected. The obstacles proved to be more formidable than the reformers had anticipated. These obstacles were not identical in the various regions. In general, the most universal weakness was failure to assess the magnitude of the problem, which day by day grew more vast. It would be like trying to hold back Niagara with bare hands to attempt by individual efforts to halt the rising tide of misery in the industrial areas.

In Germany the Kulturkampf stood in the way of effective state action to solve the social problem. When this quarrel was ended the Catholic Center and the German government co-operated to alter the social picture and to do so more rapidly than was possible elsewhere.

104. Magri, *Azione cattolica*, I, 51.
105. Soderini, *Il Pontificato di Leone XIII*, II, 117.
106. It should not be forgotten that laissez-faire individualism was also a major threat. The reformers were between these two forces. Murri was aware of the double threat. He sought to discover a new road between the two. See Mario Einaudi and François Goguel, *Christian Democracy in Italy and France* (Notre Dame, Ind., 1952), p. 5. See also Neufeld, *Italy*, p. 357.

The efforts of Ketteler awakened the consciences of many Catholics who later spoke and voted in the Reichstag. The influence of Ketteler also spread beyond the borders of Germany, to light fires in Austria, to prod the Belgians, to encourage the Swiss. It was Ketteler who influenced the Comte de Mun in France.

The French movement, so nobly begun, was held in check by two adverse factors. One was the chilling presence of the clergy in the meetings of the Workingmen's Clubs. The second was the attachment of de Mun and many of the clergy to the monarchist cause. This drew suspicion on the clubs as possible centers of antirepublican plots. The *syndicats* had more appeal for the mass of the workers.

As for Italy, the enthusiasm for reform engendered by the Association of Catholic Youth was smothered when the *Opera dei Congressi* fell into the hands of the intransigent clergy. The youth associations were salvaged, however, by the Pope's hand, and continued to study the social question systematically. The hierarchy, through dislike of the seizure of Rome in the process of unifying the peninsula, refused to work with the public authorities in the amelioration of the lot of the workingman. Political abstention remained a stumbling block. The tendency of the higher clergy to associate with the wealthy and titled, thus perpetuating the prerevolutionary system, made the task of enlisting the rank and file of parish priests in any crusade for social betterment extremely difficult. Many of the lower clergy, nevertheless, developed a genuine sympathy for the lot of the poor.

Wherever the reform movement faltered, for whatever reason, the door was left wider open for the socialists. Time would tell whether the accomplishments of the religious reformers had as yet been great enough to hold the majority of the workers under the sheltering arms of the Church.

Although the work of the Catholic reformers had invariably received the benediction of the Sovereign Pontiff, there had come as yet no authoritative pronouncement from the pen of Leo XIII. Until it should appear the path of the reformers would remain tortuous. The Pope was not yet ready for this pronouncement; much preparation would be necessary. In the meantime, a question of grave importance, but developed by His Holiness over long years, was soon to be set forth in an encyclical for the world to see. To this important pronouncement we now turn.

IX. LEO XIII IN A SCIENTIFIC WORLD

"Science did not destroy faith, did not become the sole religion, the sole law, the sole consolator of men. . . ."[1]

The later decades of the nineteenth century and the early years of the twentieth have been adjudged by many as the best in the recorded history of man. These years coincide with the pontificate of Leo XIII. After the blazing mid-century, full of wars and alarms, nationalist struggles, and revolutions, Europe settled into an era of unprecedented peace. The minds of Europeans were turned to imperialistic ventures in "heathen" lands, to scientific achievements made possible by scientific equipment which an industrial age produced, and to material well-being made possible by the new science, the new industry, the new imperialism. Exotic goods from far-away places stimulated the imagination while they added new comforts and luxuries to living. The products of applied science were eagerly accepted, while claims of greater wonders yet to come ceased to be met with derision. Trains moved; steamboats crossed oceans; balloons carried people into the air.[2] Apathy and inertia changed to optimism. Change was accepted as normal and desirable. Even the scientific hypothesis of "evolution" seemed to promise that "progress" was inevitable.

There were, nevertheless, here and there some scientific hypotheses which aroused dismay, particularly among the most religiously inclined, whether Protestant or Catholic. Geology explored the notion, popularly

1. Federico Chabod, *Storia della politica estera Italiana*, I, 265.
2. The republican leader Gambetta escaped from Paris by balloon in 1870 during the siege.

held in the Western world, of the instantaneous creation of the universe by divine fiat. Archeology pushed backward in time the beginning of the existence of man on earth. Biology postulated man's development as a two-legged animal from earlier and simpler forms of life. Hell and heaven seemed to be vanishing as a mirage which had for too long acted to restrain man's enjoyment of the here and now.

In the contest between the Catholic Church and socialism, Karl Marx had seized the initiative in the intellectual field. He had boldly based his ideology and program on "science." By "science" he had meant philosophical investigation of social and economic phenomena in human history. Using these investigations as a basis, he attempted to establish fixed and immutable "scientific" laws. In developing his economic and social theories he had pre-empted the term "science" and called his movement "scientific socialism." He would strike the "shackles" of religion from men's minds. Science viewed the world as self-explanatory. It would reveal itself, not through mysticism, but by way of the microscope, the test tube, the pickaxe and spade. Man himself was to be studied by analysis of group behavior. It was inevitable that Marxists should regard the Church as obscurantist, clinging to magic and superstition. Science represented a deeper thrust against religion than mere secularism.

Pius IX, on the other hand, listing in the *Syllabus* those aspects of the nineteenth century which aroused his animosity, branded "scientism" as heretical.[3] Leo XIII, though, realized that in his battle against socialism he would strengthen his arsenal of weapons if he appropriated the word "science" and endorsed the idea of investigative research. These concepts would not then remain the exclusive property of the socialists. The task before him was to make Catholicism intellectually respectable. At the very beginning of his pontificate he proclaimed the Church as patron and protector of learning and the arts, and insisted that it had been so throughout the centuries. Completely false, he said, were the calumnious assertions of those who would have one believe that the Church and the Roman Pontiff were "implacable enemies" of "science and progress." Enjoining the faithful not to leave the weapon of learning in the hands

3. Many attributed anticlericalism to the rise of scientism. See Vaussard, *Histoire de la Démocratie Chrétienne*, p. 220. An encyclopedic dictionary (published in 1887 throughout the English-speaking world) defined "scientism" as "the views and practices of scientists." It appended, however, the following note: "*Scientism* and *scientist* are words of recent and doubtful formation."

of the enemy, he reminded them how Julian the Apostate had discredited the Christians in the eyes of pagan society by preventing them from engaging in the "study and cultivation of letters."[4]

On the premise that truth reached by reason could never be out of harmony with truth reached by faith, Leo XIII was willing that the searchlight of rational investigation should be turned into all fields, never fearing that in a dark corner it might illuminate some embarrassing ghost. His only reservation, and it did not lie in the field of science, was that the values by which man lives and the path he must follow toward the goal of ultimate reunion with God, all of those things which lay beyond the microscope or the archeological spade, must be left under the guidance of the Church. In this he was following in the footsteps of the Popes in the greatest periods of cultural advance.

In taking his stand on the side of scientific progress Leo did not renounce the *Syllabus of Errors*. Rather, he made a distinction between the material world and the world of values. Human reason, which *Les Philosophes* of the eighteenth-century Enlightenment claimed could solve all problems, was already demonstrating that it could formulate the laws of the behavior of matter;[5] such conclusions were subject to demonstrable proof. In the realm of the human spirit, on the other hand, human reason was not, in itself, a sufficient guide. Here there was room also for faith. This distinction between the world of matter and the world of values had enabled the Church to absorb the learning of the Greeks in the first centuries and the classical learning together with Islamic contributions in the medieval renaissance. Leo XIII was following in this great tradition in clinging to the belief that reason could not be at variance with faith if both were properly understood.

The statements made verbally to the visiting scholars would not reach all ears. Leo must proclaim to the whole Church and to the world that the new learning, adequately substantiated by research and experimenta-

4. All of these points were made by Leo XIII in July in an address to a deputation of members of the Academy of the Arcades. See his address in *Univers*, July 19, 1878. To the professors of the Roman University, come to greet him at his election, he said that "the Roman Pontiff, far from combatting science and impeding its progress, on the contrary favors it and seeks to enlarge it." *Ibid.*, Aug. 13, 1878.

5. The *Philosophes* were less correct in their predictions as to the laws of human society, as the failure of the Utopians demonstrated. It would be shown later that the *nature* of matter was as elusive as ever, if, indeed, it could be said to exist at all.

tion, could not damage the inner citadel of the Church's consciousness of mission. The new intellectualism, calling in question the verbal inspiration of the Scriptures, was leading many Catholics as well as Protestants to cast religion aside as outworn superstition to be scoffed at and ridiculed. If all the Church could offer as faith was merely fetish, abhorrent to human reason, then its admonitions in this scientific age would be no more heeded than old wives' tales. Leo set out to join reason and faith together in an encyclical: the *Aeterni Patris*.

The task undertaken in the encyclical was to show that the Church throughout its history had recognized the compatibility of reason and faith. In attempting to lay the foundations for a modern synthesis the Pontiff went back to the life and teachings of St. Thomas Aquinas.[6] The synthesis of faith and reason worked out by the Angelic Doctor had been the triumph of the Middle Ages. Now the Pope would show that such a synthesis would be as possible in the nineteenth century as it had been six hundred years earlier.

Leo XIII began the *Aeterni Patris* by referring to his first encyclical, which had emphasized the importance of philosophy. False conclusions, he said, were being derived from various schools of philosophy; philosophy could not save—only religion could do that; but the natural helps with which the grace of the divine wisdom, strongly and sweetly disposing all things, has supplied the human race, are neither to be despised nor neglected; chief among these is evidently "the right use of philosophy." For the light of reason was placed in the human mind by the hand of God, and the light of faith "far from extinguishing or lessening the power of the intelligence completes it rather. . . ." Truths discovered by the pagan sages, readily admitted Leo, "with nothing but their natural reason to guide them were demonstrated and proved by becoming [suitable] arguments." He quoted from Romans (2.14): "'And the Gentiles who have not the law show, nevertheless, the work of the law written in their hearts.'" Origen had been praised because "as one snatches weapons from the enemy" he turned "to the defense of Christian wisdom

6. Aquinas had confronted the same problem in the high century of the Middle Ages, at a time when the marvels of Islamic science and learning were coming into western Europe through Spain, through southern Italy, and by way of the Crusades, building up a new intellectual world which differed from that depicted in revealed religion. St. Thomas's *Summa Theologica* resolved the differences and produced the medieval synthesis. Leo's education had been rooted and grounded in the works of Aquinas.

and to the destruction of superstition many arguments drawn from the writings of the pagans."

After speaking of the work of Basil the Great and the two Gregories, the Pontiff spoke of St. Augustine, to whom he accorded the highest praise. A "most powerful genius . . . thoroughly saturated with sacred and profane learning" and combining "the loftiest faith" with "equal knowledge," Augustine combatted errors. "What topic of philosophy did he not investigate?" What region did he not "diligently explore. . .?" Then Leo spoke of the scholastic theologians. Among them the "chief master," said His Holiness, was the angelic St. Thomas, who was said to have "inherited the intellect of all." With his spirit "at once humble and swift, his memory ready and tenacious, his life spotless throughout, a lover of truth for its own sake, richly endowed with human and divine science, like the sun he heated the world with the warmth of his virtues and filled it with the splendor of his teaching."

In showing how the fame of Thomas Aquinas had endured through the ages, Leo XIII called attention to the Council of Trent (1545-1563), where, with the Sacred Scriptures and decrees of the Pontiffs, the *Summa* of Aquinas was laid on the altar, an honor shared with none of the Catholic Doctors.

Among references to Vatican Council I one quotation in the encyclical stands boldly out: "Faith frees and saves reason from error, and endows it with manifold knowledge."[7]

Weighed at the time by the secular press, the encyclical did not come off very well. *Siècle* viewed the title as indicating at once what the *Aeterni Patris* was like.

Philosophy [said *Siècle*] is a science, it is even the science *par excellence*; it has no native land, does not depend on any sect or any religion. There can no more be a Christian philosophy than a Christian mathematics or physics, or chemistry, a Christian, Jew, or Protestant biology. Students then are being taught—by Catholic faculties—a Christian philosophy such as Dr. Thomas Aquinas taught in the Middle Ages. In the light of Leo's reputation for liberalism the encyclical seems strange. Pius IX would never have transformed human reason into the humble servant of "celestial sciences."[8]

7. Etienne Gilson, *The Church Speaks to the Modern World* (New York, 1954), pp. 31-51.

8. *Siècle*, Aug. 17, 1879. *Siècle* went on, quoting derisively (after every section it approved) Leo's words: "only, it must conform to the faith." *Ibid.*, Aug. 19, 1879.

A more moderate journal, *XIXe Siècle,* regarded the encyclical as a declaration of immobility. Other commentators said it was meant as a political move; if so it seemed to return to the policies of Pius IX. *XIXe Siècle* doubted its advisability: "Is such an act advantageous for the Holy See? Is it useful for the interest of the Catholic Church? It seems doubtful. . . ."[9]

Much more critical was *Temps*: "The encyclical . . . is not wholly a return to the past; it is intended to put a stop to the future development of human thinking." Whoever believes that the eternal search for truth is man's "greatest honor" will prefer the "free development of thought with its doubts, and its errors, but with faith in the future. . . ."[10]

République française thought it would require a good deal of naïveté to send the nineteenth century back to the "straw" of thirteenth-century schools.[11] *National* laughed at the absurdity of sending young minds back from a century of experimental science that was changing the very face of the earth to the foolish discussion of "being" and "essence." The head of the Church would give "all the discoveries of Edison, all the studies of Pasteur on fermentation . . . for a good dissertation on the 'essence of universals.' "[12]

Roussel, for *Univers,* staunchly defended the encyclical against any charge of making "unfair" attacks on modern science by quoting from the doctrine itself: " 'Nor will the physical sciences themselves, which are now in such great repute, and by the renown of so many inventions draw such universal admiration to themselves, suffer detriment, but gain very great assistance in the restoration of the ancient philosophy.' " Leo, thought Roussel, regarded it as unfair to accuse the old philosophy of putting "an obstacle to the 'progress and growth of the natural sciences.' " Underlining every word Roussel quotes: " '. . .*between the certain and*

9. Quoted in *Univers,* Aug. 19, 1879.

10. *Temps,* quoted in *Univers,* Aug. 19, 1879. It must be observed that in the past the greatest thinkers—Aristotle in ancient times and Aquinas in the thirteenth century—while constructing intellectual systems had continued to insist on the observation of reality and the exploration of all possible data. Neither had closed the door on the possibility of using proved fact constantly in modifying speculative theory. To Aristotle and Aquinas there could not be incompatible truths. The only possible irrefutable positions opposing this would be the belief in an unpredictable universe or the denial of the existence of matter.

11. Aug. 4, 1879. Quoted in *Univers,* Aug. 19, 1879.

12. *National,* Aug. 4, 1879, quoted in *Univers,* Aug. 19, 1879. So the editor of *National* thought discussion of "being" and "essence" was done with!

accepted conclusions of modern physics and the philosophic principles of the school [scholasticism] *there exists in reality no contradiction.'* "[13]

To Leo XIII the word "science" included "philosophy" as well as "natural science." He had added specifically to the statement quoted by Roussel:

For, when the Scholastics, following the opinion of the holy Fathers, always held in anthropology that the human intelligence is only led to the knowledge of things without body and matter [incorporeal things] by things sensible [capable of being apprehended by the senses], they well understood that nothing was of greater use to the philosopher than diligently to search into the mysteries of nature. . . .

In line with his own encyclical, Leo took action within the educational system provided by the Church for educating the Catholic clergy. He wrote Cardinal Luca expressing his desire to see a return to the study of St. Thomas Aquinas in the curricula of the various seminaries and academies; this was especially necessary in Rome, the religious capital of the world. He wanted the philosophical sciences to be simply, clearly, and broadly taught and cultivated according to the spirit and the principles of the Angelic Doctrine. Cardinal Luca was to organize a society for students to share the fruits of their research.[14]

National boldly attacked this action of the Pope:

The Pope wishes to renew . . . philosophical instruction! When we say renew, it is only a manner of speaking, for it is to the Middle Ages, to St. Thomas Aquinas . . . that every Catholic is to return. . . . When the minds shall have been subjected to this discipline, when they no longer reason except according to the proper formula, the Church knows that they will belong to it; there is no worse servitude than that, for one is no longer aware of it as such. . . . Whatever the Church does it will never persuade the sons of '89 that all the blood of the Revolution has been shed in vain.[15]

To the laboring man the encyclical made little difference; he was not a physicist—but he used the telegraph; he was not a biologist—but the silk-weaving industry was saved by checking the ravages of disease

13. *Univers*, Aug. 19, 1879.
14. Leo XIII to Cardinal Luca (Bishop of Praeneste), Oct. 15, 1879. *Ibid.* (French), Oct. 21, 1879 (Latin), Oct. 22.
15. *National*, quoted in *Univers*, Oct. 24, 1879. Roussel, of *Univers*, asks whether St. Thomas "who is today proposed for master and model," was reduced to the "worst of servitudes"?

in mulberry trees. So the Catholic Pasteur went on with his revolutionary studies and experiments with "microbes"; the monk Mendel went on crossing his peas. The worker was not aware of these things. It was the socialist leaders, the scornful writers and editors of the journals, who influenced the workers' thoughts.[16]

Against the view of some that Leo XIII was a Thomist only at the beginning of his pontificate[17] must be put the fact that as late as 1892 Leo directed a letter to all professors and receivers of books, with instructions to have it read every year at the beginning of every course in theology and philosophy, stating specifically that every "certain" statement (of Aquinas) was to be accepted; in case St. Thomas said nothing, then every conclusion must be in harmony with his stated opinions.[18]

All of this may sound as if Leo XIII was making no move to come to terms with the thought of his day. Expressing in scholarly fashion the age-old views of his predecessors, he seemed no less than they to be rejecting nineteenth-century liberalism. The difference lay in the gentleness with which the Pontiff's views were expressed. He did not excoriate nor anathematize. In personal interviews, too, he received amicably individuals whose views coincided with those attacked by Gregory XVI in the *Mirari vos* and by Pius IX in the *Syllabus*. This gentle manner created an atmosphere of good will between the Holy See and the secular world. One illuminating example of this kindly approach was his reception of Léon Lavedan, a publicist. *Siècle* describes the incident:

Osservatore Romano announces that M. Léon Lavedan, director of the *Correspondant*, has had the honor of being received in private audience by St. Peter on July 29. The Pope deigned to address to M. Lavedan, and thus to the review of which he was the representative, words of marked benevolence and specific encouragement.

16. As has been noted, Bishop Ketteler had found a philosophical foundation for his social program in St. Thomas; in France the Council of Studies of de Mun's Workingmen's Clubs turned to Aquinas for arguments on behalf of the rights of labor and social legislation. See Moon, *The Social Catholic Movement*, p. 158.

17. Blowitz, *Léon XIII devant ses contemporaines*, p. 257n. Francesco Crispi makes this statement: "Leo XIII appeared during the first seven years of his pontificate as a Thomist; subsequently a Jesuit." Crispi attributed the alleged change to the "fever of the Temporal Power."

18. T'Serclaes, *Léon XIII*, I, 272. T'Serclaes says that Leo subsequently condemned forty propositions from the works of Abbé Rosmini, especially on the origin of ideas on ontology and natural theology.

This evidence of esteem, says the editor of *Siècle,* is addressed to the director of a review in which "liberal Catholicism, condemned by the *Syllabus,* called a plague by Pius IX, used to publish its doctrines!"[19]

There could be no doubt that the social theories arising from the new scientific view of the universe were lessening the interest of many people in religion. Darwinism seemed to call in question the biblical account of the origin of man. The Higher Criticism, in biblical studies, used the new tools of historical and philological investigation (backed up by archeological discoveries) to portray Christianity, together with its Hebraic background, as a man-made contrivance. This view was reinforced by the philosophical developments of the age. It seemed that the man of the times was about to discard all religious ideas as childish, or that his genuflection, if retained, would be slight and perfunctory, a mere matter of conformity to propriety. The materialistic interests of the century were pushing religion aside. The numbers of the irreligious grew in the workshops as well as among the middle-class intellectuals. Sainte-Beuve, the literary critic, had predicted this development before the fall of the Empire; he said the unbelievers were deists, spiritualists, disciples of "natural" religion, "pantheists, positivists, relativists, skeptics and seekers" of every sort, devotees of "common sense" as well as "sectarians of pure science."[20] The death of Darwin in 1882 and the publication of Le Play's *Lettres historiques et sociales,* the product of a lifetime of sociological studies,[21] turned many minds in the direction of the social significance of the new scientific views. Darwin had put forth no theories as to the relation of man to God. Nevertheless, Darwin's hypothesis of the evolution of man from lower forms of life was disturbing to many Christians, both Catholic and Protestant. The new hypothesis seemed to question the Bible's account of the origins of man. The implanting of the "divine spark" in man at the "moment" of his creation, as recorded in Genesis, had seemed to ennoble the human race and raise it above the animal

19. *Siècle,* Aug. 6, 1879. The editor of the liberal journal asks with malicious glee: "What is *Univers* going to say?"

20. Sainte-Beuve in the Senate, June 25, 1867. Quoted in George Jacques Weill, *Histoire de l'idée laïque en France au XIXᵉ siècle* (new ed.; Paris, 1929), pp. 208, 214-215. Sainte-Beuve believed, however, that some became unbelievers to satisfy their appetites. *Ibid.,* p. 213.

21. More than twenty-five years had elapsed since the publication of Le Play's *Ouvriers européens.*

world. In denying this "momentary" act, Darwin's hypothesis seemed to be casting doubt on the veracity of the Book itself as the message of God to man. The Bible was the very "Word of God." To many Protestants this apparent discrediting of the Bible account seemed catastrophic. In casting aside the authority of the historical Church in the sixteenth century, they had clung more tenaciously to the Bible, literally interpreted. To Catholics, however, God still spoke through the living Church, using the voice of the Supreme Pontiff to convey the message. The Catholics were therefore less disturbed. No papal denunciation of the hypothesis appeared. Pius IX's condemnation of "scientism" in general did not single out evolution for specific condemnation in the *Syllabus*. Social theory based on Darwinism seemed difficult of acceptance. The social theory of Le Play, on the other hand, based on the method of scientific survey, could be readily accepted by Catholic and Protestant alike, by moderate or by radical. Both Darwin, the scientist, and Le Play, the social scientist, had set hypotheses based on amassing of observed facts.[22]

Whether or not these events played any part in Leo's decision to take a public step in this matter, whether he was impelled by the interest of the Protestant world in the celebration of the tercentenary of Luther, or whether the reason he assigned in the document itself was the only consideration, can only be conjectured. At any rate he did decide on a momentous step, based on the fundamental principle that the truth could not harm. He had accepted scientific truth; he had approved the scientific method, if not all the conclusions of the social scientists; now he would apply the same principle to historical studies. The step he chose to make plain this approval was a dramatic one; he wrote a letter directing that the Vatican Archives be opened for research to competent scholars.[23] Explaining in the letter that the archives were opened in order to prevent false statements and suppositions from being made and spread around to the detriment of the papacy because of the changes made in Italy, Leo XIII said it was his duty not only to vindicate the

22. A review of Le Play's *Lettres historiques et sociales* was given extended coverage in *Univers*, running through several issues.

23. Leo XIII to Antonin de Luca, vice chancellor, Jean Baptist Pitra, librarian of the Church, and Joseph Hergenroether, prefect of the Vatican Archives, Aug. 18, 1883. *Univers*, Aug. 23, 1883.

rights of the Church but to answer the unjust attacks against the Holy See. Wishing the truth to prevail, he was undertaking this task.[24]

Beginning with the Centuriators of Magdeburg, who, unable to "attack Catholic doctrine," turned their attack to the "course of history," making false and caluminous statements against those who had accomplished noble deeds for the Church and for civilization, Leo pointed out that the same sort of onslaught was initiated in the nineteenth century when the Kingdom of Italy justified on the basis of history its seizure of the Church lands. He regarded this approach as a misuse of history: it was a great evil to make history a slave of partisanship and human passion.

Becoming more specific, he went on to say that he was anxious at any cost to prevent the transforming of the "noble profession of historian into a public and domestic scourge"; history should be the mirror of truth and sincerity, based on laborious investigations carried out to maturity, "opposing to rash conclusions prudent judgment, to frivolous opinions a scholarly critique," and recognizing that *the first law of history is not ever to dare to falsify; the second, not to fear to tell the truth*, nor ever to lend oneself in the slightest to *flattery or animosity*." The Pontiff credited the Church with having saved many integral documents of men such as Eusebius (the historian), Greek philosophers, and others; without the diligence of the monks in copying there would be no knowledge of what had occurred in those centuries even with regard to civil affairs.

After mentioning some historians in the past who carried on great undertakings, amassing documents to arrive at their conclusions, Leo says that the time has come to make possible once more this same sort of scholarship.

With this plan [he concludes] We have decreed that it will be permissible to use all the resources which our literary collections afford for the development of religion and sound studies. This day We declare that, to accomplish historical works of which We have spoken, Our Vatican library will furnish the available materials.

After giving instructions to the recipients of the letter as to how to carry out their task, he concluded the letter with these words: "Truth,

24. Leo XIII believed in going to the sources. There was no danger in publishing documents. Soderini, *Il Pontificato di Leone XIII*, I, 294.

in spite of the persevering efforts against it, will break through and triumph; it may be obscured for a moment, but never extinguished."

The reception of the publication of this letter on the opening of the archives was universally favorable. The correspondent of the London *Times* noted that much of the material for the tercentenary of Luther was in the Vatican files, and the same thing was true of the bicentenary of the saving of Vienna (1683) from the Turks by the European Alliance.[25]

To render more effective the opening of the archives, Leo also established a school of paleography and comparative history to be set up by Cardinal Hergenroether, in connection with the Vatican Archives, of which the Cardinal was director.[26] The Pontiff's interest in this historical project never flagged. Eight years later, he opened a historical library to include the most important historical works sent from various countries to facilitate research. At its opening it had thirty thousand volumes and thereafter progressed steadily in size and importance.[27] The task of organizing the library was entrusted to his brother, Joseph Pecci, whose educational experience had paralleled his own.[28]

Throughout his life Leo XIII displayed daily concern for philosophical, historical, and literary studies. He spent his quiet evening hours, after his strenuous days, in intellectual pursuits. His reputation and prestige grew in Protestant, Orthodox, and Catholic lands, and even among Muslims and far-away Asiatics.[29]

The kind of science which had led the *Philosophes* of the eighteenth century to their conclusions was not the sort that Leo meant when he talked about the advantages of scientific studies.[30] He was on the point of laying out for the whole world to see how a true scientist differed

25. Letter from Rome, Sept. 18, 1883. *Univers*, Sept. 23, 1883.
26. *Journal de Rome*, Sept. 18, 1883. *Univers*, Sept. 23, 1883.
27. T'Serclaes, *Léon XIII*, I, 373.
28. Correspondence from Rome quoting *La Voce della Verità*, Sept. 23, 1878. *Univers*, Sept. 27, 1878. Joseph Pecci was called in the first year of Leo's pontificate to reorganize the library of the Vatican. Years later when the historical library was opened Joseph was chosen to become its head.
29. *Semaine religieuse* published a detailed account of a typical day of His Holiness. The description appears in *Univers*, May 3, 1884.
30. In a letter to the archbishops and bishops of France (*Noblissima Gallorum gens*) one paragraph described *Les Philosophes* as carried away by a sort of insanity resulting from a passion for "untrammeled liberty." For a summary of the letter see *Univers*, Feb. 8, 1884.

from a dangerous one. What he really had in mind as a "virus," a "pest," masquerading under the term "science," was the order of Freemasons. The Freemasons claimed to found their beliefs on science and regarded their task as one of spreading the scientific view. Here was Leo lauding science and in the same breath condemning the organization. In the nineteenth century Freemasonry was viewed as a deadly enemy of the Catholic Church. In many places it had been openly anti-Catholic. His Holiness had made some remarks about the order earlier in his encyclicals: *Quod apostolici*, *Arcanum*, and *Diuturnum illud*, as well as in the *Nobilissima Gallorum gens*;[31] now he proposed to devote a whole encyclical to it. So appeared the *Humanum genus*, and rarely has any such pronouncement received so great a flood of response and reaction, whether of praise or contradiction.

His Holiness began the document, in fact, by lining up all people on earth in two camps: God's and Satan's. St. Augustine had described them as two cities: the terrestrial and the celestial. Leo assigns the Freemasons to the camp of Satan. He accuses them of plotting maliciously to run the saints out of the bosom of the nation; for a century and a half, he insists, the Popes had had to be on guard against them.

In view of these facts, the encyclical continues, it was but natural that the Apostolic See should publicly have denounced the sect of Freemasons as a criminal association, no less pernicious to civil society than to the Church, should have called down on it the severest punishments of the Church, and should have interdicted membership in it. Some among its members, Leo recognized, had admitted that the Popes had acted legitimately in attacking them.

The Pontiff referred to the incredible progress the order had made in a century and a half in spite of laws passed against it in Holland, Austria, Switzerland, Spain, Bavaria, Savoy, and parts of Italy. This progress had extended among all classes of society. Leo's desire to move against the order, he declared, was not stirred by any fear that the Church could be broken by it, but by the conviction that the state and civil society could be damaged.

His Holiness thought one part of the appeal of the sect of Free-

31. The *Arcanum*, dealing with Christian marriage, is omitted from the present study as are the various devotional encyclicals. The *Diuturnum illud* and the *Nobilissima Gallorum gens* will be discussed below.

masonry was its secret nature, giving it a mysteriously interesting air; its hierarchy of degrees was another factor, as was its summary punishment of those who should reveal its secrets. He granted that some good people belonged to the order, but this was because these persons did not know the criminal nature of the society nor its ultimate goal, which was to destroy the papacy; their immediate goal was to separate Church and State, reduce the clergy, and disperse the religious orders. As naturalists they did not believe in God, or at least claimed that the existence of God could not be proved with certitude. "As for morality . . . in which they want youth to be 'indoctrinated' it is what they call civic morality—independent morality—free morality."

The encyclical goes on to show how sin goes unrepressed, as in the journals, theatrical performances, and works of art, where "license knows no bounds" and realism is taken as the guide, while men seek only pleasure. Leo criticizes the view that men are equal and that authority derives from the people; he does not agree that the State must be atheist. Even the pagans, he says, recognized the necessity for religion.

To combat this evil the bishops are instructed to expose the evils in society and to strengthen the people by exhortation and instruction. He praises the Third Order of St. Francis with its understanding of the true meaning of "liberty, fraternity, and equality"; he recommends to the workers that they join the Workingmen's Clubs, under the tutelage and patronage of the owners, and commends the Society of St. Vincent de Paul.[32]

That Freemasonry should be censured was to be expected; what was remarkable about the *Humanum genus* was its benevolence in tone, its gentleness of spirit. Leo was making use of the occasion to show how the Church displayed respect for the civil power, to the end that "Justice be united with clemency . . . law with moderation."[33] Even the censure

32. *Univers,* April 23, 1884.
33. See "Leo XIII, the Letter *Humanum genus* Against Freemasonry and the Spirit of the Age," April 20, 1884, and the reply for the "Ancient and Accepted Scottish Rite of Freemasonry, Grand Orient of Charleston" (1884). At the time this was no "tempest in a teapot," no "tilting at windmills"; the Church regarded Freemasonry as, next to atheistic socialism, its most dangerous enemy, especially because of the wealth, prestige, and political importance of the people who were members, in all continental Europe. This was true throughout the century. Haugwitz, chief Prussian minister and diplomat in the Metternichean era, was head of the Prussian section. See Abbé Martinet in *Univers,*

pronounced (which would prevent members of the order from receiving the rites of the Church) was postponed for one year, lest this sudden announcement should cause undue hardship in some cases.[34]

The encyclical *Humanum genus* evoked comment all over Europe, "from the Court of Berlin to London and Lisbon." In Russia it was gratefully received; the Tsar ordered it read from the pulpits of the Russian Church.[35] Germany's attitude toward Freemasonry appeared in the very fact that when the Prince Imperial came to Rome and was actually received by the Pope (as has already been noted), in spite of being first received by King Humbert, the purpose of his coming was to participate in a celebration in honor of Martin Luther and to open a Masonic lodge.[36]

Comment from the English press tended to regard the encyclical as proof that the Pope was out of step with the age and that he did not know English Freemasonry, the *Tablet* remarking that the English members of the lodges were not dangerous like those on the Continent.[37]

Dec. 14, 1878. Prince Murat of the Napoleonic house was a member; many of the French cabinet members belonged to the lodges, which were the cells of the organization. Haugwitz had left the order when he realized that its purpose was to "dominate the world, to take control of thrones, making monarchs their docile instruments." The French sect had been excommunicated by the Grand Orient of the United States, for leaving out of their discipline the belief in a supreme being. See *Univers*, Aug. 2, 1878. Ferrata (Cardinal Dominique Ferrata, *Mémoires* [Rome, 1920], p. 39) attributed the turning of young Frenchmen to Freemasonry to the fact that French Catholics identified the cause of the Church with that of the monarchist parties.

34. *Journal des Débats*, Aug. 18, 1884.

35. Correspondence from Rome. *Univers*, May 15, 1884. Coquille, of *Univers*, thought Russia, plagued by nihilism, by subversive doctrines taught in the universities (invaded by foreign professors, especially German), could not expect effective help from the Russian Church. "Only the Catholic Church," said Coquille, "effectively combats the social errors which are dragging the European order to its fall. . . ."

36. Letter from Rome, April 22, 1884; *ibid.*, April 26, 1884. Fülöp-Miller (*Leo XIII*, p. 97) calls attention to the fact that the Freemasons of Italy had been responsible for her liberation and her unification. Both Mazzini and Garibaldi had been members. Now Crispi as well as other public officials belonged to the order. Again (pp. 100-101) he speaks of Adriano Lemmi, Grand Master of the Italian Lodge, who wished to abolish the Law of Guarantees and thus do away with the Pope's extraterritoriality that "the stones of the Vatican may be scattered" and the end of the papacy brought about. See also Fonzi, *I cattolici e la società italiana*, pp. 47-48.

37. Letter from London, *Univers*, May 5, 1884. "Fine affair," commented *Univers*, "they have at their service a heretical monarchy and government." Paul Janet, writing in 1880 about socialism, mentioned a society of the illuminati (*Illuminés*) which was supposed to be a dangerous branch of Freemasonry. He stated that the objective of this organization was to destroy existing society in order to create a better one. This, he said, was one of the sources of socialism. See Paul Janet, "Les Origines du socialisme contemporaine,"

The *Courrière de Bruxelles* compared the encyclical with the *Syllabus* of Pius IX, laying them side by side in columns, and concluded that they were basically alike.[38]

The journal of the French Opportunist Government took the view that Leo XIII was entirely within his rights as head of the Church in giving advice to members to join the appropriate Catholic organizations and to emulate the Third Order of St. Francis and the Society of St. Vincent de Paul; to blame him for this would be intolerant. The journal admitted that in some French lodges atheism was predominant. As to whether the encyclical was good politics or not was another matter; he might save some people and irritate others; the Italian Liberals, said the journal, hoped he would irritate people, because they feared the rapprochement between the Vatican and Germany.[39]

A writer in *Petit XIXe Siècle* said he was profoundly stupefied; as a member of Freemasonry, not a very good one, he feared, he had been in several lodges; the dominant opinion was religious tolerance—there were Catholics, Protestants, Israelites, Moslems, and Free Thinkers; emperors and kings had been Grand Masters; he thought the "murders" and "punishments for revealing secrets pure romance."[40] Clemenceau's Extreme Left *Justice* wrote sarcastically of the confusion into which the encyclical had thrown the republican chiefs by condemning as criminal all the principles of lay society. *Siècle* thought the Pope was attacking Moslem society in "re-editing the Syllabus"; it expressed astonishment that Leo, whose conciliatory spirit had made so much impression, should appear in the role of Pius IX; a Pope could be perhaps conciliatory in detail, and even liberal as to particulars, "but when he speaks as head of the revealed religion, he stands up and becomes inflexible. One cannot correct a work which comes from the hands of God. That is why the Church and modern society are irreconcilable."[41] Antirepublican, clerical *Patrie*, on the other hand, thought the *Humanum genus* good because

---

Revue des Deux Mondes, XL (I, 1880), 397. Actually the Illuminati had inserted themselves into the Freemason lodges.

38. *Univers*, May 21, 1884.

39. *Journal des Débats*, April 26, 1884. The Triple Alliance was unpopular in Italy. "While Europe is what it is [stated the journal], the realm of Italy will never separate from the German Empire and will do nothing, absolutely nothing, without its approval. . . ."

40. Quoted in *Univers*, April 25, 1884.

41. *Justice* and *Siècle* quoted in *Univers*, April 25, 1884.

it showed how to "destroy this hidden power" and because it was directed "against the republican policy" of France.[42]

The Congress of the Association of Catholic Clubs expressed gratitude for the encyclical and promised to heed the Pope's advice. *Univers* complained that the lodges concealed their true aims under public service and charitable activities, as though they were merely a benevolent organization.[43]

In general, in France, the moderate republicans expressed disappointment, the Left ridiculed, the Right heaped praises, according to their various political affiliations. Obviously no description sent out to all the world could fit the vastly differing circumstances in all places. All of this laid the encylical open to specific attacks. As to censure against the lodges, the Grand Orient instituted a new ritual which removed that branch of Freemasonry from censure.[44]

However justified it may have been, the encyclical did not add to Leo XIII's prestige among non-Catholics or lukewarm ones. In areas where Freemasonry was innocuous or unimportant either religiously or politically, it tended to blur the new image built up consistently by His Holiness since his elevation to the Holy See. One important point seems to have been overlooked in the various analyses: Leo recognized the difference between ostensible and real goals. To Leo the ultimate goal of man was to find himself in God. To him there could be no quarrel between science and religion. He would, however, quarrel with scientists who found no room for anything not in the realm of the demonstrable. One such scientist, a professor in a medical school, put it thus before a session of French Freemasons:

The metaphysical conception of another age, which the religions of the past still stretch before the eyes of ignorant populations, will vanish promptly before the astonishing spectacle of the natural evolutions of matter and the infinite complexity of the results produced by the constant and fatal action of forces which are the very essence of nature. . . .

He thought the task of the Freemasons was to spread this scientific view.[45]

42. Quoted in *Univers*, April 26, 1884.
43. *Ibid.*, May 17, 1884. *Univers* quotes instances, to support its view, from the clerical monarchist *Chaine d'Union*.
44. *Univers*, April 26, 1884.
45. F. Blatin before the medical school of Clermont-Farrand. *Ibid.*, May 8, 1884.

As for inventions, Leo XIII said the Church was no enemy of the new; the development of science was favored as the reflection of the divine intelligence.[46] If the facts were demonstrable either by observation or by effect and the conclusions verifiable, there could be no argument. In the field of the social sciences the method might also be employed without criticism. Such was the case with regard to Le Play. The painstaking, specific, and minute survey would clearly make possible certain cautious generalizations in the developing field of sociology. Science, however, made broader claims than these. Karl Marx based his views of social change on history, deeply studied, and called his method "scientific," his program "scientific socialism"; he generalized observed trends and passed to predictions based upon these generalizations.[47] In economics, from the eighteenth-century physiocrats on, systematic studies led to generalizations which the nineteenth century regarded as scientifically proved. The word "science" made all generalizations respectable. The laissez-faire economics so derived had enriched the possessor classes without producing any Utopia for the masses. The addition of statistical method by the social sciences added a new dimension of profundity to their generalizations, conclusions, and predictions. The upper classes tended to derive from the development of science the soothing view that the ills of the masses were due to natural causes and should not be tampered with; the non-possessors found the idea of social revolution more alluring. Only religion, recognizing the evil in every heart, could encourage scientific investigation and still condemn attempts to use knowledge to exploit humanity.

One more important encyclical was to come from the pen of Leo XIII before his definitive utterances on the social question were to see the light of day. In 1888 he issued *Libertas*. While *Libertas* is more directly

46. "But as all truth must proceed from God, the Church recognizes as truth that is reached by research a trace of the divine intelligence." Quoted from Leo XIII's *Immortale Dei*. See Gilson, *The Church Speaks to the Modern World*, pp. 161-184.

47. Frédéric Le Play died in 1882. He had been influenced by the Belgian Catholic Charles Périn. Le Play was most noted for his "social survey" method of arriving at sociological truth. Marx, founder of another sociological school, had not studied specific communities in detail but had arrived at his conclusions from the study of history. Le Play's method might stir one from complacency; it was not likely to cause any storm of adverse criticism. He found the intermediary organizations, already advanced in Anglo-Saxon and Scandinavian countries, a defense of the centralizing tendency of the State. Leo XIII approved of his method. Le Play founded one of the main schools of sociological thought. See Vaussard, *Histoire de la Démocratie Chrétienne*, p. 44.

and obviously connected with the question of the relation of the individual to the government under which he lives and the society of which
he is a member, the encyclical is basic to any discussion of the right of
the individual mind to accept or reject ideas. Is man free to reach conclusions based on the evidence of his senses? Leo is here confronting the
question of questions. The year in which *Libertas* was issued was to be
one of Jubilee. He had been ordained and had celebrated his first Mass
fifty years before. He had now occupied the Chair of St. Peter for ten
years. The promulgation of *Libertas* was the outstanding event of the
year.[48]

In *Libertas praestantissimum* Leo XIII asserted that the Church was
not hostile to liberty, as many critics maintained. The use of liberty
brings forth good or evil. Man is free to choose his path, leading to good
or to destruction, and it is this which makes a man a human being. Leo
rejects the idea that man is constrained by forces over which he has no
control: the Church "at no time, and in no place . . . has . . . held truce
with fatalism." It is man's attribute of reason which puts him in the
position of being free to choose, but choice is "subsequent to a judgment
upon the truth of the good presented," and "judgment is an act of
reason." Insisting that sinning is "not freedom but slavery," he quotes
the words of Jesus: " 'Whosoever committeth sin is the slave of sin.' "
Freedom does not mean that man can disregard law: "Nothing more
foolish can be uttered than the notion that, because man is free by
nature, he is therefore exempt from law." Law includes *natural law* and
enacted law, which he calls *human law*. "Therefore," he states succinctly,
"the true liberty of human society does not consist in every man doing
what he pleases, for this would simply end in turmoil and confusion,
and bring on the overthrow of the state; but rather this, that through
the injunctions of the civil law all may more easily conform to the
injunctions of the eternal law." In stating the true aim of liberty he
says: ". . . the supreme end to which liberty must aspire is God"; the

48. During the same year Leo XIII wrote to the Brazilian bishops on the subject of
slavery. After speaking of the Church's efforts to get rid of slavery, the Pope expressed
the wish that the abolition of slavery in Brazil be accomplished, but "in such fashion as
to assure the stable welfare of the slaves themselves whose interests are at stake." See the
letter in *Univers*, May 26, 1888. It was written on May 5. While giving further insight
into the character of Leo, this letter cannot be said to have had any direct bearing on the
social question in continental Europe.

law must be no respecter of persons, as "true brotherhood" was first asserted by Jesus Christ; and His apostles reechoed His voice when they declared that in the future there was to be "neither Jew nor Gentile, nor barbarian, nor Scythian, but all were brothers in Christ." The Church, he said, used her influence "in support of any form of government which commended itself to the citizens at home, because of its justice, or was feared by their enemies without, because of its power." He said further: "But where . . . a law is enacted contrary to reason, or to eternal law . . . obedience is unlawful, lest, while obeying man, we become disobedient to God."

The Pontiff branded those who substituted "license" for "liberty" as liberals usurping the name of liberty; they operate in the field of morality and politics, as the *naturalists* or rationalists do in philosophy. This usurpation he condemned because it arose from the denial of "the existence of any divine authority to which obedience is due, and proclaims that every man is a law to himself. . . ." From this arose the concept of the "supremacy of the greater number, and that all right and all duty reside in the majority." Once God has been repudiated, all sorts of disorders follow, held back by nothing except force; he adduces as evidence "the conflict with *socialists* and members of other seditious societies, who labor unceasingly to bring about revolution." He did not believe that one had liberty to choose in religion, but must follow the one "true" Church.[49]

The other liberties cherished in the nineteenth century—speech, teaching, conscience—he denied as being absolute on the ground that one was free only to speak the truth;[50] the State may be permitted, however, to

49. Massimo Salvadori, reviewing Michael P. Fogarty, *Christian Democracy in Western Europe 1820-1953*, in *Rivista storica italiana*, LXXIV (II, 1962), 412, takes exception to Fogarty's statement (p. 151) that with the encyclical (*Libertas praestantissimum*) Catholicism accepted the liberal principles of tolerance and democracy, inasmuch as the definition of liberty given "excludes the liberty of non-Catholics."

50. This aspect of the encyclical's insistence that only the truth could be spoken, taught, or written, was in fact a reiteration of the Church's claim through the centuries that clear distinction should be made between books or journals permitted to be read by the laity and those which could be safely read only by the clergy. Romolo Murri was led to comment that this prohibition left very little to Italians to read. "Many of our journals," he said, "would have neither readers nor purchasers were it not for the clergy." He concluded that the effect of this was to foster the notion that Catholicism was for the illiterate. See Romolo Murri, *Kämpfe von Heute: Das christliche Leben zu Beginn des Zwantzigsten Jahrhunderts* (Cologne, 1908), p. 212.

tolerate some situations in order to prevent worse evils from arising. He disapproved also of the principle of separation of Church and State; he did not condemn seeking national independence or self-government, if carried out without violation of justice.[51]

The reception of *Libertas* varied according to the inclination of the different reviewers. In England, where there was no quarrel between the Church and the State, the *Saturday Review* praised the encyclical, which contained, it said, "not a single idea that cannot be accepted by all true Christians"; there was not "a trace of fanaticism or narrowness" in it.[52] *Univers*, in Paris, strongly approved of Leo's pointing out the dangers of liberalism. "Liberalism," commented Eugene Veuillot, "under all its forms . . . will have been the greatest plague of this century. Violent revolution, of which it is, moreover, one of the instruments, has produced more visible, but less profound, destruction." This encyclical should be treasured, he wrote, along with Gregory XVI's *Mirari vos* and Pius IX's *Quanta cura*; even some Catholics have been liberals; now "no illusion is possible."[53]

The *Journal des Débats* said the encyclical subordinated liberty to law in order to prevent license, socialism, and tyranny; Leo's deriving principles of liberty, equality, and fraternity from the Gospel would not sit well with the ultra-conservatives, to whom these words were anathema. The journal praised the learning of the Pope, his knowledge of philosophy as well as of the Church Fathers on which he had had time to meditate during the twenty-five years of his exile, imposed upon him by the "animosity of Cardinal Antonelli," at his bishopric of Perugia;

51. Quotations from English translation in Gilson, *The Church Speaks to the Modern World*, pp. 55-82. The Latin and French versions appeared in *Univers*, June 29, July 1, 1888. Nothing could more completely set forth the fundamental quarrel between Marx's authoritarian scientific socialism and Leo XIII than this encyclical.

52. In countries whose culture was primarily derived from England, natural law was regarded as basic and fundamental; enacted law must not attempt to set natural law aside. The Pontiff was not really addressing these areas, except incidentally. It was the Italian scene which at the moment was giving him most concern. Enacted law was striking at the time-honored customs and institutions of the Roman Church, within earshot and sight of the Vatican.

53. *Univers*, July 1, 1888. The Abbé Lagrange, editor of *Défense*, took issue with Veuillot over this statement and quoted Leo: ". . . to practice modern liberties and to make use of them to defend the Church, is sometimes, indeed, a form of liberalism, and sometimes not only a right but a duty." Veuillot replied that the Abbé was confusing liberalism and liberty, and should reread the encyclical. See *Univers*, July 18, 1888.

he was undoubtedly bound to express the traditional views of the Church, followed by a "nevertheless" (*non obstante*) permitting tolerance because not to tolerate would be to bring a greater ill; one could not reasonably expect more of the Pope than this. "In exchange for tolerance," goes on the editor of the Opportunist journal, "the liberals, at least those among whom we classify ourselves, are ready to guarantee to the Catholics the liberty of conscience which the Sovereign Pontiff energetically demands for them." The editor remarks further than an Italian journal says amusingly that the Pope could have entitled his encyclical "On the necessity of Opportunism." Probably, the article concluded, Leo was directing the encyclical against the sects, which are actually not liberal at all, but his moderation and equilibrium show the perfect measure of his spirit, and "one may think that liberalism is rather a matter of temperament than of doctrine."[54]

Before the year was out Leo XIII returned to the charge that misuse of scientific fact was responsible for many of the ills of the time. In *Jampridem* he voiced his concern. It was not science which troubled him but the materialist philosophy which claimed science as a foundation and interpreted it in atheistic fashion. "They teach," he said, "that all the world is matter, that the origins of man and beasts are the same [i.e., purely material]"; he goes on, speaking categorically: "rationalism, materialism, and atheism have engendered socialism, communism, and nihilism; all these are cruel and abhorrent plagues which must almost inescapably emanate from these principles."[55]

Five years later, when Leo XIII was eighty-three years old, the subject of the Church's attitude toward scholarship and knowledge was even more clearly set forth in a remarkable encyclical: *Providentissimus Deus*, issued on November 18, 1893. This encyclical dealt primarily with the Holy Scriptures. His Holiness was anxious to preserve "this excellent treasure of divine revelation" from corruption. Nowhere would one find, said the Pontiff, richer teachings and more ample materials for exhibiting the glory and goodness of God both to wise men and the ignorant.

54. *Journal des Débats*, June 27, 1888 (the summary); July 2, 1888 (the analysis).
55. ". . . *rationalismus, materialismus, atheismus peperere socialismus, communismus, nihilismus: tetras quidem funestasque pestes, sed quas ex iis principiis ingenerari non modo consentaneum erat, sed prope necssarium*. For the French text, see *Univers*, Jan. 2-3, 1889; for the original Latin, see *ibid.*, Jan. 6, 1889.

As to knowledge about the Saviour of the human race, he quotes St. Jerome, who said that " 'ignorance of the Scripture is ignorance of Jesus Christ.' "

Sketching the history of the Scriptures after the time of St. Jerome, the encyclical mentions the work of Bede and Alcuin in preserving the text until the eleventh century opened a new era of progress. During the age of the scholastics the Scriptures were elucidated by true scholarship. In this matter the Pope awards the palm to St. Thomas Aquinas. But he does not let the matter rest there. He points out how, in the early years of the Renaissance, Pope Clement V established chairs of oriental languages, such as Hebrew, and how in the fifteenth century the Renaissance revival of Greek and the invention of printing gave a great stimulus to scriptural studies. Editions of the Vulgate "flooded the universe," so that thanks to the work of the scholars "the illustrious age of the Fathers [i.e., of Sts. Jerome, Augustine, Ambrose, and Gregory] seemed almost to have come again." The various editions brought out would prove how wrong were the detractors of the Church in claiming that it "neglected the Scriptures." Leo then points out, without animus, that the Protestants admitted only the authority of the Scriptures, personally interpreted, rejecting the Church as an authoritative institution. The rationalists, goes on the encyclical, went far beyond the Protestants, denying both revelation and inspiration and rejecting the word "Holy." They claim, in fact, that the account is simply fiction and human invention—not an authentic narrative of real events, but pure fable and mendacious stories. According to them there were neither prophecies nor divine oracles, but rather, either predictions arranged after the event or simple intuitions of the human spirit. In miracles and manipulations of the divine power these rationalists, points out the encyclical, see only curious natural phenomena, illusions, or myths; finally, they claim that the Gospels were not written by the authors whose names are given but by others.

Having thus squarely faced the criticisms of the Scriptures emanating from the rationalists of his day, Leo mentions the constructive suggestions made by the greatest scholars of the Church in times past. St. Augustine, for example, suggested that in case of doubt as to the significance of the Vulgate rendering, it was useful to go back to the "more ancient language" of which the Vulgate was the translation;[56] indeed, the obscurity rendered a useful service by necessitating a "more searching inquiry." One may even—and here the Pontiff again quotes St. Augustine—go beyond the "unanimous agreement of the Fathers" when "reason prevents accepting it" or when necessity forces its abandonment. Even the explanations of the heterodox, maintains Leo, may be read—prudently. For the young, however, he advises the study of St. Thomas.

Coming specifically to the questions of science, the encyclical states that the Catholic interpreter must "know the natural sciences." There will never be any actual "disaccord" between the theologians and the physicists "so long as each of them remains in his own domain," taking care, the while, never to "hold as known what is unknown." His Holiness adds the sound precaution that one should accept conclusions supported by incontrovertible evidence, knowing that such conclusions "will not in any way contradict the Scriptures properly understood," but remembering that "it has happened more than once that conclusions given at first by scholars as proved have subsequently been questioned and finally rejected."[57]

Providentissimus Deus opened wider the door for the most searching scholarship in the matter of biblical studies. Encouraged to study deeply and freely, the mature scholar might make use of new linguistic knowledge and of new materials which might be brought to light through the discovery of hitherto hidden manuscripts. What more could any scholar ask?

The fame of the pontificate of Leo XIII, recognized by unbelievers as well as Christians, rests primarily upon his encyclicals on the social question and on the relation of learning to faith. The first is the main theme of this volume; the second helps to explain the first. The question of faith and learning is timeless; the social question is pertinent to a particular situation. Both questions involve the eternal problem confronting the papacy, that of preserving the tradition of the Church and

---

56. At the Council of Trent in the sixteenth century, Cardinal Reginald Pole proposed that each book of the Bible should be examined individually. He added the suggestion that the Greek and Hebrew texts be admitted with the Vulgate. These proposals were rejected. See Richard M. Douglas, *Jacopo Sadoleto 1477-1547: Humanist and Reformer* (Cambridge, Mass., 1959), p. 205.

57. Synopsis and extensive quotations from the text of *Providentissimus Deus* in T'Serclaes, *Léon XIII*, II, 602-610.

at the same time making it relevant to the human condition in a specific age. Leo XIII boldly stated that in the realm of scientific investigation, carried on in all fields, nothing could be turned up that faith need fear. Truth must be in harmony with truth. Faith and learning were but two sides of a coin. Faith without learning was speechless; learning without faith was heartless. The task of the Church was to interpret in every age the facts of science in terms of values for the human spirit. The greatest of the saints of the Church, he showed, had demonstrated throughout the Church's history this synthesis of faith and reason. He was following in their footsteps. He attacked the Freemasons because their scientific learning was untempered by faith in a Supreme Being.[58] What Leo XIII deplored was scientific knowledge proclaimed in support of unworthy ends. He backed up his position (as to the dangers of scientific conclusions arrived at by those whose spirits were arrogant and unchastened) by issuing his encyclical on "Liberty"; making a distinction between "liberty" and "license." One was free only to tell the truth.

As a demonstration of his deep conviction of the inseparability of faith and learning, Leo XIII encouraged the work of archeological investigation; opened the archives of the Vatican to competent scholars, Protestant as well as Catholic; approved the scrutiny of ancient biblical texts; and fostered the study of history. His recommendation of the study of St. Thomas Aquinas undoubtedly rested on what such study, guided by his early teachers, had done for his own intellectual awakening.

It was the materialistic philosophy of Karl Marx, with its refusal to recognize any authority higher than man himself, which seemed to Leo XIII to have made an unbridgeable chasm between Marxian socialism and Christianity.

58. He withdrew his strictures against those branches which included belief in such a Supreme Being.

X. THE SECOND INTER-NATIONAL

> "Was the International held together by a uniform dogma? On the contrary. There were communists, . . . Proudhonists, . . . Blanquists, the German Workers Party, and finally the Bakuninist anarchists. . . . There was among the early Christians the same division into countless sects, which was the very means by which discussion and later unity were achieved."[1]
>
> FRIEDRICH ENGELS

The First International had given up the ghost in the 1870's, although it can scarcely be said that it was decently interred. Throughout the decade of the eighties, while various national socialist groups were pursuing their separate ways the hope of the leading Marxists was that all might be united once more. The workers themselves, members of trade unions or *syndicats*, had never abandoned the idea of maintaining some sort of international solidarity and continued to travel to international expositions whenever the opportunity offered. Here they hobnobbed in friendly fashion, secured addresses in an effort to keep in touch, and returned home refreshed and ready for new adventures on the home front in their attempts to secure higher wages, shorter hours, or the like.

Organized meetings of workers had been held both in Paris and London, attended by a wide assortment of laborers from other lands. Such meetings were impossible in Germany, and it was apparently German pressure that persuaded one division of the French Internationalists to plan an organizational meeting for Paris which should include social-

1. Engels, "On the History of Early Christianity," Marx and Engels, *Basic Writings on Politics and Philosophy*, ed. Feuer, pp. 180-181.

ists primarily. Another socialist faction in France wanted the meeting
to be a meeting of workers' delegates, no matter what their ideological
bent. The centenary of the French Revolution of 1789 was to be celebrated in the French capital. What could be more perfect than to set
the socialist meeting to coincide with this mammoth celebration? In
point of fact, the time and place were ill-chosen. A momentous crisis in
French public life, reaching its climax before the projected meeting,
rent the French socialists' factions more completely asunder. The crisis
was the Boulanger affair.

General Boulanger, appointed Minister of War in the French cabinet
in 1886, was potentially a dangerous man, although he was not suspected
of harboring illegitimate ambitions. Immensely popular with the crowds,
making a dashing figure on his black horse, he might be used as a pawn
by any group desiring to overturn the French Republic.[2] When the
cabinet fell he retained his post in the new one, which fell in turn in
May, 1887. General Boulanger was sent back to regular army duty by
the incoming Minister of War. So great was the popularity of the Man
on the Black Horse that he was escorted to the railway station by throngs
of Parisians. Upon completion of his military duties Boulanger ran for
election, winning multiple elections in Paris and various departments.
The monarchists had originally opposed him; this made him a hero to
the masses. The French Republic had just expelled the Sisters of Mercy
from the Paris hospitals; Boulanger gained further popularity among
the people by promising to protect the Sisters and the rights of the
Church.[3]

The question must be met by the socialists: to support, to ignore, or
to reject the Boulangist threat. Guesde and the Marxists refused to take
sides in the contest; they remained neutral.[4] Brousse and his Possibilists

2. The authoritarian groups were on both sides of the republicans. Monarchists and
clericals, to the right, were in opposition to the republicans in the interest of returning
to monarchy in one form or another and halting anticlerical measures; no less authoritarian was Guesde's *Parti ouvrier*. See Adrien Dansette, *Le Boulangisme: Du Boulangisme
à la Révolution Dreyfusienne 1881-1890* (Paris, 1938), p. 375; hereinafter cited as *Le
Boulangisme*. For Leo XIII's policy in dealing with French politics, see below, chap. xii.

3. Michael Curtis, *Three Against the Third Republic: Sorel, Barrès, and Maurras*
(Princeton, 1959), p. 27. See also Ernest Alfred Vizetelly, *Republican France 1870-1912*
(Boston, 1912), p. 327. Vizetelly says the guarantee was published in *La Croix*.

4. Guesde was the avowed enemy of the middle-class capitalist state; he was no less
the avowed enemy of clericalism and monarchism. This left him in this crisis with
neutralism as the only position to take.

decided to oppose the General, concluding that the immediate danger was Boulanger and the threatened death of the Republic; they joined the Opportunist republicans and Clemenceau, leader of the Extreme Left, to support the government.[5] The Blanquists split, some joining with the Possibilists in the attempt to preserve the Republic, rather than see it slip back into monarchy.[6]

The claim has been made that modern French socialism was born in the Boulanger movement. It is certain that the affair, including its ignominious collapse, gave impetus to the entrance of socialists into public life. Not only were more socialists sent as representatives to the Chamber of Deputies, but many socialists ran in local elections, took seats in local councils, and in general assumed fuller responsibility as citizens. This was to have been expected of Brousse's Possibilists, who had all along been seeking the half-loaf by engaging in the political process; now the authoritarian Marxists led by Guesde and Lafargue[7] took to the hustings and entered political life, and not as obstructionists trying to bring the wheels of government to a grinding halt. The differences between the two groups were still too pronounced for them to coalesce.

It was just after the climax and collapse of the Boulanger affair that two gatherings of socialists from many lands were held in Paris. The Possibilists had held meetings of international character in 1883 and 1886 attended by delegates from all sorts of groups of heterogeneous character: syndicalists, trade-unionists, anarchists, and others. They held a similar international meeting at Lancre Street, Paris, in 1889. Those who were conspicuously absent from the meetings of the Possibilists were the authoritarian Marxian socialists. Following a suggestion from the German socialists, the Guesdists were now seeking to unite at the international level those who represented the Marxist point of view. In 1889 they held their international meeting in Pétrelle Hall, on Rochechouart Street, in Paris.

5. The Possibilists proclaimed: "We workers are ready to forget the sixteen years during which the bourgeoisie has betrayed the hopes of the people; we are ready to defend and to conserve by all means the weak germ of our republican institutions against military threats. Long live the social republic!" Zévaès, *Marxisme en France*, p. 116.

6. Humbert, *Les Possibilistes*, p. 38.

7. Lafargue was sent to the Palais Bourbon as deputy in 1891. Bourdeau, *Évolution du socialisme*, p. 38.

In Lancre Street the Possibilists gathered a crowd of hundreds, composed of French syndicalists and anarchists, together with members of
England's organized labor groups. Their meeting did not lead to any
permanent organization. The meeting in Pétrelle Hall, on the other hand,
although attended by fewer people, produced the Second International.

Representing German socialism at the Pétrelle Hall gathering were
Liebknecht, Bebel, Georg Heinrich von Vollmar, and Eduard Bernstein,
along with Karl Legien, the "architect" of the German trade-union movement.[8] William Morris, founder of the Socialist League, Eleanor Marx-
Aveling (Marx's daughter), and Keir Hardie of the Scotch Labor Party,
were among those who sat for Britain, while Guesde, Lafargue, and
Longuet (the latter two Marx's sons-in-law) represented the French
Parti ouvrier; Vaillant represented the Blanquists, and Sebastien Fauré
the French anarchists. Plekhanov was there from Russia; Pablo Iglesias
represented Spain; César de Paepe, Anseele, and Vandervelde were
among the Belgian delegates. Andrea Costa, Amilcare Cipriani, and
Giuseppe Croce sat for the Italians, Domela Nieuwenhuis for the Dutch,
and Victor Adler for the Austrians. Representatives were also present
from Switzerland, Poland, Bohemia, Rumania, Bulgaria, Argentina, and
the United States.[9]

This meeting in Pétrelle Hall, although numerically smaller than
its rival in Lancre Street, was no less chaotic in its make-up. Anarchists
and Blanquists, together with representatives of syndical and corporative
groups, were there with the socialists. Most of the time was taken up
with reports as to social legislation in each of the countries. Of more
than passing interest was the adoption of a resolution to hold a May
Day (1st of May) demonstration in every country, in the name of labor;
the demonstration was to be made in the interest of securing an eight-
hour day. The idea had first been suggested in the United States in 1884.
The resolution was adopted almost without notice by the group; it was
to be turned over to the various national socialist groups to be handled
separately.[10] Aside from the May Day resolution, whose future signifi-

8. Braunthal, *Geschichte der Internationale*, p. 298.
9. Émile Vandervelde, *Histoire de la IIᵉ Internationale 1889-1919* (n.p., n.d.), p. 18.
Vandervelde was there himself as a delegate.
10. Alexandre Zévaès, *La Faillite de l'Internationale* (Paris, 1917), pp. 2-3. See also his
Histoire du socialisme et du communisme en France de 1871 à 1947 (Paris, 1947), pp.
175-179. For an English translation of the text of the resolution, see Cole, *History of*

cance was unforeseen, the main work of the meeting, certainly in the opinion of those present, was the establishment of the Second International. This body was to hold regular meetings. It was designed to be permanent.[11]

The Second International was an attempt to establish, or re-establish, the cause of labor as a movement transcending national lines. The divergence of view with regard to every aspect of labor was still present: to strike or not to strike, to seek reforms or to eschew them, to enter or not to enter into legislative bodies, to preserve or to destroy the State. Opinions were as far apart as the poles. The universal bonds seemed tenuous and insubstantial. One of these bonds was the red flag. Pétrelle Hall had been decorated, in anticipation of the arrival of the delegates, with the red flag of socialism, an international symbol.[12] The delegates had adopted May Day as a day consecrated to labor. They had a gospel according to Marx and Engels, slogans from which had adorned the walls of the meeting hall. Most of all they had the meeting itself. Twenty nations speaking twelve different languages had been there assembled. They had adopted a martyr. One of the events of the meeting had been a pilgrimage to the mass grave of the Communards and to the grave of Blanqui, in Père Lachaise cemetery. Blanqui was revered as the labor leader who had spent most of his life in prison and in exile.[13]

Leadership of the revived International was in the hands of the Germans. They had the most unified group anywhere and were strongly led. The very fact of their suppression by laws directed against them since 1878 worked to their advantage. By prosecuting the Kulturkampf

---

Socialist Thought, III: *The Second International 1889-1914* (1956), Part I, 9. Nollau says (*International Communism and World Revolution*, p. 21) the last statement in the resolution was inserted at the insistence of the Germans; the statement was: "The workers of the various countries will have to accomplish the manifestation under the conditions imposed on them by the particular situation in each country."

11. Zévaès, *Faillite de l'Internationale*, p. 4. Perhaps in a sense they were right. The Second International was to die with World War I, but the Third International was soon created.

12. The red flag had been banned from Germany when the exceptional laws against the socialists had been passed. At the first German socialist Congress (Halle, 1890) after the abolition of these laws, Beck of Zurich displayed the red flag which he said had been cared for in Zurich, awaiting the day when it could be brought back to Germany. See dispatch from Halle, Oct. 15, 1890. *Journal des Débats*, Oct. 16, 1890.

13. The police had not interfered with any of this. Their attitude represented quite a change since 1878.

Bismarck had forced the Catholics from rivalry with the Social Democratic Party into an actual common political front of the two against his policies. He was, indeed, working unwittingly on the side of socialism. The virtual cessation of the Church struggle (1887) still left the socialists under the exceptional laws directed against them. Since congresses could not be held to propagandize their movement, the socialists had been reduced to individual work, winning someone in a shop who would "spread the word." Little special groups under the pretext of being singing, drinking, or walking societies, had instructed the neophytes. The Germans had held meetings abroad on freer soil, in Belgium or Switzerland. Propaganda from these gatherings could be put into print, reaching the workers inside Germany through an organized clandestine press. The speeches of the German socialists in the Reichstag (where they were immune from arrest), reported everywhere in the press, made the leaders known to everyone. The German workers turned more and more toward socialism. In 1890 they cast 1,427,000 votes for socialist candidates. The workers were trade-unionists; most of them were not socialists. Some of their unions were affiliated with the Social Democratic Party but most of them were not. The rapid rise of large-scale industry, the mushrooming of numbers of both men and women in industrial jobs, and the too rapid shift of population from rural to urban areas, ill-equipped to care for them, produced a situation for which the trade unions alone seemed to have any sort of remedy. Church and charitable efforts were neither extensive nor rapid enough to deal with the flowing sea of displaced persons.

The antisocialist laws were still in force when the German delegation returned from Paris to this repressive atmosphere. A miner who had taken part in the meeting in Paris was arrested on his return.[14] The Minister of the Interior (Bötticher), replying to a socialist speech in the Reichstag complaining of the persecution, said that the public authorities were constantly warned that dissolution of unions should not be undertaken except when theories subversive of the established order were expressed; the mere fact that a union belonged to a socialist party was not a sufficient motive for dissolving it. The Minister, however, still

14. *Rheinische Zeitung*, July 20, 1889. Quoted in *Univers*, July 31, 1889. The police were very zealous in carrying out the laws.

favored the retention of the law, especially the right conferred by it to expel agitators. The German law had never been made permanent; it had to be renewed at the end of each three-year period. In 1890 it was up again for renewal. The Minister of the Interior wanted it made permanent, even if the expulsion clause were removed. "The Socialist Party," he said, "directs its attacks against the existing order, and one may say to every partisan of this social order: *'Tua res agitur'* [your own interests are at stake]." He denied that the law bred anarchism and anarchists, as had been charged: "Does the law against housebreaking breed robbers and thieves?"[15] In the course of the debate Bebel said in memorable words: "If bourgeois society were not sick the Social-Democratic bacillus would not exist." He went on to say, his meaning unmistakable despite his biological inaccuracy, that socialism was like a serpent: if you cut off its head it immediately grew two new ones; the party had been growing for twenty years; the blows against it had been hard blows—but what did that accomplish? The party grew and became stronger than ever.[16]

In the course of his speech Bebel spoke of the Paris meeting. He described the close-knit character of international socialism as demonstrated in that gathering, held the previous summer; he concluded that "whatever the workers do is dangerous to the State." The Minister of the Interior, replying to Bebel, said the heads of the socialist party never ceased to pretend that they fought with moral arms; he did not agree; their arms corresponded with their doctrines, and they got their doctrines from London and were happy to propagate them.[17] The law against the socialists was not renewed. Even the Conservatives did not support the bill after the article permitting expulsion was removed. So an end was made to the exceptional laws against the socialists in Germany.[18] *Univers* published a letter from Berlin:

15. *Verhandlungen des deutschen Reichstags*, 7 Leg. Per., V Sess., 1889-1890, 50 Sitz., Jan. 23, 1890, LXII, 1179—1180, col. 1. The House removed the expulsion law by a vote of 166 to 111. *Ibid.*, p. 1199.

16. *Ibid.*, 52 Sitz., Jan. 25, 1890, LXII, 1225-1226.

17. *Ibid.*, 52 Sitz., Jan. 25, 1890, LXII, 1240, col. 2.

18. *Ibid.*, 52 Sitz., Jan. 25, 1890, LXII, 1255, col. 2. The National Liberals voted to retain the laws; against the bill were the Conservatives, Center, Progressists, and Socialist Democrats (socialists).

Today Bismarck must be suffering from complicated neuralgia, for today has fallen one of the foundation stones of his dictatorial policy, the law against the socialists. Opponents of this are gnashing their teeth with rage—even more because no one can any longer argue for the exclusion of the Jesuits and other religious orders struck by the law of July 5, 1872. The socialists are planning a big welcome for their exiled members "as we Catholics will for the Jesuits when they return."[19]

The news of the failure to renew the antisocialist laws in Germany produced rejoicing among German exiles everywhere,[20] one French journal commenting that now the Germans could hear their German orators, "the most loved apostles of the new religion." The Guesdists sent congratulations to their German colleagues on their emancipation:

For the first time since 1878 your Social Democratic Party will be able to meet freely in a national congress on German soil, and in its more developed and perfected organization draw upon new forces to carry out at long last its work of liberating labor. . . . You will be able to get rid of schisms exploited by the press. The French Workers' party [*Parti ouvrier*], which declares itself in solidarity with you, cannot wait to express its pleasure.[21]

With the freedom to hold national congresses won, international camaraderie increased between foreign Marxists and German socialists. Guesde, for example, attended the German Congress at Halle in 1890. With Liebknecht as interpreter, Guesde emphasized the international character of the French Commune and the solidarity of German support of that event; he hailed the Second International and said the workers' internationalism was in a declared war against capitalism.

The First of May demonstrations, resolved upon at the organizational meeting of the Second International, were to take place in 1890. Preparations were made in many cities to carry out the idea. Some *syndicats* arranged mass meetings, public balls, or concerts. Others planned to carry petitions for the eight-hour day to the local seat of government. Many workers wanted to stop all work on that day.[22] When a party head at Bordeaux asked Liebknecht's advice as to how to go about it, he was advised against a work stoppage, which (unsuccessful) might prejudice

19. *Univers*, Oct. 3, 1890.
20. *Journal des Débats*, Oct. 12, 1890.
21. *Volksblatt*, quoted in *Univers*, Sept. 20, 1890. The new *Volksblatt* could now be legally established to publicize socialism.
22. *Journal des Débats*, Oct. 20, 1890.

the situation.[23] Liebknecht said there would be evening festivities all over Germany, conferences, and other gatherings. He refused to advise France. "It is your affair," he said.

The demonstrations came off as planned on that first May Day in many important cities: Stockholm, Copenhagen, Paris, Berlin, Basle, Zurich, Milan, Madrid, Lisbon, Brussels, Amsterdam, London, and New York. There was very little violence. All were carried out so successfully that plans were immediately made to establish the affair as a yearly event.[24] The French discovered that it was a good day to hold political rallies, whether socialist or antisocialist.

The need for a resolution of the difficulties which had produced the rival congresses in 1889 led to an attempt to hold a meeting which would unite the factions. Guesde and his coterie had attended the one in Pétrelle Hall, while Brousse led his Possibilists in Lancre Street. Italians were just as divided. Andrea Costa was the head of the legalitarians; Amilcare Cipriani led the anarchists; Giuseppe Croce was the head of the Workers' Party, which had not prospered.[25] Similar divisions were present among the Belgians. With this attempt at unity in mind a Congress was held at Brussels in 1891.[26] Representatives of the various factions attended and as before they held widely divergent views on fundamental subjects.[27] One of the basic differences was the question of the general strike as the method of attaining socialist goals. Accepted by some factions, it was opposed by others. It had been suggested (at the founding meeting in Paris in 1889), during the discussion over the May Day resolution, that if the demonstrators all refused to work on that day it would be the "beginning of the social revolution." Now at Brussels the

23. The discussion of retention of the socialist laws would not come up in the Reichstag until October, 1890. For this reason the Germans were anxious not to stir up any adverse criticism. This had been in their minds in 1889 when they insisted that each country should be responsible for its own demonstrations. See Nollau, *International Communism and World Revolution*, p. 21.

24. In continental Europe it remained on May 1st. England celebrated always on Sunday, which was a day of rest anyway. In the United States the celebration moved to Labor Day, the first Monday in September. See Cole, *The Second International*, Part I, p. 16. See also Maitron, *Histoire du mouvement anarchiste*, p. 179.

25. Neufeld, *Italy*, p. 117.

26. No meeting of the International was held in 1890. An international conference sponsored by William II of Germany to discuss labor problems was held in Berlin in that year.

27. Cole (*The Second International*, pp. 18-24) analyzes the personnel of this Congress.

debate centered upon the possibility of preventing war by staging a general strike.[28]

Another of the perennial problems was the difference between the anarchists and the Marxists. The Marxists were trying to create a powerful party. Some of the anarchists came as representatives of trade unions or *syndicats* and also as representatives of anarchist organizations. There was much wrangling and waste of time over the seating or non-seating of such delegates. The decision was to let each one sit who had a mandate from a *syndicat* but to exclude any who represented only anarchist groups.[29] Some anarchists were thus seated and took part in the discussions. They insisted that both anarchists and socialists were aiming at the same thing. President Anseele of Belgium countered this claim, declaring: "Socialism wants the conquest of the State to bring about reforms by the State. Anarchists, on the contrary, want the destruction of the State. There is therefore incompatibility between the two parties." Anseele was a Marxist. The French delegation included the Marxist Guesde, the Blanquist Vaillant, Delcluze, who was deeply tinged with anarchism, and Allemane, leader of the faction of the Possibilists who opposed Brousse and his ideas. In spite of their differences of approach they brought carefully prepared agenda specifying reforms upon which they were in agreement.[30] These included labor legislation in various countries, the right to organize, universal suffrage, exchange of information (such as statistics), and other matters. The English delegation reported that England had a child-labor law with the age fixed at eleven years but that it was to be raised to twelve years in 1893. Many other questions, such as equality of wages for women and getting rid of piece work, were discussed at Brussels, but decisions were to be left to the national organizations. When the suggestion was made, during the course of the discussion, that wages should be abolished, the English delegation walked out, asserting that they had come to discuss specific reforms and were not for the class struggle. They returned at the next session.

28. Braunthal, *Geschichte der Internationale*, p. 292.

29. The anarchists never could succeed in forming an association. Such attempts as they made turned into pandemonium. See Maitron, *Histoire du mouvement anarchiste*, p. 105. Among those banished from the meeting were Rosa Luxemburg and Amilcare Cipriani. Merlino of Italy was among those seated under a decision reached by the Italian delegation. Three hundred and sixty-two delegates were seated.

30. A conference had been held in Paris for the purpose of working out these agenda.

One of the questions hotly argued was the question of nationalism. The French held to their views on patriotism; they were loyal to France. The German Liebknecht and the Blanquist Vaillant tried to satisfy them and the strongly antinationalist Nieuwenhuis. The two mediators brought in a resolution on socialism's attitude toward nationalism which avoided siding with either nationalism or internationalism and in effect said nothing. To have expected a genuinely antinationalist resolution to pass would have been the height of absurdity. French, Germans, and English were all engaged in following the legislative path. Only the anarchists were strongly antinationalist. Nieuwenhuis, himself strongly tinged with anarchism, was disgusted with the mildness of the resolution. He remarked that even the Pope could accept it if the word "Christianity" were substituted for "socialism."[31] Bebel's words were chauvinistic: "The soil of Germany, the German fatherland, belongs to us the masses as much and more than to the others. If Russia the champion of terror and barbarism went to attack Germany and destroy it . . . we are as much concerned as those who stand at the head of Germany, and we would resist Russia, for a Russian victory would mean the defeat of social democracy."[32]

Dr. Victor Adler (leader of the Austrian Labor Party) maintained that the class struggle should be emphasized rather than merely attacking the Manchester School. "It is necessary to affirm also [he said] that we want the conquest of the State by the working class."[33]

One of the specific matters attended to at the Brussels meeting was preparation for a general meeting to be held two years later at Zurich. The Brussels gathering agreed on a resolution to lay before the Zurich Congress. The resolution involved the unconditional acceptance of the tactical principles of the "need for political action."[34]

The Second International met as planned at Zurich in 1893. Again the anarchists tried to get in as delegates and again they were denied

31. James Joll, *The Second International 1889-1914* (London, 1955), p. 70. Nieuwenhuis added a paradoxical statement, which Joll calls "shockingly prophetic," in speaking against nationalism: "The international sentiments presupposed by socialism do not exist among our German brothers." Nieuwenhuis, in spite of his anarchistic leanings, had been granted a seat.

32. *Ibid.*, pp. 73, 112.

33. Braunthal, *Geschichte der Internationale*, pp. 224-225. Braunthal is encyclopedic in his coverage of the lives and contributions of all the prominent socialists.

34. *Ibid.*, p. 258.

admission. Those admitted because they represented trade unions or *syndicats* took vigorous part in the debates.[35] The prestige of the Zurich Congress was enhanced by the size of the trade-union delegation from England, led by John Hodge, a member of the Committee of Parliament and president of the Trade-Union General Association. The presence of Friedrich Engels also lent prestige to the gathering. The resolution (endorsing political action) prepared at Brussels was duly laid before the Congress. Bebel and several other German and Austrian delegates tried to amend the motion to adopt the resolution by adding: "Under political action is to be understood the workers' parties' utilization of or seeking to capture political rights and legislative machinery as power for the furthering of the interest of the proletariat and the conquest of political control." The anarchists objected vehemently to this, as did the "Young" and the "Independent" German groups. In the ensuing pandemonium during which the anarchists tried to storm the rostrum the "Young" German leaders were thrown out of the hall.[36] The amendment was accepted and the resolution passed.

Against the votes of the German delegates a resolution was passed to celebrate May Day with work stoppage and continuance of demonstrations for the eight-hour day. They also included for good measure a statement that peace was an appropriate objective for demonstration.[37] On the subject of war Nieuwenhuis attacked Bebel:

I have not forgotten how people in Germany have preached war against the "hereditary enemy" Russia, how Bebel himself has passed a sponge over all the misdeeds of his own bourgeoisie if it was a question of the hereditary foe. ... One cannot help laughing when Russia is called the champion of atrocities and barbarism, as if Germany were a protector of enlightenment and gentleness.[38]

The debate over the attitude to be assumed toward war was vigorous and practical. While agreeing that the destruction of capitalism meant

35. Maitron, *Histoire du mouvement anarchiste*, p. 105. They continued to meet in France as regional groups.
36. Braunthal, *Geschichte der Internationale*, p. 259.
37. Nollau, *International Communism and World Revolution*, p. 21.
38. Joll, *The Second International*, p. 112. All this Bebel had said at the Brussels meeting in 1891. France at this time was forming a Dual Alliance with Russia to offset the Triple Alliance headed by Germany. Nieuwenhuis, from Holland, was representing a country which lay precariously between the two alliances.

world peace (the concluding statement in the resolution that was adopted), the dangers of trying to force the issue by a general strike were pointed out by many of the delegates, from the Russian Plekhanov to the Italian Turati, from Liebknecht in Germany to Charles Bonnier in France. With the weapons of war in the hands of governments dominated by the capitalist classes any such move would be suicidal for the workers and would destroy the whole labor movement. Plekhanov, reporter for the commission on war, said the Russian government would disarm the peasants and surrender the Russian Cossacks to western Europe.[39] The resolution as adopted contented itself with urging socialists to struggle with might and main against military appropriations bills, to protest against militarism, and to work for disarmament.

Claims were made that the two congresses, at Brussels and at Zurich, had brought unity to the ranks of international labor. Such was not the case. When the Second International met in London in 1896 the old differences cropped up: the animosity of French socialists toward their fellow socialists who stuck too closely to the Germans and the eternal lack of compatibility between socialists and anarchists.[40]

Difficulties at the London meeting started with debate over the presentation of credentials. Should the French Jaurès, Millerand, and Viviani (the parliamentary group of independent socialists) be admitted? They had no letter. It was left up to the large French delegation to decide, and they were admitted. In validating the various mandates the question as to anarchism was once more posed. Jaurès made a speech on the subject, suggesting that if anarchism had been really converted to socialism it ought to be admitted, but if it "tries to insinuate itself into socialist congresses, and ventures to legislate there in disguise, that is a comedy to which we have no right to lend ourselves."

I know [continued Jaurès] that some will say that in excluding the anarchists we are repudiating also the *syndicats* which issued their mandates. We are very decidedly political and syndical partisans; we have proved this each time when the question was one of syndical rights, but one cannot defend some *syndicats* betraying or arresting the social movement by having chosen their delegates outside the ranks of socialism.[41]

39. Braunthal, *Geschichte der Internationale,* pp. 332-333.
40. Maurice Charnay, *Les Allemanistes,* Vol. V of Jaurès, *Histoire des parti socialistes en France* (Paris, 1912), p. 81.
41. Jaurès is quoted in *Univers,* July 31, 1896.

Jaurès's first speech was met with such thunderous applause and such waving of handkerchiefs and hats by the English (according to the minutes of the meeting)[42] that it was clear how highly he was to be regarded in the ranks of socialists. The Dutch Nieuwenhuis, favoring the inclusion of the anarchists, said the efforts of their opponents to exclude them only betrayed their anxiety lest "the Council of the Marxist Church Fathers might be disturbed."[43]

Millerand wanted to split the French delegation into the Guesde-Lafargue majority and the Jaurès-Millerand minority, giving a vote to each. Millerand said it was a question of *yes* or *no* as to letting the anarchists in; if they were admitted the French minority would leave. The English bewailed the loss of time in this type of wrangle. A hubbub ensued. After the stormy scenes the French minority was seated and given one vote; the antiparliamentarians and anarchists were excluded.[44] A report was adopted favoring the conquest of the public powers as the best means of emancipating the working class. The Dutch dissented from this and withdrew; they favored the strike as the better method, a view that was supported also by Bebel and the Italian Ferri.[45] To the claim that elected legislators were betraying their constituencies and supporting capitalist power Jaurès retorted that this was not true; they merely rejected syndicalist action but believed in political action. When he added that strikes bring propaganda which is of assistance when it comes to elections, he received an ovation.[46] Resolutions based on reports from the commissions were adopted, approving universal education from kindergarten to university, school meals and scholarships, socialization of land and industries, and denouncing piece work. In the realm of international relations they approved the setting up of International

42. Braunthal's report (*Geschichte der Internationale*, p. 258) is based upon the minutes.

43. *Ibid.*, p. 260.

44. Zoccoli, *Die Anarchie*, p. 455.

45. An interesting sidelight on the London Congress was a letter from George Bernard Shaw in which he said: "The Germans with their compact Democratic Party in the Reichstag are apparently far ahead of us. But then their leader, Herr Liebknecht, is going to prison [prosecuted for *lèse majesté*] for a speech which Mr. Arthur Balfour might make to the Primrose League with the approbation of England tomorrow." See Joll, *The Second International*, p. 75.

46. Jaurès's speech was quoted in *Univers*, Aug. 1, 1896.

Tribunals of Arbitration[47] and denounced standing armies. A resolution was adopted approving the extension of trade-union organization for accomplishment of specific reforms through negotiation, using the political path to legalize and protect gains so made. The Congress approved a resolution to set up a commission to establish an international secretariat.[48] Finally, a resolution was adopted that invitations to future congresses should be limited to socialist groups favoring socialization of property and production and recognizing the necessity of parliamentary legislative action. So ended the three-decades-old struggle between socialists and anarchists.[49]

The Second International met again, in 1900, in Paris. By this time an ideological rift had developed within the ranks of the socialists. The new movement came to be called Revisionism.

The Second International, until the end of the century, had no organization; it was merely a series of congresses. What was actual and real was socialism at the national level. While varying in program and procedure the national groups confronted problems which had some common factors. One was the continued development and expansion of the factory system, with its urban tendencies, its consequent social dislocation, and its uprooted masses of laborers with their families. The trend toward political democracy put a strong weapon in the hands of labor to use in improving its lot through reforms by legislative action. Of very great significance was the tendency of workers in the various countries to join labor unions of one sort or another. Anarchism, too, although excluded from the International, still posed a threat in some countries. The task of the socialists was to capitalize on the distress created by the social dislocation to gain control of the labor organizations and to use the democratic political path in gaining and maintaining this control.

47. It is interesting to note that it was in 1898 that the Russian Tsar sent out invitations to the First Hague Peace Conference, to be held in 1899. This conference established a tribunal to which international disputes could be referred.

48. When the secretariat was finally set up in 1900, the Belgian Vandervelde became the first president.

49. Braunthal, *Geschichte der International*, p. 262. The details of the decisions of the Congress appear in Cole, *The Second International*, Part I, pp. 28-35. Cole gives no citations. In his preface he thanks Julius Braunthal and James Joll for assistance in preparing the work. Joll may be consulted in his *The Second International* (1955), and Braunthal in his German work, *Geschichte der Internationale* (the first volume appeared in 1961). After World War II Braunthal was secretary of the revived International.

They must out-siren the anarchists. The workers wanted improvements. Unless these were secured by socialist leaders who represented them in the various legislative bodies labor would look elsewhere for leadership. A brief survey of some of the principal Catholic states of Europe will point up the national differences.

The dropping of the antisocialist laws in Germany in 1890 changed the whole picture of socialism and organized labor. The trade unions there differed from one another in origin and allegiance. There were "Christian Trade Unions" of two kinds, one organized by Protestants, the other by Catholics following the path laid out by Ketteler. There were some international unions also, founded by Bebel and Liebknecht. More important than any of these, numerically, were the "Free Trade Unions" which were socialist but not authoritarian in character. These "Free" unions had suffered under the antisocialist laws which had not permitted them to form a national organization. Like the socialists, they were freed from this restriction when the antisocialist laws were dropped in 1890. After that they grew slowly, unable (and unwilling) to throw off completely the leadership and control of the Marxist disciples.[50] During the period of repression the socialist leaders had played the role of martyrs, winning popular sympathy at home and gaining great personal prestige. The abrogation of the repressive laws brought new problems along with the immediate rejoicing. The *Sozialdemokrat* brought out an issue in red, in which the laborers were pictured saying: "The world is ours, let them do what they will."[51] Bismarck, who had fought both the socialists and the Catholics, was gone from the scene, dismissed by the young William Hohenzollern. Both socialists and Catholics had become more tightly knit within their respective groups as a result of the persecution. Both had progressed under Bismarck's attacks. As Liebknecht said at Halle during the first socialist Congress on German soil since the abrogation of the laws:

Have we not that which constitutes the strength of religion, faith in the highest ideals? When under the action of socialist laws we remained for years separated from wife and children, the better to serve our cause, was not ours the religion, not of the papacy, but of humanity? It was faith in the triumph of justice, of our ideal; it was the firm conviction that right must triumph

50. Gay, *The Dilemma of Democratic Socialism*, pp. 121-123.
51. Nitti, *Catholic Socialism*, p. 107.

and injustice succumb. This religion will never fail us; for it is one with socialism. While I was speaking in the Reichstag of the general injury done by the law against the socialists and foretold the fall of its author, the deputy Bamberger said to his neighbor, with a sigh: "The socialists have still faith." Yes, we still have faith; we know that we shall conquer the world.[52]

The German Marxian socialists had made truce with the Lassalleans back in 1875 at Gotha, on the basis of the Gotha Program. The labor organization wanted reform legislation. Liebknecht and Bebel preached socialist principles, needling the government and the Conservatives in brilliant speeches. The workers did not expect them to win any decisions —there were too few of them in the Reichstag—so they gave their wholehearted support to the displays of oratory. Bebel, the image of socialism, was the master orator. When the socialists and labor unions were free to organize, the demand of the majority was for labor legislation. The question confronting Liebknecht, Bebel, Vollmar, and the rest was whether to continue to menace the government and the upper classes by parading revolutionary theory, or to yield to the workers' insistence and produce a social program. The Marxist ambition to destroy the state was regarded by the workers as too revolutionary and their antireligious statements were not echoed among the members of the unions.[53] May Day demonstrations in 1890 at Hamburg brought lockouts by employers. This led to a movement to unite the unions into a federation of their own, not controlled by the Social Democratic Party.[54]

At the Congress of the German Social Democratic Party (*Sozialdemokratische Arbeiterpartie Deutschlands*) held at Erfurt in 1891 a more revolutionary program than the narrow, nationalistic Gotha Program was adopted.[55] This Marxist success over the Lassallean idea did not mean that Lassalle as a figure to be venerated was laid aside. Lassalle had brought the whole movement for labor into being and this could not be forgotten.[56] Separating their aims into long-range aims (socialistic) and

52. *Ibid.*, p. 391.
53. Mayer, *Johann Baptiste Schweitzer und die Sozialdemokratie*, p. 299. See also Carl E. Schorske, *German Social Democracy 1905-1907: The Development of the Great Schism* (Cambridge, Mass., 1955), p. 11.
54. Schorske, *German Social Democracy*, p. 9.
55. Engels published Marx's *Critique of the Gotha Program*, which he had hidden until then, in Karl Kautsky's journal: *Neue Zeit*. See *ibid.*, p. 4.
56. Braunthal, *Geschichte der Internationale*, p. 267.

immediate aims (democratic and practical), the Marxist leaders were able to hold the union members for the time being in line. The compromise nature of the program, however, met with such strong opposition from the "Young" radical, anarchistically inclined, Left, that a split developed. The "Young" were thrown out.[57]

At the party meeting in 1893 at Cologne the relation of the party to the unions again came up. Karl Legien (of the Free Trade Unions) resented what he regarded as the hostility of the socialist party leaders to the unions. The matter was smoothed over and no split occurred, but the unions were growing in size and strength and eventually cut the apron strings of the party. They adopted a formal policy of political neutrality, while individually continuing in practice to vote for socialist candidates.

Trade unionism became less revolutionary as the German government moved to improve the lot of the laborer. State labor exchanges and social security laws satisfied many of their desires. These were brought about by legislative action. As a labor organization they had no connection with the Social Democratic Party. As the decade wore along, increasing numbers of workers, as individuals, joined the Social Democrats. This action diluted the revolutionary zeal of the party and became a factor in Revisionism.[58]

Although the Social Democratic Party was the most closely knit party on the Continent, and although the Marxists had taken control of the organization, the spirit of the party was no longer thoroughly Marxist. The outstanding fact was the subtle but steady growth of Revisionism. This Revisionism will be examined in a later chapter.

There were strong supporters of the Second International in Belgium, yet a true socialist party did not develop in the constitutional monarchy. Some famous Belgian socialists were active in the International, men like de Paepe, Anseele, and Vandervelde, yet there was no real unity among them. Some were still tinged with anarchism and preferred the communal organization of society, which was characteristic in the Belgian scene. Yet they had witnessed the rapid expansion of industry and the

57. They formed an independent party for a while, from which the anarchists later dropped out, the less radical returning to the Social Democratic Party. See Cole, *The Second International*, Part I, p. 255.

58. Gay, *The Dilemma of Democratic Socialism*, p. 124.

growth of railroads and other new systems of communication. They realized that these changes demanded a more integrated economic system than the communal organization could provide. Co-operatives and mutual aid societies did prosper, however, and these were by their very nature local in organization and control. Next to England Belgium was the most highly industrialized state anywhere. It had some special problems, however, which hampered the growth of the socialist party. Two languages were spoken, the Walloons speaking French and the Flemings speaking German. Conditions in industry were very bad, which led to constant strikes, approved by anarchists but viewed with suspicion by the authoritarian socialists. The suffrage was so restricted that it seemed impossible to get reforms by legislative action except through co-operation with liberal parties. The result was that the party ultimately formed (in 1885) was a labor party, rather than one labeled "socialist."

Belgium, being Catholic, had also the problem of relations between the State and the Church to complicate the issue. When the Catholic Party took over the reins of government in 1884 (retaining them until World War I), it brought a parliamentary contest between a clerical-conservative Right, and a liberal-labor Left. The principal objective of labor became one of seeking an extension of the franchise as the *sine qua non* of securing reform legislation. There were some liberals among the higher clergy, notably Msgr. Doutreloux, and many liberals among the Catholic laity, especially among the young. Opinions held by the educated had been formed in part by the work of the social theorist, Charles Périn, who, with the French Le Play, was among the founders of sociology as a social science.

Before any outstanding progress was made toward reform, however, came Leo's pronouncements on labor and on the proper relations between Church and State.[59]

The Second International produced in France no unified socialist party, although it was undoubtedly a factor in stimulating socialist growth.[60] The same divisions as before continued to divide and divide

59. Consideration of the Belgian socialist movement must be deferred until the encyclicals on these matters have been discussed. Cole (*The Second International*, Part II, pp. 621-626) gives a résumé of some of the elements in the Belgian situation but does not mention Leo XIII.

60. Ulam (*The Unfinished Revolution*, p. 137) speaks of the growth of socialism in the nineties as "luxuriant."

again the socialist groups.[61] The Marxist *Parti ouvrier* had separated from the Possibilists, which then divided into Allemanists and Broussists.[62] The *syndicats* presently rejected subservience to the *Parti ouvrier*; they went their own way and became more anarchistic in the process; they turned to direct action. An attempt was made to unify them under the C.G.T. (*Confédération Générale du Travail*). Socialist parties were less successful in settling their disputes.

The presence of Italian representatives in the Congress which organized the Second International might lead one to assume that there was a socialist party in Italy. This was not the case. The problems confronted by the Italian socialists in any effort to establish such a party were many and complex. In spite of the extension of the suffrage in 1882, true parliamentary government did not yet exist; poverty and illiteracy continued to pervade the south and the agrarian sectors of the north; brigandage, which neither Mazzini's nor Garibldi's movements had lessened (had perhaps accentuated by making violence a national virtue), still persisted and flourished in the south; Bakunin's anarchism, while unorganized, was still deeply imbedded, influencing the rise of revolutionary syndicalism; papal reforming influence was hampered by the quarrel with the Italian state. The *Opera dei congressi* had brought about some reforms sponsored by leading churchmen and upper-class Catholics. Both the Church and the socialists suffered under repressive state action. Any national movement in Italy was hindered by provincialism.

In spite of all these difficulties Marxist socialism became organized and made substantial growth in Italy in the last decade of the century. A number of factors help to explain these socialist beginnings: the presence of German exiles in Switzerland, while the German repressive laws were in force, the publication there of their reviews, and the emergence of Italian leaders who were in contact with the German socialist stream. Among these leaders must be mentioned Turati,[63] spread-

61. This division was about to "demoralize the Western revolution *avant garde*." See Weill, *Histoire du mouvement social en France*, p. 269.

62. Useful in keeping straight these various organizational names and places of meeting is the bibliographical article by Jack Alden Clarke, "French Socialist Congresses, 1876-1914," *The Journal of Modern History*, XXXI (June, 1959), 124-129.

63. Turati refers to "our party in Germany." See Gaetano Arfé's review essay of "Ernesto Ragionieri: *Socialdemocrazia tedesca e socialista italiani, 1875-1895*" in *Rivista*

ing Marxist views through his new journal, *Critica sociale*; Labriola, who became intellectually influenced toward Marxism by his study of the documents;[64] and Bissolati,[65] the first socialist to sit in the Italian Parliament. Important also was the coming to Italy of international socialists such as Anna Kulisciov,[66] and the publication in Italian of the principal works of Marx and Engels.[67] The celebration of May Day in 1891 sponsored by the Second International and the use of the red flag as a symbol had also encouraged the Italian socialists.[68] They were impressed too with the solidarity shown by the German socialists in resisting the antisocialist laws.[69]

The Socialist Party was born in 1892 at Genoa, when a schism took place between the laborers and the anarchists.[70] The following year, at

storica italiana, LXXV (I, 1963), 189. Because of Germany's scientific prestige not only "agitators but men of letters," the young who formed the "avant-garde" of the Italian labor movement, expected to find Germany taking the lead in making socialism a science (p. 190).

64. Antonio Labriola (while teaching philosophy) studied Herbart and Hegel. When he read Marx's *Communist Manifesto* it seemed to him like a revelation. See Bonomi, *La politica italiana da Porta Pia a Vittorio Veneto*, p. 117.

65. Gaetano Arfé, "Studi recenti su democratici e socialisti italiani," *Revista storica italiana*, LXXI (III, 1959), 400. Bissolati, according to Arfé, used the *Avanti* to direct the socialist battle as a battle for liberty. The journal made its appearance on December 25, 1896.

66. Dr. Anna Kulisciov was in touch with all the leading international socialists. See Bonomi, *La politica italiana*, p. 116. She helped Turati found the *Critica sociale*. This review was presently supplemented by the *Lotta di classe*, and in 1896 by *Avanti*. See Vaussard, *Histoire de l'Italie*, p. 56.

67. Labriola to Engels, Dec. 13, 1894. Antonio Labriola, *Lettere a Engels* (Rome, 1949), p. 175. "Perhaps the 15th of this month," writes Labriola, "the *Rassegna Neapolitana* will publish the translation of your Introduction to vol. III of *Kapital*—it has practically promised." Labriola discusses other books by Marx as well as Engels' essay *Anti-Dühring* in a letter to Croce on May 17, 1895.

68. Luigi Salvatorelli, *Sommario della storia d'Italia dei tempi preistorici ai nostri giorni* (Turin, 1961), pp. 565-566.

69. Arfé, reviewing Ragionieri's *Socialdemocrazia tedesca* in *Rivista storica italiana*, LXXV (I, 1963), 190.

70. See Arfé's review of "Luigi Cortese: *La Costituzione del Partito socialista italiana*" in *Rivista storica italiana*, LXXIV (I, 1962), 205. Arfé states that the Congress at Genoa in 1892 marks the birth of the party because of two facts: (1) the "definitive separation of the workers from the anarchists," and (2) the "adoption of a program of evident Marxist inspiration" as the charter of socialism. Continuing to summarize Cortese, Arfé goes on that this charter confronts the republican currents with the principle of the class struggle and confronts the anarchists and workers with the necessity of participation in the political struggle. Arfé, reviewing Ragionieri (p. 191), says the problem in Italy was one of "orienting and accelerating the process of separation between legalitarian socialism and anarchism, which had first given the proletarian movement a faith and a flag."

Reggio Emilia, was formed the "Socialist Party of Italian Workers." While growing in numbers,[71] it failed to live up to the high hopes of its founders. An attempt to organize a workers' movement in Sicily (as "Fasci di lavoratori"), involving workers in the sulphur mines but principally agrarian in character, wanting to break up the big estates, found itself invaded by other elements of a shady nature. The organization got into serious trouble, producing arrests and severe penalties handed out in the courts, relieved only by successive royal amnesties. The lawlessness in the south discredited the law-abiding organizations in the north, with the result that Crispi resolved to dissolve all the sections of the workers' party.[72] He also dissolved all the Chambers of Labor, which had been trying against great difficulties to do for Italian labor what the Labor Exchanges (the *Bourses du Travail*) did for the French. As for his attitude toward the socialists, it is summed up in his words, uttered in the presence of the Archbishop of Venice, "From the blackest hiding places of earth has been spewed forth an infamous sect which has written on its banner, 'Neither God nor master.' "[73]

The biggest socialist explosion came in 1898. Crispi was no longer in office as Prime Minister. The crisis was preceded by poor crops and a rise in the price of bread. Taxes were increasing, making it difficult to accumulate capital, so there was no spur to economic recovery.[74] Socialists attributed the depression to the "basic weaknesses of the capitalist system"; Republicans said it proved the ineffectiveness of monarchy in looking after general welfare; clericals said it proved that a state which was an "enemy of the Church" could not "solve the social problem." The Government (now under Rudini) took no steps to alleviate the situation, and violence broke out in the south and spread to Romagna and the Marches. From May 6 to May 9 popular uprisings continued.[75] In Milan a state of siege was proclaimed; the troops were called out.

71. *Partito socialista dei lavoratori italiani.* Vaussard (*Histoire de l'Italie*, p. 56) states that while there were in 1892 26,000 socialists, of whom 10,000 were party members, by 1897 there were 138,000, of whom 36,000 were members.

72. Vaussard, *Histoire de l'Italie*, p. 57. Crispi was even going to dissolve the diocesan committees of the *Opera dei congressi*! The defeat of the Italian troops in Abyssinia had Crispi in a state of alarm. See Salvatorelli, *Sommario della storia d'Italia*, p. 566.

73. Bonomi, *La politica italiana da Porta Pia a Vittorio Veneto*, p. 135.

74. Spadolini, *Lotta sociale in Italia*, p. 131.

75. Bonomi, *La politica italiana da Porta Pia a Vittorio Veneto*, pp. 158-160.

Repression followed swiftly. The ministry fell and was succeeded by a more reactionary one under General Pelloux. Political associations were broken up. Socialists were arrested, tried, and condemned by military tribunal. Turati, Anna Kulisciov, and Lazzari were among them. Some Catholics were involved, including the well-known Don Albertario. Popular sympathy turned against the Government and was reflected in wild scenes in Parliament, where the Extreme Left adopted obstructionism.[76] The Pelloux Government fell and matters returned to a more normal situation, in which organizations were legalized once more, to the advantage of both socialists and the Church. Industry prospered, expanded, and entered new fields of manufacture.[77]

During the repressive days which preceded the uprisings of 1898, Italian Marxist theory had been developed. Labriola published in 1895 his first socialist writing in commemoration of the *Communist Manifesto*. The works of Marx and Engels were translated into Italian. The Italians were joining the mainstream. The only problem now was *which* mainstream. Division had occurred in the very heart of Marxist authoritarian socialism.

76. Salvatorelli, *Sommario della storia d'Italia*, pp. 567-568.
77. This was the era of the beginning of automobile manufacture, with an attendant growth of the rubber industry in addition to iron and steel. The twentieth century was being ushered in.

XI. RERUM NOVARUM

"De conditione opificum rerum novarum. . . ."

LEO XIII

The social question aroused both theoretical and practical responses during the nineteenth century. Sociological theory, which appeared during this period, went all the way from the atheistic approach of Auguste Comte, the founder of Positivism, and Karl Marx, with his scientific socialism, to the social theories of the religious Le Play and Périn. The combination of social theory with the eternal humanitarianism of the Catholic Church produced a slow-moving but intellectually respectable growth of enlightened opinion and consecrated effort.

The Catholic movement had been chilled, it is true, by Gregory XVI's *Mirari vos.*[1] This attack had arisen from the conservative side. As the liberal movement revived, however, it tended to be led down a blind alley which purported to lead toward a rational concept based on immutable economic laws. Social reformers should no more attempt to tinker with these laws than they would with the force of gravity. On the premise that the laws of human behavior should not be interfered with by legislative procedure, economists opposed all ameliorative measures. The laissez-faire theory was particularly agreeable to the rising industrial capitalist class. Having risen from the lower classes they were on their way up, storming the bastions of the aristocracy and the older bourgeoisie, not content with the slowness of their progress toward the stronghold. For this reason it is not surprising that the nobility, whether temporal or spiritual, came to make common cause with the working

1. Haag, "The Political Ideas of Belgian Catholics (1789-1914)," in Moody, *Church and Society*, p. 295. Haag asserts that the "majority of Catholic Belgian writers approved of Lamennais." After the encyclical they were more subdued, even though it had not been published in Belgium.

classes against their common enemy. Neither is it surprising that such a union should continue to be a paternalistic one.[2]

Catholic influence on reform and legislation varied from nation to nation, depending on local conditions. Based on the early work of Bishop Ketteler and Father Kolping, and in co-operation with Protestant leaders similarly concerned over the plight of labor, local reforms were first undertaken in Germany. These early measures, under the auspices of the factory owners, were practical, paternalistic reforms,[3] having nothing as yet to do with legislation. Side by side with Lassallean and Marxist groups appeared Christian-sponsored Workingmen's Clubs, together with associations fostered by Christian employers of labor. Many members of the Center Party were leaders in this movement which originated in paternalism.

Social theory was added to these practical attempts by a group of socially minded Catholics. The leadership of Professor Karl von Loewenstein, a Catholic prelate, resulted presently in the formation of a German Catholic Association to examine the social problem.[4] Desiring to forestall socialism, they studied the social question from a conservative and Catholic point of view. They ultimately concluded that reforms must be sought through legislation, as only state intervention could arrest the worst evils.[5] The program of individual moral regeneration, to which Bishop Ketteler and his contemporaries had been wholly committed, would be far too slow in securing beneficial results.

The development of State Socialism in Germany is thus seen to have had its beginning and ultimately its strong support from the Christian movement which preceded it. In seeking state intervention the earlier

2. The avowed egalitarian claims of the socialists were more immediately appealing to the workers.

3. The old view of Protestants and liberals was that religion was a private affair, not connected with social relations. This view was challenged in nineteenth-century Germany. The most prominent challenger was Ketteler, who said, "A Catholic cannot ignore the labor problem, without condemning himself to live as a stranger in his own time; the problem is imposed." See Gennaro Avolio, *Mons. Ketteler e il Partito Cattolico Parlamentare* (Naples, 1905), p. 16.

4. The association was to use every means of propaganda: assemblies, individual action, journals, books, etc. See "La Ligue Catholique Allemande," *Univers*, Sept. 30, 1890. This association was an outgrowth of Loewenstein's movement.

5. The German Center Party, seeking state support in the social question, sponsored a clearly social program in the Reichstag. It came to be mixed up with the Kulturkampf, which attracted greater international attention. See Avolio, *Mons. Ketteler*, pp. 22-25.

Christian paternalism was not abandoned; it was merely shifted to a new form. The State itself was now to be the fostering parent, super-seding the Church and the upper classes. Genuine democracy, proclaimed by the political revolutions of the West and claimed by Marxists as the foundation of scientific socialism, was all but ignored in the "veiled autocracy" of the German Empire. State Socialism did produce practical benefits for the enormous and swelling mass of industrial workers.[6]

Interest in social theory as well as concern for humanitarian reform spread from Germany into Austria. The movement sponsored by Bishop Ketteler at Mainz was carried to Vienna by Professor Maxen.[7] It found ready acceptance by a group of young noblemen,[8] the most prominent of whom were Prince Liechtenstein, Baron von Vogelsang (his brother), and Rudolph Meyer.[9]

The Austrian group developed around the journal *Das Vaterland*, edited by Vogelsang. Count von Blöme, originally from Mecklenburg, went to Austria because Austria under Metternich was conservative. Con-verted to Catholicism, he found a kindred spirit in Vogelsang. Blöme went to Switzerland later and established there the *Correspondance de Genève*, in order to defend Pius IX's *Syllabus*. Vogelsang and Meyer were both Prussians and Protestant in origin; both became Catholics. They played an active role in Austria in advocating state legislation for social reform. Private charity was inadequate and did not provide for justice, being sporadic by nature. The Church could not single-handedly solve the problem, but its principles translated into law could produce not only ameliorative action but justice, because they would then apply equally to all. Guilds should be established,[10] but state laws should take account of factory inspection, minimum wages, hours of labor, restric-

6. The effect of the *forms* of democracy on the German Social Democratic Party will be discussed below in chap. xiv, where Revisionism is examined. Bismarck's aban-donment of laissez-faire economics in his new tariff program, adopted largely for political reasons, was a factor in producing an atmosphere more conducive to state control in the social question.

7. Sanseverino, *Il movimento sindacale cristiano*, p. 46. Prof. Maxen was from Göttingen.

8. Nitti, *Catholic Socialism*, p. 202.

9. Moon, *The Social Catholic Movement*, p. 129.

10. The Liechtenstein brothers were especially medieval in their outlook of opposing state centralization. Their principality was a remnant of the Middle Ages. Their attitude was paternalistic and Catholic. They did agree that, leaving regulations to the guilds, the state should adjudicate differences. See Williams, *Catholic Social Thought*, p. 26.

tions on labor of women and children, social insurance, pensions, and co-operative stores. International agreements were also favored, to protect the laborer.[11] The paternalism of this group was obvious from the start. An exception was Dr. Karl Lueger, later mayor of Vienna, prominent in advocating municipal ownership of utilities.[12] The members of the group, on the whole, were opposed to the new industrial bourgeoisie. They were also violently anti-Semitic.

In Switzerland, long the place of refuge for political exiles, meeting place for congresses of all sorts from proponents of peace to proponents of anarchism, and point of origin for the dissemination of the various nationalist reformist journals, there was no dearth of social theory. Leaders in the movement to associate the Catholic Church with reform were Bishop (later Cardinal) Mermillod[13] and Gaspard Decurtins. The Swiss movement was not limited to Catholics, who formed a minority in the state, nor to conservative parties. "Hunger," said Decurtins, was "neither Catholic nor Protestant."[14] Mermillod, as early as 1868, announced his view as to the obligation of the Church to take up the social question:

This movement of the working classes appears to us as a torrent rushing down from the mountains; it may destroy everything in its passage, and scatter ruin throughout our valleys; but it must be the honor of the Catholic Church to go forth to meet these forces . . . and form them, in the nineteenth century, into a mighty and fertilizing river.[15]

The problem of labor was not as acute in Switzerland as elsewhere in Europe because of the nature of Swiss economy. Rapid progress was

11. Moon, *The Social Catholic Movement*, p. 129.

12. *Ibid.*, p. 132. Municipal ownership of public utilities was an outgrowth of the type of socialism, utopian in character, advocated by Louis Blanc in France. Municipal ownership spread widely in Europe, generally embracing transportation systems as well as utilities, and also in the larger cities of the United States, where it was always advocated by the socialists. "Collective ownership of public utilities" was item number one in the "intermediate steps to socialism." See *First Party Platform of the Socialist Party*, issued as a brochure following the "Unity Convention" (United States) in 1901. Division of Manuscripts, Duke University.

13. Nitti, *Social Catholicism*, pp. 237-238. Msgr. Mermillod was priest at Nôtre Dame in Geneva; he was made auxiliary Bishop of Lausanne and titular Bishop of Hebron. He helped to found the Sisters of the order of St. Francis de Sales. He was made Cardinal in 1890.

14. Quoted in Moon, *The Social Catholic Movement*, p. 133.

15. Nitti, *Catholic Socialism*, pp. 237-238. The Swiss Decurtins issued an invitation for an international conference on labor problems, which was applauded by Leo XIII. The conference was later shifted to Berlin.

made, however, in the matter of social legislation. In theory and practice Switzerland led the van.

The problem of labor in Belgium was of long standing. It was already acute when the future Leo XIII was sent there as nuncio to the Belgian court. Labor conditions were notoriously bad in Belgium because of the early development of the Industrial Revolution and because mining was so extensively practiced. Conditions among miners were generally worse than conditions among factory workers. At one time or another Brussels was the sheltering home of many of the important labor agitators from other lands: Marx, Engels, Bakunin, Guesde, various Blanquists, and many more. The Communist League, forerunner of the First International, had been founded there. It set up a Belgian Labor Party, made up of socialists, workers, and liberals.[16] Moderate Catholics were in a majority in Belgium, and through legislative channels provided by their constitutional government they were able to enact reforms more rapidly than in most Catholic countries. Freedom of association and of the press and a high level of literacy as compared with other Catholic states (except France) contributed to the reform movement. The Belgian bishops at first gave less attention to the solution of the social problem than they might have, because of their preoccupation with the question of retaining control over education in the democratic kingdom. Rebuked by Leo XIII[17] they were led to modify their intransigence. Social theory, as developed by Charles Périn, was moderate, avoiding the extremes of the radical Left and the clerical Right, and brought about moderate social legislation. It was paternalistic in character, fostering a "Union of Owners in Favor of Workingmen."

Nevertheless, in Belgium, as well as elsewhere in areas of rapid industrialization, the problem grew faster than the remedy. In 1886 the misery and violence accompanying the Charleroi strike shocked the Belgians into action.[18] A Catholic ministry took over the reins of government and announced a new liberal policy, inspired by Christian ideals. A liberal Belgian said it was the clergy who had pointed out the social

16. Marc-Antoine Pierson, *Histoire du socialisme en Belgique* (4th ed.; Brussels, 1953), pp. 77-79.

17. See *Univers*, Nov. 24, 1879, for the documents in the case.

18. Braunthal, *Geschichte der Internationale*, p. 218. A strike at Charleroi (1869), in which very harsh methods were used against the strikers, had turned many coal miners toward the First International. *Ibid.*, p. 131.

evils. Protection of workers was undertaken by a series of measures on wages (excessive garnisheeing of wages not to be permitted), insurance, and inspection of conditions under which laborers worked; general measures as to labor of women and children were also undertaken.[19] Strikes led to a notable growth in the movement of organizing Catholic workers; all populous centers had associations among the Flemish as well as the Walloons. Socialists, although protected, did not control labor.[20] Consumer co-operatives, on the English Rochdale plan, were also set up.[21]

Between 1866 and 1890 International Social Work Congresses were held at Liége, where workers from other Catholic countries met and discussed the problems of labor.[22] The Belgian prelate, Doutreloux, "the spirit of the Liége Congress," stood up for the demands of the workers (some thought too ardently), while Abbé Pottier presented "What is legitimate in the workers' demands."[23] Each Congress advocated with increasing vigor and vehemence the need for social legislation. This movement went so far in urging social reforms that a rival Congress (also Catholic) was set up to advocate withdrawing from the "excesses" of the Liége group. Efforts were made to reconcile the two groups. Albert de Mun was particularly active in bringing about this reconciliation.[24] Belgium remained Catholic and moderate.

In England the outstanding Catholic labor leader was Cardinal Manning, Archbishop of Westminster, who used his influence on behalf of social legislation and gave practical assistance to the laborers in the famous dock-workers' strike. Manning took the position that labor was a "social function and not a commodity."[25] England, however, was Angli-

19. Georges Goyau, *L'Oeuvre Sociale de l'état Belge: Les Catholiques au pouvoir 1884-1912* (Paris, 1912), pp. 5-7. *Kölnische Zeitung* said the clericals were afraid of the words "State Socialism." They were moving, nonetheless, in that direction.

20. The organization of labor into unions made rapid progress in 1886, having more than a hundred local unions. They formed the bulk of the Labor Party.

21. *Kölnische Zeitung*, May 3, 1886.

22. Here Mermillod declared (1887) the social paternity of the State. Asking protection of the State he recalled the words of Cavour, that "every truly liberal law must protect the weak." The worker needed the State's defense. See Soderini, *Il Pontificato di Leone XIII*, I, 347.

23. "Ce qu'il y a de légitime dans les revendications ouvrières." See *ibid*, p. 348. See also Giuseppe Mira, "I movimenti sociali di ispirazione cattolica," *Nel LXX Anniversario della "Rerum Novarum"* (Milan, 1961), p. 82.

24. Moon, *The Social Catholic Movement*, p. 156.

25. This statement of Manning was written just before the Liége Congress in 1887. See Soderini, *Il Pontificato di Leone XIII*, I, 348.

can, and the activities of the Catholics were not the deciding factor in determining the future of labor or the form which the solution of the social question would ultimately take. Manning was frequently labeled a socialist, but then, so was the conservative Albert de Mun in France, and even His Holiness, Leo XIII.

In Spain, for almost diametrically opposed reasons, social reform was not brought about by Catholic action. The eruption of sporadic violence associated with anarchist attempts to control the labor movement was not ended by the victory of Marxism over Bakuninism in the First International.[26] Violence on the Left was counteracted by extreme clericalism on the Right, which attacked the growing republicanism of the people and exhausted the radicals in the effort to ward off the attacks. (This extreme clericalism was to be reprimanded by Leo XIII.) The intellectuals became vociferously anticlerical. The social problem remained unsolved. It was particularly acute in the Catalan area of northeastern Spain, where the shift to industry occurred. The rest of the country suffered from an apparently insoluble problem of idle owners and depressed peasants.

Catholic attempts at social reform in Italy confronted the same basic problems as those which delayed the organization of socialism in the peninsula. The problem peculiar to Italy was the presence of the papacy. Italian anticlericalism was more intense in its expression because of the fear of intervention from the outside to restore the Temporal Power to the Pope. Reforming activities of Pius IX, begun in 1848, had been brought to a halt by considerations arising out of his relation to Rome as ruler. Unwillingness to accept the loss of the Temporal Power as a blessing prolonged this failure of the papacy to come to grips with the growing social problem. The *non expedit* of Pius IX prevented the Catholics from exerting political pressure toward reform. The Society of Italian Catholic Youth had, however, been formed. It seemed that here was a group which might develop a social program. The *Opera dei Congressi* was an adult movement which was an outgrowth of Catholic Youth.[27] From the beginning it was limited in its outlook.[28] Leo

26. Marx and Engels, *Marx oder Bakunin?* p. 27.
27. Fonzi, *I cattolici e la società italiana dopo l'unità*, p. 31.
28. The report of the first Congress (*Primo Congresso Cattolico tenutosi in Venezia*

XIII gave his approval to the separation of the Youth from the *Opera*. The Society of Italian Catholic Youth turned more to systematic study of the social sciences, under the leadership of such men as Toniolo, who feared that the Church, once tied to monarchy, might now tie itself to the cause of the capitalist and the employer.[29] A division of the Youth Society, known as the Christian Social Economy Group, especially interested itself in the study of and assistance to Catholic mutual aid societies and co-operatives. These societies were hampered in their growth by the principle of including employer and worker in the same organization. The societies founded by the workers themselves apart from religious controls made more rapid growth.[30]

As has been pointed out earlier, one great weakness in the movement for a Catholic confrontation of the social problem in Italy lay in the political situation. The division in the ranks of Catholics between the intransigents, who rejected any compromise with the kingdom, and the transigents, who wanted to bring about an accommodation with the realm as a foundation for creating a new society, prevented effective action. Both clergy and laity were involved in this internecine controversy. Curci and Bonomelli had from the beginning led the effort to escape from the stagnation resulting from the fundamentally different points of view. Curci had said, in the year of Leo XIII's election, "The Church establishes doctrine and government"[31] and had thus opened the door for the Catholic social movement. Msgr. Bonomelli, no less concerned about solving the labor problem in a Christian spirit, found the door to political accommodation firmly closed. His article, suggest-

---

da 12 al 16 giugno 1874, I, *Atti* [Bologna, 1874], p. 62), quoted in Fonzi (p. 32) stated: "The Congress is Catholic, nothing else than Catholic. In fact Catholicism is a perfect doctrine, the doctrine of the human race. Hence Catholicism is not liberal, nor tyrannical, nor of any other quality. It is a very great error *per se*, to link any quality whatsoever with it, implying that Catholicism either lacks something which is subsequently added to it, or contains something that is subsequently removed."

29. Soderini, *Il Pontificato di Leone XIII*, I, 425.

30. Neufeld, *Italy*, p. 355. The Christian Social Economy Group, a division of the Society for Italian Catholic Youth, should not be confused with the Union for Social Studies, whose founding Leo XIII approved in 1889. See Soderini, *Il Pontificato di Leone XIII*, p. 382.

31. Fonzi, *I cattolici e la società italiana*, p. 38. Padre Curci was a political liberal, one of the transigents. Fonzi quotes from Curci's *Il moderno dissidio tra la chiesa e l'Italia*.

ing that new conditions demanded new approaches, was placed on the *Index*, and the prelate publicly retracted his statement.[32]

The benign attitude of Leo XIII toward labor was shown on numerous occasions throughout his pontificate. His kindly reception of the great groups who came on pilgrimages to Rome and the Vatican is one evidence. Speaking to a large number of laborers from Piedmont and Liguria, His Holiness urged the formation of fraternal associations "under the protection and beneficent influence of the Catholic religion." The Church, he said, had always favored progress in the arts and professions (trades). He advocated that the laborers form associations to improve their situation, but he warned them against subversive organizations: "By flattery and great promises they try to seduce and attract workers to them. But they conceal under their outward appearances the criminal design of making use of the workers as an instrument for putting into execution their sinister projects."[33] Sound as the advice might be, something stronger was needed.

⌊ This Leo came to realize as the decade of the eighties drew to a close. Pilgrimages continued to be made to the Vatican, those from France being led by Harmel, de Mun, or Cardinal Langénieux.[34] He became convinced that it was not enough to warn workers against socialism; something more constructive was required. Whatever was to be done, however, should be solidly based on study and research.⌉

The desire for firm intellectual foundations, united with religious and humanitarian concern for the welfare of the workers, led the Pontiff to suggest the formation of a study group. At his behest such a group was organized, in the early eighties, known as the Roman Committee of Social Studies. Bishop Mermillod, exiled from Germany, was in Rome at the time, trying to form a union of Catholic exiles; he became a member of the study group. The objective of the Committee was to

32. The article in question was published anonymously in *Rassegna Nazionale* (1889), under the title "Roma e l'Italia e la realtà delle cose: Pensieri di un Prelato Italiano." See Fonzi, *I cattolici e la società italiana*, p. 49.

33. Because of the size of this delegation of workers Leo addressed them in the vast hall of the Consistory. *Journal de Rome*, May 23, 1882. Quoted in *Univers*, May 26, 1882.

34. There were French pilgrimages in 1885, 1887, 1889, and 1891. These pilgrimages laid the social problem right on the Pope's doorstep. Soderini asserts that the Pope knew the Middle Ages could not be revived, but thought the idea of harmony between employer and laborer was still possible in associations which included both. See Soderini, *Il Pontificato di Leone XIII*, I, 378, 380. See also Rollet, *Action sociale*, p. 257.

study deeply and thoroughly, from a Catholic point of view, the social and economic questions of labor, to establish principles based on that study, and secure acceptance of these principles as a basis for action. Jacobini, Prefect of the Propaganda, was president of the new group, whose members were recruited from among the Roman aristocracy.[35]

The group met at the Borghese Palace and worked out their approach to the problem.[36] It was also Jacobini's purpose, in addition to scholarly investigation, to spur the organization of Christian workers' societies all over Italy. The members of the Committee had contact with actual workers through another Roman society, "Artist-Workers' Society of Mutual Aid."[37] La Tour-du-Pin, Albert de Mun's associate in the French Workingmen's Clubs, was interested in this workers' society. It was he who suggested consultation at the international level. Up to this point various sponsors of reform in different countries had become aware of each other but had created no organization. Blöme and Kuefstein in Vienna agreed with La Tour-du-Pin that all would be stimulated by drawing together.[38] So it was that in Mermillod's study in Freiburg an international organization was formed, composed of persons from these various local groups of socially minded upper-class intellectuals.[39] The members, in addition to working for reforms in their own nations, were to carry on basic studies applicable to the international scene. They planned to meet once a year at Freiburg under Mermillod's presidency. Most of the members were lay, coming from Catholic states or states where there was a considerable Catholic minority. They were founders of Social Catholicism. La Tour-du-Pin, Albert de Mun, and Lorin were among the French members of this International Union of Social Studies. La Tour-du-Pin and de Mun were leading royalists. They traced their interest in social reform to the influence of Ketteler, to whom they had

35. Gambasin, *Il movimento sociale*, p. 200.
36. Mario Romani, "La preparazione della 'Rerum Novarum,'" *Nel LXX Anniversario della "Rerum Novarum*," p. 15, n. 16. From this group emerged the journal, *Rassegna d'Italia*, for which Soderini (a member of the group) was one of the writers. It was in this journal that the "Thoughts of an Italian Prelate," put on the *Index*, had been published.
37. Soderini, *Il Pontificato di Leone XIII*, I, 336.
38. Moon, *Social Catholic Movement*, p. 139.
39. The preliminary contributions of the various groups are enumerated in Mira, "I movimenti di ispirazione cattolica," *Nel LXX Anniversario della "Rerum Novarum*," pp. 82-83.

been directed before taking up the work of Catholic social reform in France; they were not liberal even though socially minded. The Austrian members had also been influenced by Ketteler, who may be said to have been the original inspiration of the movement.[40] Both the Liechtensteins (Alfred and Aloys) were feudal princes and wanted to combine social reform with political reaction. Jacobini had some of his Roman group join this Union of Freiburg. The international organization was to be secret and to exclude liberals.[41] There were differences of opinion among them, as was to be expected. Their national situations were quite different, from Manning of England to the Austrian feudalist Vogelsang, from Ketteler in Germany to the Swiss Decurtins.[42] They had difficulty in choosing a name for the movement; Guérin wanted the title to include "conservators"; La Tour-du-Pin wanted "Catholic" to appear, regarding "conservators" as too vague a term. Guérin said "Catholic" was vague. So they concluded that the name *"Union internationale d'études sociales"* would avoid both of these difficulties. They held seven annual sessions, until Mermillod's death, discussing and debating the issues. They denounced letting land pass into the hands of Jews.[43] Antipathy toward the new industrial capitalist class, one of the strong factors motivating the Austrian group in the beginning, was masked among lay members. They agreed that the State must redress existing abuses, while their own International Union was to foresee and prevent new ones from arising; the medieval pattern of guild organization—corporative organization—seemed most desirable to them. In this particular they occupied a middle ground between the laissez-faire liberals and the socialist collectivists.[44] Their reforms were backward-looking; the world

40. Leo XIII called Ketteler the "true precursor." Giuseppe Toniolo, *Democrazia cristiana: istituti e forme*, ser. IV, Vol. I, of *Opera Omnia* (Vatican City, 1951), pp. 47-48. See also Mira, "I movimenti di ispirazione cattolica," *Nel LXX Anniversario della "Rerum Novarum,"* p. 82. De Mun said they owed just as much to Ozanam, Lacordaire, and other early French social reformers. See Rollet, *Action sociale*, p. 114.

41. When Mermillod at one meeting, in response to a question from La Tour-du-Pin as to the basis on which the social order must rest, said, "Liberty," two frock-coated persons got up and left the hall; they were the Liechtenstiens. See Rollet, *Action sociale*, p. 118.

42. Francesco Vito, "L'economia a servizio dell'uomo," *Nel LXX Anniversario della "Rerum Novarum,"* pp. 2-3.

43. Rollet, *Action sociale*, pp. 109-111. Anti-Semitism was rising all over Europe. It was to explode in the Dreyfus affair.

44. Charles Périn, Belgian social theorist, had shown at Chartres in 1878, in talking

was moving ahead of their theories.[45] The most progressive aspect of their efforts was their conclusion that State legislation on behalf of the workingmen must be undertaken, and that for such legislation to be really effective all nations should co-operate in examining this question. Local initiative was not enough.[46] In the same year that the socialists revived their international organization the Catholic group discussed holding an international conference on the subject of needed social reforms. Albert de Mun mentioned the possibility in an interview published in the *Pall Mall Gazette*, which was widely discussed.

The Swiss, under the leadership of Decurtins, a prime mover in the International Union of Social Studies, issued the invitation for an international meeting. Leo XIII sent his congratulations for the plan. Speaking on the question in the French Chamber, de Mun objected to having the conference seem to be the triumph of freethinkers. All over Europe, he said, not only in France, but in Austria, where Prince Liechtenstein was one of the leaders of the Catholic Party, and in Belgium, it was often Catholics who took the initiative in these matters; the Swiss Decurtins was an ardent Catholic. To the accompaniment of interruptions from the Left and applause from the Right, de Mun mentioned the Pope's approval of the plan. He went on:

Why do you protest? How can it displease you that the greatest moral authority in the world, which can act most strongly and effectively on mind and will of Catholics, should manifest itself by a solemn act to recommend taking in hand the defense of the interests of the workers, to congratulate them when they do so, in order to urge them to place themselves more and more at the head of this great social movement, from which must emerge, not the triumph of free thought, but that of justice and peace.[47]

As matters turned out, the French attended another international conference, this one sponsored by the new German Emperor; the Swiss

with a group of workers, the futility of any attempt to re-establish trade guilds "today when there are no longer any trades and when large-scale industry is invading more and more the world of labor." See Lecanuet, *L'Église de France*, p. 421 n.

45. Another weakness of the movement, due to the reactionary political views of the members of the Union, was the attempt to tie the cause of the workers to the cause of the Pope as "Prisoner of the Vatican." See Fonzi, *I cattolici e la società italiana*, p. 65.

46. Members of the Second International came to the same conclusion from their first meeting.

47. *Univers*, May 9, 1889. See also Soderini, *Il Pontificato di Leone XIII*, I, 384.

project gave way. The death of the Crown Prince Frederick followed so closely after the death of William I that the Crown Prince was scarcely on his throne when he was gone, leaving the crown to young William II. The new Emperor proceeded to tackle the social question. His concern was motivated not only by the poor conditions of the laborers but also by the fact that German foreign trade was beginning to decline. If this trend should continue it would injure both workers and owners. He thought international understanding on these points would improve conditions if it did not solve the problem. In two rescripts on the matter he invited all nations interested in the labor question to participate in a conference by sending delegates to Berlin to sit in a miniature parliament. He spelled out some of the questions needing attention, saying that measures already taken had been good but did not go far enough; governments must regulate hours and conditions of labor to preserve health, morals, and sound economic conditions as well as satisfying labor's aspirations for equality before the law. Labor should be well represented at the conference along with owners and governmental authorities.[48] William II told the Prussian Council of State that he was not trying to combat the Social Democrats, but simply to satisfy the legitimate desires of the workers. William wrote to the Pope and sent him a program; Leo replied, felicitating him on having taken to heart so noble a cause; he gave his hearty approval; he was pleased that the Emperor had designated Msgr. Kopp as a delegate.[49] Members of the conference included not only political figures but workers from each of the participating states. Delegates were there from England and America as well as from continental Europe. Practical questions were

48. Agence Havas quoting *Moniteur de l'Empire Allemande*. *Univers*, Feb. 7, 1890. In the first rescript the Emperor described the situation in Europe; the second mentioned the proposed agenda.

49. Both letters quoted in *Univers*, March 25, 1890. *Siècle*, later, after admitting that the results of the Berlin Congress were not very great, expressed its views on the exchange of letters between William II and Leo XIII: "The Berlin Conference has brought into the limelight the distance which separates the Pope's letter from the rescript of the Emperor. We—free thinkers—do not hesitate to say it, William holds in his powerful hands the glaive of the law, and finds it necessary to call spiritual power to his side. What does Leo reply. . . . The Pope has affirmed, in substance, that moral causes lead the world, and the Pope is right." A visit to Alsace with its fine flowering of workers' institutions would show how superior were conditions there resting on "affection and confidence," offering this double character of being "always fruitful in promoting initiative and often sterilized by laws." *Siècle* quoted in *Univers*, April 9, 1890.

discussed, such as Sunday rest, hours of labor, and child labor. The Italians seemed on every count behind the rest of Europe in laws safeguarding labor. Italian socialists, nevertheless, found themselves heartened by the attempt of William II to study the social question "with a warm heart and a cool brain."[50]

Nothing could be legislated at such a gathering. Each country could go home and do precisely what it pleased. This the delegates all recognized. Only in Germany would the resolutions be embodied in projected laws and presented to the Reichstag.[51] But the fact that the conference had been held at all was important.

The Berlin Conference had been the first public step on labor problems resulting from the promptings of the International Union of Social Studies, whose main purpose was not merely to examine critically the accepted theories of the time and survey the changing conditions but to relate the two within the Church's view of the dignity of man. Although members of the Union had published very little of their research, they had already sent Leo XIII a memorandum.[52] This memorandum was the germ from which grew, after much study, Leo XIII's greatest encyclical. The encyclical was subjected to intense scrutiny while in preparation. Many drafts were prepared, emending, expanding, and clarifying the message.[53] Seven years had elapsed since the formation of the International Union of Social Studies.[54] The delay in promulgating the encyclical was not due to lack of interest on the part of Leo XIII but was motivated by the knowledge that an encyclical designed for all mankind must take account of the wide divergences in the various coun-

50. Benedetto Croce, *A History of Italy*, trans. Cecilia M. Ady (Oxford, 1929), p. 2.

51. Agence Havas, March 24, 1890. *Univers*, March 26, 1890.

52. The memorandum was signed by Mermillod, Kuefstein, and Lorin. See Rollet, *Action sociale*, p. 113.

53. Mario Romani, "La preparazione della 'Rerum Novarum,'" *Nel LXX Anniversario della "Rerum Novarum,"* pp. 11-12. Romani analyzes in meticulous detail the production of the encyclical, going over the various versions and sketches which preceded the authorized, definitive version, and shows the relation of the encyclical to the memoir from the Freiburg group.

54. When La Tour-du-Pin visited Rome at the same time as Harmel's first pilgrimage, in February, 1885, he had an audience with His Holiness. The French reformer said there was disagreement as to whether what they were doing was "socialist." Leo replied—"not socialism" but "Christianism." He went on: "Ah! They do not know what the Christian social order is; well, do not worry; wait for my next encyclical." See Rollet, *Action sociale*, p. 256.

tries, from the most backward to the most advanced. The words must be weighed; once spoken they could not be withdrawn.[55]

The time was ripe for the Pontiff to proclaim the Church's view of the social question to all the world. The problem of labor had reached a culmination which necessitated a clear and unequivocal statement as to Catholicism's fundamental platform. Socialism simultaneously spoke in the fifth edition of the *Communist Manifesto* and the publication of the Erfurt Program.[56] In May, 1891, Leo XIII spoke in the encyclical: *De conditione opificum rerum novarum. . . .*[57]

⎡ In opening the *Rerum Novarum*, the most famous of his encyclicals, Leo XIII plunged at once into the heart of the problem. The spirit of revolutionary change, he said, from politics had passed into the field of practical economy; unmistakable elements of conflict were apparent: industrial growth, science, the increasing gap between abject poverty and enormous wealth, the growth of labor organization, and moral deterioration. The social question was uppermost in the public mind; hence the Church must speak; remedies must be found for a situation in which the laboring man found himself little better off than in slavery, defenseless against the rapacity of callous employers.

Rejecting as futile the socialist proposal to solve the social question by removing all property from private control and turning it over to the

55. The first draft was made by the Jesuit Mathias Liberatore and the Dominican Tommaso Cardinal Zigliara, friend of Leo XIII when he was Bishop of Perugia. The draft required an immense amount of work surveying and consolidating the mass of material containing the recommendations of the different schools of social theory. To his secretaries, Gabriele Boccali, from the Seminary at Perugia, and Volpini, the leading Latinist of his day, Leo confided the task of putting the encyclical in finished form. Cardinal Mazzella also had a hand in the critical reading of the work before publication. The Pontiff himself continued to make corrections in the proofs as they came from the press. For details, see *Rivista storia della Chiesa in Italia*, XI (1950), 436-437.

56. Engels wrote the preface to this edition of the *Manifesto*. The Erfurt Program was elaborated by Karl Kautsky. See Braunthal, *Geschichte der Internationale*, p. 274. Of the Erfurt Program Engels said: "Kautsky's draft, supported by Bebel and myself, will be the basis of the program. . . . We have the satisfaction of seeing Marx's critique completely victorious." Engels to Sorge, Oct., 1891. Quoted in Gay, *The Dilemma of Democratic Socialism*, p. 47.

57. Although encyclicals are usually known by their opening phrases, this encyclical is generally referred to as *Rerum Novarum*. On May 20 *Univers* gave a résumé from *Osservatore Romano*; the Latin text appeared on May 22; the French translation came on May 24 and 25, divided because of its length. Quotations from the *Rerum Novarum* below are from Gilson, *The Church Speaks to the Modern World*, pp. 205-239. The writer has read the original and various English and French translations.

community, Leo XIII insisted on the right of all to convert their wages into property of which they would have the right of disposal, maintaining that "it is precisely in this power of disposal that ownership consists. . . ." He rejected the socialist remedy on the grounds of justice, insisting that private ownership was according to nature's law, and that man and the law of nature were older than the State, man making his by industry that portion of the earth on which he labored, the very labor becoming part of the earth itself. The right to possess is also a duty, he asserted, when one considers the obligations of a father to make provision for his family; he must not be robbed of this right and duty by the State. "The socialists, therefore," he maintained, "in setting aside the parent and setting up State supervision *act against justice*," and threaten family life. In rejecting "the main tenet of socialism, community of goods," Leo adopted as first and fundamental principle "the inviolability of private property.[58]

The second fundamental His Holiness stated no less clearly, saying that "no practical solution of this [social] question will be found apart from the intervention of religion and of the Church"; others must assist in the process: the State, employers, the wealthy, and the working people themselves. Stating with absolute clarity that "nothing is more useful than to look upon the world as it really is," he branded as false deceivers those who claimed that pain and trouble could be banished from the human race, and that society could be reduced to a level. He labeled false and irrational the view that "class is naturally hostile to class," that the rich and the working men are "intended by nature to live in mutual conflict"; rather, they are mutually interdependent, "capital" not being able to "do without labor, nor labor without capital." In preventing strife, he continued, "the efficacy of Christian institutions is marvelous and manifold," reminding groups of their duties each to the other, teaching the rich man that the working people are not his slaves and that the dignity of man as man and as a Christian must be respected. He warned: "To exercise pressure upon the indigent and destitute for the sake of gain, and to gather one's profit out of the need of another is

58. This statement is tempered, however, by a pronouncement further on that "it is one thing to have a right to the possession of money, and another to have a right to use money as one pleases."

condemned by all laws, human and divine." Moreover, he enjoined upon the wealthy the duty of exercising Christian charity. Far from concerning itself solely with spiritual matters, the Church, Leo insisted, had always been solicitous for the temporal and earthly interests of its children—feeding the needy, burying them, supporting orphans and the aged, and relieving the shipwrecked.

Leo XIII asserted that the State had also a social right and duty to perform; he said that the proper office of wise statesmanship was to make sure that the institutions and administration should be such as to produce "public well-being and private prosperity." He asserted that it was the State's duty to "benefit every class" and to "promote to the utmost the interests of the poor"; the better the State carried out this responsibility through general laws, the less need there would be for resorting to particular means to meet particular situations.

Rejecting the idea of inborn inequality among men from the standpoint of endowment by nature, the Pope emphasized that to the State the interests of all are equal. The Pontiff even said that "it is only by the labor of the working men that states grow rich"; it was incumbent on the State to intervene if religion

were found to suffer through the workers not having time and opportunity to practice its duties; if in workshops and factories there were danger to morals through the mixing of the sexes . . . or if employers laid burdens upon their workmen which were unjust . . .; if health were endangered by excessive labor, or by work unsuited to sex or age—in such cases there can be no question but that, within certain limits, it would be right to invoke the aid and authority of the law.

Speaking specifically, Leo XIII pointed out the duties of the State: it must protect private property and restrain the advocates of revolutionary change by violence; it should seek to obviate strikes by public remedial measures for the just claims of laborers; it must protect the workman's spiritual and mental interests (in which all men are equal), and to this end insist upon the day of rest—the Lord's Day.

Spelling out in detail a Great Charter of Labor to protect the worker from the "cruelty of men of greed," Leo XIII stated that the hours of labor should be restricted according to the nature of the work; children should be kept from labor in harmful trades; necessary periods of rest should be provided for workers in all agreements made between masters and their working people. Upon employers he enjoined the obligation to pay fair wages, which should rest upon the principle that wages ought not to be insufficient to support a frugal and well-behaved wage-earner. The Pontiff boldly asserted that ownership should be spread to as many workers as possible, and enjoined upon the State the obligation not to tax such ownership out of existence.

In specifying remedies to solve the social problem Leo XIII gave first place to workingmen's associations, either of workmen alone (a point subsequently neglected or overlooked by many owners, either unintentionally or deliberately) or of workmen and employers together. The state must not forbid associations to be formed to accomplish private ends (for such associations are, he maintained, a natural right) unless their purposes are "unlawful, or dangerous to the State," taking precaution not to "violate the rights of individuals, and not to enforce unreasonable regulations under pretence of public benefit." He stated succinctly that "laws only bind when they are in accordance with right reason, and hence with the eternal law of God." He advocated associations not only to "shake off courageously the yoke of . . . intolerable oppression" but also to protect the worker from irreligious associations, which would try to force him to join or starve. Leo also gave his approval to the formation of Benefit and Insurance Societies, which should be protected, but not intruded upon, by the State. The foundation of such organizations should be in religion. Funds should be created to help members in the event of accident, sickness, and old age.

The encyclical *Rerum Novarum* ended by adjuring the churchmen that each should "put his hand to the work."[59]

That the encyclical was meant to stand beside and be compared with the *Communist Manifesto* of Karl Marx is plainly evident. Yet Leo did not revile nor pour vituperative abuse upon socialists or their doctrine (the strictures he directed against the rapacity of owners were actually much sharper). Obviously he had come a long way since that first encyclical against the socialists at the beginning of his pontificate. He believed that the Christian way could stand comparison with any

59. Quotations are from Gilson, *The Church Speaks to the Modern World*, pp. 205-240.

other way of life and win approval on the basis of sheer reasonableness and knowledge of the hungers of man.

The encyclical blazed a new trail in turning away from the laissez-faire economic doctrines and insisting upon not only the right but the duty of the State to provide for human welfare. Thus he turned his back upon the popular "scientific" view of the survival of the fittest when applied to basic needs in rational and civilized society. He did not specify what he meant by "equal," in speaking of men. The Church had from the beginning emphasized the equality of all men in the eyes of God. The Napoleonic Code had long since set up as a principle the equality of all men in the eyes of the law. In this (and in other encyclicals) Leo constantly stressed the subordination of wife to husband. The socialists, on the other hand, always emphasized that women should in all things, family, suffrage, business, and politics, be regarded as the equal of men.[60] The Pontiff's concern was with the necessity for family discipline as well as for social welfare.

In the matter of spelling out the rights of labor, Leo was specific as to matters concerning wages, hours, entrance of youth into employment, and guarding women against excessive hardship. This he did without rejecting the economic theory as justifying private property, wages, and interest as essential to the capitalistic system.[61]

His claim that the worker should have "frugal comfort" was greeted sardonically by socialists and labor leaders in freer societies. In advocating that workers should have the right to acquire property, which should not be taxed out of existence, the Pontiff was endorsing what non-religious reformers were seeking and Germany was adopting: the "homestead" right.

The most revolutionary principle incorporated in the encyclical was that of permitting workers to form associations by themselves, without the presence of employers. This was the crux of the matter. In France the "mixed" associations had been viewed with suspicion by the workers. In Italy it was the dominance by non-laboring clergy that stood in the way of progress in the formation of local organizations. It may be

60. Mrs. Lydia Pankhurst, the prominent English suffragette, was to be a notable member of the Second International London meeting (1896). Many socialists regarded marriage as the enslavement of woman and recommended "Free Love" as a substitute.
61. Vaussard, *Histoire de la Démocratie Chrétienne*, p. 62.

parenthetically recalled that labor was inclined to resent the presence of the socialist leaders who earned their living by "writing" rather than by "working."

The appeal of the encyclical *Rerum Novarum* was not made to Catholics alone. Leo XIII invited all men of good will to participate.[62]

That Leo XIII's proposals in the *Rerum Novarum* did not go far enough to cure society's ills is obvious; to expect them to do so would be unjust. It would have required extraordinary foresight in 1891 to understand the power hidden in the proletarian mass, when fully aroused. Neither could anyone foresee that the State would not be able to limit itself to acting as a referee in the class struggle but must be constantly forced by the growing complexities and dangers of a scientifically and technologically awakened society to take on the role of employer; that in so doing it would also tend to lessen materially the rights of private property. What is important is not what is missing from the document but what is *there*, as an authoritative pronouncement of the Holy See. The era of speculation and theory had ended; the era of action had arrived.

There remained, to be sure, many points of obscurity. What was a "just wage?" Who should have the right to determine whether it was just or not?[63] Leo XIII favored guild organization, that is to say organization by trade and by profession. It is not clear what sort of organization he was favoring. He seemed to prefer the mixed guild (workers and employers), so strongly supported by the Union of Freiburg theory of the superiority of the medieval social and economic structure. And yet in his phrase "or workers alone" he seemed to be trying to escape from the grasp of the Freiburg Union and to confront the socialists from a more modern point of view. Because the men belonging to the Union of Freiburg were also monarchists their social theory was doctrinaire. They would tie together the paternalistic "reform from above" with medieval corporativeness and monarchy. This was true of La Tour-du-Pin, the Liechtensteins, and in general those who lived in Austria and

62. This is the first foreshadowing of the work of later Popes, John XXIII and Paul VI in removing the shackles which had bound the Church since the Council of Trent. For recent comment, see Thomas P. Neill and Raymond H. Schmandt, *History of the Catholic Church*, p. 353.
63. Nitti, *Catholic Socialism*, p. 375.

Germany. They were still influenced by notions of powerful monarchy and fixed social classes. The encyclical had gone far beyond them in confronting a world in which these presuppositions were rapidly passing away. Albert de Mun differed from La Tour-du-Pin on this matter. He was monarchist but not doctrinaire. Looking ahead in imagination de Mun saw in a society not tempered by parliamentary government the enlargement of the corporative idea ultimately posing "two terrible questions: Will this universal corporation be the owner of the instruments of labor of which the soil is the principal one? Will it own all the fruits of labor?"[64] To Albert de Mun there must always be in organized society not only religion but also the safety valve of parliament in which he had had experience now for a decade and a half.

The Enlightenment and the Revolution had demolished the medieval concept of corporative life. In resurrecting the corporative idea Leo was attacking the atomization of the individual under the all-powerful state and restoring him to economic significance as a member of a group.[65] His justification of strikes, under certain circumstances and when conducted without violence or damage to property, is further indication of Leo XIII's realization of the powerlessness of a worker as a single individual.

A proof of the significance of the *Rerum Novarum* in the life of the Catholic Church is the fact that two subsequent Popes have chosen to issue encyclicals dealing with the social problem and have promulgated these encyclicals on anniversaries of Leo XIII's *Rerum Novarum*. Pius XI did so on the fortieth anniversary, in *Quadragesimo Anno*,[66] and John XXIII did so on the seventieth anniversary, in *Mater et Magistra*.[67]

64. Quoted in Vaussard, *Histoire de la Démocratie Chrétienne*, p. 62. See also Rollet, *Action sociale*, p. 458.

65. Don Luigi Sturzo, *Pensiero antifascista* (Turin, 1923), p. 74.

66. Gilson, *The Church Speaks to the Modern World*, p. 202. Pius XI used the radio on that occasion, the Italian, French, and German versions being read; Cardinal Spellman read it in English. See George Seldes, *The Vatican Yesterday—Today—Tomorrow* (New York and London, 1934), p. 365.

67. John XXIII in his encyclical *Mater et Magistra*, said that Leo XIII spoke "in a time of radical transformations, of heightened contrasts and bitter revolt." He emphasized the fact that Leo was rejecting the classical economic theory of the nineteenth century, with its inexorable laws of interest, price, and wages, based on free competition. "This action [said John XXIII] was not without hazard, because while some alleged that the Church, face to face with the social question, should confine herself to preaching resignation to the poor and exhorting the rich to generosity, Leo XIII did not hesitate to proclaim the legitimate rights of the worker."

The response of the press to the encyclical *Rerum Novarum* was widespread and for the most part favorable. Leftist journals were somewhat skeptical as to the motive behind it; they regarded it as a "curious document," or an inexplicable "sudden switch" from "enemies to allies." More moderate papers thought it liberal conservative, animated by a "democratic breeze." The socialist journals found "nothing worth noting" in it, or warned their readers not to be "subverted" by the "socialist Pope." Ultraconservatives criticized it for leaning so far toward the side of the poor. Revolutionaries asked bitter questions about the Pope's attitude toward private property. Did one have a right to take it out of production and use great stretches for luxury? One moderate journal regarded the *Rerum Novarum* as defining a less hostile attitude toward the socialist movement:

One used to consider Catholicism an exceedingly conservative force, placing in opposition to each other the Church and the Revolution as two irreconcilable enemies, in spite of the Gospel showing itself favorable to ideas of social equality, in spite of the communist character which the Christian society showed in the early years. This antagonism was in all its violence at the moment when the Commune of Paris resolutely attacked the clergy and religion. Things have changed since that epoch.[68]

Some of the questions asked in Italy about the encyclical and its meaning sound strangely like Karl Marx, or Bakunin. What was meant by "frugal" comfort? If wages were adjusted to needs, should a *single* worker receive as much as a man with a large family? What about his future needs? Should one save up money for those? If the rich were to supply the poor out of their surplus after attending to their own necessities, just where would they begin?[69]

The *Rerum Novarum* was more than an explanation of doctrine or an expression of opinion about a debatable topic; it was also a directive

68. *France*, quoted in *Univers*, May 29, 1891. *France* went on to comment on the role of Catholics in trying to appease the conflict between labor and capital and mentioned Cardinal Manning in England, Albert de Mun in France, Decurtins in Switzerland. Eugène Veuillot gathered up all shades of opinion and published them in *Univers* on May 27 and 29.

69. Soderini surveyed journalistic expression in Italy. See his *Il Pontificato di Leone XIII*, I, 430. It will be remembered that Soderini was not only a prelate (presently becoming a Cardinal) but also a member of the Union of Freiburg and a writer, one of the two to whom the Vatican Archives were opened by Leo XIII for the purpose of writing his biography.

issued to the flock by the pastor of the faithful. Some bishops in France, trying to place a construction on the encyclical more to their liking, interpreted it to their people in less than accurate terms. *Univers*, ever faithful to the papal cause, published in parallel columns these opinions and the words of the encyclical.[70] The *Rerum Novarum* was unquestionably one of the major landmarks of the modern age.[71]

70. *Univers*, Oct. 8, 10, 13, 1894.
71. Pio Paschini, reviewing Msgr. Giovanni Antonazzi's *L'Enciclica "Rerum Novarum"* (*Testo autentico e redazioni preparatorie dai documenti originali*, with Preface by Domenico Tardini [Rome, 1957]) in *Rivista di storia della chiesa* (XI, 1957), reiterates that it is regarded as the "magna charta" of the Church's teaching in the field of the social question.

XII. LEO XIII AND THE DEMOCRATIC STATE

"The world is no longer governed by dynasties; the Holy See must now treat with the people. The more this is clearly and fully recognized, the more freely will the Church be able to exercise its spiritual authority."[1]

CARDINAL MANNING

The hierarchical structure of the Church was authoritarian. So was Marxian socialism. In the political arena the nineteenth century witnessed a shift not only toward nationalism but toward government by the people. Socialism, in spite of factionalism and for various reasons, decided to throw in its lot with universal suffrage and accept the democratic state. In Catholic countries the union of the Tiara and the Crown was traditional. Leo XIII in a series of encyclicals developed the view that the Church should work with and through existing governments, whatever their form, for its own ends which were spiritual and moral. He took his stand on the legally impeccable ground that legitimate government must be supported.[2]

Many members of the hierarchy were predisposed to cling to the principle that monarchy was the strongest wave to bear up the "bark of Peter." The tendency of the aristocracy was to agree. The middle class, rising in successive waves, was more inclined to accept the movement toward democracy as opening the door for the expansion of capitalism.

1. Nitti, *Catholic Socialism*, p. 382.
2. This, of course, does not answer the question of what constitutes legitimate government. One Catholic observer of the political scene asked how long a government (established by coup d'état) had to remain in power in order to be regarded as legitimate. The question has not yet been answered.

The strange phenomenon therefore appeared of an anticapitalist aristocracy advocating social reform based upon the "Church's view of the dignity of man." The individuals who were most active in carrying out under the aegis of the Church a new social program were the ones who adhered to the monarchist principle. If Leo XIII supported the new type of democratic state he would be at odds with the very persons who were doing the most to save the masses of workers for the Church.

Nevertheless, when the occasion demanded, he spoke out against this very group. When he urged members of the Catholic societies to be active in communal and administrative fields he was giving merely moral, not political advice; he besought them to maintain a high level of morality in the family and in society.[3] Some conservatives in Rome, however, went beyond this and proposed to seize control of the government through taking possession of the Chamber of Deputies by force. His Holiness gave them prompt and specific advice to lay aside any such dreams of seizure; they were not to think of constituting themselves the government in order to restore the Church's control. The Pontiff's words were harsh, though not delivered with harshness. The conservative plotters immediately notified him of their submission to instructions.[4]

Spurred by this incident Leo XIII made his first general pronouncement on the relations which should exist between the Church and the State: *Diuturnum illud*, issued June 21, 1881. In this encyclical Leo XIII developed the theme of man's need of a central authority, no matter how much by the virtue of "presumptuousness and massing of numbers" he sought to dispense with such a necessity; a society with no "hand, no guiding head," "would fail and not attain its goal," for the sake of which it had "arisen and founded itself." He traced the "false ideas" of political power through the centuries of reform, to issue in communism and nihilism, in the nineteenth century; all means used by secular authority to suppress such theories only aggravated the spirit of rebellion; "only religion" was efficacious in bending the human will and leading

3. Discourse of Leo XIII to the Catholic societies of Rome, April 24, 1881. *Univers*, April 29, 1881.
4. Letter from Rome, May 10, 1881. *Ibid.*, May 15, 1881. The Roman correspondent, knowing them, said that they would soon forget their submission.

it, not only to obedience, but to love of authority, "the greatest safe-guard of the social order."[5]

The words of Leo XIII sound, in isolation, as relentless as any dictum of Pius IX, showing an intention to stand fast as unbreakable as any Pope previously had exhibited; yet there is always the added advice to cherish moderation and to be charitable toward men as people even when disapproving of their actions. He expressed these thoughts at the beginning of the year 1882 to the Archbishop of Milan: "One must not depart in any manner from the moderation which should be the com-panion of all virtues. To that end no wise spirit will ever approve either a violence of style carried to excess, or malevolent insinuations or any-thing else which would rashly set aside respect and indulgence for per-sons."[6]

The *Diuturnum illud* was not to be Leo XIII's last word on the subject of the proper relations between Church and State. Finding it necessary from time to time to speak out to groups of clergy or laity, as occasion arose he expounded his ideas as to the mode of behavior suitable to follow in the individual cases in a series of letters. Other general encyclicals followed to the end of his life, as the political situa-tion in Europe continued to move toward the goals of national unity and democratic government.

Believing that legitimate authority was to be obeyed, Leo XIII gently reproved the members of the hierarchy who engaged in dissension with their secular governments. He resorted to commands only if the re-proofs went unheeded, but he insisted that legitimate secular authority must be respected. The Archbishop of Dublin he warned in 1881 about committing rash acts which might seem a refusal to submit to legitimate authority; the path of moderation should be followed lest "justice" be-come "license" and the "most just cause" degenerate, in the midst of passion, into "seditious effervescence."[7] His advice always was to use legal means for defending or forwarding the interests of the Church.

In Belgium the Catholic leaders were jeopardizing social legislation

5. Quotations from the *Diuturnum illud* taken from the French of T'Serclaes (*Léon XIII*, pp. 339-342) and the German version in Lentner (*Der Christ und der Staat*, pp. 47-48), which also gives the Latin text.
6. Quoted in *Univers*, Jan. 30, 1882.
7. Leo XIII to the Archbishop of Dublin, Jan. 3, 1881. *Ibid.*, Jan. 12, 1881.

and the progress of political representation by carrying on a quarrel with the duly constituted Liberal Government over the question of the new school law. This new law said that children must be sent to school; since public schools alone could by proper inspection be kept to a necessary standard, aid would be withdrawn from parents who sent their children to private schools or failed to send them to public institutions. The wishes of the Pope in the matter were conveyed by Cardinal Nina (Secretary of State) to the Belgian Ambassador to the Holy See, who reported in turn to the Belgian Parliament when the government was interpellated on the question. Leo agreed with the bishops as to the desirability of Catholic education, but reproved them for their way of attempting to secure it. When he learned through diplomatic channels that the Belgian government thought the "Holy See was trying to dominate the civil powers" he let it be known that, "on the contrary, he was recommending obedience to established governments, and respect for laws." This was in March, 1878, at the very beginning of Leo's pontificate. He presently became more explicit and said that the "attacks against the national institutions would receive at the Vatican neither support nor encouragement."

The Constitution has separated the State and the Churches [the document went on], proclaiming the liberty of faiths; it has interdicted the State from intervening in the nomination and installation of ministers of the faiths, in the acts and relations of the spiritual superiors with their subordinates or with the faithful.

Leo followed the giving of this advice by having Cardinal Nina instruct the Belgian nuncio to let the bishops and the Catholics know that he would approve no attack on the Belgian Constitution, nor were they "to seek any modification whatsoever in it." While some articles did not conform to the doctrines of the Church, there were many advantages in it to which the Holy See attached "a very great value." In an interview with a group of Catholics from Belgium—that country, he said, for which he had such deep affection and "living memories"—Leo XIII unveiled his platform:

The works of men are not perfect: evil is found side by side with good, error beside truth. It is thus with the Belgian Constitution; it incorporates some principles which I could not approve as Pope, but the situation of Catholicism in Belgium, after an experience of a half-century, demonstrates that, in the present state of modern society, the system of liberty established in this country is most favorable to the Church. Belgian Catholics must then not only refrain from attacking this Constitution, but they must defend it.[8]

In spite of these warnings from the Vatican, the situation in Belgium did not quiet down. The clergy asserted that the government, in possession of "all the resources of power," was "snatching the souls of children and young people out of the Church," while their opponents charged that the clerical group, "deprived of visible force," left "nothing undone to keep up the combat."[9] The Belgian Catholics now got into a heated discussion over the truth or falsity of the slogan: "All power derives from the people."[10] The Pope found it necessary, in consequence, to speak directly to the Belgian bishops. He wrote a letter, the *Licet multa*, giving specific admonitions. Concerned as he was for the maintenance of harmony, he noticed that controversies inimical to harmony were still being carried on; recent governmental changes based on the new law and not in harmony with Catholic doctrine were the object of a concerted effort, he said, to make the law conform to the doctrine; this was imprudent. His Holiness continued: "It is necessary that all Catholics, if they wish to labor fruitfully for the common good, have before their eyes and faithfully follow the prudent manner of behavior which the Church adopts in such cases." While the principles of justice should control private acts, customs, and public institutions, nevertheless the Church takes "into account the nature of things, of places, and of times," and as often happens, it is forced to "tolerate some ills" rather than open the door to "greater evils and troubles." One must be on guard, in discussions, "not to overstep the bounds of equity and charity," and must not "accuse rashly" men who otherwise were persons of devotion, especially when in positions of "authority and dignity" in the Church. "It is self-evident," he wrote, and underlined the words, "that this facility in falsely accusing no matter whom, damages the reputation of others, loosens the bonds of mutual charity and does injury to *those whom the*

8. Although these events occurred in 1878, the documents were not published until the following year. For the collection see *Univers*, Nov. 24, 1879. See also Haag, "The Political Ideas of Belgian Catholics," in Moody, *Church and Society*, p. 294.

9. *Courrier de Bruxelles* (Brussels), quoted in *Univers*, Jan. 18, 1881.

10. Lentner, *Der Christ und der Staat*, pp. 56-57.

Holy Spirit has established as bishops to govern the Church of God."
He gravely warned all Catholics to refrain from "such a manner of behavior."[11]

In Spain waves of anticlericalism appeared as a result of interference
of the clergy in political life. Their avowed support of Carlism brought
so much political bitterness that Leo XIII was forced to warn the priests
and bishops about their political activities.[12] In a letter, *Cum multa,* he
told the bishops that he did not condemn legitimate expression of political opinion but advised that Spaniards must not allow differences of
opinion to split them into hostile groups. A rumor was circulated that
Leo's Secretary of State had written a letter subsequent to the *Cum
multa* in effect countermanding the Pope's letter to the bishops. The
nuncio in Madrid contradicted this and said that the Pope's instructions
were binding on all Catholics in Spain.[13] Anticlerical students in Madrid
found their demonstrations met with bullets and imprisonment. The
path of moderation in Spain was, as always, thorny. The clergy remained
intransigent, while democratic groups became increasingly anticlerical
in opposition to them. Feeling at times ran very high. The Bishop of
Madrid was assassinated in 1886.[14] No solution of the proper relation
between State and Church in Spain was reached during the lifetime of
Leo XIII. Not only did the cause of intellectual and religious freedom
suffer in consequence, but social reform was made impossible. The door
to anarchism was thus left open.[15]

It was in France that the question of the Church and the modern
democratic state produced the most dramatic crises. France was the first

11. Leo XIII to the Belgian bishops, Aug. 3, 1881: the *Licet multa,* quoted in T'Serclaes,
Léon XIII, I, 290.

12. The Carlists, supporting a Bourbon pretender, troubled Spain through much of
the nineteenth century. The clergy were accused as Carlists of playing politics when
Cardinal Moreno organized a pilgrimage to go to Leo XIII in order to console him
for the indignities offered to the bones of Pius IX on the occasion of the removal of the
former Pontiff's remains to their final resting place, when a mob of citizens threatened
to throw the bones into the Tiber. See Giuseppe Manfroni, *Sulla soglia del Vaticano*
(2 vols.; Bologna, 1920-1925), II, 49-56.

13. Archbishop Mariano to Cardinal Archbishop of Campostello. *Univers,* July 8,
1883. Some forty Spanish disputants signed and submitted an address to the Pope;
since they signed as individuals and not as members of political parties Leo was none
too happy.

14. *Ibid.,* April 22, 1886.

15. Moody, "The Socio-Religious Problematic of Spain," in Moody, *Church and
Society,* p. 728.

great power to become republican. Its constitutional laws, adopted in 1875, provided for universal manhood suffrage. The Chamber of Deputies promptly became republican, indicating that popular approval had definitely shifted to republican views. Actually there was not *one* France; there were two. On the one hand was the France that was republican and radical—even socialist, in the thinking of many;[16] on the other hand was the France that was monarchist and ultramontane. The outstanding republican was Gambetta. In his most quoted speech he pointed out the bonds between the clerical party and the reactionaries, insisting that the question was political rather than religious; he mentioned Bishop Darboy's prophecy that the new policy of the Vatican[17] would bring about a rupture with the modern states and cause the ruin of the Concordat;[18] he ended with the words: "There is one thing which, like the Ancien Régime, is hateful to the country; it is the domination of clericalism. I only translate the sentiments of the French people in saying what my friend Peyrat once said: 'Clericalism, there is the enemy!' "[19] The dissolution of the French Chamber necessitated a national election, in which the clergy threw themselves into the fray on the side of the monarchist President of France, Marshal MacMahon.

When Leo XIII was crowned with the Triple Crown in 1878, the memory of all this was fresh in the minds of the French people. The division of France was more complete than before. Continued clerical intransigence was in evidence, as Catholic clergy sneered at, and decried, the "Marseillaise," the Republic, the 14th of July, and the heroes of the French Revolution, those "assassins."[20] The republicans on their side were carrying on an ever-increasing war against the clericals, asking

16. Émil Deschanel was quoted as saying that the terms "republican" and "socialist" were synonomous. See *Univers*, Oct. 17, 1879.

17. Pius IX and the *Syllabus*.

18. The Concordat of Napoleon I with the Holy See in 1801.

19. *Annales de la Chambre de Députés*, 1877, III, 24 f.

20. The term "clerical" had first been used in 1848 by Deschanel and Victor Hugo; about 1860 it came into occasional use; Sainte-Beuve employed it in a formal speech in the Senate in 1868, to the great anger of his opponent, Cardinal Donnet (why that word clerical?); now it was common. See Weill, *L'Idée laïque en France au xixᵉ siècle*, p. 179. At the moment of Leo's election the question of the French religious budget was the subject of debate in the Chamber of Deputies. See *Univers*, Feb. 23, 1878. Clemenceau said there was no religious budget in the United States; La Bassetière said he would be agreeable to that if France restored all the Church's property and gave all the liberty to the Church that was accorded in the United States.

whether it was not time to emancipate the clergy from the *Syllabus* and pontifical Infallibility.[21]

The quarrel went on in France not only in public meetings and the press but in the debates in the Chamber of Deputies. The main objective of the republicans[22] was to laicize the schools as the *sine qua non* of radical success. To wipe them out would, of course, leave France without any schools; lay schools did not exist.[23] This argument over schools led to discussion of relations of Church and State in general. Once started, the debate went on for the rest of the century.[24]

During the course of the debate it was also brought out that the clerical press should no more be muzzled than the journals of political opinion.[25] Baroche referred to three things which determined the situation of the Church in France; the Concordat of 1801; the Organic Laws, which set up the Republic in 1875; and the principles of 1789.[26] All was confusion; charges and countercharges were made. Meanwhile, the republicans gained control of the Senate in the election of January, 1879, and of the presidency when MacMahon resigned and was succeeded by Jules Grévy. Gambetta's republican faction continued to concern itself with clericalism, which, they said, would "subordinate French law to Catholic dogma, criticize the Constitution in the light of theology, reduce the government to the role of the secular arm charged with executing the will of the Church."[27] The republican government not

21. *Univers*, Aug. 5, 1878.
22. Gambetta was regarded as the "hidden engineer" of the constitutional machine. *Univers* claimed that even the Orleanists were supporting him. See *ibid.*, March 6, 1878.
23. *Ibid.*, Oct. 16, 1878. Publicly supported lay schools had had a beginning in the era of the French Revolution; they reappeared under the July monarchy; the Second Empire returned education to the hands of the clergy.
24. The question of the inevitability of the separation of Church and State had been raised under the Second Empire. Ollivier, Minister of State, said in the Assembly that the separation must come by mutual consent; the clergy by foregoing payment by the government (according to the terms of the Concordat of 1801) would attain complete liberty, as in America, and would be assured "a force, a dignity and independence" of such proportions as to be worth the renunciation of the budget. Such a mutual agreement would be preceded by a long period of strife.
25. *Collectio Lacensis*, VII, 1223.
26. Laws limiting freedom of the press (Art. 21, Feb. 17, 1852, and Art. 9, May 21, 1868) were still on the books. They had not been abrogated, but they were not used. See *Univers*, March 25, 1878. The articles in question dealt with publication of writings by persons who had lost their civil and political rights.
27. Loth quotes this in *Univers* (Nov. 11, 1879) and then rejects the charge.

only proceeded with the laicization of the schools but also began to attack the religious orders and to seek other ways to laicize France. It threatened an attack on the Concordat of 1801.

When Cardinal Nina, five months after Leo XIII's coronation, left the nunciature in Paris to become Secretary of State at the Vatican on the death of Cardinal Franchi, the Concordat between France and the papacy was still "weathering the storm." So sure was Nina that it was about to be liquidated that he said to his successor, "Before fourteen months, Monsignor, we shall be seeing each other in Rome."[28] Msgr. Czachi, the new nuncio, sent to improve relations with the republican government, had been Secretary of Affairs Extraordinary in Rome. He had a thorough understanding of his task as nuncio, remarking on one occasion: "I have been sent to the *de facto* government which France has provided for itself. This means . . . that I must enter into relations with the men who compose it. . . ." His personal predilections must not be allowed to interfere; his "mission of peace" admitted of no compromise.[29] Although Czachi was accused by *Siècle* of playing Polish politics,[30] he really got on well with the French ministry. Gambetta, after a long talk with him on one of several visits, remarked: "Monsignor, If I had known earlier what I have just learned, the Government of the Republic would have been able to avoid many false steps on the religious terrain."[31]

If the republicans were beginning to understand Leo XIII better because of his desire to come to terms with existing governments, so much could not be said for the French intransigents, who were alarmed at his pacific policy.[32] The interests of the Church in France were injured by these ultramontanists who sought to "exalt the Church in its most rigid form" as they sought "royal exaltation of the most absolute kind."[33]

28. Ferrata, *Mémoires,* p. 38. Ferrata was with Czachi as auditor.
29. *Ibid.,* p. 46.
30. *Siècle,* Aug. 18, 1879. The Poles (Catholics) hoped for French support in securing their independence from the Orthodox Tsar.
31. Ferrata, *Mémoires,* p. 45. Czachi was replaced by Msgr. di Rende, who did not do as well. Czachi subsequently played a role at Rome in the diplomacy of settling the Kulturkampf.
32. Fèvre, *La Défense de l'église en France sous Léon XIII,* p. 23.
33. J. Tournier, *Le Cardinal Lavigerie et son action politique 1863-1892* (Paris, 1892), p. 42. A proposed visit of Emperor William II to King Humbert, not opposed by the

Cardinal Lavigerie, Archbishop of Algiers, explained all this to Leo XIII. The Republic was taking action against the religious orders, barring them from their activities and forcing them to evacuate their houses. Believing that the Church should take a position of political neutrality, Lavigerie insisted that the regular clergy were making a mistake in turning their resistance to these moves of the state into a monarchist crusade and in making no attempt to co-operate and secure a more moderate solution.

Without doubt [the Primate of Africa continued] a time will come in which in spite of all efforts the Church will certainly be persecuted. This will be when the Commune is reestablished . . . [so that] the only reasonable policy to follow seems to me to be to defend the terrain step by step as far as conscience and honor permit, and especially to avoid the wilful faults by which they would hasten the open persecution and violent destruction of the Church in France.

Lavigerie was convinced that three-fourths of the episcopate in France agreed with him and wanted the religious congregations to abandon the terrain of political opposition.[34]

The Pope wrote to the Archbishop of Paris on October 22, 1880, calling attention to various demonstrations on the part of Catholics in favor of "Henry V," or monarchy in general. Of one such demonstration Leo commented: ". . . this declaration was made at the institgation or at least with the assent of the bishops . . . and it is evident that the faithful have to be submissive and obey them." The Church, however, His Holiness pointed out, rejected no form of government, being concerned only with religion, it being necessary "to obey those who govern, that order, which is the foundation of public security, may be preserved." He said it did not follow that in obeying one approved "what is unjust in the constitution or administration of the State." He strongly disap-

Pope, was regarded by French extremists as "insulting." See the report of the Paris correspondent of the London *Times*, sent by the Agence Havas to *Univers*, Jan. 4, 1892. This incident occurred at the climax of the French crisis.

34. Tournier, *Lavigerie*, pp. 76 ff. Paul de Cassagnac, in the debate over the amnesty issue called attention to the anomaly of a nation trying to bring back political exiles and banish the religious congregations at the same time. *Univers*, June 23, 1880. Cassagnac was a Bonapartist until the death of the Prince Imperial, Napoleon's son; after that he was a republican. His words were: "The assassins and incendiaries are returning; the priests are departing." See Curtis, *Three against the Third Republic*, p. 19.

proved of the expulsion of the religious congregations; he wished to defend the rights of the Church.[35]

The Church and secular society continued to form two separate worlds in France. *Opinion nationale,* organ of the Left Bonapartists, allying with the republicans against Church domination, said the clergy controlled their various localities in France—the clergy, 200,000 strong, bound by the same oath, the same submission to a foreign prince, held "youth among us by education and the sacraments, and old age by the fear of revolutions in this world and the devil in the next."[36]

The chief allies of the Church outside the ranks of the clergy were the aristocrats, devoted to the monarchist cause. Together with the clergy they formed the intransigent Right. Their main organ was *Univers,* utterly devoted to the papacy and the Church. It was also not only royalist but Legitimist: any word about the Count of Chambord was spread upon its pages as though it had been Holy Writ. Too fundamentally Christian to resort to subterfuge or dissimulation or to descend to vituperation, it supported the cause with dignity and devotion.[37]

Of the many moderate clergy, to whom Lavigerie referred, most kept quiet on controversial points. Occasionally one spoke out, sounding like a lone voice in a royalist chorus. One such dissenter took his episcopal seat at Poitiers in 1881: Msgr. Bellot de Minières, successor to Msgr. Pie. His predecessor had been one of the most intractable of monarchists. Bishop Pie had been friend and confidant of "Henry V"; opposed to the Tricolor, Pie had applauded the insistence of the Count of Chambord on not mounting the throne of France unless he could bring with him the white flag of the Bourbons. Bellot de Minières was

---

35. T'Serclaes, *Léon XIII,* I, 293.
36. Quoted in Weill, *Histoire de l'idée laïque,* pp. 180-181.
37. Eugène Veuillot, editor of *Univers,* maintained the family devotion to the papacy exhibited earlier by his older brother, Louis Veuillot, who guided the daily newspaper through so many of those years which witnessed the most stirring events in papal history since the Protestant Revolt. The family was about to prove that its devotion to monarchy did not outweigh its devotion to the Pope, and to prove it dramatically overnight. As for the reports of de Mun's speeches, they were verbatim, whether the orator was addressing a great Catholic gathering or debating some social issue in the Chamber, where he sat from 1879 to 1910. Stenographic reports form the most unimpeachable source for what was actually said by a public speaker, far surpassing manuscripts prepared in advance and not subject to the erasure and consequent distortion characteristic of tape recordings of today.

the very antithesis of Msgr. Pie.[38] He stated his position in his first allocution to his diocese: he did not intend to intervene in political struggles and would see that his clergy followed his example; he was honored to have been selected by the government of the Republic and said that if the duty of the government was to have religion respected, the duty of the clergy was to respect the government. The clerical press attacked him immediately for taking this stand, while the republican journals sang a paean of praise; one republican journal said these were "wise words, which we are scarcely accustomed to hearing."[39]

It would be difficult to decide who were or had been usurpers. Three lines of rulers, aside from the republican governments, had sat on the French throne during the course of the nineteenth century: the Bonapartist, the Orleanist, and the Bourbon. A Pope had graced the coronation of Napoleon Bonaparte; Napoleon III had protected Pius IX in Rome; the clerical Right supported the Bourbon line. The death of the Prince Imperial of the Bonapartist line removed for a generation the possibility of a claim from that direction.[40] The refusal of the Count of Chambord to come without his flag would seem to end the Legitimist threat, but not so; the Legitimists continued to view him as king of France and called him "Henry V." Many Orleanists went over to republican ranks, convinced that republicanism divided France least. Bishop Dupanloup was one of the liberal Catholics who took this position.[41]

38. The story of Bellot de Minières is ably told by John Burwell Woodall ("Henri Bellot de Minières, Republican Bishop of Poitiers, 1881-1888," *The Catholic Historical Review*, XXXVIII [Oct., 1952], 257-284).

39. Eugène Veuillot summed up the press comments for *Univers* (March 2, 1881). The Gambettist journals, he said, claimed that resisting the government was resisting God; Veuillot did not agree with this view; he quoted with approval the words of Balmès (*Protestantisme Comparé au catholicisme*): "Usurpation cannot claim to be a government to which such obedience is due." The republican government, in the opinion of the clerical Right, was a usurping government.

40. Adrien Dansette (*Le Boulangisme*, p. 7) remarks acutely: "But the Bonapartist spirit survived, tenacious and secretly, at the bottom of the peasant's soul. . . ." Marx and Engels (*Marx oder Bakunin?* p. 36) said that Albert Richard and Gasper Blanc appeared in London to arouse help for a Bonapartist restoration among the French refugees; they claimed to have enough control over the proletariat to say right in front of the republicans: "Long live the Emperor!" Marx and Engels thought they might really have been Bakuninists trying to insinuate themselves into Bonapartist circles, as instructed by the "Brotherhood."

41. On the occasion of the publication of a three-volume life of Dupanloup by Abbé Lagrange, a whole series of attacks against the Bishop appeared in *Univers*, written by an ultramontane Canon Maynard, whereupon the Pope ordered the cessation of *Univers*

Catholic groups not only in rural areas but in the cities showed their defiance of the republican regime in various incidents involving the different flags.[42]

One aspect of this quarrel was altered in 1883 by the death of the Count of Chambord. *Univers*, from August 27 to September 5, came out edged in black each day. A correspondent from Rome bewailed his death: "The King of France is dead."[43] One article entitled "The King" attributed all the ills of France to the refusal of the Assembly to enthrone the Bourbon "Henry V": "atheism, the menacing social question, and the imprisonment of the Pope in the Vatican." The article continued: "Founded on atheism the Republic is powerless to resolve [the social question] radically; it can only accentuate the antagonism between classes. . . ." The article suggested that the solution of the problem would be in the increase of the Catholic Workingmen's Clubs, but these would need legal sanction to be formed; if the government were Christian it would change the law; a Christian government would be a royal government, and so on and on.[44]

The Count of Paris was now assumed to be, by the monarchist Right, closest to the throne of France according to the laws of succession. Not all Catholics were agreed. Some preferred the claims of the Spanish Carlist branch of the Bourbon House. These counterclaims of rival dynasties, added to the quarrel between Catholic republicans and the antirepublican clericals, aroused a veritable furor in France. The bishops were in the midst of the furor.

The Pope took action. He addressed a letter to the bishops and archbishops of France, *Nobilissima Gallorum gens*. It was couched in the gentlest terms, expressing his love for France, calling attention to the glorious deeds of their ancestors for the Church, and suggesting that

for a month, and instructed the Catholic press not to reproduce Maynard, whose work was subsequently condemned by the Congregation of the Index. See Tournier, *Lavigerie*, pp. 190 f.

42. At Lyons a wire was stretched across the Rhone, supporting a white flag with fleur-de-lys. Opponents, presumably supporters of the Tricolor, tore it down as "seditious" and a lively fracas ensued, in which the Bourbon flag was torn to pieces. The anarchists, in the same city, hung a red flag all day by the establishment where their journal *Lütte* was published.

43. *Univers*, Aug. 27–Sept. 5, 1883.

44. *Ibid.*, Sept. 2, 1883.

differences among French Catholics be laid to rest, to the end that religion might be kept alive in France; he expressed his satisfaction with
the Concordat of 1801 and his desire not to see it destroyed; he evidenced
his regret that the new educational laws were excluding the teaching of
religion from the public schools; he enjoined the bishops to maintain
Catholic schools where Catholic faith could be taught and to support
the seminaries, recruiting new priests who might carry on the work.
As for himself, Leo XIII assured them that he had taken appropriate
action through the nuncio in Paris. He had written also to the Archbishop
of Paris and in the preceding year had written President Grévy a letter,
in which the position and attitude of the Church on the legislative questions was set forth in all Christian charity. He quoted the biblical statement that a "kingdom divided against itself will fall." In the interest of
concord, he suggested, some might have to renounce their opinions and
their judgment, but they should do so voluntarily, in the interest of
the common good.[45]

Leo XIII had reproved the clergy, but perhaps too sweetly to have
the reproof taken to heart. He had enjoined the use only of legal means
in opposing legislation and gave no comfort to any seditious plot to
change the form of government.

In the letter to President Grévy, mentioned in the *Nobilissima Gallorum gens*, the Pope showed how far he was from attempting to undermine the Republic: "We have never departed from the strictest rules of

45. Dispatch from Rome, Feb. 8, 1884. Quoted in *Ibid.*, Feb. 14, 1884. The Latin
text and the official French translation appeared in *Journal de Rome*, from which the
dispatch was taken. This was a French journal published in Rome; it had been founded
at the express wish of Leo XIII. Msgr. Galimberti became its editor. Holding a different
point of view from the staff, he resigned and became editor of the *Moniteur de Rome*.
The staff of the *Journal* held an ultra-legitimist position with regard to public affairs
both in Italy and in France. When Galimberti resigned they turned to Pitra, the
librarian of the Vatican Library, who misunderstood how devious a plan they had in
mind: to set up one of the Cardinals in Leo's place, disapproving of the Pope's policies
of moderation. Their opposition to Leo became widely known when Pitra wrote a letter
to the Dutch paper *Amstelbode*, and stirred up a polemic. When Pitra discovered to
his dismay that the object of the machinations was the Pope himself, he made complete
submission immediately to the Pope. He had been rash but not treasonable. See *Univers*,
June 23, 1885. See also Soderini, *Leo XIII, Italy, and France* (trans. Barbara Barclay
Carter; London, 1935), pp. 36-39, for an account of the whole affair. Lavigerie remarked
wittily in the midst of the polemic that it was time to inquire whether the Church
rested "on Peter or on Pitra [*super Petrum o super Pitram*]." Leo XIII subsequently
established the journal *Aurora*.

moderation and delicacy, in order not to diminish the prestige of the civil authority, now more than ever necessary for public order in a time when many subversive currents seem conspired to undermine and destroy it." He went on to express his regret that legislation was undertaken against the religious organizations; he bewailed civil marriage and military service for the clergy; he explained why the school manuals were placed on the *Index*.[46]

In his reply President Grévy expressed his regret at the growth of irreligion in society but attributed it in part to the hostility of a portion of the clergy to the Republic; if the Pontiff could keep them in the path of political neutrality, which he said was the "great and wise thought" of Leo's pontificate, it would contribute toward the pacification so much desired. President Grévy said he had passed Leo XIII's letter to the Ministry.[47] Earlier he had remarked that he was favorably impressed by the "amicable and paternal tone" of the Pope's letter. Grévy was "guardian of the Constitution" to prevent violation of it and show respect for it. He was not permitted to influence legislation, and for this reason could not be of "much value to the Pope."[48]

The response of the Archbishop of Paris to the *Nobilissima Gallorum gens* was a complete submission (for distribution to all his bishops).[49] The matter was, however, by no means settled.

It was in the encyclical *Immortale Dei* that Leo XIII set forth his general code for guidance in matters of State-Church relations. He was keenly aware that the Church, though not "of the world," was nevertheless "in the world," and that no absolute rule could be laid down, no one pattern followed; the international Church existed within the national states; the states differed in form and operation, in the position permitted to religion in public life, in education, and in countless other ways. The *Immortale Dei* was to be fitted into the conditions of the various states.

The right to command, said Leo XIII in the encyclical, was not

46. T'Serclaes, *Léon XIII*, I, 301-304.
47. *Ibid.*, p. 304. The Ferry Ministry was still in power.
48. Quoted in *Univers*, July 30, 1883. Except for this note this exchange of letters did not come to light until the time of the encyclical *Au milieu*.
49. *Journal de Rome*, May 3, 1884. Quoted in *Univers*, May 5, 1884. For comments on *Nobilissima Gallorum gens*, see also T'Serclaes, *Léon XIII*, I, 311.

necessarily linked with any specific form of government; governments, however, must take account of God as the origin of all law. "To cast aside obedience, and by popular violence to incite to revolt, is therefore treason, not against man only but against God." The Church's real power, given to it by Christ, was over religious matters. "Whatever, therefore, in things human," he wrote "is of a sacred character, whatever belongs either by its own nature or by reason of the end to which it is referred, to the salvation of souls, or to the worship of God, is subject to the power and judgment of the Church." Everything in the civil and political domain should be subject to civil authority, since Christ said: "Render to Caesar what is Caesar's and to God what is God's." A concordat should arrange matters in case of an overlapping of functions. Leo XIII did not regard as an inherent right the liberty to think or speak; this idea, he thought, was the source of many evils; "liberty is a power perfecting man, and hence should have truth and goodness for its object." He stated plainly: "Whatever, therefore, is opposed to virtue and truth may not rightly be brought temptingly before the eyes of men, much less sanctioned by favor and protection of the law." Recalling the utterances of Gregory XVI and the *Syllabus* of Pius IX, he said this did not mean that the Church opposed *just* liberty or condemned tolerance of false religions when circumstances demanded. No one should be "forced to embrace the Catholic faith against his will, for as St. Augustine wisely reminds us, 'Man cannot believe otherwise than of his own will.' "[50]

The encyclical *Immortale Dei* did not say whether Catholics should form a political party and participate in legislative matters as members of the Church rather than as simple citizens; circumstances would decide this. It was not by any means clear that His Holiness would approve this approach in France, although he had done so in the case of Germany and the Center Party.

50. T'Serclaes, *Léon XIII*, I, 394-398. The encyclical was issued on November 1, 1885. See also Gilson, *The Church Speaks to the Modern World*, pp. 161-184. In the encyclical Leo XIII also denied that the separation of Church and State was desirable. It is interesting to note that the archbishops and bishops of the United States, assembled in plenary Council at Baltimore, in a pastoral letter to their clergy and laity discussed the attacks made on the Church as the result of the Vatican Council and pointed out that in the United States there was an absence of conflict between duty to the State and to religion. See *Univers*, Jan. 12, 1885.

Some French Catholics were forming a Counter-Revolutionary League, frankly monarchist, and devoted to the purpose of destroying the French Republic. Various Catholic journals were publishing its appeal:

This union is necessary to regain our rights. The Sovereign Pontiff and the episcopacy do not cease to recommend it. It is the basis and conclusion of all the encyclicals, of all consistorial allocutions, of all the responses of Leo XIII to the different deputations he receives, and all the pastoral letters in their turn insist on this fundamental duty.

This League, together with a League of the Rights of the Pope, stirred the anger of the Liberal Catholics. They saw how such organizations could attract and provide a cloak for royalist designs; property owners, too, would find in such organizations a religious support for the maintenance of order.[51] How far the royalists were willing to go appears in this invitation from Marseilles:

The *Gazette du Midi* appeals to . . . these Catholics, to these royalists, who have fought all their lives to remain faithful to the principles. . . . We keep in our hearts the old traditional cry: "The king is dead, long live the king!" . . . Religious truth is in the infallible Holy See; political truth in France is with the traditional and Christian monarchy.[52]

Devotion to monarchism blinded the French antirepublicans to the fact that republican government may operate in the interests of the small man (the peasant, the laborer, the humble shopkeeper, the small investor) if the sincerely religious conservatives support a social program rejected by the exponents of laissez-faire liberalism.

Again in 1888, in the encyclical *Libertas* Leo XIII deplored the idea of using violence in order to gain political ends. To seek a change of government under unjust repression would not justify the use of violence to attain the end.[53] In an earlier encyclical[54] he had said that he did not disapprove of democracy per se, nor of participation in government.

The royalists of France took none of the words of caution and warn-

51. *Semaine religieuse*, quoted in *Univers*, Feb. 5, 1885.
52. *Gazette du Midi*, quoted in *Univers*, Feb. 5, 1885.
53. Gilson, *The Church Speaks to the Modern World*, pp. 55-82. See also *Univers*, June 29, July 1, 1888. See above pp. 223 ff.
54. *Immortale Dei*, issued on Nov. 1, 1885. See Gilson, *The Church Speaks to the Modern World*, p. 177.

ing to heart. The cause of royalism was becoming a burning issue. It rose to fever heat in 1889 in connection with the Boulanger affair. The prelude lay in the expulsion of the princes in 1886. Fearing the coalition of conservatives, monarchists, and many of the French clergy, the Republic decided that the heads of families who had ever occupied the throne of France, or their direct heirs, creating as they did a constant danger of intrigue and attempted coup d'état, must be expelled from France. Recalling the words of Thiers that "two governments cannot exist on the same soil," the commission that was delegated to examine the matter asked whether they were princes or citizens and concluded that they were first of all "pretenders to the throne." In spite of promises to lead private lives they had not ceased to conspire. "The princes," stated the report, "personify hostility to the Republic. They wish to substitute another form of government for the one at present existing."[55] The princes of both houses took their departure, the Count of Paris issuing a proclamation: "They are attacking in me the monarchist principle [which alone] can give to our democratic society a strong government, open to all, above all parties, and whose stability will be the gauge of a durable peace for Europe." He promised to work for the restoration of the monarchy.[56] To the Right he was a "noble exile"; to the republicans he was a "pretender."[57]

General Boulanger had been appointed Minister of War at the beginning of 1886. Potentially dangerous, he paraded his republicanism and was applauded by the Left. His popularity grew with alarming rapidity. Various groups devised plans for making use of his popularity. He might become a Leftist dictator or the precursor of a monarchist restoration. The latter would please the clergy and the religious orders. He was called the "curates' Boulanger"; his success would be the "revenge of the Jesuits." Boulanger was credited with making secret deals with the princes. He appealed also to Church supporters by guaranteeing

55. *Voltaire*, quoted in *Univers*, Feb. 21, 1886.

56. Reproduced in *Univers*, June 26, 1886. The protestation was signed: "Philippe, Comte de Paris," and dated June 24, 1886.

57. The message of readiness to carry on was received by the Rightist journals with approval: *Gaulois, Soleil, Moniteur Universelle, Patrie*, and *Gazette de France*. Quoted in *Univers*, June 27, 1886, which carried also the adverse opinions of the Leftist and Opportunist journals: *Lanterne, Petit Parisienne, France, République française*, and *Temps*.

not to tolerate religious persecution. The appeal to the spirit of revenge against Germany was quite open:

> By all the blood of France entire
> By the past, by the dead to avenge
> With the Tsar, for God, France, for the Fatherland
> Death to the Prussians and long live Boulanger![58]

Antirepublicans, reinforced by the idea of revenge against Germany, reached the point of conspiracy in a group calling themselves the "League of Patriots." To this League Boulanger seemed the answer to prayer—a military figure at whose word armed men would rise and the Republic would tremble. Boulanger did not give the word;[59] the potential tragedy became farce; the flight and suicide of Boulanger could not raise the drama from comedy to tragedy.[60]

Leo XIII reiterated in *Libertas*, while the Boulanger affair was building to its climax and fiasco, that the Church used her influence "in support of any form of government which commended itself to the citizens at home, because of its justice, or was feared by their enemies abroad, because of its power." This veiled counsel went unheeded in France.

The movement in France to solve the social problem along lines consonant with religion had become more and more hampered by the fact that so many of the leaders who were most religious and most socially minded were the very ones who were committed to the cause of monarchy and were using every opportunity to discredit the French Republic among the faithful. They mounted every public rostrum to

58. Vizetelly (*Republican France*, pp. 315, 327, 320) gives evidence as to the deals with the princes and the appeal to *Revanche*. Soderini (*Il Pontificato de Leone XIII*, II, 377) says Boulanger was well supplied with money by the "Bonapartists and Legitimists, who hoped to find in him a new Monk [Monck]. . . ." Some of the strictest Legitimists, however, thought Boulanger had treated the Duc d'Aumale shabbily. See Dansette, *Le Boulangisme*, p. 374. For the effect on socialist division, see above pp. 232 ff.

59. He proved to be a "blade of white iron in a scabbard of steel." See Dansette, *Le Boulangisme*, p. 374. Boulanger "deserved a statute," says Dansette, for "decimating and dispersing" the Republic's adversaries on the Right and "assuaging the faithful" on the Left.

60. *Figaro* said: "the comedy is ended"; *Soleil* said Boulanger would soon disappear without a trace, "Like the wake of a ship in the open sea"; *Gaulois* (which had supported Boulanger) said derisively: "Bon soir, Monsieur." See Elio Zorzi, *L'Avventura del Generale Boulanger: Storia di una rivoluzione mancata 1886-1891* (Verona, 1937), p. 307. Cf. Alexandre Zévaès, *Au temps du boulangisme* (5th ed.; Paris, 1930), p. 166 and *passim*.

this end. Although the attacks of the antirepublicans had been going on from the beginning of the Third Republic, they were now reaching a climax. The question of a monarchical restoration threatened not only to split the Church but to nullify the social movement. The specter of a monarchist plot supported by antirepublican Catholics would have to be removed. Leo XIII chose a prelate in Africa to express his views.

Cardinal Lavigerie, primate of Africa, renowned for his charity and for his sympathy with the Moslem people, for his establishment of homes for orphans, and for other missionary activities,[61] opened the campaign at the suggestion of His Holiness.[62] The occasion chosen was a very public one. On November 12, 1890, Lavigerie gave a formal luncheon to the staff of the French Mediterranean Squadron, together with leading army and administrative officials. In his toast to the naval guests the Cardinal expressed his pleasure at being able to entertain those who in Algeria represented the authority of France; he said the union of all citizens was the cherished wish of the Church. He recognized, he said, that it was hard to renounce old memories and old loyalties, but since the will of the French people had been clearly affirmed, the moment had come to give adherence to the constituted government, without looking back, and put an end to division among Frenchmen for the sake of France. He ended by drinking a toast to the French navy.[63] The band of the White Fathers played the "Marseillaise."[64]

Lavigerie had laid the groundwork for the public move by writing to the Minister of the Interior to be certain that no government action against Catholic schools or orders should be launched at the time, which would arouse Catholic opinion against the government at the critical moment when he was trying to win the clergy over to the support of

61. According to *Univers* (Jan. 10, 1882) Lavigerie fed Moslems and Jews as well as Catholics, for they were "also of God's flock being his creatures." He had received the Red Hat on April 17, 1882. *Ibid.* (May 21, 1882) published a sketch of his life and charities.

62. In October, 1890, Lavigerie had gone to Rome to confer with Leo XIII. See Soderini, *Il Pontificato di Leone XIII*, II, 391. The Pope spoke to him of "smashing the windows of the old parties." See Seldes, *The Vatican Yesterday—Today—Tomorrow*, p. 346.

63. Tournier, *Cardinal Lavigerie*, pp. 266 ff.

64. "This," said Leo when he heard of it, "I did not tell him to do." See Soderini, *Leo XIII, Italy, and France*, p. 209.

the Republic.[65] Even so, however, a storm of polemic ensued, the monarchists attacking the position of the Cardinal.[66] Lavigerie had said that "no authoritative voice" in France could contradict what he said. This left a loophole for the monarchist extremists; they could infer that the Cardinal was not speaking for the Pontiff.[67] The result was that many of the clergy affected to believe that they were free to be monarchist or not as they chose, but must work for the unity of the Church in carrying out its program.[68]

In reply to questions from his flock, Cardinal Richard, Archbishop of Paris, said the main question was to know "Whether France would remain Christian or cease to be so." The real difficulty, he maintained, lay in the anti-Christian sects; the faithful should not "waste their efforts in sterile political struggles," but attend to the "religious and social peril."[69] Cardinal Richard was more explicit in a letter to his diocese, in which he said the sects were dictating the legislative acts against the Church; he added: "for it is much more a doctrine than a form of government which they would impose on France." Cardinal Lavigerie was getting no assistance from anywhere, and as yet Leo XIII had not publicly supported him.[70]

65. Lavigerie to Constans, Minister of the Interior, Oct. 18, 1890. The advantage and necessity, he said, of the explicit adhesion of the French episcopate to the Republic were already recognized. It was merely a question of finding a suitable occasion. Quoted in Tournier, *Cardinal Lavigerie*, p. 285.

66. The extremists on the Left were also furious; the Church was cutting the ground from beneath their feet in giving support to the Republic. See *ibid.*, pp. 291 ff.

67. A letter from Rampolla (Secretary of State at the Vatican after Jacobini) to the Archbishop of Saint-Flour gave no specific orders, although asserting that the form of government was a matter of indifference to the Church, so long as it allowed the Church to operate in society. The letter was a reply to one from the Archbishop requesting advice. Msgr. Rotelli (nuncio at Paris) suggested that the "toast" was Lavigerie's idea. Rotelli was soon replaced by Msgr. Ferrata, who was more in sympathy with the Pope's views and more capable of understanding the dangers in the French situation, having been earlier a secretary in the Paris nunciature. See Soderini, *Leo XIII, Italy, and France*, pp. 210 f. See also Ferrata, *Mémoires*, pp. 244 f., where Rampolla's letter is reproduced.

68. *Univers* (March 21, 1891) quoted the Bishop of Carcassonne to the effect that Catholics should eliminate quarrels and unite for the Church, "while respecting, *today as yesterday* [italics in the original], personal preferences . . . for one as against another form of government." Leo's plan to speak through Lavigerie had not reached its goal.

69. *Ibid.*, March 4, 1891. Lavigerie felicitated Cardinal Richard on his letter (although he had fallen far short of the desired statement). See *Journal des Débats*, May 29, 1891.

70. Lavigerie was called by the Pope to Rome to confer, which gave the harassed Cardinal some encouragement. *Journal des Débats*, May 29, 1891.

Tension mounted between the bishops and the government. The formation of a Union of Christian France, composed of monarchists, filled the government with alarm. The French bishops were rebuked by the government, as a result of the incident at the Pantheon in Rome, for jeopardizing French relations with Italy.[71] Some bishops introduced electoral catechisms, giving voting instructions to their parishioners.

All of these developments were carefully scrutinized by the non-Catholic press. *Figaro* in a remarkable article analyzed the events, linking them with the social problem and the rise of labor: "The evolution of the Church toward the Republic is not the least curious phase of the profound travail of de-classing which is occurring among the masses, and, as a result, among the parties." Asserting that "this moment, confused and disoriented, begun in Boulangism, had not escaped the clairvoyance of the Church, which saw the ebb and flow of individuals from too high a point of vantage to lose track of the eddies there produced," the article declared that the Church understood "the power and significance" of this rise of the masses and planned to profit by it. "This wind, which the republican party had madly disspelled instead of using it to turn its mill . . . the Church is preparing to appropriate to turn its own." The writer draws into one net a series of seemingly disparate elements to explain this turn of events: patriotism, resistance to the Italian "complicity" in German plans, Lavigerie in Tunis, if necessary even an Italian republic, the social question, labor reform, the encyclical on labor, abandonment of the dynastic parties, adhesion to the Republic; one might imagine once more the union of patriotism and socialism which characterized the Boulangist movement. The "Voltarian bourgeoisie" took the "school away from the Church"; the Church is going to "have its revenge by taking the socialist workshop away from the bourgeois free thinkers."[72]

Such a result as that envisaged in *Figaro* could be attained only if the clergy followed the pacific advice of the Pontiff. This they had not yet done, refusing to admit that any directions had come from the Holy See. Meanwhile the situation was becoming worse. It was reaching the

71. The Archbishop of Aix sent a heated reply and was fined 300 francs. For the incident at the Pantheon, see above, p. 200.

72. Thiébaud in *Figaro*, quoted in *Univers*, July 28, 1891. The *Rerum Novarum* had come out on May 15.

point where the only choice lay between the republican policy and the clerical alliance; one must go either right or left. *Univers,* under the pen of Eugène Veuillot, said its position had never changed; it had been anchored to Catholicism. The editor quoted his brother Louis: "Wherever it [the Church] goes, we go; wherever it shall go we shall go. . . ."[73] Most of the French bishops were not of this mind. The result was not to Leo's liking; he found their intransigence more inopportune.[74]

The clerical alliance was suggesting the candidacy of a clergyman for a seat in the Chamber of Deputies. The alliance was entering the political field. *Moniteur de Rome* sought to prevent the formation of the budding Catholic party:

Is it wise [said the Roman journal], in the present circumstances to name a clergyman to the Chamber? Does it harmonize with the policy of the Pope to symbolize thus, in the eyes of France, the union, the solidarity, of the Church with a political party? To ask this question is to answer it. The Church must, more than ever, place itself above political parties and rivalries in order to fulfill its ministry of truth, peace and charity.[75]

The attempts on the part of Leo XIII to improve relations between the papacy and the temporal powers of Europe were in process of being scuttled by the French monarchists. The letters exchanged between the Pope and President Grévy a decade earlier were now for the first time brought to light and published,[76] together with quotations from *Nobilissima Gallorum gens*; they aroused much comment in the press but no shift of opinion on the part of any faction occurred.

Although a monarchist, Albert de Mun had not laid aside his interest in carrying out the message of the *Rerum Novarum.* While the State-Church quarrel was at fever pitch with accusations being publicly made only to be followed by counteraccusations,[77] he asked what Catholics were going to do about the social question:

73. *Univers,* Nov. 6, 1891.
74. The Germans thought the French were engaging in a Kulturkampf of their own. See quotation from *Journal d'Alsace* (Protestant) in *Univers,* Jan. 1, 1892.
75. Quoted in *Univers,* Jan. 2-3, 1892. Veuillot, the editor, rejected this line of reasoning. Peace was to be secured through war, or threat of war, as diplomacy well knew; one must be Catholic before everything.
76. The letters were just as *apropos* as when written. See *Journal des Débats,* Jan. 8, 1892.
77. A radical deputy said in the Chamber that an understanding between the Republic and the Church was impossible. "Monarchist regimes," he said, "served the

To hope that this crisis will pass of itself like a momentary effervescence is the height of blindness, and it is to be deplored that honest and sensible men should cherish such an illusion.

The workers today have social and political power; they seek economic power, which they have a right to possess. Remain inattentive and it will knock on your door. Then it will not be a question of knowing whether this social transformation is to be accomplished by violent means or in a pacific manner, whether it is to be revolution or evolution.

He concluded by saying that Christianity was come "to set at liberty the poor and to render him his dignity as a man."[78]

Cardinal Lavigerie in a letter to his flock mentioned the sad state of his health and his anxiety at the long trial he was undergoing; it was more than a year since the Toast of Algiers had been given at the behest of the Holy See, and still the support was far from unanimous.[79] Nevertheless, increasing pressure was being applied by Rome on the French clergy. The Archbishop of Paris received a letter from His Holiness. The normal procedure would be to publish it immediately; it was not published. The Archbishop tried to assert the right to regard it as confidential. Word leaked out as to its contents.[80]

The five Cardinals in France[81] made a declaration in the attempt to clarify the situation and allay the turmoil and confusion: ". . . in harmony with the instruction of the Holy See and Catholic tradition, we are not in any way opposed to the form of government France has adopted. We believe that the 'country has need of governmental stability and religious liberty.'[82] If we raise our voice it is to demand that the 'anti-Christian

---

Church's interests by supporting themselves on it, or they made use of it in dominating it. The Republic can accommodate itself neither to the one nor the other of these systems." Goblet in *Petite République française*, quoted in *Journal des Débats*, Jan. 19, 1892.

78. *Univers*, Jan. 18, 1892. The address was before a Catholic Association in Alhambra Hall.

79. *Journal des Débats*, Jan. 18, 1892.

80. An editor of *Éclair* talked with a "highly placed" ecclesiastic, who said Leo wanted a union of Catholics on constitutional grounds; he did not want to lose the benefits of universal suffrage; he was opposed to the idea of a Union of Christian France using known monarchists to make their speeches. It was this part of the letter that had bothered the Archbishop of Paris. See *Journal des Débats*, Jan. 19, 1892.

81. Archbishops Desprez of Toulouse, Langénieux of Reims, Place of Rennes, Richard of Paris, and Foulon of Lyons. See Soderini, *Il Pontificato du Leone XIII*, II, 415.

82. The Cardinals quote this from Cardinal Richard's "Reply to the Catholic Inquirers."

sects not pretend to identify themselves with the Republic Government, and essentially create by a congeries of antireligious laws the Constitution of the Republic.'" The promise of governmental representatives not to invade the religious domain or make any attack on the liberty of conscience was belied by recent events. "Practical atheism," the Cardinals asserted, "has become the rule of action. . . ." They must make a truce with political dissents and defend the threatened Church; they had no intention of forming a state within a state, but felt that they must resist on constitutional grounds laws that go against conscience.[83]

The declaration of the bishops was immediately analyzed[84] and commented on by the press. *Journal officielle*, comparing the declaration with recent statements made by the Count of Paris and his henchman Cassagnac ("fulminating their anathemas . . . against the Republic"), found the distance was immense; the situation of the conservatives who were loyal to the Republic would now be more bearable; they had been subjected to insult and injury; now it would be less possible to insult them in the name of religion. The question, said the journal, was one of acceptance. Would the Catholics listen to the archbishops or to Cassagnac?[85]

Siècle viewed the statement as a declaration against republicanism, with the difference that seventeenth-century Gallicanism was liberal, while "today it is ensconced in intransigence."[86] The radical press was thrown into "transports of rage," because the Extreme Left lived on "the struggle against Catholicism," having "no other policy, no other *raison d'être*; for them it is necessary that the clergy be at war with the Republic." The monarchist press preferred to view the declaration as an "attack on anti-Church legislation; in reality they were embarrassed by it."[87]

83. Declaration of the five French Cardinals, Jan. 16, 1892. Quoted in *Univers*, Jan. 21, 1892. Soderini (*Leo XIII, Italy, and France*, p. 203) says compassionately of the monarchists: "It would be unjust to say that they were monarchists first and Catholics afterwards—they had made too many sacrifices for the faith to deserve such a verdict—but it is certain that they had so identified the two causes as to render their separation difficult."

84. *Journal des Débats* (Jan. 22, 1892) approved the forthrightness of the statement but thought the Cardinals need not have said that anyone in France with an official title was an atheist—"those are big words and unfortunate exaggerations."

85. *Ibid.*

86. Quoted in *ibid.*, Jan. 23, 1892. *Débats* adds ironically: "Bossuet liberal!"

87. This is the summation by *ibid.*, Jan. 27, 1892.

Cardinal Lavigerie congratulated the Cardinals, and in more happy phraseology advised the Catholics to "make truce with dissension."[88]

The declaration brought many letters of approval. One from workers said:

And there is for us, workers, who are particularly occupied with the social question, an obligation to thank you personally, and through you the others who signed the declaration. Like you and with you we wish to lay aside these wretched party rivalries; we, like you and with you, disposed to work only for God and for France, reject all source of discord and accept in all sincerity the form of government.[89]

The clergy of France accepted, but many others remained intransigent. Leo XIII had an interview on February 14, 1892, with Henry Lorin, a prominent French sociologist, who was a member of the Union of Freiburg. In the course of the conversation His Holiness spoke emphatically: "I vow that there must be no more of these sterile quarrels which weaken you. I am of the opinion that all citizens must be united on the legal terrain. Each may keep his personal preference, but in the domain of action there is only the government which France has given itself." After a moment he went on: "The Republic is a form of government as legitimate as any other. . . ." He expressed his regret that some highly placed persons were making so difficult his efforts to secure peace and prosperity for France.[90]

Two days later came Leo XIII's letter to the French people: *Au milieu des sollicitudes*. He addressed them without any intermediary on February 16, 1892. In polished French, rather than in the customary Latin, the Pontiff stated the position of the Church: French Catholics were to support the Republic. Referring to his earlier encyclical (*Nobilissima Gallorum gens*), he reiterated his affection for the French nation and expressed his grief at certain legislative acts of recent years against the Church. He recognized two paramount duties "from which, in this life, no man can exempt himself," defense of the Catholic faith and of his native land. He was, he said, addressing his words not to "Catholics only, but all upright and intelligent Frenchmen," to "disregard all germs of political strife in order to devote their efforts solely to the pacification of

88. Lavigerie to the Archbishop of Toulouse (Desprez). *Ibid.*
89. Quoted in *Univers*, Feb. 2, 1892.
90. Soderini, *Il Pontificato di Leone XIII*, II, 420.

their country." After a theoretical analysis of religion as the foundation of the social bond and the basis of moral improvement without which "society would rise but little above the level of an aggregation of beings devoid of reason, and whose whole life would consist in the satisfaction of sensual instincts," and without which civil society might be more detriment than advantage to man, he stated that all citizens were bound to resist any attempt at "banishing God from society, thereby surely annihilating the moral sense even in the depths of the human conscience." He lauded France for her works of charity at home and the labors of the missionaries abroad, simultaneously propagating "her own renown and the benefits of the Catholic religion." Rejecting as calumnious the idea "craftily circulated" that the Church was anxious to secure *"political dominion over the State,"* he came to his principal topic: the political differences among the French with regard to the existent Republic. Various political governments, he pointed out, had succeeded one another during the century: empire, monarchy, republic. Catholics like any other citizen might prefer one type to another, but the fact remained that political power was not "found in all nations under the same form"; the form was always the combination of historical and national circumstances; individuals were "bound to accept these governments and not attempt to overthrow them"; this position had been taken by St. Peter and St. Paul from the beginning. Forms of government were not to be regarded as immutable; only the Church was to retain immutable form to the end. The changes in form might be accomplished by violent crises, followed by anarchy, necessitating the establishment of a new government—"all public order being impossible without a government"; the new government becomes the custodian of the civil power, which is itself derived from God.

Acceptance of these new governments, said Leo plainly, is not only permissible but obligatory, "being imposed by the need of the social good. . . ." The Church retains her relations with the succeeding governments, a "line of conduct" which would be "salutary for all Frenchmen"; they should not encourage political discussions. True, the Republic had shown itself animated by anti-Christian sentiments, but "one should distinguish between *constituted power* and *legislation*; the form of the government might be good and the legislation detestable, and the opposite might also be found, since the quality of the laws depends more upon the quality of these men [invested with power] than upon the form of power."

Leo XIII referred to his exchange of letters with the former head of the French state, Jules Grévy. Catholics should unite to "combat, by all lawful and honest means, these abuses of legislation." Atheism he categorized as too "monstrous an error" ever to "annihilate the consciousness in man of God's claims" and to substitute for the claims "idolatry of the State."

The letter went on to reject any thought of the abrogation of the Concordat between France and the Church; it was a bilateral pact. It also rejected the separation of Church and State, although in some cases, Leo said, such separation had some advantages. The Pontiff was confident that the elucidation of the various points in the encyclical would "dissipate the prejudice of many honest, well-meaning men, facilitate the pacification of minds, and thereby cement the union of all Catholics for the sustaining of the great cause of *Christ, who loves the Franks.*"[91]

The encyclical fell with a stunning blow on the monarchist laity in France. *Univers* published the text on February 20; on February 21 it took its stand—squarely on the Pope's side. "He to whom obedience is due," said Eugène Veuillot, the editor, "has spoken." There was no more to be said. The journal had always proclaimed itself Catholic before all else, and Catholic before all else it remained; it abandoned in a word the eulogies editorially offered to monarchism; it obeyed the order: "About face!"

Reaction of other Catholic journals was favorable and complete.[92] The republican journals went from "shouts of admiration" (*Mot d'ordre*) to the conclusion that the Pope wanted to form a Center Party (*Petite République*), pointing out that the defection from the royalist party was clear.[93] Leftist *Lanterne*, on the other hand, called the move to accept the

91. The original French version in *Univers*, Feb. 20, 1892.
92. *Monde* applauded and adhered; *Croix* said: ". . . the Pope has spoken"; *France nouvelle* stated: "Impossible henceforth to equivocate." See *Univers*, Feb. 23, 1892.
93. See quotations in *Univers*, Feb. 22, 1892. *Paix* (Opportunist) declared that there was not a "shadow of equivocation," that there could be no misunderstanding by anyone; it was a "formal condemnation" of all "monarchist agitation." *Temps* took the same view: "never had dynastic politics been so radically disavowed." *Liberté* pointed out that the party in power should administer the laws in a tolerant fashion in return, but was more likely to interpret the pacific words "in an unfavorable sense, and see in the good sentiments of the clergy merely a strategic move."

Republic a "harsh necessity," and labeled the distinction between constitutional powers and legislation a Jesuitical ruse "of which the Vatican has religiously kept the secret."[94]

The monarchist papers were divided on the subject. Imperialist *Patrie* emphasized that by legal means, on the terrain of the Republic, social and religious amelioration should be sought. Having no candidate to offer, the imperialists were already accepting the Republic, as not closing the door forever against an imperial restoration. Royalist *Autorité*, however, refused to adhere, regarding monarchists as still free to be monarchists: "Adherence to unconditional rallying to the Republic is not in any sense commanded."[95]

Another important aspect of the encyclical, making it especially significant, was brought out in *Correspondant*. As the Church had in long-past days spoken to the crowds, so now Leo XIII had spoken to the masses, using means appropriate to the new conditions of societies.[96]

French Catholics were to be divided from now on into those who rallied to the Republic—the Ralliés—and those who refused to rally, on the ground that politics was not a function of the Church.

The archbishops communicated the encyclical to their flocks, giving specific instructions as to their adherence. Desprez of Toulouse said blind submission was the more meritorious; "personal interest is effaced before that of religion and the fatherland."[97] Leo thanked the Cardinals for their replies.[98]

An unsigned Declaration of the Royal Right appeared, refusing to follow the Pope's injunctions as set forth in the encyclical. Both Albert de Mun and La Tour-du-Pin were monarchists. Both had been among the founders of the Catholic Workingmen's Clubs. La Tour-du-Pin, after the organization of the International Union of Social Studies, had given his attention more to it than to the Association of Workingmen's Clubs. He had become an Orleanist after the death of the Count of Chambord.

94. *Univers*, Feb. 22, 1892.
95. Soderini, *Il Pontificato di Leone XIII*, II, 432.
96. Feb. 25, 1892. See Soderini, *Il Pontificato di Leone XIII*, II, 421. The letter from Leo to the French had been carried in the *Petit journal*, the most widely circulated of French journals. The mass media were developing and Leo XIII was abreast of the times.
97. Quoted in *Univers*, April 18-19, 1892.
98. *Ibid.*, May 8, 1892.

Now he adhered to the Royalist Declaration, justifying that action by stating that "a government . . . without prestige" could not give "sufficient support to the realization of the profound social and political reforms" of which he, "as a Catholic," had been able to be "one of the promoters."[99] Albert de Mun, whatever his travail of spirit at breaking with the monarchists, rallied to the Republic and worked loyally to carry out the principles of the *Rerum Novarum* in the republican state. His chief concern was to improve the lot of the workingmen under the leadership of the Church.[100]

Leo's view of the continued intransigence of the royalists appeared in a letter to a French prelate who was trying to organize a Catholic Action movement. The prelate in an excess of zeal had misinterpreted the encyclical. His Holiness wrote to the Bishop: ". . . if anyone has a mission to determine the conduct which can most effectively safeguard the religious interests . . . it is the Roman Pontiff." He gave formal approbation to Albert de Mun, and confirmed the encyclical in imperative terms.[101]

This letter produced a new storm in the press. The Opportunist journals considered it a formal and absolute condemnation of Catholic Action.[102] And yet Leo XIII had not only approved but had used the Center Party in Germany as a political weapon to secure benefits for the Church. He had refused to allow the clergy in Belgium and in Spain to act politically against their respective governments. Each group held too partial a view of the situation of the Church. Leo's view encompassed all. The refusal of the intransigent royalists to heed Leo XIII's prescription was unfortunate for France. One may well conclude, indeed, with the late Federico Chabod, that the policy of Leo XIII toward France was

99. *Gazette de France*, quoted in *ibid.*, June 12, 1892. Rollet says (*Action sociale*, p. 97.) that La Tour-du-Pin in a private letter called the encyclical "majestic gibberish [*auguste bafouillage*]." *Voltaire* applauded the royalists for frankly resisting the Pope: "Between the republicans who would go along with the Pope and the royalists persecuted by him, I prefer the royalists." See *Univers*, June 15, 1892.

100. Vaussard, *Histoire de la Démocratie Chrétienne*, p. 46. Difficulties piling up in this attempt were made greater by the split between the two who had belonged to the Union of Freiburg and worked together for so long: La Tour-du-Pin and de Mun. Only workers in small establishments were being reached by de Mun. Harmel continued to organize workers in larger-scale industries. Yet in spite of the difficulties de Mun's movement lasted another decade, its end anticipating only a little the death of the Pope.

101. Leo XIII was quoting from the encyclical. Leo XIII to Amand, Bishop of Grenoble, June 22, 1892. Quoted in *Univers*, July 21, 1892.

102. *Ibid.*, July 4, 1892. Various journals are quoted.

visible proof that the Church was accommodating itself to a "marriage of reason" with the "spirit of the age."[103]

Leo XIII pursued no uniform policy in dealing with the various states. He was consistent, however, in believing that the State no less than the Church was necessary to provide for the welfare of citizens. He was willing to tolerate in some states conditions of which he disapproved, if they were conditions to which the people were accustomed and which they accepted. The Church would recognize, said Leo, any form of government to which the people gave their allegiance. Leo XIII worked with the Lutheran monarchy in Germany, the constitutional monarchy in Belgium, or the democratic government of the Third French Republic with equal good will. He would not condone conspiracy among Catholics to alter the form of government. His task, as he saw it, was not to control the State but to forward the interests of the Church.

The real enemy of the Church, in Leo XIII's view, was atheistic socialism. The socialist leaders were not subject to anathema. Verbal strictures of this sort flowed harmlessly over their heads. The Pope's weapons against them must be the Church's concern for the welfare of the laborers, in this world as in the next. The Pontiff hoped thus to stop the ears of the workers to the siren song of the Marxian prophets. To this end Leo favored state paternalism in Germany. German Catholics formed Bismarck's most consistent body of supporters in passing welfare measures. In Catholic France paternalism of employers and owners was enjoined, while the organization of labor under the guidance and blessing of the Church was promoted. Social legislation enacted by democratic majorities in Switzerland received his approval. He permitted the Belgian Catholics to form a political party.

The chief difficulty arose where those, as in France, who were most eager to help solve the social problem under the banner of the Church were the very persons engaged in the attempt to overthrow the republican form of government. To save his social program His Holiness was forced to move from mild advice to peremptory requirement that the hierarchy support the existent government. The French socialists had long since accepted the Republic and the legislative path. For the clergy to attack

103. Federico Chabod, *Storia della politica estera italiana del 1870 al 1896*, I, *Le Premesse*, 262.

the Republic was giving hostages to the enemy. As it was, tardiness on the part of many leading Catholics in carrying out the Pope's wishes resulted in unnecessarily harsh procedures adopted by the French government in laicizing public education—but the social program was saved.

In Italy, Leo's social program was less successful because of the failure of the Holy See to diagnose the political scene and come to terms with the national government. This failure will be investigated in the next chapter.

XIII. LEO XIII AND THE KINGDOM OF ITALY

"It is he who still rules in Rome; I have only the edge of the chair to sit on."[1]

KING HUMBERT OF ITALY

In the struggle *à outrance* between the Church and Marxism two powerful political forces strengthened the hands of the Church north of the Alps, but not in Italy. These forces were nationalism and democracy. They would not be at the disposal of the Church in Italy unless the Vatican and the government came to terms.

Pilgrims and visitors might come in increasing throngs to Rome to have audience with the Pope—the papacy was still the chief ornament of Rome—but the Eternal City remained during the pontificate of Leo XIII what it had been under his predecessor: a divided city. Turin was not thus divided. A magnificent exposition there, in 1884, was used as the occasion to fête a nephew of the King and Queen of Italy. The Archbishop of Turin officiated at the civil and military honors, showing deference to the royal family. The House of Savoy was, in the eyes of the Church, at Turin the most legitimate of reigning monarchs, but it was a usurper at Rome.[2] The Temporal Power continued to be the stumbling block in the relations between the Pope and the Kingdom of Italy.

Leo XIII lived in the Leonine City, outside the walls of Rome. Here were the Church of St. Peter, the tombs of the Apostles, the Vatican, and the gardens, still largely surrounded by what remained of the old walls. The area had received its name from Pope Leo IV, who had begun it,

1. Bernard Wall, *The Vatican Story* (New York, 1956), p. 50.
2. *Journal des Débats*, May 4, 1884.

and Leo V, who had reconstructed it. According to legend the bones of St. Peter were buried there.[3]

Failure to solve the problem of Rome was the gravest weakness of the pontificate of Leo XIII. This failure left the door open for the growth of revolutionary socialism in the peninsula. His Holiness recognized the validity of nationalism in France because France was as old as Gaul. That a new nation should be put together out of fragments was a phenomenon he could not understand.

When the House of Savoy had created Italy in 1861, except for Venetia and the Patrimony around Rome, France had recommended that Italy and Pius IX work out an agreement, but nothing came of the recommendation. France, in order to be rid of the responsibility for protecting Pius IX with French troops, tried again later to set up a conference of the powers to discuss the question of Rome. The powers refused to impose an agreement; one must first be worked out by Italy and the Pope, and then they would sanction it. The Italian court (at Turin) attempted in 1868 to work out a modus vivendi with the Holy See, but to no avail. The Pope was still in possession of the city of Rome and was not disposed to relinquish it. The withdrawal of the protective French troops during the Franco-Prussian war (1870) made possible the "seizure" of Rome by Italy and brought about the limitation of the Pope's territory to the Leonine City. To Pius IX the whole of Rome (and more) was rightfully his. To the Italians even the soil of the Vatican was Italian, in the same way that the land occupied by any cathedral or monastery in the peninsula was "Italian," on the principle of nationalism as a territorial concept. The proposal to leave the Leonine City to the papacy was thus unwelcome both to Pius IX (who wanted the restoration of the whole of his former possessions) and to many Italians (who wanted Italy to have the entire peninsula).[4]

A plebiscite (favorable to Italy), held in Rome before the taking over

3. See *Archives diplomatiques: Recueil de diplomatie et d'histoire* (April, May, June, 1874 [103 vols. in 112; Paris, 1861-1914]), II, 38. Twentieth-century excavation exhumed bones in the spot claimed by legend.

4. *Ibid.*, II, 37-38. On the other hand, when the nation was formed the new flags of the army were dipped while being blessed; otherwise the soldiers would not have accepted them; so the Church "looked the other way and the ceremony took place." So wrote Eugène-Melchior de Vogüé in 1887. See his "Affaires de Rome," in *Revue des Deux Mondes*, III, 820.

of the city by Italian troops, was an indication of discontent with the papal political regime which, "attentive to the things of heaven, neglected too much the good ordering of those of earth."[5] The Italian Parliament discussed and adopted the Law of Guarantees in 1871, in an attempt to settle unilaterally the question of the relations between the Kingdom of Italy and the papacy. Visconti-Venosta, Minister of Foreign Affairs, urged that the Pope be granted "jurisdictional immunity for all his residences, not out of liberality or obsequiousness," but because, exercising as he did a "jurisdiction over so great a part of their society, he *ought not to be subjected to the jurisdiction of a particular state.*" The President of the Council (Lanza) agreed: "The person of the Pontiff, recognized as sovereign, sacred and inviolable" needed to be free and independent, assured "in his residence" against any harm emanating "from any authority or jurisdiction of the state whatsoever."[6] The immunity, therefore, granted to the Pope in the Law of Guarantees was greater than that accorded to ambassadors. It even recognized, in criminal inquisitions, the right of the royal palace Tribunal to order the arrest of the King and to demand his extradition.[7] Pius IX would have none of it. He rejected the Law of Guarantees.[8] The German Emperor, William I, hoped Pius IX would accept the guarantees.[9] Visconti-Venosta wanted to keep the door open for future pacification and tranquil coexistence. When Prince Jerome (Bonaparte) urged him to "push the Pope out of Rome," the Foreign Minister replied that what he wanted was "an accord of Pope and monarchy in Rome" by a "*modus vivendi* acceptable to all."[10] Pius IX was adamant. In Rome he would be nothing other than "sovereign or prisoner." His allocution bearing this statement brought seizure of all

5. Vaussard, *Histoire de la Démocratie Chrétienne*, p. 211. Bismarck later asserted that the Italians had not entered Rome under his instructions, although they claimed to have the encouragement of his representative, Harry von Arnim. See Soderini, *Il Pontificato di Leone XIII*, II, 124. That this disclaimer by Bismarck was made when he was trying to get the Kulturkampf ended makes it somewhat suspect.

6. Soderini, *Il Pontificato di Leone XIII*, II, 92.

7. *Ibid.*, I, 94.

8. Bonghi said the Pope was right—the laws could become a dead letter. As *Nuova Antologia* put it: "Who has made can unmake." *Ibid.*, I, 97.

9. William I to Augusta, June 1, 1871, Berlin. *Vorgeschichte des Kulturkampfes*, pp. 94-95. Said William: "If the Pope does not accept the Italian Guarantees no one can help him. We shall advise him to do so."

10. Chabod, *Storia della politica estera italiana*, p. 213.

the papers carrying it, even in résumé. Pius IX asserted that this seizure proved that he was not free in Rome; Mancini (the Guard Seal) modified the ruling to prove that he was.[11]

So the city of Rome remained divided between "believing fools and unbelieving savants,"[12] as the antipapalists believed. Others realized that the Temporal Power had been a barrier standing between the Popes and religious grandeur.[13]

At the death of Pius IX there had been talk of holding the Conclave in some spot other than Rome, but the decision reached was that the customary procedure should be followed. The newly elected Leo XIII inherited, then, a quarrel with the Kingdom of Italy. He was not happy about it; he wanted the Italian people to feel that the papacy was a "great glory for Italy." To a pilgrimage of Italians received at the Vatican he said that Italy must know that "the pontificate is the first and purest glory of your fatherland" and that enduring prosperity would come only in sincere devotion to God's Vicar and "respect for the inviolability of his rights."[14] Such was his renown as a diplomat that many hoped Leo XIII would find a way out of the difficulty. This was not done. His prestige grew rapidly[15] but the gulf widened, nonetheless, between him and the Italian government.[16]

After the deplorable incident that occurred at the removal of the bones of Pius IX to their final resting place, Leo seemed more restless and disturbed.[17] He began to talk of leaving Rome, where the authorities seemed unable or unwilling to maintain order. Francis Joseph had offered asylum in 1870 to Leo's predecessor; now His Holiness wrote to the Emperor of

11. Magri, *L'azione cattolica in Italia*, I, 23.

12. Quoted in Chabod, *Storia della politica estera italiana*, p. 259.

13. This is the opinion of Egidio Vagnozzi expressed in "Leo XIII and the Problem of Human Liberty," in Gargan, *Leo XIII and the Modern World*, p. 90.

14. Gambasin, *Il movimento sociale*, p. 19.

15. Sella, in the Chamber of Deputies, said (May 14, 1881): "The influence of the Pontiff is in reality greater today in the world than when it had the Temporal Power." Quoted in Chabod, *Storia della politica estera italiana*, p. 261.

16. Bismarck remarked at the beginning of Leo's pontificate, when the papal nuncio at Kissingen attributed what was happening in Rome to the revolutionary spirit of which they were victim: "Yes, the Italians seem to want to go a long way, but then they will have a long way to come back." Quoted in Soderini, *Il Pontificato di Leone XIII*, II, 125.

17. Leo said the Catholic world must know what sort of security was left in Rome; *ibid.*, II, 53. See also Salvatorelli, *Sommario della storia d'Italia*, p. 536.

Austria mentioning the question of granting him asylum. Francis Joseph in reply said he hoped the Pope would not "be reduced to abandoning the sepulchres of the Saints Apostles" and the "Eternal City" toward which the eyes of all the world turned as to a "symbol of the unity of Our Holy Church."[18] The Emperor, nevertheless, sent Baron Hübner on extraordinary mission to Rome to discuss the matter and to offer asylum if it were really necessary.[19] Leo XIII interpreted the approaching visit of Francis Joseph to the Quirinal as evidence that Austria approved the occupation of Rome and the dethronement of the Pope.[20] He wrote again to Francis Joseph but made no mention of leaving Rome.[21]

The irreligious, the anticlericals did not throng the Pope's audiences. To this extent Leo XIII was restricted in gathering views as to the aspirations and demands of the mass of Italian people. He was also to a degree the prisoner of his entourage. But this is true of any great public figure. He did read the newspapers. He was aware of the tide of irreligion which was rising in Italy. He attributed it to materialism and indifference. Through the Italian clergy he attempted to combat this tide, addressing to them early in 1882 a letter, *Etsi Nos*.

First denouncing the error of those who represented the papacy as the enemy of the people, Leo XIII in the *Etsi Nos* proclaimed that it was actually the people's friend, at the same time being the incorruptible guardian of the doctrine without which there could be no true civilization. The perils which the Church was undergoing were particularly oppressive, he said, in Italy, where God had placed the dwelling of his Vicar "and the center of Catholic unity." He cautioned the bishops to give diligent attention to fortifying the "spirit of the people" and to surrounding them with "every manner of assistance," lest they lose "the most precious treasure, the Catholic faith"; he bemoaned the attacks on

18. Francis Joseph to Leo XIII, Sept. 13, 1881. Francesco Salata, *Per la storia diplomatica della Questione Romana*, I, *Da Cavour alla Triplice Alleanza* (Milan, 1929), 140. Hereinafter cited as *Questione Romana*.

19. Hübner reported to his government that if the Pope left the Vatican the Quirinal would be "shaken to its foundations"; if the monarch lost the Quirinal the position of the Pope would be "untenable." They needed each other. See Hübner to Kalnoky, April 26, 1882, *ibid.*, p. 169.

20. *Ibid.*, p. 172. Bismarck had already created an Austro-German alliance (1879); he was now turning it into a Triple Alliance by bringing Italy into it as third member.

21. *Ibid.*, p. 144.

the "liberty of the Church" and the efforts to "blot out from public institutions the image, the imprint of Christianity," always the source of the "glories of Italy"; he bewailed the "suppression of the religious houses," the confiscation of the property of the Church, marriages formed "outside the Catholic rites," and the removal of the "education of youth" from "religious authority." Leo expressed his regret at the loss of the principate; he deplored putting the Church under "the control and at the mercy of a foreign power [the Kingdom of Italy]." He recalled how Italy, under the leadership of the Pontiffs, had warded off the repeated "attacks of the barbarians" and stood against the "ferocious onslaught of the Turks," preserving Italy "united in a common faith." He warned that the "light of faith once extinguished," mankind usually fell into error and slipped easily down into the depths "of crass materialism." The Roman Pontiff, he insisted, "should first be put back in possession of his rights," for the attack on the Holy See was "disastrous for the cause of Italy."

Taking up the matter of how to combat pernicious influences in Italy, His Holiness continued that the clergy should "awaken the sleeping, stimulate the hesitant," encourage the founding and periodical meeting of "Christian associations" and "associations of young workers," and contribute to the institutions for the "alleviation of poverty"; he said all this should be done by every device "within the law." The clergy should also produce and publish good written works to combat with the pen the "deluge of evil books" and "journals of disorder and iniquity" which public law seemed powerless to check. A journal of instruction should be published regularly in each province of the Church, supported by contributions of the faithful, to replace the income from foundations seized by the state. He also emphasized the need of recruiting new members of the clergy, who would be virtuous, zealous, pious, and educated.[22]

One of the questions which made administration of the Church in Italy so difficult was the matter of securing governmental approval of the appointment of Church officials (the *Exequatur*). The problem arose

22. Issued on February 15, 1882, the text of *Etsi Nos* appeared in French translation in *Univers* on February 17. "The vigorous thoughts expressed in this letter, written with remarkable calm and force," were producing a "great and profound impression in Italy," according to the Roman correspondent.

because the Catholic Church was still recognized as the state church in Italy.[23] The anticlerical policies of the leftist parties controlling the government[24] used the *Exequatur* as a weapon with which to annoy the Church. Leo complained that the delay in giving approval hampered the work of the Church. He mentioned one official (Cardinal Parocchi) who for five years had vainly waited approval and had then gone to reside in Rome. The Pope asked what would happen if public authorities had to wait so long to have their administrations approved—would there not be complaint?[25]

One of the factors contributing to the growth of anticlericalism in Italy during Leo XIII's pontificate was the increase of favor shown to the Society of Jesus. It was rumored that the Pope was about to bestow the Red Hat on a Jesuit, for the first time since he had assumed the Triple Crown.[26] In 1886 he re-established all the rights of the Society, as from the beginning. This fact aroused a considerable stir in the liberal press. He also bestowed the Red Hat on his brother Joseph, a member of the Society, who was released from his perpetual vows.[27]

There was no channel of communication at the national level between the Holy See and the Kingdom of Italy. Hopes for reconciliation, early maintained by Leo, were aborted by failure of the Sacred College to support them. In the Sacred College there were three groups of Cardinals. On the right wing stood a group of extreme conservatives, the intransigents, who were clinging to the historic rights of the Church.

23. This question did not arise in countries like the United States where separation of Church and State produced no control over and no responsibility for the appointment of such officials.

24. The anticlerical Right was promonarchist, but opposed to change in social and economic fields. Had this latter group been in power, the situation would have been still more difficult for the Church.

25. Soderini, *Leo XIII, Italy and France*, p. 15. The complaint was voiced in 1882.

26. *Kölnische Zeitung*, June 1, 1886. Father Beckx, general of the Society of Jesus, was alleged to have visited the Pope regularly for two weeks, although he was old and just recovered from serious illness, and to have discussed the elevation of Mazzella, a university professor, to the cardinalate.

27. T'Serclaes, *Léon XIII*, I, 443, 520. Francesco Crispi referred to the "fever of the Temporal Power" in explaining why Leo turned more toward the Jesuits as time passed. "Leo XIII appeared," said Crispi, "during the first seven years of his pontificate, as a Thomist, subsequently a Jesuit." Leo, of course, never ceased to be a Thomist. See Adolphe Opper de Blowitz, *Léon XIII devant ses contemporains*, p. 27. Blowitz gathered estimates of Leo XIII from many prominent persons and put them together in a book when Leo was at the height of his prestige as Pope.

In their eyes everything the revolution had stood for was insupportable; the Church and the papacy were the true glory of Italy. They were opposed to monarchy, not because they were democratic but because a lay monarchy had brought Italy into being. They wanted to control the peninsula, not through the machinery of elections but through the hierarchy of the Church. This group—which had belonged to the faction of Antonelli (Joachim Pecci's opponent)—continued after the "Red Pope's" death to try to block the election of the Bishop of Perugia to the Holy See and then to thwart his conciliatory efforts toward Italy.[28] Leo XIII (certainly up to 1887) continued in spite of their efforts to hope for modification of the relations between the Vatican and the Quirinal. On the opposite wing were the conciliators, who took a realistic view of the situation. They were willing to accept the Law of Guarantees, receive the yearly stipend from the Kingdom of Italy, and live in peace.

Between these two extremes there was a middle group of Cardinals, the transigents. They were not liberals, although they were willing to go along with some liberal principles. They would be willing to relinquish even Rome in exchange for a small temporal domain, recognized as belonging to the Church, such as a portion of Rome, the Vatican to the coast at Ostia, or some other grouping. They would have preferred to keep the whole of Rome but would not insist. They were willing to take to the political path, in the interests of the Church; they pointed to the success achieved by the German Center, which the Pope had approved.[29]

One could only guess which of these groups—intransigents, transigents, or conciliators—really expressed Leo XIII's own views. In *The Intimate Thoughts of Leo XIII Confided to His Presumed Successor* (Rome, 1887), an anonymous author imagined a colloquy between the Pope and the Cardinal who should succeed him. The Pope drew a sad picture of the times—the relaxation of faith, the advance of subversive doctrines in Christendom, especially in Italy, and the question of the Temporal Power—and claimed that he was powerless to solve the latter

28. Fonzi, *I cattolici e la società italiana*, pp. 35-37.
29. Gambasin (*Il movimento sociale*, pp. 16-18, 92) analyzes these general currents in Italy. See Fonzi, *I cattolici e la società italiana*, p. 37.

problem; his pontificate was limited to the *non possumus*.[30] The volume was, of course, mere guesswork.[31]

In the government, on the other hand, the extension of the suffrage in 1882 together with the papal prescription against Catholics voting, in effect since the days of Pius IX, increased the anticlericalism of the government's policies. In 1887, as the government swung to the left, Francesco Crispi became Prime Minister.[32] He decided to hold out an olive branch to the Pope and seek an accommodation. Encouraged by the publication of a plan to create a papal zone from the Vatican to the sea,[33] Crispi entertained thoughts of solving the Roman Question to the honor of his regime as Prime Minister. Leo XIII, in Consistory, expressed his ardent desire to end the "unfortunate antagonism" without detriment to the dignity of the Holy See, "violated less by the hostility of the nation" than by the "conspiracy of the sects." A situation providing complete liberty to the Sovereign Pontiff would not only "cause no damage to the interests of Italy, but would be of powerful aid in safe-guarding her and her prosperity."[34]

Five days after the Pope's speech, Tosti, a Benedictine and Under-Archivist of the Holy See, opened negotiations with Crispi. Tosti said that in the coming year (1888) Leo XIII wanted to carry out publicly his sacred functions at St. Peter's in the customary fashion, as of old. Might he not meet the King there? The atmosphere began to thaw everywhere. In preparation for renewal of relations King Humbert had the tiara removed from the statue of Victor Emmanuel in Venice; the

30. De Vogüé, "Affaires de Rome," *Revue des Deux Mondes*, III (1887), 821-822.

31. Two years earlier a plot had been hatched to discredit and unseat Leo through the *Journal de Rome*'s constant attacks on the *Moniteur de Rome*, which carried the Pope's ideas to the outside world. The plotters had used the unsuspecting Pitra as a tool.

32. Crispi was in office from 1887 to 1891, and again from 1893 to 1896. Neufeld (*Italy*, p. 85) describes him as an Opportunist, attacking representatives of any party, Right or Left, as the exigencies of the situation seemed to demand; Neufeld says he "rolled with time and circumstances." Early in Leo XIII's pontificate Crispi had made a speech (at Palermo) lauding Mazzini and deriding the papacy as despotic. "Our Jove sat in the Vatican and his satellites on their little thrones in the peninsula," he said, and went on that the "Titan" who appeared was Mazzini who "warred against these idols. And we see them fall from their pedestals." See Francesco Crispi, *Scritti e Discorsi Politici 1849-1890* (Rome, 1890), p. 471. Leo XIII knew what Crispi had said and referred to it later.

33. Soderini, *Il Pontificato di Leone XIII*, II, 126.

34. G. Mollat, *La Question Romaine*, p. 381.

crushing of the papal tiara under the royal steed was a perpetual reminder of the triumph of the House of Savoy over the Popes. The Archbishop of Florence publicly embraced King Humbert and gave him his blessing. This blessing "came down like a dove with the olive branch of peace" upon the royal and ecclesiastical participants. Honors paid to King Humbert, Queen Margaret, and the Prince Royal by members of the clergy emphasized the "thaw" in the chill of hostility. But the King did not come to St. Peter's. According to the Law of Guarantees the Pope was not only spiritual but temporal ruler there. It would have been an act of submission going beyond religion.[35] But this is not the whole story.

Negotiations broke down and the reconciliation did not materialize. The fact is patent. No glib answer can be given as to the reason for the breakdown. The failure is attributed by some to the intervention of the Freemasons, who claimed Crispi as a member. Certainly the government anticlericals put pressure on the Prime Minister.[36] Others ascribe the failure to the machinations of the Jesuits, toward whom the Pope was turning. Perhaps the demands of the Pope were too high.[37] There were other factors involved as well, both in the Sacred College and on the international scene, as will presently appear. In the meantime the carriages of "Black" Rome continued to ignore the Quirinal while those of "White" Rome avoided the Vatican as before.[38]

When this attempt at reconciliation fell through, Crispi returned to his anticlerical program; he loudly denounced everything clerical and worked to extend still further the control of the secular government over education. Crispi's coming to power rested on the extension of the suffrage which had recently occurred. This extension practically doubled

35. Fülöp-Miller, *Leo XIII*, p. 113.

36. S. William Halperin, "Italian Anticlericalism," *Journal of Modern History*, XIX (March, 1947), 25-26. Halperin says that Adriano Lemmi, grand master of the Italian Masons, congratulated Crispi on his stand against the Curia and referred to Leo XIII as the "Pretender of the Vatican." See also Soderini, *Il Pontificato di Leone XIII*, II, 144.

37. Soderini (*Ibid.*, II, 135) mentions a letter in which Leo XIII said he was entitled to and expected to have the whole of Rome restored to him. This was, of course, far beyond anything that Crispi could offer. Soderini (II, 5) maintains that at times Leo XIII was insistent on having all of Rome but at times thought that a part would be sufficient. He wanted to be independent.

38. Fülöp-Miller, *Leo XIII*, pp. 106, 112 f.

the number of voters, even though, as Crispi said, they could "neither read, write, nor count."[39]

During the first decade of Leo's pontificate there had been slowly developing a Catholic political party, if a group could actually be called a party when it did not participate in the electoral process. This was the decade when the secretaries of state were in succession Franchi, Nina, and Jacobini, favored by the Catholic transigents. They wanted to establish a true Right (similar to the Conservative Party in England) opposed to political and economic liberalism. The developing middle class, whose rise to power the transigents intended to forestall, supported classic liberalism. This conservative group included men of title, men of landed possessions, and the transigent clergy. To this budding conservative group Leo XIII had given approval. They wanted to be able to counteract the Extreme Left and to aid in the development of a true parliamentary regime, patterned after the English system. Father Curci had given the first impetus to this development by his book: *Il moderno dissidio tra la Chiesa e l'Italia.*[40]

The breakdown of the attempted conciliation between Leo XIII and Crispi at this point made the situation worse than before, as greater rigidity developed on both sides. The Pope's demand for the whole of Rome drew from Crispi, in Parliament, these words: "We are not asking for conciliation, nor does it occur to us to do so, because we are not at war with anyone. We neither know nor care what is thought at the Vatican."[41]

Some phrases in the encyclical *Libertas praestantissimum*, issued in 1888, aroused hope among the Italian conservatives who were obeying the papal order (the *non expedit*) to refrain from participation in national elections.[42] Leo had said in the encyclical that the State might

39. *Journal des Débats*, June 30, 1888. See also Crispi, *Memoirs*, II, 515.

40. "The Modern Disagreement between the Church and Italy" (1878). See Fonzi, *I cattolici e la società italiana*, pp. 38-41. Fonzi shows how intimately Cardinals Nina and Jacobini had been involved in the formation of this group. Some of the leaders were the same ones who participated in the Roman group affiliated with the Union of Freiburg. See also Soderini, *Il Pontificato di Leone XIII*, II, 17. Soderini was himself a member of this group.

41. Mollat, *La Question Romaine*, p. 382. Crispi insisted that he was not antireligious; he had been educated in a seminary and had "written verses in honor of the Madonna." See Soderini, *Il Pontificato di Leone XIII*, II, 135.

42. Abstention had been suggested by Giacomo Margotti, approved as opportune by

tolerate some situations in order to prevent worse evils from arising. This seemed tacitly to suggest that the Holy See might also tolerate situations it did not approve. Leo added that it was lawful to seek a change of government under unjust repression, but it should not be done violently. The encyclical adds that the Holy See did not "disapprove of democracy," or "participation in government"; it did not condemn "seeking national independence" or "self-government"; this was to be accomplished "without violation of justice."[43] To the Italian Right this portion of the encyclical seemed to open once more the door to hope for participation in politics at the national level.[44] The Pope had to state again that he was not lifting the *non expedit*. The situation degenerated still further. Rumors began to be circulated that the Pope was to be made a simple citizen. This would be brought about by ceasing to recognize extraterritoriality for the Vatican. If this were carried out, contracts entered into by the Holy See would have to undergo the same regular formalities of registration as any others.[45] Although Crispi doubtless had no intention of going so far, he was proceeding rapidly with the laicization of the state.[46]

While all this had been going on in the anticlerical war, a measure was under discussion which would alter the administration of the Italian municipalities, heretofore run by moderate liberals of various sorts. The new law would put them under the radicals (Left of Center).

---

the Holy See in 1868, confirmed by the Holy See (Pius IX), and interpreted by Leo XIII as a duty of conscience in 1886. See Gambasin, *Il movimento sociale*, p. 46. According to Soderini (*Il Pontificato di Leone XIII*, II, 14) Leo XIII asked whether it might not be better to suppress the *nè eletti, nè elettori*, and thus carry the battle into the political field. *Civiltà Cattolica* favored this view. Leo XIII had tended as a Cardinal before election to favor it.

43. It was this portion of the encyclical which had aroused the factions among the French.

44. *Journal des Débats*, July 2, 1888.

45. Auguste Roussel, "La Question romaine," *Univers*, July 11, 1888.

46. *Ibid.*, July 25, 1888. The Paris journal stated the belief that the purpose of Crispi's campaign was to oblige Leo XIII to capitulate and accept, in fact if not in law, the Law of Guarantees. In the final session of the Italian Chamber (July 24, 1888) all was confusion; no one knew what question was being voted on. A liberal journal of Milan said: "Some are afraid of the clericals, the others of the republicans; all are afraid of the government. True principles are unknown." Quoted in *ibid.*, July 27, 1888.

This law would still further lessen the influence of the clergy as well as of the liberal Catholics, who were participating in local politics. In the country districts the clergy were also losing control.[47]

In the midst of this apparently inextricable tangle of cross purposes and events one significant fact may perhaps provide a clue to aid in unraveling the affair. A new force was present in the Sacred College. The new force was Cardinal Rampolla, who succeeded Jacobini as Secretary of State in 1887.[48] Rampolla subordinated other problems to the question of foreign policy. To the foreign policy of the Vatican he brought a revolutionary change, redirecting it toward solidarity with France. Incidents before his appointment had laid the foundation on which he built: the French invasion of Tunisia in 1881, the breaking of the commercial treaties between Italy and France in 1887, and the resulting economic war with France. In 1882 Italy had become a member of the Triple Alliance, joining Germany and Austria. In 1887 Italy signed a renewal of the treaty (and subsequently at five-year intervals until World War I) and broke her commercial ties with France. Crispi's stepping up of the ensuing economic war hurt France slightly but was ruinous to Italy.[49]

It was Rampolla's intention to make use of the situation and tie the Holy See to France, not to republican France but to monarchist-clerical France. The star of Boulanger was rising rapidly.[50] If war should erupt between France and Italy the armies of France would restore the Temporal Power to the Pope.[51] The Pope's new Secretary of State had no desire to see relations improve between the Pope and Italy. He was

47. *Journal des Débats,* June 30, 1888. *Débats* said that those who ceased to be governed by the Church became socialists, not moderates, nor republicans, nor liberals.

48. Gambasin (*Il movimento sociale,* p. 91) says that the "political line of the intransigents was accented, at the advent of Rampolla to the position of Papal Secretary of State."

49. Neufeld, *Italy,* p. 87.

50. Luigi Salvatorelli, *La politica della Santa Sede dopo la guerra,* in *Manuali di Politica Internazionali* (Milan, 1937), p. 10.

51. Albert de Mun told Soderini that France, whether monarchist or not, might give advice displeasing to Italy about assuring the Pope's liberty "but to speak of a war to re-establish . . . the Temporal Power would be a folly that a Sovereign, however Catholic, would not be able to commit. . . ." See Soderini, *Il Pontificato di Leone XIII,* II, 277.

hostile to Germany and Austria[52] and their alliance with Italy. Leo XIII began once more to talk of leaving Rome.[53]

Rampolla sent out a circular to the Catholic powers, pointing out the dangers of the Pope's situation, threatened by radical and sectarian elements. Even his person, it was alleged, was not safe from attack.[54] Francis Joseph was asked whether he would give Leo hospitality, and whether, if it should become necessary, the Conclave to elect Leo's successor could be held in territory belonging to His Majesty.[55] Baron Hübner went to Rome to discuss the matter with His Holiness. Leo XIII seemed less fearful for his personal security and the security of the Vatican Palace than the circular had indicated. Hübner found the Pope, however, thinking of holding an international convention, in the interest of making his position more secure. Hübner discussed this with Rampolla. "Do you believe," asked Hübner, "that bands of armed troops or ill-intentioned besiegers attacking the pontifical palace would be stopped before the display of some flags?" Rampolla was nonplussed. Hübner had a second audience with His Holiness, laying before him one objection after another to any thought of the Pope's departure from Rome. The offer of asylum from Austria seemed extremely reluctant.[56]

The general opinion in France was that the Pope's position was daily becoming more intolerable.[57] The growing intensity of the Boulanger crisis, filling all the papers, coupled with the widespread French concern over the welfare of the Pope, however thin the justification for such concern, produced a highly explosive situation. This dangerous condition persisted. France was moving toward alliance with Russia to offset the alliance of Italy with France's "enemies."[58]

52. Rampolla's candidacy for the Triple Crown was vetoed by Austria at the next Conclave, held at Leo XIII's death.

53. Crispi (Memoirs, III, 399) understood that pressure was being brought to bear at the Vatican to prevail upon the Pope to leave; Leo XIII was undecided, but the pressure would continue.

54. Salata, Questione Romana, p. 180. The circular was dated June 29, 1888.

55. Ibid., p. 181.

56. Ibid., pp. 194-197.

57. Journal des Débats, June 30, 1888.

58. Germany, of course, was meant primarily; Austria, only because of her alliance with France's chief foe. The French Foreign Minister had made the point clear (at the end of 1887) to the papal nuncio in Paris that a reconciliation between the papacy and Italy redounding solely to the credit of Italy (allied with France's enemies) would be unwelcome. See Soderini, Il Pontificato di Leone XIII, II, 125.

Leo XIII was disturbed at the same time (1888) by the news of an impending visit of Emperor William I of Germany to King Humbert of Italy. Matters were made still worse in the following spring by the erection of a statue to Giordano Bruno[59] within sight of the Vatican grounds. It was not merely the erection of the statue but the celebration which accompanied it—with banners, un-Christian effigies, and throngs of people—which so offended the Holy Father. Talk of the Pope's departure flared up as a result.

Crispi received news (he says from many sources) to the effect that France was seeking a pretext to break with Italy and was putting pressure on the Vatican to persuade the Pope to leave Rome. Lefèbvre de Béhaine was authorized to promise (according to Crispi's information) that if His Holiness would change his residence the French "would assume the entire responsibility for the 'Roman Question.' "[60] So the Italian Minister sought out Cardinal Hohenlohe. He discussed the situation with the prelate, saying that he could offer no advice to the Pontiff; as long as he stayed in Rome he would be protected. "By casting himself into the arms of France," Crispi went on, "Leo XIII has greatly benefited the Eastern Church. The Orthodox creed is gaining ground to the detriment of the Catholic. France has allowed Russia to manage things in the East, and Russia's influence there is ever on the increase. The Pope is unaware of these events, which are concealed from him because there are many whose interest it is to hide them."[61] At Crispi's request Cardinal Hohenlohe promised to seek an audience with the Pope. Rampolla said the Pope would not be able to grant an interview, alleging the Pope's health as the reason for the refusal. Thereupon Cardinal Hohenlohe wrote a letter which was delivered in person to His Holiness through the Pope's valet, not passing through Rampolla's hands. Hohenlohe's letter stated: ". . . the Church will remain unable to recover the Temporal Power. The welfare of many souls demands that we accept the inevitable. . . ."[62]

59. Bruno had been excommunicated and burned at the stake in Rome in 1600 by the Inquisition. The statue was unveiled on June 10, 1889. *Ibid.*, II, 161.
60. Crispi, *Memoirs*, II, 393 n.
61. *Ibid.*, II, 400 f.
62. *Ibid.*, II, 403. Hohenlohe also told the Pope that when he had written asking for an audience he had received a (rude) [word crossed out] reply from Rampolla. At any

An Italian deputy was sent by Crispi on a mission to Bismarck. He reported to the Minister that Bismarck felt sure the Pope would not leave Rome; papal prestige rested on "history and tradition"; outside of Rome the Pope would not be the "representative of a powerful institution . . . but a species of 'Shah of Persia, traveling about Europe at other people's expense.'" Bismarck thought he would be an "embarrassing guest," and especially to France.[63]

The Pontiff was put under constant watch to see that he did not slip away, although the Italian government affected not to be concerned: "Let the Pope remain or depart; it is a matter of complete indifference to us."[64] If the Pope did take his departure from Rome as a result of a war involving Italy it would split Rome into two completely separate factions: Italian and papal. The clerical view of the stepping up of the anticlerical measures was that Italy, backed by Austria as a member of the Triple Alliance, felt strong enough to disregard the wishes of the Catholic conservatives,[65] who could not exhibit any political weight because of the *non expedit*. The stir over the possible departure of His

---

rate, through these devious channels Crispi's view was expressed that the Pope might leave if he wished, and would be safeguarded and escorted, but that if he went he would never set foot in Rome again. When Leo sent Msgr. Salua to explain to Hohenlohe that he could not grant him an audience, Hohenlohe told the emissary that Leo should appreciate the fact that it was he, Hohenlohe, who was responsible for his ever becoming Pope in the first place, by persuading Pius IX to make him a Cardinal. *Ibid.*, II, 406.

63. *Ibid.*, II, 415. There was talk of the Pope's going to Spain. The Municipal Council of Seville invited him. See *Univers*, Aug. 2, 1889. The German Ambassador to Spain reported to Bismarck that Leo XIII was "daily expected." The Ambassador was admonished to stop reporting such "rubbish." *Univers* (Aug. 8, 1889) said England was disposed to offer Malta to the Pope as a refuge.

64. "Le Pape sous la surveillance," *Osservatore Romano*, quoted in *Univers*, Aug. 3, 1889. The Italian journal said that not only guards were watching but that carriages were also standing guard, lest the Pope drive away. Doubtless the writers in the Italian journal remembered the escape of Pius IX during the Risorgimento.

65. Domenico Farini, president of the Senate from 1887 to 1898, belonging to the constitutional Left, opposed this turn toward France. He was convinced that the Vatican was involved in the matter; "the Pope, France, and Russia, there is a new Triple Alliance," he wrote in 1891. See F. Boyer's review (Domenico Farini, *Diario di fine secolo*, ed. E. Morelli [2 vols.; Rome, 1962]) in *Bulletin de la Société d' Histoire Moderne*, 12th ser., No. 24 (1962), p. 17. Farini thought Italian unity was threatened by the clericals, the Francophiles, and the decentralizers. Anna Ginsburg, reviewing the same work (in *Rivista storica italiana*, LXXV-III [1963], 674), mentions Farini's linking of the Roman Question to Italy's adhesion to the Triple Alliance; their allies would be the very ones who would be "embroiling Rome" if Italy were not a member.

Holiness presently subsided, but it was likely to recur whenever the Triple Alliance was up for renewal.

In the struggle between the Pope and Italy, Leo's relations with other nations produced a constant anticlerical reaction in the peninsula. The Pope himself attributed anticlericalism to the Freemasons.[66] He had earlier condemned the lodges in the encyclical *Humanum genus.* According to *Civiltà cattolica* Crispi was making use of the publications of the Freemasons in his parliamentary debates on the subject of the occupation of Rome. Leo XIII thereupon had all the documents dealing with the subject assembled from the archives and put together to form a statement giving the exact situation. These documents included diplomatic notes, confidential information, and letters of sovereigns and ministers.[67]

The quarrel with Italy showed no sign of abating. At the beginning of 1890 Leo XIII issued an encyclical on the nature of man's primary allegiance, the *Sapientiae christianae.*[68] It was a bold statement on the nature of citizenship, and it was open to a variety of interpretations as to its application to specific circumstances. The encyclical said that each individual was a citizen of his state but was also a citizen of his heavenly fatherland. It was to the latter that he owed his primary allegiance. The citizen, said Leo, is not to obey unjust laws; disobedience in that case is a virtue; one may rightly suffer death in defense of his country; how much more should one be willing to endure for his soul's fatherland; "It is better to obey God than man."[69] The State has force; the Church has none, but "nothing is weaker than force when not supported by religion."[70]

Although the basic thesis of this encyclical would be unhesitatingly accepted by every theist, it obviously did not spell out in detail the

66. Schmandt ("The Life and Work of Leo XIII," in Gargan, *Leo XIII and the Modern World,* p. 23) says Leo overlooked nationalism.

67. No decision had been reached by the Pope as to how much of this was to be made public. *Civiltà cattolica,* quoted in *Univers,* Nov. 1, 1889.

68. *Univers* (Jan. 21, 1890) published the French version after the Latin text. For the English version, see Gilson, *The Church Speaks to the Modern World,* pp. 245-272. Although addressed to the faithful everywhere, it had special force in Italy, where Leo regarded himself as harassed.

69. "*Obedire oportet Deo magis quam hominibus.*"

70. "*. . . vis autem valde est infirma, praesidio religionis detracto.*"

occasions which demanded rebellion against authority.[71] It was this fact which left it open to different interpretations.

Bismarck retired from office in 1890. Neither the new Emperor nor any of those who inherited Bismarck's seat without falling heir to his power could play the subtle game of diplomacy with the skill of the Iron Chancellor. As long as his hand was at the helm the vague possibility of German intervention on Leo's behalf was left hanging. When the Kulturkampf was ended Bismarck made no move to intervene,[72] but he never actually closed the question. His retirement meant the end of any such dangling hope.[73] The realization on the part of Italy that they had nothing to fear from Germany cemented the friendship between the two monarchies. This friendship remained firm in spite of the chilling winds that from time to time swept over Italian relations with Austria, the third member of the Alliance.[74]

Relations between Italy and France continued to experience mercurial changes, as the lay monarchists in France, even after Leo XIII's warning, *Au milieu des sollicitudes,* continued to plot to overthrow the French Republic. With every rumor of monarchist plot in France the Italians were chilled. All attempts to settle colonial Mediterranean disputes were tinged with the question of the relation between the non-Ralliés in France and the Temporal Power.[75] Bank failures in Italy were attributed to the economic policies of France and the resulting conflict between the two states. Italians also resented (in 1893) the killing of

71. The encyclical should not be read as an isolated document but in connection with the letters written by Leo XIII to various groups of bishops warning them that rebellion was not always the proper response to a situation which they regarded as wrong. Note especially the letter to the Belgian bishops, *Licet multa,* the *Cum multa* to the Spanish bishops, and the *In plurimis* to the Brazilian bishops. This last has not received any attention here since it is not germane to the subject of this study.

72. Bismarck, expressing Prussian sympathies for the person of the Pope and desires for his independence, said the German cabinet could not "create difficulties for Italy." See Mollat, *La Question Romaine,* p. 363.

73. William II refused to support the idea of intervention. It would have destroyed the Triple Alliance even to discuss it. The Center Party saw this, and one of its members (Lieber) stated categorically in debate in the Reichstag that the Party was not thinking of claiming the independence of the Holy See at the risk of compromising the Triple Alliance. See Agence Havas dispatch, Dec. 14, 1892. *Univers,* Dec. 16, 1892.

74. For this aspect of the problem, see William C. Askew, "The Austro-Italian Antagonism," Wallace and Askew, eds., *Power, Public Opinion and Diplomacy,* pp. 172-183.

75. A Mediterranean accord was reached in 1902, the year preceding Leo XIII's death.

Italian imported laborers at Aigues-Mortes.[76] Relations were further strained between Italy and France by the Spanish clericals' support to the idea of restoring the Temporal Power. The question was openly discussed in the Spanish Cortes.[77]

When the King of Portugal (Don Carlos) planned to visit the King of Italy (1895), Crispi was informed that if he did so the papal nuncio to Portugal would be recalled and that diplomatic relations between the Vatican and Portugal might be broken. When Don Carlos, therefore, hesitated, Crispi threatened to recall the Italian Ambassador to Portugal if the expected visit were not carried out. The visit was canceled.[78]

There was a possibility, suggested by some, that democratic republicanism might provide a solution in Italy[79] as it was doing in France. The Pope supported the French Republic; why might he not support such a movement in Italy? The nation of Italy had despoiled him of his possessions (he said, of his freedom). The new Italian state had adopted democracy. Now, these advisers pointed out, the conservatives were his only defenders there, and it was these conservatives who despised democracy and remained aloof from national politics; the French republican statesmen whom Leo was supporting would never take up his quarrel with the Italian state or intervene to restore the Temporal Power; a remnant only of the French was committed to their program of intervention.[80]

76. Salvatorelli, *Sommario della storia d'Italia,* p. 564.

77. T'Serclaes, *Léon XIII,* I, 366.

78. Crispi, *Memoirs,* I, 225-227. Germany's attitude toward Portugal cooled as a result, and the visit of Don Carlos to Berlin brought only a simple reception at Potsdam—dinner and the opera. The opera was *Rienzi.* The German Emperor "enjoyed the opportunity of showing his guest Rome upon the stage." A delicate rebuff! *Ibid.,* I, 241.

79. Leroy-Beaulieu quotes (1892) what he had said a decade earlier in *Revue des Deux Mondes:* ". . . at the risk of scandalizing the papacy one might almost predict for it a republican evolution. Just as in the Middle Ages it often became the ally of the free boroughs against the emperors north and south, so it may some day follow the advice it refused to accept from Lamennais, and 'forsake the kings for the people'; go over, with the poor and lowly children of Christ, to democratic politics . . . nothing would prevent the Holy See from adopting the tactics . . . and turning to account the interests of the disinherited classes, of advocating before the world the economic renovation of our old societies, while preaching Christian fraternity." See his *The Papacy, Socialism and Democracy,* p. 37.

80. Chabod, *Storia della politica estera d'Italia,* p. 260. Chabod asserts that the more politically astute Italians did not think that the downfall of the monarchy would destroy the papacy; rather, that the papacy would remain and find a way to accommodation more

When in 1894 the Catholics in Rome, permitted to vote in local
elections, cast their ballots for the exposition to be held the following
year marking the twenty-fifth year since the seizure of the city by the
Piedmontese House of Savoy, Leo was much hurt.[81] He took it as a
personal affront. The hopes of the Catholics that he would be ready,
after a quarter of a century in which the national government had
weathered the storms, to recognize it as an accomplished fact, were
dashed by his refusal to alter his position. He refused to set aside the
non expedit.[82]

Leo XIII was even being criticized in some quarters for the damage
done to the Church by his preoccupation with the question of the
Temporal Power. The *Contemporary Review*, mentioning this damage,
observed: "Leo XIII considers Catholics as being exclusively members
of a Church and does not want to remember that they are citizens of
a state"; the article went on to call to mind how the Pope "ordered"
the German Catholics to vote for the military bill, in order to support
his policy with respect to the German government. *Civiltà cattolica* re-
butted this statement, insisting that the Pope "desired" but had not
"ordered" them to vote.[83]

All of this interfered with the development of a Catholic social program in Italy.[84] It is true that the group of Catholic social scientists
authorized by Leo XIII in Italy, which had become part of the International Union of Social Studies, had studied and written about the

---

easily under a republic than under the monarchy. Mistaken also, he insisted, were those
who identified the power of the Church with the Temporal Power.

81. In actuality the power of the papacy had grown during the twenty-five years since
the loss of the Temporal Power. "Catholics should rejoice at their loss," said Nitti, whose
work was published in the year of the exposition, "as at one of their victories." He spoke
of the lack of independence of the papacy before, of how the larger powers could occupy
Rome and threaten the reigning Pope, even to the point of making him act "contrary to
his convictions." See Nitti, *Catholic Socialism*, p. 385.

82. Leo XIII sent a notice to Cardinal Parocchi on May 14, 1895. See Fonzi, *I cattolici
e la società italiana*, p. 81. At the Catholic Congress of Milan (1897) the decision to support
abstention from politics was reaffirmed. Giambattista Valente's new *Il Popolo Italiano* and
Romolo Murri's new *Cultura sociale* both supported this, and insisted on social action and
political intransigence based on rigid abstentionism. See Fonzi, pp. 83-84.

83. *Univers* (Dec. 23, 1892) quoted *Civiltà cattolica*, which in turn had quoted and
editorialized on the *Contemporary Review*.

84. Leo Valiani ("L'azione di Leonida Bissolati è il revisionismo," *Rivista storica italiana*,
LXXI-IV [1959], 659) says that social action actually "oscillated invariably between
gradualism and extremism . . . ," but most of this occurred after Leo XIII's death.

social problem. They instituted a series of Social Studies Conferences[85] in which problems were discussed in depth. They realized the necessity of a network of organizations which could discuss and carry out reforms. They made a beginning and laid the foundations for a Catholic social movement.[86] Its progress was, however, slow. It maintained its anti-socialist and antisyndicalist platform, emphasizing instead mutual aid and consumer and producer co-operatives, with owners and workers in the societies, and all under ecclesiastical leadership and control.[87] The clergy and the upper classes, generally, disapproved of the workers' forming organizations exclusively of their own class; they did not want the evolution of labor organization to become social revolution. After 1890, as the growth of socialism became marked, the workers themselves tended to cast sheep's eyes at the *syndicats*, seeing in them a greater chance for rapid improvement in their economic status.[88] The fact that Leo XIII in the *Rerum Novarum* had advocated the formation of Christian organizations of owners and workers, or of *workers alone*, did give some encouragement to the rise in recruitment of members in the Catholic organizations, but they did not keep pace with the growth of socialism.[89]

The tie between political intransigence and social action was made explicit in the career of Romolo Murri. Having founded a University Catholic Circle in 1894 and having adhered to the *Opera dei Congressi* at Fiesole, he set up a Federation of Catholic Circles and after 1898 made his journal (*Cultura sociale*) the center of a Catholic group embracing adults as well as youths. He clung to the quarrel between Church and State, which he regarded as the struggle between the "Christian conception of life and civilization and the modern pagan and materialistic view. . . ."[90]

Leo XIII continued to attribute all government anticlerical measures,

85. They used the term "Social Studies Weeks" (*Settimani sociali*).
86. Mira, "Il movimenti sociali di ispirazione cattolica," *Nel LXX Anniversario della "Rerum Novarum,"* p. 86.
87. By 1891 there were 284 such societies (practically all being of the mutual aid variety); they were concentrated in northern Italy. See Neufeld, *Italy*, pp. 355 f.
88. *Ibid.*, p. 356.
89. Mutual aid societies grew from 274 (1891) to 825 (1903). They had thus tripled by the year of Leo's death. See *ibid.*, p. 357.
90. Gambasin, *Il movimento sociale*, pp. 465 f.

as well as the government's failure to take action in the solution of the social problems, to the activities of the "sects." In 1890, to a group of Italian pilgrims, he delivered a discourse in which he made the accusation specifically. "The acts which near and far touch the Church and religion," he said, "are made under the direct inspiration of the sects which all obey. . . ." He specifically inveighed against Crispi, the new code (Zanardelli), and other measures "being prepared."[91]

The anticlericalism of the Italian government was stepped up in intensity. At the beginning of 1898 circulars were sent out by Prime Minister Rudinì to the prefects, stating that any gathering of political nature held in a church must be restrained "as capable of disturbing the public peace." Associations and clerical circles were to be "considered and treated as subversive."[92] The moderates as well as the intransigents were annoyed and alarmed by the harshness of these new measures. A prominent Italian moderate, interviewed by the New York *Herald* of Paris, put it in these words:

The Roman Question, the eternal Roman Question, which short-sighted politicians foolishly believed so easy to combat . . . is at the bottom of all the present difficulties of Italy. Until it is resolved we shall never have internal peace . . . it is a question of life or death for the nation. . . . The greater part of my compatriots [he stated without endorsing] will tell you that the papal question . . . has been and is still, the cancer of Italy.

Because of the prohibition . . . against taking part in legislative elections an enormous conservative force is kept out of active politics, to the great profit of the advanced parties, socialist and republican, who are taking its place. . . .

[The clerical party] cannot be viewed simply as a religious party, as it would be in France or any other country; its anti-dynastic and anti-unitary principles tend to make it regarded by the government as a political enemy. [This is why] its circles have been closed and its parish committees dissolved, [yet] the papacy has never been more powerful than at the present hour. . . . If we had listened to its just demands in all purely religious questions . . . would we have had to fight with bayonets generations of atheists, as one has observed at the head of all disturbances in the streets of Italy?[93]

91. *Ibid.*, pp. 43 f.
92. Fonzi, *I cattolici e la società italiana*, p. 84.
93. New York *Herald* (Paris edition), quoted in *Univers*, June 4, 1898. Although the person interviewed was not identified, it was obvious that it was Visconti-Venosta, who had just withdrawn from the government because of unwillingness to support anti-Catholic laws proposed by the new minister, Zanardelli. The election had taken place on May 8.

Those who stood with Leo XIII on the Roman Question were the rich and mighty. The fact that the question remained unsettled split the liberally minded Catholics, who were interested in reforms, from those who remained entrenched in their privileged social and economic position. Both the Kingdom of Italy and the social program of the Pontiff were weakened by this situation. The result was to leave the field free for the socialists. They had had their own *non expedit* earlier. The Marxian socialists had eventually adopted a program of political participation. This greatly strengthened the Left without any counter-balancing on the Right, which alone continued to abstain.[94] The total effect of all these differences of view was an important factor in the prevention of or delay in taking adequate steps toward the solution of the social question. In consequence, the condition of the poor went from bad to worse.

The fact that the progress of democracy was more delayed in Italy than north of the Alps cannot be laid entirely either at the feet of the socialists nor of Leo XIII and his *non expedit*. A great deal of it was due to lack of education and to general poverty. Any path of modera-tion would have little chance of success. A chastened Crispi, who had returned to office in 1893, concluded that the basic question was the moral collapse of society and that the only strength lay in the two extremes, the wealthy and irreligious bourgeoisie on the Right and the atheistic masses on the Left.[95] The intransigents among the clergy would not support any efforts of Leo to alter the situation. The Far Right would not budge; the socialist Left used its political position to obstruct and prevent the orderly processes of legislation. One of the results of this impasse was to make genuine reforms slow and difficult and to dis-credit democratic processes.[96]

94. Mira, "I movimenti sociali di ispirazione cattolica," *Nel LXX Anniversario della "Rerum Novarum,"* p. 83.

95. Fonzi, *I cattolici e la società italiana*, pp. 76 f.

96. An entirely different point of view is expressed by one Italian writer who points to the fact that a Catholic party, free to participate in elections, would, had it emerged, have been controlled by the most conservative element in Italian Catholic society, joining forces with the reactionaries who were religiously indifferent. These, together with the reactionary element of the clergy and supported by those moderates who objected to the harshness of the anticlerical measures of the Left, would have dominated the Chamber of Deputies; this would have prevented the rise of any real democracy. See Fonzi, *I cattolici e la società italiana*, pp. 124-126. There is much to be said for this point of view. It would be impossible to prove.

It is possible to argue (but impossible to prove) that under the wise guidance of Leo XIII (had he accepted the Kingdom of Italy) democracy, nationalism, and concrete reforms might have acted as a deterrent against the rise of socialism, might have softened it and turned it into more moderate channels, and might have met some of the workers' most urgent demands and thus closed their ears to the promises of the protest groups. If this were true, then here, as in international affairs, insistence upon the Temporal Power was exacting a heavy toll. Leo XIII did not take this path of accommodation. On August 5, 1898, he addressed an encyclical to the clergy and people of Italy. Referring to Italy as "some countries of Italy," he complained of the attacks on the Catholic welfare societies; he recognized that they were considered subversive because they opposed the present Italy; they would not conspire against the government, even though they resented it, and hoped to see Rome restored to the Pope.[97]

There was no yielding on either side. The Pope wanted a piece of land that was not subject to any national power; Italy feared the alienation of any foot of soil that had been won with such difficulty in the Risorgimento.

A possible solution, bypassing some of the difficulties produced by this situation, was proposed during Leo's lifetime. It did not come to light until the death of the Cardinal Vicar Parocchi. It had been suggested in 1887 that the King of Italy cede a piece of land belonging to the royal estates: Castle Ponziano. In a conversation between the Chaplain and Cardinal Parocchi the feasibility of the idea was discussed; an avenue could be constructed bridging over the Roman streets to St. Paul's, which belonged to the Pope, thence easily to the hunting lodge, Castle Ponziano, and from there to the sea. Royal assent would be easy to secure; the difficulty would be to obtain Leo's approval. This might be managed, however, in view of the general situation and the realization that the present arrangement could not go on forever. This plan would offer a middle way between turning Rome over to the Pope

97. *Univers*, Aug. 9, 1898. Anna Ginzburg (reviewing Farini's diary in *Rivista storica italiana*, LXXV-III [1963], 672) quotes Farini's words to Crispi: ". . . the clergy are invading the municipalities; they are trying to take possession of the schools and charity: the brain and the stomach. What is left for the Government?"

(which is what Leo meant by "solving the Roman Question") and the Pope's relinquishing his rights to the Italian government. The Pope felt that he could not yield to Italy without risking loss of acceptance as Head of the Church, to become a sort of "glorified chaplain" of the Italian monarch. An advantage of the new proposal would be to permit the Pope to view the world with his own eyes and not through the eyes of the narrow circle of prelates who surrounded him.

One interesting aspect of this new proposal was its appeal to history, but in an unusual way. It was argued that the papacy had not been established because the Pope owned Rome (the Donation of Constantine never having existed) but because of the recognition accorded from all Christendom of the pre-eminence of the See of Peter and Paul. The essential thing was to be dissociated from the Kingdom of Italy. The proposed solution would break the connection between the papacy and the secular kingdom to their mutual advantage. It would be possible then to put into effect the Law of Guarantees passed in 1871. As proof of the feasibility of the plan, reference was made to the independence of San Marino and of the Principality of Monaco, surrounded, respectively, by Italy and France.[98]

Nothing came of the attempt to work out this way of moderation between the Italian government and the Church, and in any case, as far as Leo XIII was concerned, it was now too late. His days were nearly over. He was to remain "Prisoner of the Vatican" to the end.

98. See *Frankfurter Zeitung* (4th A.M. ed., Jan. 21, 1903) for an editorial quoting and commenting on an article by Achille Fazzari in *Patria*, which rehearsed the story of what happened when the two Catholic prelates had engaged in what seemed a very hopeful conversation. For the Law of Guarantees (*Legge per le guarentigie delle prerogative del Sommo Pontefice e della Santa Sede e per relazioni dello Stato colla Chiesa*), see Hubert Bastgen, *Die Römische Frage; Dokumente und Stimmen* (2 vols.; Freiburg, 1918), II, 68 ff.; F. Scaduto, *Guarentigie e relazioni tra stato e chiesa* (Turin, 1884), pp. 240 ff., which gives the entire text, and Andrea Piola, *La Questione Romana nella storia e nel diritto* (Padua, 1931), p. 41.

XIV. REVISIONISM: GER-MANY AND BELGIUM

"They have 'drunk much water with their wine.'"[1]

WILLIAM LIEBKNECHT

The German Marxists dominated the socialist movement from the time of the Hague Congress of the First International (1872) until the death of Leo XIII (1903). Having eliminated Bakunin's followers from that Congress by controlling the validation of credentials, Marx and Engels had taken a major step toward making the Marxist doctrine prevail. During the succeeding two decades of struggle within the different nations, recognition of Marx as founding father and acquaintance with his written works gradually extended throughout western Europe.

By the decade of the nineties, with the Second International an accomplished fact, the situation looked bright for international Marxian socialism. New editions or translations of the works of Marx and Engels continued to appear in an expanded area. The triumph of Marx's ideas and program seemed assured. At least the Marxist words were there; something, however, was happening to the tune.

REVISIONISM IN GERMANY

Before 1890 the German Social Democrats had been laboring under antisocialist laws. This very fact had produced an artificial solidarity in German socialist ranks. The controlling aim was to expunge the exceptional laws against the socialists from the legislative books. This effort

1. William Liebknecht, *Hochverrat und Revolution* ([pamphlet], Berlin, 1892).

drew together not only socialists of a wide variety of views but brought a temporary union of socialists and Catholics. The dropping of the exceptional laws in 1890 was regarded as a signal triumph. The rejoicing of the socialists was great. They were now free to organize, free to publish, and continued to be free to speak their minds in the Reichstag. Criticisms of the party, however, began to appear.[2] With freedom to publish, both criticisms and justifications found their way into print. The socialist stalwart, William Liebknecht, now took up the cudgels in the pages of his newly founded journal, *Vorwärts*. His detractors, he stated, were commonly saying that Social Democracy had become, in twenty years, something different from what it had been originally, that it had given up the revolutionary program, that he, Liebknecht, had become merely a radical, that he had succumbed to the common danger of the public speaker and become a "phrase maker."[3] All this Liebknecht strenuously denied, but in fact this was precisely what was happening. The process had begun with the compromise which joined the Lassalleans with the authoritarian Marxists. The Lassalleans had been more numerous, and the compromise was deemed a necessary one. The Marxists had already, then, embarked on the opportunist way, from which one rarely turns back. Although Liebknecht and Bebel had taken the leadership away from the Lassallean head, Schweitzer, they continued to be bound by the Lassallean majority views and to represent them in the Reichstag year after year. This was the price they paid for being elected. Basic principles, to be sure, were assumed to be unchanged and unchangeable. These basic principles were still propagated by the continued dissemination of works by Marx and Engels. From this point on the resumption of national congresses would bring discussion of theory as well as policy. Thus far opportunism was only in means and

2. In the Reichstag, for example, the Progressist von Bennigsen read a letter of Marx (now dead) which stated that during the transition period from capitalist to social democratic society a dictatorship of the proletariat would be necessary. Grillenberger (socialist) replied that Bennigsen had overlooked the fact that the Social Democratic Party did not acquiesce in this plan; they had their own program, better fitted to the German situation. *Verhandlungen des deutschen Reichstags*, 8 Leg. Per., VII Sess., 1890/1891, 77 Sitz., LXIII, 1805 (A).

3. Liebknecht, *Hochverrat und Revolution*, p. iv. This pamphlet had appeared originally as an essay in *Vorwärts* (1892). To prove his denial he reprinted word for word an article he had written in 1887.

day-to-day tactics. Some time was yet to elapse before fundamental presuppositions would be attacked.

The first Socialist Congress held on German soil, now that the socialists
were free to meet, was designed as a celebration of their victory. It
was held at Halle in October, 1890. Many socialists from other countries were present to share in the general rejoicing. Bebel spoke of the
founding of the Second International in Paris in the preceding year.
Guesde was present, bringing greetings from the French socialists and
retracing the steps in the increasing solidarity of the organization. He
deplored the impending Franco-Russian alliance as inimical to socialist
interests. A minority criticized the hegemony exercised over the Social
Democratic Party by a few Berliners, meaning, of course, Bebel and
Liebknecht. They asked for a regulatory committee to adjust matters.
Bebel presented a list of twenty-five members to be elected to such a
committee. The minority, although objecting that this list was being
"rammed down their throats," accepted it. This criticism was the first
evidence that the younger, more revolutionary members thought the
whole German party was moving away from advocacy of violent seizure
of the powers of government. Liebknecht eulogized the Gotha Program
(which had been a compromise program). He wanted the word "religion" eliminated from the socialist program.[4] The Congress, however,
did not want to give offense to the clerical Center Party. In fact, the
propaganda prepared to recruit new members for the Social Democratic
Party and to encourage the organization of labor was so opportunistic
in character that the dissident minority was "astonished and chilled."[5]

Attacks against the ruling socialist clique were renewed at Erfurt in
1891, both from the radical minority on the left (the "Young") and the
more conservative right led by the nationalist Vollmar. They managed,
however, to confirm the Gotha Program, setting forth its essentials in
a moderate statement:

The economic development of bourgeois society led by natural necessity to the
decline of small enterprise where private property of the worker, as his means
of production, was emphasized as a fundamental principle. [This decline of
small enterprise] detaches the worker from his means of production and

4. Dispatch from Halle, Oct. 15, 1890. *Journal des Débats*, Oct. 16, 1890.
5. Dispatch from Berlin, Nov. 29, 1890. *Ibid.*, Nov. 29, 1890.

changes him into a dispossessed proletarian whose production means becomes the monopoly of a relatively small number of capitalists and large land owners.[6]

The statement of their platform was concluded with these words: ". . . the Party fights not only the exploitation of wage laborers in present day society but against any kind of exploitation, be it class, party, sex, or race."[7] This statement became known as the Erfurt Program. During the course of the debate Liebknecht had defended the parliamentary approach. The goal of Marxism had not altered, he said, and not every question could be solved by legislation, "but let someone show me any other road that leads to the goal."[8] Two years later, at the party Congress in Cologne (1893), the duty of the socialists to participate in the elections to the Prussian Landtag was emphasized.[9]

Although the long-range objectives of the Erfurt Program were for social ownership to be arrived at by political means, the immediate aims were universal suffrage (including votes for women), proportional representation, referendum and recall, direct election of officials, and a graduated income tax: all of these were very practical and not visionary ambitions. In labor reform they sought the eight-hour day,[10] the extension of social insurance, restriction of child labor, and the right to organize.[11] Georg von Vollmar, leader of the Bavarian Party, unsuccessfully opposed the adoption of the Erfurt Program, and continued in subsequent years to oppose it at German party congresses. The independent peasantry, widespread in southern, Catholic Germany, would be

6. Quoted in Werner Sombart, *Sozialimus und soziale Bewegung im 19 Jahrhundert* (Jena, 1896), p. 94. On his title page Sombart states: "Je ne propose rien, je ne suppose rien: j'expose."

7. Gay, *Dilemma of Democratic Socialism*, p. 51.

8. Quoted in Cole, *The Second International*, Part I, p. 254. See also Braunthal, *Geschichte der Internationale*, p. 267. As Engels pointed out (*ibid.*, p. 274), in governments under actual democratic control, such as France, the United States, and monarchist England, it was true that socialists by achieving a majority could control the destiny of the state, but in Germany this idea was fictional because the governments of federal Germany were not under responsible ministries.

9. Edward David, "Parteitag und internationaler Congress," *Socialistische Monatshefte* (No. 9, Sept., 1900), p. 513. Because of the three-class system of voting in Prussia, the socialists could never have had a majority, but they could make their views known. Increase in socialist representation led Saxony to introduce the three-class voting system, abandoning their own earlier, freer system.

10. The eight-hour day was first demanded on a wide scale by May Day demonstrations beginning in 1890.

11. Schorske, *German Social Democracy 1905-1907*, p. 4.

crushed by large-scale agriculture, forecast by Marx's theory. As a result, they were Revisionist from the start. Vollmar represented this point of view.[12]

Karl Kautsky wrote a commentary on the Erfurt Program. The commentary was Marxist in theory but democratic in advocacy of immediate, practical steps; he did not describe the actual program which would be undertaken when the proletariat should possess themselves of the powers of the State and the means of production.[13] The practicality and absence of revolutionary proposals for immediate action annoyed the "Young,"[14] while the inclusion of the revolutionary ultimate aim held the trade unions at a distance.[15] The eventual outcome of the Marxian bid in Germany would rest with labor, organized into unions. From now on their growth was very rapid. Both Christian and "Free" trade unions were making progress (they had increased five-fold under the anti-socialist laws), although the "Free" vastly outnumbered the Christian.[16] The southern "reformer" (Vollmar) got support from the labor unions.[17] Party membership grew also, the unions acting as recruiting agencies for socialism until after 1893, when they gradually ceased to do so and became neutral.[18]

Many factors in German public life contributed to the enlargement of the proletarian class. The rapid shift to large-scale production was made possible by the fact that pioneering in this field had already been

12. *Ibid.*, pp. 7 f. See also Landauer, *European Socialism*, I, 298. The character of the membership of the German Socialist Party was changing: many were half-peasant, half-proletarian, or proletarians only one generation removed from peasant origin. They were strongly democratic and not much interested in class war.

13. Beer, *The General History of Socialism and Social Struggles*, II, 160-161.

14. *Ibid.*, II, 161.

15. Landauer (*European Socialism*, p. 311) emphasizes the unwillingness of the trade unions to subscribe to socialism's revolutionary character. They also disliked socialism's hostility to religion.

16. *Ibid.*, p. 312. Rosa Luxemburg, one of the most fiercely devoted of the "Young," called the work of the unions a "labor of Sisyphus." See Schorske, *German Social Democracy*, p. 22. The strength of the "Free" trade unions was greatly increased by their organization (1891) into a General Commission to speak for all; see Gay, *The Dilemma of Democratic Socialism*, p. 123.

17. Schorske, *German Social Democracy*, p. 8. Schorske attributes a part of the growth of the unions to the employer lock-outs as a reply to May Day demonstrations. He gives Hamburg as an example.

18. Gay, *The Dilemma of Democratic Socialism*, p. 124. See also Ulam, *The Unfinished Revolution*, p. 164.

carried out by England, slowly and without a compass. Germany was able to capitalize on the English experience and move at once to large operations. Technical excellence, due to Germany's scientific lead in the nineteenth century, had a remarkable effect in extending the scope and volume of Germany's foreign trade.[19] Superior salesmanship, analyzing market factors in different countries, increased German sales around the globe, making the Reich a serious competitor of England. The naval building program greatly increased the job opportunities of German workmen.[20] The search for colonies undertaken by the new emperor, William II, with his naval and colonial ambitions, was another factor. The unprecedently rapid growth of the proletarian class brought needed labor to the workshops but increased the uneasiness of the state's ruling clique as to the power represented by the swelling tide. If they could be prevented from making common cause with the peasants, then they could be kept down by the soldiers, armed with rifles and bullets.[21] Whatever may have been the desire of the ruling classes to "divide and rule" by keeping peasants and workers at swords' points, the Social Democrats ceased from 1895 on to emphasize differences between industrial and peasant classes.[22]

Having abandoned the pathway of antisocialist legislation, the German government turned more vigorously toward the adoption of social reforms to relieve the lot of the workingman, in the hope of taking the wind out of the sails of the socialists. Additional legal protections were provided and measures previously enacted were extended to groups not previously covered.[23] In this matter Bismarck had received the backing of Emperor William I. The accession of young Emperor William II

19. Scientifically produced lenses for telescopes and microscopes and chemically superior dyes are examples.

20. Hollyday, *Bismarck's Rival*, p. 142. Before the dropping of the laws against the socialists naval regulations required the dismissal of any worker belonging to the Social Democratic Party. See *ibid.*, p. 205. Bismarck had been reluctant to get into the naval race; his retirement in 1890 tended to enlarge the naval construction program.

21. Hollyday (*ibid.*, p. 261) quotes Admiral Stosch as saying that "despite everything," he considered the "bloody suppression of Social Democracy as imminent." Hollyday uses Stosch's unpublished memoirs.

22. Wilhelm Cohnstaedt, *Die Agrarfrage in der deutsche Sozialdemokratie von Karl Marx* (Munich, 1903), p. 257.

23. Carleton J. H. Hayes (*A Generation of Materialism*, pp. 213-214) lists some of these improvements.

did not interrupt this policy, but rather accentuated it, even though William was on the point of dismissing Bismarck from office. One of the early acts of his reign had been the calling of an International Labor Parliament in Berlin to consider the possibility of making more uniform in various countries legislation for the well-being and protection of workers.[24] He continued to favor extending benefits to the working classes. The results did not decrease the numbers or importance of the socialist leaders but had, rather, the opposite effect. The reform measures received support in the Reichstag from the Social Democrats, the Center, and other moderate parties. From participation in the legislative process the Social Democrats found themselves more and more co-operating with other parties on matters of common concern. They were not a party of political obstructionism. All of these social gains for labor brought increasing votes for Social Democratic candidates, strengthening both the party and the cause. However, the most significant result was that in the process the socialist cause was being led further and further from Marx.[25] This was a change which the radical left wing— the Young—could not support. The question was brought up in party congresses in 1897 and again in 1899. At Hamburg (1897) the majority thought that compromise with other parties should not be shut off but that decisions should be left to the local party. At Hanover (1899) Bebel's resolution sanctioning arrangements with other parties was adopted.[26] By this time the changes occurring within the ranks of Social Democracy in Germany were attracting attention from international socialists. The German Social Democratic Party was supposed to be the purveyor of the "true" belief, the custodian of unadulterated Marxism.[27]

Two events in 1899 brought the changes in German socialism squarely into view. The first was the publication of Bernstein's book, *The Preconditions for Socialism*, and the other was the entrance of Alexandre

24. Bismarck had not approved this step. See Hollyday, *Bismarck's Rival*, p. 263.
25. Schorske (*German Social Democracy*, p. 23) speaks of the "paradox" of Social Democracy whose "materialist philosophy had to be sustained largely by an idealist attitude, while the new idealist heresy battened on labor's material gains."
26. David, "Parteitag und internationaler Congress," *Socialistische Monatshefte* (No. 9, Sept., 1900), p. 513.
27. Ulam (*The Unfinished Revolution*, p. 164) says the German Socialist Party "had been considered *the* Marxist party in Europe, the official representative of the legacy of Marx and Engels."

Millerand into a non-socialist French cabinet.[28] Bernstein's book concerned itself with ideology. Millerand's move was a question of practical tactics; it received widespread attention, especially in Germany, where it was even discussed in the Reichstag. The Second International considered it at their meeting in Paris in 1900. Millerand's step, labeled "Reformism," was criticized partly on the grounds of his having made his decision without consulting other party members. The International adopted a resolution drafted by Karl Kautsky, the "pontiff of socialism," that as a "tactical measure" such a step could be approved if consultation were previously held with the local party.[29]

Bernstein produced the "Great Schism." He went beyond tactics and dared to criticize the theories of Karl Marx. This was heresy. This was Revisionism.

Many influences were operative on Bernstein in bringing him gradually to his Revisionist platform. Born in Berlin in 1850, brought up in poverty, self-educated, he grew up in the days of Lassalle, Bebel, and Liebknecht. His generation was heir to a society which had hoped so much in 1848 and become so disillusioned in 1849. He lived under the conservative constitution of Prussia, whose three-class voting system made a travesty of democracy. He was aware of the quarrel between Lassalle and the Eisenachers, who were Marxists.[30] At the age of twenty-two Bernstein became a Social Democrat.[31] He worked for the union of the

28. How the Millerand case affected the course of socialism in France will be discussed in the following chapter. Here we are concerned with its international aspect and its influence on the German movement. See Georg von Vollmar, "Zum Fall Millerand," in *Socialistische Monatshefte* (No. 12, Dec., 1900), p. 767. The *Socialistische Monatshefte*, pro-Bernstein from its inception, was not only Revisionist but Reformist, opposing violence, emphasizing ethics, and promoting trade-union activities, women's rights, co-operatives, and education. See Gay, *The Dilemma of Democratic Socialism*, p. 256.

29. Nollau, *International Communism and World Revolution*, p. 23. See also Braunthal, *Geschichte der Internationale*, pp. 265 f.

30. Carl Trautman (*Über Ferdinand Lassalle und sein Verhältnis zur Fichteschen Sozialphilosophie* [Jena, 1913], p. 98) declared that Marx and Lassalle were both recognized as Hegelians, deriving their abstract principles from the same source. Bernstein, writing in commemoration of Lassalle's death, quoted on the title page Lassalle's motto emphasizing universal, direct suffrage as the main condition for social uplift. See Eduard Bernstein, *Ferdinand Lassalle und seine Bedeutung für die Arbeiterklasse* (Berlin, 1904), title page. In his *My Years of Exile* (London, 1921), Bernstein mentions the fact (p. 158) that Marx's circle in London had little good to say about Lassalle.

31. Gay (*Dilemma of Democratic Socialism*, pp. 3-8) argues cogently that Bernstein's Revisionism did not stem from Dührung—whose views were rejected by Engels in his

two widely separated groups, and helped to bring about the early compromise between Lassalleans and Marxists known as the Gotha Propram,[32] producing the Social Democratic Party.[33] While the debate was in progress which resulted in passing the law in Germany outlawing the socialists (1878), Bernstein moved to Switzerland.[34] First at Lugano and then at Zurich, he worked in the employ of a visionary patron of Social Democracy,[35] of whom Marx and Engels were extremely skeptical. This skepticism extended, understandably, to Bernstein. Accompanied by Bebel, Bernstein went to London to meet Marx and Engels.[36] This visit improved the standing of Bernstein in the eyes of the London leaders, and he was made first provisional and then permanent editor of the *Sozialdemocrat*, published in Zurich for the benefit of the German socialists; its policy was that of the Gotha Program. Zurich was, next to London, the chief gathering ground of the German political exiles. Bernstein was able to render them service both through the journal, which gave heart to the movement, and at the congresses[37] held on foreign soil to plan the strategy for Reichstag elections and policy for the deputies. Bernstein's journal would have to be published abroad as long as the antisocialist laws were in effect. He maintained the strict Marxist line in

---

Anti-Dühring—as many believe (pp. 88-91). Bernstein said he was converted to Marxism by Engels' book.

32. Werner Sombart, *Socialismus und soziale Bewegung im 19 Jahrhundert*, p. 93. Sombart refers to the "so-called compromise of Marx and Lassalle"; he says it led step by step to domination by Marxian ideas. We have already examined evidences of the part played in this transition by the intellectually superior Marxists who held seats in the Reichstag despite the fact that they represented the minority wing of the party.

33. *Sozialistische Arbeiterpartei Deutschlands*, later to be called the *Sozialdemokratische Partei Deutschlands*, or *S.P.D.*

34. Karl Kautsky, chief theoretician of German socialism, said that Bernstein need not have left Germany. He had a secure position in a banking house and had nothing to fear from the law. His friends advised him to go to take the position with Höchberg so he would have time for his own personal development. See Karl Kautsky, *Erinnerungen und Erörterungen*, III of *Quellen und Untersuchungen zur Geschichte der deutschen und österreichischen Arbeiterbewegung* (The Hague, 1960), 409.

35. Karl Höchberg. For the details of this relationship, see Gay, *The Dilemma of Democratic Socialism*, pp. 28 ff.

36. The trip was financed by Höchberg. See Kautsky, *Erinnerungen und Erörterungen*, p. 463.

37. The first was at Castle Wyden in Switzerland (1880), the second at Copenhagen (1883), and the third at St. Gallen (1887). See Gay, *Dilemma of Democratic Socialism*, p. 36. It was at Wyden that the German socialists, becoming more revolutionary, removed from their program the "by all legal means" clause. See Schorske, *German Social Democracy*, p. 3.

editing the *Sozialdemocrat* and in supporting the left wing of Reichstag socialist delegations when the congresses discussed the party platform. The delegates were divided on the question of whether to vote against Bismarck, in order to get the exceptional laws against the socialists removed, or vote *with* him on the government-sponsored social reform bills which would bring a measure of relief to labor and would be immediately operative.[38]

Bernstein's stay in Switzerland not only brought him into contact with socialists from many areas, thus broadening his concepts, but, by his work in editing the German party journal, kept him in touch with the vast economic and social changes taking place in Germany, as well as with the legislative activities of the German deputies. When the Swiss authorities banished the staff of the *Sozialdemocrat*,[39] Bernstein went to London (1888) and edited the journal from there, until the abrogation (1890) of the exceptional laws against the socialists. Propagating socialist ideas after 1890 was no longer illegal in Germany. The journal then went home to Berlin, but Bernstein remained in London as correspondent. His source of income having been lessened, he supported himself by writing articles for socialist journals in Germany and in London.

One of the major influences on Bernstein's life, and through him on Revisionism, was England itself, its trade unions, its Fabian Socialism, its tolerance of conflicting views—the "free air of England."[40] The forced removal of Bernstein, which brought him from Switzerland to London, exposed him to this English atmosphere. The steady growth and success of the British trade unions impressed him; British Fabian Socialists[41] moved in polite society; a famous English Cardinal comforted striking dock workers; the Queen had contributed to a benefit for the widow of a Communard.[42] But Bernstein's closest contacts in London were with

38. Gay, *Dilemma of Democratic Socialism*, p. 110.

39. Bernstein, *My Years of Exile*, p. 144.

40. Quoted in Gay, *Dilemma of Democratic Socialism*, p. 56.

41. Schorske, *German Social Democracy*, p. 16. Bernstein was criticized after his return to Germany for being influenced by the Fabian Socialist views of Beatrice and Sidney Webb. They were "drawing-room socialists." See Kautsky, *Erinnerungen und Erörterungen*, p. 463.

42. This oft-quoted story is told by Bernstein himself. He had attended this particular benefit in order to hear Eleanor Marx do a reading. The program announced: "Her Majesty the Queen has headed the List with £10." See his *My Years of Exile*, p. 160.

Engels. He moved, therefore, as long as Engels lived, in the mainstream of authoritarian Marxism. Engels produced a catechism on the *Communist Manifesto*, with Bernstein providing the notes.[43] It began with the question, "What is Communism?," to which the catechism provided the answer that "Communism is the doctrine of the emancipation of the proletariat." Other answers were strictly Marxist in concept: labor is a commodity; capitalistic control is more and more centralized; abolition of private property is indispensable; the international character of Communism is the doing away with nationalism; the break with traditional ideas of religion; the wiping out of disparity between country and town. On the other hand there are some distinctly opportunistic ideas: the desirability of pacific means in abolishing private property (without ruling out revolution); the improvement of housing for workers; free education. Amazingly, the document indicated looking with favor on the bourgeois political parties in Germany because they were open to discussion and believed in the spread of ideas. This was a distinctly opportunistic note.[44]

At what time Bernstein recognized that he had left the straight and narrow path of undeviating Marxism it would be difficult to say. Few people experience the blinding light on the "road to Damascus" that converted the Apostle Paul. One moves by degrees from one position to another, ultimately discovering that he has changed direction. As a writer for socialist journals Bernstein was continually reiterating the old shibboleths. His study and writing, nevertheless, were steadily taking him away from orthodox Marxism. From 1895 on he deviated more and more toward the right.

At the party congresses all shades of opinion appeared; heated arguments took place. In spite of all this it was usually possible to come out with some kind of statement to which all would, at least grudgingly,

43. Friedrich Engels and Karl Marx, *I Fondamenti del Communismus*. The preface of the edition seen by this writer is by Angelica Balabanoff. No publication date is given but it is marked: Ancona—XIV Congreso dal Partito socialista italiano, and was published by the "Libreria sociale" of Chicago. Division of MSS, Duke University, Durham, N.C. The Marx portion of the pamphlet is the *Communist Manifesto* in Italian translation.

44. These ideas had appeared as sound doctrine in the *Communist Manifesto*. It must be remembered, however, that Marx approved them primarily for their propagandizing value. See Howard Becker and Harry Elmer Barnes, *Social Thought from Lore to Science* (3 vols.; 3rd ed.; New York), II, 662.

assent. The left was violently revolutionary; Vollmar was on the extreme right. During a discussion of free trade it was he who said: "Let us be practical and not fall into the error for which Germans have been reproached: when a German has a spot on his coat he begins by studying chemistry before removing it."[45] He remained pragmatic.

Bernstein's open break came with the publication of his *Evolutionary Socialism*.[46] In this work he took direct issue with Kautsky on the agrarian question.[47] In contradicting the Marxian "laws" on this subject Bernstein was contradicting the whole assumption that economics was a science whose "laws" were discoverable, an assumption derived from Hegel. Hegel taught that by studying history "laws" of human society could be uncovered. "No," said Bernstein; nature had no such laws. Changes occurred constantly; when change became noticeable it was labeled "law." Bernstein was of the opinion that after a few generations new "laws" would be discovered.[48] This was putting in question Marx's theory of socialism as an immanent "economic necessity,"[49] the thing which cannot *not* happen.

Here were the two chief theorists, life-long friends and collaborators, disagreeing over fundamental issues, not tactics, but basic truth. Kautsky clung to the traditional socialist view that the farmer and agricultural laborer would disappear and become "proletarians," and he would not alter the general belief that the basic aim must remain—to win the class struggle. In his view, the means of production would be socialized at the moment of seizing control of the public powers. Kautsky still included both landowners and capitalists in the possessing classes against which the attack must be made. Throughout the decade he had stood out against any attempt to extend ownership of rural land to farmers and field laborers. Such an extension would be diametrically opposed to the program of Karl Marx.[50] Kautsky insisted that both rural lands and factories

45. *Univers*, Oct. 9, 1898.
46. The German title was *Die Voraussetzungen des Sozialismus und die Aufgaben der Sozialdemokratie*, which may be translated: *The Presuppositions of Socialism and the Tasks of Social Democracy*.
47. Kautsky's book *Die Agrarfrage* had appeared in 1898.
48. Stefan Karski, "Geschichtsphilosophisches zur Bernstein- Frage," *Socialistische Monatshefte* (No. 3, March, 1900), p. 134. Karski wrote this in London for publication in the Berlin journal.
49. Braunthal, *Geschichte der Internationale*, p. 272.
50. Gay, *Dilemma of Democratic Socialism*, p. 191.

would alike require greater concentrations of capital to operate profitably, as science and technology produced new agricultural methods and factories produced more and more machines to alter the nature of labor on the farm as in the city shop. Bernstein disagreed. Originally his theories had paralleled those of Kautsky (and Engels until his death in 1895). However, from his point of view, theories should be based on fact, not fact on theory. In the nineteenth century there were no facts in rural life to support the Marxist theory and the Kautsky contention.[51] There was an extension of individual ownership, for one thing, and for another, the standard of living had been slowly rising. Kautsky could see these facts but regarded them as momentary aberrations; the theories were still "relatively true." He insisted that the interests of the peasants and the workers could not be harmonized, which would prevent their union in a political party.[52] The Social Democratic Party should not ignore the rural worker, Kautsky cautioned, but should assist him through social legislation and encourage him to look on socialism and socialization of property with a more tolerant eye.[53] Kautsky's insistence that the socialist regime did not necessarily imply violence and his approval of social legislation seemed to argue that he himself had traveled some distance on the road away from rigid interpretation of *Das Kapital*. To Kautsky, however, these were tactical changes, leaving theory still pure.[54]

Bernstein did not, of course, limit himself to criticizing socialist agrarian theory. He went on in other chapters of his book to discuss one after another the basic presuppositions which had been, in his view, proved incorrect by time. Rising prosperity cast doubts on the theory of immiseration (that the poverty and misery of the proletariat would gradually increase); the bourgeoisie were exhibiting not increasing class antagonism but sympathy and concern for the working class; where the Marxist theory proclaimed capitalism anarchic, Bernstein saw a growing order in society; where Marx had expected an economic depression to be the springboard for a taking over of the state by the workingmen, Bern-

51. Events are proving, in the second half of the twentieth century in America, that Marx was right after all in his prediction. This fact does not invalidate Bernstein's fundamental criticism of Marx: "laws" in human society are not "laws," but observable trends in a given situation.
52. Cohnstaedt, *Die Agrarfrage in der deutsche Sozialdemokratie*, p. 239.
53. Gay, *Dilemma of Democratic Socialism*, pp. 192 ff.
54. Cole, *The Second International*, Part I, pp. 265 f.

stein saw economic crisis becoming more mild; where socialist theory said only the proletariat by defeating their enemy the capitalist would usher in the new society, Bernstein said other classes would co-operate in bringing about the socializing of the state. The enemy, said Bernstein, was not capitalism but those capitalists who rejected social justice.[55] The "Young," whose most distinguished representatives were Rosa Luxemburg and Karl Liebknecht, were opposed to Bernstein. They were almost equally opposed to Kautsky, Bebel, and the rest who thought they were good Marxists. Kautsky said there were two minds in Social Democracy: the revolutionary mind, which continued to control its words, and the Revisionist, which controlled its deeds.[56] What Kautsky was trying to do in battling Bernstein's Revisionism was to try to hold the German movement in midstream. In this effort he rather dampened the enthusiasm of the German socialists and produced a stalemate.

At the meeting in 1899, at Hanover, the polemic between Bernstein and Kautsky meant that there could no longer be any pretense of harmony between the factions. Bernstein's position was rejected by the Social Democrats,[57] but without eliminating Bernstein. The altercation did not cease because of this rejection. Bernstein continued to write in support of his altered views. He showed that the doctrine of increasing poverty (immiseration) of the laborer was not working out according to Marx's predictions; Marx's "centralizing tendency" was not taking place in Germany (or elsewhere). Bernstein said such matters as education, safety devices, and sanitary inspection in industry must be taken over by the State, as should transportation. He stressed leaving future arrangements to what might seem to be required. He emphasized the importance of democracy as the road to socialism. He still clung to the idea that the

55. Schorske, *German Social Democracy*, p. 18.
56. Karl Kautsky, *Bernstein und das Sozialdemokratische Programm* (Stuttgart, 1899), p. 160. See also Friedrich Engels and Karl Kautsky, *L'International socialiste*, p. 36. Kautsky later moved closer to Bernstein's position. He admitted that the doctrine of "immiseration" was not *literally* correct, although *relatively* so. When war credits (1914) were asked in the Reichstag, he held to the middle ground and pleaded for abstention from voting rather than voting *against*; the Revisionists went all the way and voted *for*. When the Leninist revolution occurred in Russia, Kautsky refused to accept it and lined up with the West. See Gay, *The Dilemma of Democratic Socialism*, p. 275. See also Ulam, *The Unfinished Revolution*, pp. 165-166. Ulam describes the "ideological calisthenics" of the leaders of the German party.
57. William Schröder, *Handbuch des sozialdemokratische Parteitag von 1863 bis 1909* (Munich, 1910), pp. 86 f.

movement was everything, the goal unimportant.[58] In the foreseeable future he did not envisage the State's taking over the means of production.[59]

Bernstein left London and went back to Berlin in 1901, the better to fight for his cause. The reformists flocked to him, electing him to the Reichstag with a landslide vote.[60] He seemed, indeed, no longer a socialist, except in name. Perhaps it would be more accurate to say that he had made the term "socialist" at last respectable to any but reactionaries. Only the extreme left wing of the socialists drew the condemnation of moderate parties, and this more for their advocacy of violence than for their belief in the socialization of property. Those who had been regarded for so long as Marx's lieutenants, preaching the true gospel of Marx, William Liebknecht, Bebel and the rest, were moving over toward the reformist Vollmar, becoming frankly Opportunist and playing the part of sincere parliamentary deputies, eager to pass laws for the immediate and practical benefit of Germans.[61] Even their internationalism was being burned away by what they regarded as the Russian menace.

All branches of the Social Democratic Party were antimilitarist, and especially opposed to the huge expenditures for military purposes now demanded by the Government. In 1903 when the naval and military budget was debated in the Reichstag, opposition came from the Social Democrats of whatever complexion, as well as from the Progressives. After a speech from the throne and the outlining of the Government's policies by the Chancellor of the Reich, von Bülow, the arguments poured forth.

Vollmar objected to the budget on the ground that the venture into "Great Power" politics would lay its burden on the backs of "the people, who economically and politically must pay the cost."[62] He also praised a letter sent by Jaurès to the Italian deputy Costa, in which Jaurès lauded

58. Eduard Bernstein, *Zur Frage: Socialliberalismus oder Collectivismus* (Berlin, 1900), p. 13. This pamphlet was written in an attempt to settle the controversy with Kautsky.

59. *Ibid.*, p. 16.

60. One of his opponents was Karl Liebknecht, son of William Liebknecht. See Gay, *Dilemma of Social Democracy*, p. 252.

61. Jürgen Kuczynski, *Die Geschichte der Lage der Arbeiter in Deutschland von 1800 bis in die Gegenwart*, I, *1800-1932* (2 vols.; Berlin, 1947), 234.

62. *Frankfurter Zeitung*, Jan. 21, 1903.

the Triple Alliance[63] as a counterpoise to the chauvinism of France. According to Vollmar, the French desire for *Revanche* was noticeable everywhere in their press;[64] for this reason he especially appreciated the stand taken by Jaurès against "boastful patriotism" that demanded action against Germany, and went on to prove for how many millions of Frenchmen Jaurès spoke, as demonstrated by their electing him as one of the four vice-presidents of the French Chamber. Their vote, said Vollmar, showed that the Triple Alliance was not threatened by France and that Germany did not need the increased naval and military budget.[65]

Vollmar also replied to the attack on the socialists that appeared in the speech from the throne. Chancellor von Bülow thereupon spoke in defense of the Emperor as a friend of labor by reading from the report of the German Ambassador to France on his conversation in November (1901) with Millerand, the Minister of Commerce, a "political and personal friend of Jaurès, the political figure and noted orator." The Chancellor continued:

And as Jaurès, according to what I have gathered, is highly considered by Herr Vollmar . . . I think you would attach a certain importance to what M. Millerand said, as reported by our Ambassador:

> M. Millerand (says Prince Radolin) brings to our attention that in the matter of insurance for the aged among the laborers in mines, his efforts tended to establish a state of affairs similar to that which Emperor William . . . encouraged in Germany.[66]

Bebel, in a speech lasting three hours, attacked the budget.[67] Connecting the request for increased expenditure with the development (made on the preceding day) of Chancellor von Bülow's social program, Bebel asked whether the naval and artillery expenditures would not raise the price of the most essential food of the working classes.[68] After quoting

63. Renewed at five-year intervals, it had recently been renewed among Germany, Austria, and Italy.

64. *Temps*, Jan. 22, 1903. The Dreyfus affair had produced a wave of chauvinism.

65. *Frankfurter Zeitung* (2nd A.M. ed.), Jan. 21, 1903.

66. *Temps.*, Jan. 22, 1903.

67. *Frankfurter Zeitung* (2nd A.M. ed.; Jan. 23, 1903) commented on Bebel's speech, saying it exhibited a "candor and sharpness" such as had "never before occurred in the Reichstag," and added significantly, "but who would have prevented it, and, indeed, who would have wanted to?"

68. *Verhandlungen des deutschen Reichstags*, 24th Sitz., Jan. 22, 1903, col. 7468.

William II's words (which disquieted the world, and especially England): "For the trident belongs in our hand," and "Our future lies upon the water . . . ," Bebel observed that the workers provided the masses of recruits made necessary by expansion of the armed services.[69]

It is generally characteristic of the Latin peoples [Bebel declared] that actually [at present] the bourgeoisie is the most hostile, *vis-à-vis* state reforms for the working classes. So is it also in Belgium, where the powerful Catholic Party remains just as opposed to social reform through the State . . . and it is similarly the case in Italy. Here among the German peoples the ruling classes have shown themselves more obliging, particularly also the English bourgeoisie. There, Mr. Reichschancellor, there is no insurance law, as in Germany. But I do not know whether we would not sacrifice, were the choice laid before us, our social security laws for English freedom.[70]

Though the Center Party joined the Conservatives in supporting the military bill, against the opposition of the Social Democrats and the Progressists, it supported social reform also. Even Alsace and Lorraine, still sighing for their lost French nationalism, found themselves making more rapid social progress under authoritarian Germany than they would have in democratic France.

A part of the explanation of the gradual abandonment of the revolutionary path by the German Marxian stalwarts of earlier decades is to be found in the opposition of religious groups and especially the Catholics to the atheism of the socialist movement. This Catholic strand interwoven into the highly complex fabric of the German social and political situation came largely from the South German states, federally bound with Prussia in the German Empire, but never incorporated into Prussia. These states retained their kings, their religion, and their own democratically elected diets. Here the Kulturkampf of Bismarck had stimulated a greater devotion to the persecuted Church than before and had brought a new feeling of solidarity between the Holy See and the South Germans. Most of the Old Catholics ultimately gave up the attempt to maintain a separate organization. Many returned to the Roman allegiance. Others joined Protestant churches. A dwindling minority remained Old Catholics, but their organization ceased to be significant.

69. *Ibid.*, cols. 7472 and 7476.
70. *Ibid.*, cols. 7478-7479. Bebel, referring to the Millerand case, said that a German socialist, if taken into the Ministry "would have to remain a *Social Democrat*."

Also, the Kulturkampf had brought a practical partnership between the socialists and the Center in opposition to Bismarck. The Center had objected to the exceptional character of the laws against the socialists. As the number of workers grew in Germany, the number of socialist Reichstag deputies increased from the non-Prussian states. Prussia itself, although larger than all the rest of Germany put together, could restrict by its three-class voting system the number of deputies elected by the laboring class to the state Diet. Although Saxony changed over to the Prussian class-voting scheme, the Catholic states did not do so. In Bavaria Catholics and socialists co-operated politically. This co-operation was in part attributable to the support which Leo XIII gave to the democratic French Republic in the *Au milieu des sollicitudes,* addressed to French Catholics, and in part to his ultimate approach to the term "Christian Democracy."

Catholic Germany had been influenced by the early Catholic reformers, inspired by the words and acts of Archbishop Ketteler. He had not only awakened the social conscience of many German Catholics, but had also endorsed the formation of Christian labor unions. The *Rerum Novarum,* with its assertion that the labor force is not a commodity to be treated as though it were an inert mass subject to economic laws, tended to lower the barriers between socialists and Catholics. Karl Marx had said somewhat the same thing. The two were in harmony on this point. Germans had been proud of their scientific pre-eminence, and Karl Marx had called his movement "scientific socialism." Leo XIII insisted that there could be no fundamental quarrel between religious truth and scientific truth. Even the opening of the Vatican Archives, making available to Lutheran scholars the sources on which they might draw for the Luther celebration, gave Leo XIII a prestige in Germany (from the Emperor to the humblest citizen) which caused his words on the social question to be listened to and accepted by many Protestants as well as Catholics. The German socialists had found it impolitic to try to use attacks on the clerical Center as a method of propagandizing for their cause.

Catholic Germany was also the area where the peasant was improving his condition and becoming an independent owner of his small holdings. It was this area which Vollmar represented in the ranks of socialism as well as in the Reichstag. His influence on the party was always in the direction of social reform and never toward social revolution.[71]

One German anarchist living in London[72] attributed the success of the German Social Democratic Party to the nature of the government and to militarism. In other countries the socialists were split up. Only in Germany were they unified, clinging together against the government and its militarism. There is doubtless an element of truth in this conclusion. There were other factors: nationalism, the great growth of unions, social legislation. These certainly help to explain why revolutionary theory found little ground to develop and anarchism found none, but they do not tell quite the whole story. Religion and the quiet hand of Leo XIII should not be excluded from the picture.

REFORMISM IN BELGIUM

In Belgium, factors in favor of Revisionism were present almost from the time of the establishment of the Labor Party. The parliamentary path to social legislation was still closed to the socialists because of the absence of universal suffrage. Socialist action took the form of working for suffrage reform and of supporting strike activities to bring about such reform. Strikes were generally ascribed to anarchist influence, which had been slow to die in Belgium. Strikes were contrary to authoritarian Marxist principles, which took the position that conquest of the public powers could only be achieved by a revolutionary uprising (such as the Commune of 1871) or by conquest of the political structure through the electoral process. The latter could only occur under universal suffrage, where the growing numbers of workers would make them numerically dominant. Party solidarity would be essential for such an outcome. Neither of these ways seemed possible in Belgium because of the development of labor in separate communes, rather than in a state party, and because the parliamentary path was closed by the restricted suffrage. The

71. Vollmar's speeches foreshadowed the position which Bernstein eventually reached. See Gay, *Dilemma of Democratic Socialism*, p. 254 n.

72. Gustav Landauer, *Social Democracy in Germany* (London, *ca.* 1896). Although the pamphlet is undated, the author says "three years ago at Zurich," which would date it as written (if not published) in 1896.

chief issue, then, was not class war, but usually some local question, such as the endorsement of a strike or the broadening of the suffrage.[73]

Vandervelde, the faithful member of the Second International, was accused by the more rigid members of having abandoned the class war,[74] which was of course true, just as the German criticism of Bernstein, that he was deviating from the Marxist path, was pointing to an actual fact.

The Labor Party, assembled in Congress in 1891, voted to adopt the general strike as a means of securing the suffrage. Without waiting for adequate preparations to be made, some workers started a strike on May Day. It failed completely, but pointed up the need for concerted action in the matter of suffrage.

Such action was not likely to come from the government, which was completely dominated by the powerful Catholic Party. Not all Catholics were comfortable about the situation. Not only was suffrage reform ignored, but labor reform as well. By 1890, when the problems of labor were coming to be recognized as a matter of international concern, requiring international conferences sponsored by heads of state, it seemed time for Belgium to give some consideration to the social question. In reality there were three factions among the great Catholic majority. The ultraconservative element combined political control with a disinclination to change anything. A more realistic group recognized that immobility was no answer, but sought to pare to the lowest possible point the reforms that would have to be granted. Other Catholics, however, had long been favorable to reform and had taken the first steps in that direction. The outstanding leader of this group was Msgr. Doutreloux, Bishop of Liége. In 1890 a Congress was held at Liége. Doutreloux presided, with Cardinal Goosens as honorary president. Leo XIII, who was preparing the *Rerum Novarum* for promulgation in the spring of 1891, gave his blessing to the Congress.[75] The participants discussed such practical questions as types of workers' organizations, methods of propaganda, international conventions to establish principles for protection of labor,[76] and legislation. The

73. Henri De Man, *Planned Socialism: The "Plan du Travail" of the Belgian Labor Party*, trans. and ed. G. D. H. Cole (London, 1935), p. 29.
74. Karski, "Geschichtsphilosophisches zur Bernstein-Frage," *Socialistische Monatshefte* (No. 3, March, 1900), p. 134.
75. Soderini, *Il Pontificato di Leone XIII*, I, 348.
76. This was the year of William II's International Labor Parliament.

Congress after much careful discussion supported, in general, state intervention and the establishment of professional organizations (unions), but favored also a co-ordinated Catholic reform movement.[77] The Liége group was much heartened when the *Rerum Novarum* came out.

Here in Belgium as elsewhere in Catholic Europe the formation of a study group (at Liége) put constant pressure on the government and on private citizens to solve the social question not only in a Christian spirit but also intelligently, in the light of sociological and economic studies. It was this sort of study which led to the transforming of Leo's words into action.[78]

A federation of the Catholic workers' societies was established in 1891. In 1892 they adopted the name "Belgian Democratic League," and held a Congress. At their second Congress (1893) they "pronounced and defined for the first time the name *Christian Democracy*": the reclamation of the laborer under the banner of the Church.[79]

The voice of Leo XIII was powerful in Belgium, but there was still a sharp division between the conservative Catholics and the reforming group centered around Liége and Bishop Doutreloux.[80]

The broadening of the suffrage in 1893[81] led to an entirely new situation. While it enlarged the electorate among the workers, who were possible recruits for socialism, it also increased the number of voting peasants and rural workers, who were more directly under the influence of their parish priests. The contest became, in Belgium, a struggle between socialism and Catholicism.[82] The socialistically inclined Labor Party was federally organized after the franchise reform. The contest for political dominance was therefore fought out between the Church and

77. Gambasin, *Il movimento sociale*, p. 368.
78. Toniolo, *Opera omnia*, ser. iv, I, 54.
79. *Ibid.*, p. 56.
80. This division was reproved by Leo XIII. Nitti (*Catholic Socialism*, p. 387) said in 1895 that the Pope was more powerful in Belgium than the King, having at his disposal an ultra-Catholic Government and a Parliament composed mostly of Catholics. This is probably claiming too much; it was true in religious matters but not in other fields.
81. Universal suffrage was introduced, but it was tempered by a complex system of plural voting.
82. Cole (*The Second International*, Part II, p. 631) refers to it as a "mass contest between the socialists and the Church."

the socialists in each of the federal districts.[83] Liberals and socialists of necessity confronted the powerful Catholic conservatives. This enforced union of Liberals with socialists precluded any idea of left-wing, revolutionary ideology controlling the Labor Party program.[84]

As in Germany, socialists in Belgium had to confront new issues arising in the closing years of the century—colonialism and militarism. The Congo went into King Leopold's personal pocket.[85] Socialists were generally opposed to colonialism but under the circumstances had little opportunity even to protest.[86] In the matter of militarism, as in Germany, the development of nationalism and the fear of invasion softened the antimilitarist views. Strengthening the fortifications along the frontier between Belgium and Germany met with popular approval.[87]

On the international scene the influence of Vandervelde and Anseele among socialists was toward compromise and solidarity at the expense of strict Marxist tenets. They spoke no longer of expropriation. Vandervelde favored decentralized operation of a socialist economy, following in this particular the demands of the old anarchists Proudhon and Bakunin for communal development, although disavowing Bakuninist violence. Vandervelde believed in co-operatives and voluntary local organizations for mutual help that would function in everything from economic life to education and cultural life in general.[88] It was he who presented the

83. The distinction between city and country was becoming more blurred as rural factories became more common, turning farmers into industrial wage earners. Yet at the same time many small farmers continued to own their own property.

84. Both groups in the Labor Party turned to education, especially at the university level, to develop sociological theory and to pass it on to the student generation. See Cole, *The Second International*, Part II, p. 632.

85. The scandals thereafter arising leaked out through Catholic missionaries in the Congo, and Leopold was forced to turn the rich colony over to the Belgian Parliament. But this was after Leo XIII's death.

86. This failure to do something active about imperialism was regarded by later socialists as one of the mistakes of the older generation. See William Paul, *Karl Liebknecht: The Man: His Work and Message* (n.p., 1920), p. 2.

87. Belgium's neutrality, guaranteed in 1839, permitted the maintenance of a standing army (for defense) and a chain of fortifications between Belgium and Germany. As a result of the development of the rival alliances in the late nineteenth century, the situation of Belgium as a corridor of invasion became more and more a cause of alarm for the Belgian people. See Mary Elizabeth Thomas, "Belgian Neutrality and the British Press," in Wallace and Askew, eds., *Power, Public Opinion and Diplomacy*, pp. 118, 120-122.

88. Cole, *The Second International*, Part II, pp. 646 ff.

Kautsky compromise before the Second International at its meeting in Paris in 1900.[89]

Reform and compromise had taken the center of the stage in Belgium, as in Germany. Many of the factors which led to this result were the same: the growth of trade unions, nationalism, and presence of Catholicism. The most important difference lay in the fact that in Belgium the Catholic Party played the dominant role in government, representing, not the liberalizing tendency of the German Center at times in partnership with the socialists, but conservatism—political, social, and intellectual. This fact drove the Liberals in Belgium into co-operation with the socialists. This co-operation with the Liberals profoundly affected not only the public utterances of the socialists but their ideas and attitudes, drawing them away from the violence of the extreme groups at the left. The fact that the secretariat of the Second International was set up in 1900 in Belgium enabled this milder socialism to hold the party in midstream and thus to play a part in keeping the West in the path of moderation and reform. This tendency was gradually reinforced by the enlightened self-interest of the great bourgeois class, which came slowly to realize that complete rigidity in resisting reform was no longer profitable.

Certainly in Belgium the Catholic Church was the last bulwark of the old society with its toleration of inequalities in opportunity and its theological concepts so loath to yield to the dynamics of the new history and sociology.[90] Monarchy had been brought under constitutionalism and had been limited. The Napoleonic regime had early done away with the old aristocracy. Laissez-faire economics had permitted the rise of the bourgeois class to wealth and power. As Catholics the new classes were not averse to making common cause with the Belgian hierarchy. This combination controlled the state until after the end of the century. Their chief opponent was Marxian socialism, but a Marxian socialism with its antitheocratic tendencies toned down and its program little distinguishable from mere progressivism.

89. Braunthal, *Geschichte der Internationale,* pp. 278 f.
90. Hayes, *A Generation of Materialism,* pp. 133, 145.

XV. REVISIONISM: FRANCE AND ITALY

"We must never forget that we are at the same time internationalists, Frenchmen and patriots."[1]

ALEXANDRE MILLERAND

South of Belgium the social picture alters. Germanic Europe with its tendency toward methodical organization is left behind. In Latin Europe agreement on anything seems almost impossible of attainment. Here, too, the Catholic Church has not been effectively opposed by any other form of religion. Here the struggle between Leo XIII and Marxism would be in view at every moment, whether in workers' meetings or in legislative halls.

FRANCE: REFORMISM OR REVISIONISM?

The slow shift of public opinion was a necessary prerequisite in democratic France for the development of a national social program. In this respect France stood in sharp contrast with authoritarian Germany and closer to England, which moved by consensus arrived at in Hyde Park or Parliament. The shift of opinion had been further slowed in France by the chronic struggles between monarchists and republicans and by the anticlericalism of the Republic, which displeased the devout Catholics. State action was delayed by the monarchist addiction of some of the sincerest friends of labor. Leo XIII's advice in 1892 to the clergy and Catholics of France to desist from monarchist support and rally to the Republic presently clarified this situation for many but did not eliminate

1. Orry, *Less Socialistes indépendants*, p. 29.

the problem. The Church itself had gone through various stages in changing its attitudes from charity for the needy (without doing anything to alter the causes producing the need) to paternalism, which characterized the movement of de Mun. The persistence of individual or family ownership of the myriad small industrial undertakings tended to prolong the period of paternalism. Paternalism, however, by serving as a deterrent to more violent types of solutions, had given time and opportunity for Revisionism to develop.[2]

The fact that France did not succumb to Marxian doctrine cannot be attributed to the rapid development of social legislation, for this did not occur; the reasons must be sought elsewhere. They are found in the democratic form of government, the swelling tide of nationalism as the nineteenth century drew to a close, Catholic obstruction, and the unwillingness of labor groups to support a common policy with the socialists.

The aftermath of the Boulanger affair had been a turn of labor toward the left. Inclined up to this point to look to the Radicals for changes in the law, they now turned toward the socialist parties, despairing of Radical help.[3]

The general tendency to form splinter parties was characteristic of French society, not only in legislative halls and political campaigns but also in the debates occurring in the national congresses of workers and theorists. Failure to agree, instead of resulting in the adoption of innocuous statements of principle that said nothing, usually ended in a split of the organization, producing two where one had existed before. New practical organizations to meet new needs also sprang up, assuming functions similar to the trade unions in Anglo-Saxon countries. Such, for example, were the Labor Exchanges (*Bourses du Travail*), which arose to meet the need for a more mobile labor force seeking employment. Be-

2. At a socialist conference early in January, 1892, organized by Guesde and Lafargue, more than half of the three thousand present were Catholics. The statements of both these Marxists were challenged during the meeting from the Catholic point of view. See *Univers*, Jan. 19, 1892.

3. Dansette, *Le Boulangisme*, p. 382. The Radicals became "guardians of the existing order"; they became therefore *personae non gratae* to the workingmen. See also Acomb, *The French Laic Laws*, p. 66. Miss Acomb says the "Left became associated with business interests and turned to opportunism" believing that the "new social classes should be allowed to make money and become supporters of the government which permitted their enrichment."

ginning as local unemployment bureaus, they became affiliated into a national organization, speaking for labor. Syndicalism, too, pursued its own organizing way, forming a national federation of local *syndicats*. They preferred the small improvement today to the whole loaf of control of the political powers tomorrow. The undertone of anarchism, defying organization, permeated to a greater or lesser degree all groups of actual laborers[4] except those in the Catholic Workingmen's Clubs. The revolutionary spirit, which had flared into a blaze during the Commune, still smoldered, unextinguished.

The columns devoted to news of sporadic acts of violence grew in length in the journals. Leo XIII receiving Harmel, director of the pilgrimages and ultimately president of the organization of the clubs, said the growth of anarchic socialism was making the struggle of the Church extraordinarily difficult.[5]

Although these various streams of revolt had been present all along (Marxists, Blanquists, and anarchists having never merged in reality), their antagonisms became deeper and their rifts wider. The factions were never able to agree on anything, from petitions to concerts. In spite of these differences the number of socialists continued to grow.[6] The organization of the Second International acted as a spur to socialist recruitment. All of these disparate groups tended vaguely to consider themselves socialists. They sought, at any rate, admittance to socialist meetings on all sorts of occasions.

Real socialists, already divided into Possibilists under Brousse[7] and Marxists under Guesde, were not through with the process of splitting. The Possibilists divided when a faction led by Jean Allemane seceded

4. Ulam (*The Unfinished Revolution*, p. 157) says the "roots of syndicalism lie in Proudhon and Blanqui."

5. *Univers*, Nov. 16, 1889. This was before the *Rerum Novarum*. It continued to be true, although the impetus to support the Church was greatly increased after the Pope's encyclical.

6. The number of socialist votes cast in 1889 was 179,000. The number rose to 440,000 in the elections of 1893. See Braunthal, *Geschichte der Internationale*, p. 217. In Paris, in 1890, the number stood at 48,292; it rose to 66,744 in 1893. See *Univers*, May 14, 1893. One should consider in weighing these figures that the total population of France between the Franco-Prussian war and World War I virtually stood still.

7. Paul Brousse was already a Reformist when the amnesty permitted him to return to France from Switzerland where he had been working in the Jura Federation (anarchist). See Braunthal, *Geschichte der Internationale*, pp. 215 ff.

to form a separate organization.[8] The argument occurred at a regional meeting in Paris (1890) preparatory to a general national meeting of the Possibilists (*Parti ouvrier socialiste*). A Broussist speaker touched it off: "It seems to me that they are trying to make Blanquists of us—but, no, we are Possibilists and Possibilists we want to remain; we are not trying to abandon the tactics of the Socialist Workers Party." Then followed criminations and recriminations as to the part Brousse and Allemane had played in collaborating with the Opportunist Government to stop Boulanger. A tumult ensued and the whole debate descended to personalities. An Allemanist supporter objected to the intrusion of middle-class people into the workers' organization. "If the bourgeoisie want to enter our ranks," he said, "let them not try to get supremacy over the workers' majority."[9] When the general national Congress of the Possibilists was held at Châttelleraut (for which this argumentative session in Paris had been preparing), there was at the outset a wrangle over credentials. Allemane walked out with his adherents to form a new organization. The seceders were generally known as "Allemanists." The Broussists remained behind and proceeded with their meeting. Brousse described in his journal (*Proletariat*) the beating off of this intransigent new group, labeling the group's efforts a "new form of Caesarism," which was thought to have been felled when Guesde and Lafargue had walked out.[10] The seceders went back, according to their minutes, to revolutionary tactics and belief in class war.[11]

The *Parti ouvrier*, dominated by Guesde and Lafargue, held its own meeting about the same time that the Possibilists were holding theirs. Brousse had never made much of an attempt to force his way into the syndical organization, but Guesde had consistently tried to control the workers as they assembled for their national sessions. So successful had he been that now the syndicalists always met in the same city as the

8. Brousse had been advocating both municipal (not state) socialism and co-operation with bourgeois parties. Allemane, who had been a Communard, deported to New Caledonia, could not accept the fact of co-operation, although accepting municipal socialism. See Cole, *The Second International*, Part II, p. 326.

9. *Journal des Débats*, Oct. 5, 1890. Most of the socialist leaders were journalists.

10. Blum, *Les Congrès*, II, 122.

11. *Ibid.*, II, 123. Blum was aware that far from being a struggle of personalities this was a break between revolutionary elements and those inclined to political action.

Parti ouvrier, immediately following the Guesdist meeting. The Marxist leaders simply moved over from the *Parti ouvrier* gathering, carried through the same business, and adopted the same resolutions they had adopted in their own. The federation of *syndicats* followed with docility the path laid out for them.[12]

Again in 1892, meeting at Marseilles, Guesde and Lafargue attended first the Congress of the *Parti ouvrier* and then the Congress of the federation of *syndicats*. In attendance also were two foreign socialists, the Internationalist Anseele from Belgium and Liebknecht from Germany. They supported Guesde's view that the general strike was not the way to bring about control of the public powers. The *syndicats*, on the other hand, were growing restive and were favorable to the general strike. The difference over this question was now threatening to destroy harmony between Guesde's *Parti ouvrier* and the *syndicats*. The issue was postponed on this occasion[13] but was not dead.

Another socialist, Benoît Malon, had broken away from the Marxist disciples and formed a small group of intellectuals which included Alexandre Millerand and Jean Jaurès.[14] It is difficult to pin down the exact views of the leader or members of this group because they were engaged in serious study of the whole social movement set in a broad framework of society—legal, ethical, and political, as well as economic. In the course of their study they passed successively through many phases, adopting and then setting aside a variety of opinions. Finding authoritarian Marxism unsatisfactory, and not willing to go over to

12. Georges and Tintant, *Léon Jouhaux*, p. 15. Jouhaux (later the leader of the *syndicats*) was a youth in the eighties when the *syndicats* had "come under the tutelage of Guesde," becoming a "sort of appendage of the *Parti ouvrier*."

13. Blum, *Les Congrès*, II, 133-137. Aristide Briand, a disciple of Pelloutier (secretary and principal force in the syndical organization), was present. Briand was a newcomer to the cause of labor. Along with Pelloutier he favored the general strike and opposed the authoritarian Marxists. Later, Briand was to become a bitter foe of the general strike.

14. Jaurès's oratory was enthusiastically received at the London meeting of the Second International (1896). Jaurès had entered the Chamber of Deputies as a republican, sitting in the exact center. His chief interest was in the small farmer. Defeated for re-election at the time of the Boulanger crisis, he interested himself in municipal problems. He was concerned about the lot of the small man, in business, in agriculture, or as a small investor. The strike at Decazeville first turned his attention to the plight of the industrial laborer. See Alexander Zévaès, *Jean Jaurès* (Paris, 1941), pp. 33-47.

Possibilism, yet still socialist, they ultimately formed a group of Independents. Entering politics they refused to join any party and sat at the Extreme Left as Independents, achieving both national and international fame, as will presently appear.

In view of the elections coming up in 1893 the necessity of getting various socialist groups to co-operate, at least to the extent of providing for support to socialist candidates, was apparent. Before an audience of four thousand people Millerand advocated the socialist political path, nationalizing railroads, mines, and industries of a social type. Guesde, spokesman for the Marxists, agreed, and other speakers took the same line. They also agreed that the international organization of exploiters should be opposed by the international organization of labor.[15]

From this time on there was a socialist party in the Chamber of Deputies, capable of influencing, if only negatively, the legislative acts. There was no merging of the different groups of protest; there were still Guesdists, Broussists, Allemanists, and Independents; there were Blanquists, anarchists, and members of *syndicats*. All held congresses, and all claimed to be the true spokesmen of labor. The influence of the socialist groups on the rank and file of labor was reduced by the action of anarchists, working inside the *syndicats*[16] to pull them in the direction of violence and direct action. They posted placards at night which were torn down in the morning; they voted "with bombs," attracting increased notice in the press.[17]

The Guesdists, in 1894, for the first time made a serious effort to enlist the agricultural laborers in their Collectivist Party. They had made a faint beginning at the Congress of the *Parti Ouvrier* held at Marseilles in 1892; they proposed to carry out the work of propaganda at their meeting scheduled for September at Nantes. A manifesto was addressed by them to the country laborers: "Socialism alone . . . incarnated in a

15. *Univers*, Jan. 16, 1893. The socialist Millerand was by now a member of the Chamber of Deputies, where he continued to champion the rights of labor in specific cases which he laid before the Minister of Public Works. See *Univers*, Jan. 1, 1892. He had been an arbitrator in the big coal strike in 1892. The tendency of large industry was to cross international lines. This was noticeably true in the case of transportation companies, manufacturers of military equipment, and many others.

16. Bourdeau, *L'Évolution du socialisme*, p. 38.

17. *Univers*, Jan. 2-3, 1893.

minority daily growing stronger, represents order, civilization, humanity bringing enfranchisement to birth." On behalf of Marxism, Guesde repudiated any connection with the spreading anarchism.[18]

In September, the Congress of the party met at Nantes and adopted a resolution stating the reasons for complete rejection of the general strike, averring that "the Party does not see—and has never seen—in strikes anything but the natural and necessary consequences of capitalistic society based on antagonism of interests and classes." The speakers insisted that socialism did not "promote strikes." Then they turned to the question of the situation of the agricultural worker, now in many cases petty proprietors. The Guesdist group now made an abrupt shift from their earlier position with regard to agricultural laborers, although they insisted that they were not abandoning any of their earlier principles but were merely revising their application in the light of a changed set of circumstances. With Jaurès and Lafargue taking active part in the discussion, the Congress adopted a statement that "producers could not be free until they should be in possession of the means of production." The document went on to state that to the agricultural laborer the soil itself was his means of production; loss of ownership would turn him into an agricultural proletarian; the aim, therefore, of socialism was not to dispossess the peasant of his individual holding, but only idle owners of great domains, which would then be returned to the agricultural proletarians in collective form.

The Workers' Party [the statement went on], which, contrary to the anarchists, does not expect the transformation of the social order to arise out of extended and intensified poverty, and sees liberation for labor and for society only in the organization and combined efforts of the workers themselves taking possession of the countryside and the cities taking possession of the government and making the law, has adopted this agricultural program, designed to coalesce into a single struggle against the common enemy—the feudal landowner—all elements of agricultural production. . . .[19]

18. The manifesto was labeled "violent" by *Univers* (Aug. 28, 1894). Three days later Guesde was described in a series of "Portraits of Socialists" as an "absolutist, apostle and pontiff, excommunicating without hesitation whoever does not share his opinions or who wishes to change some detail of his plans . . . head of the doctrinaire German collectivists, Karl Marx in particular. . . ." *Ibid.*, Aug. 31, 1894.

19. *Ibid.*, Sept. 19, 1894.

Jaurès pointed out the absolute importance of getting the agricultural laborers into the movement. Guesde thought their enlistment would enable the socialists to gain control of the state by 1898.[20]

When the Congress of the federation of *syndicats* convened immediately after the meeting of the *Parti ouvrier*, the quarrel postponed two years before at Marseilles burst into the open at once. The issues which divided them were the general strike,[21] the question of anarchism,[22] and Guesde's attempt to win agricultural laborers to his movement, a move which was anathema to the *syndicats*.[23] When his principles were criticized, Guesde engaged in a tirade, lauding Marx and excoriating the dissidents; he was using "the old words" but not matching words with deeds. He was actually engaging in Opportunism to strengthen the party. He stoutly maintained, however, that this apparent shift was no innovation; he had always held this opinion; any attempt to suggest otherwise he labeled "as lying as it was idiotic."[24] François Veuillot, who was reporting the Congress for the Catholic daily, editorialized that in "destroying the abuses" which gave rise to the strikes and acts of violence, "in a Christian spirit, one would do more to cut through the socialist evil at its root, it would extirpate the root itself." Veuillot put his finger on the contradictions involved in the socialist statement—the very negation of their long-time claim that all property was to be collectivized.

20. *Ibid.*, Sept. 19, 1894. The position taken by Jaurès was in harmony with his general view. It was Guesde who was appearing in a new role. This shift of position on the part of Guesde was labeled by his critics as "opportunism." If the position taken by Guesde represented an actual change of view then he was becoming to some extent a Reformist, if not a Revisionist. If it were merely momentary "tactics" to gain support, it could not be so classed. At this point in his career the latter explanation would seem more appropriate. He did modify his views two decades later.

21. Pelloutier said that, in view of the fact that "armed insurrection in the presence of military power would only result in spilling the blood of the workers," the only resort left was the general strike. See Maitron, *Histoire du mouvement anarchiste*, p. 268.

22. It was the opinion of Pelloutier that at least for the militants syndicalism represented by 1895 total anarchy. See Maitron, *Histoire du mouvement anarchiste en France*, p. 251. Cole (*The Second International*, Part I, p. 336) says that Pelloutier "invented syndicalism," assigning to it the task of preparing in advance, in utopian fashion, for the society which was to emerge after the control of the powers of the state should have been taken away from the non-working classes.

23. Humbert (*Les Possibilistes*, p. 9) stated explicitly: "Karl Marx was still reproached for wishing to seize and direct the entire international movement as Citizen Jules Guesde was *reproached for wishing to impose himself on the totality of French socialism* [italics added].

24. *Univers*, Oct. 1, 1894.

If they got control of the government they could not—"imprisoned by their contradictions"—lay a finger on property without arousing the small agricultural owners against them. These contradictions, said Veuillot, the people would not perceive in advance. The only thing to do was to "satisfy their legitimate demands by other means" than those offered by the socialists.[25]

The federation of *syndicats* refused to follow Guesde's advice; on one issue after another they clung to their position. Aristide Briand, speaking on the question of the general strike, presented them with a good argument for its retention. The Guesdists "are trying today [he said] to propose to you that you reject it. But do they give you any new arguments? No . . . they regard it as Utopian. But is it not Utopian to hope to conquer the public powers by the ballot, which may be suppressed tomorrow?"[26] The *syndicat* Congress voted to retain the general strike, by a vote of 63 to 36 with 9 abstentions.[27] When the question of anarchism was brought up and one member made an anarchist profession of faith, sixteen non-anarchist members of the minority withdrew.[28]

In view of these differences the federation of *syndicats* decided not to hold their annual congresses at the same place as the *Parti ouvrier*, so the split became permanent.[29] The decision of the workers' organizations to sever their ties with the *Parti ouvrier* left them freer to pursue their own path.[30] The parliamentary democracy had not fulfilled their hopes either. The socialist group in the Chamber seemed to them "aimless and useless." The attempts to use political means to secure the

25. How perspicacious this analysis was would not be verified for almost three decades, when Lenin confronted this problem and was almost swamped by it. See Pierre Sorlin, "La crise du Parti bolchevik et les débuts du *Bol'sevik* (Avril, 1924-Avril, 1925)," *Revue d'histoire moderne et contemporaine*, IX (April-June, 1962), 81-110.

26. Blum, *Les Congrès*, II, 149 f. This speech by Briand was based on a study which he had made in 1892. See Cole, *The Second International*, Part II, p. 234.

27. Briand, a "vehement" supporter of the idea of the general strike, introduced the resolution to retain it. See Braunthal, *Geschichte der Internationale*, p. 297. For the vote see *Univers*, Sept. 22, 1894.

28. Blum, *Les Congrès*, II, 151. These sixteen had found the authoritarian character of the Guesdists too much for them so had gone over to the syndicalists. Now, finding anarchism too prominent there, they retreated slowly toward the Guesdists.

29. The "inseparable union" (in Guesde's words back in 1879 at Marseilles) was dissolved. See Braunthal, *Geschichte der Internationale*, p. 295.

30. Had the close relationship between the syndicalists and the socialists persisted, the movement, according to Lorwin's guess (*French Labor Movement*, p. 38), might have "emerged successful."

powers of the State merely "retarded class war, wore down the revolutionary strength of the proletariat and weakened good syndicalist action."[31] Proceeding on their own way, divorced from the socialists, the syndical door was still more open to anarchists. They turned even more to direct action.[32] As the laws passed against the labor of women and children left the families with less income, their plight seemed greater than before.[33]

At Limoges, in 1895, the syndicalists founded the *Confédération Générale du Travail*, the C.G.T., and continued more and more to adopt the actionist policy of the strike. Headquarters of the C.G.T. was to be in Paris; the organization was to open its doors to all the various separately organized groups, which might continue to hold their individual meetings wherever they pleased.[34] The Federation of Labor Exchanges presently joined the C.G.T., but remained only until 1898.

The *Parti ouvrier*, insisting on the parliamentary path to control of the public powers, was torn between the rigidity of the demands of the authoritarian Marxists, who were internationalists, and the modifying effects of participating in democratic procedures in the Chamber. The number of socalist deputies increased. They found themselves pulled toward the center with its policies of moderation, while at the same time the moderate Center, becoming more dependent on socialist votes, adopted measures that were more radical and anticlerical in consequence. All the socialist and labor groups were antimilitarist, although not all were internationalist. The Marxists were both. The Marxists were also anticolonialists. They were not interested in enhancing the prestige of France abroad or advancing the cause of their enemy the Church.[35]

31. Braunthal, *Geschichte der Internationale*, p. 294.
32. Maitron, *Histoire du mouvement anarchiste en France*, p. 250.
33. Georges and Tintant, *Léon Jouhaux*, p. 2. This biography of Jouhaux describes the life of a working family, dependent recurrently on the labor of mother and children to exist, and how this stood in the way of Jouhaux's education.
34. Lewis Lorwin, *International Labor Movement*, p. 24. The *syndicats* grew rapidly in numbers; from 605 in 1895 they climbed to 1,093 in 1902. See Georges and Tintant, *Léon Jouhaux*, p. 11.
35. The *Parti ouvrier* adopted an anticlerical resolution in 1896 at Romilly. French colonialism and Catholicism supported each other everywhere, as the career of any missionary demonstrated. Cardinal Lavigerie in North Africa is a striking example. Leo XIII pointed out this fact in audiences with Frenchmen. The Marxists resisted both the Church and colonialism. German Social Democrats, in contrast, rejected religion but accepted imperialism.

If as early as 1894 Revisionism might be inferred from the speeches and resolutions of the socialists, it emerged boldly into the limelight in 1896. The occasion was the Saint-Mandé socialist banquet held at Marseilles on July 11. Five or six thousand people were present. Among the participants were Guesde, Jaurès, Viviani, and Millerand. Jaurès painted a glowing picture of collectivist society. All was harmony. But then Millerand arose to speak and said: "We are at one and the same time idealists pursuing the total transformation of capitalist society, and realists demanding all the reforms immediately realizable under the present regime."[36]

Consternation appeared in the ranks of the authoritarian Marxists. This was Revisionism. This was cutting the ground from under the feet of the strict party which desired no reforms lest they postpone indefinitely—perhaps forever—the accomplishment of their aim to control the public powers. Millerand had not even mentioned the word *revolution*.[37] It is true that Millerand's speech had expressed his own views[38] and not those of any group. He saw the dangers confronting the Republic; the Boulanger crisis had just ended, but the Dreyfus affair was beginning.[39]

The *Parti ouvrier*, meeting a week later at Lille, felt it necessary to clarify its attitude. A statement was adopted to the effect that

the Party considers as socialists able to take advantage of the second scrutiny [of the electoral list] only those candidates who stand for the abolition of the capitalist regime by means of conquest of the political powers by the proletariat, the substitution of social property for capitalist property, and maintaining entente with the International labor organization.

36. Orry, *Les Socialistes indépendants*, pp. 28 f. See also Cole, *The Second International*, Part I, p. 340. Alexandre Millerand was a leader of the Independent group of socialists resisting the formation of a unified socialist party. Millerand's speech was quoted in *Univers*, July 14, 1896.

37. Bourdeau, *L'Évolution du socialisme*, p. 41. Cole (*The Second International*, Part I, p. 342) asserts that the speech was enthusiastically received—by the audience, yes. From the action of the *Parti ouvrier* a week later it was clear that the Marxists did not approve. Their own applause had been for public consumption. An impressive list of mayors graced the occasion. Bourdeau, writing much closer to the event, is undoubtedly correct.

38. Leo Valiani ("L'Azione di Leonida Bissolati e il Revisionismo," *Rivista storica italiana*, LXXI-III [1959], 657), maintains that Millerand was neither Marxist nor Revisionist; he was simply interested in reform. Reformism is thus distinguished from Revisionism.

39. Braunthal (*Geschichte der Internationale*, p. 265) sees these crises as more than merely internal affairs; both had international implications.

The "Internationale" was sung at the close of the meeting.[40]

The final sentence in the statement was immediately important. The London session of the International was about to convene. It was attended not only by Guesde and Lafargue, and other members of the authoritarian majority, but also by Millerand, Jaurès, and Viviani, the minority.[41]

Returned home from London, Guesde issued a manifesto in August addressed to the workers of France. It was published in *Petite République*. In the manifesto he congratulated the workers on having attacked two dangers: chauvinism and anarchism. He explained that unanimity had been achieved on the international level at Lille and at London, and concluded: "Long live the *Parti ouvrier*! Long live the International!"[42]

An Allemanist Congress at Paris in September fared no better than any of the rest in the matter of unity. The delegates worked out agenda to include discussion of general strikes, standing armies, free bread, how to organize society after the revolution, and the attitude socialists should take with regard to consumer co-operatives.[43] Since the Paris delegation proved hostile to the idea of free bread, the Allemanists split in 1896. The Communist Alliance was formed by the secessionists.[44] They clung to the free-bread idea.

Even the C.G.T. had not solved the question of labor unity, having to allow the separate federated groups to meet and conduct their affairs as they saw fit. In 1898 the Federation of Labor Exchanges left the C.G.T.[45]

It is thus obvious that in spite of the refusal of the syndicalists to

40. Blum, *Les Congrès*, II, 158.
41. It was here that Millerand suggested splitting the French vote, to give one vote to the minority and one to the majority. The minority was seated. Jaurès's opening oration was reproduced in *Univers*, Aug. 1, 1896.
42. Quoted in *ibid.*, Aug. 19, 1896.
43. *Ibid.*, Sept. 22, 1896.
44. Bourdeau, *L'Évolution du socialisme*, p. 36. See also Cole, *The Second International*, Part I, pp. 340, 348. Zévaès (*Socialisme en France*, p. 171n.) puts the split in 1897. They met separately, at any rate, in 1897.
45. Blum, *Les Congrès*, II, 169-172. The C.G.T. and the Federation of Labor Exchanges remained rivals for leadership of the workers. See Cole, *The Second International*, Part I, p. 340. Victor Griffuelhes, after Pelloutier's death to become the secretary of the federation of *syndicats*, was a Blanquist. The libertarian character of the Blanquists was almost as pronounced as that of the anarchists. See Georges and Tintant, *Léon Jouhaux*, p. 16.

yield to the advice or programs of the socialist parties, there was much of Marxism and of Blanquism in their basic attitudes. Blanqui had been the very spirit of the Commune in 1871; Marx had placed his blessing on it. The direct action involved in that event was permanently enshrined in the tradition of both.

Just as the Boulanger crisis had divided the ranks of socialists in France, so did the Dreyfus affair. The affair was also deeply significant in the history of the French Catholic Church. The anti-Semitic angle of the case did not so much affect the general development of socialism or the progress of the Church toward Christian Democracy, as it confused and tangled the course of events, making it more difficult to separate the essential threads.[46] It is sufficient to note here that Dreyfus, a wealthy, republican, Jewish officer in the French army, was accused (1894) of selling military secrets to the enemy (Germany), was quickly tried in a military court, and was sentenced to life imprisonment in a penal colony off the coast of French Guiana. This seemed a reasonable punishment for so heinous a crime. Another officer going over the records of the case, in the line of duty, came to the conclusion that something was amiss. He reported his misgivings to his superiors and was presently sent on duty to northern Africa, apparently to prevent a reopening of the case. From his North African post the officer continued to insist that an investigation of the Dreyfus affair was in order. The suicide of another officer who had been involved in the keeping of the records[47] cast still further doubt on the validity of the original condemnation of Dreyfus. The novelist Zola came out as champion of the Jewish officer in a pamphlet, *J'accuse!*[48] A second trial was held. This

46. The most recent study of the case appears in an essay on Millerand (Leslie Derfler, "Le 'Cas Millerand': une nouvelle interprétation," *Revue d'histoire moderne et contemporaine*, X [April-June, 1963], 81-104). The Millerand case is one of the most publicized events in the history of socialism. The Dreyfus affair made headlines around the globe.

47. Col. Henry, accused of falsifying the record, committed suicide while in prison. See Landauer, *European Socialism*, I, 322. Maurras described the act of Col. Henry as one of supreme patriotism. Paul Déroulède revived the monarchist *Ligue des Patriotes* as an anti-Dreyfus organization. See Derfler, "Le cas Millerand," p. 86.

48. Maitron points out (*Histoire du mouvement anarchiste en France*, p. 307) that the first publication in favor of Dreyfus was Bernard Lazare's *A Judicial Error: The Truth of the Dreyfus Affair*. Lazare thought Dreyfus was guilty, but that due process of law had not been observed. After Zola's *J'accuse!* the matter was seen as a social question, far bigger than Dreyfus. See Maitron, pp. 311 f.

time the verdict was "guilty" with "extenuating circumstances." The penalty was reduced. This settled nothing. The pressure became so great that Dreyfus was pardoned by President Loubet. Dreyfus was still protesting his innocence. Ultimately the matter was brought back into court, Dreyfus being exonerated and restored to his proper rank in the army.

All this was later, in 1904, a decade after the original event. Back in 1898, at the height of the affair, when no clear-cut evidence was available to the public as to what had really happened, French society was rent asunder. Many separate quarrels, religious, political, military, and social, merged into one. The significant question is: What were the ideological views and social class interests of the people who supported the Jewish officer's cause—the Dreyfusards—and of those who were his bitter enemies—the anti-Dreyfusards?[49] Most people were quite clearly one or the other, though this was not true of all.

The bourgeoisie made up the main ranks of the Dreyfusards—Dreyfus was bourgeois. Most army officers[50] were upper class, sons of the titled, antibourgeois and antirepublican. These were anti-Dreyfusards. The wealthy young Jews represented all that they detested. Anti-Semitism ran through the veins of these monarchists and Catholics[51] like a virus. The higher clergy agreed with the aristocrats and put the Church squarely into the anti-Dreyfusard column. Both the aristocrats and the clergy

49. Curtis (*Three Against the Republic*, pp. 353-356) identifies the anti-Dreyfusards as "Boulangists, the Army, the professional anti-Semites, the Church, and some intellectuals," largely a negative attitude. Curtis quotes Anatole France (*Le Parti Noir* [Paris, 1904], p. 20) as to the ultramontanism of these Catholic officers who were educated in the Jesuit schools, naming some who took "no decision without consulting [each] his confessor." Curtis (p. 39) adds the jibe of Clemenceau " 'that the incapable and ignorant knew nothing but that their sabres were sprinkled with incense.' "

50. Landauer suggests (*European Socialism*, p. 320) that the army wanted to use anti-Semitism as a counterweight against socialism, and that France was receptive to anti-Semitism because of some Jewish bankers connected with the Panama scandals. One should not, however, overlook the rising anti-Semitic tide all over Europe, making itself more and more noticeable in the press.

51. Jean-Marie Mayeur ("Congrès de la 'Démocratie Chrétienne,' " *Revue d'histoire moderne et contemporaine*, IX [July-Sept., 1962], 205) explores the relations between Catholicism, anti-Semitism, republicanism, and social reform—a tangled skein. Mayeur says: ". . . it is common to see attributed to the Jews, allies of the Freemasons, liberated by the Revolution, a large part of the responsibility in the policy of laicization, and in wider context all the ills which, since 1789, have been attacking the Church." He asserts also that anti-Semitism was not only inseparable from anti-Masonry but also inseparable from anti-Protestantism.

who took this step were those who refused to rally to the Republic when instructed to do so by Leo XIII, in his encyclical letter to the French, *Au milieu des sollicitudes*. The Ralliés among the churchmen and aristocrats were inclined on the ground of patriotism to regard the punishment of Dreyfus as reasonable for so great a crime as treason. This was, of course, the case before the whole story came to light.[52]

The socialists were just as divided as were the Ralliés from the non-Ralliés. The Independents, forming the Extreme Left in the Chamber, including Millerand, took initially a position of neutrality.[53] A manifesto to this effect included among the signatures those of Millerand,[54] Jaurès, and the Marxist Guesde.[55] The Blanquists, under Vaillant, were for neutrality.

The necessity for the socialists to get together in some sort of fashion was obvious. At Montluçon (September, 1898) they decided that while each socialist party would continue to have its own organization, that delegations from each of the groups would meet regularly together to decide on common action. They still paid deference to the international character of socialism in a world which was becoming international in production and exchange; they deplored the tendency of nationalism to arm workers of one country against their fellow workers in other countries; and they condemned anti-Semitism.[56]

52. Not all Catholics were anti-Dreyfusards. Ample proof is found in Leo XIII's comments during the course of an interview given to *Le Figaro* in 1899. He indicated that "good Catholics might support revisionism [i.e., reopening the Dreyfus case]. . . ." See Curtis, *Three Against the Republic*, p. 38.

53. Millerand said in a speech on the subject of revising or not revising the condemnation of Dreyfus, that Joseph Reinach (one of the leading Dreyfusards) ought to begin by rehabilitating his own family, who had been involved in the Panama scandal. A duel resulted between Millerand and Reinach. Neither was harmed. See Derfler, "Le 'Cas Millerand,'" *Revue d'histoire moderne et contemporaine*, X, 82.

54. Millerand said that until the documents were proved false, neutrality was the only position he could take. *Ibid.*, p. 82. Viviani and Briand were supporters of Dreyfus. See Zévaès, *Socialisme en France*, pp. 170 f.

55. Guesde and Vaillant remained aloof, fearful of what the affair was doing to French socialism. Their popularity in socialist circles waned as the "affair" waxed in popular appeal. See Derfler, "Le 'Cas Millerand,'" p. 86.

56. Blum, *Les Congrès*, II, 168 f. Zévaès (*Socialisme en France*, p. 174) says the union was a sort of "Vigilance Committee," necessitated by the Dreyfus affair and designed to give an outward appearance of unity. See also Landauer, *European Socialism*, I, 322. Up to this point the Guesdists had not been in favor of too highly unified a socialist organization; Guesde and his authoritarian Marxist friends could not have controlled it, and would have been relegated to the sidelines. Now, in the face of the

Jaurès presently wavered and then became a Dreyfusard. Why should he? Why should one abandon the class war to defend a member of the wealthy bourgeoisie? Once convinced of the innocence of Dreyfus, Jaurès made the whole affair a titanic struggle between the Republic and reaction.

If he has been condemned [said Jaurès of the accused] against all law, if he has been wrongly condemned, what a farce it is to count him among the privileged! No, he no longer belongs to that army, which by a criminal error has degraded him. . . . He is the living witness of military deceit, of political cowardice, of the crimes of authority.[57]

Jaurès was able to win over some Guesdists, who considered that socialism could take over the state more easily under the Republic than under monarchy; he won also some Blanquists, who were opponents of the militarists and who were strongly anticlerical. Other socialist groups became fearful of the danger to themselves if legal safeguards could be so set aside as in the Dreyfus trials.[58] The result was that the combined forces of clericalism, militarism, and monarchism were now arrayed against the bourgeoisie, the socialists, and many of the Blanquists.

How difficult such a position was for the socialists, in the light of their own history, must be obvious. The capitalists had been their sworn enemies. Among the Dreyfusard representatives in the Chamber and the Senate were persons who had tried to muzzle the socialist press.[59] How then could the socialists, in the future, talk loudly of the class struggle and of the necessity of destroying the wealth and power of the bourgeoisie? When it became apparent that the reactionaries were attacking the Republic itself, Millerand left his position of neutrality and came out on the side of the Dreyfusards.

Before the common peril [said Millerand] we ask no one his baptismal name nor whether he is moderately radical, or socialist. You are republican, that is sufficient; stretch out your hand, comrade, and Forward with the Republic![60]

danger of losing the Republic, this earlier opposition was withdrawn and Guesde spoke strongly for unity. See Derfler, "Le 'Cas Millerand,' " p. 87.

57. Quoted in Landauer, *European Socialism*, I, 322.

58. One aspect of the stir over the Dreyfus case was the resulting liberation of some of the anarchists who had been deported in 1894. See Maitron, *Histoire du mouvement anarchiste en France*, p. 316.

59. Derfler, "Le 'Cas Millerand,' " p. 83.

60. Quoted in *ibid.*, p. 89.

Millerand and Viviani, who agreed with him, in their reaching out toward republicanism widened the distance between themselves and the authoritarian socialists. Even the stricter socialists had come a long way from their traditional position by becoming involved in governmental affairs from which they never withdrew. In saving the Republic from the attack of its enemies the socialists created a new image of themselves in the public mind. In the forefront of the socialists now stood Jaurès and Millerand.

From the standpoint of the relation between the Republic and the Church, the effect of the years of struggle against the aristocratic, monarchist, clerical reactionaries embittered the republicans, whether moderate or socialist. They battled the Catholic Church in France and attacked the Concordat of 1801,[61] under which France had lived for a century. The responsibility for this disastrous struggle cannot be laid at the door of Leo XIII. He had warned the French clericals. Too many had not heeded his warning.[62]

There could be no question now; the socialists had accepted a political role in France; they had, however, continued to insist that socialists could not accept ministerial responsibility.[63] The departure from this rule in the case of Millerand, in 1899, who entered the ministry of Waldeck-Rousseau, came like a bombshell. Millerand was to be Minister of Commerce and Industry. Many socialists were actually willing to accept this, but there was worse. The shattering factor was the inclusion, as Minister of War, of General de Galliffet, leader of the bloody repression of the Commune in 1871.[64]

61. Acomb (*The French Laic Laws*, pp. 258 f.) concludes that the Dreyfus case "interrupted the truce between the moderate Catholics and the government"; the Radicals took vengeance on the Church.

62. Dansette, *Le Boulangisme*, pp. 380 f. Dansette, rehearsing the outcomes of the Boulanger affair leading to Leo XIII's Ralliement, asserts that "Catholicism lost at each step of this zigzag march." He maintains that the Left, which had been founded on the Jacobin tradition, had abandoned its "cult of revenge [*Revanche*]"; the Right took it up; the royalists had failed to establish a throne, had failed to secure the Church's unconditional support, and had failed to preserve the old social order; the cult of *Revanche* was the only thing left for them to adopt. They therefore dramatized the national peril.

63. While this view was held also in theory in the International, the question was not likely to come up anywhere else than in France. In Germany, where ministerial responsibility was only to the crown, the question would not arise. The Government was not likely to summon Bebel to take a place in the cabinet. In England with its two-party system it would be long before the socialists could become the second party.

64. Millerand had told the moderate socialists, Jaurès, Viviani, Briand, and one or

Millerand's step was Revisionism in practical form. Some thought that a unified party could have avoided this move by exerting its discipline over Millerand. That it was a smart move on the part of Waldeck-Rousseau all had to agree. Paul Lafargue, the uncompromising Marxist, appraised it thus:

M. Waldeck-Rousseau, who . . . tried to organize the league of great capitalists against socialism, appreciates its strength and this is why he has included one of its members in his ministry. It is a bold stroke. *Temps* and *Débats*, which represent so precisely the capitalist point of view, are still shaking from it. The entrance of Millerand into the Ministry is official recognition of the power of the Socialist Party, of its capacity to furnish men able to administer the nation's affairs.[65]

When Waldeck-Rousseau presented his Government for approval it was accepted by the Chamber. The socialists who disapproved (Guesdists, Blanquists, and the Communist Alliance—made up of seceders from the Allemanists) abstained from voting. To vote *against* would have put them at the side of the Extreme *Right*, which they could not stomach.[66] During his term of office Millerand created a Council of Labor, carried out many reforms in the interest of labor, and helped in the organization of the *syndicats*.[67] In the end he even renounced class war and advocated State Socialism.[68]

---

two others, of the talks that were in progress relative to his entering the cabinet. They approved. There was no question at that time of Galliffet. When the Galliffet decision came, Jaurès had some qualms, but concluded that the danger to the Republic would still justify the step. He continued to support Millerand strongly. The final solution of the Dreyfus affair had not yet been reached, and Galliffet would be able to hold the army officers down. See Derfler, "Le 'Cas Millerand,' " pp. 95, 98.

65. Paul Lafargue, *Le Socialisme et la conquête des pouvoirs publics* (Paris, 1899), a brochure reproduced in Zévaès, *Socialisme en France*, p. 169.

66. Their abstention gave the government a majority of twenty-five votes. See Derfler, "Le 'Cas Millerand,' " p. 101.

67. Rollet (*L'Action sociale des Catholiques en France*, p. 462) says the entrance of Millerand into the cabinet was one of the reasons for the decline of the Workingmen's Clubs. The reforms made the Catholic movement less necessary. The growth of the syndicalist movement had a similar effect. The organization of the clubs was not formally abolished until after Leo XIII's death. They had tried to stay out of politics, remaining (after the Ralliement) "clearly republican, clearly democratic, clearly Christian," as Harmel stated.

68. Landauer (*European Socialism* I, 328, 333) asserts that labor came to dislike Millerand in spite of his labor laws. See also Bourdeau, *L'Évolution du socialisme*, pp. 45 f. Waldeck-Rousseau had recognized, while still a senator, that the *syndicats* would play a decisive role in the development of labor. Although he was an enemy of socialism, he had been a key figure, back in 1884, in legalizing the *syndicats*.

Inclusion of a socialist in the cabinet scandalized both Right and Left political groups. Both took action. Under Paul Déroulède an abortive attempt was made at a coup d'état. It was promptly suppressed by Waldeck-Rousseau.[69] The socialist deputies in the Chamber, representing the Guesdist party (*Parti ouvrier*), the Social Revolutionary Party, and the Communist Alliance, refused to support the new Government, issuing a manifesto to the effect that the Socialist Party could not "under pain of suicide be or become a ministerial party."[70] The manifesto of this group continued:

It was a question of being done with a pretended socialist policy, contrived of compromises and deviations, which for too long had been forced to substitute for a policy of class. . . . The contradictions between the two policies had to show up one day or another. And by the entry of Millerand, a socialist, into the Ministry of Waldeck-Rousseau, joining hands with the killer of May, it has become evident, in conditions of gravity and scandal.[71]

The Possibilists of one sort or another who did not approve of the manifesto were thus arrayed against the combination of the Marxist leaders and the Blanquists. If they fought each other in the public arena on democratic grounds they could nullify a generation of socialist advance.[72] Appreciating this fact Jaurès called for a general Congress to found socialist unity, to lay out "precise tactics," and to "appease by its sovereign will the discords of the groups and the rivalries of the individuals"; the Congress was "equally necessary to judge the present and to organize the future."[73]

69. The occasion was the death of President Félix Faure. See Cole, *The Second International*, Part I, p. 343. President Émile Loubet succeeded Faure. It was Loubet who pardoned Dreyfus, thus returning him to civilian life, but as yet not finally settling the Dreyfus affair.

70. Blum, *Les Congrès*, II, 174. See also Braunthal, *Geschichte der Internationale*, p. 265.

71. Blum, *Les Congrès*, II, 175. The manifesto was issued July 14, 1899. See also Derfler, "Le 'Cas Millerand,'" p. 101. Many (perhaps a majority) of the *Parti ouvrier* did not subscribe to the sentiments expressed in the manifesto.

72. They were actually fighting each other in the pages of *Petite République*, of which the socialist Gérault-Richard was editor-in-chief, with Jaurès as a collaborator. See Zévaès, *Socialisme en France*, p. 172.

73. Jaurès, quoted in Blum, *Les Congrès*, II, 175. The actual summons to the Congress was issued by Gérault-Richard. See Zévaès, *Socialisme en France*, p. 177. The syndicalists were more amenable to suggestion of co-operation because their railway strike in the preceding year had proved a fiasco. See Cole, *The Second International*, Part I, p. 345.

The attempted coup d'état of the monarchist Right led by Paul Déroulède, unsuccessful though it was, frightened the socialists into making an attempt at socialist unity. Catholics had given their support to Déroulède.[74] The non-Ralliés were therefore to some extent responsible for the formation of the Unified Socialists.[75]

The First General Congress of the proposed organization of Unified Socialists was to meet in Paris in 1899. It was designed to include socialists of every shade, from Independents to the Communist Alliance, from Broussists to Blanquists. Guesde's *Parti ouvrier* held a preparatory meeting of its own in August at Épernay. Guesde hoped to get a unanimous decision at Épernay to back up his views. Thus his hand would be strengthened in the attempt to impress his authoritarian stamp on all socialist factions when the Congress should assemble. The proposed constitution, already written by a preparatory committee for presentation to the Congress, was the subject of discussion at the meeting at Épernay. Guesde did not get full support in the meeting of the *Parti ouvrier*. As a result of the Dreyfus affair, Jaurès had taken the leadership away from him. After two days and nights of arguing, the *Parti ouvrier* agreed that the constitution, as drawn up, should be presented to the Congress. They had misgivings. They knew that they meant by the "conquest of the public powers" the expropriation of the capitalist class, "whether the expropriation be accomplished pacifically or violently"; they thought this permitted occupation of political positions only if the party's own forces had secured the position (not true in the case of Millerand); they would leave to the National Council decisions as "occupation of other positions" (this would include the Millerand case); and

74. Landauer (*European Socialism*, I, 322) says the "Catholic hierarchy and the members of many religious orders had been among the chief organizers and supporters of the anti-democratic movement. . . ." This was not true of the Ralliés; whatever their personal sentiments they supported the democratic Republic. Their opposition to the laic laws should not be interpreted as anti-Republic. The non-Ralliés opposed both the laic laws and the Republic itself. Some of them supported Déroulède.

75. Soderini (*Leo XIII, Italy and France*, pp. 258 f.) asserts that the earlier policy of the Republic (under the Méline Ministry) had been to "fight the socialists openly, with the support of the Ralliés; this policy had merely increased the strength of the socialists"; now by becoming anticlerical Waldeck-Rousseau made a successful bid for socialist support. This alliance postponed to a large degree socialist insistence on their social demands.

they would be willing to approve the organizing of a central socialist body, without giving up the class struggle.[76]

The First General Congress of the Unified Socialists met as scheduled. It was composed of all the various socialist parties and workers as well. It was one thing to get together all the splinter parties under one roof; it would be another to get their adherence to a common program. Nevertheless, the desperate situation into which they had been thrust by the Dreyfus affair demanded unity. In the debate over the adoption of the constitutional formula laid before them, the leaders of the different parties and confederated groups showed in the diversity of their opinions the degree of their Revisionism. The principal argument was of course over the entrance of Millerand into the Cabinet. Were the socialists to co-operate with non-socialist parties? The Independent Socialist Viviani argued that as one marched toward an ideal he had to live in the midst of daily activities, and manifest adaptability to facts. One thus proved the possession of ability to carry on public affairs in the light of current circumstances and the great future interests of France.[77] Here was no railing at other classes but a forthright statement of willingness to be prepared for public responsibility and then to accept it in the interests of the people as a whole nation.[78] Briand disclaimed any special guilt on the part of Independents in deviating from the early program;[79] if guilt there were, then all were equally guilty and had paved the way by their own acts for the entrance of an Independent Socialist into the Government.[80] The Blanquist Vaillant insisted on sticking to the goal of realizing the impersonal dictatorship of the working class; until then socialism must remain in opposition to the government, which was controlled by the bourgeoisie.[81] The Marxist Guesde was positive that a socialist in a predominantly conservative bourgeois ministry would be a nonentity; acceptance of such an appointment could lead only to the bankruptcy of socialism; the workers, "disgusted with socialist policy as

76. Blum, *Les Congrès*, II, 177.
77. Viviani's speech quoted in Zévaès, *Socialisme en France*, pp. 178 f.
78. This was Revisionism. Viviani was not speaking idly; he was to be Premier of France during the crucial days at the beginning of World War I.
79. Deviation is here openly admitted. Briand was to be many times Premier of France.
80. Aristide Briand, quoted in Zévaès, *Socialisme en France*, p. 179.
81. Édouard Vaillant, quoted in *ibid.*, p. 179.

they are disgusted with opportunist policy . . . will fail to resist the first saber that comes along, just as they did Louis Bonaparte's 'Second of December.' "[82] Others appealed for peace and harmony.[83]

The First General Congress ultimately adopted two resolutions: one, that the entrance of socialists into government was incompatible with their program of class war, and two, that under some exceptional circumstances such an entrance would be condoned.[84] They were unanimously opposed to anti-Semitism, nationalism, reaction, clericalism, and militarism. The whole was rather a series of compromises than of agreements. Even the setting up of a General Committee (subsequently dominated by Guesde), the taking of the oath to the (socialist) constitution, and the singing of the "Internationale" by a delegate from Lille—the rest joining in the refrain—could not camouflage the basic differences, which flared up on every occasion. The "ministerial" socialists continued to side with each other against the "non-ministerials."[85]

When the First General Congress of the Unified Socialists adjourned, its affairs were left in the hands of the General Committee. Most of the groups refused to be subordinated to this committee, dominated as it was by Guesde. The General Committee became the bone of contention at the Second General Congress. At one point the Guesdists walked out, but they returned, convinced that unity was necessary at almost any price. The Congress voted to have a new General Committee.[86] At the third Congress, the following year, the motion against Millerand's membership in the French cabinet was overwhelmingly rejected—so the Blanquists led by Vaillant walked out and did not return.[87] As a result of the walkout a permanent split occurred in the Unified Socialist Party.

82. Jules Guesde quoted in *ibid.*, pp. 179 f. Even Guesde, the Internationalist, supported France in World War I and accepted cabinet rank.

83. Blum, *Les Congrès*, II, 181.

84. Braunthal, *Geschichte der Internationale*, p. 265. See also Blum, *Les Congrès*, II, 184. See also Zévaès, *Socialisme en France*, p. 180.

85. The "ministerials" were those who were willing to collaborate with non-socialist ministries. Orry, *Les Socialistes Indépendants*, pp. 49 f.

86. Blum, *Les Congrès*, II, 193-199. This second Congress was held September 28-30, 1900, just before the meeting of the Second International. See also Zévaès, *Socialisme en France*, pp. 188 f., and J. L. Breton, *L'Unité socialiste*, VII of Jaurès, *Histoire des partis socialistes* (Paris, 1912), 23-27.

87. Breton, *L'Unité socialiste*, p. 32.

Instead of one party there were now two socialist organizations in France: the French Socialist Party (*Parti Socialiste Français*), and the United Socialist Revolutionary Party, which came to be called the Socialist Party of France (*Parti Socialiste de France*). The one included the Broussists (original Possibilists), the Allemanists, and the Independents; the Guesdists and Blanquists comprised the other more radical group.[88] From then on these two parties met separately in different cities; both had yearly meetings.[89] In the election of 1902 the more moderate group polled 600,000 votes,[90] in spite of the activities of the Guesdists and Blanquists.

The socialists were welcome allies in the republican campaign against the Concordat of 1801 between France and the papacy.[91] Guesde was led to exclaim that this was short-sighted.

What has it brought us [he wrote], this war against parsons and the various gods of various parsons through the centuries? And the war against monarchies, royalty, or empires? Have we not played, without suspecting it . . . the game of the only real enemy, the bourgeoisie, too happy to see the efforts of the proletariat sidetracked against forms or phantoms?[92]

The verbal quarrels continued. Millerand denied that any socialist would accept "necessary and progressive" substitution of social property for capitalist property.[93] Guesde claimed that workers and owners alike were victims of the institution of private property, for whose existence

88. The one was made up of the *Fédération des travailleurs socialistes*, and some other autonomous federations. The other included the *Parti ouvrier français* (the Marxist party of Guesde and Lafargue), the *Parti Socialiste Révolutionnaire* (Blanquists led by Vaillant), and the *Alliance Communiste*. See Blum, *Les Congrès*, II, 105.

89. Zévaès, *Socialisme en France*, pp. 193 f. Alexandre Zévaès himself remained with the Independent group. See also Breton, *L'Unité Socialiste*, pp. 32-35.

90. Orry (*Les Socialistes Indépendants*, p. 58) makes this claim. Cole (*The Second International*, p. 353) claims that the moderate group received 400,000 votes; the more radical group (Socialist Party of France) received about the same number (400,000).

91. Georges Clemenceau, a republican, founded a journal in 1901 called the *Bloc*. He claimed that there were two blocs in France: the "theocratic Church" and the bloc of the "Revolution of justice and liberty." See Claude Lévy, "Un Journal de Clemenceau: *Le Bloc* (Janvier 1901—Mars 1902)," *Revue d'histoire moderne et contemporaine*, X (April-June, 1963), 106. Clemenceau claimed that one of the two blocs would necessarily "pulverize the other."

92. Jules Guesde, "Un Congrès modèle," *Le Petit son*, Sept. 19, 1900. Quoted in Zévaès, *Socialisme en France*, p. 184. Zévaès comments that the article was a revision of one Guesde had published a decade earlier. Zévaès said Guesde's view here expressed differed from the views of Marx expressed in *Le 18 Brumaire*.

93. Orry, *Les Socialistes Indépendants*, p. 28.

neither was responsible.[94] He rejected the idea of the State's acting as Providence,[95] claiming instead that on the contrary the State was doomed to disappear. Millerand branded as impossible the creating of a new order by "rubbing a magic ring," or setting up an entirely new society on a *tabula rasa*; it could not be accomplished by a dictator, but only by universal suffrage, by employing the right of persuasion. He claimed that internationalism did not preclude patriotism. Millerand was criticized by the uncompromising group for voting with the Government on some issues instead of abstaining. He replied that socialism would betray its most important obligation by taking refuge in a "revolutionary verbalism" in order to avoid the "responsibility implicit in the reforming method."[96] Revisionism was out in the open!

Even on the subject of militarism, about which Marx had been dogmatic, the note of Revisionism crept in. Socialists had preached international peace and disarmament for years.[97] Now, in the French Chamber, when the military budget was discussed, even socialists agreed that their doctrine did not mean that France should disarm while others armed, but that simultaneous disarmament should be sought.

Guesde remained aloof from the bloc that was conducting the affairs of France[98] and fighting the Church. He was no less opposed to the anarchists than to the moderate progressist socialists. He accused the anarchists of wanting to cure society's ills by returning to a state of nature, "man against man as the wolf of the forest is confronted with another wolf." Society, he maintained, rejecting "natural laws," developed "against the state of nature its [own] laws."[99]

The *syndicats*, which had long since parted company with the socialist

94. Jules Guesde, *Quatre ans de lutte* (2 vols., nos. VI and VII of *Bibliotèque d'études socialistes*, Paris, 1901), VI, 21.

95. *Ibid.*, p. 25.

96. *Temps*, March 5, 1903. Valiani calls Millerand a "practical reformist," not Revisionist. See *Revista storica italiana*, LXXI-IV (1959), 657.

97. The First Hague Peace Conference had been held in 1899, sponsored by Tsar Nicholas II. This conference was denounced at the meeting of the Second International (1900) because it had been called and patronized by the very powers which by their imperialism were making war inevitable. See Cole, *The Second International*, Part I, p. 44.

98. France was on the eve of forming with England an *entente cordiale*, to offset the Triple Alliance.

99. Guesde, *Quatre ans de lutte*, VI, 24.

organizations, continued their expansion over the turn of the century, still seeking direct action. Wherever large-scale industries came into being, capital and labor became sparring partners across the conference table, not to destroy each other but to gain advantage. This growth and consolidation brought another question to the fore: How far should crippling strikes be permitted to interfere with the general welfare?[100]

Revisionism is thus seen to be, in France, a gradual development, in part growing out of democratic procedures as they applied to the changing scene. The socialists were drawn steadily by the mounting pull of nationalism. They continued to respect the memory of Marx but no longer accepted his dogma as inspired. Marx had never denied that there was more than one path to the socialist goal. The French socialists chose the path opened by universal suffrage for achieving their aim through the electoral process. Participating in the legislative proceedings of government meant participating in the responsibilities that rest on legislators as well as on administrators. Responsibility had a moderating effect. Their legislative decisions resulted in tangible, visible changes in the life of all citizens. They influenced the course of events as long as their alliance with the Radicals (liberals) lasted,[101] producing improvements in the lot of the laborer. Conditions in society, especially the growth of large-scale industry,[102] set aside an earlier demand on the part of workers to own their own tools. As Jaurès pointed out, some form of collectivism was the only way for the worker to own anything. "What we want," he said, "is that no man must be at any moment, under any form, in any degree, the thing, the utensil, and the instrument of another man."[103]

100. *Temps*, Dec. 21, 1902. This question came up in connection with a shipping strike at Marseilles. The suggestion was made that an obligatory delay should occur before actually going on strike after it was announced.

101. The need of the Radicals for support from the socialists appears clearly in *Temps* (Feb. 2, 1903): ". . . a [would-be] Radical Government is trying to turn out the Government, while Jaurès, the socialist, enemy of the bourgeoisie, is trying to sustain it." The Radicals, so the journal went on, had no other program than anticlericalism while the socialists had many others in mind; for them, said the journal, anticlericalism was merely an episode. See also Lévy, "Un Journal de Clemenceau: *Le Bloc*," *Revue d'histoire moderne et contemporaine*, X (April-June, 1963), 114.

102. This was ultimately true of agriculture also, but not during the nineteenth century.

103. The encyclicals of Leo XIII on the subject of labor contain nothing that would contradict this statement. Jaurès, at the beginning of 1903, was elected one of the four vice-presidents of the Chamber of Deputies. Radicals as well as socialists voted for him.

As it became obvious that the workingman needed an education and a broader view of political and economic matters, the socialists became increasingly attached to the Republic and its democratic reforms and supported its social legislation. These new socialists, who might have approached the Church more closely still in their genuine concern for the downtrodden, were drawn instead into opposition of a bitter sort because of the violence of the quarrel between the state and the Church over the Dreyfus affair, education, and kindred subjects.[104]

During the course of the French altercation over Millerand's entry into the non-socialist cabinet of Waldeck-Rousseau, and while the Dreyfus affair was far from settled, the Second International held its fifth Congress in Paris (1900), immediately following the Second General Congress of the French Socialists. Here in Paris the International had been organized eleven years earlier. At this meeting at the turn of the century they set up an International Socialist Bureau, to function between meetings of the International. The "Millerand Case" was disturbing, but it must be settled in some way that would placate the extremes. As has already been noted, it was Kautsky who devised a compromise resolution, presented by Vandervelde. The resolution regarded the entry of a socialist into a non-socialist cabinet as a temporary and exceptional "makeshift in an emergency situation"; the minister must remain a "delegate of his party."[105] Voting on the resolution was not individual but by national delegations. The resolution was adopted by a vote of 29 to 9. The rest of the meeting was taken up with a discussion of the value of the general strike in preventing war and in the denunciation of imperialism and militarism. During the discussion of the Kautsky resolution the Italian Ferri had tried to get a stronger wording adopted

His assassination on the eve of World War I at the hands of a fanatic cut short the career of a person of brilliant mind and very sincere feeling for the welfare of the common man.

104. The quarrel with France on this question cannot be taken up in this study. The Progressist Republicans were also members of the anticlerical bloc. Paul Deschanel was their most outstanding member. He and the rest of the Progressist Republicans apparently regarded Jaurès's internationalist views as harmless. For analysis of these groupings, see *Frankfurter Zeitung* (4th A.M. ed., Jan. 22, 1903). The bloc was dependent for its life on its anticlerical policies. See *ibid.*, Jan. 29, 1903.

105. Georg von Vollmar, "Zum Fall Millerand," Socialistische Monatsheft (No. 12, Dec., 1900), p. 767. Vollmar derived his information from David and Bernstein.

on the matter of participation of a socialist in government, but he was unsuccessful.

REVISIONISM IN ITALY

Organized Marxian socialism was so late in developing in Italy that Revisionism followed close upon its heels in the peninsula. Elsewhere in western Europe Revisionism was already the order of the day in practice and rapidly becoming so in theory. Even the Second International was forced to accept it, in order to avoid disintegration. The early triumph of Italian Revisionism, however, must be attributed, partly, to the fact that many of the leading social theorists of Italy were sincerely Catholic. Through their interest in the Social Studies Circles they had become committed to an attempt to solve the social question. They were in a position to wield influence on the young, not only in the circles but in university seminars[106] and through their published works. The encyclical *Rerum Novarum* and the growth of the *Opera dei Congressi* (especially after 1889) were other factors. The number of rigid Marxists was therefore small, although it remained vocal. Their opinions expressed at international gatherings were extreme, but at home they were unable to control the party. Most of the extremists had been anarchists. The exclusion of the anarchists from the party organization left the extremists in a minority. Anarchism, not destroyed by the exclusion, moved into the workers' professional organizations, the *sindicati*. In these *syndicats* the anarchists found fertile ground, especially in the south.

Real socialist organization was limited to northern Italy and was still largely local in character. The sporadic uprisings in the south, accompanied by violence, brought the socialist movement everywhere in Italy into disrepute. The moderate socialist activities in the north were more harshly criticized and more severely repressed than would otherwise have been the case.[107] All were regarded as "subversive." Antisocialist legislation made it inexpedient to put workers' organizations and the socialist political party into organic union or even too close collaboration.

106. Vaussard, *Histoire de l'Italie*, p. 56.
107. Spadolini, *Lotta sociale in Italia*, p. 133. See also Vaussard, *Histoire de l'Italie*, p. 57.

After 1895 the expiration of the emergency laws (1894-1895) permitted the socialists to organize and to enter politics. With this entrance into political life the trend of Italian socialism toward pragmatic solutions began to take precedence over theoretical dogma. Thus it is obvious that at the very time when the views of Marx and Engels were becoming known to Italian socialist leaders[108] and followers the operation of forces drawing them toward practical application produced inevitably a tendency toward Revisionism.[109]

The socialists became a party of obstruction. After the "Terrible year" of 1898[110] the socialists decided to desist from their intransigence and collaborate with other parties of the Left. This was, of course, Revisionism, at least in practice. Socialists exiled in 1898 began to return and bolster the size of the socialist group in the Chamber, which continued its support of the Left bloc. This policy was maintained, with some increase in socialist autonomy, to the death of Leo XIII, at which time support of the Left began to dissolve. The majority in the Socialist Party was led by Ivanoe Bonomi.[111] The minority, much more extreme, was guided by Enrico Ferri.[112]

The principal question at issue among the Italian socialists was co-operation with other parties. At Emilio Reggio they had asserted that socialist deputies could not co-operate with other groups in the Chamber. In 1895 (at Parma) they decided that under some circumstances they might do so. They held to this position at the party congresses at Rome (1900) and at Imola in 1902.[113] During this period of collaboration

108. It was in 1895 that Professor Antonio Labriola published his first writing in commemoration of the *Communist Manifesto*. See Bonomi, *La politica italiana da Porta Pia a Vittorio Veneto*, p. 117.

109. Arfé (reviewing Cortesi, *La Constituzione del Partito socialista italiana* in *Rivista storica italiana*, LXXIV-I [1962]) speaks (p. 205) both of the evident Marxist inspiration of Italian socialist theory and of the necessity of participating in electoral competition and political struggle.

110. The socialists attributed the bad conditions of 1898 to the disorders of capitalist society. The republicans said it showed monarchy could not provide for the welfare of the people. The clericals said it proved that a state inimical to the Church could neither solve the social question nor provide social discipline. See Bonomi, *Politica italiana*, p. 158. A policy of too little, too late, and then violent repression did not work. See *ibid.*, pp. 159-162.

111. Neufeld, *Italy*, p. 230.

112. Neufeld speaks (*ibid.*, p. 230) of the "impulsive Enrico Ferri, who never held to one position for very long." It was he who had tried to amend Kautsky's resolution at the Paris meeting of the Second International.

113. Lémonon, *L'Italie économique et sociale*, p. 346.

some reforms were carried through,[114] notably in the administration of local government. The liberals courageously defended the socialists' rights to free speech, free association, fair trial, and free press. This defense played a conspicuous part in softening the attitude of socialists in the matter of class war; to attack middle-class liberals who were staunchly advocating civil liberties would have seemed rank ingratitude. So was formed the *Estrema*, a new grouping of republicans, radicals, and socialists, in Italian politics.[115] This union was harassed by the revolutionary wing of Italian socialism. Ill-advised strikes annoyed the public and hampered the task of the parliamentary socialists.

In the Chamber of Deputies the *Estrema* resorted to obstructionism against a government which flouted all the established procedures. Many moderates and some conservatives joined the *Estrema* in voting. Considering themselves out-gaveled and out-counted by the government, the *Estrema* even destroyed the voting urns. In this battle over democratic rights the Italian people supported the *Estrema* as the party of liberty; they voted in increasing numbers for socialist deputies. Sincere Catholics, resentful of anticlerical measures and the way the laws were enforced by the police, sympathized with the socialists, harassed by police action. The accession of Victor Emmanuel III (1900), after King Humbert's assassination by an anarchist, led Italy closer to liberty. When Zanardelli became Prime Minister in 1901, the nation entered on a new era. Zanardelli had put through a code in 1889 which permitted peaceful organization of groups, whether to right or left, and the right of workers to strike if not accompanied by violence.[116] Zanardelli appointed Giovanni Giolitti as Minister of the Interior. With sanction and support of Zanardelli, Giolitti was able to prevent police interference with the right of workers to organize and to strike, when these activities were carried out peacefully. Under Zanardelli's regime steps were taken to establish a National Labor Office and a Superior Council of Labor.

114. Workmen's compensation was made compulsory in 1890; boards of trustees were provided by legislative act (1894) to work out settlements of points of dispute between workers and employers. See Neufeld, *Italy*, p. 324.

115. *Ibid.*, p. 217. Reference is to the *Estrema Sinistra*, usually referred to simply as *Estrema*.

116. For a discussion of the parliamentary crisis, see Gaetano Mosca, *Partiti e sindicati nella crisi del regime parlamentare* (Bari, 1949), *passim*. See also Spadolini, *Lotta sociale*, p. 131.

Though theoretical Revisionism in Italy began with Benedetto Croce, in April, 1893, it was developed by Antonio Labriola,[117] Croce's philosophy professor in the University of Rome.[118] Holding orthodox views of Marxism, Labriola was partially responsible for the high esteem in which both Marx and Engels were held in intellectual circles in Italy. His correspondence with Engels (who died in 1895), pursued under difficulties,[119] is evidence. Labriola submitted the works of the two founders to keen philosophical scrutiny. He concluded that historical materialism was, in a certain sense, "the whole of Marx."[120] In discussing Marx's *Heilige Familie*, he says it showed how Marx and Engels, already freed from Hegelian scholasticism, were trying to extricate themselves from Feuerbach's humanitarianism. Labriola came to the the conclusion that the philosophic and scientific ideas of Marx and Engels were the "result of German culture, but that the social conditions they were discussing were the product of their experience in England and France as exiles." He viewed their successive writings as *progressive comments* on what they saw about them. He said they had renounced "true social-ism" by the time they wrote, "satirically," the *Communist Manifesto*. Labriola thus makes clear that he regarded both Marx and Engels as Revisionists.[121] Labriola, nevertheless, derided the attempt of the French Jaurès to reconcile the points of view of idealists and materialists.[122]

Revisionism appeared also in questioning the validity of one of Marx's most rigidly held concepts: the absence of private property in the

117. Antonio Labriola must not be confused with Arturo Labriola, also a professor, syndicalist leader, and practicing socialist.

118. Leo Valiani, "L'Azione di Leonida Bissolati e il revisionismo," *Rivista storica italiana*, LXXI-IV (1959), 655. Valiani asserts that with a few exceptions the affinity be-tween Revisionism and Reformism was always present (p. 656).

119. Labriola, writing to Engels (Nov. 23, 1894), ends his letter: "Let me hear from you on some pretext or other." See Antonio Labriola, *Lettere a Engels*, p. 175. He dis-cussed also various aliases and addresses of socialists hiding in London or Paris and how to communicate with them. This was, of course, in 1894, while Crispi was in office. As long as Crispi remained in power harassments continued, regardless of modification of the law.

120. Antonio Labriola, *Discorrendo di Socialismo e di Filosofia*, ed. B. Croce (5th ed.; Bari, 1947), p. 14.

121. *Ibid.*, pp. 15, 193.

122. *Ibid.*, p. 14. Labriola says that, according to Jaurès, the disciples of Marx recog-nized the existence of a "direction in the economic movement and in the human movement," while he himself (Jaurès) believed that "humanity seeks and affirms itself, whatever the difference of environments."

society which was inevitably to emerge. Murri, one of the outstanding leaders of the Catholic reforming movement and idolized by the young, questioned this dictum, affirming in the first place that the mass of the proletariat were opposed to the purely collective idea and, in the second place, that practical, moderate, and possible solutions attracted the leading socialists of the time in France, Germany, and Italy.[123] This fact, if Murri correctly assessed the tenor of his time, brought the thinking of workers, socialists, and Leo XIII much closer together. Leo asserted the principle of divinely ordained private property in the *Rerum Novarum*,[124] but not the right to use it as one pleased. He believed in justice, not in collectivized property.

Revisionism moved into crisis as the open controversy between Bernstein and Kautsky developed. It was the Bohemian, Thomas Masaryk, who coined the phrase: "Crisis of Marxism." Labriola quotes Masaryk:

I should like to admonish the enemies of Marxism, not to entertain any vain hopes . . . in this crisis of Marxism, which can give great strength to socialism when its leaders are willing to criticize liberally its fundamentals and overcome its defects . . . socialism has its own living fountain in the manifest imperfections of the present social order, and in its injustices and immorality, and above all in the moral, intellectual and material misery of the great mass of the people.

It would be "crazy or stupid," he concluded, "to proceed by any other path than that of parliamentary tactics."[125]

If the social problem were to be solved in Italy the Church needed to get into the fray. Some Catholics participated in elections in defiance of the *non expedit*. The intransigents among the clergy regarded the Roman Question as more significant than the "aspirations of the Italian people." The socialists, on the other hand, now parliamentary and Revisionist, seeking practical improvements in day-by-day living, had for the masses a greater appeal.[126]

123. Romolo Murri, *Kämpfe von Heute: Das christliche Leben zu Beginn des zwanzigsten Jahrhunderts*, pp. 193 f. Murri thought socialism was a "whole view of life"—as many believed—"a religion."

124. Sanseverino, *Il movimento sindacale cristiano*, p. 447. It was doubtful, thought the author, that Christian Socialism would ever give up its belief in private property.

125. Labriola, *Discorrendo di Socialismo e di Filosofia*, p. 217. He was quoting from Masaryk's *Die philosophischen und sociologischen Grundlage des Marxismus: Studien zur socialen Frage* (Prague, 1898), p. 211.

126. Gambasin, *Il movimento sociale nell'Opera dei Congressi*, p. 466.

XVI. THE LAST YEARS OF LEO XIII

" 'RERUM NOVARUM' . . . was rightly acknowledged as the Magna Carta of the economic-social reconstruction of the modern era."[1]

POPE JOHN XXIII

Leo XIII's greatest claim to fame rests on the *Rerum Novarum*. He issued it in the last decade of the nineteenth century, when he was already past eighty years of age. In it he openly and publicly espoused the cause of social welfare. In the eyes of some he was a "socialist," a "Christian socialist." From now on the term "Christian Socialism" came to be applied more and more frequently to the activities of the Church in relation to the social question. It had been used now and again in the 1880's, when the concept of "justice" was added to "charity" in concern for the welfare of the laborer.[2] Millerand, editor of *Justice*, attached the word "socialist" to Albert de Mun and referred to his movement as "Christian Socialism."[3] The designation used by the International Union of Social Studies was "Social Catholicism." The welter of terms applied to the social-action movement of the Church was not ended but rather increased by the encyclical. Both the ultraconservative Right and the socialist Left thought the encyclical advocated socialism.

In Italy, two decades had elapsed between the founding of the *Opera*

1. From the encyclical *Mater et Magistra*, May 15, 1961.
2. Francesco Nitti, Italian historian, entitled one of his books *Catholic Socialism* (*Socialismo cattolico*). By 1890 its second edition had appeared.
3. Millerand said de Mun's socialism set the rights of God as the necessary basis of institutions, laws, and customs. "That is what creates an abyss between the republican socialists and the Christian socialists." See *Univers*, July 2, 1889.

dei Congressi and the issuance of the *Rerum Novarum*. The Catholic organization had been founded at the instigation of the Society of Catholic Youth. The "Young"—in spite of massive resistance on the part of reactionary elements in the *Opera dei Congressi*—continued the attempt to leaven the resistant lump. Agreement had been reached that labor unions should be established, but always, insisted the reactionaries, under the control of the hierarchy. Medieval "corporations" of craftsmen were no answer to the problem of rescuing labor from the horrors resulting from unrestricted application of laissez-faire "laws." The "Young" advocated "free" unions, run by the laborers themselves, without the interference (or presence) of members of the clergy or employers.

The issuance of the *Rerum Novarum* strengthened the hands of the youthful Catholic reformers. A new generation of youth had grown up since the founding of the *Opera dei Congressi*. Filippo Meda, inspired and guided by Giuseppe Toniolo (professor of economics at the University of Pisa), and the young priest Romolo Murri became the leaders of the Catholic social reform movement in Italy during the last decade of Leo XIII's life. They were able to register some slight successes in the matter of labor organization,[4] working through the *Opera dei Congressi*. The success seemed infinitesimal in the face of the magnitude of the problem confronted.

Murri, in assessing the rival claims of the Church and socialism to assist the rise of the common man, took issue with the socialists' assertion that "the revolution"[5] was not anti-Catholic but un-Catholic. Leo XIII's encyclical showed that the Pope was willing to place himself at the head of a movement to accept the revolutionary implications of the changing world. The socialists, said Murri, were showing themselves adaptable to conditions which varied according to the local situation. He supported this statement by calling to mind that in Germany socialists had sided

4. Rural banks grew from 1 to 759, while mutual aid societies grew from 274 to 825 during the period from the *Rerum Novarum* to the death of Leo XIII. Even a few "free" or "simple" workers' unions were formed. Most of the 229 Catholic unions were, however, of the "mixed" variety (owners and workers). See Neufeld, *Italy*, p. 357.

5. By "revolution" is meant the revolutionary stream running from the Enlightenment to the twentieth century, embracing the Industrial Revolution, the Scientific Revolution, and the "French Revolution," which, exploding in 1789, continued to explode at intervals, in ever-widening circles, like the aftershocks and tidal waves of an earthquake. Every aspect of life was shaken and questioned.

with Catholics in the Kulturkampf. In France, on the other hand, such co-operation was not possible because the French socialists were hostile to the Church, if not frankly irreligious.[6] The Church, however, had remained, he thought, too long within the bounds of dogma and must be brought into relation with modern questions, the life of the people, the social struggle, the problems created by the new learning. This quarrel, he maintained, between old and new had been going on from the Council of Trent to the Vatican Council I, going now one way and now the other; the *Rerum Novarum* emphasized the new direction.[7]

When Toniolo established a review, *Vita Nuova* (1895), it was essentially this same point of view which emerged.[8] The *Rerum Novarum* had certainly called attention to the social function of property as an instrument of the prosperity of all.[9] The members of the Union of Freiburg had interpreted this in a paternalistic sense. What was amazing about the encyclical was that Leo XIII had gone beyond paternalism to a modern view of labor organization which could, if it chose, organize itself without the interposition of the upper classes. The propriety of state intervention in these matters of social justice was likewise affirmed.[10] This was what the intransigents could not agree to. Social legislation, or state action in any form, could not meet with their approval because it would, in Italy, necessarily imply a recognition of the legality of the state and participation of Catholics in the legislative process. They would not relinquish the *non expedit*; it became in 1895 *non oportat*. The Temporal Power blinded them to the legitimate desires of the Italian people. So

6. Murri, *Kämpfe*, pp. 187 f. Murri was interpreting socialism as having no *official* religion; he interpreted Leo XIII as coming over to views not at variance with the socialists.

7. *Ibid.*, pp. 201 f. Murri said the Church under Leo XIII had struggled for the reorganization of society and united on the basis of professional interests those who were "set adrift by political liberalism of the past hundred years." This shows Murri's antilaissez-faire attitude in economic matters, and assets that Leo's views agreed with his.

8. Vaussard, *Histoire de la Démocratie Chrétienne*, p. 222.

9. Francesco Vito, "L'economia a servizio dell uomo: caposaldo della dottrina sociale cattolico," *Nel LXX Anniversario della "Rerum Novarum,"* p. 3. Modestino R. Manfra ("La funzione sociale della proprietà," *ibid.*, pp. 95-111) devotes an entire essay to this question and its relation to the *Rerum Novarum*.

10. Vito ("L'economia a servizio dell uomo . . . ," *ibid.*, p. 3) states this as one of the important points of the encyclical, "to reduce or eliminate social injustices, whether through *social legislation* or *social policy* [italics mine]."

insistence on the Temporal Power alienated from the Church's side those who had been drawn to it by the encyclical.[11]

In France, two socialist journals warned their readers not to be subverted by a "socialist Pope."[12] La Tour-du-Pin, on the other hand, although refusing to bow to the Pope's admonition as expressed in *Au milieu des sollicitudes*, had accepted the *Rerum Novarum* as the pattern for Catholic conduct in the matter of the social question and regarded it as truly conservative in the best sense of the word. He wrote to Decurtins of Switzerland:

In the same way that Pius IX by the proclamation of the *Syllabus* turned Christianity from entering the path of revolution, so Leo XIII has accomplished the indefectible work of the Roman Pontificate in having it enter the path of social reorganization. The former has had to count on being listened to by the people; the latter on governments to second him; it is, however, one and the same policy, that of the Church, which oscillates, but never vacillates.[13]

A host of writers in Catholic Europe undertook works in the fields of sociology, morals, and law. Through their reviews and books they furnished the basis for popularizing the intent of the *Rerum Novarum* and helped to transform Leo's words into programs of action. This movement was notable in Holland and Germany as well as in Catholic states— France, Belgium, and Italy.[14]

The movement initiated in his famous encyclical was further supported by Leo in his discourses to pilgrims and in his letters to de Mun in France, to Decurtins in Switzerland, to Bishop Doutreloux and Cardinal Langénieux in Belgium. The latter two were pre-eminent leaders among the Catholic clergy on the Continent. To pastors and flocks by word of mouth papal thought was echoed in the whole world, "urging prompt and effective remedies," which would determine "whether democracy should be Christian or socialistic."[15]

11. Nitti, in 1895, wrote: ". . . the Catholic Church, whose power is daily increasing, is bound, in order to maintain its catholicity, not to stand aloof from socialism, which is the most catholic or universal fact existing in the modern world." See Nitti, *Catholic Socialism*, p. 383.

12. Quoted in *Univers*, May 28, 1891. Ultraconservative *Autorité* regarded Christian Socialism as "revolutionary and anti-social." Quoted in *Univers*, July 3, 1895.

13. *Liberté* (Freiburg), quoted in *Univers*, July 7, 1894.

14. Toniolo, *Opera omnia*, ser. iv, I, 54.

15. This movement represented a "going to the people." See *ibid.*, p. 58.

Not all agreed with Leo XIII. Some thought that he had been right in condemning the rapacity of owners, regarding his statements on this question as resembling in severity those made by the socialists themselves. They disagreed as to his placing the rights of the family as above the rights of the State. Leo regarded family rights as superior to the State's because the family as an institution was older than the State. "Just remuneration" was a "vague" term. The Pope had clarified it to the extent of insisting that it should maintain the worker and his family in "frugal comfort." Socialists scoffed, and enterprising laborers were resentful. The Revolution had promised the right of the lower classes to rise in the scale; it demanded the replacement of a closed society by an open society. The underprivileged in the end would be content with nothing less. The severest criticism was that the Pontiff underestimated the severity of the problems involved in the social revolution and therefore proposed remedies which, good as they were, were still inadequate for the changing times.[16] The miracle, to others, was that the encyclical, together with Leo's personal encouragement, untied the hands of Catholic leaders to work out social solutions in harmony with the spirit of Christianity— except in Italy.

This new spirit was particularly evident among some of the leaders in Belgium. Not all Catholics, however, heeded the Pontiff's words. In 1895 Leo XIII found it necessary to give specific advice in the case of Belgium. The Bishop of Liége, visiting His Holiness, found him saddened by the growth of socialism in the Catholic state. There were still divergences, the Bishop said, among Belgian Catholics, although they were lessening because of the discussion of doctrines and principles by economists and sociologists following the promulgation of the great encyclical. The Bishop had urged his own diocese to "concentrate their action against the enemies of religion and the social order. . . ." Such antagonisms as remained would retard reforms necessary to improve the lot of the workingmen. So Leo wrote to Archbishop Goosens and other Belgian bishops.[17] He knew, he said, what obstacles in Belgium stood in the way of carrying out the program advocated, but he believed the

16. Nitti, *Catholic Socialism*, pp. 374-379.
17. This letter is the *Permoti Nos*, written on July 10, 1895. It appeared in *Univers* on July 25, 1895.

difficulty was that in spite of advice they were "holding different opinions" from each other, embracing "different ways of acting," and were continuing to maintain these divergences; the lack of concord among the Belgian Catholics was the result. The Pope advised holding a congress to discuss the whole matter, so that in the dioceses the questions could be properly handled. He reiterated the concern which religion has with the interests of society, of domestic life, and of economic life. He went on: ". . . let the workers in no way fail in their submission and reliance on their employers, but also let the latter leave nothing to be desired as to justice, kindness, and benevolent care. . . ." They should set aside controversial discussion and mutual reproaches. "Let the clergy march at their head. . . ." When the fourth Congress of the Democratic League (Catholic) met at Ghent at the end of September, the delegates lauded Leo's letter and mourned with him "the loss of the Temporal Power."[18]

Paternalism seemed evident in Leo's advice to the Belgian Bishop. Had he revisited Belgium he would have realized its inapplicability. The political and economic changes taking place in the nineteenth century emphasized the equality of men as citizens. The Church, it is true, emphasized their equality as sons of God. The development of huge industrial plants (especially in Belgium and the Rhineland, both Catholic) rendered any possibility of paternalism outmoded.[19] That Leo XIII had gone beyond paternalism was not realized or was ignored by many of the critics of the time. This was brought out dramatically in France. The rise of social democracy there, in the absence of rigid class structure,[20] coupled with the Church's view of the dignity of man, made possible a transition through Christian paternalism to some form of collective bargaining, by *syndicats* alone, without the presence of employers. Many Catholics either did not read the words of the *Rerum Novarum* or pretended not to know that they were there. *Univers* listed[21] in parallel columns the phrases of the encyclical and the statements of the Catholic Congress of the North. When Leo said that "good will come of organization whether of workers

18. *Ibid.*, Sept. 24, 1895.
19. Shanahan (*German Protestants Face the Social Question*, p. 397) makes this point clear as to the Rhineland, which was under the German Empire; the individual proprietor was rapidly being eliminated from the scene.
20. This was in sharp contrast to the situation in Germany, where the rigidity of the class structure was maintained as long as monarchy survived.
21. Oct. 8, 10, 13, 1894.

alone" or otherwise, the congresses said: "societies composed of workers are dangerous and deadly"; they called the poverty of workers "merited," while Leo spoke of "*un*merited poverty"; they called "dangerous" and "utopic," professional *syndicats* in which the workers can discuss with the employer such questions as wages and hours of labor; Leo said it was better to discuss them rather than to bring about a situation in which the public powers would have to intervene; the congresses argued that employers were not responsible for workers out of work, whereas Leo emphasized the principle of mutual responsibilities. As the encyclical became better publicized, praise continued to pour in from everywhere for this "Magna Carta" of labor.[22]

In the field of diplomacy Leo XIII had been almost universally successful. Now, his prestige mounting as a result of the *Rerum Novarum* and his support given to the Republic of France, hope was held out that perhaps relations with the Anglican Church might be put on a better footing. It was a vain hope. His encyclical, *Satis cognitum*, on the unity of the Church,[23] stated his position without equivocation. Three quotations from earlier writers were included. Saying that the Church was unique and perpetual, and that "whoever separates himself from her ... leaves the path of safety, goes to destruction," he quoted St. Cyprian: " 'Whoever separates from the Church to be joined with an adulterous spouse is separated from the promises made to the Church, nor will he attain the rewards of Christ who abandons Christ's Church. . . .' "[24] He quoted St. Augustine: " 'There is nothing more grave than the sacrilege of schism . . . there is no legitimate necessity for breaking the unity.' "[25] Then, quoting St. Thomas: "If anyone says moreover that the one head and one pastor is Christ, who is the one spouse of the Church, this

22. Avolio, writing in the year of Leo's death (*I Democratici e'il non-expedit*, p. 27) criticized the French for resisting the pontifical advice. "Persecution in France," he said, "would not have occurred if they had tried to organize the workers on the program of democracy." According to Avolio, they "reaped" what they had sown.

23. This encyclical was issued at the very time when socialists of Europe were preparing to attend the London meeting of the Second International in the interest of proletarian unity.

24. *Quisquis ab Ecclesia egregatus adultere jungitur, a promissis Ecclesiae separetur, nec perveniet ad Christi praemia qui reliquit Ecclesiam Christi. . . ."* Univers, July 2, 1896.

25. *Non est quicquam gravius sacrilegio schismatis . . . praecidendae unitatis nulla est justa necessitas.*

response is not sufficient,' "[26] he closed the door on the possibility of reconciliation with the Church of England.[27] Relations with England remained amicable, however, throughout his pontificate.

By the summer of 1897 Leo XIII was finding the heat of Rome hard to endure. Barred by his concept of himself as "Prisoner of the Vatican" from leaving the Vatican, he could not seek relief at Castle Gandolfo, the summer refuge of his predecessors. He was an old man, now eighty-seven years of age. He had a small retreat constructed in the Vatican gardens to secure some relief. Here he could say his early morning Mass, then take a walk, reciting his breviary under the oaks; after a frugal meal he could engage in conversation with prelates and even receive, here in the gardens, pilgrimages such as those great pilgrimages conducted by Harmel, to bring the workingmen into personal contact with the Pontiff who had been so concerned for their economic and physical welfare as well as the welfare of their souls.[28]

It was probably, therefore, here in the gardens that Leo XIII held a conversation with Vice-Admiral Jules de Cuverville of the French navy, departing for his naval mission in the Orient. The conversation centered on France, but in so doing opened up the wider view of the Pope's relation to the problems of the age. The breadth of this view and the information it evidenced, together with the accessibility of the Holy Father to men of all parties, particularly impressed Cuverville. Leo's policy, according to the French admiral, as he subsequently related the conversation, was not to interfere in anything in which the welfare of the Church was not involved. The republican government (of France) was as acceptable as monarchism; French Catholics were perfectly free to hold different political views so long as these differences were not transformed into religious struggles dangerous for the government of the Church. It was the

26. *Si quis autem dicat quod unum caput et unus pastor est Christus, qui est unus unius Ecclesiae sponsus, non sufficientur respondet.*

27. *Univers*, July 3, 1896. *Univers* based its comments on the London *Times*, which saw this as a permanent check to any attempt at unifying the Anglican and the Roman churches. The *Times* also rejected the idea of considering Anglicans as being Protestants.

28. *Univers*, July 6, 1897. The construction of a private apartment in one of the towers of the wall for John XXIII to use as a "retreat" from the burdensome duties of public life emphasizes the need of public figures to escape from the tensions and fatigues of protocol.

encroaching demands "of a sectarian minority [said Cuverville] which Leo XIII wished and wishes to destroy." The absence of concessions on the part of some Catholics to the "liberal political movements" and their "intransigence of opinion" might be operating to the "detriment of the general interest"; barricading themselves behind "respectable but actually sterile traditions" they were trying to "thwart the desires of the majority of the nation." On the other hand, "the social perils caused by the abandonment of religious and moral principles" were equally dangerous to the state; if the Holy Father were asking Catholics "to forget their political differences in the face of the common enemy" and "monarchists not to engage in fratricidal strife with sincere Ralliés who loyally accept the republican form," he likewise "addresses himself to those, of whatever opinion, whose spirit thirsts for concord and care for the social order." Further, "Catholics of all classes must ally themselves with moderates of all opinions, or with independents among the public at large who are anxious for pacification"; these latter ought to accept contact with "those whose religious and charitable influence may render them suspect to men of disorder, but never to others." Cuverville quoted Leo's closing words:

I should like to see France strong within and respected abroad, and then on terms of friendship with Us; We can be useful in her colonies in Africa, in the Far East; it would be easy for them to be on good terms with the Holy See, and that [smiling] without being too clerical![29]

Leo's words, had they been universally known, might well have charted a path for twentieth-century pacification among religious groups. The ominous notes in these remarks were not seen as ominous by Leo or his visitor: the dangers of imperial rivalry leading to war; the ultimate resentment of the colonized against their imperial masters. Leo XIII and Cuverville were undoubtedly sincere in their desire to save the souls of the people in colonies. Only Marxism had denounced colonialism as incompatible with a view of the dignity of man as a human being. Fortunately for Catholicism, while Leo XIII emphasized the supreme importance of salvation of the soul he had not neglected concern for the bodily and social welfare of mankind. The breeze of the twentieth cen-

29. *Ibid.*, July 8, 1897.

tury was already stirring around the corner; it had not yet become a gale.[30]

Leo XIII's encyclical *Spesse volte*, addressed to the Italian clergy and people almost immediately after the Cuverville interview, did not display the same tolerance with regard to government. Italy was still, in Leo's eyes, a kingdom based on usurpation. He resented the presence of the House of Savoy in Rome. He said that the Church, however, would not enter into any conspiracy against it.[31]

One more major encyclical was to come from the pen of Leo XIII; at the opening of the twentieth century he issued *Graves de communi*. In this encyclical Leo looked back over his pontificate and spoke of the situation existing when he received the Triple Crown. He reviewed in this retrospective encyclical his *Quod apostolici muneris*, of December 28, 1878, in which he had attacked socialism:

At the very beginning of Our Pontificate We clearly pointed out what the peril was which confronted society on this head, and We deemed it Our duty to warn Catholics, in unmistakable language, how great the danger was which was lurking in the utterances of socialism, and how great the danger was that threatened not only their temporal possessions but also their morality and religion. . . .[In] Our encyclical *Rerum Novarum* of May 15, 1891, in which We dwelt at length on the rights and duties by which both classes of society . . . are bound in religion to each other . . . We made it evident that the remedies which are most useful to protect the cause of religion, and to terminate the contest between the different classes of society, were to be found in the precepts of the Gospel.

He went on to speak of the effect which the earlier encyclical had had, how not only Catholics but non-Catholics, "moved by the power of truth, avowed that the Church must be credited with a watchful care over all

---

30. See Braunthal, *Geschichte der Internationale*, pp. 310-318. The question of colonialism was discussed at length in every meeting of the Second International. The socialists opposed colonialism in part because it seemed to outrage every concept of human dignity. Also, it was intimately connected with capitalism, which they were pledged to destroy, and was an aspect of nationalism, which they were trying to set aside in favor of an international approach based on the solidarity of workers everywhere. The international Church, on the other hand, was convinced that imperialism would foster the growth of international religion, with all its ameliorative influences. The career of Cardinal Lavigerie in Africa was a glowing example. The idea may seem naïve in the second half of the twentieth century, but it did not seem so to either Catholics or Protestants at the close of the nineteenth.

31. *Univers*, Aug. 9, 1898.

classes of society, and those especially whom fortune had least favored."
He commented further on how the acrimony of differences of opinion
in this matter had been diminished and their works of improvement
carried to fruition; that is, "in their efforts for the elevation of the poorer
classes . . . many new enterprises were set on foot"; others "already
established were increased and all reaped the blessing of a greater stability imparted to them." Among these works he mentioned Bureaus
of the People for supplying information, savings banks, mutual aid
associations, and wisdom in the distribution of aid to the poor.

Some of these programs, he continued, were labeled "Christian Socialism," but this term was properly allowed to fall into disuse, although
in a few countries the name "Christian Socialists" was retained by some
groups. "Elsewhere the movement is described as Christian Democracy
in contradistinction to those who are designated Socialists, and whose system is known as Social Democracy." Many found the term "Christian
Democracy" ambiguous, tending to disparage any political forms other
than democracy and appearing to restrict the scope of religion "to the care
of the poor, as if other sections of society were not of its concern";
furthermore, the name might cast the shadow of its protection over
some "design to attack all legitimate power either civil or sacred"; the
purpose of the encyclical is therefore to show how the movement might
"extend its scope and be made more useful to the Commonwealth."

What Social Democracy is and what Social Democracy ought to be assuredly
no one can doubt. The first . . . is carried to such an excess by many as to
maintain that there is nothing really existing above the natural order [and that
the] acquisition and enjoyment [of material goods] constitutes man's happiness.

It seeks to abolish class, says Leo flatly, and finally to introduce "community of goods," abrogating the right of private ownership of property.
"Christian Democracy," on the other hand, seeks to better the masses
in material ways in such fashion as to turn men's minds to what is
"everlasting,"[32] and therefore Christian Democracy must regard justice

32. This point of difference has been captured in a phrase coined by the twentieth-
century Jacques Maritain (*Primauté du spirituel* [Paris, 1927]): "the primacy of the
spiritual" as against the "primacy of the material." Pope John XXIII, in the encyclical
Mater et Magistra, devoted a section (Respect for the Hierarchy of Values) to this idea.

as sacred, maintain the right of possessing property, and guard such distinctions and degrees in society as are indispensable in "every well-ordered commonwealth." Social and Christian Democracy have nothing in common; "they differ from each other as the sect of socialism differs from the profession of Christianity." The encyclical closed with an exhortation to Catholics to unite in the bonds of fraternal charity.[33]

A great polemic had been stirred up in Italy over the name "Christian Democracy" before approval was publicly given by Leo XIII. In the effort to bring about harmony some ardent Christian Democrats had suggested altering the name. But it was not *just a word*; it was a way of life; it was the new against the conservative. In the ears of the workers it had "a magic charm."[34] Putting the seal of approval on the term "Christian Democracy" was far more important than merely seeking a felicitous phrase to put in an essay.[35]

Some have regarded the *Graves de communi* as the completion and achievement of the *Rerum Novarum*.[36] Others have pointed out its significance in explaining how the Church has been able to live under such a variety of regimes. Professor Toniolo, evaluating the encyclical, wrote at the time: ". . . finally, the imperious insistence of the encyclical, calling on Christian Democracy to engage in decisive struggle for the amelioration and redemption of people of all social classes, passes from the realm of ideas to the realm of concrete reality."[37]

It was actually too late to pre-empt the term "socialism" for the Catholic movement; it was too closely associated with the names of Karl Marx, Bebel, and William Liebknecht.

One may regret [said a member of the faculty of the Belgian University of Louvain] that this name has fallen to them, just as I, for my part, regret that the name Liberalism has become the property of the Liberals; but these would be useless regrets. The term Democracy has not yet been confiscated, and as it

33. Quotations taken from Gilson, *The Church Speaks to the Modern World*, pp. 315-328.

34. Soderini, *Il Pontificato di Leone XIII*, I, 425.

35. Gilson (*The Church Speaks to the Modern World*, p. 313) points out in his introduction to the encyclical that since several political parties claimed Leo XIII as their inspiration, this authoritative pronouncement proved to be extremely useful.

36. Henri Joly, *Les Crises sociales de l'Italie* (Paris, 1924), p. 28.

37. Giuseppe Toniolo (*Rivista internazionale de' Scienze Sociali* [Feb., 1901], pp. 214-217) is quoted in Joly, *Les Crises sociales de l'Italie*, p. 28.

conveys an idea that is in keeping with the Gospel, let us appropriate it, lest it be taken from us; we shall know how to justify it.[38]

Christian Democracy, in the view of the Italian Catholic reformers, could not function except under conditions of the civil and political liberties of speech, press, assembly, and universal enfranchisement. It would be dependent on the existence of a parliament for debate. It must distinguish between the executive, legislative, and judicial functions of the State.[39] The Anglo-Saxon influence is plain here. It is doubtful whether such concepts, without considerable modification, could be exported to areas of different cultural and historic background. The papal insistence, however, on the dignity of man as a human being, as a child of God, was exportable. The socialists would have agreed in part with this view.

Toniolo regarded the *Graves de communi* as the answer to those who emphasized the *democracy* without the *Christian*. He regarded Revisionist Socialism as more dangerous to Catholicism than radical socialism had been.[40] He was accused, as a result of his Christian concept of democracy, of sponsoring a political program. This he denied, and protested his unconditional obedience to the Holy See in religious and in political and social matters.[41] His idea spread rapidly in Italy. Murri's attempt to construct a political party to carry out the new social ideas, although approved in the beginning by Leo XIII, was presently rejected, as going too far[42] in trying to modernize Church dogma for modern minds by reinterpreting basic creeds in terms of mystic symbolism.[43] Dom Sturzo took up reform, but he was careful to avoid the pitfalls of his predecessors. Neither Toniolo nor Murri was excommunicated during Leo XIII's lifetime. It is significant that none of the controversial writings were placed upon the *Index*.[44]

Leo XIII, at any rate, had approved the term "Christian Democracy," with whatever implications might attach to it. In so doing he had

38. *Quoted* in Leroy-Beaulieu, *Papacy, Socialism and Democracy,* pp. 72 f.
39. Luigi Sturzo, *Presupposti e carattere della Democrazia cristiana* (Rome, 1947), pp. 1-4. (Part of the Piccola Biblioteca di Cultura Politica.) The leading Catholic reformers were Toniolo, Meda, Murri, and (later) Sturzo himself.
40. Toniolo, *Opera Omnia,* ser. iv, II, 68-73.
41. Gambasin, *Il movimento sociale nell'Opera dei Congressi,* p. 469.
42. Bonomi, *Politica italiana,* p. 221.
43. Neufeld, *Italy,* p. 255.
44. Nitti, *Catholic Socialism,* p. 371.

certainly laid the foundation of the Church's policy with regard to the common man.

In the last year of Leo XIII's life one final act in the relations between Germany and the Vatican registered a vindication of the policy of kindliness and diplomacy exhibited in the settlement of the Kulturkampf. The major issues had been worked out fifteen years earlier. Now the support which the Center continued to give to the military budget against the opposition of the Liberals and the Social Democrats received its reward.[45] In 1902 the Vatican signed a convention with Germany with reference to the operation of the seminary at Strasburg. *Temps* reported the outcome: the "nomination of professors" was to be made "after a previous agreement with the bishop."

The government will have to replace [*Temps* continued] the professors whose orthodoxy and conduct would not offer sufficient guarantees; these concessions on the part of Germany are regarded as a great success for the Vatican.[46]

As the end of the year 1902 approached it seemed that Leo XIII might well complete his twenty-fifth year in the Pontificate, thus "seeing the years of Peter," as only his predecessor, Pius IX, had done. Preparations were under way to hold a pontifical jubilee. Not only would the Church be there but representatives from the secular monarchs. Leo had held out the friendly hand to rulers whether they were Catholic, Protestant, or Orthodox. Diplomatic relations had been restored with Orthodox Russia under Tsar Alexander III.[47] Now, under Nicholas II, Russia would be represented. Protestant William II of Germany had been on amicable terms with His Holiness.[48] Edward VII of England would be represented by Lord Denbigh.[49] This was not, to be sure, Leo XIII's first pontifical jubilee. One had been held at the end of his first decade, in

45. Avolio (*I Democratici Cristiani*, p. 27) attributed the Center's success to its solid base, resting on the people, and its positive program.

46. *Temps*, Dec. 22, 1902.

47. Alexander Isvolsky was appointed as semi-official agent of Russia to the papacy in 1893; the next year he was made Envoy Extraordinary and Minister Plenipotentiary to the Vatican. See Graham, *Vatican Diplomacy*, p. 69.

48. When the Emperor visited the Quirinal, just before the issuance of the *Au milieu* to the French Catholics, Leo made no opposition. The very idea of such a visit was regarded by French Catholic extremists as "insulting." See the report of the Paris correspondent of the London *Times* sent by the Agence Havas, *Univers* (Jan. 4, 1892).

49. Sir Alec Randall, *Vatican Assignment* (London, 1956), p. 10.

1887,[50] and a second ten years later, in 1897. On the latter occasion even the Sultan of Turkey sent a pasha to the celebration.[51]

As the year drew to a close His Holiness was in good health and was anticipating the Jubilee.[52] He received the Cardinals and Roman prelates bringing him Christmas greetings. The presentation of his discourse was begun by him but the reading of the remainder was delegated to another.[53] The text as published differed somewhat from the one delivered, being more general in nature.[54] To the disappointment of the leaders of Italian Christian Democracy it gave no encouragement to their going beyond the field of social amelioration to engage in political life as a party.[55] Leo's preoccupation with the Temporal Power still tied the hands of Italian Catholics.

The day of the Golden Jubilee, the twenty-fifth anniversary of Leo's coronation, went off well. His Holiness was equal to the occasion although the elaborate ceremony conducted at St. Peter's before a great throng was long and fatiguing. Cardinal Rampolla gave a state dinner to the diplomatic corps and the Vatican prelates; at night Prince Colonna gave a vast reception.[56]

It is understandable that in these last years Leo's thoughts should have gone back to his youth. On one occasion, to a group of the faithful from his old diocese of Perugia, he had voiced his sentiments that Perugia had never been effaced from his heart and spirit: "Often, indeed, in the midst of my new solicitude it has been and still is comforting to carry myself back in thought to the countryside of Trasimene and to see again in imagination your beautiful San Lorenzo, in whose protective shadow Providence was perhaps intending to prepare Our humble person for a higher ministry."[57] Now he was ninety-three years old.

50. The earlier jubilee had coincided with Queen Victoria's own celebration of her fiftieth year as ruler. Leo had sent a special mission on that occasion to congratulate the Queen; she sent a special mission to congratulate him. The Queen's letter had been addressed "Most Eminent Sir"; Leo's was begun "The Most Serene and Powerful Victoria, Queen of the United Kingdom of Great Britain and Ireland, and other regions, Illustrious Empress of India." See Randall, *Vatican Assignment*, pp. 10 f.

51. Fülöp-Miller, *Leo XIII*, p. 118.
52. Dispatch from Rome, Dec. 19, 1902. *Temps*, Dec. 20, 1902.
53. Dispatch from Rome, Dec. 23, 1902. *Ibid.*, Dec. 24, 1902.
54. Dispatch from Rome, Dec. 24, 1902. *Ibid.*, Dec. 25, 1902.
55. Neufeld, *Italy*, p. 232.
56. Dispatch from the Holy See. *Temps*, March 5, 1903.
57. *Univers*, May 1, 1898.

In scholarly matters Leo XIII kept an open mind to the end. He advanced with the advances of science and archeological research. Even in the matter of biblical exegesis he kept abreast of the times. A decade before his death he had issued an encyclical on the matter, the *Providentissimus Deus*. In this remarkable document he had advocated going back to the earliest sources in Hebrew and Greek from which the accepted Latin Vulgate had been drawn, even when conclusions based on such study contradicted the consensus of the Fathers. Leo himself continued the sort of study he had recommended in this encyclical. Of one such subject of research he remarked almost at the close of his life: "I should like to have ten years to resolve this question in harmony with the needs of the Church and the exigencies of science."[58]

While the Vatican, in the spring of 1903, was busy trying to surmise who would replace the late Parocchi, protector of the Workingmen's Clubs, the question of Leo's successor inevitably came up. Cardinal Serafina Vannutelli was mentioned as probably aspiring to the position. Cardinal Rampolla, Papal Secretary of State, and Cardinal Segna were also suggested. It was all speculative, but it was generally believed that the successor would be an Italian.[59]

Stricken on July 3, 1903, Leo XIII entered his last illness. In spite of physical weakness he continued to confer with the Cardinals about necessary matters and was interested in the publication of one of his Latin poems, proofs of which he had been reading earlier in the day on which he was taken ill.[60] He lasted until July 20, when he said his last farewell to the members of the Sacred College. He knew that preparations were in progress for the Conclave, which must be assembled at once. He recalled the scene twenty-five years before, when as *camerlengo* he had had charge of all the preparations for the Conclave (1878) at which he had been elected Pope. On that earlier occasion Cardinal Oreglia had whispered that Pecci was "beating the recruiting drum." Now Leo said, "When I am dead, Oreglia will touch my temples very gently with the

58. Dispatch from the Holy See. *Temps*, Feb. 4, 1903. The Pope was referring to a particularly acrid polemic which had been stirred up over the views of Alfred Loisy, a professor who had lost his chair in 1893 at the Catholic Institute of Paris. Leo XIII died before taking any sanctions against Loisy. See Paschini, *Storia ecclesiastica*, III, 574 and 576, n. 1.
59. Dispatch from Rome, Feb. 3, 1903. *Frankfurter Zeitung*, Feb. 11, 1903.
60. Fülöp-Miller, *Leo XIII*, pp. 145 f.

silver hammer, for fear he might awaken me."[61] He died at four o'clock while thousands thronged before the Vatican. The *camerlengo* took up his duties, arranging for the procession to the Vatican Basilica, where the body of the Pope would lie in state while the faithful passed in review. They came in an endless stream.[62]

When the Conclave assembled, Cardinal Mariano Rampolla's name was vetoed by Emperor Francis Joseph of Austria through the pronouncement of Cardinal Puzina, Bishop of Cracovia.[63] On August 4, 1903, Giuseppe Sarto, Cardinal Patriarch of Venetia, was elected and assumed the name Pius X.[64] The new Pope inherited from his predecessor Leo XIII an unsolved Roman Question and with it the continued refusal to permit Italian Catholics to participate in national elections. The choice of Pius X seems to have rested on the widespread sentiment that Leo XIII had been a "political" Pope and that his successor ought to be a "spiritual" one. That Pius X lived up to that expectation is, of course, a matter of record, he having been canonized in 1954. No Pope since the sixteenth century had been so designated.[65]

61. Harden, *Monarchs and Men*, p. 66. Oreglia was the only Cardinal left who had been appointed by Pius IX. All the others were appointees of Leo XIII. The two Popes' pontificates had spanned fifty-seven years. See Humphrey Johnson, *The Papacy and the Kingdom of Italy*, p. 27.

62. Fülöp-Miller, *Leo XIII*, p. 146. Fülöp-Miller asserts that the Fisherman's Ring was taken from the dead Pope's finger and broken according to custom; the prescribed rite symbolized the descent of the Holy Spirit upon the Sacred College as a whole. Harden (*Monarchs and Men*, p. 67) insists that the ring was not on Leo's finger and could not be found. The story of its later showing up in a fish brought to the Vatican kitchen is doubtless apocryphal.

63. France, Spain, and Austria by tradition had the right of veto. It was used against Cardinal Rampolla for the last time, however, as Pius X ended this privilege. See E. L. Woodward, "The Diplomacy of the Vatican," *Journal of the British Institute of International Affairs*, III-IV (1924-25), 117

64. Paschini, *Storia ecclesiastica*, III, 565. The new Pope, says Paschini, condemned the doctrines of Loisy, the apostle of modernism from whom Leo XIII had withheld condemnation.

65. James A. Corbett, *The Papacy: A Brief History* (Princeton, 1956), p. 82. Pius V, who died in 1572, had been the last.

THE CONCLUSION

XVII. CONCLUSIONS

"History seeks the truth and makes such research without prejudice or moral constrictions whatever."[1]

FEDERICO CHABOD

The death of Leo XIII marked the end of an era. The century of his life-time witnessed the coming of age of science, covering every aspect of the physical world and man himself as part of it; it witnessed the rising tide of demand for democracy, yielding on the political scene only to the demand for nationalism, which proved emotionally stronger. It was the century of the rise of Marxism, claiming to be "scientific" socialism. Marxist science was primarily economic and social theory based on the history of the human race, philosophically investigated. It rejected nationalism and took its stand on internationalism. The Marxist view of man and history led inescapably to atheism. Not content with mere secularism, which tinged every aspect of nineteenth-century life, setting up material values and goals, Marxism went beyond this to reject even the idea of the existence of God, regarding God as a notion conjured up by the minds of men. Many scientists, social theorists, and economists were inclined to agree, or to insist that if God existed he was unknowable, and so to put the affairs of man on a mundane level. In the search for the perfect society Marxism claimed that such a society should be classless, a society in which there should be neither exploiter nor exploited. In Europe the Marxist movement came to be called "Social Democracy."

The century was one in which the Catholic Church took the measure of the age and attempted to come to grips with it. Leo XIII was at the forefront of this attempt. The Church claimed that it had existed as a

1. *Rivista di storia della chiesa in Italia,* XIV (Rome, 1960), 481.

perfect society from its inception. The actual image it projected, however, seemed not to have kept pace with changing intellectual, political, and social needs. A new image must be created, not by changing its basic concept, which had personified the relationship of man with God and man with man in terms of humanity, but by stating the precepts of the Church in a form more suited to the age.

Prepared by his education for such an approach and basing his conclusions on the axiom that truth could never harm, Leo XIII succeeded in making Catholicism intellectually respectable. Politically he made it clear that any form of government was acceptable provided it left the Church free to accomplish its work of grace. The growth of democracy was no stumbling block for him; he ultimately accepted "Christian Democracy" as the name for his regeneration of society. In the realm of social theory and practice he recalled the Church to its duty to study the needs of human society in terms of both spiritual and temporal welfare, working through the institutions which an increasingly democratic society was creating for itself.

In the rise of Marxian socialism Leo XIII met the most formidable foe the Church had ever contended with and one no less authoritarian than the Church itself. The Church regarded its authority as from God; Marxism regarded its authority as inherent, proclaiming man as the be-all and end-all. Leo reiterated the view held by the Church that no manmade institution could triumph over God and God's chosen vessel; Marxism proclaimed the inexorability of history in determining the ultimate success of the proletariat in achieving dictatorship over human society. Leo called Christian society to more diligent practice of Christian virtues. The admonition was badly needed and long overdue.

The struggle between Marxism and the Church outlived both Marx and Leo XIII. Neither was destroyed. Until the death of Leo, Marxists had not succeeded in possessing themselves of the public powers in any state, nor did they seem on the verge of doing so anywhere in the West. Many writers have stated the factors which forestalled success on the part of Marx and his program: nationalism, democracy, trade unionism in a variety of forms, the social state, the tendency toward Revisionism. Leo XIII and the Church should not be omitted from this list, although one could compile a long list of writers on socialism who never mention Leo or Christian Democracy. Human need and science were the allies of Marxism. By championing the cause of labor and opening the door to science Leo XIII plucked two arrows from the quiver of Karl Marx. The Pope regarded nationalism as a natural expression of man's political nature and did not oppose its rise (except in Italy). He refused to sanction any attacks upon democratic principles (although he did not approve carrying these principles into Church affairs); rather, by supporting the republican government of France he gave more than tacit approval to the democratic ideal. By approving the international meeting in Berlin in 1890 to discuss the social question, the Pontiff gave open acceptance to the idea of state-administered reforms. The *Rerum Novarum* gave active support to the idea of labor organization. By all of these means he was able to use the Church as a holding force employing delaying tactics which by the end of the century permitted the inner revision and reform of the Marxist movement to unfold.

Wherever the admonitions of Leo XIII were earnestly carried out, authoritarian Marxism failed. Wherever, for whatever cause, they were ignored, Christian Democracy was less successful in vanquishing the foe. This was especially true wherever economic backwardness and lack of education provided little basis for democracy or for state-sponsored reform. Italy and Spain furnished conspicuous examples of this fact.

It would be too much to claim that there were no weaknesses in the program of Leo XIII. While accepting democracy as legitimate political procedure, he failed to realize that the removal of Rome from papal control solved for the Church the problem of applying the democratic principle to the temporal possessions of the Church; the Pope could not have granted democracy in any case. He did not actually understand the pull of nationalism, accepting it as a fact already present in existing states; he did not realize that it would of necessity operate against the unity of the Austrian Empire and in favor of the unity of Italy; he continued to refer to the several states of Italy, refusing to recognize their nationhood. As an internationalist and religious head he commended peace, but he hoped for armed intervention which would restore Rome to him. His foreign policy was more favorable to France after he recognized that Germany was not going to force Italy to give the Eternal City back to him.

Of the many reasons for the failure of Marxism in the West, various writers assign priority of significance to one or another. This seems a futile procedure. Nothing less than the total movement of history with its interplay of forces can provide a valid explanation. The story could be written from the standpoint of the rise of democracy, subordinating other factors to this one. One would concentrate thus on the role of the new bourgeoisie, who in trying to mount the ladder toward financial and political control played a crucial part in extending the suffrage. With some justification, therefore, one could write the whole account from the point of view of social mobility. Democracy, in its turn, by enfranchising both country and town, produced legislators who spoke for the universal demand of the rural population to retain or secure ownership of land. It took Revisionism (or sophistry) to recognize this property as the rural workers' "means of production" and to accept the rural owners into the proletarian movement *with their property*. This idea was to have tremendous future significance. The account of the failures and successes of Marxism could be written from the standpoint of the influence of the rural voter, whether he voted with ballots or bullets, for most of the world was still more rural than urban.[2]

Most popular among the reasons assigned has been the growth of nationalism. There is much to be said for it. Authoritarian socialism declared itself antinationalist (and anti-imperialist, a closely associated idea). Presently the leaders of strict Marxism found themselves swayed by this feeling. The leading Social Democrats in Germany discovered that they were still Germans (although the "Young" did not share this sentiment)[3]; and so it was elsewhere, at least wherever men were free. The founders of scientific socialism had been men without a country; they became a League of the Banished; London, Geneva, or New York might shelter them, but they remained uprooted. Since each national socialist group had local autonomy, the feeling of separatism grew. French socialists referred to "those Germans" with resentment. Nevertheless, although nationalism was a potent factor in defeating rigid Marxism in Germany or France, it certainly could not explain its failure in England or America.

2. In the late twentieth century the sprouting of Marxist systems from rural soil is almost too obvious to be worth mentioning.

3. See Rosa Luxembourg, *Réforme ou révolution* (Paris, 1932).

Social reforms carried out by the State proved to be the overriding factor in many cases. Vollmar, Bebel, and William Liebknecht were no longer mere agitators but deputies seeking constructive reforms. Coupled with the bargaining power of organized labor, this public movement produced immediate improvements, judged by labor as better than waiting for some distant Utopia.

Under all the motives which operated in different countries and in different individuals, however, lay the more basic factor of man's desire to feel emotionally attached to a cause. Increasingly at the end of the nineteenth century nationalism represented such a cause. It is true, on the other hand, that during the days of persecution the young socialists found in socialism a cause worth suffering for. Life was worth living in order to engage in the struggle. They were not won to socialism by statistical studies or cold logic, but by the warm feeling of resentment against injustice. They were attracted by the revolutionary character of the socialist doctrine.[4]

It was this same quality of attachment to a soul-satisfying cause that made the Church the most formidable and implacable foe of Marxism. The Marxists inveighed against the Church as the "opiate" of the people, against its preaching of love instead of class hatred; they reviled the Church as a conspirator with monarchy and aristocracy to keep the poor in ignorance and poverty; they called the Church obscurantist, clinging to magic and holding out rewards in a future world as substitute for justice in this world.

After the advent of Leo XIII these claims could no longer be made against the Church. Leo agreed with his opponents that the poor wage earner should not be put off with promises of future bliss. He called upon the faithful—and all men of good will—to reorder industrial conditions in the interest of justice. He restored to the workingman his dignity as a man and his dignity as a son of God.[5]

It was impossible that Marxism and the social movement in the

4. Lenin (Vladimir Ilich Lenin, *Marx, Engels, Marxism* [New York, 1935], p. 70) explained Marxism as a world view "continuing and carrying to fruition, with genius, the three principal currents of ideas of the XIXth century . . . classic German philosophy, classical English political economy, and French socialism, in liaison with French Revolutionary doctrines in general."

5. Barrès said that after reading the *Rerum Novarum* no one could ever again be

Church should coalesce.[6] It was impossible also for them not to influence each other. They were frequently parliamentary allies; in Germany during the Kulturkampf and in France after Leo's acceptance of the Republic the harshness of socialist criticism was toned down. Said one of the socialists,[7] "If the Church wishes to give us a helping hand and put her shoulder to the wheel for us, we will let her priests alone." Pressure from the socialists, on the other hand, forced the Church not to postpone adopting a social program. Leo XIII, de Mun, Ketteler were all moved to action by the plight of the workers; the rise of socialism pointed up the immediacy of the problem and moved Catholics to rouse themselves from lethargy to combat the new foe. As an enemy of socialism the Church was already organized.[8] What is often overlooked is the beneficial effect produced on the Church by the socialist attack. Overlooked also, all too often, is the part played by the Church in the development of socialist Revisionism. Could Bebel ever really recover from having translated, while in prison in Zwickau, *The Social Teachings of Christianity?*[9] It was Bebel who took to the parliamentary path and refused to go along with the revolutionary violence of the "Young." The same effect was noticeable in France, not only in the case of Guesde but of Lafargue. "Have we not heard," said a contemporary, "at the Palais Bourbon, amid the stamping of the scandalized Radicals, the son-in-law of Karl Marx, the collectivist member for Lille, declaring in his maiden speech that he placed himself under the patronage of Leo XIII?"[10] Not only did the Church influence the Revisionists, it also

anticlerical. This was the attitude even among the skeptics. See Blowitz, *Léon XIII devant ses contemporaines*, p. 221.

6. When the *Rerum Novarum* was first issued, a member of the Institute, Leroy-Beaulieu, wrote (*Papacy, Socialism and Democracy*, p. 222): "You could marry the Republic of Venice to the Grand Turk, even the French Republic to the autocratic Tsar; but you cannot unite the papacy to socialism. . . . We are not likely to see the keys of St. Peter upon the red flag."

7. Leroy-Beaulieu (*ibid.*, p. 220) thought it was Jules Guesde.

8. Barrès said that in the struggle against socialism the Church could muster "the most formidable organization of cadres" which any "congress of organizers could possibly glimpse, and had, furthermore, the gift of turning mathematical reasons into a matter of feeling." See Blowitz, *Léon XIII devant ses contemporaines*, p. 222.

9. Bebel was in prison in 1875-1876. The work was by Yves Guyot and Sigismond Lecroix. Bebel, as has earlier been noted, was first aroused to interest in the social problem by a Catholic priest.

10. This is Leroy-Beaulieu's own comment, written in 1892. See his *Papacy, Socialism and Democracy*, p. 219.

helped to modify the attitude of the bourgeoisie. By precept and example employers were led to realize that economic prosperity for themselves might more reasonably be achieved through raising the standard of living of the employed and through meeting their demands for improved conditions in industrial establishments.[11]

Certainly in the late nineteenth century the belief was widely held that the "strongest and most insurmountable obstacle" to the propagation of socialism was Catholicism.[12] It was variously phrased: "only the Catholic Church" could snatch the workmen from the influence of the socialist party;[13] in the "absence of Christian sentiment" perhaps the "only power strong enough to prevent [social war] was the national sentiment."[14] Some went further and advised the Church to ally itself with the Revolution, to make the Vatican the center of the social movement and the "headquarters of the new International." This was, of course, impossible for the time being; the words themselves, "socialism," "revolution," "international," had taken on a living existence, sinister in character, which would be difficult to forget. Thus are movements imprisoned by language.

It thus appears that Leo XIII in ranging himself on the side of nationalism (except in Italy) greatly strengthened the resistance of the West to social war while lending the weight of his office to a social crusade. Both socialism and Leo embarked on a pathway of Revisionism. Wherever the clergy, heedless of advice, ranged themselves on the side of privilege and the old order, as in southern Italy, Spain, and Latin America, the end desired by the Pope was not attained, or was reached only in part. In such areas class war might still erupt.

In eastern Europe, into which for the most part the voice of Leo XIII did not reach and where the path of moderation was not followed, no effective dike was built against revolutionary socialism and class war. It would have taken clairvoyance to foresee at Leo's death what the

11. This was especially true in France and Catholic Germany. When Belgian employers were resorting to coercive measures such as the lock-out, *Bien Public* said this was neither Christian nor just; so Belgium was also affected, although more tardily. See *Univers*, Sept. 24, 1895.

12. *Osservatore Romano*, quoted in *Univers*, Oct. 13, 1894.

13. This statement from *Nuova Gazzetta* quoted in *Le Monde* appears in Soderini, *Socialism and Catholicism* (London, 1896), p. 324.

14. Leroy-Beaulieu, *Papacy, Socialism and Democracy*, p. 190.

next two decades would produce in Russia.[15] It would have taken a clairvoyant indeed to foresee the world struggle that was to emerge in the new century. Such a clairvoyant was Leroy-Beaulieu, historian and publicist, who wrote in 1892, when the Pope had still another decade of life before him:

A great struggle is preparing in our midst—a long and hard struggle. I do not think our children will witness the end of it. Social war is declared, and it will last for generations. It will not be a war of thirty years, confined to France and our old Germano-Latin Europe, but a war of a hundred years and perhaps more, which will simultaneously set on fire the two extremities of the world.[16]

Leo XIII by cutting the cord of dead politics had brought into reality a movement demanded in vain by Comte and the philosophical Positivists, by Saint-Simon and the Utopians, and by the liberal Catholics. He, whose words no power on earth could reverse or label heretical, had championed the cause of the laborers. He richly deserved the title of "the workingman's Pope."

15. "History was to show," says Ulam (*The Unfinished Revolution*, p. 167), "that Marxism would come to power not as the heir of democracy or as the receiver of bankrupt liberalism but *as the heir of anarchism*." (Italics in original.)

16. Leroy-Beaulieu, *Papacy, Socialism and Democracy*, p. 189. Leroy-Beaulieu, by virtue of his historical studies carried on in Russia as well as his studies in Catholic history and the history of the papacy, was more qualified than most to predict what the twentieth century was soon to witness.

BIBLIOGRAPHY

BIBLIOGRAPHY

PRIMARY SOURCES

Acta et Decreta Sacrorum Conciliorum Recentorium: Collectio Lacensis. Vol. VII. Friburgi Brisgoviae, 1890.

Annales de la Chambre de Députés. Paris, 1871.

Archives diplomatiques. Recueil de diplomatie et d'histoire.

BAKUNIN, MICHAEL. *Beichte aus der Peter-Paul Festung an Zar Nikolaus I.* Gefunden im Geheimsrank des Chefs der III Abteilung der Kanzlei der früheren Zaren zu Leningrad. Trans. and with a foreword by W. Polonski.

————. *Correspondance de Michel Bakounine: Lettres à Herzen et à Ogareff 1860-1874.* Publiée avec préface et annotations par Michel Dragomanov. Trans. Marie Stromberg. Paris, 1896.

————. [BAKOUNINE, MICHELE.] *Dio e lo Stato.* Prefazioni di Filippo Turati e Leonida Bissolati (1887); Cenni biografici di Cafiero e Reclus (Geneva, 1882). Milan, 1914.

————. [BAKUNIN, MICHAIL.] *Oeuvres.* 6 vols.; 4th ed. Paris, 1902-1913.

————. [BAKUNIN, MICHAIL.] *Sozial-politischer Briefwechsel mit Alexander Herzen und Ogarjov.* Stuttgart, 1895.

BASTGEN, HUBERT. *Die Römische Frage; Dokumente und Stimmen.* 2 vols. Freiburg, 1918.

BERNSTEIN, EDUARD. *Ferdinand Lassalle und seine Bedeutung für die Arbeiterklasse.* (Commemorating the 46th anniversary of his death.) Berlin, 1904.

————. *My Years of Exile.* London, 1921.

————. *Zur Frage: Sozialliberalismus oder Collectivismus.* Berlin, 1900.

BISMARCK, OTTO, FÜRST VON. *Gedanken und Erinnerungen.* 2 vols. in one. New York and Stuttgart, 1898.

BLANC, LOUIS. *Le Socialisme: Droit au travail.* Paris, 1848.

BLANQUI, LOUIS AUGUSTE. *La Patrie en danger*. Paris, 1871.

BLOWITZ, ADOLPHE OPPER DE. *Léon XIII devant ses contemporaines*. Paris, 1892. This collection of opinions by prominent people in several countries was designed to honor Leo XIII's fifteenth year in the pontificate.

BLUM, LÉON. *Les Congrès ouvriers et socialistes français*. 2 vols. Paris, 1901. Minutes of the meetings are quoted and summarized.

BROGLIE, DUC DE. "Mémoires," *Revue des Deux Mondes,* VII (1932).

BUSCH, MORITZ. *Our Chancellor: Interviews with Bismarck*. Leipzig, 1884.

Ce qui c'est que L'Internationale; sa raison d'être, son but, ses moyens, ses tendances; où elle nous conduit. Brussels, 1869. Apparently written by a Belgian socialist.

Ce qui se passe au Concile. Paris: Henri Plon, 1870. A running account of what was happening during Vatican Council I.

Christian Socialist. London, April 26, 1851.

Civiltà Cattolica, La, Series VII, Vol. V, *Acta et Decreta: Collectio Lacensis*.

CRISPI, FRANCESCO. *Memoirs*. Trans. Mary Prichard-Agnetti from the documents collected and edited by Thomas Palmengo-Crispi. 3 vols. London, 1912-1914.

DA COSTA, CHARLES, and ÉDOUARD VAILLANT. *Blanquist Manifesto. Daily Telegraph*, Feb. 8, 1878.

DAVID, EDWARD. "Parteitag und internationaler Congress," *Socialistische Monatshefte* (1900). In consecutive numbers.

DE MAN, HENRI. *Planned Socialism: The Plan du Travail of the Belgian Labor Party*. Trans. and ed. G. D. H. Cole. London, 1935.

DE MUN, COUNT ALBERT. *Combats d'hier et d'aujourd'hui*. 4 Series. Paris, n.d.

Débats, Journal des, 1878-1892.

Documents diplomatiques français. 1st Series, I, II. Paris, 1929.

DUBREUILH, LOUIS. "La Commune." Part II of Vol. XI of Jean Jaurès, *Histoire Socialiste*. Rev. ed. Paris, 1922.

ENGELS, FREDERICK. *Ludwig Feuerbach and the Outcome of Classical German Philosophy*. Vol. XV of the Marxist Library: Works of Marxism-Leninism. N.Y. [1888]. This is the probable original publication date; n.d. for the reissue by the Marxist Library. It was written and published between the death of Marx (1883) and the death of Engels (1895).

―――. "On the History of Early Christianity," in Marx and Engels, *Basic Writings on Politics and Philosophy*. Lewis S. Feuer, ed. Garden City, N.Y., 1959.

―――, and KARL KAUTSKY. *Histoire de l'Internationale socialiste*. Brussels, 1924.

FERRATA, CARDINAL DOMINIQUE. *Mémoires*. Rome, 1920.

FÈVRE, MSGR. JUSTIN, PROTONOTARY APOSTOLIC. *La Défense de l'Église en France sous Léon XIII*, 2nd ed. Paris, 1894.

Figaro, 1892.

First Party Platform of the Socialist Party. U.S., 1901. Division of MSS, Duke University Library.

Founding of the First International: A Documentary Record. New York, 1937. From the archives of the Marx-Engels-Lenin Institute.

Frankfurter Zeitung, 1903.

FRIBOURG, E. E. *L'Association Internationale des Travailleurs*. Paris, 1871. Fribourg was one of the founders.

FRIEDBERG, EMIL. *Sammlung der Achtenstücke zum ersten vaticanischen Concil*. Tübingen, 1872.

FRIEDRICH, JOHANNES. *Tagebuch während des vaticanischen Concils*. Nördlingen, 1873.

Germania. June 24, 1871.

GERTH, HANS. *The First International: Minutes of the Hague Congress of 1872 with Related Documents*. Madison, Wis., 1958.

GILSON, ÉTIENNE, ED. *The Church Speaks to the Modern World: The Social Teachings of Leo XIII*. New York, 1954. Encyclicals are quoted in English translation.

GUESDE, JULES. *Essai de Catéchisme socialiste*. Brussels, 1878.

―――. *Quatre ans de lutte*. 2 vols. Paris, 1901. These are Vols. VI and VII of *Bibliothèque d'études socialistes*.

GUILLAUME, JAMES. *L'Internationale: Documents et souvenirs 1864-1878*. 4 vols. Paris, 1905, 1907, 1909, 1910.

HEGEL, G. W. F. "Man and the State," Vol. IV of *Political Philosophers* in *The World's Great Thinkers*. New York, 1947.

HERZEN, ALEXANDER. *My Past and Thoughts: The Memoirs of Alexander Herzen*. Trans. Constance Garnett. 4 vols. Edinburg, 1924.

HOHENLOHE. *Memoirs of Prince Chlodwig of Hohenlohe-Schillingsfürst*. Ed. Friedrich Curtius and George W. Chrystal. 2 vols. New York, 1906.

HUMBERT, SYLVAIN. *Le Mouvement syndical*. Paris, 1912. Vol. IX of Jaurès, *Histoire Socialiste*.

———. *Les Possibilistes*. Paris, 1911. Vol. IV of Jaurès, *Histoire Socialiste*.

JANET, M. PAUL. "Les origines du socialisme," *Revue des Deux Mondes* XL (1880).

JAURÈS, JEAN. *Le Conclusion: Le Bilan social du XIXe siècle*. Paris, 1922. Vol. XII of Jaurès, *Histoire Socialiste*. Jaurès also wrote the first volume of the set, giving historical backgrounds.

JOHN XXIII. *Mater et Magistra*. The Vatican, May 15, 1961.

KAUTSKY, KARL. *Bernstein und der Sozialdemokratische Programm: Antikritik*. Stuttgart, 1899.

———. *Erinnerungen und Erörterungen*. Vol. III of *Quellen und Untersuchungen zur Geschichte der deutschen und österreichischen Arbeiterbewegung*. The Hague, 1960.

KETTELER, WILHELM VON. *Die grossen socialen Fragen der Gegenwart*. Mainz, 1849. Ketteler was at this time a priest; later he became a bishop.

———. *Liberalismus, Socialismus und Christenthum: Rede gehalten auf der XXI General Versammlung der katholischen Vereine Deutschlands*. 2nd ed. Kirchheim, 1871.

Kölnische Zeitung, 1884-1886.

LABRIOLA, ANTONIO. *La concezione materialistica della storia*. Foreword by Benedetto Croce. Bari, 1946.

———. *Discorrendo di Socialismo e di Filosofia*, ed. B. Croce, 5th ed. Bari, 1947.

———. *Lettere a Engels*. Rev. ed. Rome, 1949.

LAFARGUE, PAUL. *Le Socialisme et la conquête des pouvoirs publics*. Paris, 1899.

LANDAUER, GUSTAV. *Social Democracy in Germany*. London, ca. 1896. (Landauer says, "three years ago in Zurich. . . .")

LASKI, HAROLD J. *Communist Manifesto: Socialist Landmark; A New Appreciation Written for the Labor Party; Together with the Original Text and Prefaces.* 3rd impression. London, 1954.

LENIN, VLADIMIR ILICH. *Marx, Engels, Marxism: A Collection of Articles by V. I. Lenin.* New York, 1935.

LEO XIII. *The Church and Civilization: A Pastoral Letter for Lent, 1877, by Cardinal Pecci, now Leo XIII.* Perugia, Feb. 6, 1877; Dublin, 1878. (Treasure Room, Duke University.)

——. *The Great Encyclical Letters of Leo XIII.* See Wynne.

——. *The Letter "Humanum Genus" against Free-Masonry and the Spirit of the Age* (April 20, 1884); and the *Reply for the Ancient and Accepted Scottish Rite of Free-Masonry; Gr. Orient of Charleston* (1884).

LEROY-BEAULIEU, Anatole. *Papacy Socialism and Democracy,* followed by the *Papal Encyclical on the Condition of Labour.* Tr. from the French by B. L. O'Donnell. London, 1892. (This is the *Rerum Novarum,* beginning: *De conditio opificum.*)

LIEBKNECHT, WILHELM. *Hochverrat und Revolution.* Berlin, 1892.

LUXEMBOURG, ROSA. *Réforme ou révolution?* Paris, 1932.

MANFRONI, GIUSEPPE. *Sulla soglia del Vaticano: Reminiscences recorded by Camillo Manfroni.* 2 vols. Bologna, 1920-1925.

MANNING, HENRY EDWARD, CARDINAL. "True Story of the Vatican Council," *Nineteenth Century,* I (April, 1877), 190.

MANSI, GIAN DOMENICO, ED. *Collectio conciliorum Recentorium Ecclesiae Universae.* Series VII; Vol. V. Paris, 1911.

MARX, KARL. *Der Achzehnte Brumaire des Louis Bonaparte.* 3rd ed. Hamburg, 1885.

——. *Civil War in France.* New York, 1933.

——. *Excerpt from "A Contribution to the Critique of Political Economy." Basic Writings on Politics and Philosophy.* Lewis Feuer, ed. Garden City, N.Y., 1959.

——, and FRIEDRICH ENGELS. *Briefwechsel.* Vol. III: *Der Briefwechsel zwischen Marx und Engels 1861-1867.* Berlin, 1930.

——. *Communist Manifesto.* Preface by Harold Laski. London, 1954.

——. *Karl Marx oder Bakunin? Democratie oder Diktatur? Eine Kampfschrift gegen den Vorläufer des Bolschewismus.* Stuttgart, 1920.

————. *I Fondamenti del Communismus.* Preface by Angelica Balabanoff. n.p., n.d. Ancona—XIV Congreso dal Partito socialista italiano. The Marx portion is the *Communist Manifesto* in Italian. Division of MSS, Duke University Library.

MAZZINI, GIUSEPPE. *Scritti editi ed inediti.* 94 vols. Imola, 1906-1943.

METTERNICH, PRINCE. *Mémoirs, documents et écrits divers.* 7 vols. Paris, 1881.

MONTANELLI, GIUSEPPE. *Memorie sull Italia e specialmente sulla Toscana dal 1814 al 1850.* 2 vols.; 2nd ed. Turin, 1855.

MURRI, ROMOLO. *Kämpfe von Heute: Das christliche Leben zu Beginn des Zwantzigsten Jahrhunderts.* Authorized trans. from the Italian. Cologne, 1908.

Nel LXX Anniversario della "Rerum Novarum." Milan, 1961.

OLLIVIER, EMILE. *L'Église et l'État au Concile du Vatican.* 2 vols. in one; 4th ed. Paris, 1879.

ORRY, ALBERT. *Les Socialistes indépendants.* Paris, 1911.

Pall Mall Gazette. Oct. 9, 1889.

PANTALEONO, D. "L'Italia e'il Papato Spirituale," *Nuova Antologia* XV (Nov., 1870).

PECCI, JOACHIM. *See* Leo XIII.

PIRRI, PIETRO. "L'amnistia di Pio IX nei documenti ufficiali," *Rivista di storia della chiesa,* VIII (1954).

PROUDHON, P. J. *Les Confessions d'un Révolutionnaire pour servir à l'histoire de la Révolution de Fevrier.* 3rd ed. Paris, 1851.

Provinzial Correspondenz. Feb. 8, 1878.

RANDALL, SIR ALEC. *Vatican Assignment.* London, 1956.

ROUSSEL, AUGUSTE. "La Question Romaine," *Univers,* July 11, 1888.

Sacrorum conciliorum nova et amplissima collectio. Gian Domenico Mansi, ed. Editing continued by Venetian and Florentine editors through 31 volumes. Publication brought down to date by Ludovico Petit and Joanne Baptiste Martin. 53 vols. in 57. Paris, 1903-1927. Vol. LII.

SCADUTO, F. *Guarentigie e relazioni tra stato e chiesa.* Turin, 1884. The Law of Papal Guarantees is given.

SCHRÖDER, WILLIAM. *Handbuch der sozialdemokratische Parteitage von 1863 bis 1909.* Munich, 1910.

Siècle, 1878-1879.

SODERINI, EDUARDO. *Il Pontificato di Leone XIII*. 3 vols. Milan, 1932-1933. Soderini was one of the two prelates to whom Leo XIII opened the archives of his pontificate.

———. *Leo XIII Italy and France*. Trans. Barbara Barclay Carter, London, 1935. This is a translation of Vol. I of the *Pontificato*.

SORLIN, PIERRE. "La Crise du Parti bolchevik et les débuts du *Bol'ševik* (avril, 1924-avril, 1925)," *Revue d'histoire moderne et contemporaine* IX (April-June, 1962).

STURZO, (DOM) LUIGI. *Pensiero antifascista*. Turin, 1925.

———. *Presupposti e caratteri della democrazia cristiana*, in *Piccola Biblioteca di Cultura Politica*. Rome, 1947.

Temps, 1903.

TESTUT, OSCAR. *Association Internationale des Travailleurs*. Lyons, 1870.

THOMAS, ALBERT. *Le Second Empire 1852-1870*. Vol. X of Jaurès *Histoire Socialiste 1789-1900*. Paris, 1922.

Times (London), Feb. 8, 1878.

TONIOLO, GIUSEPPE. *Capitalism and Socialism*. Vatican City, 1947.

———. *Democrazia cristiana: Istitute e forme*. Vatican City, 1951. Series IV, Vol. I of *Opera Omnia*.

———. *Opera Omnia*. Vatican City, 1947-

T'SERCLAES DE WOMMERSOM, MSGR. DE. *Le Pape Léon XIII: Sa vie, son action religieuse, politique et sociale*. 2 vols. Paris, 1894. A third volume appeared in the 20th century. It is not available. Facsimiles of Leo's letters are scattered through the work and assembled in appendix. T'Serclaes was one of the two prelates to whom Leo XIII opened the archives of his pontificate.

Univers, 1847-1848, 1869-1898.

VALBERT, G. "L'Allemagne nouvelle jugée par un Allemand [Bruno Bauer]," *Revue des Deux Mondes*, XLI (1880).

VANDERVELDE, ÉMILE. *Histoire de la IIe Internationale 1889-1914*. Pamphlet, n.d., n.p. Presumably Brussels.

———. *Souvenirs d'un militant socialiste*. 7th ed. Paris, 1939.

Verhandlungen des Haus der Abgeordneten, Landtag, Stenographische Berichte über die. Berlin.

Verhandlungen des deutschen Reichstages, Stenographische Berichte über die. Berlin, 1871-1903.

VOGÜÉ, EUGÈNE MELCHIOR. "Affaires de Rome," *Revue des Deux Mondes.* Paris. A regular feature in the journal.

VOLLMAR, GEORG VON. "Zum Fall Millerand," *Socialistische Monatshefte,* No. 12, Dec., 1900.

Vorgeschichte des Kulturkampfes, Die. Quellenveröffentlichung aus dem Deutschen Zentralarchiv. Adelheid Constabel ed.; introduction by Fritz Hartung. Issued by Germany (the Democratic Republic of 1949) through its State Archives Section of the Ministry of the Interior.

SECONDARY SOURCES

ACOMB, EVELYN M. *The French Laic Laws 1879-1889.* New York, 1941.

ACTON, JOHN EMERICH EDWARD, LORD. "The Vatican Council," *North British Review,* LIII (Oct., 1870).

ALEXANDER, EDGAR. "Church and Society in Germany; Social and Political Movements and Ideas in German and Austrian Catholicism 1789-1950," in Joseph N. Moody, ed., *Church and Society; Catholic Social and Political Thought and Movements 1789-1950.* New York, 1953.

ARFÉ, GAETANO. Essay review of Luigi Cortesi: "La Costituzione del Partito socialista italiana (Milan, 1961)," in *Rivista storica italiana,* LXXIV-I (1962).

———. Review of E. Ragionieri, "Socialdemocrazia tedesca e socialisti italiani," *Rivista storica italiana,* LXXV-I (1963).

———. "Studi recenti su democratica e socialisti italiani," *Rivista storica italiana,* LXXI-III (1959). Raffaele Colapietra's *Leonida Bissolati* (Feltrinelli Editore, 1958) is reviewed.

ASKEW, WILLIAM C. "The Austro-Italian Antagonism," in Lillian Parker Wallace and William C. Askew, eds., *Power, Public Opinion and Diplomacy: Essays in Honor of Eber Malcolm Carroll.* Durham, N.C., 1959. Askew's essay is written from unpublished documents.

AVOLIO, GENNARO. *I Democratici Cristiani è il non-expedit.* Naples, 1903.

———. *Mons. Ketteler è il Partito Cattolico Parlamentare.* Naples, 1905.

BALLERINI, P. RAFAELLO. *Les Premières pages du Pontificat de Pie IX.* Rome, 1909.

BECKER, HOWARD, AND HARRY ELMER BARNES, *et al. Social Thought from Lore to Science.* 3 vols, 3rd ed. New York, 1961.

BEER, M. *The General History of Socialism and Social Struggles.* 2 vols. New York, 1957.

BONOMI, IVANOE. *La politica italiana da Porta Pia a Vittorio Veneto 1870-1918.* Turin, 1944.

BOURDEAU, JEAN. *L'Évolution du socialisme.* Paris, 1901.

BOYER, F. Review of Domenico Farini, *Diario di fine secolo* (E. Morelli, ed., 2 vols., Rome, 1962) in *Bulletin de la Société d'Histoire Moderne.* 12th Ser., No. 24, Paris, 1962.

BOYER D'AGEN, A. J. B. *La Jeunesse de Léon XIII d'après sa correspondance inédite. De Carpineto à Bénévent 1810-1838.* Tours, 1896. Facsimiles of the letters are included.

BRAUNTHAL, JULIUS. *Geschichte der Internationale.* Vol. I (2 vols. planned). Hannover, 1961. Written from the documents.

BRETON, J. L. *L'Unité socialiste.* Vol. VII of Jean Jaurès, *Histoire des partis socialistes en France.* Paris, 1912.

BUTLER, E. C. (DOM). *The Vatican Council: The Story Told From Inside in Bishop Ullathorne's Letters.* London, 1930.

CARR, E. H. *Michael Bakunin.* London, 1937.

CESARE, RAFAELE DE. "Il Dottor Schloezer e la Fine del Kulturkampf," *Nuova Antologia,* CXXXVI (July, 1894), 22.

CHABOD, FEDERICO. *Storia della politica estera italiana dal 1870 al 1896.* Vol. I: *Le Premesse.* Bari, 1951.

CHARNAY, MAURICE. *Les Allemanistes.* Vol. V of Jaurès, *Histoire des partis socialistes en France.* Paris, 1912.

CLARKE, JACK ALDEN. "French Socialist Congresses 1876-1914," *The Journal of Modern History,* XXXI, No. 2 (June, 1959).

COHNSTAEDT, DR. WILHELM. *Die Agrarfrage in der deutsche Sozialdemokratie von Karl Marx.* Munich, 1903.

COLE, G. D. H. *Socialist Thought: Marxism and Anarchism 1850-1890.* London, 1954. Vol. II of *A History of Socialist Thought.*

———. *The Second International.* Parts I and II. London, 1956. Vol. III of *A History of Socialist Thought.*

COLLINS, JAMES. "Leo XIII and the Philosophical Approach to Modernity," in Edward T. Gargan, ed., *Leo XIII and the Modern World*. New York, 1961.

COMPÈRE-MOREL. *Jules Guesde: La Socialisme fait homme 1845-1922*. Paris, 1937.

CORBETT, JAMES A. *The Papacy: A Brief History*. Princeton, 1956.

CORNU, AUGUSTE. *Karl Marx et Friedrich Engels: Leur vie et leur oeuvre*. Vol. I: *Les Années d'enfance et de jeunesse: La Gauche Hégélienne*. 1818/1820-1844. Paris, 1955.

———. *The Origins of Marxian Thought*. Springfield, Ill., 1957.

COTTIER, GEORGES M-M. *L'Athéisme du jeune Marx: Ses origines hégéliennes*. Paris, 1959.

CROCE, BENEDETTO. *A History of Italy 1871-1915*. English ed. trans. Cecilia M. Ady. Oxford, 1929.

CURTIS, MICHAEL. *Three against the Third Republic: Sorel, Barrès, and Maurras*. Princeton, 1959.

DALSÈME. *Les Mystères de l'Internationale*. Paris, 1871. (Published anonymously but catalogued as by Dalsème.)

DANSETTE, ADRIEN. *Le Boulangisme: Du Boulangisme à la Révolution dreyfusienne 1886-1890*. Paris, 1938.

———. *Les Origines de la Commune de 1871*. Paris, 1944.

DAY, HENRY C. *Catholic Democracy, Individualism, and Socialism*. Preface by Francis Cardinal Bourne. New York, 1914.

DERFLER, LESLIE. "Le 'Cas Millerand'; une nouvelle interprétation." *Revue d'Histoire moderne et contemporaine*, X (April-June, 1963), 81-104.

DESCHANEL, PAUL. *Gambetta*. Paris, 1919.

DETTMER, GÜNTER. *Die Ost- und Westpreussischen Verwaltungsbehörden im Kulturkampf*. Heidelberg, 1958.

DOUGLAS, RICHARD M. *Jacopo Sadoleto 1477-1547: Humanist and Reformer*. Cambridge, Mass., 1959.

EGGERS, KURT. *Rome gegen Reich*. Stuttgart, 1937.

EINAUDI, MARIO, AND FRANÇOIS GOGUEL. *Christian Democracy in Italy and France*. Notre Dame, 1952.

FOGARTY, MICHAEL P. *Christian Democracy in Western Europe 1820-1953*. London, 1957.

FONZI, FAUSTO. *I cattolici e la società italiana dopo l'unità.* 2nd ed. Rome, 1960.

FRANTZ, CONSTANTIN. *Über den Atheismus mit besonderer Bezugname auf Ludwig Feuerbach.* Vol. II of *Speculative Studies.* Berlin, 1844.

FRANZ, GEORG. *Kulturkampf: Staat und Katholische Kirke im Mitteleuropa von der Säkularisation bis zum Abschlüss des Preussischen Kulturkampfes.* Munich, 1954.

FÜLÖP-MILLER, RENÉ. *Leo XIII and Our Times.* Trans. Conrad Bonacina. London, 1937.

GAMBASIN, ANGELO. *Il movimento sociale nell'Opera dei Congressi 1874-1904: Contributo per la storia del cattolicismo sociale in Italia. Analecta Gregoriana. Series facultatis historiae ecclesiasticae. Section B* (n.16). Rome, 1958.

GARGAN, EDWARD T., ED. *Leo XIII and the Modern World.* New York, 1961.

GEORGES, BERNARD, AND DENISE TINTANT. *Léon Jouhaux: Cinquante ans de Syndicalisme. I: Des origines à 1921.* Paris, 1962.

GINZBURG, ANNA. "Domenico Farini: Diario di fine secolo (E. Morelli, ed.)," *Rivista storica italiana,* LXXV-III (1963), 671-680.

GOYAU, GEORGES. *Bismarck et l'Église: Le Culturkampf 1870-1887.* 4 vols.; Paris, 1918-1922.

———. *L'Oeuvre sociale de l'État Belge: Les Catholiques au pouvoir 1884-1912.* Paris, 1912.

GRAHAM, ROBERT A. *Vatican Diplomacy.* Princeton, 1959.

GRÉGOIRE, FRANZ. *Aux sources de la pensée de Marx: Hegel: Feuerbach.* Paris, 1947.

HAAG, HENRY. "The Political Ideas of Belgian Catholics 1789-1914," in Joseph N. Moody, *Church and Society: Catholic Social and Political Thought and Movements 1789-1950.* New York, 1953.

HAHN, LUDWIG. *Geschichte des Kulturkampfes im Preussen.* Berlin, 1881.

HALES, E. E. Y. "Cardinal Consalvi: The Tragedy of Success," *History Today,* X (Sept., 1960), 618-620.

———. *Pio Nono: Creator of the Modern Papacy.* New York, 1954.

HALÉVY, DANIEL. *La Fin des notables.* Paris, 1937.

HALPERIN, S. WILLIAM. "Italian Anticlericalism 1871-1914," *Journal of Modern History,* XIX (March-Dec., 1947).

————. *Italy and the Vatican at War: A Study of Their Relations from the Outbreak of the Franco-Prussian War to the Death of Pius IX.* Chicago, 1939.

————. "Leo XIII and the Roman Question," in Edward T. Gargan, ed., *Leo XIII and the Modern World.* New York, 1961.

HANOTAUX, GABRIELLE. *Histoire de la France contemporaine 1871-1900.* 4 vols., Paris, 1903.

HARDEN, MAXIMILIAN. *Monarchs and Men.* London, 1912.

HAYES, CARLETON J. H. *A Generation of Materialism 1871-1900.* 2nd ed. New York, 1941.

HELMREICH, ERNST C., ED. *A Free Church in a Free State? The Catholic Church, Italy, Germany, France, 1864-1914.* Boston, 1964. (*Problems in European Civilization.*)

HOLLYDAY, FREDERIC B. M. *Bismarck's Rival: A Political Biography of General and Admiral Albrecht von Stosch.* Durham, N.C., 1960.

HOOK, SIDNEY. *From Hegel to Marx: Studies in the Intellectual Development of Karl Marx.* New York, 1936.

HOSTETTER, RICHARD. *The Italian Socialist Movement.* I: *Origins (1860-1882).* Princeton, 1958.

JOHNSON, HUMPHREY. *The Papacy and the Kingdom of Italy.* London, 1926.

JOLL, JAMES. *The Second International 1889-1914.* London, 1955.

JOLY, HENRI. *Les Crises sociales de l'Italie.* Paris, 1924.

KAMINSKI, H. E. *Michel Bakounine: La Vie d'un révolutionnaire.* Paris, 1938.

KARSKI, STEFAN. "Geschichtsphilosophisches zur Bernstein Frage," *Socialistische Monatshefte* (No. 3, March), Berlin, 1900.

KELLER, REV. JOSEPH E., S.J. *The Life and Acts of Pope Leo XIII* preceded by a sketch of *The Last Days of Pius IX* and *Laws of The Conclave.* New York, 1879.

KIEFER, WILLIAM J., S.M. *Leo XIII: A Light from Heaven.* Milwaukee, 1961.

KUCZYNSKI, JÜRGEN. *Die Geschichte der Lage der Arbeiter in Deutschland von 1800 bis in die Gegenwart.* I, *1800-1932.* Berlin, 1947.

LABOUSQUIÈRE, JOHN. *La Troisième République 1871-1900.* Part I of Jaurès, *Histoire Socialiste,* Vol. XII. Rev. ed. 1922.

LANDAUER, CARL. *European Socialism: A History of Ideas and Movements*. I: *From the Industrial Revolution to Hitler's Seizure of Power*. Berkeley, 1959.

LAVELEYE, ÉMILE DE. *The Socialism of To-day*. Trans. Goddard H. Orpen. London [1885].

LECANUET, E. *L'Église de France sous la Troisième République 1870-1878*. Paris, 1907.

LEFÈBVRE DE BÉHAINE, ÉDOUARD. *Léon XIII et le Prince de Bismarck: Fragments d'histoire diplomatique avec pièces justicatifs*. (Munich, 1872-1879, Rome, 1882-1887.) Paris, 1898.

LÉMONON, ERNEST. *L'Italie économique et sociale 1801-1912*. Paris, 1913.

LENTNER, LEOPOLD. *Der Christ und der Staat*. Vienna, 1952.

LÉVY, CLAUDE. "Un Journal de Clemenceau: *Le Bloc* (Janvier 1901-Mars 1902)," *Revue d'histoire moderne et contemporaine*, X (April-June, 1963), 105-120.

LORWIN, LEWIS L. *The International Labor Movement: History, Policies, Outlook*. New York, 1953.

LORWIN, VAL R. *The French Labor Movement*. Cambridge, Mass., 1954.

MAGRI, FRANCESCO. *L'Azione Cattolica in Italia*. Vol. I, 1775-1939. Vol. II, 1939-1951. Milano, 1953.

MAITRON, JEAN. *Histoire du mouvement anarchiste en France 1880-1914*. Paris, 1951.

MARITAIN, JACQUES. *Primauté du spirituel*. Paris, 1927.

MAYER, GUSTAVE. *Johann Baptist von Schweitzer und die Sozialdemokratie: Ein Betrag zur Geschichte deutschen Arbeiterbewegung*. Jena, 1909.

MAYEUR, JEAN-MARIE. "Congrès de la 'Démocratie Chrétienne,'" *Revue d'histoire moderne et contemporaine*, IX (July-Sept., 1962), 171-206.

McCARTHY, JUSTIN. *Pope Leo XIII*. 2nd ed., New York, 1899.

MEHRING, FRANZ. *Karl Marx: Geschichte seines Lebens*. Leipzig, 1933.

MICHELS, ROBERT. *Italien von Heute: politische und wirtschaftliche Kulturgeschichte von 1866 bis 1930*. Zurich and Leipzig, 1930.

MIRA, GIUSEPPE. "I movimenti sociali di ispirazione cattolica," *Nel anniversario della "Rerum Novarum."* Milan, 1961.

MOLLAT, G. *La Question romaine de Pie VI à Pie XI*. Paris, 1932.

MOODY, JOSEPH N. *Church and Society: Catholic Social and Political Thought and Movements 1789-1950*.

MOON, THOMAS PARKER. *The Labor Problem and the Social Catholic Movement in France*. New York, 1921.

MOSCA, GAETANO. *Partiti e sindacati nella crisi del regime parlamentare*. Bari, 1949.

MÜNZ, SIGMUND. *Aus Quirinal und Vatikan*. Berlin, 1891.

NADA, NARCISO. *L'Austria e la Questione Romana della Rivoluzione di Luglio alla fine della Conferenza diplomatica romana, agosto 1830-luglio 1831*. Vol. 5, *Publicazioni della Facoltà di Lettere e Filosofia della Università di Torino*. Turin, 1953.

———. *Metternich e le Riforme nello Stato Ponteficio: La missione Sebregondi a Roma 1832-1836*. Turin, 1957.

NEILL, THOMAS P., AND RAYMOND H. SCHMANDT. *History of the Catholic Church*. Milwaukee, 1957.

NEILSEN, FRIEDRICH. *History of the Papacy in the Nineteenth Century*. 2 vols.; London, 1906.

NEUFELD, MAURICE F. *Italy: School for Awakening Countries; The Italian Labor Movement in Its Political and Economic Setting 1800-1960*. Ithaca, N.Y., 1961.

NITTI, FRANCESCO S. *Catholic Socialism*. Trans. Mary Mackintosh. 3rd ed.; London, 1911. The first edition was in 1895.

———. *Sul Bilancio di agricoltura, industria e commercio*. Rome, 1909.

NOLLAU, GUNTER. *International Communism and World Revolution: History and Methods*. New York, 1961.

PANTALEONE, D. "Libertà o Giurisdizione nel regime della chiesa," *Nuova Antologia*, XXXI (Jan., 1876), 41.

PASCHINI, MSGR. PIO. *Lezioni di storia ecclesiastica*. 3 vols. Turin, 1955.

———. Review of Msgr. Giovanni's *L'Enciclica* "Rerum Novarum" (*Testo autentico e redazioni preparatorie dai documenti originali*) with preface by Domenico Tardini, *Rivista di storia della chiesa*, XI (Rome, 1957).

PAUL, WILLIAM. *Karl Liebknecht: The Man, His Work and Message*. n.p., 1920.

PIERSON, MARC-ANTOINE. *Histoire du Socialisme en Belgique*. 4th ed., Institut Émile Vandervelde. [Brussels ?], 1953.

PIOLA, ANDREA. *La Questione Romana nella storia e nel diritto*. Padua, 1931.

PIOU, JACQUES. *Le Comte Albert de Mun: Sa Vie Publique*. Paris, n.d.

PLAMENATZ, JOHN. *The Revolutionary Movement in France 1815-1871*. London, 1950.

PURCELL, EDMUND SHERIDAN. *The Life of Cardinal Manning*. 2 vols. London, 1896.

RIASANOVSKY, NICHOLAS. *Russia and the West in the Teaching of the Slavophiles: A Study of Romantic Ideology*. Cambridge, Mass., 1952.

ROLLET, HENRI. *L'Action sociale des Catholiques en France (1871-1901)*. Paris, 1947.

ROMANI, MARIO. "La preparazione della 'Rerum Novarum,' " in *Nel LXX Anniversario della "Rerum Novarum."* Milan, 1961.

ROMANO, ALDO. *Storia del movimento socialista in Italia*. I: *L'unificazione nazionale e il problema sociale (1861-1870)*. 2 vols. (9 vols. projected). Rome, 1954.

RUHENSTROTH-BAUER, RENATE. *Bismarck und Falk im Kulturkampf*. Heidelberg, 1944.

SALATA, FRANCESCO. *Per la storia diplomatica della Questione Romana*. I: *Da Cavour alla Triplice Alleanza*. Milan, 1929.

SALVADORI, MASSIMO. Review of M. P. Fogarty: *Christian Democracy in Western Europe* (Notre Dame, 1957), *Rivista storica italiana*, LXXIV-II (1962), 409-416.

SALVATORELLI, LUIGI. *La Politica della Santa Sede Dopo la Guerra*. No. 3 from *Manuale Di Politica Internazionale*. Milan, 1937.

———. *Sommario della storia d'Italia dai tempi preistorici ai nostri giorni*. Turin, 1961.

SANGNIER, MARC. *Albert de Mun*. Paris, 1932.

SANSEVERINO, LUISA RIVA. *Il movimento sindacale cristiano dal 1850 al 1939*. Rome, 1950.

SCHILLING, WERNER. *Feuerbach und die Religio*. Munich, n.d.

SCHIROKAUER, ARNOLD. *Lassalle: The Power of Illusion and the Illusion of Power*. London, 1931.

SCHMANDT, RAYMOND H. "The Life and Work of Leo XIII," in Edward T. Gargan, ed., *Leo XIII and the Modern World*. New York, 1961.

SCHORSKE, CARL E. *German Social Democracy 1905-1907: The Development of the Great Schism*, Cambridge, Mass., 1955.

SCHUMANN, HARRY. *Karl Liebknecht: Ein Stück unpolitischen Weltanschauung*. Dresden, 1923.

SELDES, GEORGE. *The Vatican Yesterday Today Tomorrow*. New York and London, 1934.

SHANAHAN, WILLIAM O. *German Protestants Face the Social Question*. South Bend, Ind., 1954.

SODERINI, EDUARDO. "Per la genesi della 'Rerum Novarum' nel suo venticinquesimo anniversario," *Nuova Antologia*, May 16, 1916.

———. *Socialism and Catholicism*. Trans. Richard Jenery Shea. London, 1896.

SOMBART, WERNER. *Der Proletarische Sozialismus* ("Marxismus"). 2 vols. I: *Die Lehre*; II: *Die Bewegung*. Jena. 1924.

———. *Sozialismus und soziale Bewegung im 19 Jahrhundert*. Jena, 1896.

SPADOLINI, GIOVANNI. *Lotta sociale in Italia*. Florence, 1948.

SPELLANZON, CESARE. *Storia del Risorgimento e del unità d'Italia*. 5 vols. Milan, 1933-1950.

STARCKE, C. N. *Ludwig Feuerbach*. Stuttgart, 1885.

———. *Histoire du mouvement social en France 1852-1924*. Paris, 1924.

WEISS, JOHN. *Moses Hess: Utopian Socialist*. Detroit, 1960.

WILLIAMS, MELVIN J. *Catholic Social Thought: Its Approach to Contemporary Problems*. New York, 1950.

WOODALL, JOHN BURWELL. "Henri Bellot de Minières, Republican Bishop of Poitiers 1881-1888," *The Catholic Historical Review*, XXXVIII (Oct., 1952), 257-284.

WOODWARD, E. L. "The Diplomacy of the Vatican under Popes Pius IX and Leo XIII," *Journal of the British Institute of International Affairs*, III-IV (May, 1924).

ZANNINI, GIAN LUDOVICO MASETTI. "La spiritualità di Pio IX prima del Pontificato," *Rivista storia della chiesa in Italia*, XIV (1960).

ZÉVAÈS, ALEXANDRE. *Au Temps du Boulangisme*. 5th ed. Paris, 1930.

———. *De l'introduction du Marxisme en France*. Paris, 1947.

———. *La Faillite de l'Internationale: Faits et documents*. Paris, 1917.

————. *Jean Jaurès*. Paris, 1941.

————. *Le Socialisme en France depuis 1871*. Paris, 1908.

————. *Histoire du socialisme et du communisme en France de 1871 à 1947*. Paris, 1947.

ZOCCOLI, HEKTOR. *Die Anarchie: Ihre Verkünder—Ihre Ideen—Ihre Taten: Versuch einer systematischen und kritischen Übersicht sowie einer ethischen Beurteilung*. Trans. from the Italian by Siegfried Nacht. Leipzig, 1909. Zoccoli quotes from Nettlau on Bakunin. Nettlau not available in libraries in Europe. Zoccoli had his own copy.

ZORZI, ELIO. *L'Avventura dal Generale Boulanger: Storia di una rivoluzione mancata 1886-1891*. Verona, 1937.

INDEX

intransigent clergy: in France, 94, 283, 285; in Italy, 261, 330, 331; in Sacred College, 92, 94, 104, 203, 315, 321n
intransigent Right, 287, 288
"iron" law of wages; *see* laissez-faire
Islam's contributions to culture, 208, 209
Israelites, 221
Isvolsky, Alexander, Russian Envoy to the Vatican, 401n
Italian Catholics, 383
Italian Chamber of Labor, 252
Italian clergy, 11, 180, 180n, 313
Italian Court, 310
Italian Left (*Sinistra*), 180, 331, 382
Italian Liberals, 221
Italian Marxist theory, 253
Italian Ministry, 253
Italian Parliament, 311
Italian people, 179
Italian republicanism, 130, 252, 327
Italian Right (*Destra*), 91, 319, 331
Italian socialism, 73, 179, 251, 251n, 260, 267, 384, 384n
Italian Socialist Party, 251, 384
Italian uprisings (May, 1898), 252
Italy, Kingdom of, 16, 22, 93, 202, 216, 298, 309-333, 409; aid of Freemasons in unification of, 220n; king of, 309, 311, 327, 333, 334; laws against Freemasons in, 218; mutual-aid associations in, 181, 261, 329, 389, 397n; queen of, 309; social reforms in, 260; in Triple Alliance (1882), 321, 324

Jacobi, Polish physician, 62
Jacobini, Cardinal: nuncio at Vienna, 127; Vatican Secretary of State, 136, 138, 263, 264, 319, 319n, 321
Jampridem (Leo XIII, Jan. 6, 1889), 227
Japan, Bakunin in, 46
Jaurès, Jean, French Independent socialist, 348, 349, 361, 363, 364, 364n, 367, 368, 371-373, 374n, 375, 376, 381, 381n, 382n, 386, 386n; at Second International, 243-244
Jerome, Saint, 228
Jesuit Order; *see* Society of Jesus
Jewish bankers, 370n
Jewish religion, 35
Jews, 225, 296n, 370
John XXIII, Pope, 273n, 274, 388, 395n, 398n
Joseph II, of Austria, 13
Josephism, 13n, 108, 118n
Jouhaux, Léon, Secretary of Syndicalists, 361n
Journal de Rome (ed. Galimberti), 317n
Journal des Débats, 121
Journal officielle, 301
Julian the Apostate, 208
July Monarchy; *see* Bourgeois Monarchy
July Revolution (France, 1830), 18
"June Days," 16
Justice (ed. Clemenceau), 198, 221

Kapital, Das, 42n, 50, 346

Temporal Power, 17, 83, 85, 91, 121, 138n, 141n, 191n, 213n, 260, 309, 312, 315n, 316, 321, 321n, 323, 326-328, 332, 390, 391, 393, 402
Temps, French Protestant journal, 211, 304, 374, 401
Thierry, Jacques, French historian, 39
Third Estate, 174
Third French Republic, 66, 103, 164-166, 173, 198; anticlericalism in, 119, 283-285; clericalism in, 283, 285; crisis in, 151, 169; and Dreyfus, 367; Leo XIII's support of, 394, 412; monarchism in, 198, 286, 293-296, 300-308, 357; relations of with Italy, 326, 327; and socialism, 372, 373
Third International, 235n
Third Order of St. Francis, 219, 221
Thomas, Saint; *see* Aquinas, St. Thomas
Thomism; *see* Aquinas, St. Thomas
Tiara and the Crown, union of, 277
Times, London, 217
"Toast of Algiers," 296, 296n, 300
tombs of the Apostles, 309, 313
Toniolo, Professor Giuseppe, of Society of Italian Catholic Youth, 261, 264n, 389, 390, 399, 400
Tosti, Under-Archivist of the Holy See, 317
trade guilds, 256, 265n
trade unions, 153, 234, 242, 358; in Belgium, 356
"transigents": in Italy, 261; in Sacred College, 316, 319
Trasimene, Perugia, 402
Trent, Council of; *see* Council of Trent
Triple Alliance, 130n, 140n, 242n, 313n, 321, 322, 324, 324n, 325, 326, 326n, 349, 349n
Triple Crown, 12, 84n, 141n
Tsar of Russia; *see* names of individual Tsars
Turati, Filippo, Italian socialist, 243, 250, 251n, 253
Turin, 309; Archbishop of, 309
Turkey, Sultan of, 402
Turks, 217
Tuscany, 17n

ultra-conservatives, 275, 388; in Belgium, 353
ultramontanism, 163, 370n
Ultramontanists: in epoch of Gregory XVI, 14-16, 18n; in Republican era, 163, 285
Umbria; *see* Perugia
Unified Socialists in France, 376, 377, 378, 382
Union for Social Studies, Italy, 261
Union of Christian France (monarchist), 298
Union of Owners in Favor of Workingmen, Belgium, 258
United States of America, 54n, 239n; separation of Church and State in, 292n, 315
Univers, French ultramontane journal, 211, 276, 287, 289, 299, 304, 364, 393
University Catholic Circle, Italy, 329
Utopian socialism, 49, 56, 208n
Utopians, 29-31, 37, 42, 44, 46, 414

Vagnozzi, Archbishop Egidio, Apostolic Delegate to the United States, 312n
Vaillant, Éduard, 70, 172; at Second International, 234, 240, 241, 371, 377, 378
Vandervelde, Emile, Belgian socialist, 234, 248, 353, 355, 382
Vannutelli, Cardinal Serafina, 97, 403
Vaterland Das (ed. Vogelsang), 256